The Horse Flies of Europe

(Diptera, Tabanidae)

By

Milan Chvála, Leif Lyneborg
& Josef Moucha

Copenhagen 1972

Published by the Entomological Society of Copenhagen

Sole agent:
E. W. Classey Ltd., 353 Hanworth Road,
Hampton, Middlesex, England

E. W. Classey Ltd.

ISBN 0 900848 57 x

Printed by

Vinderup Bogtrykkeri, 7830 Vinderup, Denmark

Contents

Chapter 1

Introduction

The family Tabanidae (Diptera) includes some 3500 species throughout the world, of which 166 are known to occur in Europe. This is a group of insects of great economic importance. The females of most species are well-known as unpleasant or even dangerous blood-sucking flies. Tabanids are therefore of interest from both theoretical and practical points-of-view.

For this reason Horse Flies have been rather intensively studied in almost all countries, and several valuable monographs have been published on individual countries or on large regions. Among the most important are the monograph by Oldroyd (1952, 1954, 1957) on the »Horse-flies (Diptera: Tabanidae) of the Ethiopian Region«, Olsufjev's (1937) revision of Tabanidae in the series »Fauna of the USSR«, and Leclercq's (1960, 1967) review of the Palaearctic species »Révision Systématique et Biogéographique des Tabanidae Paléarctiques«.

No monograph of the European fauna exists at present. For almost 20 years we have been devoting ourselves to the study of the Tabanidae, particularly of the European fauna, but the study of European material has been made more difficult by the fact that papers on individual countries are scattered throughout the literature which is itself often difficult to locate. Our task has been to make good this deficiency. Above all else, a modern key for identification is necessary for the study of the Tabanidae of Europe, together with thorough descriptions of the species and illustrations of the most important characters. In order to revise the fauna of European Tabanidae, we have therefore joined forces.

M. Chvála has written the systematic part, including the keys for identification, prepared the outlines for the drawings, and contributed to the chapters on life-history and collecting methods. L. Lyneborg has written the general part of the book except for those chapters written by J. Moucha, contribured to the systematic part including the drawings, checked the synonymies, and arranged the whole book for publication. J. Moucha has written the chapters on history, zoogeography and importance of European Tabanidae, prepared the bibliography, and contributed to the paragraphs on distribution in the systematic part.

Europe is here used in the geographical sense. The eastern boundary of the region under study conforms with the generally accepted boundaries of Europe: the eastern foot of the Ural Mountains, and the Emba River as far as its mouth in the Caspian Sea. The south-eastern boundary between Europe and Asia is formed by the River Terek, as far as its mouth in the Caspian Sea, and the River Manych, which joins the River Don to the northeast of Rostov-on-Don; it continues through Kerch, the Bosphorus and the Dardanelles. In our revision we have included those species which are recorded from the northern slopes of the Caucasus Mountains. In the section reviewing individual countries we have not given any account of the very small states because no comprehensive data were available: Andorra, Liechtenstein, Monaco, San Marino and Vatican City. This is also true for Gibraltar and Malta. Data on the larger Mediterranean islands are included under the relevant states.

It is clear to us that further studies will entail certain additions and corrections to our monograph, but such is the fate of all works such as ours. In spite of this, however, we hope that all those interested in the European Tabanid fauna will find all the most important information that is needed for the correct identification of their species in the present work. We hope that entomologists, parasitologists, zoological technicians, hydrobiologists and other specialists in biological sciences who need to use Tabanids in their research will find all the most necessary information in this monograph.

The authors are grateful to the following persons for valuable help: Dr. A. Kaltenbach, Naturhistorisches Museum, Vienna, Austria; Dr. Fr. Kühlhorn, Zoologische Sammlung des Bayerischen Staates, München, Germany; Dr. M. Leclercq, Beyne-Heusay, Belgium; Prof. Dr .E. Lindner, Staatliches Museum für Naturkunde, Ludwigsburg, Germany; Dr. I. M. Mackerras, Canberra, Australia; Dr. G. Morge, Deutsches Entomologisches Institut, Eberswalde, Germany; Mr. H. Oldroyd, British Museum (Natural History), London, England; Prof. Dr. N. G. Olsufjev, Moscow, USSR; Prof. C. B. Philip, California Academy of Sciences, San Francisco, USA; Dr. H. Schumann, Zoologisches Museum der Humboldt-Universität, Berlin, Germany; and Dr. L. Tsacas, Muséum National d'Histoire Naturelle, Paris, France. Mr. D. M. Ackland, Oxford, and Mr. A. C. Pont, London, have kindly offered their help correcting the manuscript.

The authors also acknowledge the careful work done by the two artists, Mrs. Grete Lyneborg who prepared all the line drawings, and Mr. Henning Anthon who is the master of the colour plates.

The Carlsberg Foundation has offered generous financial support, both for payment of the artistic work and for the printing of the book. The Danish State Research Foundation has also supported the printing of the book. The Rask-Ørsted Foundation has supported the linguistic correction and the translation of several parts.

Chapter 2

Historical review of research on European Tabanidae

The history of our knowledge of the Tabanidae of Europe can be studied from two points-of-view, neither of which is mutually exclusive.

The taxonomic study of European Tabanidae really began in 1758. In the 10th edition of his »Systema Naturae«, Linné described five European species of Tabanidae. Later he described a further two (1761) and two (1767) species. Some of these were incorrectly interpreted by later authors, but Lyneborg (1961) studied the historic material in the Linnéan collection which is preserved in London. The work of Scopoli (1763) was also published in this period, but unfortunately it has been overlooked by subsequent workers. Whilst revising the types of Fabricius, Chvála and Lyneborg (1970) drew attention to this work. Both these authors made a thorough study of Fabricius' types and proposed several alterations in the nomenclature of European species. They also gave redescriptions of many of the species first described by Fabricius.

This initial period lasted from 1758 until the beginning of the 19th century. In addition to Linné and Fabricius, new taxa were described by Scopoli, Herbst, Villers and Rossi.

Many authors worked on Tabanidae during the 19th century. The classical works on Tabanidae by Meigen, Fallén, Coquebert, Macquart, Wiedemann, Zetterstedt, Zeller, Wahlberg, Walker, Loew, Egger, Jaennicke, Schiner, Brauer, Gobert, Pandellé, Costa and Mik were published during this period. The most significant advances were made in the works of Meigen (1804, 1820), Loew (1858, 1859) and Brauer (1880).

The outstanding monograph by Brauer (1880) dealt not only with the taxonomy but also with the faunistics of »Tabanus-species« of the present tribes Tabanini and Diachlorini, but not the Haematopotini and Chrysopsini.

In the period from 1758 to 1900 a large number of species was described, of which 103 are now regarded as valid species of European Tabanidae.

In the first half of the 20th century many authors published individual descriptions of European species, for example Becker, Strobl, Verrall, Pleske, Surcouf, Frey, Villeneuve and Séguy. Szilády, Kröber, Austen and Enderlein are among those who devoted themselves particularly to the study of this family, and this period is characterised by a series of monographs by Kröber. Among the most basic monographs that were published shortly before the Second World War must be mentioned the revisions by Olsufjev (1937) and Kröber (1938).

Since the Second World War rather little has been written on the taxonomy of European Tabanidae. In the main single descriptions have been published within the framework of faunistic papers, especially by Leclercq (1956–1967). Among the most important taxonomic papers of this period should be mentioned the revision of Danish *Hybomitra*-species (Lyneborg, 1959), the revision of the *Tabanus bovinus*-group (Olsufjev, Moucha and Chvála, 1967) and the revision of the genus *Therioplectes* (Moucha and Chvála, 1958–1964).

This period is characterised by the publication of Leclercq on the Palaearctic Tabanidae (1960a, 1967a). Between 1901 and the present day, 64 valid species of the family Tabanidae have been described or named.

A chronological review of taxonomic work on European Tabanids is given in the following table:

DATES OF DESCRIPTION OF THE EUROPEAN SPECIES: a chronological review. Species marked with an asterisk (*) are known to us in Europe only from records in the literature (except *Hybomitra macularis)* and have not been seen by us in any materials or collections from Europe.

1758 Linné	*Chrysops caecutiens, Hybomitra tarandina, Hybomitra tropica, Tabanus bovinus, Haematopota pluvialis.*
1761 Linné	*Tabanus bromius, Tabanus autumnalis.*
1763 Scopoli	*Silvius alpinus.*
1767 Linné	*Pangonius mauritanus, Atylotus rusticus.*
1776 Fabricius	*Heptatoma pellucens.*
1781 Fabricius	*Pangonius haustellatus, Hybomitra borealis.*
1787 Herbst	*Therioplectes gigas.*
1789 Villers	*Glaucops hirsutus.*
1790 Rossi	*Dasyrhamphis ater.*
1794 Fabricius	*Chrysops sepulcralis, Chrysops viduatus, Hybomitra vittata, *Hybomitra macularis, Tabanus lunatus, Philipomyia graeca, Dasyrhamphis nigritus.*
1804 Coquebert	*Tabanus barbarus.*
1804 Meigen	*Pangonius ferrugineus, Chrysops italicus, Chrysops flavipes, Hybomitra micans, Haematopota italica.*
1805 Fabricius	*Pangonius variegatus, Silvius variegatus.*
1817 Fallén	*Hybomitra lurida, Atylotus plebeius.*

1820 Meigen	*Pangonius micans, Chrysops relictus, Chrysops rufipes, Nemorius vitripennis, Hybomitra auripila, Hybomitra aterrima, Hybomitra montana, Hybomitra solstitialis, Atylotus fulvus, Tabanus quatuornotatus, Tabanus nemoralis, Tabanus glaucopis, Tabanus cordiger, Tabanus spodopterus, Haematopota grandis, Philipomyia aprica, Dasyrhamphis anthracinus, *Dasyrhamphis carbonarius, Dasyrhamphis umbrinus.*
1826 Macquart	*Hybomitra bimaculata.*
1828 Wiedemann	**Atylotus agricola.*
1830 Meigen	*Silvius algirus.*
1838 Zetterstedt	*Chrysops nigripes.*
1839 Macquart	**Tabanus rousselii, *Dasyrhamphis algirus.*
1842 Zetterstedt	*Hybomitra nigricornis, Atylotus sublunaticornis, Tabanus maculicornis.*
1842 Zeller	*Chrysops parallelogrammus, Therioplectes tricolor, Tabanus sudeticus.*
1845 Macquart	*Pangonius funebris, Dasyrhamphis tomentosus.*
1846 Macquart	*Silvius appendiculatus.*
1848 Wahlberg	*Haematopota crassicornis.*
1850 Walker	*Tabanus tinctus.*
1858 Loew	*Chrysops divaricatus, Chrysops connexus, Chrysops concavus, Chrysops hamatus, Hybomitra decora, Hybomitra pilosa, Hybomitra acuminata, Atylotus pulchellus, Tabanus bifarius, Tabanus unifasciatus, Tabanus spectabilis, Tabanus rectus.*
1859 Loew	**Pangonius griseipennis, Pangonius pyritosus, Pangonius fulvipes, *Pangonius obscuratus, Pangonius fumidus, Pangonius affinis, Pangonius dimidiatus.*
1859 Egger	*Tabanus tergestinus.*
1866 Jaennicke	*Tabanus regularis, Tabanus paradoxus.*
1868 Schiner	*Tabanus eggeri.*
1870 Loew	*Haematopota pallens.*
1874 Loew	*Tabanus sabuletorum, Atylotus quadrifarius.*
1880 Brauer	*Hybomitra muehlfeldi, Hybomitra erberi, Atylotus latistriatus, Tabanus rupium, Tabanus miki.*
1881 Gobert	*Haematopota bigoti.*
1883 Pandellé	*Hybomitra expollicata, Tabanus obsolescens, Tabanus exclusus, Haematopota subcylindrica.*
1893 Costa	*Chrysops mauritanicus.*
1898 Mik	*Chrysops melichari.*
1900 Becker	*Hybomitra aequetincta.*
1906 Strobl	**Pangonius escalerae, Pangonius granatensis.*
1909 Verrall	*Hybomitra distinguenda.*
1910 Pleske	*Chrysops ricardoae.*
1912 Surcouf	*Hybomitra morgani.*
1914 Szilády	*Hybomitra sareptana, Hybomitra peculiaris.*
1915 Szilády	*Atylotus flavoguttatus.*
1915 Frey	*Hybomitra polaris.*

1920 Austen	*Tabanus leleani.*
1920 Villeneuve	*Atylotus loewianus.*
1921 Villeneuve	*Haematopota lambi.*
1921 Kröber	*Stonemyia hispanica, *Pangonius brevicornis, Pangonius hermanni.*
1922 Kröber	**Haematopota caenofrons, Haematopota turkestanica, Haematopota ocelligera, Haematopota pallidula.*
1922 Szilády	*Haematopota csikii.*
1923 Szilády	*Pangonius striatus, Hybomitra caucasi, Hybomitra arpadi, Tabanus cuculus, Tabanus prometheus, Haematopota gallica, Haematopota pseudolusitanica, Haematopota graeca.*
1923 Hine	*Hybomitra sexfasciata.*
1925 Austen	*Silvius inflaticornis, Tabanus fraseri, Haematopota latebricola.*
1925 Enderlein	*Hybomitra caucasica, *Dasyrhamphis denticornis.*
1925 Kröber	*Tabanus caucasius.*
1927 Enderlein	*Tabanus holtzianus.*
1927 Szilády	*Therioplectes tunicatus.*
1928 Kröber	*Hybomitra media, Tabanus decipiens, Tabanus armeniacus, *Tabanus martinii.*
1932 Enderlein	*Tabanus tenuicornis.*
1934 Séguy	*Pangonius sobradieli.*
1936 Kröber	*Tabanus shannonellus, Haematopota pandazisi.*
1936 Olsufjev	*Atylotus pallitarsis, Tabanus brunneocallosus.*
1937 Olsufjev	*Silvius latifrons, Nemorius caucasicus, Therioplectes tricolor pallidicaudus, Haematopota longeantennata, Philipomyia rohdendorfi.*
1937 Séguy	*Hybomitra ciureai.*
1939 Hauser	*Tabanus indrae.*
1941 Olsufjev	*Tabanus subparadoxus.*
1952 Olsufjev	*Hybomitra ukrainica.*
1956 Leclercq	*Tabanus marianii.*
1957 Leclercq	*Hybomitra valenciae.*
1959 Leclercq	*Tabanus simovae.*
1959 Lyneborg	*Hybomitra lundbecki.*
1959 Moucha & Chvála	*Therioplectes tricolor kirchbergi.*
1962 Leclercq	*Tabanus briani.*
1962 Olsufjev	*Tabanus smirnovi.*
1964 Leclercq	*Tabanus darimonti.*
1964 Olsufjev, Moucha & Chvála	*Haematopota scutellata.*
1966 Leclercq & French	*Hybomitra bryanensis.*
1967 Leclercq	*Atylotus venturii.*
1967 Olsufjev, Moucha & Chvála	*Tabanus spodopterus ibericus, Tabanus spodopterus ponticus.*
1969 Olsufjev, Moucha & Chvála	*Tabanus spodopteroides.*
1970 Chvála & Lyneborg	*Hybomitra kaurii.*
1971 Chvála & Moucha	*Hybomitra nitidifrons confiformis.*
In this volume is described	*Silvius latifrons graecus.*

Since the period of the classical works of the last century, we regard the monographic revisions of Olsufjev (1937), Kröber (1938) and Leclercq (1960a, 1967a) as being the most fundamental contributions to the knowledge of European species. These works are of importance for the faunistics of Tabanidae as well as for the taxonomy.

Faunistic papers where data on European Tabanidae are given can also be divided into two groups.

In the first group are those works which are devoted to the whole of the Diptera. Such works have a limited value for the faunistic study of individual European countries.

Because of its economic importance the family has been studied in almost every European country since the Second World War. Thanks to this we now have not only faunistic lists of the species in each European country, but also several monographs on this subject.

In the following review only the most important and, above all, the most recent faunistic works are included. The results of these researches are reflected in the chapter »Geographical distribution of Tabanidae in Europe«.

Review of faunistic work in the individual countries of Europe

Some years ago one of the present authors (Moucha) dealt with this subject and presented his results at the International Congresses (1st International Congress of Parasitology, Rome, 1964, and 13th International Congress of Entomology, Moscow, 1968).

The fauna of Portugal is little worked. Arias (1914) only mentioned four species from this country, and by an error one of these was not Palaearctic. The only modern work on the Tabanid fauna here is by Leclercq (1964b).

In Spain, Strobl (1898, 1906) and Arias (1914) have been active, as has been Leclercq more recently who has published seven papers between 1957 and 1966 on the Tabanids of this country. Smaller faunistic contributions on Spain can be found in the lists of Moucha and Chvála (1960, 1965) and of Lyneborg (1970). There are thus substantially more papers on the fauna of Spain than on the fauna of Portugal, but nevertheless new discoveries can also be expected here.

The area between Spain and France, the Pyrenees, has been recently studied by Leclercq in two publications in 1970. His papers have appeared under the title »Tabanidae (Diptera) des Pyrenées«.

France is also a country where Leclercq has been active faunistically. From 1955 to 1961 he published seven papers, one of which (1957d) also gave a zoogeographic analysis of French Tabanids. Further faunistic contributions have also been published, for example by Roman (1959), by

Mirouse (1958) and by other authors. The French species were monographically treated by Surcouf (1924a) and Séguy (1926).

The family is rather well known in Italy on account of the publication of a monograph by Ghidini (1937). Recently Leclercq has also paid attention to this country (1956a, 1965b) and has also worked up material from Sicily (1965a).

Further Mediterranean islands were studied by Leclercq (1967d). In his revision this author also includes a table giving the recorded species from Cyprus, Rhodes, Crete, the Greek Archipelago, Corfu, Sicily, Sardinia and Corsica. The fauna of the last two islands had been studied earlier by Philip and Aitken (1958), and that of the Balearic Islands by Compte-Sart (1958).

Greece was studied faunistically before the war by Shannon and Hadjinicolaou (1936), and later by Leclercq (1958c) and Moucha and Chvála (1967b). Much faunistic information on the Tabanids of Greece is contained in the taxonomic works of Kröber and Enderlein.

Faunistic studies on the fauna of Albania have been published by Szilády (1922), Moucha (1962), and Moucha and Chvála (1963b). The country is still inadequately worked, but one can hardly expect to find species that are not already known from Greece or Jugoslavia.

The fauna of Jugoslavia has been worked by several authors: two papers each have been published by Coe (1958, 1960), Leclercq (1959, 1960c) and Moucha (1959b, 1965). Further contributions are found in a later paper by Leclercq (1968) in which he deals with the Tabanids of Jugoslavia, Greece and Italy. Faunistic work in Jugoslavia is complicated by the fact that certain areas were formerly part of Austro-Hungary and so a great deal of relevant information is scattered through the older Austrian literature.

In Bulgaria a comprehensive monograph was published many years ago by Drenski (1929a), and more recently there has been a faunistic contribution by Moucha and Chvála (1961).

The fauna of Turkey has been recently dealt with by Leclercq in three papers (1966 b, 1967 b &c), but there are very few references to the European part of the country. Moucha and Chvála (1957 b) have also published some information on this area. The species of the Dardanelles region were studied earlier by Austen (1925).

In spite of the publication of the volume on Tabanidae in the series »Fauna of Rumania« (Dinulescu, 1958), the Rumanian fauna is still very incompletely known faunistically. This revision clearly shows that the author had a restricted and predominantly old material before him.

The situation is similar in Hungary. In spite of Aradi's (1958) revision, the faunistics of the Horse Flies are contained in a few and mainly rather old publications.

In Czechoslovakia the Tabanid fauna has been systematically worked by Moucha and Chvála (since 1955). A series of faunistic papers has been published not only by these two authors but also by Čepelák, Gunárová, Minář, etc.

The foundations of our knowledge of the Austrian Tabanids were laid by the classical authors. The faunistic data in Brauer's monograph (1880) are of interest. Since the war the fauna of Austria has been studied above all by Moucha (1964, 1970b) who has given the most recent review of the species recorded from Austria in his second paper.

The fauna of Switzerland was recorded in a series of papers by Galli-Valerio (1922–1940). Bouvier (1945) published a comprehensive review of the Swiss Tabanidae, and Leclercq (1966 c) has recently summarised all the data from this country.

In the series »Tierwelt Deutschlands«, a revision by Kröber was published (1932 b). Not a great deal has been published on the fauna of this country since that time. In 1966 Fischer revised the Horse Flies in the Fauna of Swabia. Comparable lists of the species of the German Federal Republic (DBR) and the German Democratic Republic (DDR) have been published by Moucha (1969).

The Polish fauna of Horse Flies was revised by Trojan (1959). This work contains keys for the identification of species. A precise faunistic review of this country is still needed.

Recently the Benelux countries have been thoroughly revised by Leclercq, who has dealt with the fauna of Belgium (1952), Luxemburg (1957e) and the Netherlands (1967 e).

No work on the Tabanid fauna of Ireland is known. The data on this country have been kindly placed at our disposal by H. Oldroyd, British Museum (Natural History), London.

Oldroyd (1939, 1970) has given comprehensive accounts of the fauna of Great Britain. Further data can be found in the papers listed in our bibliography.

The Horse Flies of Denmark have been thoroughly studied since 1959 by Lyneborg, so that this country is rather well explored from the faunistic point-of-view.

Similar researches have been carried out in the other Scandinavian countries by Kauri since 1951. He has published a series of papers on the Tabanids of Finland, Sweden and Norway. A new summary of our knowledge of the fauna of Finland has been given by Karvonen (1969).

The fauna of the USSR is well-known thanks to the papers of Olsufjev. His most important work was published in 1937: it is a revision of the Tabanidae in the series »Fauna of the USSR«. Since then some additions and corrections have been published. The species of the European part of the USSR have recently been summarised by Olsufjev (1969a) in the form of a key for the identification of species. Among the most important contributions to knowledge of the European part of the USSR is the recently published book by Lutta (1970) on the Horse Flies of Karelia.

In conclusion it must again be stressed that the Tabanid fauna in virtually all European countries has been intensively studied during the last 20 years. Nonetheless several areas have only been superficially examined, and many new faunistic and taxonomic observations can be expected. Comprehensive data on the fauna of individual countries together with lists of the older faunistic literature can be found in the papers referred to above.

Chapter 3

Systematical list of all taxa with tables indicating occurrence in the European countries

The following pages present a combination of a systematical list of the taxa of European Tabanidae arranged in the same way as in the taxonomical section, and a tabular review of their occurrence in the individual countries. The species marked with an asterisk (*) are known from Europe only from old literary records, or are only expected to be European.

The authors are well aware that the tabular review must be very incomplete. Faunistic research is still in its infancy. A further difficulty is that many changes in the systematics and nomenclature of Tabanids have taken place during recent years, and for this reason it has been almost impossible to interpret many older records correctly. We have only used those records which we have been able to check or which have been published in reliable sources. Amongst other things the tabular review also shows the present state of research on the family Tabanidae in the individual countries of Europe. In 27 states of Europe, or in their European parts, a minimum of eight species (Ireland) and a maximum of 89 species (European part of the USSR) have been established.

As it has already been emphasised, the figures are only approximate and largely depend on the intensity of faunistic researches in the individual countries.

Among other things the tables show the striking increase in the number of species from north to south and from west to east. There are three exceptions to this, European Turkey, Albania and Portugal, and this emphasises that the Tabanid fauna of these areas has not been well studied.

The number of species of Tabanidae in individual countries is as follows:

Ireland 8
Luxemburg 17
Turkey (European part) 28
Norway 30
Great Britain 30
Netherlands 31
Portugal 31
Finland 35
Denmark 36
Belgium 39
Sweden 41
German Democratic Republic (DDR) 43
Albania 43
Hungary 44
Poland 45
Switzerland 51
Bulgaria 57
German Federal Republic (DBR) 57
Austria 60
Rumania 60
Czechoslovakia 61
Greece 64
Jugoslavia 75
Italy 77
Spain 81
France 83
USSR (European part) 89

PANGONIINAE

PANGONIINI

	Portugal	Spain	France	Italy	Greece	Albania	Jugoslavia	Bulgaria	Turkey, Eur. part	USSR, S Eur. part	USSR, C Eur. part	Rumania	Hungary	Czechoslovakia	Austria	Switzerland	Germany, GFR	Germany, GDR	Poland	Luxemburg	Belgium	Netherlands	Ireland	Great Britain	Denmark	Sweden	Norway	Finland	USSR, N Eur. part
Stonemyia Brennan, 1935																													
hispanica (Kröber, 1921)		+																											
Pangonius Latreille, 1802																													
(*Melanopangonius* Szilády, 1923)																													
brevicornis Kröber, 1921		+																											
griseipennis Loew, 1859		+																											
micans Meigen, 1820	+	+	+	+	+		+										+												
haustellatus (Fabricius, 1781)		+	+	+	+	+	+	+	+				L																
funebris Macquart, 1845						+	+	+	+																				
(*Pangonius* s. str.)																													
pyritosus Loew, 1859					+		+	+	+	+		+																	
fulvipes Loew, 1859				L	+		+		+																				
* *obscuratus* Loew, 1859	L	L			L			L																					
mauritanus (Linné, 1767)		+	+	+																									
sobradieli Séguy, 1934		+																											
striatus Szilády, 1923				+																									
escalerae Strobl, 1906		+																											
hermanni Kröber, 1921	+	+																											
variegatus Fabricius, 1805	+	+		+	+																								
granatensis Strobl, 1906	+	+																											
fumidus Loew, 1859		+																											
affinis Loew, 1859		+																											
ferrugineus (Meigen, 1804)	+	+			L																								
dimidiatus Loew, 1859		+																											

+ = occurrence in the respective country.

L = occurrence in the respective country according to the literary records.

CHRYSOPSINAE
CHRYSOPSINI

Chrysops Meigen, 1803
(*Chrysops* s. str.)

	sepulcralis (Fabricius, 1794)	*nigripes* Zetterstedt, 1838	*divaricatus* Loew, 1858	*caecutiens* (Linné, 1758)	*viduatus* (Fabricius, 1794)	*relictus* Meigen, 1820	*ricardoae* Pleske, 1910	*parallelogrammus* Zeller, 1842	*concavus* Loew, 1858	*rufipes* Meigen, 1820	*melichari* Mik, 1898	*flavipes* Meigen, 1804	*italicus* Meigen, 1804	*connexus* Loew, 1858	*mauritanicus* Costa, 1893
Portugal				+	+							+			
Spain				+	+	+						+	+	+	+
France	+			+	+	+		+		+		+	+		
Italy				+	+	+		+		+	+	+	+	+	
Greece				+	+	+						+	+		
Albania				+	+	+						+	+		
Jugoslavia	+			+	+	+		+		+	+	+	+		
Bulgaria				+	+	+		+				+	+		
Turkey, Eur. part				+	+	+						+	+		
USSR, S Eur. part	+			+	+	+	+	+	+	+		+	+		
USSR, C Eur. part	+		+	+	+	+		+	+	+					
Rumania				+	+	+		+		+		+	+		
Hungary				+	+	+		+		+		+			
Czechoslovakia	+		+	+	+	+		+		+		+			
Austria	+			+	+	+		+		+		+			
Switzerland	+		+	+	+	+				+	+				
Germany, GFR	+		+	+	+	+		+		+	L	L			
Germany, GDR	+			+	+	+		+		+					
Poland	+		+	+	+	+		+		+					
Luxemburg				+	+	+									
Belgium	+			+	+	+				+					
Netherlands	+			+	+	+				+					
Ireland						+									
Great Britain	+			+	+	+									
Denmark	+		+	+	+	+				+					
Sweden	+	+	+	+	+	+				+					
Norway	+	+		+		+				+					
Finland	+	+	+	+	+	+				+					
USSR, N Eur. part	+	+	+	+	+	+				+					

\+ = occurrence in the respective country.
L = occurrence in the respective country according to the literary records.

CHRYSOPSINAE

CHRYSOPSINI

	(*Petersenichrysops* Moucha & Chvála, 1970) *hamatus* Loew, 1858	*Silvius* Meigen, 1820 *algirus* Meigen, 1830	*alpinus* (Scopoli, 1763)	*appendiculatus* Macquart, 1846	*inflaticornis* Austen, 1925	*latifrons latifrons* Ols., 1937	*latifrons graecus* ssp. n.	*variegatus* (Fabricius, 1805)	*Nemorius* Rondani, 1856 *caucasicus* (Olsufjev, 1937)	*vitripennis* (Meigen, 1820)
Portugal										
Spain			+	+				+		+
France		+	+							+
Italy			+							+
Greece		+	+				+			
Albania		+	+							+
Jugoslavia		+	+							
Bulgaria	+	+	+							+
Turkey, Eur. part		+	+		+					+
USSR, S Eur. part			+			+			+	+
USSR, C Eur. part			+							+
Rumania			+							
Hungary			+							
Czechoslovakia			+							
Austria			+							L
Switzerland			+							
Germany, GFR			+							
Germany, GDR			+							
Poland			+							
Luxemburg										
Belgium										
Netherlands										
Ireland										
Great Britain										
Denmark										
Sweden										
Norway										
Finland										
USSR, N Eur. part										

+ = occurrence in the respective country.
L = occurrence in the respective country according to the literary records.

TABANINAE

TABANINI

Hybomitra **Enderlein, 1922**

	tarandina (Linné, 1758)	*aequetincta* (Becker, 1900)	*micans* (Meigen, 1804)	*auripila* (Meigen, 1820)	*aterrima* (Meigen, 1820)	*caucasica* (Enderlein, 1925)	*caucasi* (Szilády, 1923)	*decora* (Loew, 1858)	*polaris* (Frey, 1915)	*borealis* (Fabricius, 1781)	*sexfasciata* (Hine, 1923)	*kaurii* Chvála & Lyneborg, 1970	*arpadi* (Szilády, 1923)	*pilosa* (Loew, 1858)	*nigricornis* (Zetterstedt, 1842)	*lurida* (Fallén, 1817)	*nitidifrons confiformis* Chvála & Moucha, 1971
Portugal																	
Spain			+	+	+	+											
France			+	+	+	+						+		+		+	
Italy			+	+	+	+						+		+			
Greece					+			+				+		+			
Albania														+			
Jugoslavia			+	+	+							+		+		+	
Bulgaria								L									
Turkey, Eur. part																	
USSR, S Eur. part						+	+										
USSR, C Eur. part				+						+			+			+	+
Rumania			+	+	+	L								+	+		
Hungary														+	L	+	
Czechoslovakia			+	+						+		+	+	+	+	+	+
Austria	+		+	+	+	+				L		+		+	+	+	
Switzerland			+	+	+	+						+			+		
Germany, GFR	+		+	+	+	+				+		+	+	+		+	+
Germany, GDR	+		+	+						+		+				+	+
Poland	+		+	+	+							+			+	+	+
Luxemburg			+											+			
Belgium			+									+	+			+	+
Netherlands			+												+	+	
Ireland																	
Great Britain			+													+	
Denmark			+									+				+	
Sweden	+			+	+				+	+	+	+	+		+	+	+
Norway	+				+					+	+	+	+		+	+	+
Finland	+				+					+	+	+	+		+	+	+
USSR, N Eur. part	+	+							+	+		+	+		+	+	+

+ = occurrence in the respective country.
L = occurrence in the respective country according to the literary records.

TABANINAE

TABANINI

	Portugal	Spain	France	Italy	Greece	Albania	Jugoslavia	Bulgaria	Turkey, Eur. part	USSR, S Eur. part	USSR, C Eur. part	Rumania	Hungary	Czechoslovakia	Austria	Switzerland	Germany, GFR	Germany, GDR	Poland	Luxemburg	Belgium	Netherlands	Ireland	Great Britain	Denmark	Sweden	Norway	Finland	USSR, N Eur. part
bryanensis Leclercq & French, 1966																	+												
sareptana (Szilády, 1914)										+																			
lundbecki Lyneborg, 1959			+	+		+	+				+	+	+	+	+	+	+	+	+		+	+			+	+	+	+	+
tropica (Linné, 1758)		+	+				+							+	+		+	+			+	+			+	+	+	+	
montana (Meigen, 1820)		+	+	+			+			+	+	+		+	+	+	+	+	+		+	+	+	+	+	+	+	+	+
muehlfeldi (Brauer, 1880)				+			+			+	+	+	+	+	+	+	+	+	+		+	+		+	+	+		+	+
bimaculata (Macquart, 1826)		+	+	+			+			+	+	+	+	+	+	+	+	+	+	+	+	+		+	+	+	+	+	+
solstitialis (Meigen, 1820)		+	+																		+			+	+	+		+	
distinguenda (Verrall, 1909)		+	+				+	+		+	+	+	+	+	+	+	+	+	+		+	+	+	+	+	+	+	+	+
ciureai (Séguy, 1937)		+	+	+	+	+	+	+	+	+	+	+	+	+	+	+	+	+	+		+	+		+	+	+		+	+
ukrainica (Olsufjev, 1952)										+		+																	
valenciae (Leclercq, 1957)		+																											
expollicata (Pandellé, 1883)		+	+	+						+	+				+	+		+			+	+		+	+	+			
morgani (Surcouf, 1912)										+															+				
erberi (Brauer, 1880)			+	+	+					+																			
peculiaris (Szilády, 1914)					L					+		L																	
acuminata (Loew, 1858)			+				+			+		+	+	+	+														
media (Kröber, 1928)					+								L																
vittata (Fabricius, 1794)		+	+																										
* *macularis* (Fabricius, 1794)																													

+ = occurrence in the respective country.
L = occurrence in the respective country according to the literary records.

TABANINAE
TABANINI

	Atylotus Osten-Sacken, 1876 *sublunaticornis* (Zetterstedt, 1842)	*plebejus* (Fallén, 1817)	*venturii* Leclercq, 1967	*latistriatus* (Brauer, 1880)	* *agricola* (Wiedemann, 1828)	*fulvus* (Meigen, 1820)	*loewianus* (Villeneuve, 1920)	*rusticus* (Linné, 1767)	*quadrifarius* (Loew, 1874)	*pallitarsis* (Olsufjev, 1936)	*flavoguttatus* (Szilády, 1915)	*pulchellus* (Loew, 1858)	*Therioplectes* Zeller, 1842 *gigas* (Herbst, 1787)	*tunicatus* Szilády, 1927	*tricolor tricolor* Zeller, 1842	*tricolor pallidicaudus* (Olsufjev, 1937)	*tricolor kirchbergi* Moucha & Chvála, 1959
Portugal				+					+								
Spain				+		+	+	+	+								
France	+	+		+		+	+	+	+		+		+				
Italy	+	+	+			+	+	+				L	+	+	+		
Greece				+			+	+	+				+	+			+
Albania														+			
Jugoslavia	+			+		+	+	+					+	+			
Bulgaria				+	L	+	+	+					+		+		
Turkey, Eur. part								+			+						
USSR, S Eur. part		+		+		+	+	+	+	+	+	+			+	+	
USSR, C Eur. part	+	+				+		+									
Rumania		+		+		+	+	+			+		+		+		
Hungary						+	+	+					+				
Czechoslovakia	+	+		+		+	+	+					+				
Austria	+	+				+	+	+			+		+				
Switzerland	+					+	+	+					+				
Germany, GFR	+	+		+		+	+	+					+				
Germany, GDR		+				+		+									
Poland		+				+		+									
Luxemburg	+							+					+				
Belgium	+					+	+	+					+				
Netherlands	+					+		+					+				
Ireland						+											
Great Britain		+		+		+		+									
Denmark	+	+				+		+									
Sweden	+	+				+		+									
Norway	+	+						+									
Finland	+	+				+		+									
USSR, N Eur. part	+	+				+		+									

+ = occurrence in the respective country.
L = occurrence in the respective country according to the literary records.

TABANINAE

TABANINI

***Tabanus* Linné, 1758**

	quatuornotatus Meigen, 1820	*nemoralis* Meigen, 1820	*decipiens* (Kröber, 1928)	*rupium* Brauer, 1880	*simovae* (Leclercq, 1959)	* *rousselii* Macquart, 1839	*lunatus* Fabricius, 1794	*marianii* (Leclercq, 1956)	*bifarius* Loew, 1858	*tenuicornis* (Enderlein, 1932)	*holtzianus* Enderlein, 1927	*glaucopis* Meigen, 1820	*shannonellus* Kröber, 1936	*obsolescens* Pandellé, 1883	*caucasius* Kröber, 1925	*exclusus* Pandellé, 1883	*fraseri* Austen, 1925	*cuculus* Szilády, 1923
Portugal		+					+											
Spain	+	+		+			+		+			+				+		
France	+	+		+			+		+			+				+		
Italy	+	+		+			+	+	+			+				+		
Greece	+		+	+			+	+	+	+	+	+	+	+		+		+
Albania	+			+			+		+			+				+	+	
Jugoslavia	+	+		+	+	L	+		+			+	+			+		+
Bulgaria	+						+		+	+		+	+			+	+	
Turkey, Eur. part	+					L	+					+					+	
USSR, S Eur. part				+					+			+			+			
USSR, C Eur. part												+						
Rumania	+						+		+	+		+						
Hungary	+								+	+		+				+		
Czechoslovakia	+								+	+		+						
Austria	+			+					+	+		+						
Switzerland	+	+		+								+						
Germany, GFR	+			+					+			+						
Germany, GDR	+											+						
Poland	+											+						
Luxemburg		+																
Belgium	+											+						
Netherlands																		
Ireland																		
Great Britain												+						
Denmark																		
Sweden												+						
Norway												+						
Finland																		
USSR, N Eur. part	+											+						

+ = occurrence in the respective country.
L = occurrence in the respective country according to the literary records.

TABANINAE TABANINI	*cordiger* Meigen, 1820	*smirnovi* Olsufjev, 1962	*leleani* Austen, 1920	*unifasciatus* Loew, 1858	*brunneocallosus* Olsufjev, 1936	*sabuletorum* Loew, 1874	*briani* Leclercq, 1962	*armeniacus* Kröber, 1928	*miki* Brauer, 1880	*indrae* Hauser, 1939	*regularis* Jaennicke, 1866	*darimonti* Leclercq, 1964	*bromius* Linné, 1758	*maculicornis* Zetterstedt, 1842	*tergestinus* Egger, 1859	* *martinii* Kröber, 1928	*paradoxus* Jaennicke, 1866	*subparadoxus* Olsufjev, 1941	*spectabilis* Loew, 1858
Portugal	+			+							+	+	+						
Spain	+			+			+		+		+		+	+	+		+		+
France	+			+			+		+		+		+	+	+		+		+
Italy	+			+			+		+		+		+	+	+		+		+
Greece	+			+					+		+		+		+		+		+
Albania	+			+					+				+	+	+		+		+
Jugoslavia	+			+			+		+	+	+		+	+	+		+		+
Bulgaria	+			+			+		+	+	+		+	+	+				+
Turkey, Eur. part	+		+										+						+
USSR, S Eur. part	+	+	+	+	+	+		+	+	+			+	+	+			+	+
USSR, C Eur. part	+								+				+	+	+				
Rumania	+			+					+				+	+	+	L			+
Hungary	+			+					+				+	+	+		+		+
Czechoslovakia	+			+			+		+		+		+	+	+		+		
Austria	+			+					+				+	+	+		+		
Switzerland	+								+				+	+	+		+		
Germany, GFR	+			L					+				+	+	+		+		
Germany, GDR	+								+				+	+					
Poland	+								+				+	+			+		
Luxemburg													+	+					
Belgium	+								+				+	+					
Netherlands	+												+	+					
Ireland																			
Great Britain	+								+				+	+					
Denmark									+				+	+					
Sweden	+								+				+	+					
Norway													+	+					
Finland	+												+	+					
USSR, N Eur. part	+								+				+	+					

+ = occurrence in the respective country.
L = occurrence in the respective country according to the literary records.

TABANINAE
TABANINI

	rectus Loew, 1858	*autumnalis* Linné, 1761	*spodopteroides* Olsufjev, Moucha & Chvála, 1969	*spodopterus spodopterus* Meigen, 1820	*spodopterus ibericus* Olsufjev, Moucha & Chvála, 1967	*spodopterus ponticus* Olsufjev, Moucha & Chvála, 1967	*prometheus* Szilády, 1923	*sudeticus* Zeller, 1842	*bovinus* Linné, 1758	*tinctus* Walker, 1850	*eggeri* Schiner, 1868	*barbarus* Coquebert, 1804	*Glaucops* Szilády, 1923 *hirsutus* (Villers, 1789)
Portugal	+	+						+			+	+	
Spain	+	+			+			+	+		+	+	
France	+	+		+	+			+	+		+		+
Italy	+	+	+	+				+	+	+	+		
Greece		+		+				+	+	+			
Albania		+							+	+	+		
Jugoslavia		+		+				+	+	+	+		
Bulgaria		+		+		+	+	+	+	+	+		
Turkey, Eur. part		+											
USSR, S Eur. part		+		+				+	+				
USSR, C Eur. part		+		+				+	+				
Rumania		+		+				+	+	+			
Hungary		+		+				+	+				
Czechoslovakia		+		+				+	+				+
Austria		+		+				+	+				+
Switzerland	+	+		+				+	+				+
Germany, GFR		+		+				+	+				
Germany, GDR		+		+				+	+				
Poland		+		+				+	+				+
Luxemburg		+						+					
Belgium		+						+	+				
Netherlands		+						+	+				
Ireland								+					
Great Britain		+						+	+				
Denmark		+						+	+				
Sweden		+						+	+				
Norway		+						+	+				
Finland								+	+				
USSR, N Eur. part		+						+	+				

+ = occurrence in the respective country.
L = occurrence in the respective country according to the literary records.

TABANINAE
HAEMATOPOTINI

	Heptatoma Meigen, 1803 *pellucens* (Fabricius, 1776)	*Haematopota* Meigen, 1803 * *caenofrons* (Kröber, 1922)	*pallens* Loew, 1870	*grandis* Meigen, 1820	*pandazisi* (Kröber, 1936)	*italica* Meigen, 1804	*longeantennata* (Olsufjev, 1937)	*lambi* Villeneuve, 1921	*gallica* Szilády, 1923
Portugal						+		+	
Spain				+	+	+		+	L
France	+			+	+	+		+	+
Italy				+	+	+			L
Greece				+	+	+	+		L
Albania				+	+	+	+		
Jugoslavia	+			+	+	+			+
Bulgaria				+	+	+			
Turkey, Eur. part									
USSR, S Eur. part		L	+	+		+			
USSR, C Eur. part	+					+			
Rumania	+			+	+	+			
Hungary	+			+		+			
Czechoslovakia	+			+		+			
Austria	+			+		+			
Switzerland	+			+		+			
Germany, GFR	+			+		+			
Germany, GDR	+					+			
Poland	+					+			
Luxemburg						+			
Belgium	+					+			
Netherlands	+					+			
Ireland									
Great Britain				+		+			
Denmark	+			+		+			
Sweden	+			+		+			
Norway	+								
Finland	+								
USSR, N Eur. part	+					+			

+ = occurrence in the respective country.
L = occurrence in the respective country according to the literary records.

TABANINAE HAEMATOPOTINI	* *latebricola* Austen, 1925	*turkestanica* (Kröber, 1922)	*csikii* Szilády, 1922	*pseudolusitanica* Szilády, 1923	*ocelligera* (Kröber, 1922)	*pluvialis* (Linné, 1758)	*scutellata* (Olsufjev, Moucha & Chvála, 1964)	*subcylindrica* Pandellé, 1883	*bigoti* Gobert, 1881	*graeca* Szilády, 1923	*crassicornis* Wahlberg, 1848	*pallidula* (Kröber, 1922)
Portugal				+	+	+			+			
Spain			+	+	+	+			+		L	
France				L	+	+	+	+	+		+	
Italy					+	+	+		+		+	
Greece					+	+				+		
Albania			L		+	+						
Jugoslavia						+					+	
Bulgaria			L		+	+	+					
Turkey, Eur. part						+						
USSR, S Eur. part		+				+		+				+
USSR, C Eur. part						+		+			+	
Rumania			L		+	+		+	+		+	
Hungary						+		+			+	
Czechoslovakia						+	+	+	+		+	
Austria			L			+	+	+	+		+	
Switzerland						+	+				+	
Germany, GFR						+	+	+			+	
Germany, GDR						+	+	+	+		+	
Poland						+	+	+	+		+	
Luxemburg						+					+	
Belgium						+		+			+	
Netherlands						+		+			+	
Ireland						+			+		+	
Great Britain						+			+		+	
Denmark						+		+	+		+	
Sweden						+		+	+		+	
Norway						+					+	
Finland						+						
USSR, N Eur. part						+		+			+	

+ = occurrence in the respective country.

L = occurrence in the respective country according to the literary records.

TABANINAE DIACHLORINI	*Philipomyia* Olsufjev, 1964 *aprica* (Meigen, 1820)	*graeca* (Fabricius, 1794)	*rohdendorfi* (Olsufjev, 1937)	*Dasyrhamphis* Enderlein, 1922 *ater* (Rossi, 1790)	*anthracinus* (Meigen, 1820)	* *carbonarius* (Meigen, 1820)	*nigritus* (Fabricius, 1794)	*umbrinus* (Meigen, 1820)	*tomentosus* (Macquart, 1845)	* *denticornis* (Enderlein, 1925)	* *algirus* (Macquart, 1839)
Portugal	+			+			+				
Spain	+	+		+			+			L	
France	+	+		+	+		L		+		L
Italy	+	+		+	+	L	L	+			
Greece	+	+		+			L	+			
Albania	+	+		+				+			
Jugoslavia	+	+		+				+			
Bulgaria	+	+		+	+						
Turkey, Eur. part	+			+				+			
USSR, S Eur. part	+		+								
USSR, C Eur. part											
Rumania	+	+		+				+			
Hungary	+	+									
Czechoslovakia	+	+									
Austria	+	+									
Switzerland	+	+		+							
Germany, GFR	+										
Germany, GDR	+										
Poland	+	L									
Luxemburg											
Belgium	+										
Netherlands											
Ireland											
Great Britain											
Denmark											
Sweden											
Norway											
Finland											
USSR, N Eur. part											

+ = occurrence in the respective country.
L = occurrence in the respective country according to the literary records.

CHAPTER 4

Geographical distribution of Tabanidae in Europe

The dipterous family Tabanidae is almost cosmopolitan in distribution. Our researches have shown that some 3500 species and more than 100 subspecies are known throughout the world. This large number of species is divided among 121 genera and 77 subgenera. In Europe there are 14 genera and 2 subgenera.

The centre of distribution of the recent species lies in the tropics. Outside the tropics the number of species decreases very strikingly. In the Palaearctic region we know of about 490 species, of which 176 species and 5 subspecies are recorded from Europe.

The genus *Pangonius* is a circum-Mediterranean group of 30 species which are found exclusively in South Europe, North Africa and the Near East. The origin of one species from »China«, *P. sinensis,* needs to be checked. With the exception of *P. obscuratus,* which is only known from Turkey, 13 species of *Pangonius* s. str. are known in Europe of which 10 (!) are found in Spain. The centre of distribution of this genus thus lies in South-West Europe (Spain, Portugal). The subgenus *Melanopangonius* has a similar distribution, and is represented in Europe by five species. The species of this subgenus are found everywhere around the Mediterranean coast of Europe, from Spain to Greece, and some extend as far as Rumelia (the European part of Turkey), Bulgaria and Rumania (along the Black Sea coast). A single species, *P. micans,* has been found at an isolated area in South-West Germany (Kaiserstuhl). *P. haustellatus* was recorded from the area of Budapest, but has not been found there since 1880 and the specimens in question have not been seen by us.

The genus *Stonemyia* is represented in Europe only by a single species, *S. hispanica* from Spain. The centre of distribution of this genus is in North America (4 species) and in the Far East (Japan, 2 species).

The genus *Chrysops,* with two other genera, *Silvius* and *Nemorius,* belongs to the tribe Chrysopsini. Altogether the genus *Chrysops* s. str. includes 245 species of which 40 are found in the Palaearctic region. The centre of distribution of this genus lies in the New World (Nearctic region with 73, Neotropical region with 68 species). The most widely distributed of the 15 European species are *C. caecutiens, C. relictus* and *C. viduatus* which with few exceptions are found in all European countries. Two further species,

C. sepulcralis and *C. rufipes,* are also widely distributed but are absent from the South of the continent. Apart from these widely distributed species, four patterns of distribution can be discerned in the genus:

South European species of Mediterranean distribution: *C. mauritanicus, C. connexus, C. italicus* and *C. flavipes.* One of these, *C. flavipes,* extends as far north as Central Europe and is known from South Slovakia, Hungary and Austria. *C. melichari* has a Central European distribution, and is known only from the eastern parts of the Alps. *C. parallelogrammus* also seems to be a European species, and is rather widely distributed though nowhere common. Two species are mainly northern: *C. nigripes,* which is Holarctic and circumboreal, and *C. divaricatus,* whose southern limit runs through Central Europe.

C. concavus and *C. ricardoae* are West or Central Asian species, which are found only in the eastern parts of Europe.

The subgenus *Petersenichrysops* has a conspicuously East Mediterranean distribution. The single European species, *P. hamatus,* is endemic in Asia Minor, and one isolated locality in Bulgaria has been recorded.

Six of the 18 known species of the genus *Silvius* occur in Europe, of which only one, *S. alpinus,* is rather widely distributed. It is known from Central and South Europe. *S. algirus* is locally common in the south of the continent. The remaining four species occur only in the south; two are known only from Spain, *S. appendiculatus* and *S. variegatus,* and one only from the region of the Dardanelles, *S. inflaticornis.* The distribution of *S. latifrons* is most interesting. It was known only from the Caucasus and from Turkish Armenia, but was discovered a few years ago in an isolated region of Greece *(S. latifrons graecus).*

The genus *Nemorius* is a Mediterranean-Central Asian group of seven species, of which only two have been found in Europe. *N. vitripennis* is found in the Mediterranean region from Spain to eastern Central Europe (Transcarpathian Ukraine, USSR). *N. caucasicus* is endemic in the Caucasus and its northern foothills.

The tribe Tabanini is represented by five genera altogether. *Hybomitra* is one of the richest in species, with 174 species of which 36 occur in Europe. In Europe there are six species of Eurasian distribution, and these are amongst the commonest species of the genus: *H. lundbecki, ciureai, distinguenda, muehlfeldi, bimaculata* and *montana. H. tropica* is also widely distributed but seems to be more local. The centre of distribution of *Hybomitra* undoubtedly lies in the Holarctic region, and very few species are known from outside this zoogeographic region. Among the European species there are six that are Holarctic and circumboreal: *H. aequetincta, polaris, sexfasciata, arpadi, lurida* and *montana. H. tarandina* is found in the north of Eurasia, and is also known from certain narrowly restricted localities in Central Europe.

Another group is formed by species which are found in the North of Europe, or of Eurasia, and are sometimes also common in Central Europe. At the southern limits of their distribution they are above all found either in the mountains or in certain well-defined localities such as moors, swampy meadows, etc. This group includes: *H. micans, auripila, borealis, kaurii, arpadi, lurida* and *nitidifrons* (ssp. *confiformis* in Central Europe). Most of these species can be found in Central Europe, but some of them also occur in the mountains of Southern Europe: *H. auripila, micans* and *lurida.* Three species are found in the mountains or even high mountains of Central Europe: *H. caucasica, aterrima* and *nigricornis.* One little-known species, *H. bryanensis,* has not been found since it was originally described from West Germany.

Only six species are South European in distribution: *H. vittata, valenciae, decora, pilosa, erberi* and *acuminata.* The East Mediterranean species *H. decora* has also been recorded from Bulgaria and Greece, but these are older records which have not been confirmed more recently. Two of these species, *H. pilosa* and *acuminata,* penetrate from the south into Central Europe. At their northern limits, in South and East Slovakia, Hungary and Austria, they only occur in isolated pockets.

H. caucasi is one the endemic species of the Caucasus Mountains, and a further four species reach the western or north-western limit of their distribution in South-East Europe: *H. sareptana, ukrainica, peculiaris* and *morgani.*

Eleven of the 63 known species of the genus *Atylotus* are found in Europe. *A. rusticus* and *fulvus* are found almost throughout the entire continent. *A. loewianus* is widely distributed, but is absent from the north. *A. sublunaticornis* and *plebeius* are also widely distributed, but both are found in narrowly defined biotopes, above all on moors and in damp places where *Sphagnum* mosses dominate. The remaining species of *Atylotus* are only known from the South and Central of Europe. *A. venturii* was described from Italy, but has not been found again since the original description. *A. pulchellus* and *pallitarsis* are known from the southeastern regions of the USSR, where the western limits of their distribution run. *A. latistriatus* is also known from Great Britain.

The genus *Therioplectes* contains only seven species, of which three are known from Europe; one occurs in three subspecies. It is *tricolor* which is known in Europe only from the area of the Black Sea (Bulgaria, Rumania, USSR) and from Greece (Samos Island: ssp. *kirchbergi),* and we have also seen old specimens from Italy (Sicily). The ssp. *pallidicaudus* has been described from the Crimea and from the northern foothills of the Caucasus. *T. tunicatus* is known from the Balkan Peninsula: Greece, Albania and Jugoslavia, and has also been recorded from Italy. *T. gigas* has the widest distribution. From the south it penetrates as far as Central Europe, to Czechoslovakia, Austria and Hungary, but in the west it reaches further north, to all the Benelux countries.

On a world basis the genus *Tabanus* contains about 1050 species. Only 45 of these have been recorded from Europe, which means that the genus is represented here by only 4 % of the total number of species. No European species is Holarctic in distribution. Within the European framework, there are only eight species which are recorded from 20 or more countries: *T. bromius, sudeticus, autumnalis, maculicornis, cordiger, bovinus, glaucopis* and *miki*. Two mountain species are known from the Caucasus: *T. caucasius* and *subparadoxus*. It is interesting that in Europe there are no species that have a predominantly northern distribution such as is the case in for example *Hybomitra* or *Chrysops*. On the other hand the number of species of *Tabanus* increases considerably towards the south. Eight species are known to us which have a principally South European distribution but which also extend into Central Europe: *T. quatuornotatus, rupium, bifarius, tenuicornis, unifasciatus, tergestinus, paradoxus* and *spodopterus*. We also include *T. briani* in this group, which has been recently described and whose distribution is therefore not yet really known.

Of the 27 known South European species and subspecies, only three species and one subspecies are confined to the Western Mediterranean: *T. rectus, barbarus, darimonti* and *spodopterus ibericus*.

On the other hand the number of species known from the Eastern Mediterranean area of Europe is much larger and consists of 14 species and one subspecies. Most of these are known from the broad area of the Balkan Peninsula and adjacent countries: *T. shannonellus, leleani, fraseri, indrae, spodopterus ponticus, cuculus* and *tinctus*. Three further species should also be placed in this group although until now they have only been recorded from Greece *(T. decipiens, holtzianus* and *obsolescens)* as should also be one species from Jugoslavia *(simovae)*, Bulgaria *(prometheus)* and the Crimea *(smirnovi)*.

Three species extend into Europe from the adjacent areas of Asia: *T. sabuletorum, brunneocallosus* and *armeniacus*. These are endemic in Asia and reach the western or north-western limits of their distribution in Europe.

Widely distributed South European species of Mediterranean distribution occur in almost all South European countries: *T. nemoralis, lunatus, exclusus, regularis, spectabilis* and *eggeri*. Several of these are also known from narrowly limited areas of Central Europe, for example *T. spectabilis* and *T. exclusus* in Hungary and *T. regularis* in South Slovakia. So far little is known of the distribution of *T. simovae,* which was described from Jugoslavia. *T. prometheus,* known in Europe only from Bulgaria, is endemic in Transcaucasia.

The Holarctic genus *Glaucops* consists of only three species, one of which is known in Europe, *G. hirsutus.* It is known from two of the European mountain ranges: the Alps of France, Switzerland and Austria, and the Krkonoše Mountains of Poland and Czechoslovakia. It seems to be a very rare species.

The tribe Haematopotini contains 4 genera with 394 species, of which 382 belong to the genus *Haematopota.* Two genera are known from Europe. The monotypic *Heptatoma* with the species *H. pellucens* is distributed throughout most of Europe and is only absent in the South.

The genus *Haematopota* is represented in Europe by 19 species. *H. pluvialis,* which is recorded from all countries, is the most widely distributed of all the European Tabanidae. *H. italica* is also widely distributed, and is only absent from Ireland and the north of Scandinavia. Its occurrence in the European part of Turkey is also likely though it has not yet been recorded from there. *H. subcylindrica* is more of an East European species and extends as far as Central and North Europe, but is replaced by the closely related *H. ocelligera* in the South-West. *H. bigoti* has been recorded from many countries, but is local. Along the sea-coast it penetrates far to the north, to England, Denmark and Sweden. This distribution is reminiscent of, but not identical with, that of *H. grandis, Hybomitra expollicata* or *H. solstitialis.*

It is difficult or almost impossible to interpret correctly the distribution of most species of *Haematopota* at present. The taxonomic status of many of them has only been clarified during recent years (Lyneborg and Chvála, 1970) and few collections have yet been examined in the light of these results. Among these species belongs for example the recently described *H. scutellata.*

H. crassicornis is North European in distribution, and has also been found in the mountains of South Europe. *H. caenofrons,* described from the »Caucasus«, has not been found again since and is known to us only from the literature.

Among the typically West Mediterranean *Haematopota*-species are *H. lambi, pseudolusitanica* and, probably, *ocelligera.* The following species have been found in South and South-East Europe: *H. pandazisi, gallica, longeantennata* and *graeca.* Three Central Asian species, otherwise known only from the USSR, are known from the adjacent areas of Europe: *H. pallens, turkestanica* and *pallidula.*

As stated above, this division of *Haematopota*-species according to their geographical distribution is not yet definitive and many additions should be expected.

The tribe Diachlorini includes many genera and is known from all continents. It is particularly numerous in the Neotropical region. On a world basis the tribe consists of 45 genera and 720 species.

In Europe only two genera and eight species are known. All three species of the genus *Philipomyia* are present in Europe though one of them, *Ph. rohdendorfi,* is known only from the USSR. The other two are widely distributed in the South. *Ph. graeca* seems to be a typical Mediterranean species, and also extends into Central Europe, to South Slovakia and Hungary. The other species, *Ph. aprica,* is more closely bound to hilly areas and the mountains. In the north it extends as far as Belgium.

Eleven species are known in the genus *Dasyrhamphis,* five of which occur in Europe. They are all confined to South Europe, and the northern limit runs through Switzerland *(D. ater).* Two species, *D. ater* and *umbrinus,* are well-known, but the others, *D. anthracinus, nigritus* and *tomentosus,* have only been recorded from a few countries.

This chapter on the geographical distribution of Tabanidae in Europe is concluded with a list of species. Unreliable records, which are those known to us only from published sources, have been omitted from this review. Rather a large percentage of the species (29.8 %) is known in Europe from only one country. These are not exclusive endemic species but are also those that impinge upon the peripheral areas of Europe from outside. Many species that are known from only one country can be expected from others. The European area has still been very unevenly surveyed. For this reason we have not given a zoogeographic analysis, as would be possible with Lepidoptera or Coleoptera, but have only given a review of geographical distribution.

Species distributed through almost the whole of Europe

Chrysops caecutiens	*Hybomitra distinguenda*	*Tabanus maculicornis*
Chrysops viduatus	*Hybomitra ciureai*	*Tabanus autumnalis*
Chrysops relictus	*Atylotus fulvus*	*Tabanus sudeticus*
Hybomitra lundbecki	*Atylotus rusticus*	*Tabanus bovinus*
Hybomitra tropica	*Tabanus glaucopis*	*Haematopota italica*
Hybomitra montana	*Tabanus cordiger*	*Haematopota pluvialis*
Hybomitra muehlfeldi	*Tabanus miki*	*Haematopota bigoti*
Hybomitra bimaculata	*Tabanus bromius*	*Heptatoma pellucens*

Species distributed throughout Europe, but in Southern Europe only in the mountains

Chrysops rufipes
Hybomitra micans
Hybomitra auripila
Hybomitra kaurii
Hybomitra lurida
Atylotus sublunaticornis
Atylotus plebeius
Haematopota crassicornis
Haematopota subcylindrica

European montane species

Hybomitra caucasica
Glaucops hirsutus

Endemics of the Caucasus Mountains

Nemorius caucasicus
Silvius l. latifrons
Hybomitra caucasi
Tabanus caucasius
Tabanus subparadoxus
Haematopota caenofrons

Central European species

Chrysops melichari

North European species

Hybomitra aequetincta
Hybomitra polaris
Hybomitra sexfasciata

North and Central European species

Chrysops sepulcralis
Chrysops divaricatus
Hybomitra tarandina
Hybomitra aterrima
Hybomitra borealis
Hybomitra arpadi
Hybomitra nigricornis
Hybomitra nitidifrons confiformis

Central and South European species

Chrysops parallelogrammus
Chrysops flavipes
Silvius alpinus
Hybomitra pilosa
Hybomitra acuminata
Atylotus latistriatus
Atylotus loewianus
Therioplectes gigas
Tabanus quatuornotatus
Tabanus bifarius
Tabanus rupium
Tabanus tenuicornis
Tabanus unifasciatus
Tabanus briani
Tabanus tergestinus
Tabanus paradoxus
Tabanus spodopterus
Haematopota grandis
Haematopota scutellata
Philipomyia aprica
Philipomyia graeca

South-West European species

Stonemyia hispanica
Pangonius brevicornis
Pangonius griseipennis
Pangonius micans
Pangonius mauritanus
Pangonius escalerae
Pangonius hermanni
Pangonius variegatus
Pangonius granatensis
Pangonius fumidus
Pangonius affinis
Pangonius ferrugineus
Pangonius dimidiatus
Pangonius sobradieli
Chrysops connexus
Chrysops mauritanicus
Silvius appendiculatus
Silvius variegatus
Hybomitra valenciae
Tabanus darimonti
Tabanus rectus
Tabanus spodopterus ssp. *ibericus*
Tabanus barbarus
Haematopota lambi
Haematopota ocelligera
Haematopota pseudolusitanica
Dasyrhamphis nigritus
Dasyrhamphis tomentosus

South European species

Pangonius haustellatus
Pangonius fulvipes
Pangonius striatus
Chrysops italicus
Silvius algirus
Nemorius vitripennis
Hybomitra decora
Hybomitra erberi
Hybomitra vittata
Atylotus quadrifarius
Atylotus venturii
Tabanus nemoralis
Tabanus lunatus
Tabanus exclusus
Tabanus regularis
Tabanus spectabilis
Tabanus spodopteroides
Tabanus eggeri
Haematopota pandazisi
Haematopota gallica
Haematopota csikii
Dasyrhamphis ater
Dasyrhamphis anthracinus
Dasyrhamphis umbrinus

Asiatic species, which extend into East Europe

Chrysops concavus
Chrysops ricardoae
Tabanus brunneocallosus
Tabanus sabuletorum
Tabanus armeniacus
Haematopota turkestanica
Haematopota pallens
Haematopota pallidula

Other types of distribution

Hybomitra solstitialis (principally along the sea-coast)
Hybomitra expollicata (on the coast and in halophile biotopes)
Hybomitra morgani (South-East Europe and Denmark)

Chapter 5

Life history

Seasonal activity of the adults

The adult stage is relatively short compared with the larval stage, and last only about six weeks. Emergence of the earliest specimens depends on the geographic latitude of the areas studied. In Central Europe the first species emerge in the second half of May, and these are usually *Hybomitra nitidifrons confiformis, H. lurida, H. tropica* and *Tabanus quatuornotatus.* At the beginning of June other species of *Hybomitra (bimaculata, muehlfeldi, lundbecki)* emerge and so do some species of *Chrysops;* these are followed by *H. borealis, H. kaurii,* and then by most of the species of *Tabanus, Atylotus, Chrysops* and *Haematopota.*

In the mountains and northern regions the first specimens occur later, usually about the middle of June, whilst in the northern tundra and in high mountains they do not fly until the first half of July. The late appearance of Tabanids in these regions is caused by the low temperature of the soil during May, which induces late pupation of the larvae. On the other hand, in the warm regions of southern Europe the first specimens emerge as early as March and April. The swarming of the economically important Tabanids takes place from the second half of June through to the end of August; in northern regions the period is much shorter, and usually lasts from the end of June until the end of July. Some of the most important economic species, such as *T. bromius* and most of the *Haematopota*-species, maintain their maximum populations to the end of August and individuals are often collected throughout the whole of September. The dates of occurrence given in the taxonomic part under each species apply, of course, to the whole of Europe and will be quite different in the extreme north and south.

Daily activity of the adults

There are usually two different periods of daytime activity at the time of the mass occurrence of Tabanids. Firstly, there is the activity of hovering males which is associated with mating. This seems to be restricted to the early morning and the evening hours. It involves both sexes, and is discussed in more detail below in the relevant section. The second and economically more important activity is connected with the feeding habits of the females. The females of all European Tabanids except one are diurnal feeders, attacking livestock and man between sunrise and sunset. Feeding starts before 7 a. m. and some individuals, especially those of *Chrysops* and *Haematopota* species, may be found on livestock as late as 9 p. m. Swarming is usually between 11 a. m. and 3 p. m., with a singly peak in northern regions from about 1 to 2.30 p. m. (Lutta, 1970) and with two distinct peaks in southern regions, one before noon about 11 a. m. and the second one about 2 p. m. This bimodal activity is also typical of Central European populations, even if these peaks are not as distinct as in the south.

The only undoubtedly nocturnal feeder in Europe is *Tabanus paradoxus,* observed several times on the wing only after the point of almost complete darkness. One of the authors (Chvála) observed this species on August 10, 1964, in a pasture meadow in South Slovakia. Several females were flying in complete darkness, just above the ground among small bushes, and resembled humble-bees. No feeding on man was observed, although the females were flying slowly in small circles around the legs of the observer. Unfortunately, no livestock were present in the pasture on this occasion.

Factors affecting activity

The most important factor influencing the adult Tabanids seems to be temperature. This has also been verified by Blickle (1959) when studying the hovering and mating activities of the Nearctic *Tabanus bishoppi.* He showed that temperature was the main factor affecting the beginning of the hovering activity. The adults do not usually fly when the air temperature is below 13° C, and there is a distinct reduction of activity when the temperature fluctuates around 15° C. Swarming starts when the temperature is above 17° C, and the optimum temperature seems to be about 25° C. Relative humidity is closely related to temperature: when the humidity is high, then the temperature is lower and there is less flying activity among the Tabanids.

Wind influences the activity of Tabanids very greatly. Windless days are best for adult activity, and on windless days swarming reaches its peak. With a wind-speed of 4—5 m per sec. activity decreases very much, especially in open areas.

The light intensity is a very important factor, though it is not as decisive as the temperature. Most European Tabanids are exclusively diurnal (except *T. paradoxus),* with the highest activity at about noon, but some *Chrysops* and particularly some *Haematopota* also feed at dusk or when it is clouded: swarming has never been observed under such conditions. In general the activity of Tabanids is much lower when it is cloudy, and females are much less aggressive compared than on warm sunny days. Some of the Asiatic species, for instance *T. sabuletorum* and *H. peculiaris,* are known to be active feeders even after sunset in very southern regions, and several species in Africa or Central America are nocturnal feeders. This phenomenon is, however, most probably caused by the very warm nights in tropical regions, and the influence of temperature thus seems to be the decisive factor.

The occurrence and activity of Tabanids depends, of course, on the presence of the host animals, and also on the presence of water and trees. It is known that Tabanids in the dry southern areas of Europe and Asia are abundant along the large rivers that are fringed with forest and other vegetation, whereas they are practically absent in dry areas away from the rivers.

Feeding of the adults

Females only seek a blood meal after mating, as was observed in 99.9 % of 293 dissected specimens (Lutta, 1970). Most of the European species are obligatory haematophagous flies in the female sex, but a few species (*Atylotus sublunaticornis, A. plebejus, Glaucops hirsutus* and possibly all *Pangonius* species) apparently never seek a blood-meal and feed on flower nectar like the males. However, some females of the typical blood-sucking species are occasionally found on flowers as well, particularly species of *Atylotus* and *Dasyrhamphis.*

Females mainly attack livestock, which are evidently preferred before man except by *Haematopota* species. The different species usually differ strikingly in their choice of feeding-site on the host. Species of *Chrysops* usually prefer to feed on the head and neck; when attacking man they usually fly very quietly in small circles around the head. The large species of *Tabanus* prefer the legs and the belly, most species showing preference for special areas on the host. The main reasons for this are probably variations in the thickness of the skin, in the density of the blood-vessels, and in the density and length of the hairs. Attacking females are most attracted to black animals as well as to man in black clothes, and also prefers perspiring animals. They are also attracted to large black objects, a fact which is used when devising trapping methods. The large species make direct attacks and attempt to feed immediately, unlike the small species which usually hover around the animal before feeding.

Females of the smaller species suck about 20–30 mg of blood, of the larger species up to 200 mg; the Nearctic *Tabanus lasiophthalmus* takes up to 352 mg according to Tashiro and Schwardt (1949). Fully-fed females often fly very heavily, and small drops of blood can often be seen in the anal opening.

Emergence

Adults usually emerge during morning, often in large numbers if the preceeding days are warm. Eclosion from the pupa lasts about 10–20 min. and after three hours the adult is able to fly. The longevity of the individual adult is very short in comparison with that of the larva, and is only about 2 or 3 weeks. Males usually live for a shorter time and it is thought that they die soon after mating. Males usually emerge earlier than females, and mating occurs just after the emergence of the female.

Hovering and mating

The characteristic hovering by the males and its association with mating is a phenomenon which has been studied several times and about which many papers have been published. However, hovering and mating is insufficiently known in the European species. All the literature on this subject up to 1947 was reviewed by Bailey (1948 b) and since then several more papers have appeared, e. g. Blickle, 1955, 1959; Wentges, 1952; Corbet, 1964; Corbet & Haddow, 1962; and Lutta, 1970. The hovering and mating of the Nearctic *Tabanus bishoppi* was described in great detail by Blickle (1959). Hovering of the males of *Tabanus* and *Hybomitra* is usually observed in the early morning hours after sunrise. Males usually hover in forest clearings or in the open tree canopies in the same way as Syrphid flies, facing into the wind with sudden darts forwards and sideways, or chasing each other around the hovering area, sometimes causing »chain reaction« as described by Bailey (1948 b). A few to several dozen specimens usually hover in the same place, but cases of a single or two specimens are not rare, especially during the first or last days of the hovering period. Females fly into the hovering areas and couple with one of the males. Copulation begins in the air and ends on nearby vegetation or on the ground, where the copulating pair rest. The whole process takes about 5 min. The present authors have observed on several independent occasions the hovering or also the mating of *Hybomitra lundbecki, H. bimaculata, H. muehlfeldi, H. tropica, Tabanus bromius* and *T. maculicornis.* Brauer (1880) observed the hovering of males of *T. sudeticus* on high peaks in the Tyrolian Alps. The same observation including mating has been reported from the Tatra Mts., Czechoslovakia, by Kramář (1929). Males of *Chrysops* and *Haematopota* have been observed several times swarming above water or close to it, usually in the morning hours, as reported for instance by Surcouf (1921), Goffe (1931) and Cameron (1930, 1934).

Oviposition

Females usually lay eggs 4 to 7 days after feeding, and two such cycles have been observed in a single female (Lutta, 1970). When ovipositing the head of the female is directed downwards and the abdomen is recurved ventrally and anteriorly. The female usually places the egg-masses on vertical objects close to or just above water; the cement coating is a product of the accessory vaginal glands. The oviposition of one egg-mass takes about 40 to 100 minutes. The female usually lives a further 5 to 20 days after oviposition.

Eggs

The eggs are laid in masses which consist of one layer in several *Chrysops*-species, two or three layers in *Haematopota*-species, and three or four layers in other Tabanids. The egg-masses are rather deep in *Tabanus, Hybomitra* and *Atylotus,* and they usually contain about 400 eggs in the small species to 1000 eggs in the large species. The eggs are laid at higher angle to the substrate, i. e. at an angle of 45 to 50°. The egg-masses in *Haematopota* are rather flat, the eggs are less numerous (about 100), and they are laid at a lower angle, i. e. about 15–20° to the substrate. When first laid, the eggs are milky-white to very pale yellow in colour, but soon they become darker. The final colour of the egg is dark grey to deep black.

The egg stage lasts about 1 to 3 weeks, and its length depends mainly on the weather conditions. The relative humidity is the most important factor for the eggs; when the humidity is rather low, under 70 %, the egg stage lasts much longer.

Larvae (See plate 5)

The larvae usually hatch during the morning, and almost at the same time all the larvae from one egg-mass fall directly into water or onto damp soil. The first instar larva possesses a black labral hatching-spine, but very soon after hatching, often still whilst on the egg-mass, it moults into a second instar larva. Neither the first nor the second instar feeds, but the young larva subsists on stored yolk in the mid-gut. The second instar is still positively phototropic and usually crawls on the water surface or on the soil, a moist environment being essential. Small larvae, perhaps with exceptions (see below), need water or moist soil immediately after hatching, otherwise they will not survive. Usually after 3 to 6 days the second instar larva moults into the third instar which is negatively phototropic; it crawls down into the water, or under moss and into the soil. The third instar larva begins to feed actively. The greatest mortality takes place in this instar, possibly because of the fundamental changes and adaptations necessary for the different environment.

The following instars are very active predators, feeding on worms, Mollusca and especially on the larvae of other Diptera. They never attack small Crustacea or the larvae of Coleoptera. Further larval development depends on a number of factors such as food, temperature, humidity, and it is strange that in this family not only the length of the larval period, but also the number of instars vary, even in the same species. In European species the number of instars usually ranges from 7 to 11, and in *Chrysops*-species it may be 6 to 7. It is very difficult to recognize the individual instars. Even the number of paired bodies in Graber's organ is not decisive, although this character has been used in the literature on several occasions. We have observed larvae moulting and no additional pair of circular bodies has appeared, especially when one of the last instars is involved. The larvae originating from a single egg-mass vary in the length and the number of instars.

Tabanid larvae are very adaptable. They can survive for a long time without food, up to several months, and they can hibernate several times with additional subsequent instars, if the living conditions are unfavourable, and especially in the laboratory. In the South, and usually also in Central Europe, the larvae hibernate only once, but in North Europe it is often twice or sometimes three times. Diapause is not connected with hibernation, the larvae being active practically throughout the winter, particularly those species living in water. Diapause takes place in a rather short final (prepupal) instar (Lutta, 1970). Some Tabanids in Africa are bivoltine, and Isaac (1924, 1925) recorded up to three generations a year in several species of *Tabanus* in India. This adaptability of Tabanid larvae enables them to survive even in very cold regions. The larvae are typical eurybionts, unlike the egg, pupa and adult which are stenobionts.

The larvae of Tabanids may be roughly separated into three ecological groups: 1) Hydrophilous larvae, which develop only in water. These are mainly larvae of *Chrysops* and of some *Hybomitra;* the larvae of the former genus can also be found in streams and rivers, but those of the latter genus only in standing water. 2) Semihydrophilous larvae, which include the majority of European Tabanids. The first two instars crawl on a water-surface or on moist soil, and in the third instar they migrate into soil close to water. 3) Edaphic larvae, which live in drier soil, usually far from water, as for instance some *Haematopota*-species. There seems to be a further group of typically xerophilous larvae. In May 1958 one of the authors (Chvála) observed early morning emergence of females of *Tabanus quatuornotatus* at a very dry limestone biotope in South Slovakia. The nearest water reservoir was about 0.5 km away. Perhaps most of the species of the *quatuornotatus*-group *(bifarius, nemoralis, rupium, lunatus,* etc.) and the species of *Dasyrhamphis* have xerophilous larvae.

Pupae (See plate 5)

The prepupal larval instar migrates to a drier place and pupation usually takes place at night. At first the pupae have a whitish-yellow to a pale greenish colour, but become dark brown later on when exposed to light. Pupae which are deeper in the soil preserve their pale colour. Before emergence the pupa actively crawls to the surface of the soil or to the upper layers of grass tufts. The pupal stage lasts from one to three weeks, the length depending mainly on the temperature. The larvae always pupate in late spring, and pupae are never found hibernating.

CHAPTER 6

Collecting methods and rearing techniques

ADULTS

When Tabanids occur in large numbers, as for example in June and July in pastures, marshy areas or forests, and particularly in forest clearings near water, the simplest method for collecting them is to use a host as bait, such as horses, horned cattle or man. It is usually quite sufficient to walk through wooded areas where Tabanids are abundant and to collect flies by swinging the net around one's own head or legs. This method is adequate for faunistic or taxonomic studies but not for quantitative studies of seasonal and daily activity.

For quantitative work several types of collecting trap have been described in the literature. At least two of them seem to us to be very effective. Firstly there is a helio-thermal trap (Thorsteinson, 1958) where use is made of the well-known phenomenon that Tabanids are attracted to open motor-car cabs where the inside temperature is much higher than the outside. The helio-thermal trap is very simple, being based on the greenhouse principle, and uses the thermal attraction and the positive phototaxis of adult females. It consists of a painted black funnel which leads to a killing jar below, the whole being covered by a plastic cone which is open below. The temperature within the trap is about 15° C higher than the ambient temperature.

The Manitoba trap (Thorsteinson, Bracken & Hanec, 1964) is rather similar, and consists of a plastic cone with a killing jar placed on the top. A large black sphere, usually a painted ball, is hung under the cone. The flies are attracted by the black ball, but cannot escape from the plastic cone and fly into the killing jar. All such traps are incredibly effective, especially when combined with carbon dioxyde. Experiments in trapping Horse-flies with special traps have been carried out recently in the USA, Japan and Czechoslovakia, and several papers on this subject have been published.

A feature of the traps just described is that they are specific only for the females. However, there is another type of trap that is effective for both males and females. The fact that adults need a great deal of water during their activity and that they often visit the water-surfaces of reservoirs to drink during flight is the basis for the so-called »pools of death« described by Portschinsky (1915). These are pools or small water basins of one to several square metres and with a thin film of oil or petrol on the surface.

The flies are unable to escape and will be killed there. It is, of course, much more convenient to prepare such traps far from water or marshy places, but care must be taken to prevent cattle from drinking from them. Species of *Haematopota* are not attracted as much as are other Tabanids.

Using the same principle, Blickle (1955) devised another method, the so-called »watering can« method. This method proved specially effective for collecting males and females in dry areas or in years with low rainfall. Blickle prepared artificial pools on dirt roads and collected Tabanids around these damp areas with the net. This method was also rather successful in periods of wet weather and even when there was more water in swamps on both sides of the road.

The males can easily be collected on flowers or by sweeping grass and bushes near the places where the larvae live. They can also be collected in large numbers in the early morning hours when they rest on sun-lit wooden walls or palings, or the canvas of tents or cabs of motor cars, or when hovering after sunrise in forest clearings or over forest pathways.

In all cases the flies should be pinned as soon as possible. We do not recommend preserving them in alcohol.

Eggs

The best time for collecting egg-masses is during the swarming of adults. The egg-masses are easily seen because of their black colour, and they are usually found in large numbers on the leaves of weeds, on grasses or on stakes in water or near the edge of water, and they are usually laid on vertical objects. However, females also lay eggs on the leaves of trees and bushes near water, usually on branches just above the water surface. In such cases the egg-masses are laid mainly on the undersides of the leaves. The eggs are laid from just above the water-level to about 80 cm above water-level, but can also be found on branches of trees up to 2 or 3 metres above the ground or the water-surface.

Larvae

The best time for collecting fully-grown larvae is from April to June. However, they can be collected throughout the year, even in the winter months if the ground or water is not frozen too hard. The most effective collecting is, of course, from known or suspected breeding sites. Usually an ordinary sieve is used for sorting out the larvae from soil or grass-roots and other plants, stirring it in water until the larvae float to the surface. The same method is used for collecting larvae directly from water or from roots of water plants. Jones and Anthony (1964) used special racks for obtaining larvae from soil samples; the larvae crawl through funnels out of the drying material into pans of water. This method provides a large number of uninjured larvae for further rearing, which cannot be expected when sifting soil and larvae together on a sieve. Bailey (1948) and Anthony (1958) collected larvae by applying pyrethrum on and below the soil-surface. The larvae are irritated by the pyrethrum and migrate to the surface where they can be easily collected.

Pupae

The pupae can be found just under the soil-surface or among roots of grass and plants, and usually in drier places than the larvae. The best time for collecting pupae is in the second half of May and the beginning of June, though of course earlier in the southern regions. The sieving method as used for collecting larvae is quite suitable for collecting pupae as well. Pupae are not damaged by contact with water. However, by searching grass tufts and by breaking up grass tussocks in moist places or near water, large numbers of pupae can be obtained.

Rearing techniques

Rearing the eggs and pupae is not a complicated matter, but a moist atmosphere is always necessary. Rearing larvae through to adult is most important in order to obtain information on the life-history and morphology of the immature stages, and in order to obtain males which is not always easy by normal collecting in the field.

There are several methods for rearing larvae collected wild or hatched from eggs. The type of container, whether jars or shallow dishes, is not as important as the rearing medium. Larvae are usually reared on wet sand or on soil from the natural habitat. However, we have found it most convenient to rear larvae in Petri dishes with 2 or 3 pieces of moistened filter-paper of the same shape as the dish. The main advantage of this method is that one can easily observe the larvae moulting, or at least the larval exuviae cannot be overlooked as in sand or soil. The larvae crawl and feed on the filter-paper, or more often they are concealed between two sheets, as in other rearing media. Earthworms, dipterous larvae, larvae of *Tenebrio molitor* (cut into pieces), snails, beef liver or boiled egg yolk, are the best and most easily obtainable foods. The food must be changed every second day, otherwise it becomes mouldy.

When collecting larvae in the field we place them individually in serological test tubes, which are very convenient for this purpose. Larvae must be reared individually because of the cannibalism which has been observed in all larvae except for some *Chrysops*. When several larvae are kept together in one dish, only one will survive.

The pupae can be kept in the same dishes as the larvae. The preservation of the larval exuviae from each instar is important, not only to know the number of instars, but also because the exuviae present good characters for studies of external larval morphology.

CHAPTER 7

Medical and economic importance of Tabanidae

The females of most species attack mammals, principally Equidae, Bovidae and Camelidae, and man. Some species have been observed sucking the blood of pigs (North America), crocodiles (Africa), sand lizards (Western Sahara), turtles (Seychelles) and tortoises (Galapagos). Freshly killed game may also be attacked. Like other blood-sucking flies, Tabanids have an important effect on milk production in those areas where they are common.

Many authors have studied the economic, medical and veterinary importance of Horse Flies, but there are numerous problems that have not yet been definitively solved. Many discoveries can be expected in this field of research.

Olsufjev (1937) and subsequent authors have considered the damage done by Tabanids under the following categories:

(1) Adults bite wild and domestic animals, and man. The damage arises not only from the fact that they suck blood but also because the small bleeding wounds are visited by other flies. In this way the possibility of further infection taking place is increased.
(2) Whilst biting, secretions from the salivary glands are introduced into the wound, with toxic effects.
(3) Horse Flies disturb cattle by biting. As a result the animal no longer increases in weight and eventually milk-production also decreases.
(4) It has been established that Horse Flies act as vectors of various diseases. During mass-occurrences of the adults, Horse Flies swarm in unbelievably large numbers and make it difficult even for man to live in areas affected in this way. It is not possible to work out-of-doors at the height of the season for Tabanid swarms.

All these aspects have been relatively well studied during the last few decades. There is however still no summarising review of these problems.

It is difficult or quite impossible to compare individual observations. Different workers have used different methods. Some results are published from areas where Horse Flies swarm in enormous numbers, whilst others are published from areas where the flies are not particularly abundant. Areas where the adults swarm are often restricted within very narrow limits.

Lutta (1970) observed in Karelia that 500 adults were attracted to one animal (horse or cow) during the course of one hour. In the Moscow region this figure is considerably higher, and Soboleva (1956) established that some 280 specimens were attracted to one animal during the course of five minutes (the maximum figure was much higher: 492 specimens).

Horse Flies cause freely bleeding wounds at the places where they bite. The quantity of blood taken varies. Several authors report about 20—30 mg of blood for the small species, but this figure rises up to 40 mg for the larger species. The robust representatives of the genera *Tabanus* L., *Hybomitra* End. and others need up to 200 mg of blood during a meal. Oldroyd (1964) recorded that a single grazing animal might lose as much as 100 cc of blood during a long summer's day.

The introduction of saliva into the wound is also dangerous. After biting irritating swellings arise which disappear in man after 3—4 hours. In many people however they persist for 10—15 hours or longer. Milk-production shows a marked decrease in cattle. The available figures are high: during heavy infestations of Horse Flies milk-production is 11—15 % lower, but in some areas these figures are even higher, being 19—25 %. In many areas where cattle are allowed to graze freely in the open these losses are rather high.

Attacks are naturally not confined to cattle but also affect other domestic animals, for example horses, camels, reindeer, etc.

All the damage listed so far is of particular importance for zoological technique and animal husbandry. Horse Flies are also of great importance for veterinary medicine, medicine and epidemiology. For this reason we have prepared a short review of the diseases for which Tabanids are known to act as vectors:

LOIASIS IN MAN (agent *Loa loa:* Nematoda): *Chrysops silaceus* Austen and *C. dimidiatus* Wulp in West Africa.

LOIASIS IN MONKEYS (agent *Loa loa:* Nematoda): *Chrysops centurionis* Austen and *C. langi* Beq. in West Africa.

ONCHOCERCIASIS (agent *Onchocerca gibsoni:* Nematoda): in muscular tissues of cattle, in Australia.

SURRA, MBORI, EL DEBAB (agent *Trypanosoma evansi:* Flagellata): all continents, chiefly warm regions; definitive hosts are equines, camels, elephants, monkeys, dogs, ruminants, etc.

MAL DE GADERAS (agent *Trypanosoma equinum:* Flagellata): in S. America, a disease of equines.

DERRENGUERA, MURINA (agent *Trypanosoma hippicum:* Flagellata): in Panama and (probably) Colombia; as hosts are recorded equines, bats and vampires.

SLEEPING SICKNESS and NAGANA (agents *Trypanosoma* spp.: Flagellata): mechanical transmission to zebra, impala, bubale; tropical Africa.

SU-AURU (agent *Trypanosoma ninae:* Flagellata): in C. Asia; an infection of camels and equines.

DOURINE (agent *Trypanosoma equiperdum:* Flagellata): in all continents, a disease of equines.

TRYPANOSOMIASIS of cattle (agent: *Trypanosoma theileri:* Flagellata): in all continents; an infection of cattle, wild ruminants, antilopes.

TULARAEMIA (agent *Francisella tularensis:* Bacteria): northern hemisphere, geographically the most distributed disease of animals and man, transmitted by the Horse Flies. As hosts were recorded: rabbits, hares, rodents, certain wild birds, etc.

ANTHRAX (agent *Bacillus anthracis:* Bacteria): an infection of animal and man. All continents.

HAEMORRHAGIC SEPTICAEMY of buffalos (agent *Bacillus bipolaris balisepticus:* Bacteria): South-East Asia, Egypt, some regions of Europe.

INFECTIOUS ANEMIA of horses, SWAMP FEVER (agents Arboviruses): in all continents.

VESICULAR STOMATITIS (agents Arboviruses): in N. America recorded in horses, bovines, pigs, mouses and man.

ENCEPHALITIS (agents Arboviruses): it was recorded an isolation of neurovirus from *Tabanus* sp. in the Khabarevsk region, USSR.

PIROPLASMOSIS of reindeer (agent *Gonderia tarandi rangiferis:* Piroplasma): in northern regions, an infection of reindeer.

CUTANEOUS MYIASES: the Tabanids may transport the eggs of *Dermatobia hominis,* causing cutaneous myiases in South America.

From the epidemiological point-of-view TULARAEMIA is the most important disease under European conditions. Much work has been published on this subject. The following species have been proved to act as vectors of tularaemia:

Genus *Chrysops* Meigen: *aestuans* Wulp, *caecutiens* Linné, *discalis* Williston, *flavipes* Meigen, *fulvaster* Osten-Sacken, *italicus* Meigen, *noctifer* Osten-Sacken, *relictus* Meigen, *ricardoae* Pleske.

Genus *Tabanus* Linné: *autumnalis* Linné, *bromius* Linné, *golovi* Olsufjev.

Genus *Hybomitra* Enderlein: *erberi* Brauer, *peculiaris* Szilády, *ciureai* Séguy, *turkestana* Szilády.

Genus *Atylotus* Osten-Sacken: *agrestis* Wiedemann, *flavoguttatus* Szilády, *karybenthinus* Szilády, *pulchellus* Loew.

Genus *Haematopota* Meigen: *pluvialis* Linné, *turkestanica* Kröber.

ANTHRAX is another serious disease which is transmitted by Horse Flies. This is known from all continents. The following species have been proved to act as vectors:

Genus *Chrysops* Meigen: *caecutiens* Linné, *flaviventris* Macquart.

Genus *Tabanus* Linné: *atratus* Fabricius, *autumnalis* Linné, *bicinctus* Ricardo, *bovinus* Linné, *bromius* Linné, *indianus* Ricardo, *rubidus* Wiedemann, *striatus* Fabricius.

Genus *Hybomitra* Enderlein: *bimaculata* Macquart, *lundbecki* Lyneborg, *lurida* Fallén, *montana* Meigen, *nitidifrons* Szilády, *ciureai* Séguy.

Genus *Atylotus* Osten-Sacken: *rusticus* Linné.

Genus *Haematopota* Meigen: *montana* Ricardo, *pallens* Loew, *pluvialis* Linné.

Future investigations will undoubtedly show that further species can act as vectors of these and other diseases. This short review is not a complete account of Horse Flies as vectors of disease. The authors have rather tried to draw attention to the economic and epidemiological importance of these flies.

CHAPTER 8

Adult morphology

HEAD

Most of the more or less hemispherical head is occupied by the large facet-eyes. In the males the eyes are normally touching or are only narrowly separated. The upper facets of the males of many species are enlarged in comparison with the lower facets, and there may be a sharp line of demarcation between the larger and the smaller facets. The eyes may have a shorter or longer pile or may be bare. It is characteristic of many Tabanidae to have a colour-pattern of spots or stripes on the eyes.

In the female (Fig. 1) the eyes are separated by a frontal stripe. This consists of a broader or narrower band which is limited anteriorly (below) by the antennal sockets (=subcallus) and posteriorly by the vertex. The frons usually has a distinct pattern formed by raised areas that are free of tomentum and hairs. Such areas are termed calli and the rest of the frons that surrounds them is pruinose and haired normally. The face and even the genae may also have such calli. These calli are of great importance for the recognition of species.

The frontal calli (see fig. 1) consist basically of a so-called lower callus, which is strongly variable in shape and is situated on the anterior (lower) part of the frons, and a so-called upper callus which is often present on the middle of the frons. This may be comparatively large and separated from the lower callus as in some species-groups of *Tabanus*, or may be more linear and connected with the lower callus as in other species-groups of *Tabanus* and in *Hybomitra* (Fig. 1d) and *Dasyrhamphis*. *Atylotus* (Fig. 1e) has the lower and the upper calli reduced or even absent, and they are absent in *Pangonius* (Fig. 1a) and *Stonemyia*.

Three distinct ocelli are present in Pangoniinae (Fig. 1a) and Chrysopsinae (Fig. 1c). In the Tabaninae, however, there is a tendency towards reduction of the ocelli. Species of the genus *Hybomitra* (Fig. 1d) have an oval or triangular ocellar tubercle, or three vestigial ocelli are present, whereas in the other genera functional ocelli are absent though the ocellar area itself is often marked by a different colour.

The area between the antennae and the frons is called the subcallus (or frontal triangle), and is formed by the united antennal sockets, as is clearly shown by the presence of a suture dividing the subcallus. The subcallus is

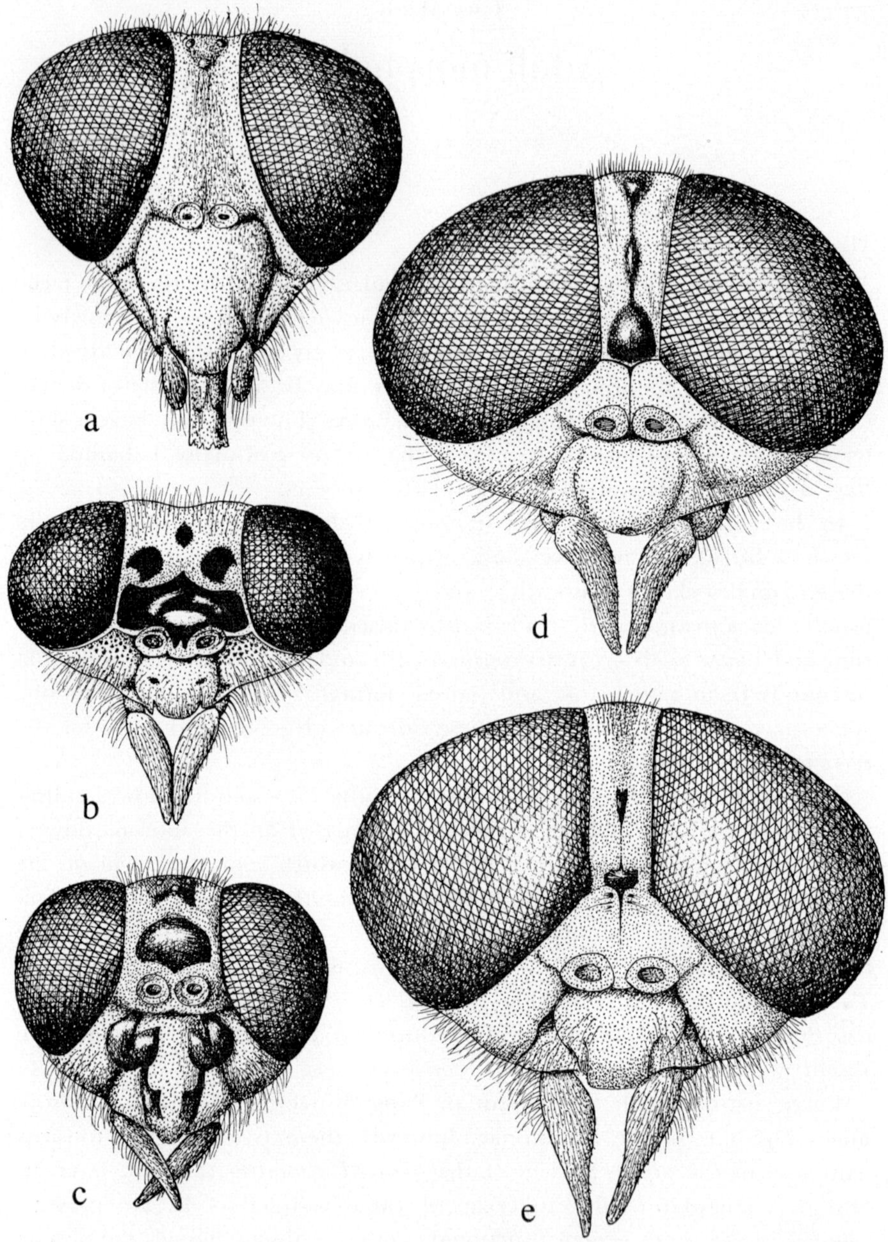

Fig. 1. Heads of female Tabanidae, a. *Pangonius mauritanus* (L.), b. *Haematopota pluvialis* (L.), c. *Chrysops relictus* Meig., d. *Hybomitra lundbecki* Lyneb., e. *Atylotus rusticus* (L.). Colour-pattern and pubescence of eyes omitted.

normally free of hairs and is entirely pruinose, but in some species of several genera may appear shiny (without tomentum) like the lower frontal callus. The area below the antennae, reaching down to the proboscis and limited laterally by the foveal grooves running from the antennal bases to the tentorial pits, consists mainly of the clypeus, but is here termed the face. The strips lying between the eye-margins and the foveal grooves are termed the cheeks. They lead imperceptibly below into the genae (or jowls) under the eyes. In Pangoniinae and Chrysopsinae the facial and rostral regions are often produced into a snout and at the same time are provided with calli of similar nature as the frontal calli, i. e. without tomentum and hairs.

The antennae (Fig. 2) are of major importance for the classification at all levels. They consists of scape, pedicel and flagellum. The scape, or antennal segment 1, is highly constant in most Tabanini and also in (e. g.) *Pangonius* (Fig. 2a), but shows more variation in shape and coloration in genera like *Chrysops* (Fig. 2b) and *Haematopota* (Fig. 2d). The pedicel, or antennal segment 2, is still more constant. It is usually very short, and is only elongated in genera like *Chrysops* (Fig. 2b) and *Nemorius*.

The rest of the antennae is the flagellum which consists fundamentally of numerous similar segments. In most Tabanidae the most basal of these flagellar segments is clearly longer and wider than any of the following flagellar segments. We term this segment antennal segment 3, although it is evident that it is an amalgamation of several flagellar segments in all higher Tabanidae (Chrysopsinae and Tabaninae). In *Pangonius* (Fig. 2a), antennal segment 3 is only slightly longer and wider than the next flagellar segment and must certainly only represent the basal flagellar segment. In *Chrysops* (Fig. 2b) it is usually clear that antennal segment 3 is a fusion probably of 4 flagellar segments, but it differs in shape from the 4 terminal flagellar segments. In Tabaninae (Figs. 2c–e) the complexity of what is termed antennal segments 3 cannot be clearly seen, and the number of flagellar segments beyond the antennal segment 3 varies from 4 to 3 or even 2 only. Following this reduction there is a tendency towards a less distinct annulation of the terminal flagellar segments. In the following descriptions the flagellar segments beyond the ones forming antennal segment 3 are termed terminal flagellar segments.

The proboscis of female Tabanidae consists of the following elements: a labium, a pair of mandibles, a pair of maxillae with two-segmented palpi, labrum and hypopharynx. The labium is the largest component and forms a sheath for the mouthparts. It consists of a stalk of varying lengths, and a pair of lobes apically, the labella. These labella vary strongly in size through the family and on their inner surfaces are provided with half-open tubes, the pseudotracheae. In many genera the stem of the labium and the labella are very flexible, and their shape can therefore vary greatly from one specimen to another. This flexibility is of importance during feeding, but the various shapes can often be noticed in dried specimens. In other genera, e. g. *Pangonius,* the labium and its stem are more rigid and of little flexibility. These forms are adapted for extracting nectar from flowers but are blood-suckers as well.

The mandibles and maxilles (= the stylets) are drawn out into stylet-like organs which are adapted for piercing. These four components and the hypopharynx with its salivary duct lie in a groove on the dorsal surface of the labium, reach to the base of the labella, and are covered dorsally by the labrum with its food-channel. When piercing and blood-sucking, the stylets are pushed into the skin, while the labella are folded back. The latter are then able to suck up the blood flowing from the wound. In *Pangonius* the stylets are normally much shorter than the labium, i. e. extend only a short way along the stem of the labium. How these organs work together is not known exactly. Mandibles have been lost in all male Tabanidae, and also in the females of some exotic genera, where tendencies to a reduction also occur.

The palpi are two-segmented, and the basal segment is often short. The apical segment is longer, often curved in the females, and more club-shaped in the males. The shape of the apical palpal segment may be of importance when identifying the species of certain groups.

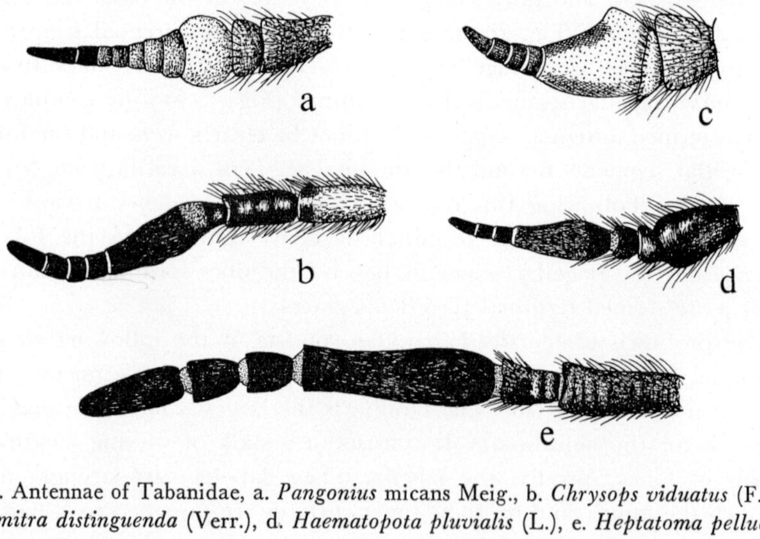

Fig. 2. Antennae of Tabanidae, a. *Pangonius* micans Meig., b. *Chrysops viduatus* (F.), c. *Hybomitra distinguenda* (Verr.), d. *Haematopota pluvialis* (L.), e. *Heptatoma pellucens* (F.).

Thorax

This section of the body is remarkably stable in structure. Macrochaetae never occur, either on the mesonotum or on the scutellum. The mesonotal pattern consists of broad dark bands which are separated by paler stripes or vittae. There is a dark median band which may be divided by a narrow paler stripe along the midline and which is limited laterally by similar paler stripes. Outside these stripes are sublateral dark bands. There are thus 3 or 4 bands depending on whether a pale middle stripe is present or not. The lateral areas of the mesonotum are not separated morphologically from the sublateral bands but are often differently coloured. Laterally there are two well-developed notopleural lobes on the mesonotum. The mesonotal pilosity is composed of longer, erect hairs and shorter, adpressed hairs. The erect pile is usually darker coloured than the adpressed one. The pleural sclerites are remarkably constant and do not have any distinct pattern. The pilosity may vary in length and is evenly distributed on all pleural sclerites except the hypopleura.

Wings

The venation is remarkably constant in the Tabanidae. Four radial veins are present. Vein R_4 and R_5 are widely separated and terminate on either side of the wing-tip. An appendix to vein R_4 may be present or absent. The anal cell may be open or closed. The presence of setulae on the basicosta (see fig. 3) at the base of the costa is an important character for separating the tribes Diachlorini and Tabanini. Vein Sc may have setulae, or may be bare as in all Pangoniinae.

The shape and pattern of the wings is more diverse. The shape tends to be longer and more pointed in the Pangoniinae, while in the Tabaninae the wings are broader and more blunt-tipped. The majority of Tabanidae have the wings clear or with a greyish or brownish tinge. *Chrysops* has distinctive wings which are strongly banded. In *Haematopota* the wings are dark and have a characteristic pattern of hyaline rosettes.

Legs

These only vary a little throughout the family. The middle tibia always has two spical spurs. In Pangoniinae and Chrysopsinae the hind tibia also has apical spurs, which are absent in Tabaninae.

Abdomen

The abdomen in Tabanidae is usually broadly built and often has a distinctive colour pattern. The lateral areas of the first tergites often have a

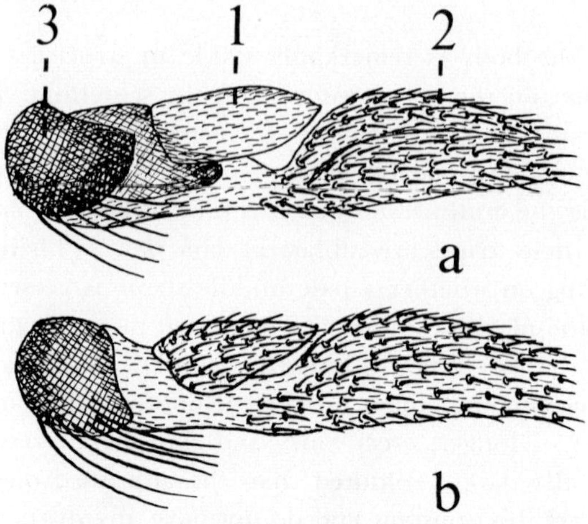

Fig. 3. Base of wing in: a. *Limata capensis* (Tribe Diachlorini) and b. *Tabanus taeniola* (Tribe Tabanini), 1 = basicosta, 2 = costa, 3 = tegula. (Redrawn after Oldroyd, 1954).

paler ground colour than the rest. A pale median line, that usually consists of pollinose areas, is another common feature. Paler hind margins of the tergites and sublateral rows of paler spots also have a common occurrence.

MALE GENITALIA (FIG. 4)

These are important for the classification of the higher categories, but cannot usually be used for the separation of genera and species. The genitalia are never rotated. The epandrium, which may include both tergites 9 and 10, is situated dorsally. It forms a cover above the other genital structures. The epandrium may form a single shield as in the Pangoniinae (Fig. 4a), or may be divided into two separate sclerites as in the other two subfamilies (Figs. 4b–c). Caudally the epandrium carries the paired cerci, and below these there is an unpaired sclerite. The anus is situated between these elements. The unpaired ventral sclerite may represent the paraprocts. It is an interesting fact that an intersegmental membrane is present between the paraprocts and the anteriorly situated margin of the dorsal portion of aedeagus. This may indicate that this dorsal part of the aedeagus contains elements of sternite 10.

Sternite 9 is fused with the bases of the gonocoxites, forming a continuous ventral sclerite. This may well be the plesiomorph condition in the Brachycera and in Diptera in general. It belongs to the ground-pattern of many Nematocera, and is found in Xylophagidae, all (?) Stratiomyidae and most Rhagionidae. This contradicts an earlier view of one of the authors (Lyne-

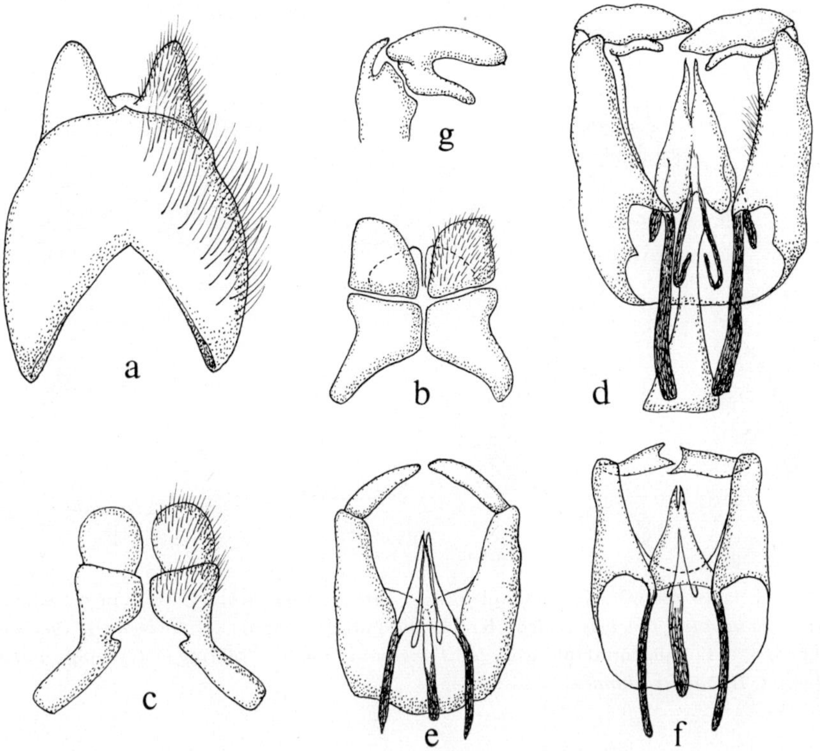

Fig. 4. Male genitalia in Tabanidae, a–c. Epandrium and cerci in dorsal view of: a. *Pangonius funebris* Macq., b. *Chrysops italicus* Meig., and c. *Hybomitra lundbecki* Lyneb. – d–f. Gonocoxites, styli and aedeagus in dorsal view of: d. *Pangonius funebris* Macq., e. *Chrysops italicus* Meig. and f. *Hybomitra lundbecki* Lyneb. – g. Stylus in caudal view of *Pangonius funebris* Macq.

borg, 1968). The question is connected with the presence or absence of a sclerotized bridge between the dorsal edge of the gonocoxite and the dorsal part of aedeagus. Such a bridge seems to occur in all Tabanoidea. Its occurrence in some groups of Therevidae and Asilidae (Lyneborg, 1968) was previously regarded as apomorphic, but seems to be a plesiomorphic character. The occurrence of a sclerotized element on the dorsal edge in some Therevidae and Asilidae, e. g. *Thereva* and *Dioctria,* then leads to the assumption that it has evolved secondarily, and the term »gonapophysis« is thus quite misleading. We propose to term this »dorsal gonocoxal process«.

Apically the gonocoxites carry the styli which are bifid in all European Pangoniinae (Figs. 4d & g), simple and bluntly tipped in Chrysopsinae (Fig. 4e) and truncate in Tabaninae (Fig. 4f).

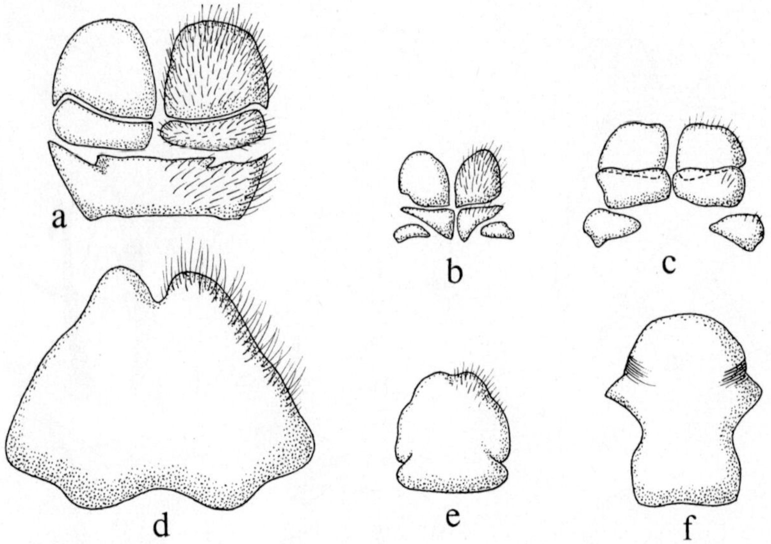

Fig. 5. Female genitalia in Tabanidae, a–c. Terminal tergites and cerci in dorsal view of: a. *Pangonius funebris* Macq., b. *Chrysops italicus* Meig., c. *Hybomitra lundbecki* Lyneb. – d–f. Subgenital plate of: d. *Pangonius funebris* Macq., e. *Chrysops italicus* Meig., f. *Hybomitra lundbecki* Lyneb.

The aedeagus (Figs. 4d–f) itself is rather uncomplicated in the Tabanidae. The phallic part is funnel-shaped but open ventrally. Long sclerotized sticks are loosely attached to the point where the aedeagus is connected with the gonocoxite. The homology of these sticks is unclear. A well-developed ejaculatory apodeme is present. At the proximal end of the ejaculatory apodeme two pairs of structures are attached, viz. a pair of small medial sclerites and a pair of long, flagellum-like structures which reach through the lumen of the aedeagal funnel. These so-called flagella (an unfortunate term) are strongly developed and strongly curved in e. g. *Pangonius* (Fig. 4d), but are weaker and straight in e. g. *Chrysops* (Fig. 4e).

Female genitalia (Fig. 5)

These are usually dorsoventrally compressed, and are never rotated. Tergite 9 shows the same differences as in the male, consisting of a transverse bar in the Pangoniinae (Fig. 5a) but of a pair of widely separated sclerites in the Chrysopsinae (Fig. 5b) and the Tabaninae (Fig. 5c). Tergite 10 is nearly always divided and shows variation in the degree of sclerotization. The cerci are 1-segmented. Sternite 8 and the gonapophysies form a shield ventrally. The shape of this complex (Figs. 5d–f) shows some interesting variations, in both higher and lower systematic categories. The genital fork or furca lies dorsally of sternite 9 and is usually large and irregular in shape. Three spermathecae are present. These are oval or fusiform in shape and lie at the level of segment 6 or 7. The spermathecal ducts are very long, slender, and lightly sclerotized and pigmented. At first they are directed anteriorly, but then double back and run to the tip of abdomen, where they meet in an ampulla on the dorsal surface of the genital fork. The posterior ends of the ducts, just before they enter the ampulla, are thickened in a characteristic manner. This thickening is straight and cylindrical in the Pangoniinae and Chrysopsinae, or at most with slight funnel-shaped expansions apically, whereas in the Tabaninae there is a characteristic mushroom-shaped expansion at the apex of this thickened part.

CHAPTER 9

Classification

Modern workers on Tabanidae now generally accept the classification elaborated by Mackerras (1954, 1955). He divides the family into three subfamilies, Pangoniinae, Chrysopsinae and Tabaninae. All three subfamilies are represented in the European fauna.

The subfamily Pangoniinae is regarded as containing the more primitive Tabanidae, that is to say its members have the largest number of plesiomorphic characters. These can be summarized as follows:

Antennae short and subulate (Fig. 2a).
Flagellum composed of 6–8 segments, of which the basal one is larger than the following flagellar segments (Fig. 2a).
Proboscis well-developed, sometimes strongly elongate.
Ocelli usually well-developed (Fig. 1a).
Hind tibia nearly always with paired apical spurs.
Vein Sc bare above and below.
Tergite 9 of ♂ forming a complete undivided shield (Fig. 4a).
Tergite 9 of ♀ normally forming a narrow transverse bar (Fig. 5a).
Stylus of ♂ simple or bifid (Fig. 4d & g).
Caudal ends of spermathecal ducts of ♀ without mushroom-like expansions.

The Pangoniinae is divided into four tribes, Pangoniini, Scionini, Philolichini and Scepsidini. The Pangoniini is regarded as the more primitive of these tribes, and the two European Pangoniine-genera, *Stonemyia* and *Pangonius,* belong to this tribe. The tribe is characterized by having ocelli well-developed, eyes usually bare, and vein R_4 nearly always with a strong appendix. The stylus of the ♂ is bifid and the gonapophyses of ♀ (Fig. 5d) are close together. The members of this tribe are distributed in the Palaearctic, Nearctic, Neotropical and Australasian regions.

The subfamily Chrysopsinae, together with the Tabaninae, may be the sister-group of the Pangoniinae. The characters of this subfamily are:

Antennae short or long (Fig. 2b).
Flagellum composed of what is usually termed antennal segment 3 and some terminal flagellar segments; segment 3 represents a fusion of probably 4 flagellar segments and often shows traces of annulation (Fig. 2b).
Ocelli well-developed (Fig. 1c).
Frontal callus usually well-developed (Fig. 1c).
Hind tibia with paired apical spurs.
Vein Sc bare or setulose.
Vein R_4 rarely with appendix.

Tergite 9 divided in both sexes (Figs. 4b & 5b).
Stylus of ♂ simple, more or less bluntly tipped (Fig. 4e).
Caudal ends of spermathecal ducts of ♀ forming simple tubes, without mushroom-like expansions.

The Chrysopsinae are divided into three tribes, Bouvieromyiini, Chrysopsini and Rhinomyzini. The three European genera *(Silvius, Nemorius* and *Chrysops)* belong to the Chrysopsini. These are slender forms, with long and slender antennae, a wide frons with a large callus and often with additional facial and genal calli, and the eyes bare with a characteristic pattern. Most Chrysopsini are found in the tropics of South America and Africa, but the tribe is also well represented in the Nearctic and Palaearctic regions.

Whether the subfamily Tabaninae is the sister-group of the Chrysopsinae is unclear and is probably too simple a solution. The Tabaninae are characterized as follows:

Antennae mainly as in Chrysopsinae, but the complexity of what is termed antennal segment 3 is more concealed (Figs. 2c–e).
Ocelli usually absent, but when present poorly developed and inconspicuous (Figs. 1b, d, e).
Frontal calli usually well-developed (Figs. 1b, d, e).
Hind tibia never with apical spurs.
Vein Sc setulose at least below, in all genera except *Heptatoma.*
Vein R_4 often with an appendix.
Tergite 9 as in the Chrysopsinae (Figs. 4c & 5c).
Stylus of ♂ truncate (Fig. 4f).
Caudal ends of spermathecal ducts of ♀ with expansions like inverted mushrooms.

The three tribes of the Tabaninae are the Diachlorini, Haematopotini and Tabanini. All three tribes are represented in Europe. The European species of the Diachlorini belong to *Philipomyia* and *Dasyrhamphis.* They have the basicosta bare (Fig. 3b), the antennae are short, often with a strong dorsal hook on segment 3, the frons is comparatively narrow, and the wings are often infuscated or patterned. Both genera are found only in the southern part of Europe. The tribe as a whole is well represented in the tropics of the Old and New World.

The Haematopotini consists of one large genus, *Haematopota,* with numerous species in Africa and the Palaearctic and Oriental regions, and three further monotypic genera of which one, *Heptatoma,* is European. The tribe is characterized by the sparsely setulose basicosta, the very wide female frons (Fig. 1b) with a lower callus and paired velvety spots, the very long and slender antennae (Fig. 2d—e), and the characteristically mottled wings.

Finally, in the Tabanini are found the majority of the European Tabanidae, divided among the genera *Therioplectes, Atylotus, Glaucops, Hybomitra* and *Tabanus.* In this tribe the basicosta is strongly setulose, the frons

(Fig. 1d–e) of medium to narrow width in the female and usually has distinct calli, the antennae (Fig. 2c) are short and stout and nearly always with a distinct dorsal tooth on segment 3, the terminal flagellar segments are normally 4 in number, and the wings are never mottled but are sometimes infuscated.

CHAPTER 10

Key to subfamilies and genera of European Tabanidae

1 Hind tibiae with apical spurs. Vertex usually with functional ocelli on distinct tubercle 2

– No apical spurs to hind tibiae. No functional ocelli present, vertex at most with ocellar swelling. Subfamily *Tabaninae* 6

2 (1) Flagellum of antennae composed of 7 or 8 segments, basal segment of flagellum not much differentiated from the following segments. Labella very small and narrow. Proboscis conspicuously long, longer than head is high. Subfamily *Pangoniinae* 3

– Flagellum composed of only 5 segments, terminal four segments distinctly shorter and narrower than basal segment (= antennal segment 3). Labella rather large and swollen, occupying about one-third of length of proboscis. Proboscis much shorter. Subfamily *Chrysopsinae* 4

3 (2) First posterior cell open. Labrum slightly longer than head is high. Ocelli absent (Fig. 6a) .... *Stonemyia* Bren.

– First posterior cell closed. Labrum usually much longer than head is high. Ocelli present .... *Pangonius* Latr.

4 (2) Antennal segments 1–2 long and narrow, nearly equal in length. Face with distinct facial and genal calli, or at least facial calli slightly developed. Wings with brown pattern .... *Chrysops* Meig

– Antennal segment 2 distinctly shorter than segment 1. Face without calli, wings clear 5

5 (4) Antennal segment 1 long and slender, segment 2 shortened but about twice as long as deep. Mostly greyish species, eyes with central spot or isolated bar when relaxed .... *Nemorius* Rond.

– Antennal segment 1 shortened and stout, segment 2 very short, as long as deep. Mostly yellow or yellowish-brown species with freckled eyes when relaxed .... *Silvius* Meig.

6 (1) Flagellum of antennae composed of 5 segments, basal segment (or antennal segment 3) being a fusion of 4 flagellar segments and having a more or less developed dorsal tooth, sometimes strongly hooked 7

– Flagellum of antennae composed of 4 segments, basal segment (or antennal segment 3) being a fusion of 5 flagellar segments and slender, without dorsal tooth (except for *Glaucops*) 12

7 (6) Basicosta bare. Rather robust species with flat, broad abdomen. Ocellar tubercle absent 8

– Basicosta strongly setulose. Species of various size, abdomen rather elongated (except for *Therioplectes*). Ocellar tubercle sometimes developed 9

8 (7) Eyes bare, frontal calli of female joined into a single keelshaped callus. Wings always clear, abdomen yellowish-brown to dark brown .... *Philipomyia* Ols.

– Eyes usually at least microscopically pubescent, frontal calli well developed. Mostly blackish species with more or less clouded wings .... *Dasyrhamphis* End.

9 (7) Eyes in living specimens light yellowish to pale green-grey, usually with one incomplete narrow band, or unbanded; in dry specimens eyes light to reddish-brown coloured. Frontal calli in female reduced, very small or absent. Generally smaller, light grey or yellowish-brown species .... *Atylotus* Ost.-Sack.

– Eyes in living specimens bright green to dark reddish-brown, with 1 to 4 bands or unbanded; in dry specimens eyes blackish. Frontal calli in female well developed. Dark or light species of various size 10

10 (9) Posterior four tibiae very stout and densely whitish haired. Eyes pubescent, unbanded. Large blackish and bright coloured species, densely black, pale and rufuous haired, resembling humble-bees .... *Therioplectes* Zell.

– Posterior four tibiae slender and never conspicuously whitish haired. Smaller or larger, usually uniformly black, grey or reddish-brown species, only seldom bright coloured 11

11 (10) Vertex with usually well developed shining ocellar tubercle. Eyes more or less haired, usually with 3 bands. Mostly blackish species, often with striking reddish-brown sidemarkings on anterior tergites .... *Hybomitra* End.

– Ocellar tubercle absent, eyes bare (except for the *quatuornotatus*-group) with 1 to 4 bands or unbanded. Usually greyish or brownish species of various sixe (see also paragraph 14, *Glaucops*) *Tabanus* L.

12 (6) Wings with distinct grey-brown pattern of small spots and rosettes. Basal part of antennal segment 3 slender but distinctly differentiated from three terminal flagellar segments. *Haematopota* Meig.

– Wings clear, without any pattern 13

13 (12) Antennae very long and slender, more than twice as long as head is deep. Flagellum with basal segment not clearly differentiated from the three terminal flagellar segments. Antennae look like six-segmented .... *Heptatoma* Meig.

– Antennae short, tabanine-like, basal part of first flagellar segment with a distinct dorsal tooth; terminal flagellar segments short, stout and indistinctly separated .... *Glaucops* Szil.

Chapter 11

Subfamily Pangoniinae

TRIBE PANGONIINI

GENUS *STONEMYIA* BRENNAN, 1935

Kans. Univ. Sci. Bull., 22: 360.

Type species: *Pangonia tranquilla* Osten-Sacken, 1875.

Diagnosis. Rather smaller species with bare eyes, frons in female convergent above or almost parallel-sided. Vertex with more or less developed ocellar tubercle, ocelli present or absent. Frontal calli usually absent. Face more or less prominent, polished or dusted. Antennae almost as long as head is deep, flagellum consists of 8 slightly differentiated segments. Legs long and slender, hind tibiae with apical spurs. Wings clear or clouded, usually a long appendix to vein R_4, first posterior cell always open. Proboscis long as in *Pangonius* Latr., usually longer than head is high.

Remarks. The genus is distributed in the Holarctic region, altogether 9 species have recently been placed in this genus, 5 species are North American and 4 species Palaearctic. From this number only one species is known from Europe, viz. *S. hispanica* (Kröb.), which was described from Spain and is still known only from the female type.

STONEMYIA HISPANICA (KRÖBER, 1921)

Fig. 6.

Corizoneura hispanica Kröber, 1921, Arch. Naturgesch., Abt. A, 87 (1): 14.

Diagnosis. Smaller species with abdomen mostly black, wings slightly yellowish-brown tinted, all posterior cells including the first open. Frons greyish dusted without calli, ocelli absent. Labrum slightly longer than head is high, legs uniformly brownish.

Description. ♀. *Head* slightly broader than thorax, frons and face pinkish-brown in ground colour. Frons densely greyish dusted and finely pale haired, distinctly convergent above. Vertex with only indistinctly visible ocellar tubercle, ocelli absent. Occiput densely whitish-grey dusted, only finely pale haired above neck, below with long whitish hairs. Face only thinly greyish dusted, clothed with long whitish hairs on lower parts and at sides. Antennae brownish, segment 3 darkened towards tip, basal two segments with some long greyish hairs. Palpi dark brown, apical segment slender and pointed, bare. Labrum mostly black, brownish at base, slightly longer than head is high.

Thorax black in ground colour and entirely densely whitish-yellow haired, mesopleura with some more yellowish-brown hairs. Notopleural lobes and postalar calli rather reddish-brown. *Legs* uniformly brown, coxae somewhat greyish dusted and with long whitish-yellow hairs as on thoracic pleura, otherwise legs only short black haired. *Wings* very faintly yellowish-brown tinted, veins yellowish-brown, but costa blackish; a long appendix to vein R_4. First posterior cell narrowed apically but open; fourth posterior cell likewise narrowed apically, second and third posterior cells broadly open. Squamae yellowish, halteres yellow, stem brownish.

Abdomen brown on anterior two segments, following segments black with indefinite dark brown to reddish-brown posterior margins. Tergite 2 with a small and narrow perpendicular black median spot, blackish at sides. Sternite 2 blackish at middle. Whole of abdomen short but rather densely pale haired.

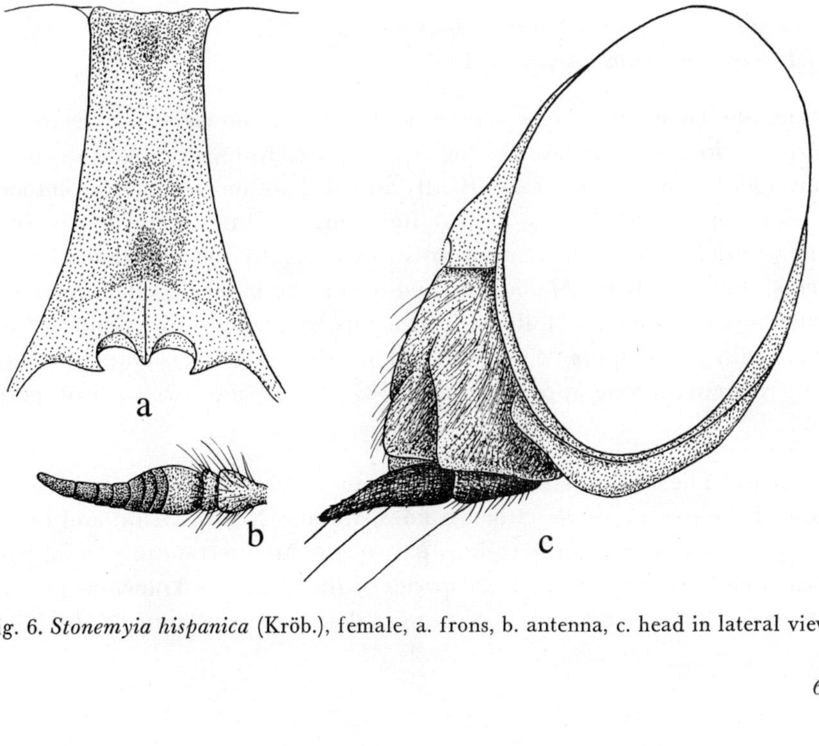

Fig. 6. *Stonemyia hispanica* (Kröb.), female, a. frons, b. antenna, c. head in lateral view.

♂. Unknown.
Length. 14 mm.

REMARKS. This species is still only known from the female holotype deposited in the Zoologische Staatssammlung, München, labelled »Type«, »Type von Kröber ex coll. Engel«, »Corizoneura ♀ hispanica Kröber, det. O. Kröber, 1919«, »888«, »aperta Lw. ex coll. Lw., Spanien« and »lateralis«. The above description is based on this specimen.

DATES. Unknown.

DISTRIBUTION. Spain.

GENUS *PANGONIUS* LATREILLE, 1802

Hist. nat. Crust. Ins., 3: 437.

Pangonia auct. nec Latreille.
Tanyglossa Meigen, 1804, Klass., 1: 174.
Tacina Walker, 1850, Ins. Saunders., 1: 9.
Dasysilvius Enderlein, 1922, Mitt. zool. Mus. Berl., 10: 343.
Taeniopangonia Szilády, 1923, Biologica hung., 1 (1): 30.

TYPE SPECIES: *Tabanus proboscideus* Fabricius, 1794
(=*Tabanus mauritanus* Linné, 1767).

DIAGNOSIS. Generally larger species with long proboscis which is usually distinctly longer than head is high. Eyes bare, frons in female distinctly convergent above, frontal calli usually absent. Face more or less prominent, polished or dusted. Vertex with 3 functional ocelli. Antennae almost as long as head is deep, flagellum consists of 8 usually not differentiated segments; only in subgen. *Melanopangonius* Szil. the basal flagellar segment is differentiated from the following segments. Legs long and slender, hind tibiae with apical spurs. Wings often clouded or distinctly spotted on forks and crossveins, a long appendix to vein R_4, first posterior cell closed, petiolate.

REMARKS. The genus is distributed mainly in the Mediterranean region, most of the species are described from Spain and North Africa, and only 8 species are known from the eastern part of the Mediterranean region, from Syria and Turkey. More than 25 species of the genus are known at present, but only 2 rather uncertain species were described from outside the Mediterranean region, viz. *senegalensis* Macquart, 1834, from Senegal and *sinensis* Enderlein, 1922, from China. Altogether 18 species in 2 subgenera have been found so far in Europe.

The genus *Pangonius* Latr. has not been revised recently except for the species described by Fabricius, which have been studied by Chvála and Lyneborg (1970), but the genus calls for a precise modern revision. Only a little is known on the biology and life history of *Pangonius* species, and the immature stages are still unknown. Females of European *Pangonius* have not been observed as being blood-suckers, although some Pangoniinae with similar very long proboscis are blood-sucking, viz., species of the genus *Philoliche* Wied. They are collected together with males on flowers, especially on *Knautia, Scabiosa, Lavandula, Echium, Salvia, Silybum, Centaurea, Galactites, Eupatorium,* etc. The females when sucking on flowers may be taken very easily.

Key to European species of *Pangonius*

1 Flagellum broadened at base, basal segments distinctly broader than following segments, and basal two segments short, not as long as broad. Generally black species, at most with only small brownish sidemarkings on anterior segments (subgen. *Melanopangonius* Szil.) 2

– Flagellum not so distinctly broadened at base, basal two segments at least as long as broad and not differentiated from following segments. Usually more or less brownish coloured species on abdomen, if blackish, then densely pale haired (subgen. *Pangonius* s. str.) 6

2 (1) Face covered with yellow tomentum, only extreme apex reddish-yellow. Antennae reddish-yellow, flagellum darkened towards tip. Legs reddish-yellow, wings faintly spotted on forks and crossveins .... *brevicornis* Kröb. ♀

– Face polished black or blackish-brown at least on apical third to quarter. Antennae black or reddish-brown 3

3 (2) Abdomen polished black, anterior three tergites with small reddish-brown sidemarkings. Wings faintly uniformly clouded. Generally smaller species, 15.5–16 mm in length .... *griseipennis* Loew ♀

– Abdomen entirely polished black, no brownish sidemarkings. Generally larger species, 15–21 mm in length 4

4 (3) Wings yellowish-brown clouded or almost clear, veins brown; squamae pale yellowish. Antennae (Figs. 7b–c) mostly reddish-brown. Lower part of head, thorax and part of abdomen covered with pale greyish hairs. Femora brown in female .... *micans* Meig.

– Wings darker brown clouded with dark brown veins. Antennae (Figs. 8b–c, 9b–c) black, at most segment 3 slightly brownish at extreme base. Femora black in both sexes 5

5 (4) Lower part of head, thorax including mesonotum and part of abdomen with mostly pale yellowish-grey hairs. Legs bicoloured, tibiae dark brown to blackish-brown .... *haustellatus* (F.)

– Pilosity on head, thorax and abdomen unicolorous blackish-brown, only 3–4 posterior abdominal segments with short reddish hairs. Legs entirely black including tibiae .... *funebris* Macq.

6 (1) Face (Figs. 10c, 11c, 12c) entirely polished black or blackish-brown with no trace of greyish tomentum (*pyritosus*-group) 7

– Face (Figs. 13c, 21b) more or less covered with greyish tomentum, at least on basal third to quarter 9

7 (6) Legs unicolorous yellowish-brown to brown 8

– Legs bicoloured, femora black or at least darker than tibiae. Wings distinctly brownish, especially on costal half, dark grey infuscated along veins on apical part and dark spotted. ♀: Abdomen black coloured and densely silvery-grey haired, anterior two tergites with slightly brownish small areas at sides. ♂: Tergites 1–3 mostly orange to reddish-brown, blackish median spots very small .... *pyritosus* Loew

8 (7) Yellowish-grey species in ground colour, face polished blackish-brown to brown. Legs yellowish-brown to reddish-brown. Wings tinted yellowish-brown with rather yellowish veins, faintly dark spotted. ♀: Abdomen mostly brownish and covered with dense greyish-yellow tomentum and concolorous hairs, anterior 2 or 3 segments translucent orange at sides. ♂: Abdomen orange on anterior tergites, black median spots small .... *fulvipes* Loew

– Greyish to dark grey species in ground colour, face polished black. Legs rather brown. Wings brown clouded especially on costal half, veins dark brown, only very faintly spotted. ♀: Abdomen rather polished black and densely black and silvery-grey haired; anterior two tergites with only a trace of brown coloration at extreme sides. ♂: Tergites 1–3 orange at sides, black median stripe broad .. .. *obscuratus* Loew

9 (6) Face (Figs. 13c, 14d) entirely covered by greyish tomentum, at most extreme tip slightly subshining (*mauritanus*-group) 10

– Face (Fig. 21b) distinctly dusted at base, at least apical third to quarter polished black to brown (*variegatus*-group) 13

10 (9) Legs unicolorous yellowish-brown to light brown, femora not darker than tibiae 11

– Legs with femora extensively darkened, always distinctly darker than tibiae 12

11 (10) Face very conical and strongly protruding (Fig. 13c). ♂: Abdomen mostly orange-brown, dark grey spots reduced or absent on tergite 3 and following tergites .... *mauritanus* (L.)

– Face low and rounded (Fig. 14b). ♂: Abdomen orange-brown, without dark grey spots in median line .... *sobradieli* Séguy

12 (10) Wings almost clear with small, faintly brown spots on forks and crossveins. Antennae yellowish-brown, segment 3 slightly darkened towards tip. Abdomen unicolorous brownish in both sexes, tergites black haired on anterior halves, posteriorly and on median triangles with silvery-white hairs .... *striatus* Szil.

– Wings brownish clouded, not spotted. Antennal segment 3 mostly black, brownish at base. Abdomen mostly black, anterior two tergites with large orange sidemarkings in both sexes, male with smaller lateral spots also on following tergites .... *escalerae* Strobl

13 (9) Wings spotted on forks and crossveins, at least distinctly infuscated along veins 14

– Wings almost clear or uniformly tinted, not spotted 16

14 (13) Abdomen unicolorous black to dark olive-brown in ground colour, only tergite 1 almost entirely brownish. Wings brownish clouded and distinctly dark spotted. Palpi, legs and antennae (Fig. 15b) reddish-brown to brown .... *hermanni* Kröb.

– Lighter species with large orange-brown sidemarkings on anterior tergites, blackish on median stripe only 15

15 (14) Femora reddish-brown to dark brown, antennae (Fig. 16a) reddish-brown. Wings slightly tinted brownish and distinctly dark brown spotted. Mesonotum unstriped, halteres brown .... *variegatus* F.

– Femora shining black, antennal segment 3 (Fig. 17a) black, brownish at extreme base only. Wings somewhat yellowish and only faintly brown spotted. Mesonotum more or less striped, halteres whitish-yellow .... *granatensis* Strobl

16 (13) Face (Fig. 18c) rather short and rounded, not very conical; anterior polished part brown to blackish. Wings almost clear or very slightly greyish-brown. Femora mostly blackish, abdomen orange-brown at sides in both sexes, in female on anterior two tergites only .... *fumidus* Loew

– Face conical, polished black at least on apical third. Wings more or less clouded 17

17 (16) Smaller species, 13–16 mm in length. Venter of abdomen mostly orange, at least on anterior four sternites at sides. Apical segment of palpi and antennal segment 1 with pale hairs, halteres yellowish .... *affinis* Loew

– Larger species, 16.5–18.5 mm in length. Venter of abdomen entirely black. Apical segment of palpi and antennal segment 1 with black hairs. Halteres dark brown 18

18 (17) Paler, more orange coloured species. ♀: Black median stripe on abdomen narrowest on tergite 2, occupying there at most one-third of tergite. ♂: Black median stripe on abdomen narrow .... *ferrugineus* (Meig.)

– Darker species with sidemarkings reddish-brown. ♀: Black median stripe evenly broad on anterior three tergites, leaving only small lateral reddish-brown spots. ♂: Black median stripe on abdomen broad .... *dimidiatus* Loew

SUBGENUS *MELANOPANGONIUS* SZILADY, 1923

Biologica hung., 1 (1): 30.

Generally black species with flagellum broad at base, basal flagellar segment enlarged and somewhat globular, distinctly separated from the following flagellar segments.

The subgenus comprises 5 species distributed only in the Mediterranean region, all have been found in South Europe.

PANGONIUS (MELANOPANGONIUS) BREVICORNIS KRÖBER, 1921

Pangonia brevicornis Kröber, 1921, Arch. Naturgesch., Abt. A, 87 (1): 19.

DIAGNOSIS. Small blackish species with abdomen black, face almost entirely yellowish dusted, dull reddish-yellow apically. Wings faintly brownish tinted and brownish spotted. Antennae and legs reddish-yellow.

We have not seen this species and therefore we present a translation of the original *description.*

♀. »Frons ochreous-yellow dusted, in front of ocellar tubercle with several black setae. Ocellar tubercle grey with some short black hairs. Ocelli yellowish. Occiput grey, sparsely short whitish haired. Antennae light reddish-yellow, laterally very compressed. Segment 1 1.5 times as long as deep, laterally rounded, with some short black setae. Segments 2 half as long as segment 1, black haired. Flagellum composed of eight segments. First flagellar segment large, circular in lateral view, much deeper than first and second antennal segments. Apical three flagellar segments brownish. Apical flagellar segment long conical and armed with several black hairs at tip. Flagellum lanceolate in lateral view. Face as long as diameter of eye, yellowish dusted, apex reddish-yellow, almost dull, dorsal part greyish. Cheeks with very sparse whitish-yellow hairs. Lower part of head with long whitish-yellow hairs. Palpi reddish-yellow, very short. Palpal segment 1 style-like, with short, erect black hairs, segment 2 scarcely three times as long as deep and clothed with very short, adpressed black setae. Proboscis reddish-yellow, about 1.5 times longer than head.

Thorax. Mesonotum black in ground colour, densely grey dusted, paler longitudinal stripes hardly visible. Pilosity woolly, pale rufuous-yellow. Postalar calli brown. Scutellum black, sparsely greyish haired. Pleura black, grey dusted. Squamae pale ochreous-yellow with whitish hairs. Halteres pale reddish-yellow, knob somewhat brownish.

Abdomen very arched, short, entirely black, slightly shining with greyish tint. Segment 1 entirely dull. All posterior margins narrowly yellowish with fine, adpressed, shining white pubescence. Venter agrees with the dorsum but due to tomentum is generally olive coloured. *Legs* reddish-yellow, fine black haired. Coxae black, greyish-brown dusted, long whitish haired; fore coxae with long black hairs intermixed. Tips of all tarsal segments somewhat darkened. *Wings* faintly brownish tinted. Anterior margin with a broad yellowish-brown clouding up to second basal cell. There is a hyaline quoin-like area at base of first basal cell, and another one on a vein between both basal cells. All crossveins brown clouded, likewise the fork of vein R_4

including an appendix and apex of the closed first posterior cell. The appendix is shorter than basal part of upper branch. Veins yellow, partly black.«

♂. Unknown.

Length. 11 mm.

REMARKS. The species was described from a single female from Casablanca, Morocco; the female holotype should be deposited in the Museum in Berlin.

DATES. June.

DISTRIBUTION. Morocco and Spain.

PANGONIUS (MELANOPANGONIUS) GRISEIPENNIS LOEW, 1859

Pangonia griseipennis Loew, 1859, Neue Beitr., 6: 31.

DIAGNOSIS. Blackish species, abdomen black with anterior three tergites slightly yellowish laterally at hind corners, all tergites with whitish haired posterior margins and more or less visible median triangles. Face prominent, polished black at tip above and at sides, otherwise greyish dusted. Wings greyish clouded especially on costal half towards apex. Antennae mostly black; legs bicoloured, femora black, tibiae yellowish-brown.

We have not seen this species and therefore present a translation of the original *description.*

♀. »Face very strongly prolonged, black, the arched median part greyish dusted, dull and armed with several fine yellowish hairs, polished black at sides and at mouth-opening. First palpal segment black with yellowish hairs, second segment dark brown, not very long. Proboscis black, brown at base. Narrow lateral parts of face, cheeks, occiput, and the comparatively broad frons, dulled by yellowish-grey dust. The hairs on occiput and cheeks pale yellowish. Antennae black, only extreme base of flagellum reddish. Segments 2 and 3 grey dusted; short hairs on segment 1 mainly yellowish, black on segment 2.

Thorax, scutellum, pleura and coxae light yellowish haired. *Abdomen* entirely black, only the extreme posterior corners of segments 1—3 often yellowish; segment 2 and following segments with short, almost white haired posterior margins, which form rather obtuse-angled median triangles reaching the anterior margins; segment 1 with similar whitish pubescence at middle; otherwise the pubescence on anterior two segments is pale yellowish, on following segments yellowish-white at sides, and mostly black on anterior parts. Venter blackish with whitish pubescence especially on posterior margins of segments. Femora black. Pubescence yellowish, on anterior pair mostly black. Tibiae brown-yellow. *Wings* greyish clouded; the clouding is more intensive anteriorly on apical half, becoming there more brownish; discal cell and basal cells more hyaline in contrast to basal parts of wing.«

♂. Unknown.

Length. 15–16 mm.

REMARKS. The type material should be deposited in the Museum in Berlin.

DATES. June and July.

DISTRIBUTION. Spain; described by Loew from Spain, Arias (1914) and Leclercq (1966a) recorded it from several Spanish localities.

PANGONIUS (MELANOPANGONIUS) MICANS MEIGEN, 1820

Fig. 7; pl. 1: fig. b.

Bombylius haustellatus Olivier, 1789, Encycl. Méth., 4: 329 (nec Fabricius, 1781).
Pangonia micans Meigen, 1820, Syst. Beschr., 2: 25.
Pangonia ornata Meigen, 1820, Syst. Beschr., 2: 26.

DIAGNOSIS. Large blackish species with yellowish-brown tinted wings, light yellow squamae and brown legs, only femora in male sometimes darkened. Face polished black on apical third, antennae reddish-brown. Pubescence on head and thorax silvery-grey to yellowish-grey, abdomen black with paler pattern of light pubescence.

DESCRIPTION. ♀. *Head.* Frons grey to yellowish-grey dusted, distinctly convergent above. Face likewise dusted on basal two-thirds, apical third polished black. Occiput and lower part of head whitish-grey haired. Antennae reddish-brown, basal segments and tip of flagellum often darkened. Palpi dark brown, apical segment almost naked, basal segment pale haired. Labrum black, distinctly longer than head is high.

Thorax blackish in ground colour, rather thinly greyish dusted; mesonotum short pale haired, pleura with longer, mostly yellowish-grey hairs. *Legs* with coxae concolorous with pleura and similarly long pale haired, otherwise legs uniformly reddish-brown to brown coloured. *Wings* more or less uniformly yellowish-brown clouded, sometimes only very faintly, almost clear. Veins dark brown, base of wing including both basal cells somewhat yellowish. Squamae light yellowish, halteres light brown with very darkened knob.

Abdomen black in ground colour and rather shining, tergite 1 densely light grey dusted. Sides of tergite 2 and large median triangles on tergites 2 – 3 or to 4 silvery-grey haired, the median triangles usually form a median stripe; posterior margins of all segments (very broad on apical tergites) and sides of posterior tergites yellowish-grey haired. Venter with broader yellowish-grey haired posterior margins on sternites 3 – 6, sternite 2 predominantly with silvery-grey hairs.

♂. Resembling female in all characters including the abdominal hairing, but femora sometimes extensively darkened. Eye-facets almost equal in size.

Length. 15.5–20 mm.

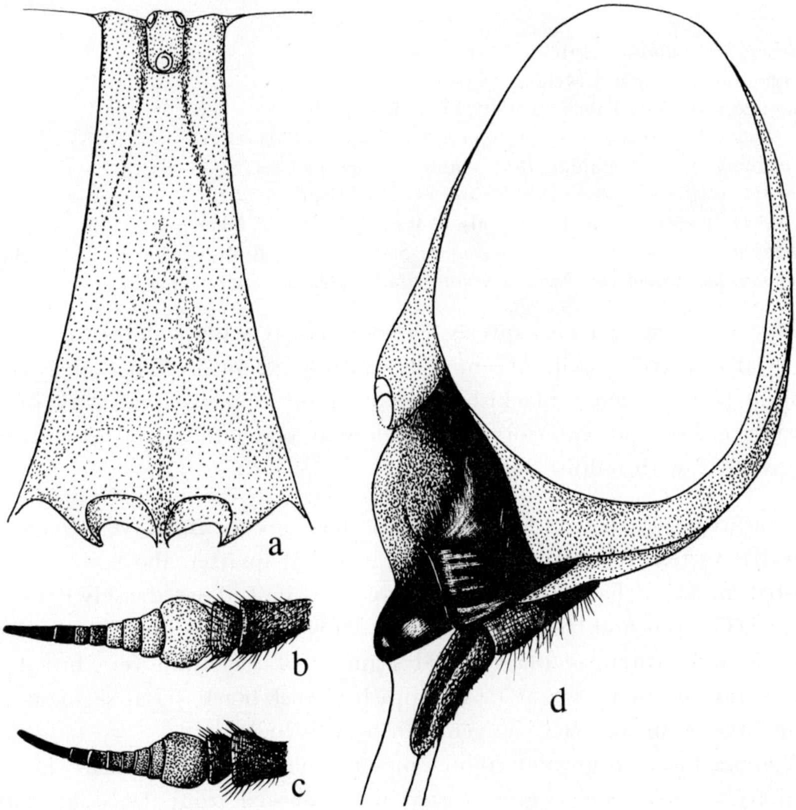

Fig. 7. *Pangonius (Melanopangonius) micans* Meig., a. female frons, b. female antenna, c. male antenna, d. female head in lateral view.

Dates. From May until August.

Distribution. A South European species known from Portugal, Spain, France, South West Germany, Italy, Jugoslavia and Greece including Corfu; from North Africa it is known only from Morocco. It is the only one species of the genus which penetrates far northwards to Central Europe (South West Germany) but not recorded from Switzerland or Austria. We have seen documentary material from South France, Spain, Italy and Germany (Kaiserstuhl).

PANGONIUS (MELANOPANGONIUS) HAUSTELLATUS (FABRICIUS, 1781)

Fig. 8.

Tabanus haustellatus Fabricius, 1781, Spec. Ins., 2: 455.
Tanyglossa mauritanica Meigen, 1804, Klass., p. 176.
Pangonia marginata Fabricius, 1805, Syst. Ant., p. 90.
Pangonia cellulata Brullé, 1832, Exped. Sci. Morée, 3: 303.
? *Pangonia aterrima* Dufour, 1853, Annls Soc. ent. Fr. (Ser. 3), 1: 388.
Pangonia atrifera Walker, 1860, Trans. ent. Soc. Lond., 5: 272.
Pangonia marginata var. *tenuipalpis* Kröber, 1921, Arch. Naturgesch., Abt. A, 87: 22.
Pangonia marginata var. *medioargentata* Szilády, 1923, Biologica hung., 1 (1): 23.
Pangonia marginata var. *basiargentata* Szilády, 1923, Biologica hung., 1 (1): 23.

Diagnosis. Large blackish species, wings extensively blackish-brown clouded especially on costal half. Antennae blackish, segment 3 often slightly brownish at base; squamae blackish. Legs black on femora, tibiae dark brown. Head, thorax and anterior two abdominal segments silvery-grey haired, tergites 3–7 with reddish hairs.

Description. ♀. *Head.* Frons grey to dark grey dusted, very narrowed towards vertex. Face polished black on apical quarter above, very thinly dusted on apical half and at sides, only basal half above densely dark grey dusted. Occiput and cheeks rather dark brownish-grey coloured and silvery-grey haired. Antennae black, basal segment of flagellum very broad and often translucent brown at base. Palpi brownish-black, basal segment with pale hairs. Labrum black, longer than head is high.

Thorax black in ground colour, mesonotum subshining black when viewed from above, silvery-grey dusted when viewed from the side; clothed with short silvery-grey hairs; humeri and lateral margins of mesonotum often brownish. Pleura and coxae subshining black from some points of views, densely light grey haired. *Legs:* Femora black with short rufuous hairs, tibiae and tarsi dark brown to blackish-brown. *Wings* blackish-brown clouded, leaving posterior margin paler; veins blackish. Squamae blackish, halteres blackish-brown with paler knob at tip.

Abdomen entirely black, rather shining, anterior two tergites densely short silvery-grey to whitish-grey haired, following segments with reddish-brown to rufuous hairs.

♂. Closely resembling female but pubescence on thorax usually more yellowish-grey. All facets almost equal in size. Abdomen with the same pattern of coloration and pubescence as in the ♀.

Length. 15–21 mm.

DATES. From the end of May until July.

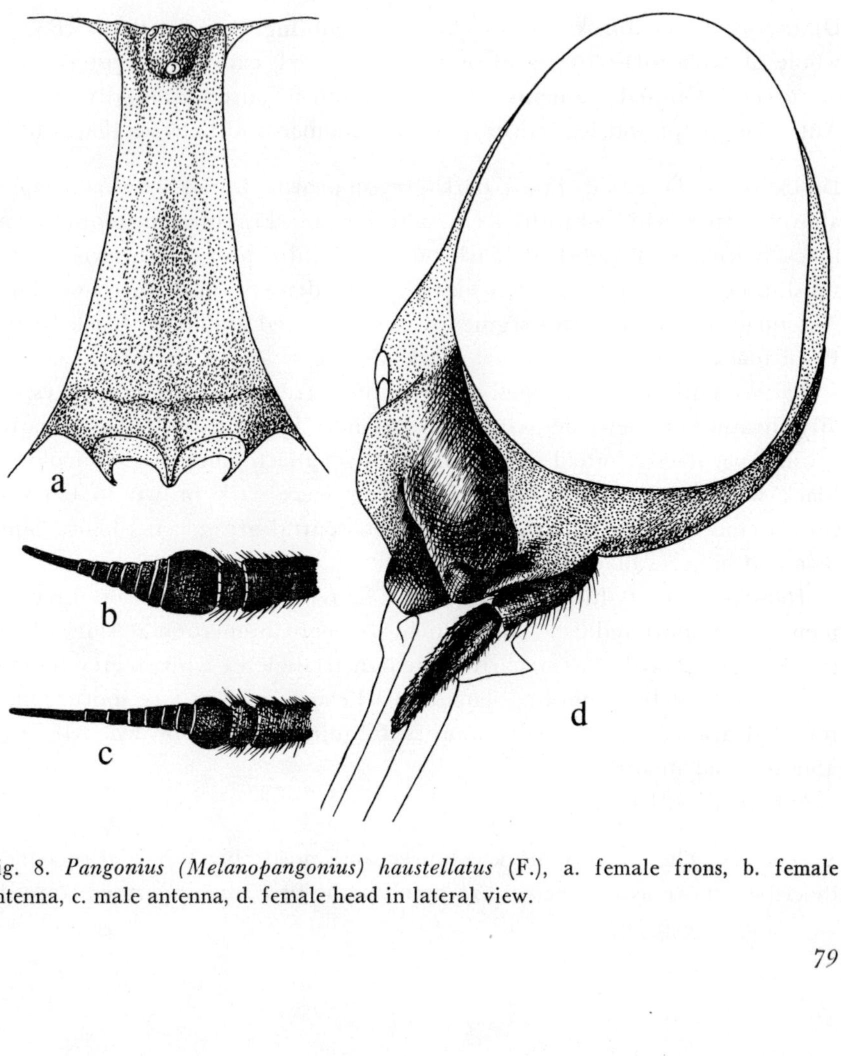

Fig. 8. *Pangonius (Melanopangonius) haustellatus* (F.), a. female frons, b. female antenna, c. male antenna, d. female head in lateral view.

Distribution. A widely distributed species in South Europe from Spain eastwards to as far as Bulgaria and Turkey. In North Africa it is known from Morocco, Algeria and Tunisia. We have seen the documentary material from Algeria, Spain, France, Italy, Greece and Albania.

PANGONIUS (MELANOPANGONIUS) FUNEBRIS MACQUART, 1845

Figs. 4a, d & g; 5a & d; 9.

Pangonia funebris Macquart, 1845, Dipt. exot. Suppl., 1: 23.
Pangonia aterrima Dufour, 1853, Annls Soc. ent. Fr. (Ser. 3), 1: 388.

Diagnosis. Large black species closely resembling *P. haustellatus* (F.) but whole of body including head only black haired, except for posterior two or three abdominal segments which are reddish haired especially at sides. Antennae, palpi and legs entirely black, squamae and halteres blackish.

Description. ♀. *Head.* Frons dark greyish-brown dusted, very convergent above, vertex with whitish ocelli. Occiput blackish-brown coloured and black haired. Face polished black on apical third above, otherwise rather subshining, thinly dark brown dusted, more densely dusted at base above. Antennae black, basal two segments greyish dusted and short black haired. Palpi blackish, labrum polished black, distinctly longer than head is high.

Thorax entirely black, mesonotum thinly greyish-brown dusted, especially in anterior view, densely but very short black haired. Pleura rather subshining black, clothed with tufts of longer black hairs. *Legs* unicolorous black with short concolorous hairs. *Wings* very dark brown to blackish-brown clouded, cells often semihyaline in central areas, veins black. Squamae and halteres blackish.

Abdomen rather shining black, black haired, posterior two or three segments with short reddish hairs which are more numerous at sides. Sometimes tergite 2 with a very narrow median triangle of whitish-grey hairs.

♂. Very closely resembling female in all characters but face shorter, more rounded apically and usually more subshining blackish-brown. All facets almost equal in size.

Length. 17–21 mm.

Synonymy. The entirely black coloured and mostly black haired specimens described above as *P. funebris* are here for the first time seperated from the common *P. haustellatus.* The species, which is also mentioned by Kröber (1921:23), occurs very probably in the same area of distribution as *haustellatus* and we have adopted for it the first available name on the basis of the original descriptions, which is *funebris* of Macquart. *P. aterrima* Duf., listed as another synonym of *haustellatus,* is very probably identical with *funebris.*

Dates. June and July.

Distribution. Both *funebris* Macq. and *aterrima* Duf. were described from Algeria and we have seen numerous specimens from Jugoslavia, Albania, Bulgaria and from the European part of Turkey. A South European and North African species which probably has the similar pattern of distribution as *haustellatus* (F.).

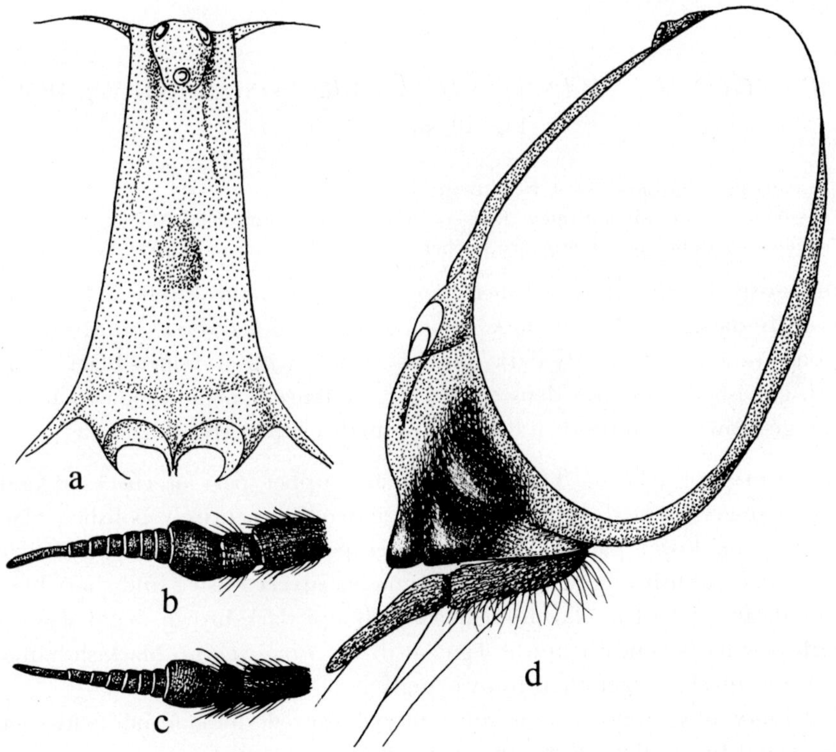

Fig. 9. *Pangonius (Melanopangonius) funebris* Macq., a. female frons, b. female antenna, c. male antenna, d. female head in lateral view.

SUBGENUS *PANGONIUS* S. STR.

DIAGNOSIS. Generally yellowish-brown to silvery-grey or dark olive-grey species with flagellum rather slender at base, basal flagellar segment not distinctly separated from the following flagellar segments.

REMARKS. Over 20 species are known so far of the nominate subgenus, 13 species of which have been found in Europe. The species are separated into three groups of species, viz. *pyritosus*-group, *mauritanus*-group and *variegatus*-group, the differentiation is based upon the type of dusting of the face.

PYRITOSUS-GROUP

Species with entirely polished black or blackish-brown face without any trace of greyish tomentum. Usually also cheeks at least partly polished.

PANGONIUS (PANGONIUS) PYRITOSUS LOEW, 1859

Fig. 10; pl. 1: fig. a.

Pangonia pyritosa Loew, 1859, Neue Beitr., 6: 27.
Pangonia pyritosa var. *decipiens* Kröber, 1921, Arch. Naturgesch., Abt. A, 87 (1): 54.
Pangonia pyritosa var. *hirsutipalpis* Kröber, 1921, Arch. Naturgesch., Abt. A, 87 (1): 56.

DIAGNOSIS. Face entirely polished black, antennae reddish-yellow, flagellum apically darkened. Wings dark grey infuscated along veins, faintly brown along costa and distinctly dark spotted. Female with abdomen black coloured, greyish dusted and densely silvery-grey haired; male abdomen mostly orange-brown on anterior four tergites, small median spots blackish.

DESCRIPTION. ♀. *Head.* Frons, occiput and upper part of cheeks densely yellowish-grey dusted, frons convergent above. Face entirely polished black likewise on lower part of cheeks. Lower part of head long pale haired. Antennae reddish-yellow, basal two segments silvery dusted and short black haired, apical half of flagellum blackish. Palpi dark brown, basal segment with pale hairs beneath, apical segment in var. *hirsutipalpis* blackish haired. Labrum black, longer than head is high.

Thorax olive-grey to light olive-brown dusted, mesonotum with very short and fine yellowish-grey hairs, pleura with tufts of longer concolorous hairs. *Legs.* Coxae with the same dusting and hairing as pleura. Femora mostly shining black, dorsum on the whole length and apices often brownish. Tibiae and tarsi brown. *Wings* brownish tinted especially on costal half, veins dark grey infuscated, forks and crossveins dark spotted. Squamae yellowish-brown, halteres brown with darker grey knob.

Abdomen black in ground colour, densely dark grey dusted and silvery-grey haired, anterior part of each tergite short black haired. Anterior two tergites translucent brown on a small area posteriorly at side. Venter uniformly darker grey coloured and similarly haired as on the dorsum.

♂. Generally smaller, abdomen mostly orange to reddish-brown on anterior four tergites, leaving only rather small median spots black. Dorsum mostly yellowish-grey haired with some additional black hairs anteriorly on each tergite. Venter uniformly yellowish-brown on anterior four sternites, posterior sternites blackish-grey. Sternite 1 with a broad darker median patch. Anterior parts of posterior four sternites with black hairs, otherwise venter with pale hairs. All facets almost equal in size.

Length. 14.5—19 mm.

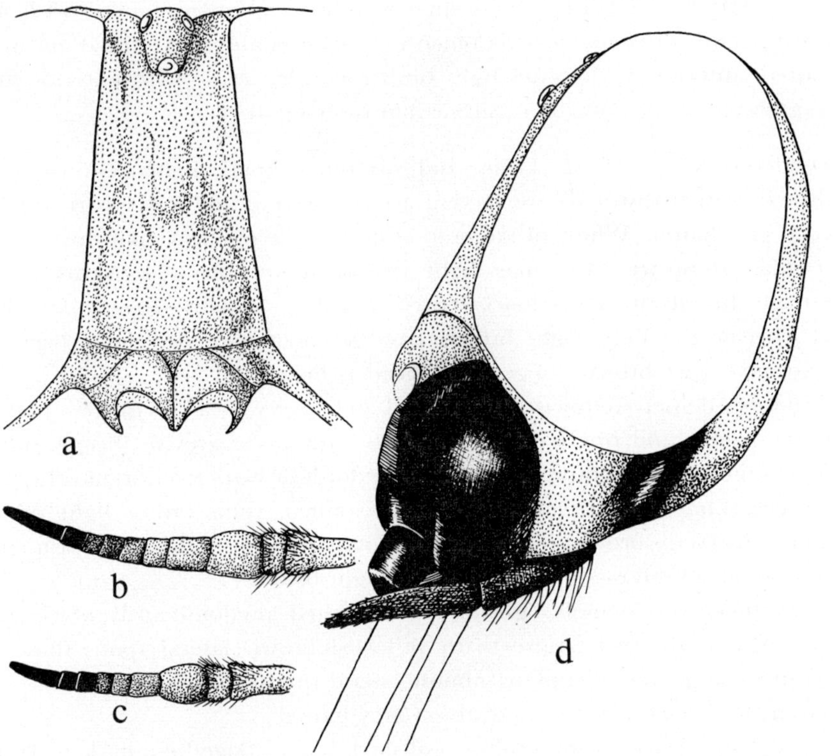

Fig. 10. *Pangonius (P.) pyritosus* Lw., a. female frons, b. female antenna, c. male antenna, d. female head in lateral view.

DATES. June and July.

DISTRIBUTION. South Europe (Jugoslavia, Greece, Bulgaria, Rumania), South of the European part of the U.S.S.R. (Ukraine, North Caucasia), and Turkey. Rather a common species on the coast of the Black Sea. We have seen documentary material from Rumania, Bulgaria and Jugoslavia.

PANGONIUS (PANGONIUS) FULVIPES LOEW, 1859

Fig. 11.

Pangonia fulvipes Loew, 1859, Neue Beitr., 6: 26.
Pangonia sulcata Bezzi, 1909, Broteria, 8: 41.
Pangonia fulvipes var. *palpalis* Kröber, 1921, Arch. Naturgesch., Abt. A. 87 (1): 50.

DIAGNOSIS. Resembling *pyritosus* Loew but legs including femora unicolorous yellowish-brown to reddish-brown. Face entirely polished black to brown (often in female), wings slightly yellowish-brown clouded with less distinct faint brown spots. Abdomen in female lighter grey dusted and pale haired, anterior two tergites light brown at sides. Male with anterior four tergites reddish-yellow, blackish median spots small.

DESCRIPTION. ♀. *Head.* Frons and occiput densely light yellowish-grey dusted, former distinctly convergent above. Occiput and lower part of head light grey haired. Whole of face and almost whole of cheeks polished brown to blackish-brown. Antennae light reddish-yellow, basal segments thinly greyish dusted and short black haired, flagellum usually slightly darkened at extreme tip. Palpi light brown, basal segment with pale hairs beneath. Labrum rather brown, longer than head is high.

Thorax densely yellowish-grey dusted and silvery to yellowish-grey haired, more densely and finely on pleura. *Legs* with coxae greyish dusted, otherwise unicolorous yellowish-brown to reddish-brown, femora mostly pale haired. *Wings* faintly yellowish-brown clouded, veins rather light brown and indistinctly brownish infuscated, crossveins only faintly brownish spotted. Squamae yellowish-brown, halteres light brown.

Abdomen very densely light olive-grey dusted, predominantly silvery-grey haired, anterior two tergites with yellowish-brown lateral spots, those on tergite 2 large and occupying almost lateral quarter of tergite. Venter uniformly darker grey dusted and silvery-grey haired.

♂. Face and labrum usually polished black, flagellum darkened and palpi rather dark brown. Facets on the lower third of eyes somewhat smaller, sharp separation absent. Abdomen yellowish-brown to reddish-brown on anterior four tergites, median black spots small. Posterior tergites dark grey. Venter dark grey, sternites 2–4 yellowish-brown, tergite 2 with a small dark median spot anteriorly.

Length. 14–19 mm.

DATES. June and July.

DISTRIBUTION. An East Mediterranean species known from Italy including Sicily, Greece including Corfu, Jugoslavia, Turkey and Syria. We have seen the documentary material from Jugoslavia, Greece and Turkey.

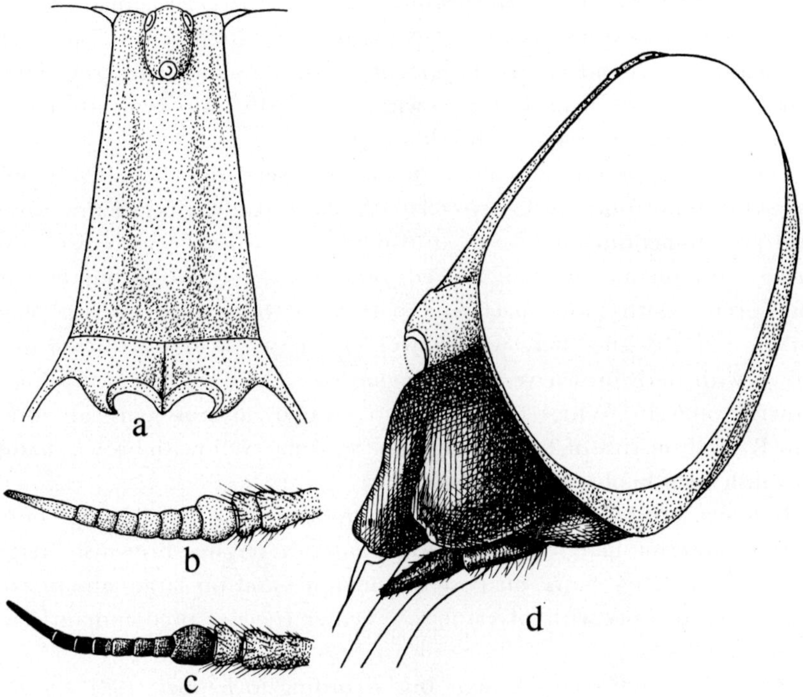

Fig. 11. *Pangonius (P.) fulvipes* Lw., a. female frons, b. female antenna, c. male antenna, d. female head in lateral view.

PANGONIUS (PANGONIUS) OBSCURATUS LOEW, 1859

Fig. 12.

Pangonia obscurata Loew, 1859, Neue Beitr., 6: 27.

DIAGNOSIS. Blackish species with entirely polished black face and cheeks, antennae and legs unicolorous reddish-brown to brown. Wings smoky brown with only very faintly infuscated crossveins and fork of vein R_4. Abdomen rather shining blackish, covered with a dense black and whitish pile.

Description. ♀. *Head.* Frons distinctly widening out below, greyish dusted but somewhat darkened and slightly shining on median part, subcallus plain, only indistinctly differentiated from frons. Face including cheeks polished black to blackish-brown, only a small patch on the upper part of cheeks close to eye-margin greyish dusted. Occiput light greyish dusted with short pale hairs becoming much longer on lower part. Antennae yellowish-brown, basal two segments fine black haired, flagellum very slightly darkened. Palpi very slender, apical segment yellowish-brown with very minute dark hairs, basal segment dark grey with longer pale hairs ventrally. Labrum blackish, slightly longer than head is high.

Thorax black in ground colour, mesonotum very slightly dulled, more or less subshining, unstriped, covered with short pale hairs. Pleura covered with grey tomentum and long whitish-grey hairs. *Legs* with coxae concolorous with pleura and pale haired, otherwise legs unicolorous brownish and covered with short black and pale hairs, only four anterior femora darker ventrally and there with longer pale hairs. *Wings* distinctly smoky brown with dark brown veins, darker on costal half and more hyaline on posterior margin. Wings faintly brown spotted on crossveins, on fork of vein R_4 and on tips of both basal cells. Squamae yellowish-brown, halteres brownish with knobs blackish-brown.

Abdomen uniformly black to blackish-brown, rather shining, only a narrow posterior margin especially on anterior tergites brownish; tergites covered with black hairs, on posterior margins and on large, almost triangular median spots with silvery hairs. Venter covered predominantly with silvery-grey hairs.

♂. We have not seen the male but according to Kröber (1921:45) it can be distinguished as follows: Eyes meeting for a long distance, facets almost equal in size. Basal antennal segments black, flagellum dark reddish-brown, almost black. Palpi short, black, both segments equal in length. Mesonotum dull black, olive dusted and densely golden-brown haired. Abdomen dark reddish-yellow with very broad black median spots on anterior three tergites, the spot on tergite 3 the smallest, following tergites mostly black, narrowly reddish-yellow at sides and on posterior margins.

Length. 15.5–18.5 mm.

Remarks. We have seen only a single female deposited in the Vienna Museum and labelled »Asia Minor, Alte Sammlung, Schiner 1869 / ♀ obscurata det. Schiner / P. obscurata Lw., Type, det. Szilády« which, however, cannot belong to the type series. The above description of the female is based on this specimen. According to Kröber (1921: 45) the type female from the island of Rhodos is deposited in the Museum in Berlin.

DATES. Unknown to us.

DISTRIBUTION. The species has been recorded from Asia Minor, from the islands of Rhodos and Corsica, and from Bulgaria and Greece; Arias (1914) also recorded it from Portugal and Spain. We have seen documentary material from Asia Minor.

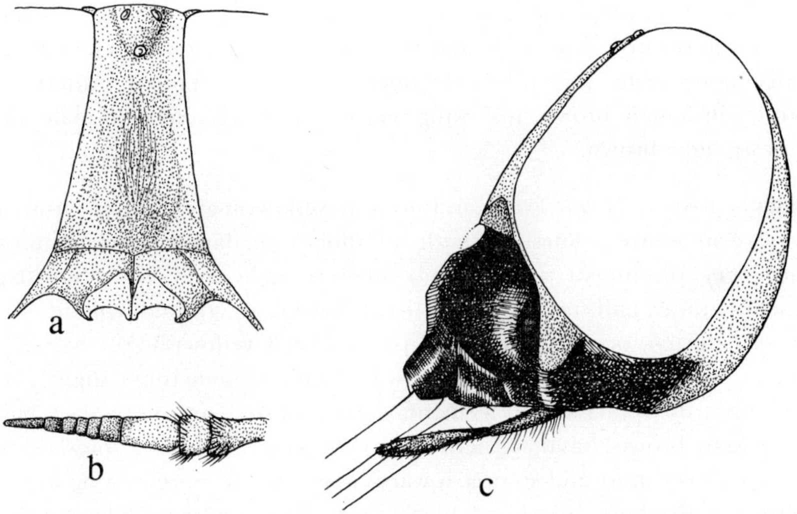

Fig. 12. *Pangonius (P.) obscuratus* Lw., female, a. frons, b. antenna, c. head in lateral view.

MAURITANUS-GROUP

Species with face entirely covered by greyish or brownish tomentum, at most only extreme apex of face slightly subshining.

PANGONIUS (PANGONIUS) MAURITANUS (LINNÉ, 1767)

Figs. 1a; 13; pl. 1: fig. c.

Tabanus mauritanus Linné, 1767, Syst. Nat., 12: 999.
Tabanus proboscideus Fabricius, 1794, Ent. Syst., 4: 362.
Pangonia maculata Fabricius, 1805, Syst. Ant., p. 90.
Pangonia tabaniformis Latreille, 1805, Hist. nat. Crust. Ins., 14: 318.
Pangonia varipennis Latreille, 1811, Encycl. Méth., 8: 705.
? *Pangonia maculata* var. *basalis* Macquart, 1847, Dipt. exot. Suppl., 2: 10.
? *Pangonia maculata* var. *aethiops* Szilády, 1923, Biologica hung., 1 (1): 27.
Pangonia proboscidea var. *maroccana* Surcouf, 1924, Tab. de France, p. 202.
Pangonius acuminatus Enderlein, 1931, Sber. Ges. naturf. Freunde Berl., 1930: 383.

DIAGNOSIS. Brownish species with prominent and entirely greyish dusted face. Antennae, palpi and labrum reddish to yellowish-brown, legs including femora unicolorous brown. Wings brownish to darker brown clouded, especially along veins, and distinctly brown or darker spotted. Anterior two tergites in female brown, following tergites black; abdomen in male almost entirely light brown.

DESCRIPTION. ♀. *Head.* Frons and occiput yellowish-grey dusted, frons very convergent above, sometimes with an indefinite darker patch at middle. Face very prominent and entirely densely light grey to yellowish-grey dusted, apical half usually translucent brown in ground colour; cheeks entirely dusted, occiput and lower part of head yellowish-grey haired. Antennae orange-yellow to reddish-brown, flagellum sometimes slightly darkened towards tip, basal two segments greyish dusted and short black haired. Palpi light brown, basal segment long pale haired beneath, apical segment conspicuously short and stouter towards apex, about twice as long as broad, clothed with short, adpressed black hairs. Labrum reddish-brown, much longer than head is high.

Thorax dark brown in ground colour and densely olive-grey to brown-grey dusted; light grey to yellowish-grey haired, shorter on mesonotum and with longer hairs on pleura. Coxae concolorous with pleura, otherwise legs unicolorous brown to reddish-brown and predominantly short black haired. *Wings* slightly brown to dark brown clouded along veins, crossveins with distinct brown to dark grey spots. Squamae whitish-yellow, halteres brown with paler tip to knob.

Abdomen dull brown to yellowish-brown on anterior two segments, following segments rather shining black; both tergite 3 and sternite 3 with several brownish patches at sides. Tergite 2 with a narrow dark median spot which occupies the whole length of tergite. Abdominal hairing black, silvery-grey on posterior margins.

♂. Eyes very narrowly separated on frons, or touching for a very short distance; all facets almost equal in size. Basal antennal segments with long blackish hairs; head, legs and wings as in the ♀. Abdomen mostly yellowish-brown to light reddish-brown, tergite 1 darkened anteriorly, following tergites often with hardly visible darker median cloudings, posterior three tergites sometimes dark grey or concolorous with foregoing tergites. Pubescence pale, posterior sternites with black hairs.

Length. 11–15 mm.

Remarks. The variety *aethiops* Szil. with entirely black abdomen probably refers only to extremely black coloured females and cannot be, considering its occurrence in Morocco, a different subspecies as stated by Leclercq (1960a: 22).

Dates. From the end of April until June.

Distribution. A West Mediterranean species known from North Africa (Morocco, Algeria, Tunisia) and in Europe from Spain, France and Sardinia. We have seen the documentary material only from Algeria and Tunisia.

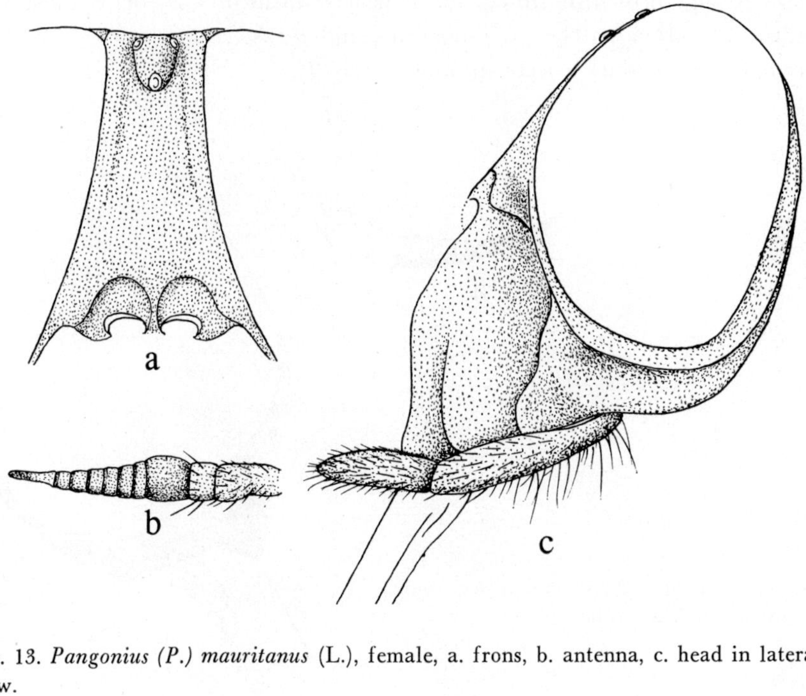

Fig. 13. *Pangonius (P.) mauritanus* (L.), female, a. frons, b. antenna, c. head in lateral view.

PANGONIUS (PANGONIUS) SOBRADIELI SÉGUY, 1934

Fig. 14.

Pangonius sobradieli, Séguy, 1934, Mems. Acad. Cienc. exact. fis.–quim. nat. Zaragoza, 3:21.

DIAGNOSIS. Brownish species in general appearance similar to *mauritanus* (L.), but easily recognized by the low, rounded face and the unspotted abdomen.

DESCRIPTION. ♂. (♀ unknown). *Head.* Face low and rounded, entirely and rather densely brownish-grey dusted. Also cheeks and occiput entirely dusted, and all parts of head yellowish-grey haired. Antennae orange-yellow, flagellum only slightly darkened towards apex; basal two segments light dusted and short black haired. Palpi greyish-brown, apical segment more reddish-brown towards apex and very slender, 4—5 times longer than broad, not widening at apex, clothed with short, adpressed black hairs. Labrum dark brownish, about as long as height of head.

Thorax dark brownish in ground colour and densely brown-grey dusted and yellowish-grey haired. *Legs:* Coxae concolorous with pleura. Legs otherwise uniformly brownish to reddish-brown and mainly with short, black hairs. *Wings* brownish tinted, often nearly uniformly so, or at most with indistinct darker patches at cross-veins and forks. Halteres with darkened knob, distinctly darker than in *mauritanus* (L.).

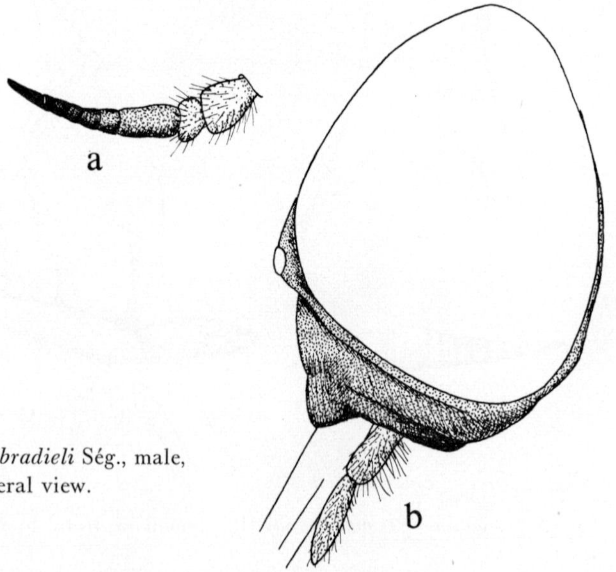

Fig. 14. *Pangonius (P.) sobradieli* Ség., male, a. antenna, b. head in lateral view.

Abdomen yellowish-brown without darker patches on middle of tergites. Posterior tergites hardly darkened. Pubescence composed of pale and black hairs, the latter dominating on middle parts of anterior tergites and on whole surface of posterior tergites.

Length. 11 mm.

REMARKS. Séguy (1934: 21) described this species on a male specimen which is deposited in the Paris Museum and has been seen by the present authors. It bears a label of »Sobradiel, Zaragoza, 11.VII. 1932«. The species is also recorded from Morocco but we doubt the distinction between *sobradieli* and *powelli* Séguy, 1930, also described from Morocco.

DISTRIBUTION. Spain, Morocco.

PANGONIUS (PANGONIUS) STRIATUS SZILÁDY, 1923

Fig. 15.

Pangonia striata Szilády, 1923, Biologica hung., 1 (1): 28.
Pangonia kraussei Surcouf, 1921, Genera Insect., 175: 128 (nomen nudum).

DIAGNOSIS. Face rather short, not very convex, entirely greyish dusted. Antennae reddish-brown, darkened on flagellum, segment 3 rather broad at base. Legs brown, femora darkened. Wings rather clear or very light brownish smoky with distinct faint brown infuscations. Abdomen unicolorous brown, densely black and silvery haired.

DESCRIPTION. ♀. *Head.* Frons and occiput greyish dusted, frons slightly convergent above, subcallus inconspicuous. Face very short and entirely greyish dusted. Occiput with minute whitish hairs which are much longer on lower part of head. Basal antennal segments yellowish-brown coloured and silvery-grey dusted, covered with fine black hairs; flagellum distinctly broader than usual at base; reddish-brown at base and brown to dark brown towards the apex. Palpi reddish-brown, basal segment more greyish-brown, apical segment with minute black hairs. Labrum light brown, scarcely longer than head is high.

Thorax dark brown in ground colour, mesonotum covered with short whitish hairs and greyish tomentum, and with three, rather shining brown, distinct longitudinal stripes; median line very narrow and hardly visible on anterior third of mesonotum, sublateral stripes broad and distinct for whole length, reaching from the somewhat paler humeri to scutellum.

Scutellum more densely whitish-grey dusted, with slightly shining brown median patch. Pleura densely greyish dusted and clothed with tufts of long whitish hairs. *Legs* unicolorous light brown except for femora which are considerably darkened, mostly short pale haired. *Wings* rather clear or very faintly brownish tinted on costal half, veins dark brown. Fork of vein R_4, discal and both basal cells at tip, faintly brown infuscated. Squamae whitish-yellow, halteres dark brown with paler stems.

Abdomen mostly brown, somewhat darker on posterior segments; all tergites mostly black haired on anterior two-thirds, posterior margins and median triangles whitish-grey haired. Venter uniformly whitish-grey haired, posterior three to four sternites extensively darkened.

♂. Eyes touching for a long distance on frons, basal two antennal segments darkened and more densely black haired. Proboscis longer than in the ♀, almost twice as long as head is high. Legs darker brown on femora, abdomen rather reddish-brown on tergites 2–4 anteriorly.

Length. 13—14.5 mm.

REMARKS. Szilády described this species from Tempio, Sardinia. The types were deposited in the Hungarian National Museum, Budapest but were very probably destroyed in 1956. We have found a couple of syntypic specimens in the Museum in Vienna, the male is labelled »Sardinia, Tempio,

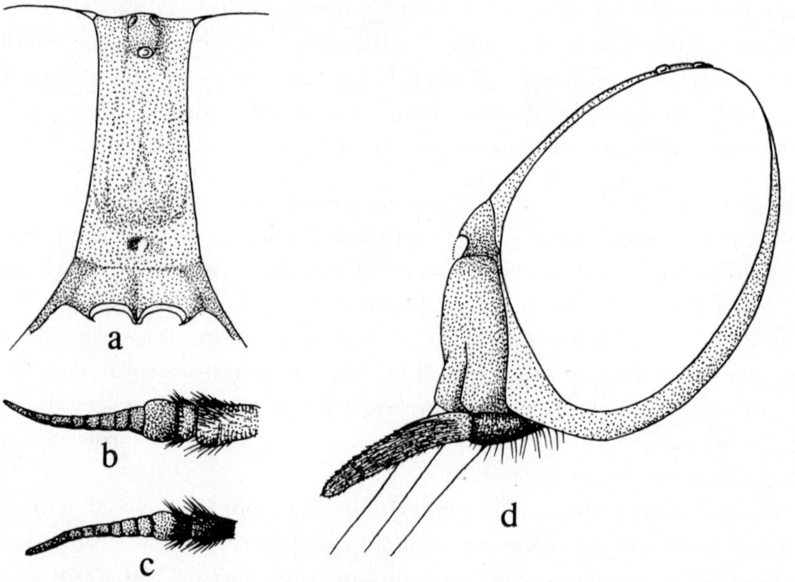

Fig. 15. *Pangonius (P.) striatus* Szil., a. female frons, b. female antenna, c. male antenna, d. female head in lateral view.

Krausse« and »striata m., det. Szilády«; the female bears only the identification label but is undoubtedly of the same origin; the male could be selected as lectotype if necessary. The above given description was based on this material. There is another male in coll. Bezzi, Milano, labelled »Dorigliano 6.05 / P. striata m., det. Szilády« which is identical with the above mentioned pair but does not belong to the syntypic series.

SYNONYMY. The synonymy with *P. kraussei* Surcouf is obvious. *P. kraussei* was mentioned by Surcouf (1924: 203; as *krausei).* Surcouf (1921: 128) refers in »Genera Insectorum« to the description in »Annls Soc. ent. Belg.« of 1921 but, however, there is neither a description of this species nor any paper written by Surcouf, *P. kraussei* Surcouf, 1921, thus being a nomen nudum.

DATES. June.

DISTRIBUTION. Sardinia, Italy.

PANGONIUS (PANGONIUS) ESCALERAE STROBL, 1906

Pangonia Escalerae Strobl, 1906, Mems. R. Soc. esp. Hist. nat., 3 (1905): 278.

DIAGNOSIS. A species of the *mauritanus*-group with entirely grey dusted face which is rather short, semiglobular and reddish-brown in ground colour. Antennae and femora black. Wings greyish clouded and darker spotted. Abdomen blackish, only anterior two tergites broadly reddish-yellow at sides.

A very little known species described by Strobl (1906) from Spain (females only); later Arias (1914) also recorded the male sex. We have not seen this species, the type material of which is deposited in coll. Strobl at Admont. Therefore we present a translation of the short original *description:*

♀. »Long. 16 mm. Differt a *granatensi* antennis obscuris, rostro breviore, facie breviore, rufobrunnea, tota pollinosa.«

This species cannot be mistaken for any others already described. It agrees with *granatensis* in the blackish-brown palpi and entirely black femora, it differs, however, in the almost pitchy-black antennae; only segment 3 at base narrowly reddish-yellow; further the face is shorter and more convex, almost semiglobular, not black but reddish-brown and everywhere, even at mouth, densely grey dusted. Proboscis shorter, 5 mm (in *maculata* 7—8 mm); abdomen still more blackish, only sides of anterior two segments broadly reddish-yellow, following segments at sides and on posterior margins only narrowly pale. I cannot find any differences in venation and spotting of the rather intensively grey wings which are more reddish on anterior margin.«

♂. The male sex was recorded by Arias (1914: 52) who found 1 ♂ and 3 ♀ of *escalerae* in the Museum in Madrid. According to Arias, who did not present any description, the male agrees quite well with the female except for sexual differences. No other records are available.

Length. 16—16.5 mm.

DATES. Unknown.

DISTRIBUTION. Spain.

VARIEGATUS-GROUP

Species with face partly dusted, partly polished; at least apical third to quarter of face polished black to brown, and base of face always densely dusted. Wings very faintly to very distinctly clouded, sometimes spotted on forks and crossveins.

PANGONIUS (PANGONIUS) HERMANNI KRÖBER, 1921

Fig. 16.

Pangonia Hermanni Kröber, 1921, Arch. Naturgesch., Abt. A, 87 (1): 37.
Pangonia Hannibal Szilády, 1923, Biologica hung., 1 (1): 26 – syn. n.

DIAGNOSIS. Blackish species, abdomen entirely black except for yellowish-brown tergite 1. Face greyish dusted on basal half, apical half polished black. Wings brownish tinted anteriorly, veins darker brown clouded, forks and crossveins dark infuscated. Antennae and legs brown.

DESCRIPTION. ♀. *Head.* Frons dark grey dusted, convergent above, mesally with more or less visible black, double line-shaped patch simulating median callus. Subcallus somewhat brownish. Face dark grey dusted on basal half, apical half to third polished black. Cheeks partly polished black. Occiput grey with paler hairs. Antennae brown, basal segments yellowish-grey dusted and finely black haired, flagellum sometimes slightly darkened. Palpi dark brown, basal segment with dark hairs beneath. Labrum blackish, longer than head is high.

Thorax black in ground colour, humeri and narrow sides of mesonotum brownish. Mesonotum subshining black, only thinly dusted, with two indefinite greyish sublateral stripes and a narrow black median stripe on posterior half. Whole of thorax rather short pale haired, pleura with longer and more greyish pile. Coxae concolorous with pleura, otherwise legs unicolorous brown, pale and black haired. *Wings* light brown on anterior half, all veins distinctly brown clouded, forks and crossveins darker brown infuscated. Squamae yellowish-brown, halteres light brown, knob very darkened.

Abdomen rather shining black to blackish-brown except for tergite 1 which is distinctly light brown coloured. All tergites and sternites whitish-grey haired on posterior margins, tergites with rather small median triangles of concolorous pubescence; otherwise abdomen short black haired.

♂. Unknown.

Length. 13–16.5 mm.

SYNONYMY. We have seen one type female of the syntypic series of *P. hannibal* Szil. deposited in the Naturhistorisches Museum, Vienna, which is undoubtedly identical with *P. hermanni* Kröb. Szilády (1923) when describing *P. hannibal* from Spain did not see the Kröber's species *P. hermanni* and placed the latter by mistake in a different group of species with striped mesonotum (his group »C« = *Taeniopangonia* Szil.).

Both original descriptions of *hermanni* Kröb. and *hannibal* Szil. clearly show that only one species is involved.

DATES. June and July.

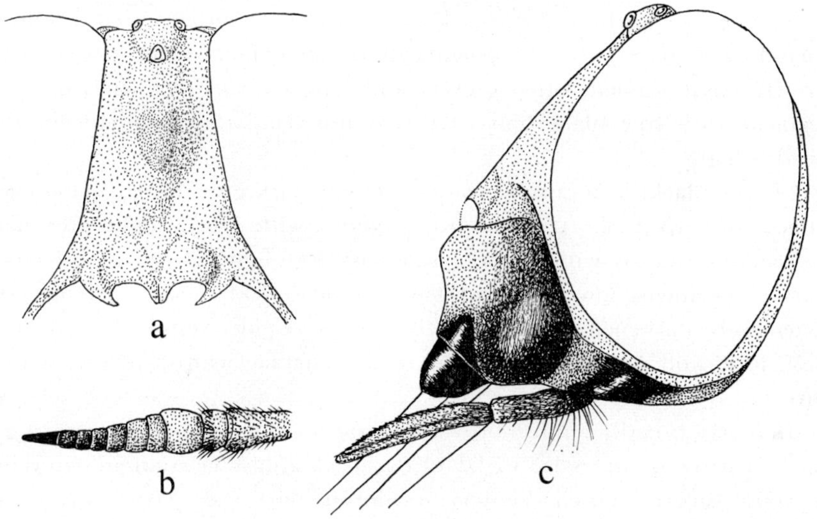

Fig. 16. *Pangonius (P.) hermanni* Kröb., female, a. frons, b. antenna, c. head in lateral view.

Distribution. Spain; we have seen females collected by A. Kricheldorff on 2.VII. 1929 at Manteegas, Serra da Estrela, and by G. Hesselbarth on 22.VII. 1961 at Cord. Cantabrica, Pto. del Ponton, 1250 m. Leclercq (1964b: 7) recorded it also from Portugal.

PANGONIUS (PANGONIUS) VARIEGATUS FABRICIUS, 1805

Fig. 17.

Pangonia variegata Fabricius, 1805, Syst. Ant., p. 92.
Pangonia variegata var. *acutipalpis* Kröber, 1921, Arch. Naturgesch., Abt. A, 87 (1): 33.
Pangonia variegata var. *brunneipes* Szilády, 1923, Biologica hung., 1 (1): 26.

Diagnosis. Reddish-brown species with brown legs, face greyish dusted usually on more than basal half, apical part of face polished black to dark brown. Antennae reddish-brown, wings faintly brownish clouded and darker brown spotted. Abdomen reddish-brown to yellowish-brown on at least anterior three tergites in both sexes, the dark grey median stripe occupying at most one-third of tergites.

Description. ♀. *Head.* Frons grey dusted, convergent above, occiput concolorous and pale haired. Face greyish dusted on basal two-thirds to half, at least apical third polished black to dark brown. Antennae reddish-brown including flagellum, basal segments short but densely black haired. Palpi brown, basal segment often greyish and long pale haired beneath, apical segment with fine black hairs. Labrum usually dark brown, longer than head is high.

Thorax blackish in ground colour, densely dark grey dusted; mesonotum almost unstriped, short pale haired, pleura with longer light grey hairs. Coxae concolorous with pleura, otherwise legs light brown to brown; in darker specimens lower part of femora and apical tarsal segments often extensively darkened. Wings faintly brown clouded especially on costal half, forks and crossveins brown spotted. Squamae whitish-yellow, halteres brown.

Abdomen broadly reddish-brown on anterior three to four tergites, a grey median stripe occupies 1/3 to 1/5 of tergites 2 and 3. Dorsum golden-yellow to yellowish-grey haired. Venter unicolorous dark grey, rather silvery-grey haired, sternites anteriorly with some black hairs. Sometimes venter translucent dark brown, especially on anterior sternites.

♂. Facets on lower third of eyes smaller but not sharply differentiated from larger facets above. Basal antennal segments with longer dark hairs. Head, thorax and abdomen longer pale haired, otherwise as in the ♀. Abdomen with dark median stripe on tergites 2 and 3 usually narrower, often forming seperate dark median spots; venter yellowish-brown on anterior two or three sternites.

Length. 13–16 mm.

SYNONYMY. We have seen 2 female types of *variegatus* var. *brunneipes* Szilády, 1923, from the coll. Bezzi at Milano, Italy; one female was labelled »Campobasso Leoni«, the second »Macerati, 18.VII.95«. Both bear a label »P. variegata F. v. brunneipes m., det. Szilády« and are identical with *variegatus* F., having only lighter, yellow-brown coloured legs.

DATES. June and July.

DISTRIBUTION. A widely distributed South European species known from Morocco and Spain through South Europe as far as Asia Minor. It has also been recorded from Italy including Sardinia, Greece and Corfu. We have seen the documentary material from Italy and Corfu.

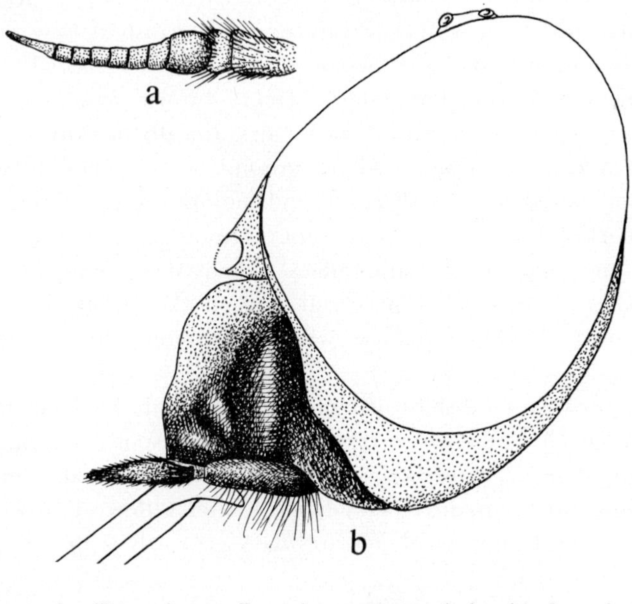

Fig. 17. *Pangonius (P.) variegatus* F., male, a. antenna, b. head in lateral view.

PANGONIUS (PANGONIUS) GRANATENSIS STROBL, 1906

Fig. 18.

Pangonia granatensis Strobl, 1906, Mems. R. Soc. esp. Hist. nat., 3 (1905): 277.

DIAGNOSIS. Resembling *variegatus* F. but femora black, antennae extensively blackish and halteres whitish-yellow. Wings only faintly greyish-brown clouded on costal half, the darker spots on forks and crossveins less distinct. Abdomen mostly reddish-brown on anterior tergites in both sexes.

DESCRIPTION. ♀. We have not seen females of this species and present therefore a more detailed description of the male sex only. According to Strobl (1906) both sexes are quite identical in all main characters including the abdominal pattern. Anterior segments reddish-yellow with moderately broad blackish median stripe which is broader on following segments, forming either anterior bands on tergites or tergites are mostly blackish except for lateral margins. Pilosity rather dense, whitish, forming distinct whitish posterior margins when viewed from above.

♂. *Head.* Subcallus and cheeks greyish dusted, face polished blackish-brown on apical half and at sides, basal half above densely grey dusted. Lower part of head with long whitish-grey hairs, occiput with shorter hairs. Eyes meeting on frons for a shorter distance, facets on more than lower third of eye small but not sharply differentiated from larger facets above. Antennae blackish, basal segments translucent brownish at base, segment 1 clothed with longer dark hairs; segment 2 short black haired; flagellum slightly brownish at base. Palpi dark blackish-brown, basal segment pale haired, apical segment with minute dark hairs, apically brownish.

Thorax black to blackish-brown in ground colour, very densely light yellowish-grey haired. *Legs* with coxae and femora rather shining black to very dark blackish-brown in ground colour, femora with longer pale hairs. Tibiae and tarsi light brown, short black haired. *Wings* only slightly greyish-brown clouded especially on costal half, darker spots on forks and crossveins faintly brown. Squamae whitish, halteres whitish-yellow with brownish stem.

Abdomen broadly reddish-brown on dorsum, a blackish median stripe on tergites 2 and 3 in a form of triangular median spots, widening on posterior tergites. Sides of tergites densely whitish-yellow haired, central parts of tergites with predominantly black hairs. Venter yellowish-brown on sternites 2–4, sternite 1 and apical sternites dark grey, whole of venter mostly whitish-yellow haired.

Length. 15—16.5 mm.

DATES. From April until July.

DISTRIBUTION. The species is known only from Spain and Portugal.

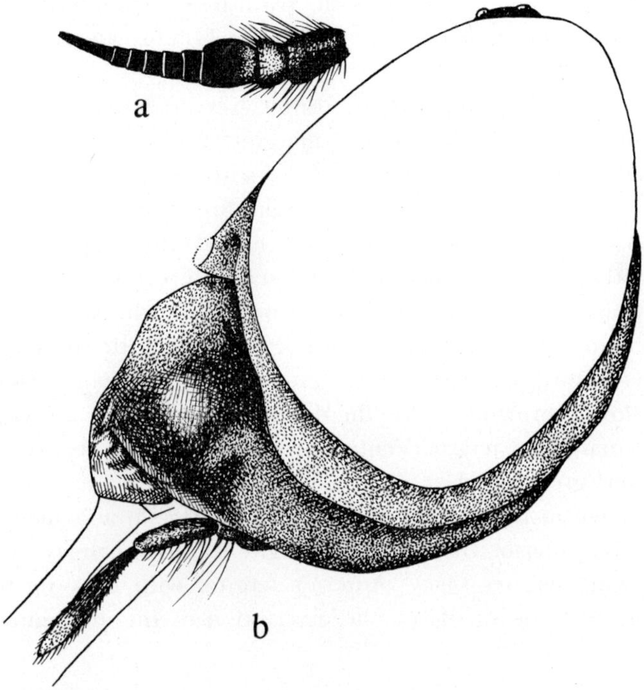

Fig. 18. *Pangonius (P.) granatensis* Strobl, male, a. antenna, b. head in lateral view.

PANGONIUS (PANGONIUS) FUMIDUS LOEW, 1859

Fig. 19.

Pangonia fumida Loew, 1859, Neue Beitr., 6: 28.
? *Pangonia Loewii* Kröber, 1921, Arch. Naturgesch., Abt. A, 87 (1): 35.

DIAGNOSIS. Face not very convex, mostly densely greyish dusted, only apical quarter above polished black to brown. Wings at most only slightly tinted along costal margin, no distinct spots or cloudings along veins. Antennae darkened, femora blackish. Abdomen brownish at sides, in female on anterior two tergites.

DESCRIPTION. ♀. *Head.* Frons and occiput light grey dusted, frons distinctly convergent above. Occiput whitish-grey haired, hairs on lower part of head much longer. Face light grey dusted at sides and on almost basal three-quarters above, small apical area polished brown to black. Antennae blackish-brown, basal segments thinly greyish dusted and clothed with longer pale hairs; flagellum mostly blackish, reddish-brown at base. Palpi dark brown, basal segment pale haired. Labrum blackish-brown, distinctly longer than head is high.

Thorax black in ground colour, thinly greyish dusted on mesonotum, more densely on lateral mesonotal margins, pleura and coxae. Pilosity whitish-grey, pleura longer haired. *Legs* with femora extensively black coloured and pale haired, slightly translucent brownish especially at middle. Tibiae and tarsi light brown, short black haired, tibiae apically darkened. *Wings* slightly greyish-yellow tinted on costal half, veins dark, not clouded. Squamae whitish-yellow, halteres light brown, knob whitish.

Abdomen mostly black, rather shining, clothed with short silvery-grey pubescence, tergites on posterior margins with longer hairs. Anterior two tergites yellowish-brown at sides, the dark patch on tergite 2 occupies more than three-quarters of tergite. Venter extensively blackish-grey coloured and densely silvery-grey haired.

♂. Unknown to us. According to Kröber (1921: 33) abdomen light reddish-yellow on anterior three tergites, tergite 4 only narrowly brownish at sides, following tergites black. Anterior tergites with dark median spots, that on tergite 3 the smallest. The description of the abdominal pattern

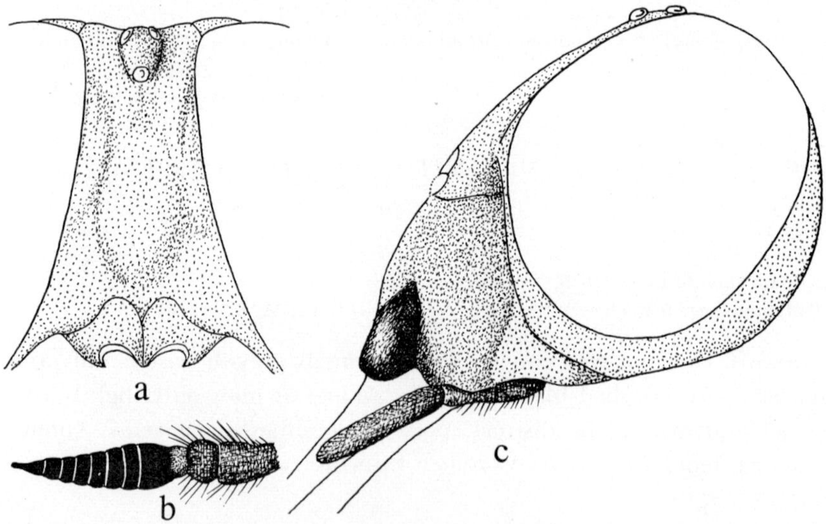

Fig. 19. *Pangonius (P.) fumidus* Lw., female, a. frons, b. antenna, c. head in lateral view.

given by Leclercq (1960a: 11) and figured on his plate III, fig. 17c is, however, quite different.

Length. 12–16 mm.

SYNONYMY. Szilády (1923: 24) recorded *P. loewi* Kröb., 1921, as a variety of *fumidus* Loew, but according to the original description and the figure of head, *loewi* is probably more closely related to, and perhaps identical with, *affinis* Loew.

DATES. July.

DISTRIBUTION. The species is known so far only from Spain.

PANGONIUS (PANGONIUS) AFFINIS LOEW, 1859

Fig. 20.

Pangonia affinis Loew, 1859, Neue Beitr., 6: 29.
? *Pangonia Loewii* Kröber, 1921, Arch. Naturgesch., Abt. A., 87 (1): 35.

DIAGNOSIS. Face polished brown to black, densely greyish dusted on basal third to half above. Antennae extensively blackish, femora black to blackish-brown. Wings slightly brownish tinted along anterior margin, veins in female distinctly brownish clouded. Abdomen yellowish-brown at sides on at least anterior four segments; with the dark dorsal median stripe very broad in female, in male in a form of median spots.

DESCRIPTION. ♀. *Head.* Frons greyish dusted, usually with indefinite brown median patch, distinctly convergent above. Occiput lighter grey dusted and yellowish-grey haired, lower part of head with longer hairs. Face mostly polished brown to black, densely greyish dusted on only basal third to half above. Antennae translucent brown on basal segments, slightly greyish dusted and pale haired; flagellum black, narrowly brownish at extreme base. Palpi dark brown, basal segment pale haired beneath, apical segment very short, shorter than basal segment. Labrum dark brown, distinctly longer than head is high.

Thorax black, mesonotum rather shining and sparsely pale haired, pleura and coxae more densely greyish dusted and longer yellowish-grey haired. Femora black or blackish-brown in ground colour, sometimes more brownish dorsally, only pale haired. Tibiae and tarsi yellowish-brown, short black haired, tibiae often darkened towards tip. *Wings* slightly brownish clouded on costal half, veins blackish, distinctly but only narrowly brown clouded. Squamae whitish, halteres whitish-yellow.

Abdomen black in ground colour, anterior four tergites yellowish-brown at sides; blackish median stripe broad, occupying at least 1/3 or more of tergite 2, posteriorly widening, apical three tergites black. Venter with the same pattern as on dorsum, whole of abdomen mostly whitish-grey haired, tergites 3 and 4 anteriorly mostly black haired.

♂. Eyes meeting for a long distance on frons, facets on the lower third of eyes distinctly smaller, not very sharply but distinctly separated from larger facets above. Wings less tinted and veins not clouded as in the ♀. Abdomen mostly yellowish-brown, a blackish median stripe in the form of median spots which are broader anteriorly, occupying about one-third of tergites, posteriorly pointed and separated from following tergite by yellowish posterior margin. Venter entirely yellowish on anterior four sternites, apical sternites dark grey. Sternite 1 mostly greyish, sternite 2 with a very small greyish spot anteriorly at middle.

Length. 12—16 mm.

REMARKS. The female of *affinis* Loew is described here for the first time. We have seen, in addition to several specimens of both sexes collected by V. S. v. d. Goot in Spain in 1965, a male deposited in the Naturhistorisches Museum, Vienna, and labelled »A / Hispania / 1857—59 Reise / Ferruginea,

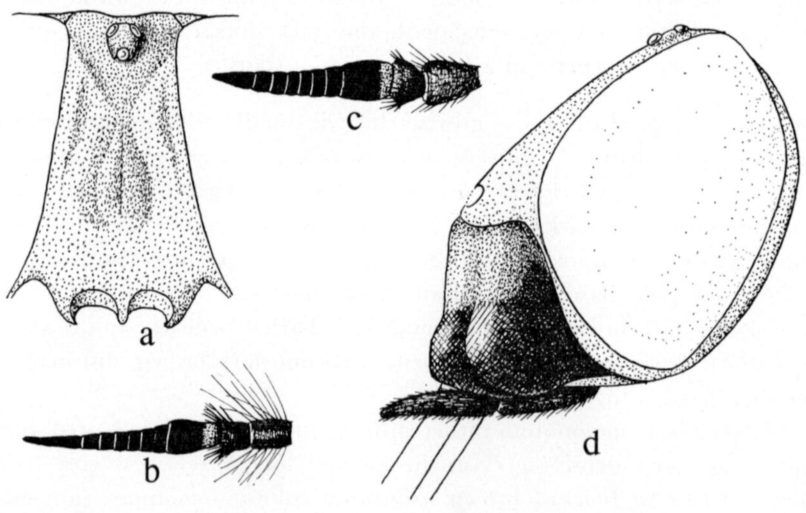

Fig. 20. *Pangonius (P.) affinis* Lw., a. female frons, b. female antenna, c. male antenna d. female head in lateral view.

Alte Sammlung / P. affinis Lw. det. Szilády« and a pair labelled »Albaracin / affinis det. Szilády 1936«.

SYNONYMY. The female described as *loewi* (Kröber, 1921) from Spain is, according to the original description, very probably identical with *affinis* Loew. We have not seen the type material of *loewi* which is deposited in the Museum in Berlin. Szilády (1923: 24) considered it to be a variety of *fumidus* Loew.

DATES. July and August.

DISTRIBUTION. The species is known so far only from Spain.

PANGONIUS (PANGONIUS) FERRUGINEUS (MEIGEN, 1804)

Fig. 21.

Tanyglossa ferruginea Meigen, 1804, Klass., p. 175.

DIAGNOSIS. Face mostly polished black, greyish dusted on basal half above, wings uniformly tinted brownish. Basal antennal segments and palpi with minute black hairs. Closely related to *dimidiatus* Loew, venter of abdomen also entirely blackish, but dorsum more orange-yellow coloured and black median stripe rather narrow on tergite 2, occupying distinctly less than one-third of tergite in female, widening out on tergite 3.

DESCRIPTION. ♀. *Head.* Frons densely greyish dusted, distinctly convergent above. Face polished black on apical half above, at sides right up to ocular margins, only basal half above greyish dusted and covered with sparse, fine pale hairs. Cheeks thinly greyish dusted, lower part of head long and densely pale haired. Antennae black, flagellum brownish at extreme base; basal two segments greyish dusted and short black haired, segment 1 above with several longer pale hairs. Palpi very dark reddish-brown, almost black towards tip on apical segment, clothed with fine black hairs. Labrum black, about one and a half times longer than head is high.

Thorax thinly greyish-brown dusted on mesonotum, almost unstriped and densely covered by short greyish to grey-yellow hairs. Pleura rather subshining black or only very thinly dusted, long whitish-grey haired. Coxae concolorous with pleura. *Legs* with femora blackish and finely pale haired; tibiae and tarsi unicolorous brown, very short but densely black haired, which gives them a darker brown appearance. *Wings* brownish tinted, costal cell yellowish, veins dark brown. Squamae pale yellow, halteres dark brown.

Abdomen rather bright orange at sides of tergites 1–3, posterior tergites blackish, dorsum of abdomen covered by golden-yellow adpressed hairs. The black median stripe on anterior three tergites not so broad and parallel-sided as in *dimidiatus* Loew, occupying almost one-third of tergite 1, much narrower on tergite 2, slightly widening posteriorly, and evenly broader on tergite 3, occupying there about one-half of tergite on posterior margin. Venter entirely black coloured and densely whitish to silvery-grey haired, posterior margins on apical sternites more densely haired.

♂. We have not seen the male but according to Kröber (1921:41) it resembles the female except for the abdominal pattern and the pale haired basal segment of palpi. Dorsum of abdomen reddish-yellow on anterior four tergites, tergites 2–4 with only small dark median spots situated close to anterior margin, posterior tergites darkened but densely yellowish haired.

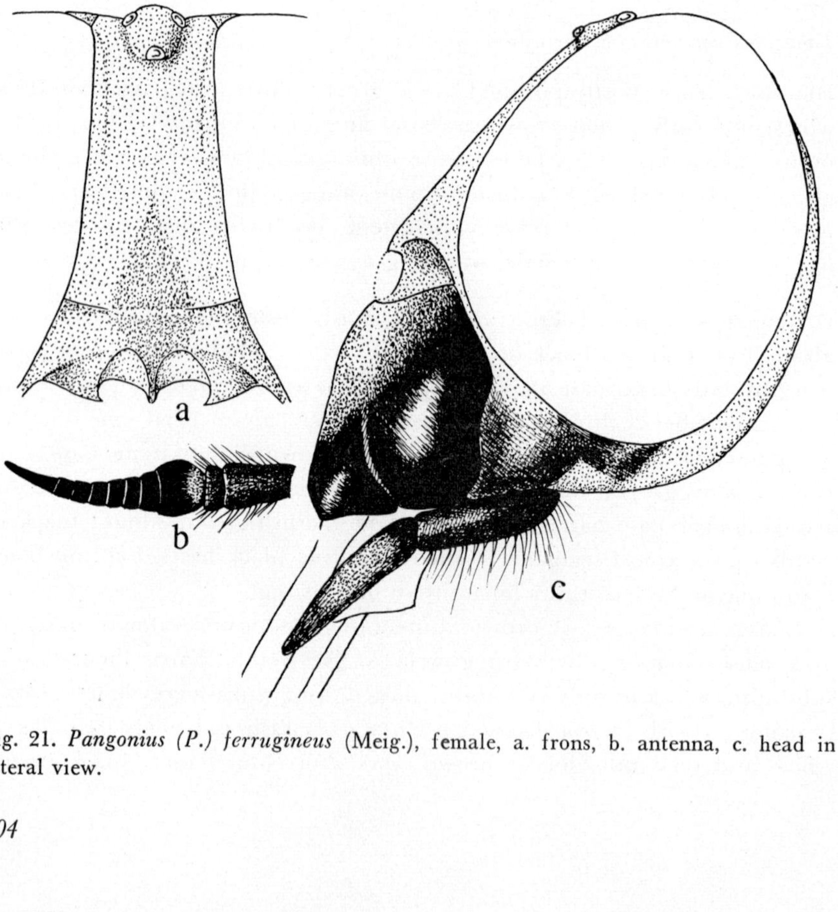

Fig. 21. *Pangonius (P.) ferrugineus* (Meig.), female, a. frons, b. antenna, c. head in lateral view.

Venter reddish-yellow on anterior sternites in contrast to female; the same character was also mentioned by Szilády (1923: 24).

Length. 14.5–17 mm.

DATES. From May until the beginning of August.

DISTRIBUTION. A West Mediterranean species known from Spain, Portugal and Gibraltar. Kröber (1921) also recorded it on the basis of two males from Greece. We have seen a single female collected on 22.–27. V. 1925 by Zerny at Algeciras, Spain, deposited in the Museum in Vienna.

PANGONIUS (PANGONIUS) DIMIDIATUS LOEW, 1859

Fig. 22.

Pangonia dimidiata Loew, 1859, Neue Beitr., 6: 50.

DIAGNOSIS. Larger species with abdomen rather dark, dorsum only narrowly reddish-brown on tergites 1–3 at sides, venter entirely blackish. Face polished black, greyish dusted on almost basal half above, legs blackish-brown. Palpi and basal antennal segments short black haired. Wings tinted brownish. Male with abdominal tergites 2 and 3 mostly reddish-yellow, only median spots dark.

DESCRIPTION. ♀. *Head.* Frons dark grey dusted, distinctly convergent above. Face mostly polished black, only the upper part on almost basal half greyish dusted and finely dark haired. Occiput greyish dusted and short pale haired, lower part of head with long pale hairs. Basal antennal segments blackish-brown and clothed with minute black hairs; flagellum missing on both antennae but according to Kröber (1921) black, only basal flagellar segment brownish. Palpi very dark brown, apical segment more brownish, very long and slender, and clothed with minute black hairs. Labrum black, slightly longer than head is high.

Thorax black in ground colour, greyish dusted especially on mesonotum, latter densely light grey haired. Pleura with longer and somewhat yellowish-grey hairs. *Legs* very dark, coxae concolorous with pleura. Femora subshining blackish-brown, very finely and short pale haired. Tibiae and tarsi brown, tibiae at tip and tarsi somewhat darkened, short black haired. *Wings* tinted brownish, more distinctly along costa. Veins dark brown. Squamae pale yellow, halteres dark brown.

Abdomen mostly blackish, rather subshining, clothed with rather dense, adpressed yellowish-grey hairs. Anterior three tergites narrowly reddish-brown at sides, a very broad black median stripe which occupies more than one half of tergites 2 and 3. Venter entirely black without any brown coloration, rather densely silvery-grey haired, posterior margins of all sternites more densely haired.

♂. We have not seen the male but the description given by Kröber (1921: 52) corresponds quite well with the above description of the female except for abdominal pattern: Abdomen light reddish-yellow with brown median spots. Tergite 1 reddish-yellow only on posterior margin and on hind corners; tergite 2 with a large rectangular median spot, posterior margin greyish dusted; tergite 3 with a small more or less triangular spot which reaches the greyish dusted posterior margin; following tergites blackish-brown with greyish posterior margins and yellow sides. Pubescence long, adpressed, yellow, the blackish spots on anterior tergites with some black hairs. Venter light reddish-yellow on anterior three sternites, posterior sternites blackish with yellowish sides. Wings according to Kröber brownish with all crossveins including the appendix to vein R_4 brown clouded. The latter mentioned character points, however, to a different species!

Length. 15–17 mm.

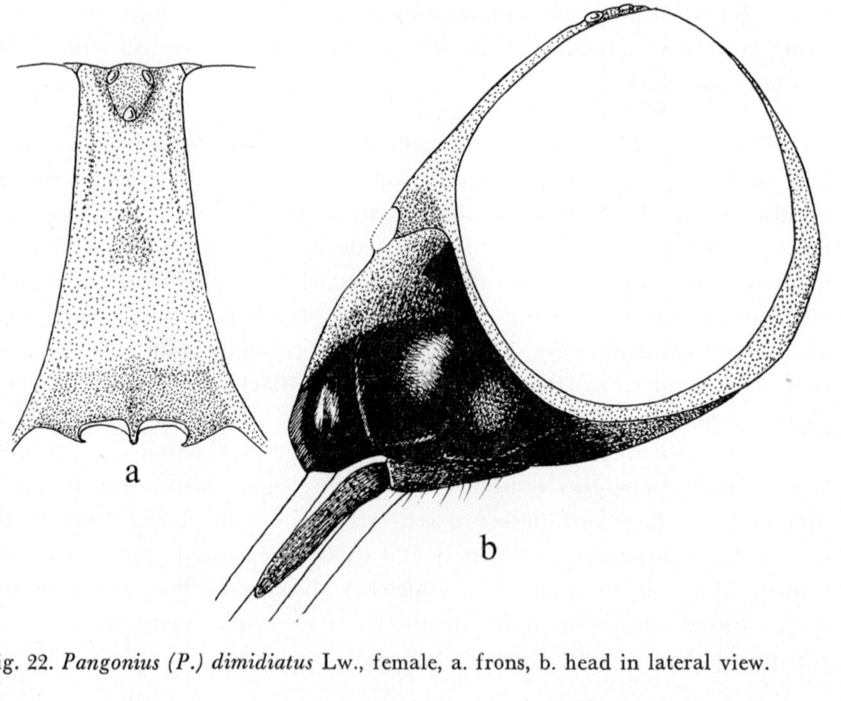

Fig. 22. *Pangonius (P.) dimidiatus* Lw., female, a. frons, b. head in lateral view.

Remarks. *P. dimidiatus* Loew is a very little known species. We have seen a single female specimen in the Vienna Museum labelled »22/5«, »Staudg. Andal. 1869«, »Griseipennis, Alte Sammlung« and »P. dimidiata Lw. Type, det. Szilády« which, of course, cannot be the type specimen. Kröber (1921) described this species from the damaged female type deposited in the Museum in Berlin, and a single male from Bosdagh. Szilády (1923: 24) referred to this species as a possible dark variety of *ferrugineus* (Meig.).

Dates. May.

Distribution. Andalusia, Spain.

CHAPTER 12

Subfamily Chrysopsinae

TRIBE CHRYSOPSINI

GENUS *CHRYSOPS* MEIGEN, 1803

Illig. Mag. Ins., 2: 267.

Heterochrysops Kröber, 1920, Zool. Jb., 43: 50.
Neochrysops Szilády, 1922, Annls Mus. nat. hung., 19: 126.
Psylochrysops Szilády, 1926, Zool. Anz., 66: 328 (nom. nov. for *Neochrysops* Szil. nec Walton, 1919).

TYPE SPECIES: *Tabanus caecutiens* Linné, 1758.

DIAGNOSIS. Medium-sized to small, usually yellow and black coloured or entirely black species. Wings with brown design which consists usually of a dark margin along costa, a middle cross-band and an apical spot. Frons in female relatively broad, slightly divergent. Frontal callus prominent, rounded or oval in shape. Facial part usually with facial, rostral and genal calli, which may be more or less reduced. Antennae very long and slender, much longer than head is deep, all segments nearly equal in size; basal two segments only exceptionally slightly swollen. Eyes metallic, emerald green or golden yellow and dark spotted in life.

REMARKS. The genus *Chrysops* Meig. belongs among the tabanid genera with the largest number of species. Most of the species belong to the subgenus *Chrysops* s. str., the other three subgenera include only a few species and only one them, subgen. *Petersenichrysops* Moucha & Chvála, 1970 (2 species), belongs to the European fauna. Subgen. *Turanochrysops* Stackelberg, 1926 with its 2 known species inhabits Central Asia, and the subgenus *Liochrysops* Philip, 1955, is a monotypical subgenus of the Nearctic region.

SUBGENUS *CHRYSOPS* S. STR.

The subgenus *Chrysops* s. str. is distributed mainly in the Nearctic (73 species and 24 forms) and Neotropic (68 species and 3 forms) regions. Altogether 40 species and 2 forms are known from the Ethiopian region, 26 species and 2 forms from the Oriental region, and 40 species with 15 forms from the Palaearctic region.

The European fauna of the subgenus *Chrysops* s. str. is represented by only 15 species with a more or less large area of distribution, and only a few species inhabit a small area on the border of the Continent, where they penetrate from neighbouring geographic regions; e. g. *C. concavus* Loew and *C. ricardoae* Pl. penetrate to Europe from western parts of Asia, *C. mauritanicus* Costa from North Africa to South Spain, and finally *C. connexus* Loew is a typical species of the western Mediterranean.

Some of the species of the subgenus are very important in human medicine, especially in the Ethiopian region, where they are vectors of *Loa loa*. *C. silaceus* Aust. and *C. dimidiatus* Wulp are important vectors of human loiasis, *C. langi* Beq. and *C. centurionis* Aust. are vectors of monkey loiasis. Several European species are known (usually in laboratory conditions) as vectors of *Pasteurella tularensis* which causes tularaemia.

The European species of the subgenus *Chrysops* s. str. can be separated into 4 rather natural groups of species, viz. *sepulcralis*-group, *relictus*-group, *rufipes*-group and *italicus*-group. The species are arranged in the keys and in the following text in the corresponding groups of species.

Key to European species of *Chrysops* s. str.

FEMALES

1 Legs including tibiae all black (*sepulcralis*-group) 2
– Legs with at least four posterior tibiae brownish 5
2 (1) Frons and face (Fig. 23a & c) uniformly shining black, abdomen (Fig. 23d) mostly black .... *sepulcralis* (F.)
– Frons and face yellow or grey in ground colour with distinctly marked polished calli 3
3 (2) Frons and face (Fig. 24a–b) grey to greyish-yellow with enlarged shining black calli. Tergite 2 (Fig. 24d) black, only slightly yellowish at sides. Sternite 2 blackish .... *nigripes* Zett.
– Frons and face yellow to yellowish-grey. Tergite 2 yellow with distinct black design. Sternite 2 yellow, usually with only a small dark patch 4
4 (3) Apical spot on wing (Pl. 6, fig. d) very narrow, reaching only to vein R_4. Tergite 2 (Fig. 25d) with black design in the form of an inverted widely open letter »V«, not connected with tergite 3. Following tergites with distinct yellow border at posterior margins .... *divaricatus* Loew
– Apical spot on wing (Pl. 6, fig. f) large, occupying nearly three quarters of vein R_4. Black design on tergite 2 (Fig. 26f) in the form of a narrow inverted letter »V«, connected below with tergite 3. Following tergites mostly black without pale borders .... *caecutiens* (L.)
5 (1) Discal cell (Pl. 7, figs. g–l) with clear central area (*italicus*-group) 12
– Discal cell clouded, at most only very indistinctly hyaline in central part ... 6

6 (5) Tergite 2 yellow with a single or paired black spots at middle. Anal cell closed, wings clear with distinct brown pattern (*relictus*-group) 7

– Tergite 2 except for side margins black with greyish median triangle. Anal cell open, wings tinted brown with indefined brown pattern (*rufipes*-group) 11

7 (6) Tergite 2 (Fig. 27d) with a small square or oval black spot at middle near anterior margin. Apical spot on wing (Pl. 6, fig. h) large, occupying about three quarters of vein R_4 .... *viduatus* (F.)

– Tergite 2 with two larger black central spots of usually triangular shape 8

8 (7) The two black spots on tergite 2 (Fig. 28e) connected anteriorly, reaching anterior margin of the tergite. Apical spot on wing (Pl. 6, fig. k) large, occupying nearly the whole vein R_4 .... *relictus* Meig.

– Black spots on tergite 2 widely separated and not reaching anterior margin of the tergite. Apical spot on wing not so large, occupying at most apical half of vein R_4 9

9 (8) Apical spot on wing (Pl. 6, fig. l) very narrowly connected with median cross-band, leaving most of cell R_1 clear. The two black spots on tergite 2 (Fig. 29c) only small and rather circular .... *ricardoae* Pleske

– Apical spot on wing broadly connected with median cross-band, whole cell R_1 clouded. The two black spots on tergite 2 larger and elongated 10

10 (9) Femora black. The two black spots on tergite 2 (Fig. 30e) rather close. Facial calli (Fig. 30b) large, broadly connected with black ventral callus and only narrowly separated from eye-margins .... *parallelogrammus* Zell.

– Femora yellowish-brown. The two black spots on tergite 2 (Fig. 31d) widely separated dividing the tergite into thirds. Facial calli (Fig. 31b) not so large, more narrowly connected with brownish and often denuded rostral callus .... *concavus* Loew

11 (6) Darker species with indefined striped thorax and brownish legs, base of femora darkened. Facial and genal calli (Fig. 32a–b) large, genal calli touching eye-margins and usually connected with facial calli .... *rufipes* Meig.

– More yellowish species with predominantly yellow legs. Mesonotum with three broad, shining black longitudinal stripes. Calli on head (Fig. 33a–b) smaller, genal calli separated from eye-margins and no connection with facial calli .... *melichari* Mik

12 (5) Facial calli (Fig. 34b) large, broadly connected with rostral callus, genal calli large 13

– Facial calli (Fig. 36b) small, broadly separated from eye-margins and only indistinctly connected with rostral callus, if present. Usually no genal calli . 14

13 (12) Apical spot on wing (Pl. 7, fig. g) small, occupying one third to one half of vein R_4. The two black spots on tergite 2 (Fig. 34d) smaller and rather perpendicular. Smaller species, 6–9 mm .... *flavipes* Meig.

– Apical spot on wing (Pl. 7, fig. i) large, occupying three quarters of vein R_4. The two black spots on tergite 2 (Fig. 35d) large, rather oblique, directed to posterior corners of the tergite. Larger species, 8.5–10 mm ...... *italicus* Meig.

14 (12) Apical spot on wing (Pl. 7, fig. k) very large, occupying the whole vein R_4, not connected with cross-band along costa. Palpi shortened, at most half length of proboscis. Abdomen (Fig. 36d) yellow with paired black spots on tergites 2 to 4 .... *connexus* Loew

– Apical spot on wing (Pl. 7, fig. l) not so large, occupying about three-quarters of vein R_4 and narrowly connected with median cross-band along costa; cross-band with deep outer incision in first posterior cell. Palpi longer than half length of proboscis. Abdomen (Fig. 37d) mainly greyish ... *mauritanicus* Costa

MALES[1]

[1] The male of *concavus* is unknown.

1 Legs unicolorous black (*sepulcralis*-group) 2

– Legs bicoloured, at least posterior four tibiae brownish 5

2 (1) Face entirely polished black, no trace of pale ground colour. Abdomen black .. .. *sepulcralis* (F.)

– Face with distinctly separated polished black calli on yellowish to greyish ground colour 3

3 (2) Tergite 2 (Fig. 25e) yellow with distinct black design in the form of an inverted and widely open letter »V«. Apical spot on wing very narrow, of the same width as cell R_1 and reaching only to vein R_4 .... *divaricatus* Loew

– Abdomen black, anterior two tergites at most with small yellowish patches at sides. Apical spot on wing distinct, at least slightly broader than width of cell R_1 4

4 (3) All tergites with distinct, narrow greyish to greyish-yellow posterior margins and median triangles. Apical spot on wing narrow, occupying only one-third of vein R_4, outer margin of cross-band with distinct projection towards base of vein R_4 .... *nigripes* Zett.

– Abdomen (Fig. 26e) entirely black with usually only a small lateral patch on tergite 2. Apical spot on wing (Pl. 6, fig. e) large, occupying three-quarters of vein R_4 and no projection to outer margin of median cross-band *caecutiens* (L.)

5 (1) Discal cell with clear central area (*italicus*-group) 11

– Discal cell brown, at most only slightly paler in central part 6

6 (5) Eyes meeting on frons. Tergite 2 yellow with large black central patch. Anal cell closed (*relictus*-group) 7

– Eyes narrowly separated on frons. Abdomen predominantly black, all tergites with yellow posterior margins, tergites 1–2 with small yellowish patches at sides. Anal cell open (*rufipes*-group) 10

7 (6) Apical spot on wing only very narrowly connected with median cross-band, leaving most of cell R_1 clear. Tergite 2 (Fig. 29d) with large black patch at middle leaving only sides yellow .... *ricardoae* Pleske

– Apical spot on wing broadly connected with median cross-band, whole cell R_1 clouded 8

8 (7) Palpi (Fig. 28d) very short and blunt ended, shorter than half length of proboscis. Tergite 2 (Fig. 28f) with two black triangular spots broadly connected anteriorly .... *relictus* Meig.

– Palpi (Fig. 27f) long and pointed, much longer than half length of proboscis . 9

9 (8) Tergite 2 (Fig. 27e) with large square central spot which is only very narrowly separated from posterior margin. Tergites 3 and 4 black with yellow stripe at posterior margins .... *viduatus* (F.)

– Tergite 2 (Fig. 30d) with two black triangular spots at middle which are connected anteriorly, tergites 3 and 4 with similar black design .... *parallelogrammus* Zell.

10 (6) Antennal segment 1 (Fig. 32f) swollen but rather short, as long as two-thirds of depth of head. Mesonotum indistinctly striped. Legs extensively darkened .... *rufipes* Meig.

– Antennal segments 1–2 (Fig. 33e) long and very stout, segment 1 about as long as head is deep. Mesonotum apparently striped. Legs mostly yellowish .... *melichari* Mik

11 (5) Eyes narrowly separated on frons. Abdomen (Fig. 34e) yellow with black design 12

– Eyes meeting on frons even if for a short distance. Abdomen (Fig. 35e) mostly black 13

12 (11) Antennae mostly black, subcallus dulled. Apical spot on wing (Pl. 7, fig. g) rather small, occupying about half length of vein R_4 .... *flavipes* Meig.

– Antennal segments 1–2 yellowish brown, subcallus polished black. Apical spot on wing (Pl. 7, fig. k) very large, occupying whole vein R_4 .... *connexus* Loew

13 (11) Eyes meeting for a short distance. Antennae black. Abdomen (Fig. 35e) black, tergite 2 (or also 1) with a very small yellow patch at sides, second and following tergites with small greyish median triangles at posterior margins .... *italicus* Meig.

– Eyes meeting for a long distance. Antennal segment 1 mostly brown. Abdomen (Fig. 37e) black, tergite 2 with three greyish triangles at posterior margin, forming on following segments greyish posterior borders .. *mauritanicus* Costa

SEPULCRALIS-GROUP

Legs including tibiae all black. Abdomen usually black coloured or tergite 2 yellow with a black pattern in a form of an inverted letter »V« *(divaricatus* and ♀ *caecutiens).* Facial calli well developed, sometimes merged forming entirely black face. Wings with enlarged, distinct dark pattern. Generally northern species in distribution.

CHRYSOPS (CHRYSOPS) SEPULCRALIS (FABRICIUS, 1794)

Fig. 23; pl. 1: fig. f; pl. 6: figs. a—b.

Tabanus sepulcralis Fabricius, 1794, Ent. Syst., 4: 374 (*sepulchralis* auct.).
Chrysops maura Siebke, 1863, Nyt Mag. Naturvid., 12: 108.

Diagnosis. A small species with frons, face, legs and abdomen entirely black. Wings tinted with brownish but distinct brown cross-band and narrow apical spot are present.

Description. ♀. *Head.* Frons with a wide polished black frontal callus which reaches as far as vertex. Calli of face and jowls coalescent, so that whole face is polished black leaving only a very small, downwards narrowed yellowish patch just below antennae. Antennae and palpi black, latter long and pointed.

Thorax entirely black, densely covered with fine black hairs, mesonotum with some yellowish-golden hairs. Pleura and especially mesopleura usually yellowish-golden haired. *Legs* black, fine black haired. *Wings* with a distinct dark brown cross-band. Apical spot evenly wide, occupying the whole width of cell R_1 and disappearing just behind vein R_4. First basal cell nearly whole brownish, hyaline only before apex, second basal cell except for basal quarter entirely hyaline. Otherwise wings faintly tinged with brownish, especially on costal half. Halteres black.

Abdomen entirely black, tergites shining black, densely covered with short black hairs, only on hind margins predominantly with golden hairs. Sternites black, yellowish-golden haired.

♂. Resembling female but wings more brownish coloured and both basal cells hyaline only before apex.

Length. 6–9.5 mm.

VARIABILITY. The pilosity of thoracic pleura and of abdomen is rather variable. Entirely black haired specimens were described by Siebke (1863) as *Chrysops maura*, which has in fact no taxonomic value. There is a continuous sequence with all intermediate forms from yellowish-golden to entirely black haired specimens, the last mentioned are usually named by present authors as f. *maurus* Siebke. At some localities in Central Europe (Bohemia) the dark haired to entirely black specimens are more often to be found, especially in the male sex.

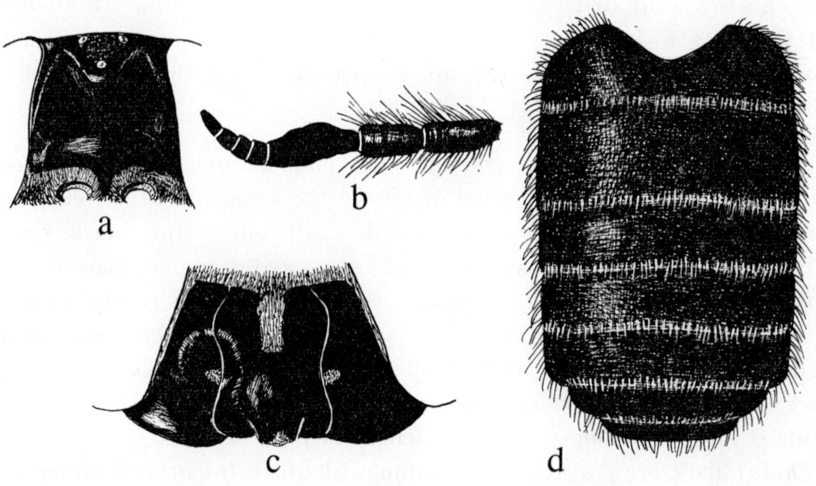

Fig. 23. *Chrysops (C.) sepulcralis* (F.), female, a. frons, b. antenna, c. face, d. abdomen.

DATES. From the end of June to August.

BIOLOGY. The species occurs on swampy biotopes, especially on peat bogs and therefore its occurrence in the whole area of distribution is comparatively isolated. Similarly as in other species of this genus the adults do not fly far from the places where the larvae live. The females attack man.

DISTRIBUTION. A typical European species but it does not occur in the south. *C. sepulcralis* is known from Great Britain, eastwards as far as West Siberia. It is well known from all Scandinavian countries including Denmark, in the European part of the U.S.S.R. northwards to Murmansk and Archangelsk. From the Asiatic part it is known only from West Siberia (river Ishim near Tjumen) and from North Kazakhstan (Akmolinsk). The southern border of its area of distribution in Europe lies in France (Masif Central), Switzerland, Jugoslavia (Bosna) and South Ukraine. Not yet recorded from Hungary, Rumania, Albania, Greece and Bulgaria.

CHRYSOPS (CHRYSOPS) NIGRIPES ZETTERSTEDT, 1838

Fig. 24; pl. 6: fig. c.

Chrysops nigripes Zetterstedt, 1838, Ins. Lapp., p. 519.
Chrysops lapponicus Loew, 1858, Verh. zool.-bot. Ges. Wien, 8: 624.

DIAGNOSIS. A small black species with black legs, abdomen predominantly shining black, only first two tergites slightly yellowish at sides. All abdominal segments with narrow greyish-yellow border on hind margin. Dark brown pattern on wings distinct, apical spot narrow, of the same width as cell R_1.

DESCRIPTION. ♀. *Head.* Frons greyish with a large shining black frontal callus, which is only narrowly separated from the eye-margins; vertex black around ocelli. Facial part grey to grey-yellow, all calli shining black. Facial calli large and roundish, very narrowly separated from eye-margin, and broadly connected with rostral callus; the latter sometimes connected with the polished black lower part of genae. Antennae black, segment 1 sometimes slightly brownish on basal half; segments 1—2 with fine black hairs. Palpi black, sometimes brownish on the inner side, narrow and very pointed, about as long as or longer than half length of proboscis.

Thorax dark grey dusted, mesonotum with three broad and rather shining black longitudinal stripes which occupy nearly the whole mesonotum;

scutellum nearly shining black. Pleura, margins of mesonotum and scutellum with longer yellowish hairs. *Legs* entirely black, only base of posterior four tarsi sometimes slightly brownish, middle and hind femora with very long and fine pale hairs beneath, the hairs being distinctly longer than femora are wide. *Wings* with distinct dark brown pattern, both basal cells brownish at base, first basal cell clear in only apical third, the second one in apical two-thirds. Cross-band reaches hind wing-margin only in anal cell, apical spot narrow, connected with cross-band in the whole width of cell R_1, apically not widened, occupying only apical third of vein R_4. Outer margin of cross-band with distinct tooth pointing to base of vein R_4. Halteres blackish-brown.

Abdomen predominantly shining black with sparse pale hairs. Tergites 1–2 with small yellowish patch at sides, all tergites with narrow greyish-yellow to pale grey hind margin and median equilateral triangle, that on tergite 2 the largest. Sternites black with somewhat broader greyish hind margin, sternites 1–2 sometimes slightly tinged with yellow at sides.

♂. Eyes meeting on a short distance, facets on upper two-thirds larger but not sharply separated from the lower third. Calli on face and genae larger and more broadly connected than in female. Antennal segments 1–2 with long black hairs. Palpi very pointed and about as long as half length of proboscis. Thoracic pleura with predominantly black hairs. Wings more infuscated than in female, both basal cells with small clear area in apical third only and cross-band widened towards hind margin. Legs and abdomen as in female, median triangles on tergites smaller.

Length. 8–9 mm.

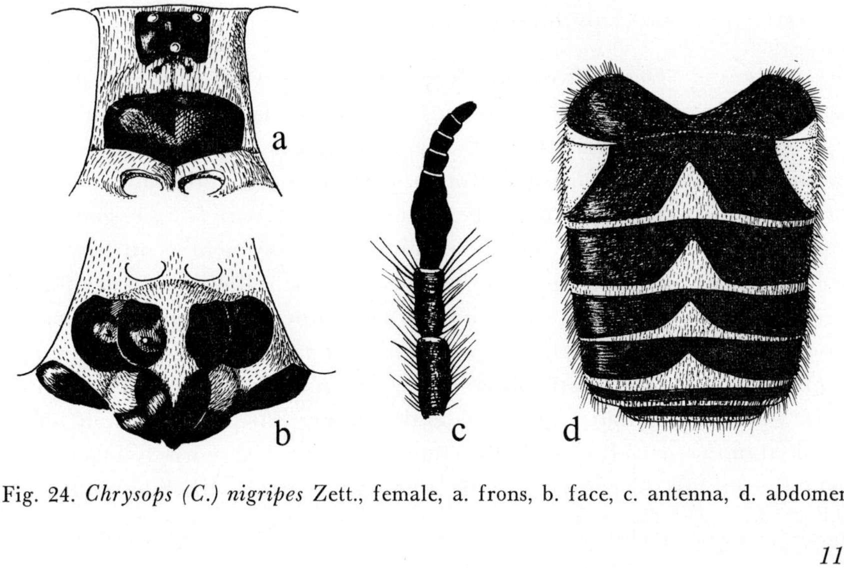

Fig. 24. *Chrysops (C.) nigripes* Zett., female, a. frons, b. face, c. antenna, d. abdomen.

VARIABILITY. Only a very slightly variable species.

DATES. June and July.

BIOLOGY. A typical species of swampy biotopes, especially near rivers and brooks. Rather a common species in northern taiga, it forms at the time of its maximal occurrence in the Siberian taiga as much as 15.3 % of the tabanid population (Violovič, 1968). The population rapidly decreases southwards, e. g. in Kazachstan it is very rare species.

DISTRIBUTION. A Holarctic species known from North America from Alaska to as far as Labrador, in the United States as far as Idaho and Maine. In Europe a typical northern species known from Scandinavia exclusive of Denmark, in northern parts of the U.S.S.R. from the Kola Peninsula as far as Kamtchatka, Sachalin and the Japanese island of Hokkaido. It is recorded also from Korea and North East China.

CHRYSOPS (CHRYSOPS) DIVARICATUS LOEW, 1858

Fig. 25; pl. 6: fig. d.

Chrysops divaricatus Loew, 1858, Verh. zool.-bot. Ges. Wien, 8: 624.

DIAGNOSIS. Face yellow with black calli, legs entirely black. Wings with narrow apical spot which reaches only to R_4. Tergite 2 yellow with black design in the form of a widely open inverted letter »V«. Other tergites with distinct yellow border on hind margin.

DESCRIPTION. ♀. *Head.* Frons and face yellowish grey to yellow dusted, former more greyish. Frontal callus large, polished black and only narrowly separated from the eye-margins. Vertex shining black on the whole width. Facial calli narrowly separated from the eye-margins and connected with the small rostral callus. Calli on genae large; lower part of face, genae and vertex with longer yellow hairs. Antennae black, segment 1 on basal half and usually on the inner side on the whole length yellow-brown, segment 3 brownish at base. Palpi long and narrow, inner side reddish-brown to brown-yellow, outside black, and with fine pale hairs at base.

Thorax black in ground colour with grey dust, only mesonotum shining black with two median and two lateral pale grey stripes; scutellum black. Whole thorax fine yellowish haired, most on sides. *Legs* entirely black, only metatarsi slightly brownish; middle and hind femora with long pale hairs beneath, rest of legs black haired. *Wings* very clear, dark brown pattern restricted to dark border along costal margin, to middle cross-band which reaches hind wing-margin only at tip of anal cell, and to a very narrow apical spot of the width of cell R_1, disappearing just behind vein R_4. Halteres black.

Abdomen. Tergites 1–2 yellow, the first with black central spot, the second with a black design in the form of an inverted widely open letter »V«, the apices of which do not reach tergite 3. Following tergites black with distinct yellow border on hind margins and small triangular spots at middle. Sternites 1–3 yellow with rounded black central spot, last sternites greyish, yellowish on hind margins.

♂. Facets on upper two-thirds larger and distinctly separated from lower third. Dark pattern on wings is more extended at base, so that both basal cells are mainly dark. Dark design on tergite 2 is rather similar to that of

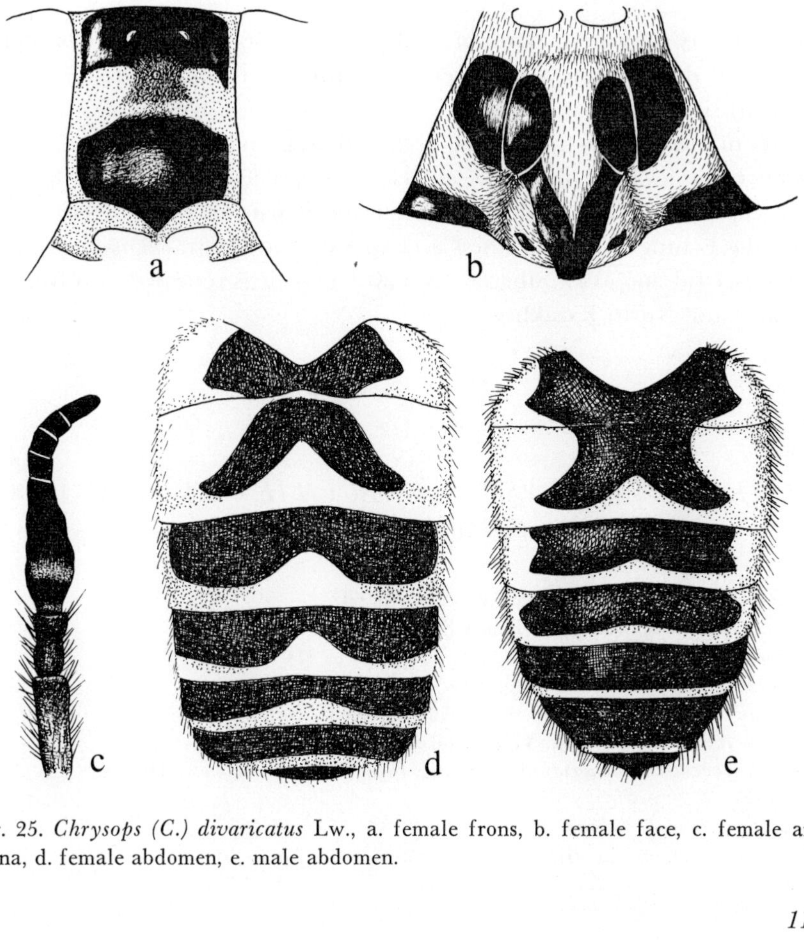

Fig. 25. *Chrysops (C.) divaricatus* Lw., a. female frons, b. female face, c. female antenna, d. female abdomen, e. male abdomen.

female, yellow bands on hind margin of following tergites are broader at sides. Otherwise as in female.

Length. 8–12 mm.

VARIABILITY. The dark design on tergite 2 in female is rather variable; the black design is only distinct in some specimens on the upper part of the tergite, resembling in this way more the pattern of the common *Chrysops relictus* Meig.; this, however, differs in the brown tibiae and in the broad apical spot on wings.

DATES. June to August.

BIOLOGY. *C. divaricatus* occurs in swampy regions, especially on peat bogs, near large lakes and ponds, in the north it is a typical species of taiga and above all of forest taiga. The females attack man, horses, horned cattle and dogs.

DISTRIBUTION. Northern parts of Europe and Asia. The western border of its area of distribution lies in Central Europe in Germany (Bayern, Oberfranken), the southern border in South Bohemia, where it is a common species in a few isolated biotopes; it should be found also in Austria. A very common species in Scandinavia, especially in Sweden and Finland, but only once captured in Denmark. In the European part of the U.S.S.R. known from the Leningrad region, the Carelian SSR and Central Russia eastwards as far as Ural and West Siberia (river Kolyma); it is recorded also from the Ukraine and North Kazakhstan.

CHRYSOPS (CHRYSOPS) CAECUTIENS (LINNÉ, 1758)

Fig. 26; pl. 6: figs. e–f.

Tabanus caecutiens Linné, 1758, Syst. Nat., p. 602.
Tabanus lugubris Linné, 1761, Fauna Suec., p. 464.
Tabanus maritimus Scopoli, 1763, Ent. Carniol., p. 374.
Tabanus nubilosus Harris, 1782, Expos. Engl. Ins., p. 28.
Chrysops crudelis Wiedemann, 1828, Ausser. zweifl. Ins., 1: 195.
Chrysops ludens Loew, 1858, Verh. zool.-bot. Ges., Wien, 8: 628.
Chrysops caecutiens f. *meridionalis* Strobl, 1906, Mems. R. Soc. esp. Hist. nat., 3 (1905): 277.
Chrysops hermanni Kröber, 1920, Zool. Jb., 43: 117.
Chrysops caecutiens var. *trifenestratus* Kröber, 1920, Zool. Jb., 43: 119.

DIAGNOSIS. Face yellow with black calli, legs predominantly black. Wings with large apical spot occupying three quarters of vein R_4. Tergites 1–2 in female yellow, tergite 2 at middle with black pattern in form of an inverted letter »V«. Abdomen in male predominantly black.

DESCRIPTION. ♀. *Head.* Face greyish-yellow to yellow dusted, all calli well developed, shining black to black-brown. Facial calli connected with rostral callus and with eye-margin. Frons greyish to yellowish, frontal callus large, only narrowly separated from eye-margins and usually joined with polished black vertex. Antennal segment 1 often slightly brownish at base, rest of antennae black. Palpi black, long, narrow and pointed.

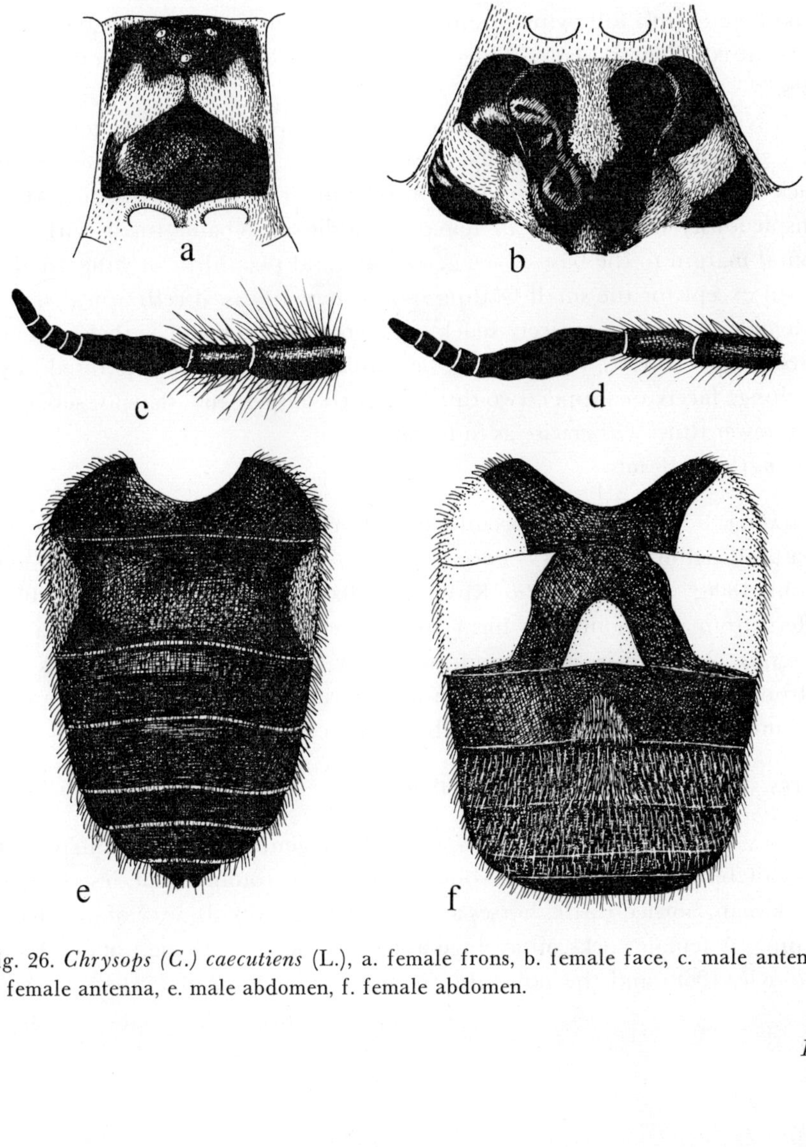

Fig. 26. *Chrysops (C.) caecutiens* (L.), a. female frons, b. female face, c. male antenna, d. female antenna, e. male abdomen, f. female abdomen.

Thorax black with greyish tomentum, gold-yellow haired, especially on notopleural lobes and on mesopleura. Mesonotum with two broad shining black lateral stripes, hind part of mesonotum and scutellum shining black. *Legs* black, only tibiae sometimes slightly brownish at extreme base, and first two tarsal segments of posterior two pairs more or less brown-yellow. Legs covered with fine black hairs, posterior four femora with paler hairs beneath. *Wings* with distinct dark brown pattern. Middle cross-band wide and reaches as far as posterior wing-margin; apical spot large, occupying three quarters of vein R_4, and broadly connected with cross-band on the whole width of cell R_1. Halteres black, paler at base.

Abdomen. Tergites 1–2 yellow, first with black central spot, second with black pattern in the form of a slender inverted letter »V« which is connected at both ends with following tergite. The rest of the tergites black, yellowish-grey haired. Venter blackish-grey, first two or three sternites yellowish at sides.

♂. Not resembling the female; abdomen entirely black, only tergite 2 at sides slightly yellowish and first three or four tergites clothed with only black hairs. The yellow coloration on sternites 1—2 is more distinct. Wings conspicuously darker than in female; middle cross-band fused with dark frontal margin to the base of wing, so that basal two-thirds of wing are dark brown except for the small hyaline spot at base of discal cell; apical spot as in female. Antennae entirely black, segment 1 stouter and with long black hairs. Palpi shorter, half as long as proboscis, black and pointed. Eyes touching, facets on upper two-thirds slightly larger and sharply separated from lower third. Otherwise as in female.

Length. 7—10 mm.

VARIABILITY. A pale form occurs very often in the southern parts of the area of distribution which is known as f. *ludens* Loew, 1858 (= *meridionalis* Strobl, 1806; = *trifenestratus* Kröber, 1920; = *hermanni* Kröber, 1920). It differs from the nominate form in the reduction of the black pattern on tergite 2, which is usually indicated only by a small rounded black spot at frontal margin of the tergite, but all intermediates to the nominate form are known. The male differs in the black haired sides of thorax.

DATES. May to beginning of September.

BIOLOGY. One of the commonest species of the genus which inhabits various types of biotopes near water, sometimes a very common species. Females attack man, horned cattle, horses and wild living animals, very often till late evening. A female sucks on average about 42 mg. (30—55 mg.) of the blood (Violovič, 1968) and the possibility of the transmission of *Pasteurella tula-*

rensis was demonstrated in the laboratory (Olsufjev, 1935). *Machimus atricapillus* Fall. (Diptera), *Mellinus arvensis* L., *Bembex rostrata Fabr.* and *Ectemnius cavifrons* Thoms. (Hymenoptera) are known to be predators. *Trichogramma evanescens* Westw. is a parasite of the eggs, *Eurymermis chrysopidis* Müll. parasites in the larvae. The larva was described by Beling (1888), Stammer (1924), Bischoff (1925), Vimmer (1925), Skufin (1967) and Ježek (1970), the last mentioned author also described the pupal stage.

Distribution. A well known species throughout Europe, from Great Britain to as far as East Asia. In the north it is known from the vicinity of Archangelsk and Murmansk, and from North Scandinavia. The eastern border lies in the Jakutsk region and in Mongolia. In Southern Europe it is well known from all the countries from Portugal through the Balkan Peninsula (including Sicily, all Greek Islands and the Baleares) to the European part of Turkey, in the non European regions from Transcaucasus, Kazakhstan and Iran but not yet recorded from Afghanistan. The southern form *ludens* Loew occurs on the same biotopes together with the nominate form. *Caecutiens* has been recorded from all the European countries except for Ireland.

RELICTUS-GROUP

Legs not entirely black, at least four posterior tibiae brown, facial calli always well developed and distinct. Wings clear with distinct dark pattern. Abdomen always yellow on tergite 2 with a single or paired small black median spots. Species occurring usually throughout Europe.

CHRYSOPS (CHRYSOPS) VIDUATUS (FABRICIUS, 1794)

Fig. 2 b; Fig. 27; pl. 1: fig. d; pl. 6: figs. g–h.

Tabanus viduatus Fabricius, 1794, Ent. Syst., 4: 374.
Chrysops pictus Meigen, 1820, Syst. Beschr., 2: 70.
Chrysops quadratus Meigen, 1820, Syst. Beschr., 2: 70.
Chrysops novus Schiner, 1868, Novara Reise, Dipt., p. 103.
Chrysops minor Szilády, 1917, Arch. Naturgesch., Abt. A, 83 (4): 119.

Diagnosis. Four posterior tibiae brown, apical spot on wing large, occupying about three quarters of vein R_4. Tergite 2 in female yellow with a small dark isolated spot at middle near front margin. In the male the dark spot is enlarged and occupies nearly the whole midpart of tergite 2.

Description. ♀. *Head.* Frons and face yellowish-grey to gold-yellow, facial calli widely joined with large rostral callus, calli on genae small. Frontal callus large, it reaches nearly to the eye-margins, and is usually very narrowly connected with shining black vertex. Antennae black-grey, segment 1 more or less brownish, segment 3 slightly brownish at extreme base. Palpi long and rather slender, blackish-grey on the inner side and nearly reddish-brown on outer side.

Thorax blackish-grey in ground colour. Mesonotum with three indistinct, wide longitudinal polished black stripes, scutellum black. Thorax wholly golden haired, especially dense at sides of mesonotum and on pleura. Fore *legs* black, only tibiae at extreme base slightly brownish. Tibiae and first tarsal segment of posterior two pairs brown, apical tarsal segments and femora black, the latter often brownish at tip. *Wings* with distinct dark pattern, sharply separated from the clear parts; middle cross-band wide and reaches on the whole width the hind wing-margin; apical spot, connected with cross-band in the whole cell R_1, rather large, occupying about three quarters of vein R_4, but not sharply separated from the clear area of wing. Both basal cells clear, only on both tips brown. Halteres black.

Abdomen. Tergites 1–2 yellow, first black at middle, second with small black, round to square spot at middle near front margin. The following tergites black, at hind margins with yellow to greyish-yellow fringe forming a small triangular spot at middle and widening at sides. Last tergites nearly greyish. Sternites 1–3 yellow, first with small dark spot at middle, third with a large one; last sternites blackish-grey.

♂. Facets on upper half of eyes enlarged and sharply separated from those on the lower half. Antennal segment 1 with long black hairs. Palpi long and slender, pointed, longer than half length of proboscis. Wings on basal third predominantly brown, both basal cells slightly hyaline only before tip. The dark spot on tergite 2 occupies nearly the whole middle third of the tergite, from the following tergite it is only narrowly separated by yellow stripe. The yellow coloration on following tergites is more distinct than in female, especially at sides. Sternite 2 with large, dark roundish spot at middle. Otherwise as in female.

Length. 7–11 mm.

Variability. Only a slightly variable species except for the shape of the small black spot at middle of tergite 2 in female; the spot is round, triangular to square *(quadratus* Meig.).

Dates. June to August.

Biology. A species inhabiting various types of biotopes. It can be found in wet meadows, in forest clearings but also in dry places. In comparison with other common European species of the genus it seems to prefer warmer regions, and it is rather rare in Siberian taiga. Females attack man, horned cattle, horses, red deers, etc. Skufin (1967) described the larva, Ježek (1970) both larva and pupa.

Distribution. A rather widely distributed species in Europe, and very common in suitable localities; known from England to as far as West Siberia but is there very rare (up to the present known only from the environment of Tomsk). In the north it is known from Carelia and from southern parts of Scandinavia (Sweden, Finland), but not yet recorded from Ireland and Norway. In South Europe it is a common species from Portugal as far as to the Balkan Peninsula including the Mediterranean isles, and it penetrates through Turkey to the Caucasian coast of the Black Sea; not yet recorded from the Transcaucasus.

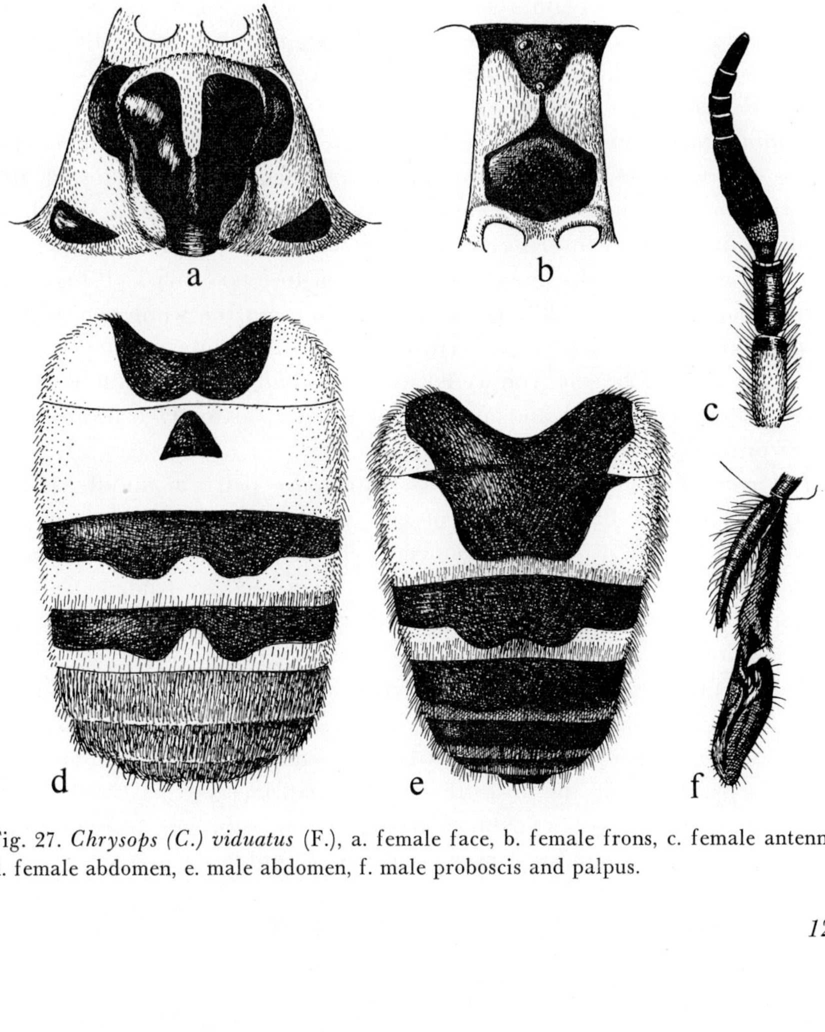

Fig. 27. *Chrysops (C.) viduatus* (F.), a. female face, b. female frons, c. female antenna, d. female abdomen, e. male abdomen, f. male proboscis and palpus.

CHRYSOPS (CHRYSOPS) RELICTUS MEIGEN, 1820

Fig. 1 c; fig. 28; pl. 6: figs. i–k.

Chrysops relictus Meigen, 1820, Syst. Beschr., 2: 69.
Chrysops melanopleurus Wahlberg, 1848, Öfvers. K. Vetensk Akad. Förh., 9: 200.
Chrysops morio Zetterstedt, 1849, Dipt. Scand., 8: 2942 (nomen nudum).

DIAGNOSIS. A species with brown tibiae and very large apical spot on wing occupying nearly the whole vein R_4. Tergite 2 in both sexes yellow with two short black spots, which are connected at front margin.

DESCRIPTION. ♀. *Head.* Face yellow dusted, facial calli roundish, distinctly separated from the eye-margin and narrowly connected with small paired rostral calli. Genal calli small. Frons greyish-yellow, frontal callus shining black, large and roundish, with its upper side more or less connected with a polished black patch on vertex. Antennae black, segment 1 sometimes brown-yellow beneath and on the inner side, segment 3 occasionally slightly brownish at base. Palpi long and pointed, pale brown, on the outside dark brown to black.

Thorax. Mesonotum blackish-grey, pale grey dusted and with three more or less distinct wide black longitudinal stripes. Scutellum grey dusted, thorax with only fine pale hairs. *Femora* black; fore tibiae except apical third, whole of middle and hind tibiae, and first two tarsal segments, brown-yellow. Apical three tarsal segments and whole of fore tarsi black. *Wings* with distinct dark pattern, middle cross-band reaching on the whole width hind wing-margin; apical spot large, occupying more than three-quarters of vein R_4, nearly the whole vein, connected with cross-band in the whole width of cell R_1. Both cross-band and apical spot usually distinctly translucent in center of individual cells. Halteres black.

Abdomen. Tergites 1–2 yellow, first with black patch at middle, second with characteristic black pattern of two short black spots triangular or rectangular shaped, which are connected in front. The following tergites black with wide greyish-yellow band and large median triangle at hind margin. Venter greyish-yellow, first two or three sternites at sides predominantly yellowish.

♂. Antennal segment 1 more swollen than in female and with longer dark hairs. Palpi black and very short, not reaching to middle of proboscis, blunt ended. Facets in upper two-thirds of eyes not very much enlarged, but sharply separated from the lower third with small facets.

Tergite 2 yellow with two black triangular spots broadly connected in front, the following tergites darker with greyish middle triangular spots on tergites 2–5, last tergites black. Venter of abdomen yellow, sternites 2–4 with black central spot at front margin, last sternites black. Thorax, legs and wings as in female.

Length. 6–11 mm.

Variability. Only a slightly variable species, no distinct forms are known.

Dates. June to August.

Biology. One of the commonest species of the genus in Europe inhabiting various types of biotopes, the adults are to be found most often near water but also in forests. The bionomy and life history of *relictus* have been stu-

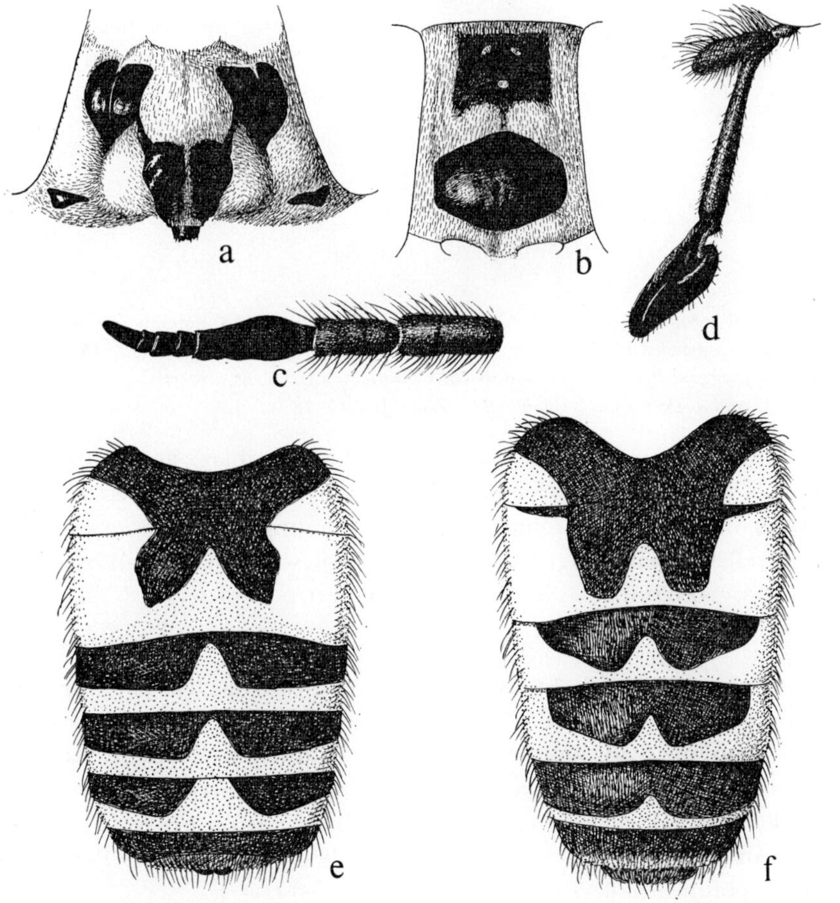

Fig. 28. *Chrysops (C.) relictus* Meig., a. female face, b. female frons, c. female antenna, d. male proboscis and palpus, e. female abdomen, f. male abdomen.

died by many authors, the flight period in Central Europe is from about 50 to 80 days. The females attack man, horned cattle, horses, camels, red deer, but also rodents, and are known as vectors of tularaemia. *Dysmachus forcipula* Zett. (Diptera, Asilidae) and *Ectemnius continuus* Fabr. (Hymenoptera) are recorded as predators. The eggs are often parasitized by *Trichogramma evanescens* Westw. (Violovič, 1968). The larva was described by Beling (1882), Marchand (1920), Skufin (1967), Vimmer (1925), Tamarina (1956) and Ježek (1970); the last three named authors also described the pupal stage.

Distribution. Very often the commonest species of the genus in Central and North Europe. Its area of distribution runs from Ireland and Great Britain eastwards to the Jakutsk region, northwards to Murmansk. It is recorded from all Scandinavian countries including the northern parts of Lappland. A rather common species also in South Europe but not yet known in Portugal or on the Mediterranean isles.

CHRYSOPS (CHRYSOPS) RICARDOAE PLESKE, 1910

Fig. 29; pl. 6: fig. 1.

Chrysops ricardoae Pleske, 1910, Annls Mus. Zool. Acad. Sci. St. Petersb., 15: 461.
Chrysops przewalskii Pleske, 1910, Annls Mus. Zool. Acad. Sci. St. Petersb., 15: 464.
Chrysops wagneri Pleske, 1910, Annls Mus. Zool. Acad. Sci. St. Petersb., 15: 466.
Chrysops pseudoricardoae Kröber, 1920, Zool. Jb., 43: 78.

Diagnosis. A medium-sized species with brown tibiae, apical spot only narrowly connected with median cross-band, the brown connecting stripe between these two in the form of brown clouding only close to costa, the rest of cell R_1 clear. Tergite 2 in female yellow with two median oval black spots near posterior margin; male with central part of tergite 2 black, leaving only the sides yellow.

Description. ♀. *Head.* Frons and face yellowish, ocellar swelling shiny black, triangular, lower frontal callus large, narrowly separated from eye-margins, oblong oval, polished black. Facial calli shiny black to brownish, narrowly separated from eye-margins and widely contiguous to yellowish rostral callus, which is often dusted apically. Calli on genae large, shiny black. Antennae black, or segments 1–2 nearly yellowish brown. Palpi dark, apically pointed, half as long as the black proboscis.

Thorax black in ground colour, sides of mesonotum and parts of pleura yellowish. Mesonotum occasionally with two narrow grey longitudinal stripes. Scutellum black. *Legs.* Fore coxae, four posterior tibiae and base of fore tibiae yellowish, otherwise legs dark brown. Tarsi nearly black, the first or first two segments on posterior two pairs yellowish. *Wings.* Clear with distinct brown-grey markings. Median cross-band reaching posterior margin at fourth posterior cell like a greyish shadow. Apical spot only faint and small, only very narrowly connected with median cross-band in cell R_1, more than a half of the cell being clear. Apical spot rather narrow occupying only apical third of vein R_4. Both basal cells nearly clear, only indistinctly clouded at extreme apex. Squamae yellowish-brown, halteres dark brown.

Abdomen mostly yellow on tergites 1–2, tergites 1 with small black median spot which is hardly as broad as scutellum, tergite 2 with two black oblong patches near posterior margin. Tergites 3—5 with black anterior bands which are interrupted in middle and at sides, leaving rather narrow posterior margin yellow; posterior tergites nearly blackish and rather densely yellowish haired as whole abdomen. Venter unicolorous yellow on first three segments, posterior segments blackish.

♂. Eyes touching on frons, antennae black, segments 1—2 rather long black haired. Facial calli more prominent than in ♀ and polished black. Palpi long, distinctly longer than half length of proboscis. Thorax mostly black including mesonotal margin and pleura. Legs extensively darkened, usually only middle tibiae distinctly brownish. Wings as in ♀, the dark pattern is more distinct, the brown pattern occupies most of both basal cells, at most only apical thirds clear. Abdomen black, only tergite 2 yellow at sides, the median spot very large on the whole width of the tergite; ster-

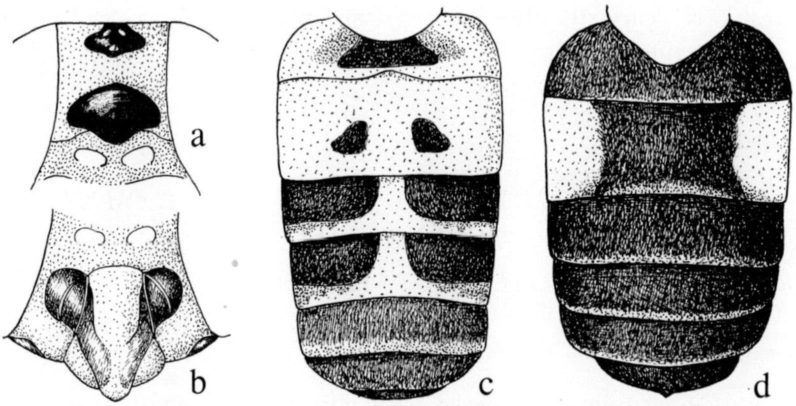

Fig. 29. *Chrysops (C.) ricardoae* Pl., a. female frons, b. female face, c. female abdomen, d. male abdomen.

nite 2 yellow with only narrow black medial spot reaching both anterior and posterior margins.

Length. 8–10 mm.

VARIABILITY. The paired black spots on tergite 2 in ♀ are rather variable; usually in the form of large oval spots but they are replaced sometimes by only two blackish points. The apical spot on wings is enlarged in some specimens, occupying nearly the whole apical half of vein R_4.

This species is well distinguished from all the European species, because of the narrow connection of the apical spot on wing in cell R_1, but it could be easily mistaken for the Asiatic *Chrysops dissectus* Loew. The latter has, however, an even narrower spot on the wing, the median black spot on tergite 1 in female is much more enlarged, occupying the whole width of the segment, and the abdomen in ♂ is mostly yellow with only a small, posteriorly bifurcated black median spot.

DATES. From late May to early September.

BIOLOGY. The species occurs in meadows and on banks of rivers and lakes, and is in some suitable localities a common species. The adults are on the wing from late May (environs of Alma-Ata) until early September (central part of the river Ili) but the main emergence lasts about three weeks in late June and early July. Females attack man and domestic animals, males are to be found on flowers, especially on Euphorbiaceae. Shevtshenko (1961: 47) records species of the dipterous family Asilidae, the hymenopteran genus *Bembex* and occassionally also Odonata as predators.

DISTRIBUTION. The Asiatic part of the U.S.S.R., China (Manchuria) and Mongolia. It penetrates also to the European part of the U.S.S.R. in the Astrachan region along the lower part of the river Volga.

CHRYSOPS (CHRYSOPS) PARALLELOGRAMMUS ZELLER, 1842

Fig. 30; pl. 7: figs. a–b.

Chrysops parallelogrammus Zeller, 1842, Isis, 2: 823.

DIAGNOSIS. A medium-sized species with brown tibiae; tergite 2 in female yellow with two separate, dark elongated triangular spots at middle; in male these spots are larger and connected in the front half of the tergite.

Wings with distinct apical spot, which is connected with the cross-band in whole width of cell R_1.

DESCRIPTION. ♀. *Head.* Frons whitish-grey dusted with large shining black frontal callus, which is only narrowly separated from the eye-margins. Face yellowish, all calli shining blackish-brown. Facial calli widely connected with rostral callus; genal calli relatively small. Antennae blackish-brown, only segment 1 except tip yellow-brown. Palpi long and slender, pointed, dark brown.

Thorax greyish dusted, mesonotum with three broad shining black longitudinal stripes, median stripe not so distinct. Whole of thorax finely pale haired, margins of mesonotum with longer yellowish hairs. All femora blackish-brown to black, fore legs except for brown basal third of tibiae, black. Tibiae and tarsi of posterior two pairs brown to yellow-brown, last 3 to 4 tarsal segments darker. *Wings* with distinct dark brown pattern, the middle cross-band reaches hind margin in the whole width. First basal cell brown in basal half, second at extreme base only. Apical spot connected

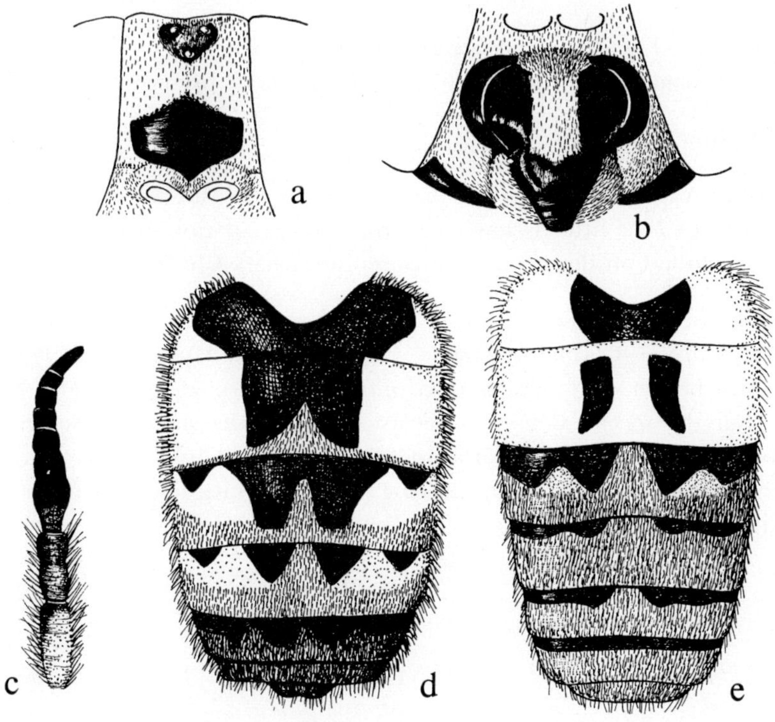

Fig. 30. *Chrysops (C.) parallelogrammus* Zell., a. female frons, b. female face, c. female antenna, d. male abdomen, e. female abdomen.

with cross-band in the whole width of cell R_1, occupying apical third of vein R_4 and a cloud nearly half of its length. Halteres dark brown.

Abdomen. Tergites 1–2 yellow, tergite 2 with two dark, narrow, longitudinal median triangular spots, which do not reach front margin of the tergite. Following tergites greyish, tergites 3—4 with irregular dark lateral spots on anterior margin. Sternite 2 yellow with small rounded median spot, following sternites greyish.

♂. It differs in a stouter, long haired and entirely blackish-grey antennal segment 1, in blackish palpi, in clouding of both basal cells, which are clear in apical third only, and in pattern of abdomen. Tergite 1 yellow at sides only, tergite 2 with two broad dark triangular spots, which are anteriorly connected and reach the front margin. Tergites 3—4 yellowish with two larger median and two smaller lateral triangular spots, last tergites greyish. Sternites 1—3 yellow with greyish median spots, following sternites greyish-black. Resembling male of *relictus* Meig. in pattern of abdomen but is readily distinguished by long and pointed palpi extending distinctly for half length of proboscis.

Length. 8—10 mm.

Variability. The shape and size of dark median spots on second abdominal tergite in female is rather variable, especially their distance.

Dates. June to August.

Biology. A rather rare species which does not occur anywhere in large numbers. Only a little is known of the biology of this species, the males are to be found on flowers of Asteraceae (Moucha & Chvála, 1955).

Distribution. A typical European species. Its center of distribution lies in Central Europe (Germany, Austria, Czechoslovakia, Hungary and Poland). The west border of its area of distribution runs through France and North Italy but the species is not yet recorded from Switzerland. In South East Europe recorded from Bulgaria and Rumania, and from the central and southern regions of the European part of the U.S.S.R.; not known from the Asiatic part of the U.S.S.R.

CHRYSOPS (CHRYSOPS) CONCAVUS LOEW, 1858

Fig. 31; pl. 7: fig. c.

Chrysops concavus Loew, 1858, Verh. zool.-bot. Ges. Wien, 8: 622.

DIAGNOSIS. A medium-sized pale species resembling *parallelogrammus* Zell. All femora and tibiae yellow, tergite 2 in female yellow with two small dark and widely separated triangular spots. Apical spot on wings indistinct but rather large, occupying one half of vein R_4 and connected with middle cross-band in the whole width of cell R_1. Male unknown.

DESCRIPTION. ♀. *Head.* Frons pale grey, frontal callus egg-shaped, shining black to blackish-brown, rather widely separated from the eye-margins. Facial calli smaller, shining blackish-brown, only narrowly connected with brownish rostral callus, which is sometimes partly reduced. Genal calli shining black, touching the eye-margins. Antennal segment 1 yellow, segment 2 dark brown, both segments with short black hairs. Antennal segment 3 black, slightly brownish at base only. Palpi yellowish or yellow-brown to dark brown, rather narrow and sharply pointed, longer than half length of proboscis.

Thorax entirely greyish dusted, mesonotum with three broad, more or less shining black longitudinal stripes, scutellum dark. Mesonotum and scutellum finely short pale haired, margins of mesonotum and pleura on the upper part with dense longer yellowish hairs. *Legs* predominantly yellow; only tip of fore coxae, whole middle and hind coxae, knees, whole of fore tarsi and apical three segments of four posterior tarsi, dark. Fore tibiae at tip slightly darker. *Wings* with paler brown pattern, middle cross-vein reaches hind margin along veins only, fourth posterior cell distinctly narrowed towards tip. First basal cell brownish in basal third and at tip, second basal cell entirely clear. Discal cell usually with greyish or nearly clear cen-

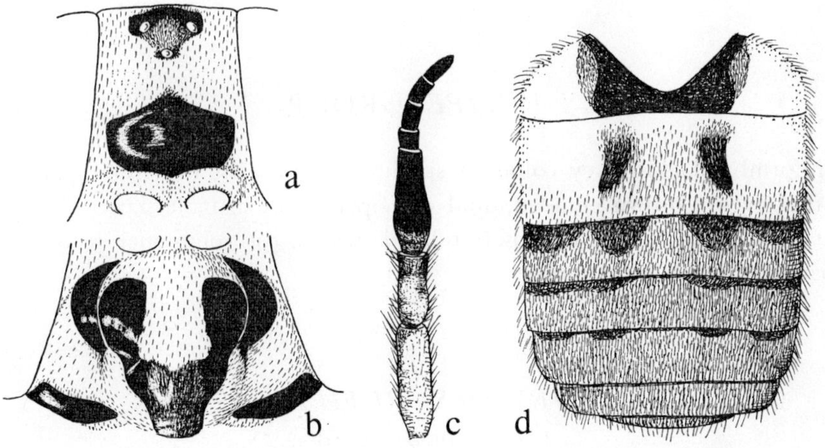

Fig. 31. *Chrysops (C.) concavus* Lw., a. female frons, b. female face, c. female antenna, d. female abdomen.

ter, as well as first submarginal cell near apex. Apical spot not very distinct, rather indefinite, widely connected with cross-band in the whole cell R_1 and occupying about half length of vein R_4. Halteres dark brown.

Abdomen. Tergite 2 yellow with two smaller dark and widely separated triangular spots, dividing the tergite into thirds. The following tergites greyish, tergite 3–4 with dark patches at front margin and at sides. First two or three sternites yellow, sternite 2 with small greyish median spot, the following sternites greyish.

♂. Unknown.

Length. 8.5–11 mm.

VARIABLITY. Coloration of palpi rather variable, as well as size of brownish rostral callus.

DATES. June and July.

BIOLOGY. The species occurs along large rivers in lowlands in forest and forest-steppe zones but is rather rare in steppe zone. The flight period is from the middle of June to the second half of July. Females attack man, horned cattle, camels, but also wild living animals, e. g. wild pig *(Sus scrofa).*

DISTRIBUTION. An East European and West Siberian species which occurs in Europe only in the European part of the U.S.S.R. It has been recorded from Austria (e. g. Leclercq, 1960a: 46) and from Germany (Violovič, 1968: 48) but these records are either mistakes or misdeterminations. The whole area of distribution covers the area from Saratov and Kazaň eastwards to Barnaul and Irkutsk. Never a common species.

RUFIPES-GROUP

Uniformly blackish-grey coloured species. Wings with indefinite pattern, rather evenly brown clouded, anal cell open. Eyes in male narrowly separated on frons. Only two closely related species, the commoner *rufipes* distributed throughout Europe.

CHRYSOPS (CHRYSOPS) RUFIPES MEIGEN, 1820

Fig. 32; pl. 7: figs. d–e.

Chrysops rufipes Meigen, 1820, Syst. Beschr., 2: 71.

Diagnosis. A smaller dark-brown species, legs brownish-yellow, femora darker at base. Wings entirely brownish clouded with only slightly differentiated darker middle cross-band. Abdomen predominantly blackish. Facial and genal calli reach the eye-margins, eyes in male not meeting.

Description. ♀. *Head.* Eyes in dried specimens black-grey to black-brown, frontal callus wide, shining black and only narrowly separated from eye-margins. Vertex predominantly shiny black. Face yellowish-grey dusted with large and distinct shining black calli; facial calli touching the eye-margins and widely connected with rostral callus; genal calli large, touching the eye-margins as well and sometimes connected along eyes with facial calli. Antennae black, sometimes segments 1–2 brownish to brown-yellow; segment 1 slightly swollen, cylindrical; segments 1–2 short black haired. Palpi brownish-black, pointed, longer than half length of proboscis.

Thorax black, mesonotum with slightly visible longitudinal stripes and rather shiny, pleura brownish dusted. Whole of thorax fine yellowish-brown haired. *Legs* predominantly brownish-yellow, femora at base, knees and apical three tarsal segments, darker. *Wings* wholly brown clouded, veins distinctly blackish-brown; darker cross-band and large apical spot indistinctly defined. Halteres blackish-brown.

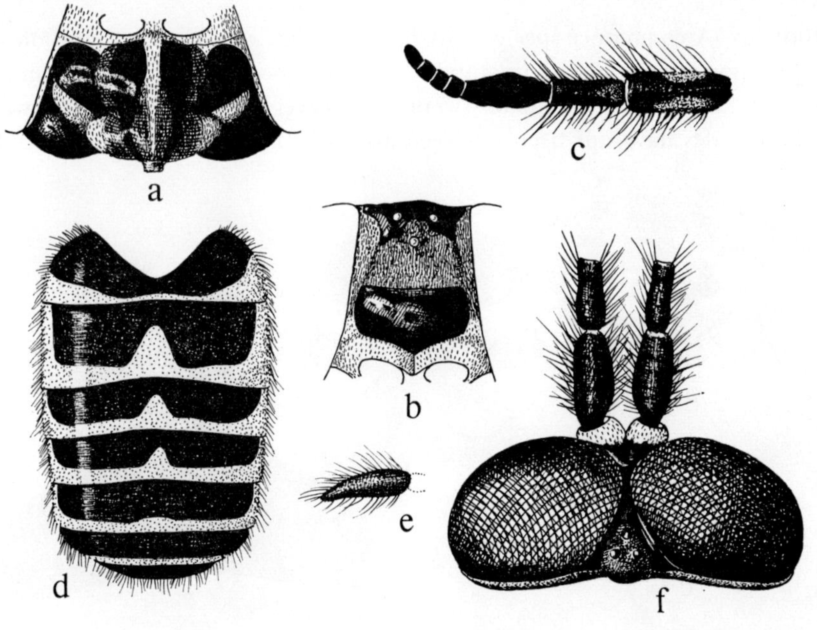

Fig. 32. *Chrysops (C.) rufipes* Meig., a. female face, b. female frons, c. female antenna, d. female abdomen, e. male palpus, f. male head from above.

Abdomen predominantly black, slightly shining. Tergites 1—2 with indication of small yellowish patches at sides, all tergites with narrow yellow posterior margin; tergite 2 with yellowish-grey median triangle on hind margin, smaller median triangles are to be seen also on following two tergites. Venter black with narrow yellowish posterior margin on all segments, sternite 2 sometimes slightly yellowish at sides.

♂. Eyes not meeting in front, very narrowly separated; all facets nearly of same size. Facial and genal calli distinctly enlarged as in female. Antennae black, segments 1–2 long black haired; segment 1 distinctly swollen but rather short, about as long as two-thirds of height of head. Palpi black with long black hairs, slender and narrowly pointed at tip, longer than half length of proboscis. Legs extensively darkened, femora yellowish usually only at tip and sometimes whole of fore legs blackish-brown. Wings more brown clouded than in female, usually only apical quarter of basal cells and wing-apex below apical spot lighter. Abdomen as in female.

Length. 6—9 mm.

VARIABILITY. Often slightly variable are the coloration of frons, the width of connection of facial and genal calli, coloration of legs and size of the median triangles on anterior abdominal tergites.

DATES. June and July.

BIOLOGY. A commoner species only on peat bogs, wet meadows, and on shores of ponds and lakes. On suitable localities occasionally a very common species. The adults are to be swept on the vegetation close to the water. The females have not been observed attacking either man or animals. The

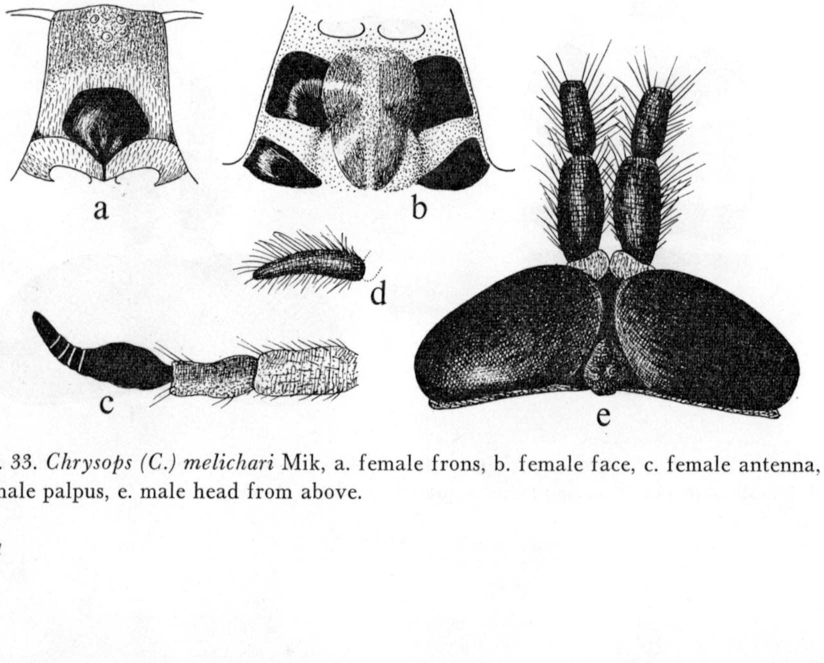

Fig. 33. *Chrysops (C.) melichari* Mik, a. female frons, b. female face, c. female antenna, d. male palpus, e. male head from above.

larvae and pupae were described by Tamarina (1956) and Ježek (1970), a description of the larva is also given by Skufin (1967).

DISTRIBUTION. A European species well known from Central Europe but also from Scandinavia and Denmark. The west border of its area of distribution lies in Netherland, Belgium, France, Switzerland and North Italy, the southern border in Jugoslavia (Bosna) and Rumania. Rather a common species in the European part of the U.S.S.R., known from Carelia as far as to the Crimea, eastwards it penetrates through Siberia to Altai and to the river Jenisej 63° North.

CHRYSOPS (CHRYSOPS) MELICHARI MIK, 1898

Fig. 33; pl. 7: fig. f.

Chrysops Melicharii Mik, 1898, Wien. ent. Ztg, 17: 158.

DIAGNOSIS. A smaller species closely resembling *rufipes* Meig. but general coloration is more yellowish. Legs predominantly yellow; mesonotum with three dark longitudinal stripes; wings tinged brown with indefined darker pattern; abdominal tergites distinctly yellow at sides and along posterior margins; facial calli smaller. Eyes in male narrowly separated on frons as in *rufipes* but antennal segments 1–2 elongated and stouter.

DESCRIPTION. ♀. *Head.* Frons greyish-yellow with a shining black and almost circular callus, which is widely separated from the eye-margins; vertex with ocellar tubercle and its surroundings darker. Face yellowish dusted, facial calli polished black on the outside, touching the eye-margins, on the inner side yellowish-brown and widely connected with yellowish-brown rostral callus. Genal calli black, separated from both eye-margins and facial calli. Antennal segments 1–2 yellow to yellowish-brown, segment 2 darker at tip, both segments with short black hairs. Antennal segment 3 black, slightly brownish at base. Segment 2 slightly swollen, about as broad as base of segment 3. Palpi brown to dark brown, pointed, longer than half length of proboscis.

Thorax thinly greyish-yellow dusted, pleura with fine pale hairs. Mesonotum with three broad, shining black, well separated longitudinal stripes. Scutellum more or less shining black. *Legs* yellow to yellow-brown, only coxae of posterior two pairs, knees and apical two to three tarsal segments, dark. *Wings* predominantly brown, with the same pattern as in *rufipes* Meig. Vein R_4 sometimes with indication of appendix. Halteres blackish-brown.

Abdomen. Dorsum shining black to black-brown, sparsely pale pubescent. All tergites with distinct narrow yellow border at sides and at hind margin; tergite 2 with yellow median triangle which reaches to middle of tergite, tergite 3 with only indication of median triangle. Sternites 1—2 or 1—3 yellowish to brown-yellow, the following sternites dark with narrow yellowish posterior margin.

♂. Eyes not meeting, narrowly separated, all facets of the same size. Facial and genal calli as in ♀. Antennae black, segments 1—2 with long black hairs. Segment 1 elongated and distinctly swollen, about as long as head is deep. Segment 2 swollen as well. Palpi black-brown, long black haired, slightly stouter but pointed at tip, about as long as half length of proboscis. Thorax and legs as in ♀. Wings more intensively brown clouded, both basal cells paler in apical third only. Abdomen yellowish-brown with long yellowish and black hairs. Tergite 1 dark at middle; tergite 2 with paired, blackish-brown, large triangular spots, which are connected anteriorly and reach with apex to posterior margin of the tergite. On following two tergites these triangular spots are smaller and more broadly connected, on apical tergites forming only a dark band at anterior margin. Tergites 2—4 with distinct pale median triangle at hind margin.

Length. 7.5—10 mm.

DATES. Unknown to us.

BIOLOGY. Because of a limited area of distribution and rare occurrence nothing is known on its biology. The adults are to be found probably on swampy and peat bogs biotopes.

DISTRIBUTION. *Melichari* is one of the European species with a more limited area of distribution, known so far only from Switzerland, North Italy and North Jugoslavia. The records from Bayern, Germany (Kröber, 1932b, 1938; Leclercq, 1960a) need verification.

ITALICUS-GROUP

Facial calli often less developed, wings with distinct dark pattern but always with a clear patch in discal cell. Eyes in male sometimes narrowly separated on frons. The species of this group were previously separated into the subgenus *Heterochrysops* Kröb. The distribution of the species of this group is restricted to the southern parts of Europe.

CHRYSOPS (CHRYSOPS) FLAVIPES MEIGEN, 1804

Fig. 34; pl. 1: fig. g; pl. 7: fig. g.

Chrysops flavipes Meigen, 1804, Klass., 1: 159.
? *Chrysops pallida* Macquart, 1838, Dipt. exot., 1 (1): 162.
Chrysops punctifer Loew, 1856, Neue Beitr., 4: 24.
Chrysops perspicillaris Loew, 1856, Neue Beitr., 4: 25.
Chrysops maculiventris Becker, 1912, Annls Mus. Zool. Acad. Sci. St. Petersb., 17: 587.
Chrysops flavipes var. *askahabadensis* Szilády, 1917, Arch. Naturgesch., Abt. A, 83 (4): 111.
Chrysops beckeri Kröber, 1920, Zool. Jb., 43: 135.
Chrysops punctifer var. *abdominalis* Kröber, 1920, Zool. Jb., 43: 141.
Chrysops simillima Austen, 1923, Bull. ent. Res., 13: 278.
Chrysops flavipes gedrosiana Abbassian-Lintzen, 1964, Annls Parasit. hum. comp., 39: 297.

DIAGNOSIS. A smaller species with clear patch in discal cell, apical spot rather narrow, occupying one-third to one-half of vein R_4, and only narrowly connected with cross-band. Eyes not meeting in male.

DESCRIPTION. ♀. *Head.* Frons and face yellow-grey, frontal callus rather small, shining blak, widely separated from eye-margins. Vertex with shining black ocellar callus. Facial calli shining black to black-brown, rather small but broadly connected with rostral callus, which is divided by yellow tomentum into two narrow stripes. Genal calli shining black, small. Anten-

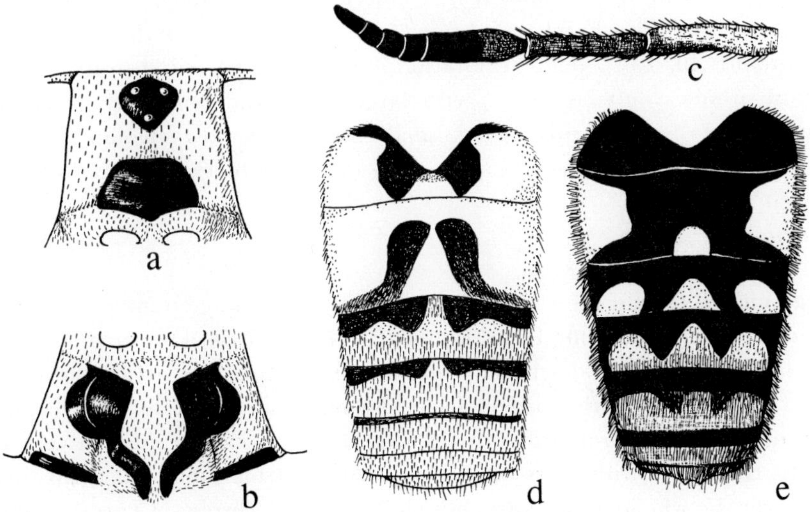

Fig. 34. *Chrysops (C.) flavipes* Meig., a. female frons, b. female face, c. female antenna, d. female abdomen, e. male abdomen.

nae long and slender; segment 1 yellow-brown, segment 2 and base of 3 black-brown, rest of segment 3 black. Palpi yellow-brown, long and pointed.

Thorax greyish dusted and wholly short but fine pale haired, mesonotum with five shining black longitudinal stripes; two narrow sublateral, two broad lateral and one median, which is very narrow. Scutellum mostly shining black. *Legs* yellow; fore coxae at tip, whole of four posterior coxae, apex of four anterior femora, apical half of fore tibiae, extreme apex of four posterior tibiae, whole of fore tarsi, and apical segments of posterior tarsi, blackish-brown to black. *Wings.* Both basal cells nearly clear, middle cross-band reaches posterior margin nearly on the whole width, discal cell with clear patch at middle. Apical spot rather small, occupies one-third to one-half of vein R_4; its connection with cross-band only narrow, occupying frontal half of marginal cell. Halteres blackish-brown.

Abdomen predominantly yellow, posterior tergites somewhat greyish; tergite 2 with two black, narrow and separated spots, which are sometimes connected with both anterior and posterior margins of tergite. Following tergites with black seam at sides and on anterior margin, dark patches on last segments hardly visible. Posterior four sternites very dark.

♂. Eyes not meeting on frons, distinctly separated by a narrow shining black stripe. Facets on upper two-thirds larger than on lower third and distinctly separated. Antennae mostly black, segment 1 often brownish on the inner side. Palpi pointed, longer than half length of proboscis, black. Apical spot on wing larger than in ♀, connected with cross-band in the whole marginal cell. Both basal cells brown at base. Legs darker than in ♀, predominantly blackish, yellow coloration distinctly restricted. Tergite 1 black, yellow at sides only; tergite 2 with large black and posteriorly widening central spot, leaving only a very small rounded yellow median patch at posterior margin; following tergites with extensive black design at anterior margin.

Length. 6–9 mm.

VARIABILITY. One of the very variable species with a large number of named forms. There is only one form, f. *punctifer* Loew, 1856, known in Europe; the other forms were described from eastern parts of the area of distribution. Loew's f. *punctifer* differs from the nominate form in larger apical spot on wings, which occupies in ♀ one-half and in ♂ one third of vein R_4 and is connected with cross-band in the whole of marginal cell. This form occurs in the whole area of distribution from Spain through Central Europe to as far as Central Asia, but more often in southern regions.

C. beckeri Kröber, 1920, also belongs within the range (?Spain) of variability (see also Olsufjev, 1937: 104). Extreme dark males were described from Central Asia as f. *abdominalis* Kröber, 1920, and Szilády (1917) described a very pale form with narrow apical spot on wing as *askahabadensis*. From Iraq and Iran f. *simillimus* Austen, 1923, is recorded, and from Iran f. *gedrosiana* Abbassian-Lintzen, 1964.

DATES. May to September.

BIOLOGY. The species is typical of warm regions, the flight period lasts about 60 days (Shevtshenko, 1961: 51). Females attack man, camels, as well as other domestic and wild animals. Males have been observed on flowers, e. g. on *Butomus umbellatus, Calamagrostis epigejos,* etc. The species has been ascertained as a vector of tularaemia (Boženko, 1941).

DISTRIBUTION. A Mediterranean species penetrating to Central Europe, the northern border of its area of distribution in Europe lies in Czechoslovakia (South Slovakia), Hungary, Austria and Rumania. The records from Germany (Kröber, 1932) are problematical, no documentary material has been found. *Flavipes* is well known from France, Italy (incl. Sicily), Spain, Portugal and from all countries of the Balkan Peninsula, and it penetrates eastwards over Turkey, Syria, Israel and Iraq as far as to Iran, Afghanistan and to the Central Asiatic republics of the U.S.S.R. It is also recorded from Cyprus and from North Africa (Morocco, Algeria).

CHRYSOPS (CHRYSOPS) ITALICUS MEIGEN, 1804

Fig. 4 b & e; fig. 5 b & e; fig. 35; pl. 1: fig. e; pl. 7: figs. h–i.

? *Tabanus salinarius* Scopoli, 1763, Ent. Carniol., p. 373.
? *Tabanus marmoratus* Rossi, 1790, Fauna Etrusca, 2: 322.
? *Tabanus fenestratus* Fabricius, 1794, Ent. Syst., 4: 373.
Chrysops italicus Meigen, 1804, Klass., 1: 158.
Chrysops nigriventris Loew, 1856, Neue Beitr., 4: 26.

DIAGNOSIS. Resembling closely *flavipes* Meig. but larger, apical spot on wings enlarged and occupying distinctly more than one half of vein R_4. Discal cell enlarged with clear central area. Black pattern on tergite 2 in female enlarged and more distinct; eyes meeting in male.

DESCRIPTION. ♀. *Head.* Face and frons greyish-yellow dusted, all calli shining black to black-brown. Frontal callus rather small, transversely oval and widely separated from eye-margins. Shining ocellar tubercle only a little smaller than the frontal callus. Facial calli large, only narrowly separated from eye-margins and broadly connected with the divided rostral callus. Genal calli rather large. Antennae long and slender, segments 1–2 more or less brownish, or whole of antennae blackish-brown to black. Palpi brown to black-brown, slender and pointed at tip, only slightly longer than half length of proboscis.

Thorax greyish dusted and short grey haired, mesonotum with three black longitudinal stripes as in *flavipes* Meig., scutellum predominantly shining black. *Legs* yellow-brown to dark brown; coxae black-grey, fore coxae at base sometimes paler; femora brownish, darkened towards tip or mostly black-brown. Fore tibiae on apical half and fore tarsi black, tibiae otherwise yellow-brown with extreme tip dark, last tarsal segment black. *Wing* pattern as in *flavipes* Meig. but apical spot larger, occupying nearly two-thirds of vein R_4 and discal cell distinctly larger. Halteres dark brown.

Abdomen. Black pattern on tergites more distinct. Both central spots on tergite 2 enlarged at sides, forming a wide border along posterior margin. Venter dark grey, only two basal sternites sometimes yellowish at sides.

♂. Eyes distinctly meeting for a short distance, facets on upper two-thirds larger and sharply separated from those on lower third. Antennae black or black-grey; palpi brownish, very pointed and longer than half length of proboscis. Wings more brownish, especially on basal third. Both cross-band and apical spot as in ♀ but they are more broadly connected, in the whole

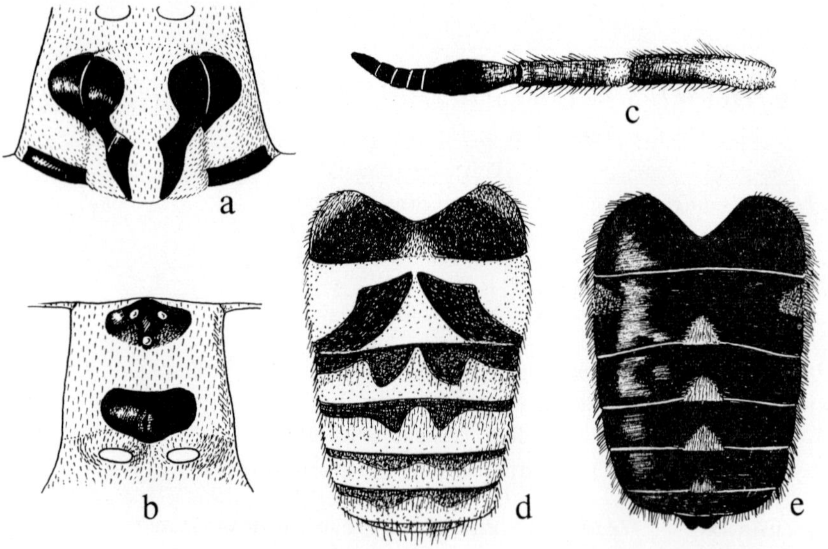

Fig. 35. *Chrysops (C.) italicus* Meig., a. female face, b. female frons, c. female antenna, d. female abdomen, e. male abdomen.

of marginal cell. Basal cells predominantly brown, with clear patch only in apical third before tip. Tergites mostly black, tergite 2, or 1—2, at sides more or less yellowish, following tergites with small yellowish or greyish medial triangles on posterior margin. Hairs concolorous. Venter yellowish at base, blackish-grey on last segment.

Length. 8.5—10 mm.

VARIABILITY. Conspicuously darkened males are named as f. *nigriventris* Loew, 1856. It differs from the nominate form in black antennae, palpi and legs, the mesonotum is predominantly blackish-brown with only slightly indicated longitudinal stripes; both tergites and sternites are unicolorous blackish-brown and black haired, only tergites 2–4 or 2—5 with small yellowish median triangle at posterior margin.

DATES. May to August.

BIOLOGY. The adults are to be found most often on marshy sea-shores, especially near gulfs with brackish water and on salt marches. Females attack especially man, males are often swept on the low vegetation. On suitable localities in South Europe sometimes a very common species. Larva and pupa were described by Boško (1968).

DISTRIBUTION. A South European species penetrating to Central Europe but the north border of its area of distribution here lies more southern in comparison with *flavipes* Meig. *Italicus* is recorded from France (incl. Corsica), Italy (incl. Sardinia and Sicily), from all countries of the Balkan Peninsula and from Rumania. The records from Germany (Kittel & Kriechbaumer, 1872) are probably mistakes and they have not been later verified by new captures, as well as the record from Bavaria (Kröber, 1938). The same problem is with the record from Poland (Trojan, 1956) which is unreliable. *Italicus* is a very common species on the coast of the Black Sea and it penetrates eastwards to Turkey, Iran and Cyprus; it is recorded also from North Africa (Tunisia, Algeria, Morocco).

CHRYSOPS (CHRYSOPS) CONNEXUS LOEW, 1858

Fig. 36; pl. 7: fig. k.

Chrysops connexus Loew, 1858, Verh. zool.-bot. Ges. Wien, 8: 629.
Chrysops aurantiacus Jaennicke, 1866, Berl. ent. Z., 10: 88.

DIAGNOSIS. A medium-sized yellowish species, calli on head only little developed. Discal cell with light central area. Apical spot on wing large, distinctly separated from the cross-band along costa, but connected with it along vein R_4. Dark pattern on tergite 2 as in *parallelogrammus* Zell. Eyes not meeting in male.

Description. ♀. *Head.* Face and frons yellow-grey, frontal callus small, shining black, with small projection below. Vertex yellowish-grey dusted and without trace of shining area. Facial calli small, widely separated from the eye-margins and narrowly elongated towards the rostral callus, which is often absent, as well as genal calli are. Antennae yellow-brown, segment 3 dark; segment 1 slightly swollen. Palpi yellowish, sharply pointed but short, about as long as half length of proboscis.

Thorax yellow-grey dusted, mesonotum with three dark and slightly shining longitudinal stripes, middle stripe anteriorly widened. Scutellum dark. *Legs* mostly yellow-brown, fore coxae at tip, all knees and last 3 to 4 tarsal segments, black-brown. Fore tibiae on apical quarter dark. *Wings* with distinct brown pattern, cross-band reaches hind margin on the whole width, dark clouding is more distinct along veins. Discal cell in central area lighter but not entirely clear. Both basal cells brown in basal third and at extreme apex. The conspicuously large apical spot is separated from cross-band at costal margin by a clear area in marginal and submarginal cells, but is narrowly connected with it lower down along R_4. Halteres dark brown.

Abdomen predominantly yellow and yellowish haired. Tergite 1 with dark median spot, tergite 2 with two longitudinal central spots as in *parallelogrammus* Zell. Similar spots are distinct also on tergites 3–4. Following tergites greyish. Venter yellowish on sternites, otherwise greyish.

♂. Eyes not meeting, but very narrowly separated. Subcallus shining black, palpi black. Legs darker than in ♀, especially femora. Tergite 1 black, tergites 2—4 with yellow median triangle and additional small yellow spots on posterior margin, forming on following two tergites a narrow yellow margin posteriorly. Wing pattern as in ♀ but the clear area separating apical spot from cross-band is distinct in submarginal cell only.

Length. 9—10 mm.

Dates. July.

Biology. Nearly nothing is known on the biology of this rare species.

Distribution. *C. connexus* is a species of the Western Mediterranean, it is recorded from South Italy (incl. Sicily), Spain and from Morocco. Séguy (1926) recorded this species also from France but its occurrence there has not been verified by any further captures (Leclercq, 1960a: 51). Not yet recorded from Portugal but its occurrence there is very probable.

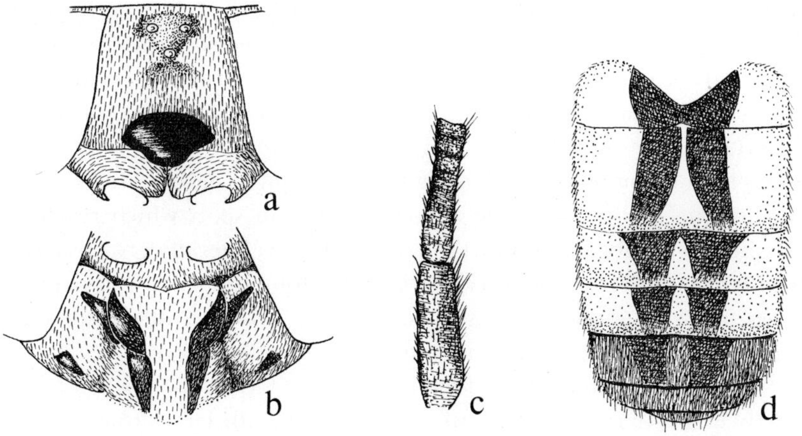

Fig. 36. *Chrysops (C.) connexus* Lw., female, a. frons, b. face, c. antenna, d. abdomen.

CHRYSOPS (CHRYSOPS) MAURITANICUS COSTA, 1893

Fig. 37; pl. 7: fig. 1.

Chrysops mauritanicus Costa, 1893, Rc. Accad. Sci. fis. mat., Napoli (2), 7: 101.
Chrysops mauritanicus var. *Chobauti* Villeneuve, 1934, Revue fr. Ent., 1: 182.
Chrysops mauritanicus var. *Surcoufi* Villeneuve, 1934, Revue fr. Ent., 1: 182.

Diagnosis. A medium-sized, predominantly greyish coloured species. Discal cell with clear area in apical two-thirds, outer margin of brown cross-band with deep incision in first posterior cell. Facial calli small, separated from the divided rostral callus. Eyes in male meeting for a long distance.

Description. ♀. *Head.* Face and frons grey-yellow dusted, densely and fine pale haired. Frontal callus shining black, rather small and widely separated from the eye-margins. Ocelli on small shining black tubercle. Facial calli very small, oval and shining brown, separated by two linear patches from rostral callus; no genal calli. Antennae long and slender, segment 1 yellowish-brown, segment 2 dark brown, segment 3 blackish except at base. Palpi gold-brown and sharply pointed, longer than half length of proboscis.

Thorax yellow-grey dusted and wholly covered with dense, fine pale hairs. Mesonotum more greyish with three dark longitudinal stripes, the middle one very narrow, lateral stripes wide and predominantly shining black. Scutellum dark and slightly polished. *Legs* including coxae light brown to brown, only all knees, apical third of fore tibiae and all tarsi, darkened. *Wings* with distinct brown pattern, discal cell with clear area in apical one to two-thirds. Cross-band on the outer margin with deep incision in first posterior cell; apical spot large, narrowly connected with cross-band in anterior half of marginal cell, and occupies at least three quarters of vein R_4. First basal cell clear in apical third, second basal cell clear except for both tips. Halteres pale brown.

Abdomen predominantly greyish coloured; tergite 1 nearly entirely black-brown; tergite 2 with two wide triangular median spots which reach with their apices posterior margin of the tergite. This is laterally grey or slightly yellowish. The following tergites greyish with four triangular dark spots on posterior margin, on last tergites these spots are hardly visible. Venter greyish, first two sternites at sides sometimes slightly yellowish.

♂. Eyes meeting for a considerable distance, facets of upper two-thirds distinctly larger than those on lower third. Facial calli larger than in ♀ and widely connected with rostral callus. Antennae brownish at base, palpi dark, long, considerably longer than half length of proboscis. Abdomen predominantly shining black, tergite 1 laterally greyish dusted, tergite 2 with greyish median triangle on posterior margin and another two small triangles at sides. The following tergites with greyish patches on posterior margin forming paler border, which is only indistinct on last tergites. Wings as in ♀, only both basal cells predominantly brownish.

Length. 8—11 mm.

VARIABILITY. Villeneuve described in 1934 two forms of this species (f. *cho-*

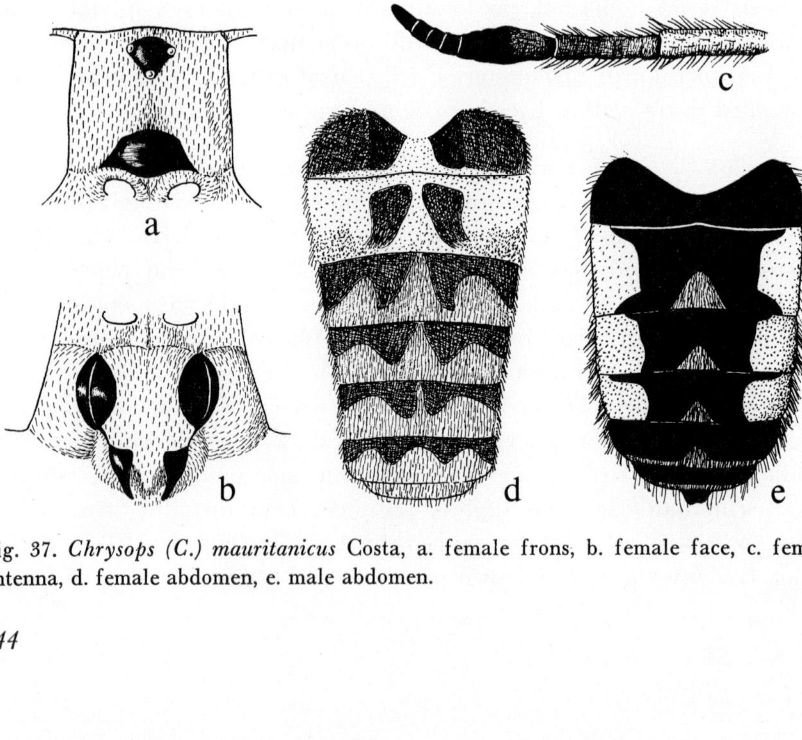

Fig. 37. *Chrysops (C.) mauritanicus* Costa, a. female frons, b. female face, c. female antenna, d. female abdomen, e. male abdomen.

bauti and f. *surcoufi)*, which are recently correctly taken for identical with the nominate form (Leclercq, 1960: 53).

DATES. Unknown to us.

BIOLOGY. Nothing is known on the biology of this species.

DISTRIBUTION. A North African species known from Morocco, Algeria and Tunisia, from where it penetrates to southern regions of Spain (Andalusia).

SUBGENUS *PETERSENICHRYSOPS* MOUCHA & CHVÁLA; IN MOUCHA, 1970

Acta ent. Mus. Nat. Pragae, 38: 261.

Pseudochrysops Moucha & Chvála, 1957, Acta ent. Mus. Nat. Pragae, 31: 159 (nec Nabokov, 1945 – Lep., Lycaenidae).

TYPE SPECIES: *Chrysops hamatus* Loew, 1858.

DIAGNOSIS. Antennae long and very slender, segments 1–3 of about equal length. Calli on lower part of head very reduced; female with only facial calli, the rostral callus and genal calli absent; in the male all calli absent. Wing pattern only slightly developed, the median cross-band does not reach the posterior wing margin, apical spot absent.

REMARKS. The subgenus is represented by three species of the east Mediterranean; only one of them, *hamatus* Loew, penetrates to South East Europe (Bulgaria). The other species of the subgenus, *compactus* Aust. and *buxtoni* Aust., are known only from Iraq.

CHRYSOPS (PETERSENICHRYSOPS) HAMATUS LOEW, 1858

Fig. 38; pl. 7: fig. m.

Chrysops hamatus Loew, 1858, Verh. zool.-bot. Ges. Wien, 8: 617.

DIAGNOSIS. A medium-sized yellowish species with only slightly developed dark pattern on wings, antennae very long and slender. Calli on lower part of head very reduced, only facial calli present in female sex.

DESCRIPTION. ♀. *Head.* Frons greyish dusted, distinctly broader than high, with narrow but large polished black lower callus which reaches the eye-margin, and is very often connected in central part or also along eye-margins with polished black vertex. Face yellow-brown, genae greyish with long whitish hairs. Facial calli very reduced, rather narrow in median part of face, rostral and genal calli absent. Antennae apparently long and slender, about twice as long as head. Segment 1 very slender, brownish, segments 2—3 black; segment 3 somewhat brownish at base and slightly broader than segments 1—2. Palpi dark brown, slender and pointed, longer than half length of proboscis.

Thorax. Black in ground colour and greyish dusted, finely pale haired. Mesonotum with three broad, shining black longitudinal stripes. Scutellum mostly shining black. *Legs* with coxae and femora mostly blackish-grey, anterior four femora slightly brownish at middle, tibiae yellowish-brown, only apical half on anterior pair and apices on posterior two pairs, dark. Tarsi dark, first or first two basal segments brownish. *Wings* mostly clear with dark brown veins; the wing pattern only slightly developed, only costal and subcostal cells, and a narrow median cross-band, brown. The latter very narrowed apically, it reaches to only a short distance behind discal cell below, occupying apices of both basal cells and base of discal cell. Apical spot absent. Halteres dark brown.

Abdomen. Tergites 1—2 mostly yellow, tergite 1 black in central part, tergite 2 with widely open black central spot as in *divaricatus* Loew. The following tergites dark. Sternites 1—2 yellow with dark pattern at middle, following sternites dark and likewise tergites with narrow, yellow border at posterior margins.

♂. Eyes meeting on frons for a longer distance, facets on upper three-quarters large and sharply separated from the lower quarter with small facets; the two parts are in dried specimens of different colour, upper part with large facets being light brown, lower part dark brown. Apex of subcallus and ocellar swelling shining black, latter with long and fine black hairs, hind part with some whitish hairs. Face densely covered with long whitish-grey hairs, all calli on head absent except for slightly visible remains of facial calli. Antennae blackish-grey to black, segment 1 indistinctly stouter than in female, brownish below and with long pale hairs. Palpi yellowish with darker circular patch beneath near tip, covered with long whitish hairs; slender but rather short, about as long as one third of proboscis. Thorax, legs and wings as in female. Abdomen mostly yellow, covered with dense, fine whitish hairs, all tergites bear a circular black spot at middle. Venter yellow with dark median stripe.

Length. 8—9 mm.

VARIABILITY. The intensity and shape of median cross-band on wings seems to be rather variable, in some specimens the cross-band reaches nearly to posterior wing-margin. In paler specimens it does not go beyond discal cell.

DATES. July.

BIOLOGY. Nothing is known on the biology of this species.

DISTRIBUTION. *Hamatus* was described by Loew from Asia Minor, where it has ben collected also later, about 10 km N of Iskenderun near Sariseki (Moucha & Chvála, 1957). In the collections of the Naturhistoriska Riksmuseet, Stockholm, there is a single female from the island of Rhodos. The first record from Europe is from Bulgaria where the species has been collected in the valley of the river Struma near the village Sandanski (Moucha & Chvála, 1961). No further records from Europe are known to the authors.

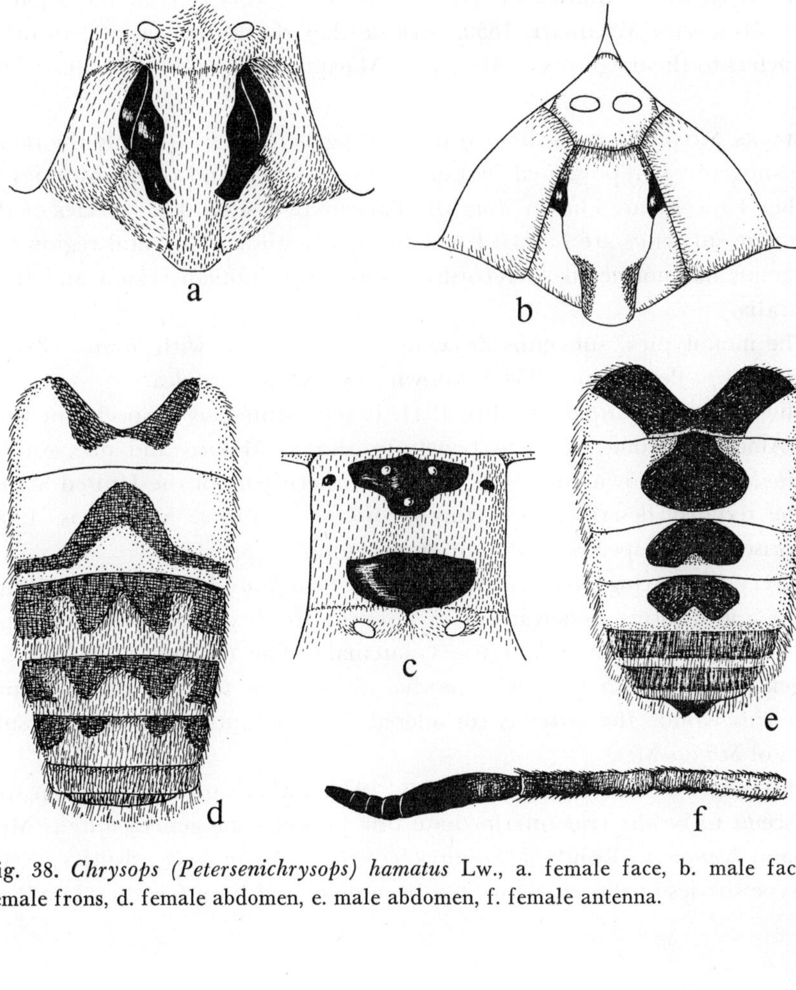

Fig. 38. *Chrysops (Petersenichrysops) hamatus* Lw., a. female face, b. male face, c. female frons, d. female abdomen, e. male abdomen, f. female antenna.

GENUS *SILVIUS* MEIGEN, 1820

Syst. Beschr., 2: 27.

TYPE SPECIES: *Tabanus vituli* Fabricius, 1805.

DIAGNOSIS. Mostly medium-sized species, yellow to brownish coloured, seldom with darker pattern; wings clear or only slightly clouded. Head with usually well developed frontal callus, face without calli except in the Asiatic subgenus *Heterosilvius* Olsufjev, 1970. Antennae rather short, about as long as head is deep (when viewed from above) or rarely longer; first segment usually thickened, segment 2 short, as long as deep or only very slightly longer. Eyes in living or relaxed specimens metallic green to greenish-yellow with dark spots, naked or haired. We do not place the species with haired eyes, *inflaticornis* (Aust.) and *variegatus* (F.), in the separate genus *Mesomyia* Macquart, 1850, because they do not correspond in other characters to the diagnosis of *Mesomyia* Macq. given by Oldroyd (1957: 202).

REMARKS. *Silvius* Meig. is divided into 5 subgenera, of which only the nominate subgenus is represented in Europe by 6 species and one subspecies. A further 4 species are known from the Palaearctic region. Five species of the nominate subgenus are known from the poorly studied Oriental region but the genus has not yet been recorded from the Ethiopian region and from Australia.

The monotypical subgenus *Zeuximyia* Philip, 1941, with *Silvius (Zeuximyia) philipi* Pechuman, 1938, is known from North America.

The subgenus *Assipala* Philip, 1941, is represented by 4 species in Central America. Some of them penetrate also to Mexico and one, *Silvius (Assipala) ceras* Townsend, 1897, to the southern part of the United States.

The recently described subgenus *Neosilvius* Philip & Mackerras, 1960, comprises only 2 species of the Oriental region.

A very interesting Nearctic subgenus *Griseosilvius* Philip, 1961, with 7 species and 2 forms, penetrates with 2 species to Mexico and with one species to as far as Central America, Guatemala. The representatives of this subgenus are greyish species somewhat resembling the Palaearctic genus *Nemorius* Rond., the latter is considered by some authors as another subgenus of *Silvius* Meig.

The subgenus *Heterosilvius* Olsufjev, 1970, with its 6 non European species seems to be the real intermediate link between the genera *Silvius* Meigen and *Nemorius* Rondani. *Silvius (Heterosilvius) zaitzevi* Olsufjev, 1940, the type species of the subgenus, has been described from Georgia, USSR.

The importance of the genus *Silvius* Meig. in economy and epidemiology has not yet been studied. Most of the species occurs only here and there, and only 2 of the European species, *alpinus* Scop. and *algirus* Meig., occur occasionally in large numbers. Nothing has been published up to present on the life history of *Silvius*. Males are often to be found on flowering Asteraceae.

Key to European species of *Silvius*

1 Eyes naked in both sexes 2

– Eyes pilose, in the female at least microscopically 6

2 (1) Abdomen (Pl. 1, fig. h) unicolorous yellowish-brown, at most with indefinite brownish or grey pattern. Frons (Fig. 39a & g) narrow, about twice as high as broad; antennae (Figs. 39b–c & e–f) yellow on basal segments, rather short 3

– Abdomen (Figs. 41e, 42e) black with yellow pattern. Frons (Figs. 41a–b & 42b) very broad, broader than high; antennae (Fig. 41c–d) entirely black, conspicuously long and slender 5

3 (2) Abdomen (Fig 40c) with indefinite grey median spots on tergites 1–4, usually a long appendix to vein R_4. Rather smaller species, at most 10 mm in length .... *appendiculatus* Macq. ♂

– Abdomen yellowish to brownish, sometimes a very short appendix to vein R_4. Generally larger species, 9–13 mm in length 4

4 (3) Abdomen unicolorous yellowish-brown; antennae (Fig. 39e–f) short, terminal flagellar segments shorter than antennal segment 3. Male with a row of rather shorter pale to dark hairs on vertex .... *alpinus* (Scop.)

– Abdomen on dorsum covered with short dark pilosity, giving to it a more brownish appearance and forming distinct yellow median triangles. Antennae (Fig. 39b–c) longer, terminal flagellar segments together at least as long as antennal segment 3. Male with a row of very long, densely set black hairs on vertex .... *algirus* Meig.

5 (2) Frons (Fig. 41a) above as broad as high, frontal callus rather small, broadly separated from the eye-margins. Antennae (Fig. 41d) with segment 1 three times as long as deep. Segment 2 as long as deep. Palpi yellowish-brown with pale hairs .... *latifrons latifrons* (Ols.)

– Frons (Fig. 41b) broader, distinctly broader above than frons is high, frontal callus large, only very narrowly separated from the eye-margins. Antennae (Fig. 41c) longer, segment 1 four times as long as deep, segment 2 longer than deep. Palpi brown with black hairs .... *latifrons graecus* ssp. n.

6 (1) Basal antennal segments dark grey. Abdomen black on anterior three tergites with only extreme sides yellowish .... *inflaticornis* Aust.

– Basal antennal segments (Fig. 42c–d) yellowish-brown. Abdomen (Fig. 42a & e) mostly yellow on dorsum, tergite 1 with large black central spot, following tergites with double black spot anteriorly, which is divided into 2 rhomboic spots on tergite 2 .... *variegatus* (F.)

SILVIUS ALGIRUS MEIGEN, 1830

Fig. 39a–d.

Silvius Algirus Meigen, 1830. Syst. Beschr., 6: 319.
Silvius bicolor Bigot, 1892, Mém. Soc. zool. Fr., 5: 625.

DIAGNOSIS. Medium-sized species resembling *Silvius alpinus* (Scop.) but generally darker coloured, dorsum of abdomen with paler median triangular spots forming more or less distinct narrow median stripe. Antennae long, terminal flagellar segments together at least as long as basal flagellar segment (= segment 3). Male with long black hairs on vertex.

DESCRIPTION. ♀. *Head.* Frons and face ochraceous-yellow coloured and pale haired, former with predominantly black hairs on upper half. Frons rather narrow, about twice as high as broad, somewhat widened below. Frontal callus shining black, rather large, slightly oval to circular. Antennae light brown, only terminal flagellar segments blackish. Antennal segments 1–2 with black hairs, segment 1 2,5 times as long as deep, segment 2 very short, hardly as long as deep. Terminal flagellar segments together very long, at least as long as antennal segment 3, and usually distinctly longer. Palpi yellowish-brown to brownish, long and slender, with sparse black hairs.

Thorax greyish with yellowish-grey tomentum, mesonotum with indication of paler longitudinal stripes, mostly yellowish haired, pleura with longer and more greyish hairs. Notopleural lobes usually yellow. *Legs* yellowish-brown, mid and hind coxae greyish dusted, apex of fore tibiae and apical 2 to 4 tarsal segments black, similarly likewise tibiae covered with short and dense black pubescense. *Wings* clear, slightly yellowish near base, along costal margin, and in the lower part of second basal cell. Veins dark, R_4 often with a short appendix. Halteres yellowish-brown with paler knob.

Abdomen yellowish-brown in ground colour, tergites nearly dark brown. All tergites except for the first one with high, pale median triangles reaching on each tergite the posterior margin of the foregoing tergite but often confluent, forming in this way a narrow pale median stripe. The darker brown coloration of tergites is caused by a very dense, adpressed black pubescense. Sternites light brown, basal three sternites with pale and dark hairs, the following sternites with only black hairs.

♂. Eyes naked, the upper two-thirds with large facets sharply separated from the lower third with small facets. Vertex with a row of densely set, long black hairs. The two basal antennal segments with long black hairs, palpi long and slender. Mesonotum darker, the whole of thorax clothed with long pale brown hairs.

Length. 9–13 mm.

VARIABILITY. The mesonotum and scutellum are nearly dark grey in some specimens, in other specimens, with dominant yellow tomentum and pale hairs, nearly yellowish. The size of median triangles on abdominal tergites is also variable, the triangles reach the foregoing tergites usually with a pointed apex, but they can often be much prolonged above, forming in this way a distinct median stripe.

DATES. Late May and June (29 May: Krapina, Jugoslavia; 21 June: Oraison, France).

DISTRIBUTION. A Mediterranean species; it is recorded also from North Africa (Algeria and Morocco: Leclercq, 1960). Not yet recorded from the Near East. In Europe *Silvius algirus* is known from Bulgaria (Asenovgrad), Jugoslavia (Krapina), Albania (Shkodër) and from the European part of Turkey (Edirne). The occurrence in Southern France (Oraison: Moucha and Chvála, 1967a: 28) is very interesting from the zoogeographic point of view, so much more so in that *Silvius alpinus* (Scop.) has also been found in the same locality. This is the only one locality known to us where both these species have been collected. *Silvius algirus* has not been recorded from other South European countries but it is very probable that it has been misidentified as another species of this genus. *Silvius algirus* is usually well separated

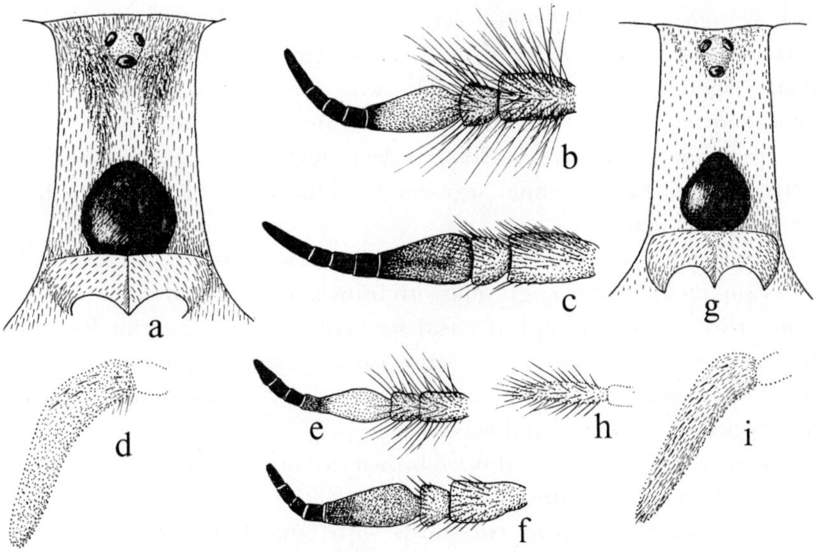

Fig. 39. a–d. *Silvius algirus* Meig. and e–i. *Silvius alpinus* (Scop.) a. female frons, b. male antenna, c. female antenna, d. female palpus, e. male antenna, f. female antenna, g. female frons, h. male palpus, i. female palpus.

in older collections from *alpinus*, but it is very often determined as *Silvius alpinus* Drapiez (nec Scopoli), which is, however, a synonym and also a homonym of *Silvius alpinus* (Scop.).

SILVIUS ALPINUS (SCOPOLI, 1763)

Fig. 39e–i; pl. 1: fig. h.

Tabanus alpinus Scopoli, 1763, Ent. Carniol., p. 372.
Tabanus italicus Fabricius, 1781, Spec. Ins., 2: 457.
Tabanus vituli Fabricius, 1805, Syst. Ant., p. 97.
Tabanus alpinus Drapiez, 1819, Ann. Gén. Sci. Phys., 1: 136.
Tabanus decisus Walker, 1848, List Dipt. Brit. Mus., 1: 171.
Silvius hirtus Loew, 1858, Wien. ent. Monatschr., 2: 350.

Diagnosis. Medium-sized, yellowish-brown species; eyes naked in both sexes; frons in the female higher than broad. Abdomen unicolorous yellowish to yellowish-brown, without any pattern. Terminal flagellar segments shorter than antennal segment 3, vertex in the male with a row of longer pale or darker hairs.

Description. ♀. *Head.* Frons and face orange-yellow, clothed with fine, short yellow hairs. Frons rather narrow, slightly widening below, nearly twice as high as broad. Frontal callus rather small, circular, shining black. Vertex concolorous with frons, ocelli dark. Antennae yellowish-brown, terminal flagellar segments blackish-brown. Antennal segments 1–2 with sparse, short black hairs. Antennae rather short, segment 1 twice as long as deep, segment 2 scarcely as long as deep, terminal flagellar segments distinctly shorter than antennal segment 3. Palpi yellowish-brown to brown, very long and slender.

Thorax yellowish-grey dusted and short yellowish haired, no longitudinal stripes on mesonotum. *Legs* yellowish-brown, only tip of fore tibiae, the whole of fore tarsi, and apical tarsal segments of four posterior legs, blackish-brown to black. *Wings* clear, yellowish at base and along costal margin; veins brown, paler near base and along costa. Vein R_4 sometimes with a short appendix. Halteres yellowish.

Abdomen unicolorous yellowish-brown to orange-yellow, clothed with short black hairs but without any pattern.

♂. Eyes with the upper two-thirds with large facets sharply separated from the lower third with small facets. Vertex with a row of rather long, mostly golden-yellow or even darker hairs. Antennae shorter than in the female, segment 1 distinctly stout. Antennal segments 1–2 with very long, black and pale hairs. Palpi yellowish, rather shorter, slender and sharply pointed at tip, of about half length of the proboscis. All other characters as in the female but whole of thorax, including mesonotum, conspicuously long pale haired.

Length. 9–13 mm.

VARIABILITY. The coloration of the hairs forming a row on vertex is rather variable, both in male and in female; some males have only dark hairs on vertex without any pale hairs intermixed. The frons is very pale greyish and mesonotum greyish-yellow in some females, mesonotum seldom with very indefinite paler longitudinal stripes; humeri and notopleural lobes sometimes yellow.

SYNONYMY. This species has been for a long time very well known as *Silvius vituli* (Fabricius, 1805). The synonymy of this species has been discussed in detail by Chvála & Lyneborg (1970). *Silvius vituli* (F.) is antedated by *Tabanus italicus* Fabricius, 1781, and there is no reason not to use the name *Silvius alpinus* (Scopoli, 1763) which has been quoted as a possible senior synonym of *Silvius vituli* (F.). The type material of *Tabanus alpinus* Scop. has obviously been lost but according to the original description it cannot be anything other than the species known up to the recent time as *Silvius vituli* (F.). The same may be said about *Silvius alpinus* (Drapiez, 1819) which has already been previously quoted as a junior synonym of *Silvius vituli* (F.). The material determined by Szilády and other authors as *Silvius alpinus* (Drapiez) in the Naturhistorisches Museum, Vienna is partly *Silvius alpinus* (Scop.), partly *Silvius algirus* Meig.

DATES. May to September.

BIOLOGY. *Silvius alpinus* (Scop.) occurs in suitable localities usually singly, only rarely in large numbers. It inhabits pastures, females attack horned cattle and man. The species can be easily recognized in the field from other species of the family by the yellow coloration and very green eyes. The males are to be found on flowering Asteraceae.

DISTRIBUTION. A European species with a large area of distribution from North East France to as far as the Ural Mts. It has not been recorded from England, Scandinavia, Denmark and the countries of Benelux. The northern border of its area of distribution in the European part of the U.S.S.R. lies in the District of Jaroslavl, 58° North. In South Europe it is known from Spain (not yet recorded from Portugal) to Bulgaria, and is a well known species in all Central European countries. Its occurrence in North

Africa should be verified, in view of possible misidentification with other species of the genus (*Silvius algirus* Meig. and *S. appendiculatus* Macq.). Eastwards it penetrates to Turkey (Abant-Sea) and the Transcaucasus.

SILVIUS APPENDICULATUS MACQUART, 1846

Fig. 40.

Silvius appendiculatus Macquart, 1846, Dipt. exot. Suppl., 1: 45.

DIAGNOSIS. Smaller yellowish species with yellow palpi and antennae, the latter with only terminal flagellar segments black. Vertex with long black outstanding hairs. Legs yellow, only tips of tibiae (more broadly on fore tibiae) and whole of tarsi blackish. Abdomen yellow, with indefinite greyish spots on tergites 1 to 3, and mostly greyish on posterior tergites.

DESCRIPTION. ♀. Unknown.

♂. *Head.* Eyes naked, the lower third with small facets (placed more laterally and black coloured in dried specimens) is sharply separated from the upper two-thirds with large facets (light brown in dried specimens). Vertex with a row of very long black hairs, occiput dark grey tomented and covered with minute pale hairs. Face yellow in ground colour and thinly silvery-grey dusted, clothed with long yellowish hairs. Antennae yellow, only extreme tip of the segment 3 together with terminal flagellar segments deep black. Antennal segments 1–2 clothed with very long black hairs, segment 2 short and square. Palpi with rather long and narrow apical segment, basal segment broader and darkened; both segments with long yellowish hairs. Proboscis black.

Thorax blackish in ground coloration, mesonotum thinly yellowish-grey tomented, pleura with denser coating of grey tomentum. The whole of thorax rather densely yellowish haired, the hairs are on both mesonotum and pleura nearly of the same length. *Legs* including fore coxae yellow, four posterior coxae greyish dusted like pleura, only apical third of fore tibiae, extreme tip of posterior four tibiae, fore tarsi, and terminal tarsal segments of four posterior tarsi, black. Legs covered with fine hairs, the hairs are mostly pale on femora, predominantly black and shorter on tibiae and tarsi. *Wings* clear, yellowish tinted basally and in costal cell, veins yellow to yellowish-brown on basal half, apically black. A distinct appendix to vein R_4. Squamae whitish with pale fringes, halteres yellowish.

Abdomen yellow with indefinite pale grey pattern consisting of anterior

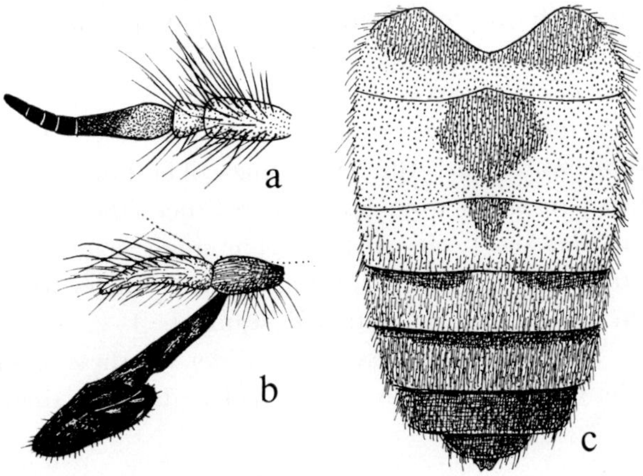

Fig. 40. *Silvius appendiculatus* Macq., male, a. antenna, b. proboscis and palpus, c. abdomen.

border on tergite 1, a large irregular median spot on tergite 2, and smaller rounded to triangular median spot on tergite 3. Posterior tergites mostly greyish, covered predominantly with short black hairs, posterior margins with paler hairs. Sternites 2 to 4 with a very narrow, dark grey median line, posterior sternites mostly greyish, at least anteriorly. Sternites 1 and 2 only short pale haired, sternite 3 and following sternites with some black hairs mostly mesally.

Length. Body: 9.3—10.0 mm, wing 8.5—9.3 mm.

REMARKS. The male of *Silvius variegatus* (F.) (= *singularis* Meig.) differs in the darkened antennal segment 3, in the black coxae and the tips to all femora, the mesonotum bears 3 broad polished black longitudinal stripes, and the distinct black pattern on dorsum of abdomen is quite different, the median spot on tergite 2 resembling somewhat the pattern of the female of *Chrysops relictus* Meig.

Macquart described this species in 1846 on the male sex from Algeria, where it was collected by M. Lucas. We did not succeed in finding the type material but there is one male from Syria and two males from Spain in the Naturhistorisches Museum in Vienna. These three males quite correspond to the original description and were all identified by Szilády as »*appendiculatus* Mcq.«. According to the short original diagnosis: »Thorace cinereo. Abdomine antice rufo, maculis dorsalis nigris, postice nigricante. Alis flavidis«, and according to the further longer original description, *Silvius appendiculatus* Macq. is rather closely related to *Silvius alpinus* (Scop.) or

S. algirus Meig., differing mostly in the dark pattern on basal four abdominal tergites.

The single male from Syria is labelled: »Dr. F. Leuthner, Djobslakra 6.85, N. Syrien«, the two males from Spain bear a label »Novara 1857–59 Reise« and »*appendiculatus*, Alte Sammlung«. The latter two males represent the material recorded from Spain by Schiner (1868: 97), and quoted later by Arias (1914) and Leclercq (1960). The single male from Syria agrees quite well with the original description, while the males from Spain have paler hairs on vertex and on antennal segments 1–2, and have a very long appendix to R_4. Nevertheless, we consider all these specimens to be conspecific. The redescription, given here, is based on the single male from Syria.

DATES. June.

DISTRIBUTION. Described from Algeria, later recorded by Schiner (1868) from Spain. Now it has been found also in Syria. *Silvius appendiculatus* Macq. seems to be a very rare Mediterranean species.

SILVIUS INFLATICORNIS AUSTEN, 1925

Silvius inflaticornis Austen, 1925, Bull. ent. Res., 16: 6.

DIAGNOSIS. Smaller species with finely haired eyes and antennal segments 1–2 greyish. Anterior three tergites narrowly yellow at sides. This rather problematic species is still known only from the female holotype. Therefore we give the original *description* published by Austen.

♀. »Frons (front) rather broad and conspicuously broader below, with shining black callus somewhat cordate or roughly triangular in outline with upwardly-directed apex; front, subcallus and face, when head is viewed in profile, somewhat prominent; eyes clothed with minute hairs; first segment of antenna noticeably incrassate; dorsum of abdomen (in case of type) for most part black, but lateral extremities of first three (visible) tergites ochraceous-tawny; wings with light but distinct sepia coloured tinge; legs (so far as visible in case of type) for most part ochraceous-tawny.

Head. Occiput borders deep (as seen when head is viewed from above); front (frons), occiput and jowls in case of type, sooty-black, jowls with a trace of olive-grey or smoke-grey pollinose covering; ground-colour of subcallus and face vinaceous-buff or pinkish cinnamon, but central area and lateral extremities of subcallus infuscated; face, jowls and proximal segment of palpi clothed with fine pale yellowish hair; ocelli in female rather wide apart, anterior ocellus further from posterior pair of ocelli that latter are from each other; proximal segment of palpi dusky, distal segment orange-cinnamon coloured, laterally compressed and knife-shaped; first and second segments of antennae dark mouse-grey (third segment missing in case of type), orange-cinnamon coloured on inner side of base in each case, first segment distinctly swollen, more or less cylindrical, its inner margin as seen from above strongly (cf. fig. 1 and b), second segment small and somewhat rounded, little more than one-third of length of first segment, both first and second segments sparsely clothed below with fairly long, brownish or blackish hair.

Thorax. Dorsum, including scutellum, in case of type discoloured, sooty-black, entirely devoid of markings and almost completely denuded, but with pale yellow (Naples yellow or straw yellow) hairs on lateral borders of scutum, pleurae and pectus dark mouse-grey or dark neutral grey, clothed with Naples yellow or straw yellow hairs.

Abdomen. Hind borders of second (visible) and following tergites, as well as lateral margins in case of fourth and succeeding tergites, yellowish (dark olive-buff); lateral extremities of first three tergites clothed with pale yellowish hairs (remainder of dorsum completely denuded in case of type); ground-colour of venter agreeing generally with that of dorsum, though ochraceous-tawny lateral extremities of first three sternites rather more extensive than those of corresponding tergites; venter clothed for most part with fine yellow hair. *Wings.* Veins for most part mummy-brown, fifth and sixth longitudinal veins, and base of anterior branch of former paler (ochraceous buff); anterior branch of third longitudinal vein, at least in case of type, without slightest trace of an appendix; anal cell open; stigma cinnamon-rufous, narrow, elongate and fairly conspicuous. Squamae cream-buff, small and inconspicuous. Halteres cream-buff, distal extremities of knobs slightly brownish. *Legs.* Coxae and trochanters iron-grey, front coxae ochraceous-buff at base; tips of all femora blackish-brown, femora likewise coloured like those of front femora (middle tibiae missing in case of type), hind tibiae dark brown only at tips, apical spines of moderate size; front tarsi uniformly blackish brown (middle tarsi missing in case of type), hind tarsi blackish-brown, first segment, except tip, paler (mummy brown), coxae and femora clothed for most part with pale yellowish hairs, frons femora also with blackish hairs below; front and hind tibiae clothed partly with minute, appressed, naples yellow and partly with black hairs; front and hind tarsi clothed above with minute black hairs.

Length (one specimen): 10 mm.

N.B. In the case of the typical specimen, excessive exposure to damp during the process of pinning or mounting has caused the more or less complete disappearence of pollinose covering, while the dark areas on head, thorax and abdomen, instead of being greyish-olive or dark greyish-olive, as is very possible the case in life, are sooty black.«

NOTE. The holotype female in the British Museum (Natural History), London is rather damaged. The third antennal segment, a part of left wing, and the two posterior legs on the left side are missing; abdomen with the two basal segments very damaged.

DATES. July.

DISTRIBUTION. The holotype female has been collected in the vicinity of »Gallipoli, near Anzac Cove (leg. Major W. M. J. Martin)« on the European shore of the Dardanelles, Turkey. The modern transcription of the type locality is Gelibolu. No further specimens have been collected.

SILVIUS LATIFRONS LATIFRONS OLSUFJEV, 1937

Fig. 41a & d–e.

Silvius latifrons Olsufjev, 1937, Fauna SSSR, 7: 116, 371.

DIAGNOSIS. Medium-sized blackish-yellow species with very broad frons in female and with very long and slender black antennae. Wings tinted brownish, abdomen with striking yellow and black pattern. Eyes naked in both sexes.

DESCRIPTION. ♀. *Head.* Frons blackish-grey, broad, narrowed towards vertex; frons is much broader below than high, above (on vertex) slightly broader or as broad as high. Frontal callus broad, rather straight on lower edge and touching subcallus, semiglobular above, broadly separated at sides from the eye-margin. The lower part of frons with pale hairs, the upper part above a deep excision above frontal callus with black hairs. Face and cheeks coated with greyish tomentum and pale yellow haired. Antennae black, long and slender, basal two segments greyish dusted and covered with short black hairs; segment 1 three times as long as deep, segment 2 as long as deep. Palpi brownish-yellow to yellow, short pale haired, rather long and slender, about as long as three-quarters of the proboscis.

Thorax black, pleura and scutellum greyish dusted; mesonotum with short, pleura with longer, dense, grey to yellowish hairs. *Legs.* Coxae and femora dark and greyish dusted, tibiae yellowish, fore tibiae on apical third and posterior femora just at tip dark; tarsi black, posterior four tarsi near base brownish. *Wings* faintly brownish clouded, veins brown, stigma brown. Sometimes a short appendix to vein R_4. Halteres blackish-brown.

Abdomen yellowish-brown on anterior two tergites; tergite 1 with a broad black median spot, tergite 2 with two black triangular spots which are connected anteriorly, and with a large light grey triangular spot on posterior margin. Following tergites black with narrow greyish-yellow posterior margins, forming small median triangles. Sternites dark grey dusted and pale haired, anterior two sternites slightly yellowish at sides.

♂. Eyes naked, the upper two-thirds with large facets sharply separated from the lower third with small facets. Vertex with a row of short black hairs and a tuft of long black hairs on ocellar swelling. Basal two antennal segments with long hairs, palpi brown and rather slender. Thorax with long and densely set yellowish hairs. Other characters as in the female but the black pattern on tergite 2 enlarged.

Length. 10–12 mm.

DATES. May to July.

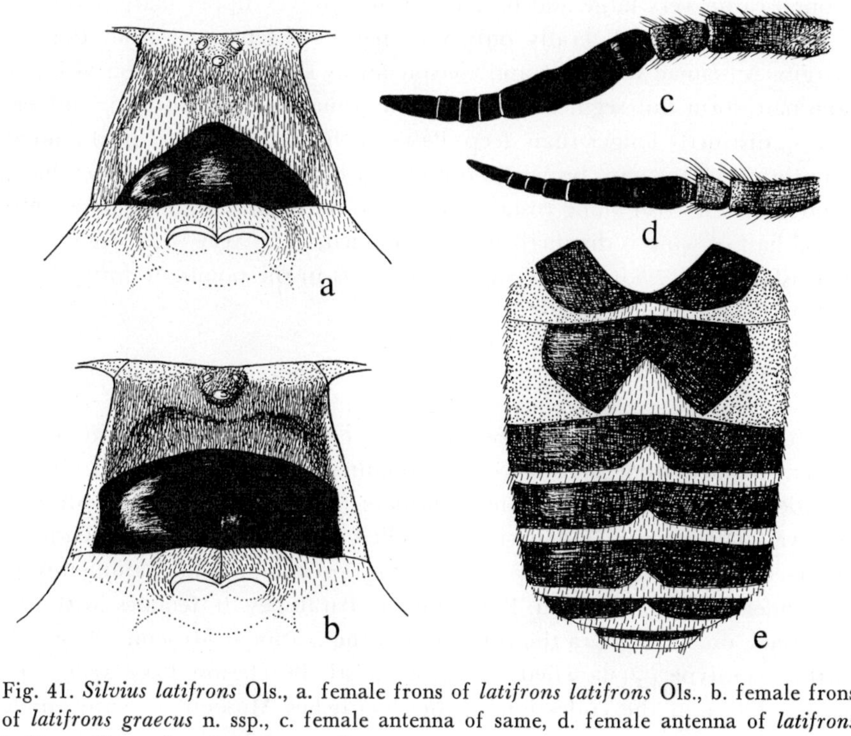

Fig. 41. *Silvius latifrons* Ols., a. female frons of *latifrons latifrons* Ols., b. female frons of *latifrons graecus* n. ssp., c. female antenna of same, d. female antenna of *latifrons latifrons* Ols., e. female abdomen of same.

DISTRIBUTION. A species with a very interesting pattern of distribution. It has been described from the Caucasus Mts., where it inhabits both the European part (environment of Majkop in the region of the river of Kuban) and the Asiatic part (Daghestan, Georgia). Southwards it penetrates as far as the Turkish part of Armenia (Sur mali; Olsufjev, 1937: 117) but it also has an isolated occurrence as a distinct subspecies in Greece.

SILVIUS LATIFRONS GRAECUS SSP. N.

Fig. 41b–c.

The specimens, females only, of *Silvius latifrons* collected in the Oiti Mts., Greece, differ very conspicuously from the nominate form of the Caucasus and, therefore they are described here as a distinct subspecies.

DESCRIPTION. ♀. *Head.* Frons distinctly broader than in the nominate form, narrowed towards vertex but still much broader here than frons is high. Frontal callus very large and broad with less convex upper margin and not so pointed mesally, laterally only very narrowly separated from the eye-margin. Antennae very long and conspicuously slender, coloration as in the nominate form but segment 1 about four times as long as deep, and segment 2 distinctly longer than deep. Palpi of the same shape as in the nominate form but they are brown coloured and clothed with short black hairs. *Wings* are yellowish along costal margin and on basal half along basal cells, apical half of wing is distinctly greyish clouded; veins very pale, stigma very blackish brown. *Thorax, legs* and *abdomen* as in the nominate form.

Length. 11–13 mm.

DATES. May to June.

DISTRIBUTION. This subspecies has an isolated area of distribution in Greece quite separated from the area of the nominate form. It has been already recorded under the name of the nominate form from Greece by Moucha & Chvála (1967c: 271). Our series is labelled as follows: Holotype: Graecia, Oiti-Gebirge 1500 m, ♀, 18–25.5. 1956, leg. Borchmann und Mannheims, in Alexander Koenig Museum Bonn/Rhein. Paratypes: 4 females with the same data, one of them in the collection of the National Museum, Prague; a further paratype (♀) labelled: »Florina, westl. Pisoderion Pass 2000–2100 m, 3.6. 1965« in the collection of the Staatliches Museum f. Naturkunde Stuttgart, Germany.

SILVIUS VARIEGATUS (FABRICIUS, 1805)

Fig. 42.

Haematopota variegata Fabricius, 1805, Syst. Ant., p. 109.
Chrysops singularis Meigen, 1838, Syst. Beschr., 7: 60.
Diachlorus maroccanus Bigot, 1892, Mém. Soc. zool. Fr., 5: 623.

DIAGNOSIS. Medium-sized species with eyes haired in both sexes, in female only microscopically. The eye pattern is reduced in living specimens to a small cross-band. Basal antennal segments yellow, tergites yellowish-brown with black anterior margins.

DESCRIPTION. ♀. *Head.* Eyes microscopically haired, frons yellowish with short pale pubescence, slightly higher than broad. Frontal callus black to blackish-brown, rather prolonged, pointed above. Antennae rather short, yellowish-brown, segment 3 dark. Basal segments covered with short black hairs, segment 2 as long as deep. Palpi yellowish-brown, very long and slender, about as long as proboscis.

Thorax blackish-grey in ground colour, brownish dusted; mesonotum with short, pleura with long, pale hairs. Mesonotum with three shining black longitudinal stripes which are distinctly separated by a brownish tomentum; central stripe continues on scutellum, only sides of scutellum

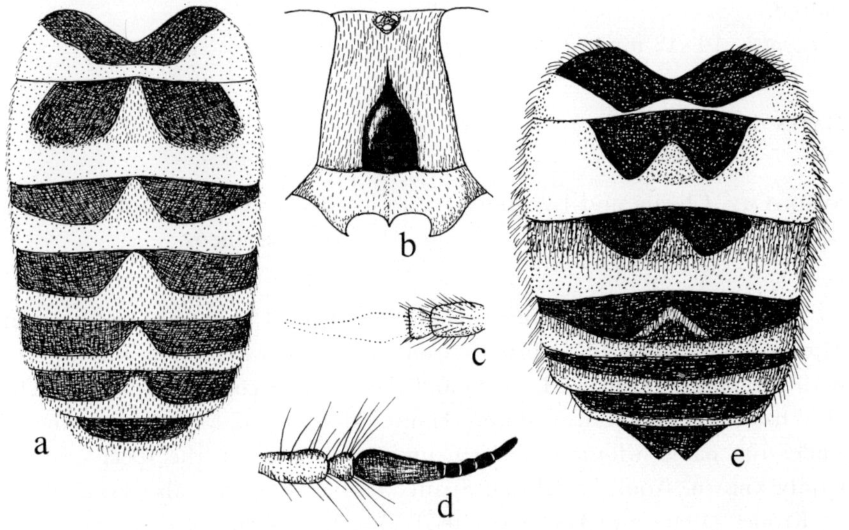

Fig. 42. *Silvius variegatus* (F.), a. female abdomen, b. female frons, c. female antenna, third segment missing, d. male antenna, e. male abdomen, a–c. from female holotype.

dusted. *Legs* mostly yellowish-brown, coxae, knees and tarsi black, fore legs darker. *Wings* clear, somewhat darker along costal margin, veins brownish. No appendix to vein R_4, halteres brown.

Abdomen with tergite 1 yellowish laterally and with black median patch, following tergites yellowish to yellow-grey. Tergite 2 with two separeted black rhomboic spots anteriorly. On the following tergites similar spots which are connected anteriorly, leaving distinct light grey median triangles. Sternites yellowish-brown with greyish pattern.

♂. Eyes densely light brown haired, meeting on frons for a long distance. The upper two-thirds with large facets are sharply separated from the lower third with small facets. The dark cross-patch is placed near the upper margin of the lower third of eyes. Subcallus yellowish-brown dusted and distinctly convex. Face with long pale hairs, cheeks with some additional black hairs. Basal two antennal segments yellowish-brown with long black hairs. Palpi yellowish, slender, about as long as half length of proboscis, clothed with long whitish hairs; basal segments dark. Thorax and wings as in the female. Femora blackish-grey on basal third to half, apical half of fore tibiae and fore tarsi black; basal two tarsal segments on posterior two pairs brown, darker at tips only. Tergite 2 yellow with two triangular black spots anteriorly, tergite 3 with an oval black spot near anterior margin, yellow laterally. Following tergites black with narrow yellowish posterior margins. Sternites 2 and 3 yellow with a greyish median spot, following sternites mostly greyish. Whole of the abdomen densely and rather long yellowish haired.

Length. 10—12 mm.

DATES. May.

SYNONYMY. Chvála and Lyneborg (1970) discuss fully the complicated synonymy of this species and give notes on the type specimens.

DISTRIBUTION. The species has been collected until now only in Spain and Morocco. Described by Fabricius from Morocco, where it is known from both the Mediterranean (Tanger) and the Atlantic coasts (Rabat, Salí), but also from the mountains (Hzér, Haute Moulouya). Meigen described it under the name *Silvius singularis,* under which name the species is commonly known, from Andalusia, Spain. This finding has also been quoted by Kröber (1938) and Leclercq (1957f). We have seen a good series of males from Sevilla, Lebrija-Trebujena, 10.5., deposited in the Museum at Leiden, Netherlands, collected by the Museum Leiden expedition in 1960.

GENUS *NEMORIUS* RONDANI, 1856

Dipt. Ital. Prodr., 1: 171.

Haemophila Kriechbaumer, 1873, Verh. zool.-bot. Ges. Wien, 23: 69.
Haematophila Verrall, 1882, in Scudder Nomencl., p. 152 (nom. nov. for *Haemophila* Kriechb., nec Reichenbach, 1850).

TYPE SPECIES: *Chrysops vitripennis* Meigen, 1820.

DIAGNOSIS. Medium-sized to small, nearly unicolorous greyish species with entirely clear wings without any pattern, and with completely absent facial and genal calli. Antennae long and slender, distinctly longer than head is long, antennal segment 1 about 4 times as long as deep, segment 2 usually twice as long as deep (only in two non European species, *N. irritans* Ric. and *N. shapuricus* Abb.-L., nearly as long as deep). Eyes naked, in living or relaxed specimens with distinct pattern consisting of a narrow border along the margin and a cross-band in female; in male the same type of pattern is present only on the lower part with smaller facets.

REMARKS. Not all students of tabanidology agree about the position of the genus *Nemorius* Rond. Some authors consider it as a valid genus (e. g. Moucha and Chvála, 1959; Leclercq, 1960a; Philip, 1961), the other only as a synonym of *Silvius* Meig. (Olsufjev, 1937, 1969b), or as a subgenus of *Silvius* Meig. (Shevtshenko, 1961).

Similarly the validity of some species is not accepted by all specialists. On the basis of the most recent studies it seems to us that there are 7 valid species in this genus with one subspecies and one form. Only one species, *Nemorius vitripennis* (Meig.), is widely distributed in Europe. *Nemorius caucasicus* (Ols.) penetrates only to the European part of the Caucasus and its center of distribution lies in adjacent part of Asia. The genus *Nemorius* Rond. is known from South West Europe (Spain) to as far as Himalaya, from where a very distinct species, *Nemorius himalayanus* Chvála, 1969, has been recently described. Almost nothing is known about the biology and economic importance of the species.

Key to European species of *Nemorius*

1 Antennal segment 2 (Fig. 43a) long, at least twice as long as deep; frontal callus (Fig. 43c) large, nearly globular. Parantennal calli large, touching the eye-margin .. .. *vitripennis* (Meig.)

– Antennal segment 2 (Fig. 43b) shortened, only slightly longer than deep; frontal callus (Fig. 43d) smaller, oval in shape, higher than broad. Parantennal calli reduced .... *caucasicus* (Ols.)

NEMORIUS CAUCASICUS (OLSUFJEV, 1937)

Fig. 43b & d.

Silvius caucasicus Olsufjev, 1937, Fauna SSSR, 7: 115.

DIAGNOSIS. Closely resembling *N. vitripennis* (Meig.) but antennal segment 2 is shorter and frontal callus in female narrow, higher than broad. Parantennal calli reduced.

DESCRIPTION. ♀. *Head.* Frons light grey dusted, slightly broader than high and somewhat widening out below. Shining black frontal callus rather small, oval, higher than broad. Vertex entirely grey dusted without any black areas. Parantennal calli partly reduced on the inner side, outer tips nearly touching the eye-margin. Face and cheeks whitish-grey dusted and finely whitish haired, cheeks with fine black punctuation. Antennae black, long and slender, first two segments covered by a greyish tomentum and short dark hairs. Segment 2 rather short, only slightly longer than deep. Palpi light brown, rather slender and pointed at tip, longer than half ot the proboscis.

Thorax dark, greyish dusted, pleura with sparse, short greyish hairs, mesonotum with three indistinct darker longitudinal stripes. *Legs* with coxae and femora greyish, fore tibiae brownish on basal half, the rest, including tarsi, black. Four posterior tibiae yellowish except for tip; tarsi black, basal segments yellowish with dark apices, more or less annulated. *Wings* clear, veins brown, somewhat yellowish near base and along costal margin. Stigma distinctly brown, sometimes a very short appendix to vein R_4. Halteres dark brown, lighter at base.

Abdomen dark grey, both tergites and sternites with narrow paler borders on posterior margins. Tergites 1—3 (or 1—4) with a pair of large, dark median triangular spots, on tergite 2 reaching nearly the posterior margin, becoming smaller on next two tergites, on tergite 4 hardly visible.

♂. The area with large facets on the upper part of the eyes sharply separated from the small facets below. Antennae black, basal two segments greyish dusted and long black haired. First segment slightly stout, second segment short, as long as deep or slightly longer. Face and cheeks grey with concolorous hairs, cheeks with fine black spots, on the upper part with long black hairs. Palpi brownish with long grey hairs, apical segment very short, blunt ended and slightly directed downwards at tip. Thorax, legs and wings as in the female, thoracic pleura with longer greyish and black hairs. Abdomen dark, tergites 2 and 3 yellowish at sides. First three sternites yellowish, sternite 1 and partly also sternite 2 with dark median spot, apical four sternites grey dusted.

Length. 6–9 mm.

VARIABILITY. The specimens without parantennal calli were described from the Transcaucasus as a ssp. *molitor* Bogačev & Samedov, 1949; the same form has been described by Leclercq (1960a) from Iran as *Nemorius abbassianae.*

DATES. June–August.

DISTRIBUTION. The whole Caucasus including its northern European parts in the region of Majkop, from where it has also been described. The center of its area of distribution probably lies in Georgia and Azerbaijan and the species penetrates south to Armenian SSR (Nachitchevan region) and to Iran, from where the ssp. *molitor* Bog. & Sam. is recorded.

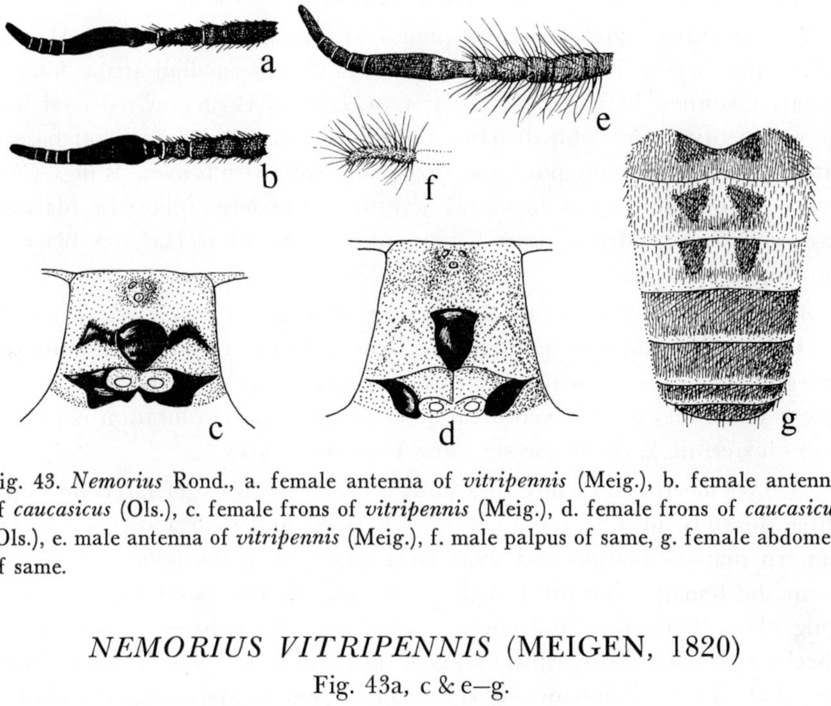

Fig. 43. *Nemorius* Rond., a. female antenna of *vitripennis* (Meig.), b. female antenna of *caucasicus* (Ols.), c. female frons of *vitripennis* (Meig.), d. female frons of *caucasicus* (Ols.), e. male antenna of *vitripennis* (Meig.), f. male palpus of same, g. female abdomen of same.

NEMORIUS VITRIPENNIS (MEIGEN, 1820)

Fig. 43a, c & e–g.

Chrysops vitripennis Meigen, 1820, Syst. Beschr., 2: 74.
Chrysops Ranzonii Schiner, 1858, Verh. zool.-bot. Ges. Wien, 8: 34.
Haemophila Fallotii Kriechbaumer, 1873, Verh. zool.-bot. Ges. Wien, 23: 69.
Nemorius Horváthi Szilády, 1926, Annls. Mus. nat. hung., 24: 597.
Nemorius klapperichi Moucha & Chvála, 1959, Acta Soc. ent. Čechoslov., 56: 317.
Nemorius bouvieri Philip, 1961, Bull. Annls Soc. r. ent. Belg., 97: 232.

Diagnosis. Smaller grey species, antennal segment 2 about twice as long as deep, wings clear without any pattern. Frontal callus shiny black, very often with some black at sides (so called »nebencalli«). Parantennal calli shining black, large, touching the eye-margin.

Description. ♀. *Head.* Frons greyish dusted, slightly broader than high; frontal callus not very large, rounded, very often with more or less reduced black triangular spots (»nebencalli«) at sides. Vertex greyish dusted without any black. Rather large shining black parantennal calli reaching from antennae to the eye-margin. Face whitish-grey, covered with sparse, short whitish hairs, cheeks finely black spotted. Antennae long and slender, basal two antennal segments greyish dusted, segment 3 black. Segment 2 long, at least twice as long as deep, segment 1 more than 4 times as long as deep. Palpi yellowish-brown, greyish below, sharply pointed at tip and slightly swollen near base, longer than half length of proboscis.

Thorax entirely greyish haired, pleura with longer whitish hairs. Mesonotum with three darker, broad longitudinal stripes, median stripe longitudinaly disunited by a narrow paler strip. *Legs* blackish-grey, covered with grey tomentum and whitish hairs, only tibiae except for tip, and base of first tarsal segment on posterior two pairs, yellowish-brown. *Wings* clear, veins yellowish-brown along costal margin and at base, otherwise blackish-brown. No appendix to vein R_4 or only a trace of it. Halteres blackish-brown, paler at base.

Abdomen greyish, basal three tergites with more or less developed large, dark, broadly triangular paired spots, which do not reach to the posterior margins. Each tergite with a narrow pale border on posterior margin, tergite 2 sometimes slightly yellowish at sides, the yellow coloration is present also on sternite 2, otherwise sternites unicolorous grey.

♂. Eyes meeting on frons for a short distance; with larger facets on upper three quarters, lower quarter with small facets and with a reduced darker pattern (narrow margin and short cross band) as in the female. Antennae as in the female, segment 1 slightly stouter, the two basal segments with long black hairs. Face and cheeks with long greyish hairs, upper part of cheeks with black hairs. Apical segment of palpi short, slender, blunt ended and slightly turned downwards at tip. The whole of apical segment clothed with long grey hairs, likewise a longer basal segment. Thorax, legs and the dark pattern on abdomen as in the female. Abdomen and thorax uniformly clothed with long, densely set whitish and dark grey hairs. Tergites 2 and 3 yellowish at sides, corresponding sternites mostly yellowish.

Length. 8–10 mm.

Variability. A very variable species; frontal callus often with very well developed so called »nebencalli« which are broadly connected with frontal callus in some specimens, sometimes missing at all. The intensity of black punctuation on cheeks, the stoutness of palpi near base, the broadness of the postocular rim, the size and shape of dark spots on basal tergites, as well as the intensity of yellow coloration on tergite 2 and on corresponding sternite, are also rather variable.

Nemorius fallottii (Kriechbaumer, 1873) has been for a long time recorded as synonymical with *N. vitripennis* (Meigen, 1820) but again redescribed by Philip in 1961 and considered as a valid species. In the last few years we have had the opportunity to study a large number of specimens of *Nemorius vitripennis* (Meig.) from the whole area of its distribution, as well as specimens, including the type specimen identified as *Nemorius fallottii* and deposited in the Zoologisches Sammlung des Bayerischen Staates in München, Germany. We found them to be conspecific.

Dates. May–August.

Biology. The adults are rather seldom found, only exceptionally in large numbers (Shevtshenko, 1961). Females attack horned cattle, horses and camels. From the Kara-Tau region in the U.S.S.R. this species has been recorded from 300 to 1400 m but it has been taken in Afghanistan at 2200 m. The flight period recorded is about 70 days.

Distribution. A Mediterranean species, it penetrates eastwards through Turkey to as far as Iran and Afghanistan. The northern border of its area in Europe lies in North Italy, Austria (only old records) and in the Transcarpathian Ukraine (Chust, leg. Boško). In Southern Europe it is a well known species from Spain, France, Italy and Bulgaria including the Mediterranean isles of Sardinia and Corsica. In the U.S.S.R. it is recorded from all Central Asiatic republics including Kazakhstan.

Chapter 13
Subfamily Tabaninae

TRIBE TABANINI

GENUS *HYBOMITRA* ENDERLEIN, 1922
Mitt.zool.Mus.Berl., 10: 347.

Therioplectes auct. nec Zeller, 1842.
Dasyommia Enderlein, 1922, Mitt. zool. Mus. Berl., 10: 346.
Tylostypia Enderlein, 1922, Mitt. zool. Mus. Berl., 10: 347.
Didymos Szilády, 1923, Állatt Közl., 21: 4.
Tylostypina Enderlein, 1923, Dt. ent. Z., 1923: 545.
Sipala Enderlein, 1923, Dt. ent. Z., 1923: 545.
Sziladynus Enderlein, 1925, Zool. Anz., 62: 181.
Aplococera Enderlein, 1933, Dt. ent. Z., 1933: 144.

Type species: *Tabanus solox* Enderlein, 1925 = *Hybomitra rhombica* (Osten-Sacken, 1876).

Diagnosis. Medium-sized to larger species, usually densely haired on thorax and abdomen. Predominantly species with brownish sidemarkings on anterior abdominal segments, or mostly greyish-black to black species, sometimes with paler dusted and pubescent posterior margins of abdominal segments. Eyes always pubescent, usually rather long and very densely, or the hairs only indistinctly visible in the female sex (*erberi*-group). Males with longer and more densely haired eyes, facets on the upper part of eyes either more or less enlarged and sharply separated from lower part with small facets, or all facets almost equal in size. Eyes in living specimens mostly greenish with three purple bands, only very rarely unbanded or with one or two bands. Ocellar tubercle always present in both sexes, or vertex sometimes with three small vestigial ocelli. Frons usually narrower, frontal calli well developed; median callus usually linear and connected with a larger circular, square to rectangular shaped lower callus; only exceptionally calli reduced or missing. Wings clear or slightly clouded especially anteriorly, rarely with darker patches on crossveins and bifurcations; exceptionally a very short appendix to vein R_4.

Remarks. The genus *Hybomitra* End. is one of the Tabanid genera with a large number of described species, forming at the same time an essential part of the Holarctic fauna of this family. Most of the species occur in the

Palaearctic and Nearctic regions and only a few species inhabit the adjacent areas; 3 species occur in Mexico, 12 species are recorded from the Ethiopian region (some of them may not be congeneric) and only one species is known from the Oriental region. On the other hand there are at least three endemic and common species in the Himalaya Mts., on the border between the Palaearctic and Oriental regions.

The genus is distributed mostly in the cold and temperate zones of the Holarctic region, the number of species and individuals conspicuously decreases towards the south. A large number of species are very common in northern tundra and taiga, and on peat-bogs and foggy biotopes in the temperate zone, for instance in Central Europe.

Altogether 54 species are known from the Nearctic region, and 93 species from the Palaearctic region. From this number only seven species are known to be Holarctic in distribution, viz. *H. aequetincta* (Beck.), *H. polaris* (Frey), *H. sexfasciata* (Hine), *H. arpadi* (Szil.), *H. lurida* (Fall.), *H. montana* (Meig.) and *H. epistates* (Ost.-Sack.); the first six of them are also known from Europe. Altogether 37 species have been found in Europe.

In contrast to the genus *Tabanus* L. the genus *Hybomitra* End. tends to have an increasing number of species. The *Hybomitra* species are generally more closely related, forming groups of very relative species which are often very difficult to separate without an examination of the female genitalia (i. e. cerci and subgenital plate). The study of the female genitalia in the taxonomy of *Hybomitra* species has been first used successfully by one of the present authors (Lyneborg, 1959) and this has enabled the precise separation of complicated groups of species such as the *bimaculata*-group. In addition *Hybomitra* species inhabit high mountains and some mountainous regions are still unsufficiently known, as has been found for instance in Nepal (Chvála, 1969).

Olsufjev in 1967 separated the subgenus *Tibetomyia* for three Central Asiatic mountainous species.

The immature stages have for a long time been little known, the few records in older literature were rather confused because of the inaccurate determination and complicated nomenclature. The first detailed and available description of the larvae and pupae were published by Roberts & Dicke (1964), Chvála & Ježek (1969) and by Teskey (1969).

The economic importance of *Hybomitra* species is considerable regarding their regular mass occurrence on suitable biotopes. The epidemiological importance of the species is discussed in the general chapter and under respective species.

All species can be separated into more or less natural groups of species; the separation is based on the female sex but males correspond well to these subdivisions. The European species are separated in the present study into 9 groups of species which more or less correspond to those proposed by Olsufjev in 1937 in his Fauna SSSR. The nine groups are as follows: *tarandina*-group, *aterrima*-group, *decora*-group, *borealis*-group, *montana*-group, *bimaculata*-group, *erberi*-group, *acuminata*-group and *vittata*-group. The species are arranged in the following text under these groups.

Key to European species of *Hybomitra*

Females

1 Larger blackish species (Pl. 2, fig. a) with broad, conspicuously whitish dusted and silvery-yellow to golden-yellow pubescent posterior margins to all tergites. Legs extensively orange-yellow, palpi long and slender (*tarandina*-group) .. 2

– Not as above 3

2 (1) Antennae (Fig. 44e) and palpi (Fig. 44c) orange-yellow. Lower callus (Fig. 44a) and subcallus above subshining reddish-yellow. Generally larger species, 17–22 mm in length .... *tarandina* (L.)

– Antennae (Fig. 45b) darkened apically and on terminal flagellar segments, palpi (Fig. 45c) blackish. Lower callus (Fig. 45a) and subcallus polished black. Generally smaller species, 15–19 mm in length .... *aequetincta* (Beck.)

3 (1) Legs unicolorous black. Medium-sized blackish species (Pl. 2, fig. b) (*aterrima*-group) 4

– Legs bicoloured, at least posterior tibiae brownish. Reddish-brown or blackish-grey species (Pl. 2, figs. c–d) 7

4 (3) Subcallus (Fig. 46a) polished black. Antennae (Fig. 46e) and palpi (Fig. 46c) blackish. Abdomen black with indefinite greyish pattern, tergite 2 largely greyish at sides .... *micans* (Meig.)

– Subcallus (Fig. 47a) dull greyish dusted. Abdomen (Pl. 2, fig. b) with paler haired posterior margins to all tergites or entirely black, no greyish sublateral spots 5

5 (4) Abdominal tergites (Pl. 2, fig. b) more or less distinctly golden-yellow pubescent on posterior margins .... *auripila* (Meig.)

– Abdomen entirely black with concolorous hairs, or with indistinctly greyish haired median triangles or posterior margins at sides 6

6 (5) Palpi (Fig. 48c) blackish with black hairs, rather equal in width. Face black haired, antennal bows high. A distinct darker patch on wing at base of vein R_4 .... *aterrima* (Meig.)

– Palpi (Fig. 49c) yellowish-brown, pale haired and rather stout at base. Face predominantly pale haired, antennal bows narrow. No dark patch at base of vein R_4 on wing .... *caucasica* (End.)

7 (3) Frons (Fig. 77a & d) very broad, index 1: 1.5–2. Abdomen conspicuously broad and flat, light grey, with three brown longitudinal stripes (*vittata*-group) .. 39

– Frons usually much narrower, index at most 1: 2.5 and abdominal pattern different. Abdomen of usual tabanine-like shape, never dorsoventrally compressed 8

8 (7) Halteres whitish-yellow. Eyes clothed with only sparse, minute hairs, sometimes almost naked; if densely pubescent, then abdomen pointed at tip. Reddish-

brown species. Ocellar tubercle vestigial and extensively black antennae ... 34
– Halteres blackish-brown to brownish or knob slightly paler at tip. Eyes more or less densely pubescent. Reddish-brown or blackish-grey species 9

9 (8) Apical segment of palpi long and slender, more than 3.5 times as long as deep, whitish-yellow or dark brown 10
– Apical segment of palpi distinctly stout at base, at most 3 times as long as deep, always whitish-yellow to light brown 16

10 (9) Palpi (Figs. 50c, 51c) whitish-yellow to very light brown, entirely pale haired. Eyes clothed with very long whitish hairs, with 1 to 3 bands or unbanded. Subcallus finely haired at sides (*decora*-group) 11
– Palpi very dark brown to brown, black haired, or at least with some black hairs. Eyes clothed with densely set, short greyish to brown hairs, always with 3 bands. Subcallus naked (*borealis*-group) 12

11 (10) Abdomen entirely black, tergite 2 greyish dusted at sides, pubescence black and pale. Basal antennal segment (Fig. 50e) with long pale hairs. Eyes with 1 band. Generally larger species, 13.5–16 mm in length .... *caucasi* (Szil.)
– Abdomen yellowish-brown at least on tergite 2 at sides, mostly pale haired. Basal antennal segment (Fig. 51e) almost naked. Eyes with 1 to 3 bands or unbanded. Generally smaller species, usually about 12 mm in length .... *decora* (Loew)

12 (10) Conspicuously reddish-brown species on anterior three to four tergites at sides, resembling *H. distinguenda* (Verr.). Antennae (Fig. 56b) chestnut-brown with segment 3 very broad. Frons (Fig. 56a) narrow, index 1: 4–4.5 ... *arpadi* (Szil.)
– Blackish-grey species or anterior tergites chestnut-brown at sides and all tergites with whitish posterior margins 13

13 (12) Abdomen black with more or less distinct greyish pattern of sublateral spots, median triangles, and indefinite paler borders on posterior margins to all tergites 14
– Abdomen shining black with conspicuous, narrow whitish borders to all tergites posteriorly; at least tergite 2 at sides distinctly chestnut-brown coloured ... 15

14 (13) Frons (Fig. 52a) broad, index about 1: 2.5. Antennae (Fig. 52b) mostly black, palpi lighter brown. Grey sublateral patches very distinct and rather light grey .... *polaris* (Frey)
– Frons (Fig. 53a) narrower, index about 1: 4. Antennae (Fig. 53e) brown except on terminal flagellar segments, palpi dark brown. Greyish abdominal pattern rather indistinct .... *borealis* (F.)

15 (13) Antennae (Fig. 54b) extensively black, segment 3 rather slender, reddish-brown at most on basal half. Frons (Fig. 54a) broader, index about 1: 2.5. Generally darker and smaller species, usually only tergite 2 chestnut-brown at sides .... *sexfasciata* (Hine)
– Antennae (Fig. 55e) brown except for black terminal flagellar segments, segment 3 broader with rectangular dorsal tooth. Frons (Fig. 55a) narrower, index about 1: 3.5. Generally larger species, extensively lighter chestnut-brown on anterior three tergites at sides .... *kaurii* Chv. & Lyneb.

16 (9) Frons broader, index 1: 2.5–4, rather parallel-sided. Lower callus large, plain and polished (except *nitidifrons confiformis* and *sareptana*) (*montana*-group) 17
– Frons narrower, index 1: 4–6, usually distinctly widened above. Lower callus usually small and distinctly wrinkled, not polished, except *valenciae* (*bimaculata*-group) 27

17 (16) Dorsum of abdomen entirely blackish-grey, without reddish-brown sidemarkings 18

– Abdomen largely reddish-brown at sides, brownish sidemarkings at least on tergite 2 20

18 (17) Frons (Fig. 57a) very broad, index about 1: 2.5, lower callus very large. Abdomen with distinct light grey pattern, tergite 2 largely greyish at sides .... *pilosa* (Loew)

– Frons narrower. Greyish abdominal pattern less distinct, sublateral patches on all tergites equal in size, oval 19

19 (18) Subcallus (Fig. 58a) low, not higher than frons is broad below, slightly convex. Frons broader, index 1: 3–3.5. Antennal segment 3 (Fig. 58e) very slender with hardly visible dorsal tooth .... *nigricornis* (Zett.)

– Subcallus rather high, of usual shape, not convex. Frons narrower, index 1: 3.5–4. Antennal segment 3 not so slender, dorsal tooth more distinct .... *montana* (Meig.) var. *flaviceps*

20 (17) Subcallus (Figs. 59a, 60a) at least at middle or on the upper part polished brown to black 21

– Subcallus entirely dulled by greyish dust 22

21 (20) Subcallus (Fig. 59a) distinctly convex and entirely polished black to blackish-brown. Lower callus plain, usually polished black. Generally smaller species, 11.5–15 mm in length .... *lurida* (Fall.)

– Subcallus (Fig. 60a) shining brown to blackish-brown at middle or on the upper part, not convex. Lower callus usually brownish, only slightly shining and distinctly wrinkled. Generally larger species, 14–18 mm in length .... *nitidifrons confiformis* Chv. & Mch.

22 (20) Frons golden-yellow dusted. Lower callus polished black, rectangular, wider than high and with entire lateral edges touching the eye-margins. Palpi robust, short and thickened, with blunt tip, 2.5–3 times longer than deep .... *bryanensis* Lecl. & French

– Not as above 23

23 (22) Apical segment of palpi very stout and rather short, less than 2.5 times as long as deep. Lower callus wrinckled 24

– Apical segment of palpi not so stout, almost 3 times as long as deep. Lower callus plain and polished 25

24 (23) Antennal segment 3 (Fig. 60e) reddish-brown, terminal flagellar segments black. Eyes brownish pubescent .... *nitidifrons confiformis* Chv. & Mch.

– Antennal segment 3 (Fig. 61e) black, often brownish at base. Eyes whitish pubescent. Abdomen with greyish pattern of sublateral spots and median triangles, at most anterior three tergites at sides light reddish-brown coloured and silvery-grey pruinose .... *sareptana* (Szil.)

25 (23) Antennal segment 3 (Fig. 62e) broad, mostly reddish-brown. Notopleural lobes blackish .... *lundbecki* Lyneb.

– Antennal segment 3 rather slender and more or less darkened. Notopleural lobes brown 26

26 (25) Antennal segment 3 (Fig. 63e) rather slender, brownish at base. Thorax at sides and abdomen mostly golden-yellow haired. Generally larger species, 15.5–18 mm in length .... *tropica* (L.)

– Antennal segment 3 (Fig. 64b) conspicuously slender, often slightly brownish at extreme base. Thorax at sides and abdomen with greyish and black hairs.

Generally smaller species. 12.5–16 mm in length .... *montana* (Meig.)

27 (16) Dorsum of abdomen unicolorous blackish-grey with greyish pattern, at most anterior two tergites at sides with a trace of brown coloration .... *bimaculata* (Macq.) var. *bisignata*

– Abdomen with reddish-brown sidemarkings at least on anterior two tergites 28

28 (27) Larger species, 17–19 mm in length. Palpi (Fig. 71c) whitish-yellow, apical segment very stout at base and only pale haired. Abdomen broadly yellowish-brown at sides on anterior four tergites, tergite 2 at sides only pale haired .... *ukrainica* (Ols.)

– Generally smaller species, usually about 15 or 16 mm in length. Apical segment of palpi not conspicuously stout at base, and at least with some black hairs . 29

29 (28) Lower frontal callus polished black, square of shape. Frontal index 1: 5–5.5 .... *valenciae* (Lecl.)

– Lower frontal callus always dulled and more or less wrinkled 30

30 (29) Reddish-brown sidemarkings (Pl. 2, figs. d & g) on not more than anterior three tergites, or if small sidemarkings also on tergite 4, then basal antennal segments distinctly grey dusted 31

– Reddish-brown sidemarkings (Pl. 2, figs. e–f) on anterior four tergites, or if only on anterior three, then basal antennal segments and notopleural lobes light brown 33

31 (30) Notopleural lobes brown. A dark median stripe on dorsum of abdomen (Pl. 2, fig. g) narrower, occupying at most 1/3 of tergites. Cerci distinctly longer than deep, subgenital plate (Fig. 65d) very narrow with a deep excision above .... *muehlfeldi* (Br.)

– Notopleural lobes blackish. Cerci short and broad, subgenital plate broad, apically rounded 32

32 (31) Basal antennal segments (Fig. 67e) greyish-black. A dark median stripe on abdomen (Pl. 2, fig. d) broad, occupying more than 1/3 of tergites. Sidemarkings dark yellowish-brown and not sharply separated from the median stripe. Pleura mostly dark grey and black haired .... *bimaculata* (Macq.)

– Basal antennal segments (Fig. 68e) lighter, always grey dusted, but the brown ground coloration can be seen. Dark median stripe on abdomen narrower, occupying less than 1/3 of tergites. Sidemarkings light (almost whitish) yellowish-brown and sharply separated from the median stripe. Pleura light grey haired . ... *solstitialis* (Meig.)

33 (30) Basal antennal segments (Fig. 70e) and notopleural lobes yellowish-brown, lower frontal callus often brown. Tergite 2 at sides with pale and black hairs .. .. *ciureai* (Ség.)

– Basal antennal segments (Fig. 69e) greyish-black, notopleural lobes dark brown or blackish; lower callus black. Tergite 2 at sides unicolorous golden-yellow haired without any black hairs .... *distinguenda* (Verr.)

34 (8) Posterior abdominal segments conspicuously laterally compressed, abdomen distinctly pointed when viewed from above. Postocular margin on vertex deep. Eyes short but rather densely haired (*acuminata*-group) 38

– Posterior abdominal segments not laterally compressed, abdomen of usual shape, broadly rounded apically. Postocular margin on vertex narrow. Eyes very indistinctly haired, almost naked (*erberi*-group) 35

35 (34) Reddish-brown sidemarkings at most on anterior three tergites. Venter with a distinct, broad, blackish median stripe on anterior sternites . *expollicata* (Pand.)

– Abdomen with reddish-brown sidemarkings on anterior four to five tergites. Anterior sternites yellowish, at most with a dark median patch on sternite 2; no median stripe 36

36 (35) Ocellar tubercle (Fig. 73a) well developed, oval to triangular in shape. Blackish median stripe narrow, occupying almost 1/8 of tergites, with a distinct, light grey median line of high median triangles. Sternite 2 with a dark median patch .... *morgani* (Surc.)

– Ocellar tubercle reduced into three vestigial ocelli which are more or less covered by greyish dust. Eyes with very minute hairs, almost naked 37

37 (36) Abdomen with a broad dark median stripe occupying 1/5 to 1/3 of tergite 2, mesally with a distinct light grey line. Ocelli almost circular, or the upper two slightly linear. Sternite 2 with a dark median patch .... *erberi* (Br.)

– Abdomen with a narrow greyish median stripe occupying 1/6 to 1/10 of tergite 2, no paler median line. Upper two ocelli linear, lower one circular and much smaller. Sternite 2 unicolorous yellowish, no darker median patch .... *peculiaris* (Szil.)

38 (34) Frons (Fig. 76a) narrower, index about 1: 4.5, median callus present, connected with lower callus. Posterior three abdominal segments distinctly laterally compressed. Basal antennal segments dark grey .... *acuminata* (Loew)

– Frons broader, index about 1: 3.5, median callus absent. Only posterior two abdominal segments laterally compressed. Basal antennal segments reddish .... *media* (Kröb.)

39 (7) Eyes unbanded. Frontal calli (Fig. 77a) absent .... *vittata* (F.)

– Eyes with three bands. Frontal calli (Fig. 77d) more or less developed, blackish .... *macularis* (F.)

Males

1 Larger blackish species with broad and conspicuously silvery-yellow to golden-yellow pubescent posterior margins to all tergites. Legs extensively orange-yellow (*tarandina*-group) 2

– Not as above 3

2 (1) Antennae (Fig. 44f) and palpi (Fig. 44d) orange-yellow, subcallus densely greyish dusted. All facets almost equal in size. Generally larger species, 17–20 mm in length .... *tarandina* (L.)

– Antennae and palpi extensively darkened, subcallus polished black. Upper facets enlarged. Generally smaller species, 15–19 mm in length .... *aequetincta* (Beck.)

3 (1) Black species, with legs unicolorous black and venter of abdomen shining black in ground colour. Anterior tergites often translucent dark brown at sides (*aterrima*-group) 4

– Reddish-brown to greyish-black species, legs brown at least on posterior tibiae. Venter brownish anteriorly, only exceptionally uniformly blackish-grey (*pilosa*) or posterior margins distinctly whitish 7

4 (3) Palpi black to blackish-brown. Wings with a darker patch at base of vein R_4 . 5

– Palpi light brown or greyish. Wings without a darker patch at base of vein R_4. All facets almost equal in size .... *caucasica* (End.)

5 (4) Fore tarsi with very long, black erect hairs. Subcallus (Fig. 46b) somewhat blackish above, facets almost equal in size. Abdomen somewhat bluish-grey

dusted when viewed from behind, anterior tergites with sublateral greyish patches .... *micans* (Meig.)

– Fore tarsi short haired, subcallus entirely greyish. Upper facets slightly enlarged. Abdomen dull blackish-brown when viewed from behind 6

6 (5) Abdomen with more or less distinctly golden-yellow pubescent posterior margins on tergites and sternites. Posterior tibiae rather short haired .... *auripila* (Meig.)

– Abdomen black haired with more or less distinct silvery-grey pubescent median triangles. Hind tibiae with longer black hairs anteriorly and posteroventrally .. .. *aterrima* (Meig.)

7 (3) Halteres whitish-yellow 26

– Halteres blackish-brown to brown 8

8 (7) Thorax and abdomen lighter grey with distinct darker brown longitudinal stripes (*vittata*-group) 30

– Thorax black or greyish-black, sometimes with paler longitudinal stripes. Abdomen black to greyish, with more or less developed reddish-brown to yellowish-brown sidemarkings on anterior tergites 9

9 (8) Eyes with conspicuously long whitish or light grey hairs, subcallus distinctly pale haired at sides. Palpi (Figs. 50d, 51d) long and slender, at least twice as long as deep, whitish-yellow. Facets almost equal in size, basal antennal segments (Figs. 50f, 51f) with very long pale hairs (*decora*-group) 10

– Eyes with shorter brown or pale hairs, subcallus always naked. Basal segments of antennae short haired or with longer dark hairs above 11

10 (9) Abdomen extensively blackish, tergite 2 (or partly tergite 3) with reddish-brown sidemarkings; venter unicolorous black and grey dusted. Generally larger species, 13.5–16 mm in length .... *caucasi* (Szil.)

– Abdomen very light grey, anterior four to five tergites broadly yellowish-brown at sides. Venter yellowish on anterior four sternites. Generally smaller species, usually about 12 mm in length .... *decora* (Loew)

11 (9) Apical segment of palpi slender, rather cylindrical in shape, blackish-brown to brown (*borealis*-group) 12

– Apical segment of palpi very stout or if elongated, then whitish-grey to yellowish-brown 14

12 (11) Palpi (Fig. 56e) rather lighter brown. Facets almost equal in size, only indistinctly enlarged above. Reddish-brown sidemarkings on anterior three to five tergites, a dark median stripe occupying 1/4–1/3 of tergite 3 .... *arpadi* (Szil.)

– Palpi (Figs. 53d, 55d) blackish-brown to dark brown. Facets on the upper part distinctly enlarged. Anterior three tergites darker brown at sides, a dark median stripe occupying about 1/3 of tergite 3 13

13 (12) Facets on the upper part of eyes very large and sharply separated from small facets. All tergites with distinct, narrow, whitish-grey posterior borders, venter unicolorous blackish-grey. Larger species, 14–16 mm in length .... *kaurii* Chv. & Lyneb.

– Facets on the upper part enlarged but not sharply separated from small facets. Tergites without conspicuous whitish posterior margins, venter yellowish-brown on anterior sternites. Smaller species, 11–13 mm in length .... *borealis* (F.)

14 (11) Eyes (Fig. 57b) meeting on frons for a shorter distance, equal to one and a half times the height of subcallus 15

– Eyes meeting on frons for a longer distance, equal to twice the height of subcallus 19

15 (14) Antennal segment 3 (Figs. 57f, 58f, 61f) black, at most slightly brown at base 16

– Antennal segment 3 (Figs. 59f, 60f) reddish-brown, at most terminal flagellar segments black. All facets almost equal in size 18

16 (15) Facets almost equal in size. Tergites 2 and 3 broadly silvery-grey pollinose at sides .... *sareptana* (Szil.)

– Facets on the upper part of eyes distinctly enlarged, sharp division absent .. 17

17 (16) Eyes long whitish-brown pubescent. Tergites 2 and 3 with less distinct dark chestnut-brown sidemarkings. Venter uniformly blackish-grey ... *pilosa* (Loew)

– Eyes long dark brown pubescent. Tergites 2 and 3 with more distinct brown sidemarkings, sternites 2 to 4 brownish .... *nigricornis* (Zett.)

18 (15) Dark median stripe on abdomen broader, occupying 1/3 to 1/5 of tergite 3, slightly widened posteriorly or parallel. Scutellum with black hairs. Smaller species, 12–14 mm in length .... *lurida* (Fall.)

– Dark median stripe narrower, occupying 1/8–1/5 of tergite 3, posteriorly narrower. Scutellum apically with pale hairs. Larger species, 14–17 mm in length .... *nitidifrons confiformis* Chv. & Mch.

19 (14) Antennal segment 1 (Fig. 67f) above with long black hairs which are as long as or longer than basal two segments combined. Palpi (Fig. 67d) distinctly stout, almost globular. Vertex with a tuft of long hairs behind ocellar tubercle. Antennal bows (Fig. 67b) of equal width (*bimaculata*-group) 22

– Antennal segment 1 (Fig. 62f) above with short black hairs which are much shorter than basal segments combined. Palpi (Fig. 62d) rather oval, not very stout. Vertex at most with a few shorter hairs. Antennal bows (Fig. 62b) broader at middle (*montana*-group) 20

20 (19) Antennal segment 3 (Fig. 62f) reddish-brown except for terminal flagellar segments, rather broad, with distinct dorsal tooth. Notopleural lobes blackish .. .. *lundbecki* Lyneb.

– Antennal segment 3 (Figs. 63f, 64c) extensively blackish and rather slender, dorsal tooth slightly developed. Notopleural lobes brown 21

21 (20) Antennal segment 3 (Fig. 63f) rather slender, slightly brownish at most on basal half, dorsal tooth slightly developed. Abdomen predominantly with golden-yellow hairs. Generally larger species, 15.5–17 mm in length ...... *tropica* (L.)

– Antennal segment 3 (Fig. 64f) very slender and almost black, dorsal tooth indistinct. Abdomen mostly greyish and black haired. Generally smaller species, 13–15 mm in length .... *montana* (Meig.)

22 (19) Facets almost equal in size, median facets only slightly larger than lower facets. Notopleural lobes blackish. Brown sidemarkings on anterior three tergites, dark median stripe broader, occupying 1/5 to 1/3 of tergite 3 23

– Upper facets considerably enlarged. Brown sidemarkings as a rule on anterior four tergites or if only on anterior three tergites, then notopleural lobes brownish; dark median stripe narrow, occupying about 1/8 of tergite 3 24

23 (22) Thorax, especially on pleura, light grey haired. Dark median stripe on abdomen rather narrower, occupying about 1/5 of tergite 3. Brown sidemarkings very light, without greyish shadows .... *solstitialis* (Meig.)

– Thorax dark grey and black haired. Dark median stripe broader, occupying 1/4 to 1/3 of tergite 3. Brown sidemarkings with greyish shadows .... *bimaculata* (Macq.)

24 (22) Upper facets very enlarged and sharply separated from the lower small facets. Basal antennal segments (Fig. 70f) brownish. Notopleural lobes brown .... *ciureai* (Ség.)

– Upper facets less strongly enlarged and gradually smaller downwards. Basal antennal segments grey or greyish-black 25

25 (24) Dark median stripe with broad and low whitish-grey median triangles, sharply separated from brown sidemarkings. Tergite 1 broadly golden-yellow haired on posterior margin. Notopleural lobes blackish, only occasionally brownish ... . *distinguenda* (Verr.)

– Dark median stripe with less distinct and high paler median triangles, not very sharply separated from brown sidemarkings. Tergite 1 at most with a narrow posterior border of golden-yellow hairs. Usually only anterior three tergites brown at sides, notopleural lobes usually brownish .... *muehlfeldi* (Br.)

26 (7) Head considerably large, semiglobular. Abdomen more or less laterally compressed and pointed at tip. Generally smaller species, about 13 mm in length (*acuminata*-group) .... *acuminata* (Loew)

– Head not very large, about as broad as thorax. Abdomen not laterally compressed on posterior segments and not conspicuously pointed apically. Generally larger species, about 15 mm in length (*erberi*-group) 27

27 (26) Venter of abdomen with a broad, deep black median stripe on anterior sternites, occupying 1/3 of sternites. Black median stripe on dorsum broader, occupying about 1/4 of tergites 2 and 3 .... *expollicata* (Pand.)

– Anterior sternites yellowish-brown, at most sternite 2 with a darker median spot, no median stripe. Dark median stripe on dorsum very narrow, greyish, sometimes interrupted or absent posteriorly 28

28 (27) Sternite 2 unicolorous yellowish, no dark median spot. A dark median stripe on dorsum of abdomen very narrow or absent .... *peculiaris* (Szil.)

– Sternite 2 with a distinct greyish median spot 29

29 (28) Femora almost wholly blackish-grey. Facets on the upper part of eyes slightly enlarged, about 2–3 times as large as small facets, sharp division absent (according to Olsufjev, 1937) .... *morgani* (Surc.)

– Apical third of femora yellowish-brown. Upper facets very enlarged, about 5–6 times as large as small facets, and sharply separated from the lower area with small facets .... *erberi* (Br.)

30 (8) Eyes meeting on frons for a long distance. Antennae broad (according to Leclercq, 1967) .... *vittata* (F.)

– Eyes meeting on frons in a point. Antennae long and slender (according to Leclercq, 1967) .... *macularis* (F.)

TARANDINA-GROUP

Larger species resembling species of the *Tabanus chrysurus*-group. Abdomen black with conspicuous pale coloured and densely golden-yellow pubescent posterior margins on tergites and sternites. Legs extensively orange-yellow coloured. Subcallus more or less polished. Apical segment of palpi very long and slender, orange-yellow or blackish. Species inhabiting northern parts of the Holarctic region.

H. aequetincta (Beck.) is provisionally placed here because of its general similarity to *H. tarandina* (L.), but it has much more in common with the Asiatic *astur*-group with species *H. stigmoptera* (Ols.), *H. tatarica* (Portsch.), *H. zonata* (Szil.), *H. mouchai* Chv., *H. astur* (Erichs.), *H. olsufjevina* (Mch. & Chv.) and *H. lyneborgi* Chv.

HYBOMITRA TARANDINA (LINNÉ, 1758)

Fig. 44; pl. 2: fig. a.

Tabanus tarandinus Linné, 1758, Syst. Nat., p. 601.
Tabanus karafutonis Matsumara, 1911, J. Coll. Agric. Hokkaido Imp. Univ., 4: 64.

Diagnosis. Large blackish species with orange-yellow antennae, palpi and legs. Lower frontal callus and subcallus above subshining reddish-yellow, median callus black. Abdomen blackish with conspicuously whitish-yellow dusted and golden-yellow pubescent posterior margins of all segments. Male resembling female, all facets almost equal in size, subcallus greyish dusted.

Description. ♀. *Head.* Eyes rather short but densely greyish to greyish-brown pubescent, with three narrow bands. Frons rather broader, index 1: 3—3.5, almost parallel-sided, yellowish-grey dusted. Lower callus not very large, distinctly separated from the eye-margins, subshining reddish-yellow. Median callus black, spindle-shaped dilated, connected with lower callus. Ocellar tubercle oval, shining reddish-brown. Subcallus subshining reddish-yellow at least on apical half, antennal bows rather narrow. Face and cheeks greyish dusted and densely light golden-yellow haired. Antennae unicolorous orange-yellow, basal segments with some shorter black hairs; segment 3 broad with a distinct, pointed dorsal tooth. Palpi orange-yellow, apical segment long and slender, clothed with short adpressed pale hairs and with some additional fine black hairs.

Thorax black, very thinly dark grey dusted; mesonotum unstriped, subshining, densely golden-yellow pubescent. Notopleural lobes and partly lateral margins of mesonotum yellowish-brown. Pleura densely golden-yellow pubescent, sternopleura usually mainly dark haired. *Legs* orange-yellow except blackish-grey coxae and basal part of femora. Tarsi sometimes darkened. Legs golden-yellow haired but coxae and blackish base on femora mostly black haired. *Wings* slightly yellowish tinted on costal half and at base; veins yellowish-brown, slightly brownish clouded on apical half of wing. Halteres light brown.

Abdomen black in ground colour and mostly black haired, posterior margins of all segments both dorsally and ventrally broadly whitish-yellow dusted and golden-yellow pubescent. Anterior two tergites slightly translucent brown at sides.

♂. Head rather small, not broader than thorax. Eyes densely greyish-brown pubescent, all facets almost equal in size. Subcallus greyish dusted. Antennae more slender on segment 3, dorsal tooth rectangular, distinct; basal segments mostly short pale haired, segment 1 at tip above with a tuft of short black hairs. Apical segment of palpi orange-yellow, long oval and rather slender, about twice as long as deep, clothed with fine, short pale hairs, and with some darker grey hairs at tip. Mesonotum longer pale haired, otherwise including legs and wings as in the ♀. Abdomen with the same pattern but anterior three tergites dark reddish-brown coloured and black haired at sides, a black median stripe occupying one-third of tergites 2 and 3. Anterior sternites only slightly brownish at sides.

Length. 17–22 mm.

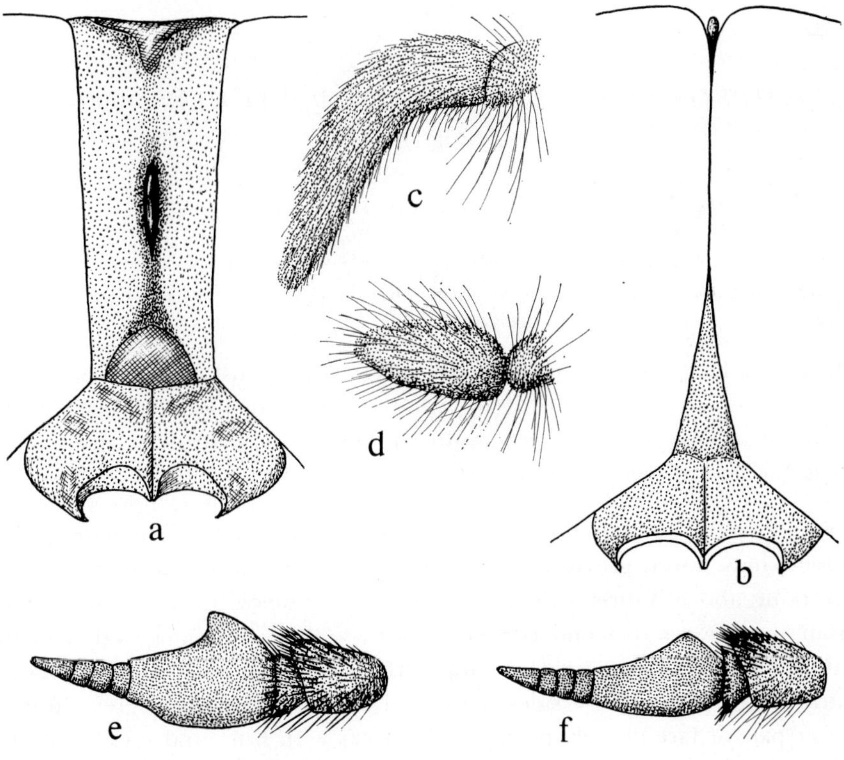

Fig. 44. *Hybomitra tarandina* (L.), a. female frons, b. male frons, c. female palpus, d. male palpus, e. female antenna, f. male antenna.

Biology. A typical species of North European and Siberian taiga; in the region of Tomsk *H. tarandina* (L.) is a dominant species of Tabanids in late summer. Females fly for long distances, Violovič (1968: 132) recorded that Samko observed adults flying over the Irtys river which is 1200—1500 m broad. Soboleva (1965) described the egg-clusters; the pupa was described by Portschinsky (1915). The larva is still undescribed though often observed in nature.

Dates. From June until August.

Distribution. A widely distributed species from Scandinavia through Siberia to the Far East of the U.S.S.R. and Japan with the centre of distribution lying in North Europe and North Asia. While the area of occurrence in the north is continuous, in Central Europe the species occurs only rarely in several isolated localities. The western and southern border of its distribution in Europe lies in Germany, Austria and Poland. It has not yet been found in Czechoslovakia.

HYBOMITRA AEQUETINCTA (BECKER, 1900)

Fig. 45.

Tabanus flavipes Wiedemann, 1828, Aussereur. zweifl. Ins., 1: 137 (nec Gravenhorst, 1807).

Therioplectes aequetinctus Becker, 1900, Acta Soc. Sci. fenn., 26 (No. 9): 8.

Tabanus nigrotuberculatus Fairchild, 1934, Occ. Pap. Boston Soc. nat. Hist., 8: 139 (nom. nov. for *flavipes* Wied. nec Gravenh.).

Diagnosis. Larger species with slender black palpi, polished black subcallus, femora reddish-brown at least on apical third, and abdomen black with broad, silvery-yellow posterior margins of tergites. Legs mostly orange-yellow including apical part of femora.

Description. ♀. *Head.* Eyes with short but densely set brown hairs, with three bands. Frons greyish, rather broad, index about 1: 2.5, more or less diverging above. Lower callus polished black, convex, distinctly separated from the eye-margins and connected with a short and long-oval median callus. Ocellar tubercle oval, shining dark brown. Subcallus polished black, narrowly grey dusted at sides. Face and cheeks rather dark grey dusted, lower part of face densely pale haired, cheeks with finer and smaller blackish hairs. Antennae reddish-brown, segment 3 towards tip and terminal flagellar segments darkened or black; basal segments short black haired;

segment 3 very broad, plate as long as deep, with prominent rectangular dorsal tooth. Palpi blackish, apical segment long and slender, more than 4 times as long as deep, clothed with short, adpressed black hairs.

Thorax black, mesonotum unstriped, somewhat shining and densely clothed with longer pale hairs, especially long haired in front and on scutellum. Notopleural lobes rarely slightly brownish at middle. Pleura very thinly greyish dusted and mostly pale haired except for pteropleura and sternopleura. *Legs* black on coxae and at least on basal third of femora, rest of femora reddish-brown. Tibiae and tarsi orange-yellow, fore tarsi darkened. Coxae, fore femora, darkened parts on posterior femora, and fore tarsi black haired; otherwise legs pale haired. *Wings* slightly tinted yellowish-brown, costal cell and extreme base of wing yellowish; veins brown, paler on costal margin and at base. Halteres dark brown.

Abdomen black in ground colour, anterior two tergites light brown at sides. All tergites whitish dusted and densely silvery-yellow pubescent on posterior margins. Venter densely pale haired except sternite 1, and with distinct, broadly paler posterior margins.

♂. We have not seen the male sex but according to Kröber (1925a: 64) resembling very much the female, facets on the upper part of eyes distinctly enlarged, and anterior two tergites brownish.

Length. 15–19 mm.

BIOLOGY. A species inhabiting northern tundra; the adults fly for long distances from the biotopes where the larvae live. A very common species at suitable localities, forming on some biotopes in tundra in the middle of

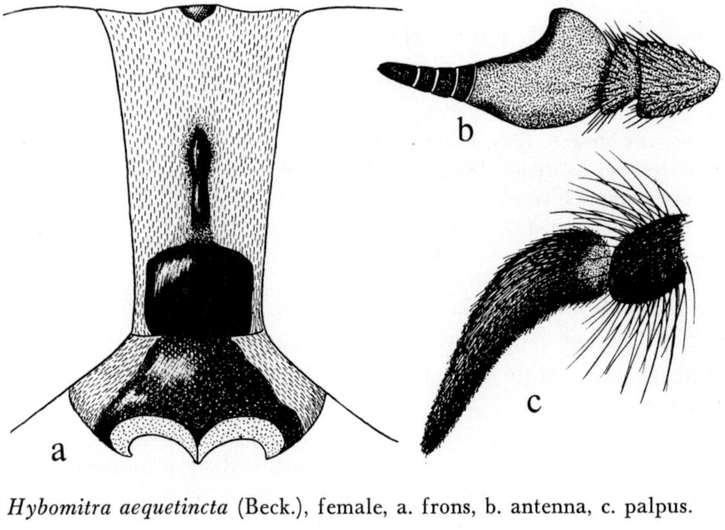

Fig. 45. *Hybomitra aequetincta* (Beck.), female, a. frons, b. antenna, c. palpus.

July as much as 42 % of the Tabanid population. A rare species in mountainous tundra. Females attack man and large animals.

DATES. From June until August.

DISTRIBUTION. A Holarctic species known from the northern parts of America (Quebec, Labrador) and Eurasia. In Siberia it is known from the lowlands of the river Ob, Yenisei, Kolyma and Anadyr, and it penetrates from the Arctic part of Asia to an adjacent European part of the U.S.S.R. (Olsufjev 1969a: 487). Is has not yet been recorded from North Scandinavia. Leclercq (1967a: 107) recorded this species from North Mongolia; the original records are not known to us and this is very probably an inaccurate interpretation of Olsufjev's (1937: 153) record from the Bujato-Mongolian A.S.S.R.

ATERRIMA-GROUP

Medium-sized black species with entirely black legs, apical segment of palpi usually blackish (except *caucasica* (End.)), more or less slender. Abdomen entirely black with concolorous hairs, often with a few silvery-grey hairs forming indefinite median triangles and indistint posterior margins, or posterior margins to all tergites narrowly golden-yellow pubescent. Species inhabiting northern parts of the Holarctic region and high mountains in the south.

HYBOMITRA MICANS (MEIGEN, 1804)

Fig. 46.

Tabanus micans Meigen, 1804, Klass., 1: 167.
Tabanus austriacus Fabricius, 1805, Syst. Ant., p. 96.
Tabanus nigerrimus Gravenhorst, 1807, Vergl. Übers. Zool. Syst., p. 363.
Tabanus niger Donovan, 1813, Nat. Hist. Brit. Ins., 16: 47.
? *Tabanus signatus* Meigen, 1820, Syst. Beschr., 2: 34.

DIAGNOSIS. Medium-sized black species with silvery-grey lateral patches on tergite 2. Antennae, palpi and legs black. Subcallus polished black, in male on the upper part. Male with all facets almost equal in size, fore tarsi with long black hairs.

DESCRIPTION. ♀. *Head.* Eyes densely greyish-brown pubescent, with three bands. Frons grey, rather broad, index about 1: 3, almost parallel-sided.

Lower callus broadly rectangular, polished black, touching the eye-margins. Median callus subshining black, spindle-shaped, often connected with lower callus and with polished brown ocellar tubercle. Subcallus entirely polished black, antennal bows rather narrow. Face and cheeks long whitish haired. Antennae black, basal segments greyish dusted and short black haired; segment 3 rather slender with a slightly developed dorsal tooth. Palpi blackish-grey, apical segment stout at base and sharply pointed at tip, about three times as long as deep at base; densely black haired and with some longer whitish hairs at base.

Thorax blackish-grey, mesonotum with short black hairs and some additional whitish hairs, scutellum at tip and pleura with long whitish-grey hairs. *Legs* entirely black and black haired. *Wings* brownish clouded at base and in costal cell; veins blackish; a small dark patch at base of vein R_4. Halteres black.

Abdomen shining black when viewed from above but somewhat bluish-grey when viewed from behind. Large sublateral patches on tergite 2 and small median triangles to all tergites greyish dusted and pale haired, otherwise abdomen black haired. Tergite 1 usually greyish at sides. Venter greyish and predominantly whitish haired.

♂. Eyes densely brownish pubescent, all facets almost equal in size, some larger facets at middle of eyes. Subcallus polished black on the upper part.

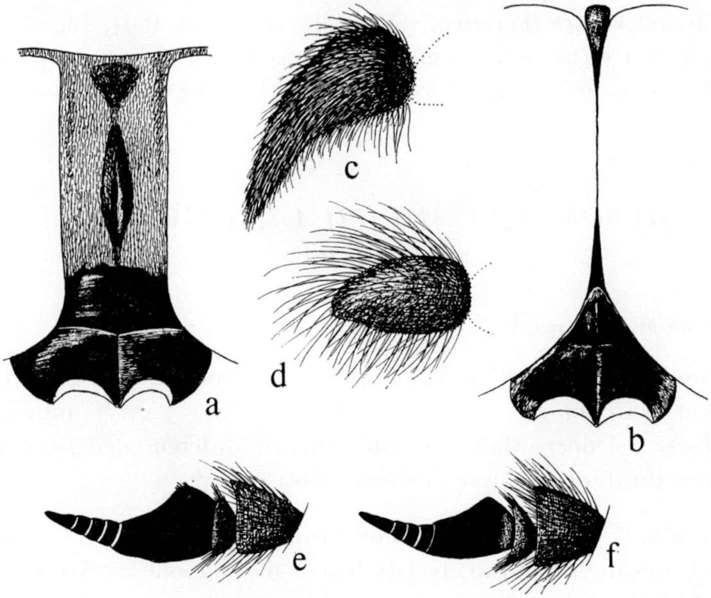

Fig. 46. *Hybomitra micans* (Meig.), a. female frons, b. male frons, c. female palpus, d. male palpus, e. female antenna, f. male antenna.

Antennae black, segment 1 enlarged, greyish dusted and clothed with long black hairs; segment 3 slender. Palpi blackish-grey, short and conical, black haired. Posterior part of mesonotum and scutellum only black haired. Legs black, basal four segments on fore tarsi with conspicuously long and erected black hairs. Abdomen black with concolorous hairs, an indefinite greyish pattern as in the ♀.

Length. 13—17 mm.

Biology. Occasionally a common species on peat-bogs and in foggy biotopes; also in the mountains but uncommon. It has been taken in the Slovak Carpathians over 2000 m (High Tatra Mts., Ždiarská Vidla 2148 m). Kröber (1932b: 73) states that the species can be met with along roads with flowering hedges, and in the early morning both males and females can be seen on flowers, especially of *Heracleum*. It has been several times taken in England on honey dew (from aphids) and it has also been seen drinking on damp soil and at small streams (Lyneborg, 1959: 91). Females attack man and animals.

Dates. From May until September.

Distribution. A European species inhabiting the British Isles except Ireland, Denmark (Jutland) and countries of Benelux, Germany and all countries of Central Europe. The southern border of its area of distribution lies in Spain and France (Leclercq, 1967a: 112), in North Italy, Jugoslavia and Rumania. Not yet recorded from Scandinavia and the European part of the U.S.S.R. In southern areas it occurs especially in the mountainous regions.

HYBOMITRA AURIPILA (MEIGEN, 1820)

Fig. 47; pl. 2: fig. b.

Tabanus auripilus Meigen, 1820, Syst. Beschr., 2: 41.

Diagnosis. Blackish species, all tergites with more or less golden-yellow pubescent posterior margins. Legs black, subcallus greyish dusted. Palpi blackish-grey, slender. Male with only slightly differentiated facets on the upper two-thirds of eyes, fore tarsi only short haired.

Description. ♀. *Head.* Eyes with short brown hairs and with 3 bands. Frons yellowish-grey dusted and finely dark haired, index about 1: 3.5. Lower callus polished black, rectangular to triangular in shape, usually slightly separated from the eye-margins. Subcallus greyish dusted, face and frons greyish and long golden-yellow haired. Antennae black, segment 3 with plate usually dark brown to blackish, terminal flagellar segments always black. Palpi blackish-grey to very dark brown, apical segment slender and slightly pointed at tip, clothed with short black hairs.

Thorax black, mesonotum and scutellum clothed with fine black and some pale hairs, pleura and coxae long greyish-yellow haired. *Legs* entirely black with fine black hairs, femora and posterior four tibiae predominantly golden-yellow haired. *Wings* rather clear, veins black, on basal half of wing brownish; a small brownish patch at base of vein R_4. Halteres black.

Abdomen rather shining black, all tergites at sides and along posterior margin golden-yellow pubescent. Sternites dark grey and mostly greyish haired. Cerci nearly rectangular with straight margins. Subgenital plate broad on basal half with straight lower margin, anterior part small, oval-shaped, slightly higher than broad.

♂. Eyes densely brownish pubescent, facets on the upper two-thirds, but especially at middle, indistinctly enlarged. Antennae entirely black, segment 1 finely greyish dusted and clothed with long black hairs. Apical segment of palpi dark brown and mostly black haired, short conical. Mesonotum and scutellum long black haired; legs black, fore tarsi only short haired.

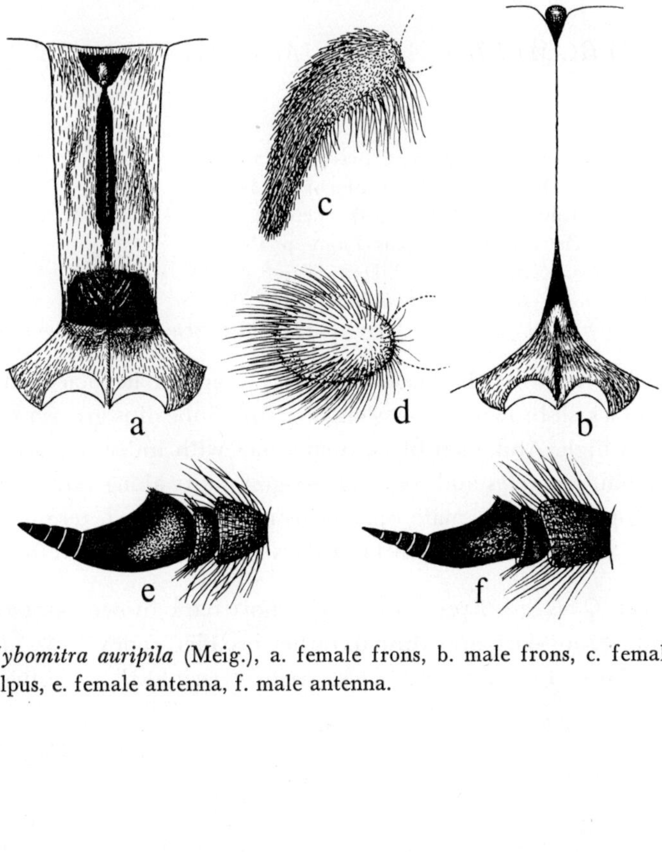

Fig. 47. *Hybomitra auripila* (Meig.), a. female frons, b. male frons, c. female palpus, d. male palpus, e. female antenna, f. male antenna.

Abdomen black, the golden-yellow pubescent posterior margins are more distinct at middle and at sides, sternites on the whole length on posterior margins.

Length. 13—16 mm.

Biology. A typical species occurring on peat-bogs, in marshy biotopes and on mountains. Sometimes a very common species in suitable localities, its occurrence in Europe is rather isolated. Nothing is known of the immature stages but we have observed an emergence of the species in the morning hours on 28. V. 1968 near a brook in the High Tatra Mts., Czechoslovakia.

Dates. From the end of May until August.

Distribution. A European species known from Scandinavia (North Sweden) as far as Spain (Huesca), in Central Europe sometimes a very common species but rather rare in the south; it occurs in mountains often at higher altitudes over 2000 m (Carpathian). The eastern border of its area of distribution lies in the Carpathians (Hoverla), the western border lies in the Pyrenees. It has been recorded from all parts of the Alps, and also from Belgium and Luxemburg.

HYBOMITRA ATERRIMA (MEIGEN, 1820)

Fig. 48.

Tabanus aterrimus Meigen, 1820, Syst. Beschr., 2: 33.
? *Tabanus signatus* Meigen, 1820, Syst. Beschr., 2: 34.
Tabanus aethiops Ljungh, 1823, K. svenska Vetensk.-Akad. Handl., 44: 265.
Tabanus lugubris Zetterstedt, 1838, Ins. Lapp., p. 515.
Tabanus nigerrimus Zetterstedt, 1842, Dipt. Scand., 1: 115.
Tabanus Heydenianus Jaennicke, 1866, Berl. ent. Z., 10: 68.
Therioplectes aterrimus var. *jacobi* Bouvier, 1945, Mitt. schweiz. ent. Ges., 19: 425.

Diagnosis. Entirely black species with black antennae, black haired face, and with blackish-brown, rather slender palpi. Subcallus greyish dusted, antennal bows high. Abdomen black, sometimes with indistinct, small, silvery haired median triangles and some silvery-grey hairs along posterior margins at sides. Upper facets in male only indistinctly enlarged, tergite 2 translucent brown at sides. Wings with faint dark patch at base of vein R_4.

Description. ♀. *Head.* Eyes densely but short dark brown pubescent, with three bands. Frons dark grey dusted, rather broader, index 1: 3—3.5, slightly widening above. Lower callus black, slightly wrinkled, touching the eye-margins and connected with a linear black median callus. Ocellar swelling oval, light brown and slightly shining. Subcallus dark grey dusted, yellowish antennal bows high. Face and cheeks very dark grey, face clothed with long black hairs. Antennae black, basal segments with black hairs; segment 3 rather broad, with a distinct dorsal tooth. Palpi blackish-brown to dark brown, apical segment rather slender, clothed with small black hairs.

Thorax entirely black with concolorous hairs, pleura thinly dark grey dusted. *Legs* black and black haired, coxae and femora clothed with longer and fine hairs. *Wings* slightly tinted dark grey, costal cell brownish; veins very dark, a small dark patch at base of vein R_4 distinct. Halteres blackish.

Abdomen black, densely clothed with rather short black hairs. Tergites sometimes with very small silvery-grey haired median triangles and indistinct, narrow posterior margins at sides.

♂. Eyes with longer brown pubescence, meeting on frons for a long distance. Upper facets only slightly larger, about twice as large as small facets. Antennae with segment 3 more slender and sometimes indistinctly brownish at base, dorsal tooth very small and placed near base; basal segments with

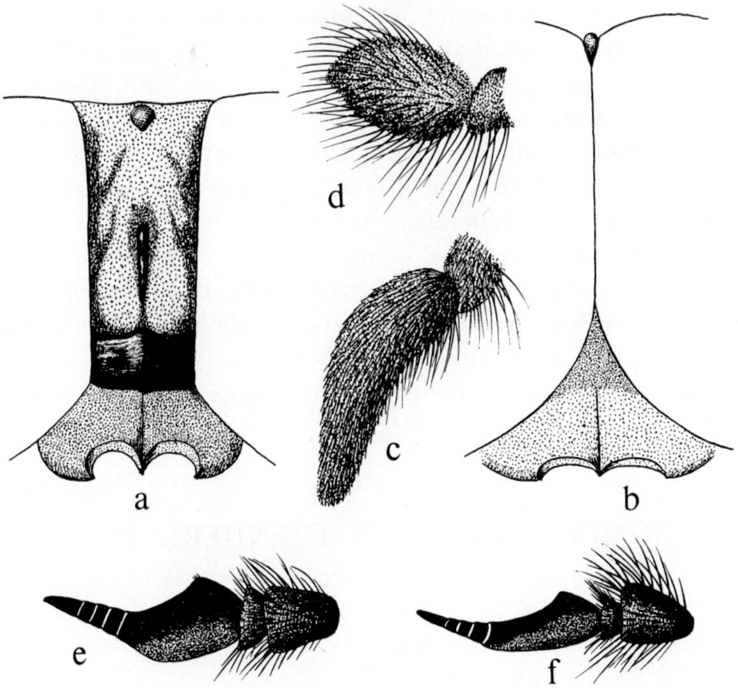

Fig. 48. *Hybomitra aterrima* (Meig.), a. female frons, b. male frons, c. female palpus, d. male palpus, e. female antenna, f. male antenna.

long black hairs which are longer than basal two segments combined. Palpi blackish-brown, apical segment rather broadly oval, about 1.5 times as long as deep, densely clothed with longer black hairs. Pleura sometimes with some paler hairs. Legs black, hind tibiae with distinct hairs in anterior and posteroventral rows. Wings as in the ♀, halteres usually more brownish. Abdomen translucent brown on tergite 2 (sometimes also on tergite 3) at sides; pubescence as in the ♀, small median triangles usually present.

Length. 13–16 mm.

VARIABILITY. The abdominal pubescence is usually entirely black, sometimes there are more or less distinct small median triangles and narrow posterior lateral margins of silvery-grey pubescence. The specimens with distinct silvery pattern were named by Bouvier (1945) as a variety *jacobi* which has, of course, no taxonomic value.

DATES. June and July.

DISTRIBUTION. A boreo-mountainous species known from North Europe from Scandinavia (Norway, Sweden and Finland to as far as 70° north) and from the mountains of Central and South Europe. It is known from the Alps (also at an altitude of about 2400 m) from all countries from France and Switzerland through Germany and Austria to North Jugoslavia and North Italy. The species has been recorded from the Spanish and French Pyrenees including Andorra and from the Carpathians. We have seen the documentary material from the Pyrenees and the Alps and also from the Black Forest Mts. (Schwarzwald) in Western Germany. On the other hand we cannot confirm the recorded occurrence in the Carpathians, in the Polish Tatra Mts. and in Rumania. Leclercq (1967a: 102) recorded this species by mistake from Bohemia, Czechoslovakia. All the specimens we have seen from the Carpathians are either *H. auripila* (Meig.) or males of *H. micans* (Meig.). The species is not known from East Europe and from the Caucasus.

HYBOMITRA CAUCASICA (ENDERLEIN, 1925)

Fig. 49.

Tabanus (Therioplectes) tetricus Szilády, 1914, Annls. Mus. nat. hung., 12: 661 (nec Marten, 1883).

Therioplectes bimaculatus Enderlein, 1925, Mitt. zool. Mus. Berl., 11: 358 (nec Macquart, 1826 – secondary homonym).

Therioplectes caucasicus Enderlein, 1925, Mitt. zool. Mus. Berl., 11: 358.

Sziladynus aterrimus auripilus f. *palpalis* Kröber, 1938, Acta Inst. Mus. zool. Univ. athen., 2: 172 – syn. n.
Sziladynus hariettae Muschamp, 1939, Entomologist's Rec. J. Var., 51: 52 – syn. n.
Hybomitra olsoufievi Philip, 1956, J. sanit. Zool., 7: 230 (nom. nov. for *tetricus* Szil. nec Marten) – syn. n.
Hybomitra olsufjevina Philip, 1961, Pacif. Insects, 3: 479 (nom. nov. for *olsoufievi* Phil. nec Bog. et Sam., unnecessary change) – syn. n.

DIAGNOSIS. Entirely black species including legs and antennae, resembling *H. aterrima* (Meig.) but it differs in the yellowish-brown palpi, mostly pale haired face and in the wings which are uniformly slightly tinted brownish without a dark patch at base of vein R_4. Subcallus dusted grey with narrow antennal bows. Male with all facets almost equal in size.

DESCRIPTION. ♀. *Head.* Eyes densely light grey pubescent, with three bands. Frons greyish dusted, rather broader, index 1: 3—3.5, sometimes almost 1: 4, slightly widened above. Lower callus polished black to dark brown, connected on lower half with the eye-margins and subcallus, upper margin usually rounded; median callus linear, black, connected with lower callus. Ocellar tubercle broadly oval, shining brown. Frons at vertex black haired, postocular margin rather deeper laterally, whitish-grey dusted and pale

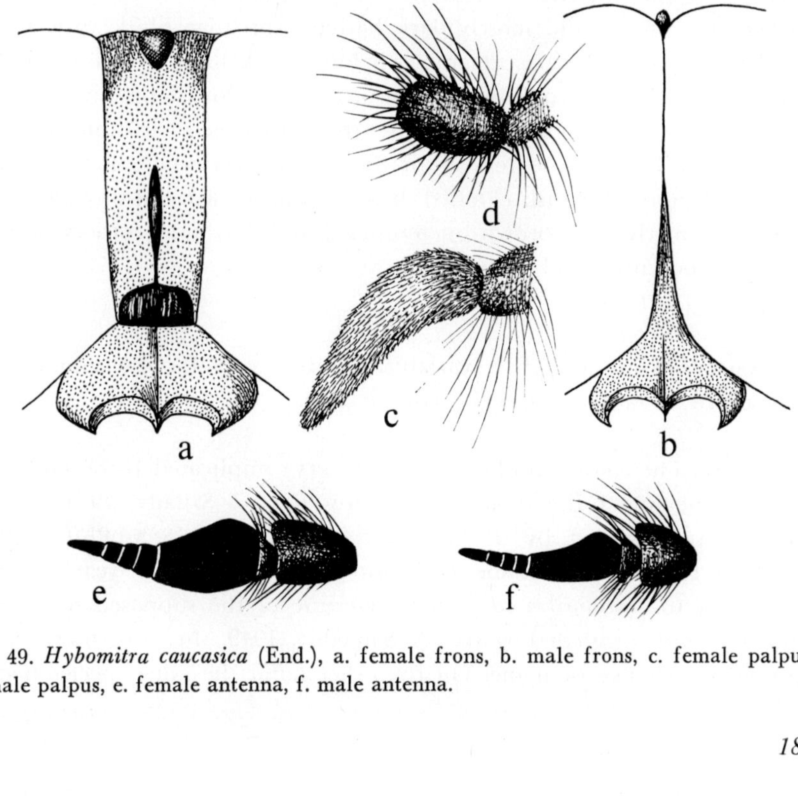

Fig. 49. *Hybomitra caucasica* (End.), a. female frons, b. male frons, c. female palpus, d. male palpus, e. female antenna, f. male antenna.

haired similarly as occiput. Subcallus grey dusted with narrow yellowish antennal bows. Face and cheeks lighter grey dusted and long pale haired. Antennae black, segment 3 brownish at extreme base, basal segments greyish dusted and clothed with longer black hairs; segment 3 rather slender with obtuse and somewhat rounded dorsal tooth, flagellum blunt ended. Palpi yellowish-brown, apical segment stout at base and rather shorter, clothed with adpressed pale hairs, usually some additional black hairs present.

Thorax black with concolorous hairs, humeri sometimes yellowish-brown, notopleural lobes exceptionally translucent dark brown. Prothoracic part of pleura including base of fore coxae, sometimes also pteropleura, with some pale hairs. *Legs* unicolorous black and black haired, femora with fine, long hairs beneath; hind tibiae with longer hairs in row anteroventrally. Posterior tarsi reddish pubescent beneath. *Wings* uniformly slightly tinted brownish, veins blackish, more brown at base of wing and along costal margin. No darker patch at base of vein R_4. Halteres blackish-brown.

Abdomen black with concolorous hairs, tergite 2 sometimes indistinctly translucent dark brown at sides anteriorly. Abdomen distinctly silvery-grey dusted when viewed from behind. Venter black with greyish dusting, short but densely black haired.

♂. Eyes rather longer and densely greyish-brown pubescent, meeting on frons for a long distance. All facets almost equal in size. Face and cheeks darker grey dusted and mostly dark haired. Antennae black with a more slender segment 3, basal segment with long black hairs which are as long as basal two segments combined. Palpi brown to yellowish-brown, apical segment broadly oval, slightly pointed at tip, and clothed with longer, mostly black hairs. Thorax and legs as in the ♀ but everywhere longer haired, wings still more brownish clouded, base to vein R_4 without any patch. Abdomen distinctly dark brown on tergites 2 and 3 at sides, otherwise black coloured and entirely black haired.

Length. 13—17 mm.

Variability. Only a slightly variable species except for the coloration of pubescence on face and anterior part of pleura.

Synonymy. The synonymy of this species is very complicated. It was known for a long time under the name of *Tabanus tetricus* Szilády, 1914 but this name is preoccupied by *Tabanus tetricus* Marten, 1883. Philip (1956) proposed for it a new name *Hybomitra olsoufievi* but 5 years later he changed it to *Hybomitra olsufjevina* because of the supposed homonymy with *Tabanus olsufievi* Bogatčev & Samedov, 1949, this was, however, an unnecessary change of name. On the other hand the same species had already been described in 1925 by Enderlein as *Therioplectes caucasicus* (which is not preoccupied by *Tabanus caucasius* Kröber, 1925) and which should be a valid and available name for this species.

We have seen two of Enderlein's female type specimens of *caucasica* in the Zoological Museum, Berlin. They are labelled: »Caucasus, Brandt S.«, »Type«, and »Therioplectes caucasicus Type Enderl. / ♀ / Dr. Enderlein det., 1923«. These females are conspecific and identical with the species hitherto known as *tetricus* Szil. or *olsoufievi* Phil. One female has a black lower frontal callus, but the antennal segments 3 are missing. The second female has a brownish lower frontal callus and is very well preserved. It is hereby designated as the lectotype of *H. caucasica* (Enderlein) and has been labelled accordingly.

In the same collection there is the holotype male of *Therioplectes bimaculatus* Enderlein (nec *T. borealis* var. *bimaculata* Enderlein) labelled »Kurusch, Christoph«, »coll. H. Loew«, »aterrimus Mg. var., det. Szilády«, »Type«, and »Therioplectes bimaculatus Type Enderl. / ♂ / Dr. Enderlein det. 1923«. The holotype is well preserved, as only antennal segment 3 on right antenna is missing, and it undoubtedly represents the holotype of Enderlein's *bimaculatus* and is identical with Enderlein's *caucasicus* described in the same paper from the female sex.

H. auripila f. *palpalis* (Kröber, 1938) described from Carinthia, Austria and *H. hariettae* (Muschamp, 1939) described from the French Savoy Alps are, on the basis of their original descriptions, other synonyms; we did not succeed in finding the type material of the last two mentioned taxa.

Dates. From June until August.

Distribution. A European mountainous species known from the Alps from Austria, North Italy, Germany (Südbayern) and Switzerland, but it is also recorded from the Pyrenees and from other French and Spanish mountains. It is also recorded from the Rumanian Carpathians but we have not seen any documentary material. *H. caucasica* (End.) also occurs in the Caucasus, from where it was described, and all records of *H. aterrima* (Meig.) from the Caucasus refer to this species (Olsufjev, 1937: 173). Neither Shevtshenko (1961) nor Violovič (1968) recorded this species from Kazakhstan and Siberia respectively.

DECORA-GROUP

A very distinct group of usually smaller light grey or blackish species with conspicuously long pale haired eyes in both sexes. Subcallus greyish dusted and distinctly pale haired at least at sides. Apical segment of palpi very long and slender, whitish-yellow coloured and pale haired. Eyes with one to three bands or unbanded, the number of eye-bands varies in one species. Antennae black, segment 1 in male always with very long pale hairs. Species inhabiting southern parts of the Palaearctic region.

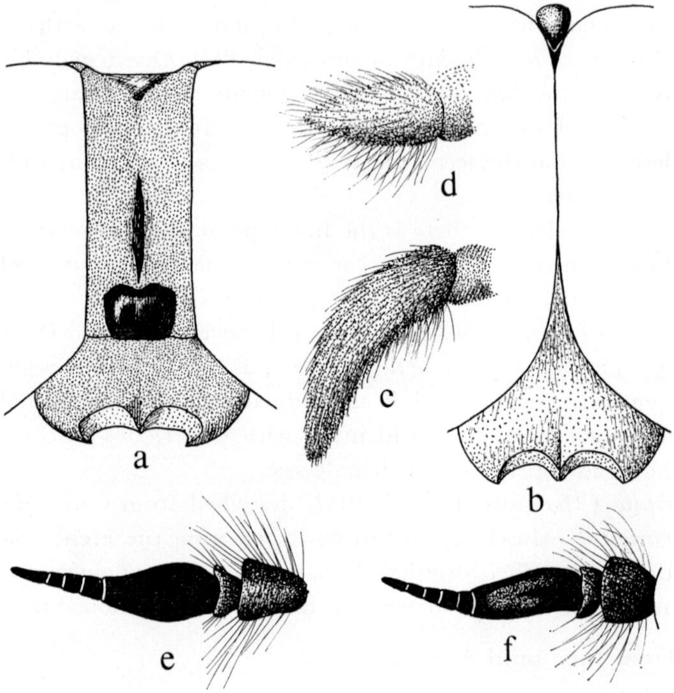

Fig. 50. *Hybomitra caucasi* (Szil.), a. female frons, b. male frons, c. female palpus, d. male palpus, e. female antenna, f. male antenna.

HYBOMITRA CAUCASI (SZILÁDY, 1923)

Fig. 50.

Tabanus (Therioplectes) caucasi Szilády, 1923, Biologica hung., 1 (1): 5.

Diagnosis. Blackish species with long haired eyes and slender black antennae; basal segments long pale haired. Palpi light brown, face and thorax mostly grey haired. Frons rather broad, all tibiae yellowish-brown. Abdomen black, tergite 2 greyish dusted, venter uniformly greyish. Facets in male almost equal in size.

Description. ♀. *Head.* Eyes long pale haired with one band. Frons broad, index 1: 2.5, dark brown in ground colour and densely black haired above, lower quarter with pale hairs. Lower callus polished black, rather plain, distinctly separated from the eye-margins, and with a deep excision at middle above. Median callus very narrow, rather indistinct, connected with lower callus. Ocellar tubercle, together wih a triangular patch on vertex, polished light brown. Subcallus greyish dusted with fine pale hairs at sides. Face densely dark grey dusted, covered with long light grey hairs. Antennae entirely black, segment 3 rather slender, at most with only an indication of dorsal tooth; basal segments densely greyish dusted, segment 1 with long light grey hairs. Palpi light brown to yellowish, clothed with long pale adpressed hairs, long and slender.

Thorax dull black on mesonotum, pleura thinly greyish dusted and long pale haired. Mesonotum covered with shorter and fine pale and black hairs. *Legs* black but basal two-thirds of fore tibiae and whole of posterior tibiae yellowish-brown. Coxae greyish dusted as pleura and long pale haired; femora only thinly dusted and very densely clothed with fine pale hairs, the hairs being ventrally much longer than femur is deep. Tibiae with shorter pale hairs, tarsi very short black haired. *Wings* clear, only very indistinctly yellowish-brown tinted along costa, veins dark brown. Squamae whitish, halteres blackish-brown.

Abdomen very black on dorsum and mostly black haired, some pale hairs present at sides of anterior tergites, on a very narrow median stripe on all tergites, but posterior two or three tergites mostly pale haired. Tergite 2 thinly light grey dusted except at middle. Venter mostly greyish dusted and uniformly densely, long pale haired.

♂. Eyes with very long light grey hairs, all facets almost equal in size. Subcallus greyish dusted, concolorous with face, and covered with fine pale hairs except central part. Antennae black, segment 3 very slender; segment 1 rather large, distinctly greyish dusted and long pale haired. Apical segment of palpi light brownish, long oval, and clothed with long pale hairs. Thorax long yellowish-grey haired, legs and wings as in the ♀. Abdomen mostly black, tergite 2 and usually also tergite 3 chestnut-brown at sides; tergite 2 with a large greyish sublateral patch, and all tergites except first with distinct greyish triangles which are, likewise posterior margins, pale greyish haired; otherwise pubescence black. Venter entirely black in ground colour, rather densely grey dusted and pale haired.

Length. 13.5–16 mm.

Remarks. We were able to revise the type female deposited in the Naturhistorisches Museum, Vienna, labelled »Caucasus, Kussari 5.84, Mik« and »Tabanus caucasi m., det. Szilády«. The above description of the female sex is based on this specimen.

DATES. May.

DISTRIBUTION. Described from the Caucasus, later recorded also from Transcaucasus from Armenia, South Georgia, Daghestan, Azerbaijan, from the Turkish Armenia, and from Turkey (Ankara).

HYBOMITRA DECORA (LOEW, 1858)

Fig. 51.

Tabanus decorus Loew, 1858, Verh. zool.-bot. Ges. Wien, 8: 588.
Tabanus decorus var. *defasciatus* Szilády, 1923, Biologica hung., 1 (1): 11.
Tabanus (Therioplectes) decorus var. *amani* Szilády, 1926, Annls Mus. nat. hung., 24: 600.

DIAGNOSIS. Closely resembling *H. pilosa* (Loew) but smaller, lower frontal callus broadly separated from the eye-margins, palpi long and slender, whitish-yellow and pale haired; tibiae yellowish, and abdomen at least on tergite 2 slightly yellowish-brown at sides. Eyes very long whitish haired, with 1 to 3 bands or unbanded. All facets in male almost equal in size.

DESCRIPTION. ♀. *Head.* Eyes with long whitish hairs, with one to three bands or unbanded. Frons light grey, broad, index about 1: 2.5, almost parallel-sided. Lower callus polished dark brown to brown, distinctly convex, pointed above and connected with a linear black median callus; broadly separated from the eye-margins. Ocellar tubercle oval, and similarly as whole of vertex, polished brown. Subcallus darker grey dusted and clothed with fine pale hairs at sides; antennal bows rather narrow. Face and cheeks darker grey dusted and clothed with long, dense whitish pubescence. Antennae black, basal segments conspicuously naked, only a few whitish hairs on segment 1 beneath; segment 3 with indistinct dorsal tooth, rather slender. Apical segment of palpi whitish-yellow, clothed with sparse whitish hairs; long and slender, about 4 times as long as deep.

Thorax rather polished black on mesonotum with pale hairing, pleura and coxae densely light grey dusted and whitish haired. Notopleural lobes greyish with some black hairs. *Legs:* Femora darker grey dusted and clothed with long whitish hairs beneath; tibiae yellowish with pale hairs, apical third of fore tibiae and fore tarsi extensively darkened or almost black; posterior tarsi brownish and short black haired. *Wings* clear with dark veins, veins along anterior margin and at base of wing yellowish-brown. Halteres dark brown.

Abdomen black in ground colour and only pale haired, more densely on posterior tergites and on venter. Anterior two tergites densely whitish-grey dusted; tergite 2 with indefinite black median patch and with a larger, light grey median triangle; usually more or less yellowish-brown at sides, the slight brown coloration may be found sometimes also on tergites 3 and 4. All tergites more or less light grey dusted along posterior margins, there are sometimes indefinite median triangles on tergites 3 and 4. Venter unicolorous light grey dusted and pale haired.

♂. Eyes very long and densely whitish haired, all facets almost equal in size. Antennae light grey dusted on basal segments and covered with very long and densely set pale hairs; segment 3 very slender with indistinct dorsal tooth near base, mostly blackish. Palpi whitish-yellow to very light yellowish-brown, clothed with rather shorter pale hairs; oval in shape, rather slender, slightly more than twice as long as deep. Thorax with longer pale hairs especially on mesonotum; legs and wings as in the ♀. Abdomen extensively yellowish-brown on anterior three tergites at sides, a black median stripe occupying hardly one-third of tergite 2. Posterior tergites rather shining black, light grey posterior margins and median triangles indistinct. Venter yellowish-brown on sternites 1 to 4, apical sternites greyish dusted.

Length. 11–14.5 mm, usually about 12 mm.

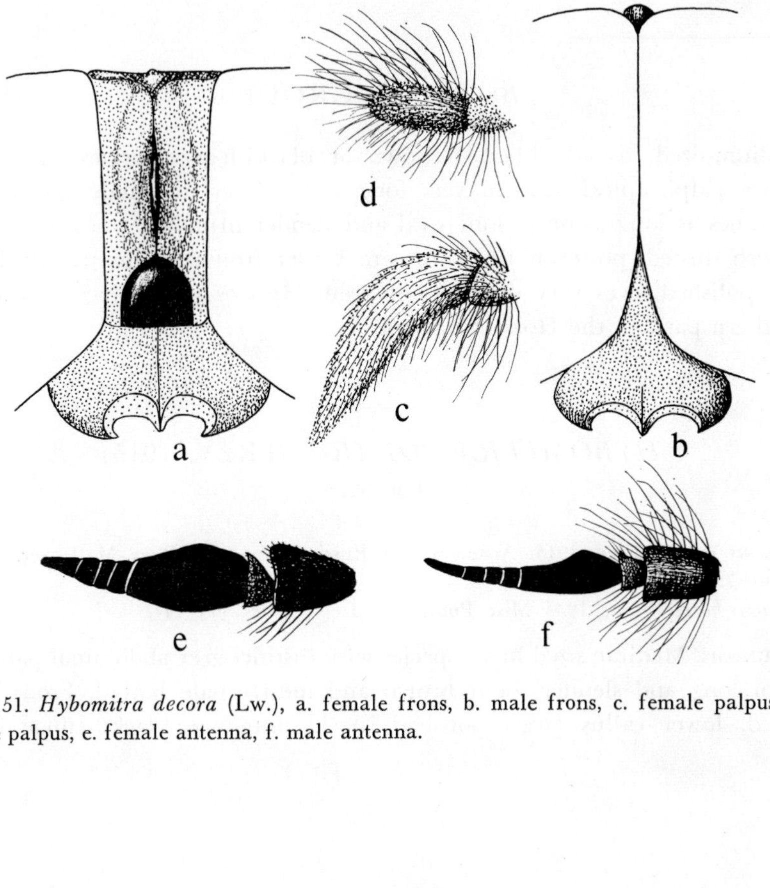

Fig. 51. *Hybomitra decora* (Lw.), a. female frons, b. male frons, c. female palpus, d. male palpus, e. female antenna, f. male antenna.

Variability. The yellowish-brown sidemarkings vary in the female in size and intensity, sometimes only tergite 2 translucent yellowish anteriorly at side, but in very pale specimens all anterior four tergites distinctly yellowish-brown at sides. The number of eye-bands varies from one to three, some specimens (var. *defasciata* Szil.) have no eye-bands. Both var. *defasciata* Szil. (only female sex) and var. *amani* Szil. (only male sex) probably represent very individual forms and have no taxonomic value.

Dates. From April until June.

Distribution. The centre of the area of distribution lies in the East Mediterranean (Israel, Lebanon, Syria, Jordan, Turkey) from where it penetrates to Iraq. The record from North Africa (Algeria) needs verification. In Europe it is recorded from Crete and Bulgaria. The occurrence in Bulgaria needs also to be verified; we have revised an extensive collection of Tabanidae from Bulgaria in the past ten years but we did not find this species. According to Drenski (1929) *H. decora* (Loew) was observed in 1925 in the vicinity of Ajtos, South East Bulgaria. Theodor (1965) recorded it from Israel to be distributed in the coastal plain, the Valley of Yizréel and the northern part of the Valley of the Jordan river, in Jerusalem, and in Sinaii.

BOREALIS-GROUP

Medium-sized, usually blackish-brown or blackish-grey species with dark brown palpi, apical segment very long and slender in female, more than 3.5 times as long as deep, long oval and slender in male. Subcallus always greyish dusted, posterior tibiae brown. Lower frontal callus usually large and polished, eyes very densely pubescent. Species inhabiting exclusively northern parts of the Holarctic region.

HYBOMITRA POLARIS (FREY, 1915)

Fig. 52.

Tabanus polaris Frey, 1915, Acad. Sci. de Russie, Mém., Cl. Phys.-Math. ser. 8, 29 (10): 7.

Tabanus boreus Stone, 1938, Misc. Publs U. S. Dep. Agric., 305: 147.

Diagnosis. Medium-sized black species with distinct grey abdominal pattern; palpi long and slender, light brown and mostly pale haired. Frons very broad, lower callus large, polished black; antennae black; tibiae light brown. Closely allied to *H. borealis* (Fabr.) (= *lapponica* Wahlbg.) but the latter has narrower frons, brownish antennae and less distinct greyish abdominal pattern. Both *H. kaurii* Chv. & Lyneb. and *sexfasciata* (Hine) have brown sidemarkings on anterior tergites.

DESCRIPTION. ♀. *Head.* Eyes clothed with minute greyish hairs, with three bands. Frons grey, broad, index about 1: 2.5, almost parallel-sided or very slightly widened above. Lower callus polished black to blackish-brown, largely rectangular, very narrowly separated or almost touching the eye-margins. Median callus spindle-shaped, polished black, usually narrowly connected with lower callus. Ocellar tubercle rather large, oval, polished reddish-brown. Rather a deep postocular margin on vertex whitish-grey dusted and finely pale haired. Subcallus greyish dusted, slightly convex, antennal bows narrow. Face and cheeks light grey dusted, clothed with almost whitish hairs. Antennae black or slightly brown on segment 3 at extreme base and on segment 2; basal segments densely greyish dusted and short, mostly black haired; segment 3 rather short with blunt dorsal tooth; terminal flagellar segments form a short and stout complex. Palpi brown to light brown, apical segment long and slender, about 4 times as long as deep, clothed with minute pale and some black hairs.

Thorax black in ground colour, mesonotum and scutellum subshining black and only thinly greyish dusted, mesonotum with distinct grey longitudinal stripes. Notopleural lobes dark. Pleura densely paler grey dusted and mostly pale haired, pteropleura with blackish hairs. *Legs* almost black on femora, thinly greyish dusted and very pale haired, tibiae lighter brown. Fore tibiae on apical third and all tarsi blackish-brown. *Wings* clear with brown veins, costal margin very slightly tinted yellowish-brown. Halteres blackish-brown.

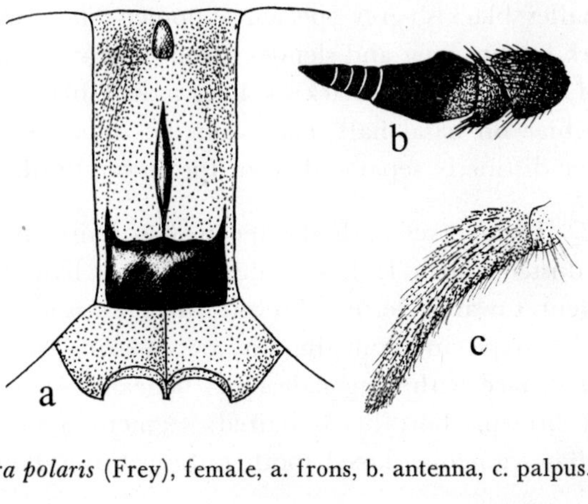

Fig. 52. *Hybomitra polaris* (Frey), female, a. frons, b. antenna, c. palpus.

Abdomen rather shining black including tergite 2, with distinct light grey pattern consisting of large sublateral patches on all tergites (usually confluent with paler posterior margins) and of less distinct but large median triangles. Pubescence black, pale on greyish areas and along posterior margins. Venter uniformly grey dusted and rather densely pale haired.

♂. Unknown.

Length. 12–14.5 mm.

Biology. The species is known from the tundra zone and from the mountainous districts of Siberia. It occurs mainly in summer, everywhere a rare species.

Dates. From June until August.

Distribution. A species inhabiting northern parts of the Holarctic region. It has been recorded in North America only from Alaska, in Europe in North Scandinavia from where it penetrates through the Kola Peninsula and Siberia (Verkhoyansk and along the Yana river, 71° north) as far as Kamtchatka.

HYBOMITRA BOREALIS (FABRICIUS, 1781)

Fig. 53.

Tabanus borealis Fabricius, 1781, Spec. Ins., 2: 457.
Tabanus albo-maculatus Zetterstedt, 1838, Ins. Lapp., p. 516.
Tabanus lapponicus Wahlberg, 1848, Öfvers. K. Vetensk Akad. Förh., 5: 199.
Tabanus Komurae Matsumara, 1911, J. Coll. Agric. Hokkaido imp. Univ., 4: 65.

Diagnosis. Smaller blackish-grey species, abdomen black with greyish pattern. Palpi dark brown, long and slender. Frons narrower, index 1: 4, lower callus polished dark brown to blackish. Legs mostly black, tibiae brownish at base, mid tibiae on basal half. Facets on the upper two-thirds in male enlarged, rather distinctly separated from the lower third.

Description. ♀. *Head.* Eyes with shorter greyish hairs and with 3 bands. Frons greyish dusted, index 1: 4, very densely black haired at middle and slightly divergent towards vertex. Lower callus polished dark brown to black, square in shape and touching the eye-margins. Subcallus and face dark grey dusted, face with long pale hairs beneath. Antennae with basal segments light brown, short black haired; segment 3 brown with black terminal flagellar segments, dorsal tooth rather obtuse. Palpi dark brown, apical segment long and slender, about 4 times as long as deep at base, densely clothed by short black hairs.

Thorax blackish-grey, mesonotum with three paler longitudinal stripes and mostly black haired, pleura pale haired with some black hairs intermixed. *Legs* black but mid tibiae on basal half, and fore and hind tibiae at base, brown. *Wings* slightly tinted brownish along costal margin, veins blackish. Halteres dark brown.

Abdomen shining black with indefinite greyish pattern consisting of lateral patches on tergites 1 to 5, becoming smaller posteriorly. All tergites with light grey posterior margins, pale median triangles only indicated on tergites 2 and 3. Tergite 2 sometimes slightly brownish at sides. Venter polished black, anterior sternites greyish dusted, sternites 2 and 3 sometimes translucent brownish at sides, and distinct pale posterior margin to all sternites. Cerci long, semiglobular. Subgenital plate as in *kaurii* Chv. & Lyneb., lower part uniformly clothed by densely set black hairs.

♂. Eyes densely clothed by rather long reddish-brown hairs, touching on frons for a rather long distance. Facets on the upper two-thirds larger and rather distinctly separated from the small facets on the lower third of eyes. Subcallus rather small and convex, silvery-grey dusted. Antennae brown,

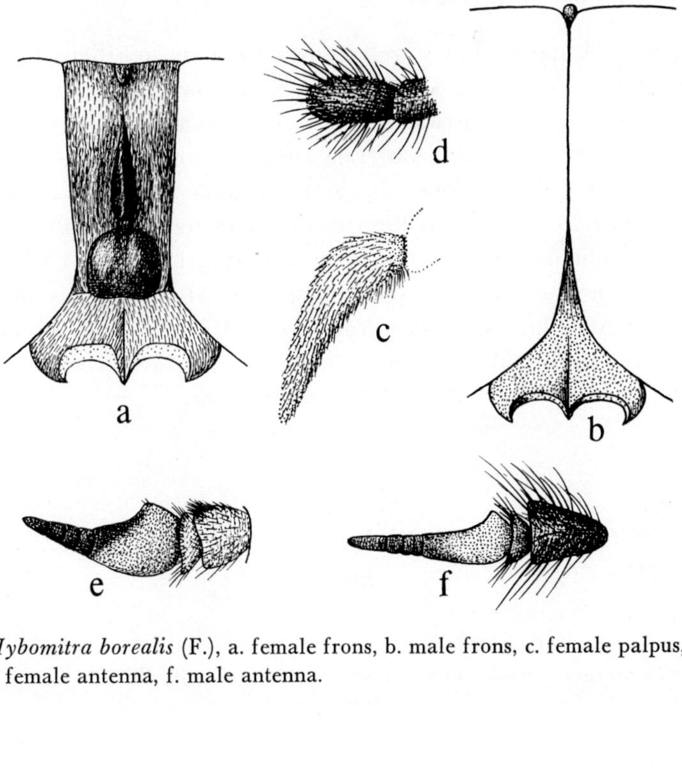

Fig. 53. *Hybomitra borealis* (F.), a. female frons, b. male frons, c. female palpus, d. male palpus, e. female antenna, f. male antenna.

basal segment with long black hairs which are longer than basal two segments combined; segment 3 rather slender with a small dorsal tooth at base, blackish above and on terminal flagellar segments. Apical segment of palpi blackish-brown, clothed with black hairs; oval, about twice as long as deep. Mesonotum with fine, long black hairs. Legs black with tibiae partly brown as in the ♀. Abdomen black, tergites 2 and 3 brownish coloured and silvery dusted at sides, a dark median stripe occupies about one-third of the tergite. Tergites 2 to 4 with small pale median triangles, both tergites and sternites with narrow pale posterior margins. Sternites 2 and 3 brownish, sternite 2 with a large greyish median patch.

Length. 10—13 mm.

Biology. A typical taiga species, at the time of its optimal occurrence forming about 10 % of the tabanid population, only exceptionally a dominant species; according to Violovič (1968) sometimes forming over 43 % in the region of Tomsk. The species is much less common in forest-tundra and it occurs only individually on forest-steppe. In Europe mostly on peat-bogs and on foggy biotopes. Females lay the eggs in several egg-clusters, altogether 140—340 eggs. The immature stages are not yet described. Females attack man and animals.

Dates. From June until August.

Distribution. A species fairly well known from the northern parts of Europe and Asia. It is recorded throughout Scandinavia but not known from Denmark and England. Eastwards it penetrates to as far as Kamtchatka and the Japanese island of Hokkaido. The southern border of its area of distribution lies in Central Europe, in Czechoslovakia and in South Germany. The occurrence in Austria has been recorded several times in the literature but we have not seen any documentary material. Leclercq (1967a: 109) recorded it from Austria from »Starnberg« but Starnberg lies in Bavaria, South Germany. The species has been recorded several times by mistake as Holarctic, the only Holarctic species of this group of species are *H. sexfasciata* (Hine), *H. arpadi (Szil.)* and *H. polaris* (Frey).

HYBOMITRA SEXFASCIATA (HINE, 1923)

Fig. 54.

Tabanus sexfasciatus Hine, 1923, Can. Ent., 55: 144.
Tabanus (Tylostypia) borealis anderi Kauri, 1951, Opusc. ent., 16: 101.

Diagnosis. Resembling very much *H. kaurii* Chv. & Lyneb. but generally smaller and darker, antennae extensively blackish. Frons broader, with a large, usually reddish-brown, rectangular lower callus. Apical segment of palpi very long and slender, blackish-brown.

Description. ♀. *Head.* Eyes clothed with minute but densely set grey hairs, with three bands. Frons rather bluish-grey dusted, broad, index about 1: 2.5, parallel-sided. Lower callus polished reddish-brown to blackish, convex and plain, broadly rectangular, touching the eye-margins. Median callus black, linear, connected with lower callus. Ocellar tubercle oval, polished reddish-brown. Subcallus slightly convex and with the same dusting as frons, antennal bows higher, occupying about one-third of subcallus. Face and cheeks greyish dusted and pale haired, cheeks above with some dark hairs. Antennae black; segment 3 reddish-brown at base or on basal half, rather slender, dorsal tooth blunt; basal segments thinly greyish dusted and rather short black haired. Palpi blackish-brown, basal segment pale haired; apical segment short black haired, long and very slender.

Thorax blackish-grey dusted, mesonotum with indefinite paler longitudinal stripes, clothed with longer dark and pale hairs. Notopleural lobes dark. Pleura concolorous with mesonotum, pteropleura mostly dark haired, otherwise pleura long pale haired. *Legs* rather shining black coloured and pale haired on femora; fore tibiae on basal third, whole of mid tibiae, and hind tibiae on basal half, dark brown; otherwise legs blackish with concolorous hairs. *Wings* clear with blackish-brown, somewhat brownish clouded, veins. Usually an indistinct darker patch at base of vein R_4. Halteres very dark brown.

Abdomen mostly shining black with concolorous hairs, all tergites with less distinct greyish dusted and pale haired narrow median triangles, and

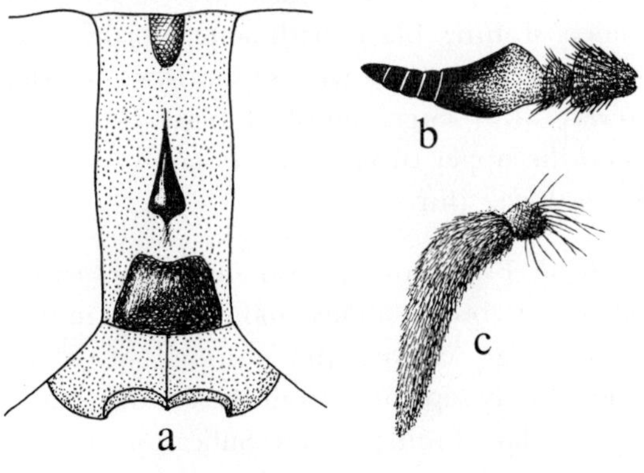

Fig. 54. *Hybomitra sexfasciata* (Hine), female, a. frons, b. antenna, c. palpus.

with conspicuous whitish-grey borders on posterior margins. Tergite 2 usually slightly chestnut-brown at sides, the dark brown coloration spread sometimes to all three anterior tergites, forming on tergites 1 and 3 only small patches. The abdominal pattern on dorsum is very similar to that of *H. kaurii* Chv. & Lyneb. Venter mostly dark grey dusted and pale haired with distinct pale posterior margins.

♂. Unknown.

Length. 11–15 mm.

DATES. July.

DISTRIBUTION. The species was originally described from North America where it is distributed over a wide area in the north from Alaska and to North East Manitoba in Canada. In Europe is was discovered only recently by Kauri (1951) from the northern parts of Scandinavia (Sweden, Norway, Finland); it was originally described by Kauri as ssp. *anderi* of *H. borealis* auct. (= *kaurii* Chv. & Lyneb.). The species has not yet been recorded from the north of the European and Asiatic parts of the U.S.S.R. but it probably occurs there. Violovič (1968: 124) mistakenly synonymized *H. sexfasciata* (Hine) with *H. borealis* Loew (= *borealis* auct. nec. Fabr.) but it is difficult to say if he had specimens of *H. sexfasciata* from Siberia.

HYBOMITRA KAURII CHVÁLA & LYNEBORG, 1970

Fig. 55.

Tabanus borealis auct. nec Fabricius, 1781.
Hybomitra kaurii Chvála & Lyneborg, 1970, J. Med. Entomol., 7: 546.

DIAGNOSIS. Medium-sized species with dark brown, long and slender palpi in female; abdomen shining black with anterior three tergites chestnut-brown at sides and all tergites with whitish, narrow posterior margin. Frons rather broad, lower callus large, polished black. Posterior tibiae brown. Male with facets on the upper two-thirds very large and distinctly separated from small facets on lower third.

DESCRIPTION. ♀. *Head.* Eyes short greyish pubescent, with 3 bands. Frons light grey dusted, rather broad, index about 1: 3.5, indistinctly widening above. Lower callus large, convex and polished black, nearly square in shape and only indistinctly separated from the eye-margins. Ocellar tubercle very small, nearly circular, shining brown. Subcallus, frons and cheeks light grey dusted, face and cheeks with long pale hairs. Antennae brown to dark reddish-brown except for blackish terminal flagellar segments, basal segments covered with greyish dust and minute black hairs. Segment 3 with a distinct and nearly rectangular dorsal tooth. Palpi dark brown, long and slender, more than four times as long as deep at base; covered with short black hairs, lower part with fine pale hairs.

Thorax black including notopleural lobes, whole of mesonotum thinly grey dusted and covered with short, mostly black and some pale hairs. Pleura including coxae more light grey pollinose and mostly long pale haired. *Legs* black, rather shiny, only posterior four tibiae brown, apical half of posterior four femora and extreme base of fore tibiae blackish-brown. *Wings* clear or somewhat tinted brownish especially along costal margin, veins blackish; base of vein R_4 with an indication of a small brownish patch. Halteres very dark brown, base of stem paler.

Abdomen shining black, tergites 1 to 3 largely chestnut-brown at sides, posterior margins of all tergites and a large median triangle on tergite 2 whitish with light grey dusting. Venter mostly black, whitish posterior margins to all sternites broad. Sternites 1 to 4 thinly greyish dusted; sternite 1 mesally, and sternite 2 narrowly at sides and along posterior margin, slightly reddish-brown. Cerci broadly rectangular, slightly convex at sides. Subgenital plate straight on lower margin, lateral lobes pointed, upper margin with a slight excision.

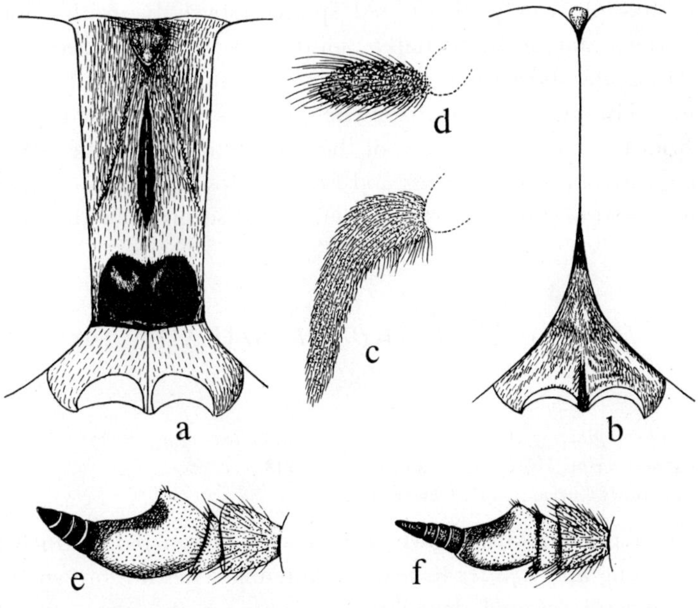

Fig. 55. *Hybomitra kaurii* Chv. & Lyneb., a. female frons, b. male frons, c. female palpus, d. male palpus, e. female antenna, f. male antenna.

♂. Eyes covered with long light brown hairs, meeting for a distance of one and a half times height of subcallus; facets on the upper two-thirds very large and distinctly separated from the lower third with small facets. Face with long pale hairs, cheeks mostly black haired. Antennae dark brown, segment 3 rather yellowish-brown with blackish terminal flagellar segments, dorsal tooth distinct; segment 1 with longer black hairs which are not longer than segment is long. Apical segment of palpi blackish-brown, clothed with long black hairs; long and slender, rather conical. Thorax mostly long black haired. Legs black, covered by long, fine black hairs except fore tibiae; posterior tibiae and base of fore tibiae brownish, posterior femora often blackish-brown. Abdominal pattern as in the ♀, anterior three tergites chestnut-brown at sides, a black median stripe occupies one-third of the tergites.

Length. 13–16 mm.

BIOLOGY. A typical inhabitant of northern tundra, sometimes a very common species in northern parts of its area of distribution. In Central Europe it occurs usually only infrequently on peat-bogs, in foggy places and in open places in forests, sometimes on mountains up to 2500 m. Females attack man, horses, horned cattle, dogs and other animals.

DATES. From June until August.

DISTRIBUTION. A widely distributed species especially in the north from Scandinavia as far as Kamtchatka, southwards it is recorded from Altai, North Mongolia and China. In Europe it is known from all Scandinavian countries including Denmark, from Belgium, Germany, Poland, Czechoslovakia, from the northern regions of the European part of the U.S.S.R., and from the Austrian, Italian, Swiss and French Alps. The records from Greece from the island of Tinos (Leclercq, 1967a: 103) seems to be unlikely.

HYBOMITRA ARPADI (SZILÁDY, 1923)

Fig. 56.

Tabanus (Therioplectes) Árpádi Szilády, 1923, Biologica hung., 1 (1): 7.
Tabanus gracilipalpis Hine, 1923, Can. Ent., 55: 143.
Tabanus cristatus Curran, 1927, Can. Ent., 59: 81.

DIAGNOSIS. Larger reddish-brown species with brown palpi which are conspicuously long and slender in female. Antennae chestnut-brown, segment 3 very broad with pointed dorsal tooth. Facets on the upper two-thirds in male only indistinctly larger and hardly differentiated from the lower third.

Description. ♀. *Head.* Eyes very short brownish pubescent. Frons yellowish-grey dusted, index 1:4—4.5, slightly widened above. Lower callus polished dark brown to black, narrowly separated from the eye-margins, somewhat rounded above and connected with linear median callus. Ocellar tubercle largely oval, polished brown, with distinct ocelli. Subcallus and face light yellowish-grey dusted, face and cheeks long pale haired. Antennae chestnut-brown, segment 1 densely greyish dusted; segment 3 very broad at base with distinct pointed dorsal tooth, terminal flagellar segments blackish. Palpi brown, apical segment long and slender, about 4 times as long as deep at base, tip rather obtuse; clothed with short black and pale hairs.

Thorax blackish-grey, notopleural lobes sometimes slightly brown. Mesonotum mostly black haired with some pale hairs, scutellum and pleura predominantly long pale haired. *Legs* black, fore tibiae on basal quarter dark brown. Posterior four femora at tip and whole of tibiae and metatarsi brown. *Wings* clear with costal cell slightly brownish, veins dark brown. Halteres blackish-brown.

Abdomen black in ground colour, anterior three or four tergites reddish-brown at sides; a black median stripe on tergite 2 occupying one-quarter to one-third of the tergite. Whole of abdomen densely clothed by short black hairs, only posterior margins to all tergites and small median triangles with pale hairs. Anterior four sternites brownish, following sternites greyish.

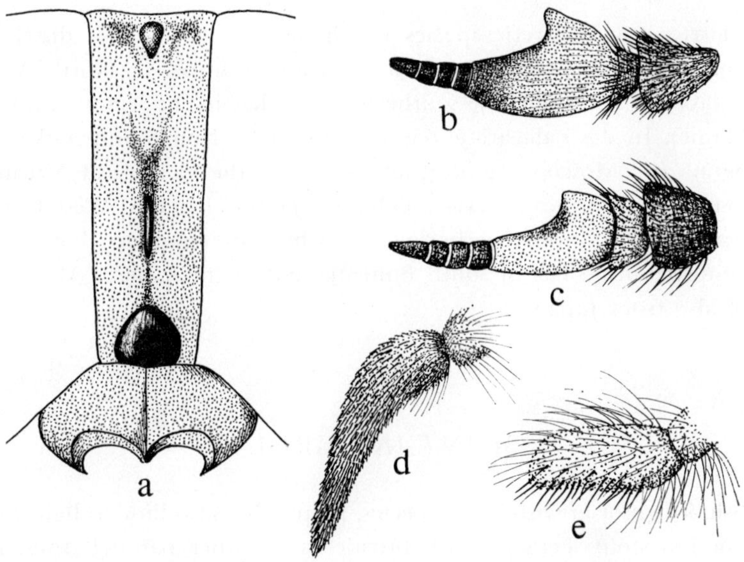

Fig. 56. *Hybomitra arpadi* (Szil.), a. female frons, b. female antenna, c. male antenna, d. female palpus, e. male palpus.

Sternite 1 greyish at middle, sternite 2 with grey triangular patch anteriorly at middle. Cerci long, semiglobular, nearly as long as deep; subgenital plate with straight lower margin, upper margin rounded with distinct excision.

♂. Eyes with long brown hairs, facets on the upper two-thirds only slightly larger and indistinctly separated from the lower third. Antennae with segment 1 short black haired, segment 3 more slender with less distinct dorsal tooth. Apical segment of palpi light brown, rather slender and blunt ended, mostly black haired. Mesonotum with long black hairs, scutellum pale haired. Abdomen with brownish sidemarkings on anterior three tergites, exceptionally reaching tergite 5; black median stripe rather broad, occupying one-third to one-quarter of the tergites. Venter brownish-yellow except for sternite 1 and apical three sternites, sternite 2 with dark median patch.

Length. 13.5–18 mm.

BIOLOGY. A species occurring mostly in taiga and in forests in the north, in Central Europe on peat-bogs and in hilly countries. Occasionally a common species in Siberian taiga, representing there a major part of the Tabanid population. An uncommon species also in the mountainous taiga of Altai, Tuba and Saian. Females attack man, horses, horned cattle, elks and dogs. The larva and pupa were described by Teskey (1969).

DATES. From June until August.

DISTRIBUTION. A Holarctic species which has a wide area of distribution covering northern parts of America, Asia and Europe. In North America from Alaska to Labrador, the southern border lies in the U.S.A. (Minnesota and Maine). In the Palaearctic region it is known from Kamtchatka to the Leningrad and Moscow regions, northwards to the vicinity of Murmansk. It is recorded from Scandinavia, Belgium (Hautes-Fagnes), West Germany (Grafenwöhr) and from Czechoslovakia, where the southern border of its area of distribution lies in South Bohemia and in the Şumava Mts. It is recorded also from Japan.

MONTANA-GROUP

Reddish-brown or greyish-black species, palpi whitish-yellow to light brown, more or less stout. Females with broader and rather parellel frons, index 2.5–4. Lower callus large, polished black and distinctly plain (except *nitidifrons confiformis* Chv. & Mch. (= *conformis* Frey) and *sareptana* (Szil.)).

Males with basal antennal segment usually short haired and with rather slender palpi. Halteres dark brown, eyes distinctly pubescent in both sexes.

The species with very stout palpi and a usually at least partly polished subcallus, viz. *H. lurida* (Fall.), *H. nitidifrons* (Szil.) and *H. sareptana* (Szil.) are provisionally placed here but very probably form a distinct group of species. This group was erected for the species with rather broad and almost parallel-sided, or only very slightly widened above, frons in female, contrary to the *bimaculata*-group. The species are widely distributed in the Holarctic region.

HYBOMITRA PILOSA (LOEW, 1858)

Fig. 57.

Tabanus lateralis Meigen, 1820, Syst. Beschr., 2: 58 (nec Fourcroy, 1785) – syn. n.
Tabanus pilosus Loew, 1858, Verh. zool.-bot. Ges. Wien, 8: 587.

DIAGNOSIS. Medium-sized blackish-grey species, abdomen shining black with distinct grey pattern on tergites 2–7. Posterior tibiae brownish. Frons broad, lower callus large, polished black. Antennae mostly black, segment 3 slender. Eyes densely long pale pubescent, facets on the upper two-thirds in male enlarged but sharp division absent. Male with tergites 2 and 3 chestnut-brown at sides.

DESCRIPTION. ♀. *Head.* Eyes long pale pubescent, with three bands. Frons whitish-grey and broad, index about 1: 2.5, almost parallel-sided. Lower callus shining black, rounded above, below touching the eye-margins. Median callus polished black, spindle-shaped dilated and connected both with the lower callus and with a large, polished black ocellar tubercle which is broadly triangular in shape. Subcallus and face light greyish dusted, face with long whitish-grey hairs. Antennae mostly black, basal two segments greyish dusted, sometimes almost brown, segment 1 mostly pale haired; segment 3 with only a small dorsal tooth, sometimes translucent brownish beneath at base. Palpi light greyish-yellow, apical segment stout, mostly pale haired and with some black hairs on apical half.

Thorax blackish-grey dusted and wholly densely yellowish-grey pubescent, mesonotum with some black hairs. Notopleural lobes blackish. *Legs* black, posterior four tibiae except tip brown, fore tibiae brownish on basal third. *Wings* clear, slightly tinted yellowish at base and in costal cell. Veins dark, sometimes a short appendix to R_4. Halteres blackish-brown, knob often paler at tip.

Abdomen shining black with distinct light grey pattern consisting of median triangles and sublateral patches, which are small and rounded on tergites 3 to 7, but very large on tergite 2. Abdomen black haired, greyish median triangles and sublateral patches with yellowish hairs. Venter densely greyish dusted and entirely golden-yellow pubescent, apical sternites darkened.

♂. Eyes with all facets almost equal in size, only the median facets slightly enlarged. Antennae black, segment 3 dark brown at base, long and slender with slightly developed dorsal tooth; segment 1 greyish dusted and clothed with long black hairs. Apical segment of palpi brownish-yellow, oval but rather stout, long black haired. Legs black, all tibiae brown but fore tibiae at tip blackish. Abdomen black, tergites 2 and 3 chestnut-brown at sides. All tergites except the first with silvery dusted small median triangles and with larger, nearly circular sublateral patches. Venter black, densely silvery-grey dusted and clothed with rather long dark grey and whitish hairs.

Length. 13–16 mm.

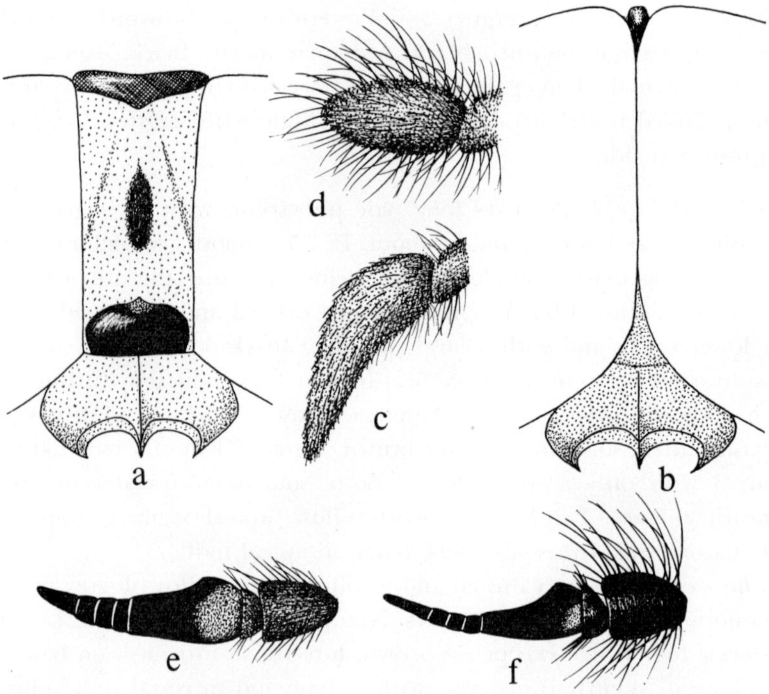

Fig. 57. *Hybomitra pilosa* (Lw.), a. female frons, b. male frons, c. female palpus, d. male palpus, e. female antenna, b. male antenna.

SYNONYMY. This species is fairly well known under the name of *Hybomitra lateralis* (Meig.), described by Meigen in the genus *Tabanus* L. The name, however, cannot be used in future, because it is a primary homonym of *Tabanus lateralis* Fourcroy, 1785. *Tabanus pilosus* Loew is the only available name for this species.

BIOLOGY. Never a common species, the adults occur rather individually in forest clearings and in forest ways, and are on the wings for a short period from the end of May usually until the middle of June. Females attack man and animals.

DATES. From May until July.

DISTRIBUTION. A European species known from the Balkan Peninsula including the island of Corfu, from France northwards to Luxemburg, and in Central Europe (Germany, Austria, Czechoslovakia and Hungary). The northern border of its area of distribution lies in Central Europe in South Germany and in South Slovakia. Not yet recorded from the European part of the U.S.S.R.

HYBOMITRA NIGRICORNIS (ZETTERSTEDT, 1842)

Fig. 58.

Tabanus nigricornis Zetterstedt, 1842, Dipt. Scand., 1: 112.
Tabanus alpinus Zetterstedt, 1842, Dipt. Scand., 1: 116.
Tabanus engadinensis Jaennicke, 1866, Berl. ent. Z., 10: 75.
Tabanus (Therioplectes) altainus Szilády, 1926, Biologica hung., 1 (7): 20.

DIAGNOSIS. Medium-sized to larger blackish species, posterior tibiae brownish. Subcallus rather low and convex, greyish dusted. Frons rather broad; antennae black with slender segment 3; palpi whitish-yellow, stout. Abdomen black in female with indistinct greyish pattern, male with brown side-markings on tergites 2 and 3. Upper facets in male enlarged but not sharply separated from the area with small facets.

DESCRIPTION. ♀. *Head.* Eyes finely and short pale haired, with three bands. Frons greyish-yellow dusted, rather broad, index 1: 3—3.5, almost parallel-sided. Lower callus polished black to blackish-brown, semiglobular to rectangular, below touching the eye-margins. Median callus black, linear, connected with lower callus. Ocellar tubercle shining dark brown, broadly oval. Subcallus greyish-yellow dusted, low and distinctly convex, antennal bows rather narrow. Face and cheeks greyish dusted and with long yellowish hairs. Antennae black, basal segments greyish dusted and rather short black haired; segment 3 slightly brownish at base, slender, with only slightly developed dorsal tooth. Palpi whitish-yellow, apical segment stout, apically pointed; mostly pale haired with some additional black hairs.

Thorax blackish-grey, mesonotum and scutellum with fine black hairs, pleura mostly yellowish haired. Notopleural lobes sometimes slightly translucent brown, usually blackish. *Legs* blackish-grey, fore tibiae on basal half and posterior four tibiae except tip brown. Apical half of fore tibiae and fore tarsi black, posterior tarsi darkened. *Wings* clear with blackish veins. Halteres blackish-brown, stem paler.

Abdomen blackish-grey with paler grey pattern consisting of a row of median triangles, of circular sublateral patches and a narrow posterior margin on all tergites. Tergite 2 sometimes very indistinctly translucent brownish at sides. Venter unicolorous greyish dusted and densely yellowish pubescent.

♂. Eyes with long brownish hairs, facets on the upper two-thirds distinctly enlarged, sharp division absent. Eyes meeting on frons for a distance corresponding to one and a half height of subcallus. Latter greyish dusted, face yellowish-grey dusted and clothed with pale and black hairs. Antennal segment 3 still more slender, segment 1 with long black hairs about as long

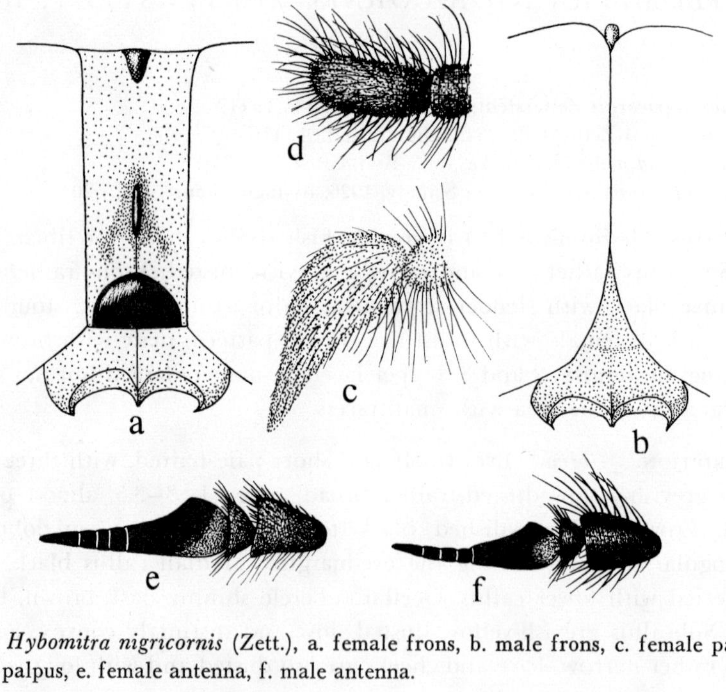

Fig. 58. *Hybomitra nigricornis* (Zett.), a. female frons, b. male frons, c. female palpus, d. male palpus, e. female antenna, f. male antenna.

as basal two segments combined. Apical segment of palpi yellowish, rather stout, apex pointed and downcurved; mostly black haired. Abdomen black, tergites 2 and 3 brown at sides, sometimes also tergite 4 with an indication of brownish coloration anteriorly. A blackish median stripe occupying about one-third of tergites. All tergites with distinct grey posterior margins and median triangles. Venter black, sternites 2 to 4 brownish, sternite 2 with a dark median spot.

Length. 14—18 mm.

BIOLOGY. A common species especially in the mountainous regions of West and Central Siberia but only a rare species in Europe. Violovič (1968: 151) observed oviposition on the leaves of the Common Reed *(Phragmites communis)* in Siberia, up to 570 eggs in one female. Females readily attack man and animals.

DATES. From May until August.

DISTRIBUTION. A species inhabiting the northern parts of the Palaearctic region from Scandinavia to as far as Kamtchatka and Sakhalin, the southern border lies in Asia in Kazakhstan, Mongolia, North West China and the Ussuri region. In Europe it is known from Scandinavia except Denmark, and isolatedly on high mountains of Central Europe, more often in the Alps. Kröber (1932b) recorded it from Germany but we did not succeed in finding the documentary material.

HYBOMITRA LURIDA (FALLÉN, 1817)

Fig. 59.

Tabanus luridus Fallén, 1817, Dipt. Suec., Tabanii, p. 5.
Tabanus borealis Fabr.; Zetterstedt, 1842, Dipt. Scand., 1: 113.
Tabanus depressus Walker, 1848, List Dipt. Brit. Mus., 1: 167.
Tabanus punctifrons Wahlberg, 1848, Öfvers. K. VetenskAkad. Förh., 5: 200.
Tabanus hirticeps Loew, 1858, Wien. ent. Monatschr., 2: 105.
Tabanus metabolus McDunnough, 1922, Can. Ent., 54: 239.

DIAGNOSIS. Smaller reddish-brown species with distinctly convex and entirely polished blackish-brown to black subcallus in female. Apical segment of palpi yellowish, short and stout. Male with subcallus dulled by greyish dust, all facets almost equal in size, and abdomen with a broad black median stripe on dorsum.

DESCRIPTION. ♀. *Head.* Eyes short reddish pubescent, with three bands. Frons dark grey dusted, rather broad, index 1: 2.8—3.5, slightly widened above. Lower callus plain, polished dark brown to black, semiglobular, below touching the eye-margins. Median callus linear, connected with lower callus. Subcallus polished black to blackish-brown, distinctly convex. Ocellar tubercle circular, polished light brown. Face whitish-grey dusted and long yellowish haired. Basal antennal segments greyish with short black hairs, segment 3 brown, terminal flagellar segments black; dorsal tooth distinct, almost rectangular. Apical segment of palpi yellowish coloured and long whitish-yellow haired, apical half with some short black hairs; very short and stout at base, apically pointed.

Thorax blackish-grey, mesonotum and scutellum shining, densely yellowish and black pubescent; pleura greyish dusted and mostly pale haired. Notopleural lobes black or brown. *Legs* with coxae and femora blackish-grey, fore tibiae on basal half and whole of posterior tibiae including apical tip of all femora brown. Tarsi black but posterior four metatarsi dark brown. *Wings* clear with brownish costal cell, veins dark, narrowly brownish clouded on basal two-thirds of wing; a small dark patch at base of vein R_4. Halteres brown, knob darkened.

Abdomen shining black, tergites 2 and 3 (or to 4) brown at sides, black median stripe very broad, occupying at least 1/3 of tergite 2. All tergites with large, silvery-grey sidemarkings. Venter mostly blackish-brown, sternites 2 and 3 (or to 4) predominantly reddish-brown, sternite 2 with a dark median patch of various shape.

♂. Eyes long dark brown pubescent, all facets almost equal in size. Subcallus greyish dusted, eyes meeting on frons for a short distance, equal to about one and a half times height of subcallus. Antennae with segment 3 more slender, segment 1 with long black hairs about as long as basal two segments combined. Apical segment of palpi yellowish-grey, distinctly stout and mostly long black haired. Thorax and abdomen black, anterior three tergites reddish-brown at sides. Venter mostly yellowish-brown, apical two or three sternites darkened; sternite 1 and a median patch on sternite 2 dark grey.

Length. 11.5—15 mm.

Synonymy. The species has been considered for a long time to be a Palaearctic species but recently Pechuman & Stone (1968) synonymized the North American *H. metabola* (McDunnough) with *H. lurida* (Fall.).

Biology. A species of forest-tundra and taiga, in Europe especially on peatbogs and on foggy biotopes. Rather a common species but it occurs only individually in the western parts of its wide area of distribution. In Europe one of the earlier spring species; Violovič (1968: 138) published a general table about its occurrence in West and Central Siberia. Females attack man, horses, horned cattle, elks, reindeer and dogs.

DATES. From May until August.

DISTRIBUTION. A Holarctic species with a wide area of distribution from England through Siberia as far as Kamtchatka, Sakhalin and the Japanese island of Hokkaido, recorded also from North East China and Mongolia; in North America it is well known under the name of *metabola* from Alaska to as far as Labrador, southwards to Colorado and New York. In Europe it is known from England, throughout Scandinavia including Denmark, from western European countries except Portugal and Spain, and from all Central European countries eastwards to Carelia. The southern border of its area of distribution in Europe lies in France, Germany (Bavaria), Czechoslovakia, Hungary and Ukraine.

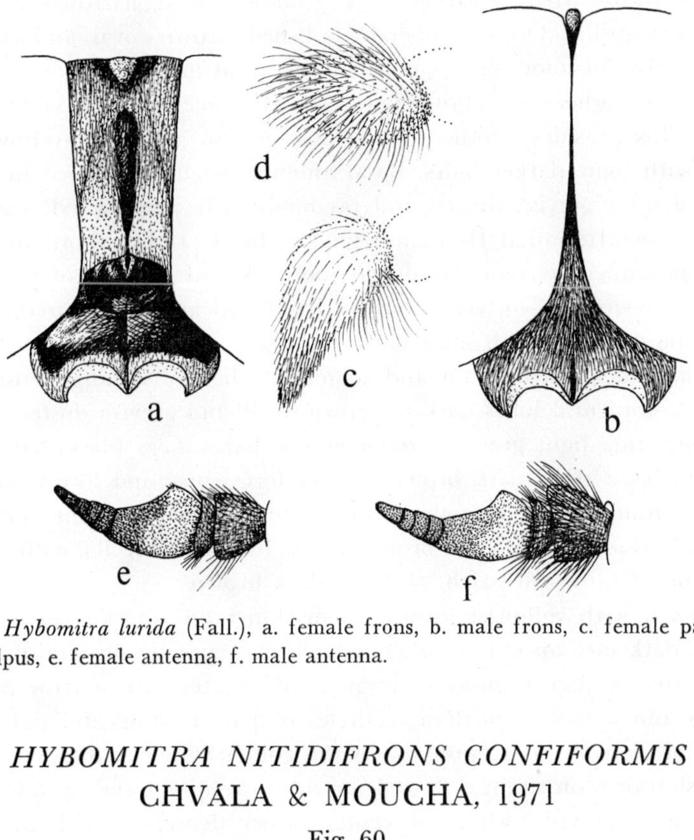

Fig. 59. *Hybomitra lurida* (Fall.), a. female frons, b. male frons, c. female palpus, d. male palpus, e. female antenna, f. male antenna.

HYBOMITRA NITIDIFRONS CONFIFORMIS CHVÁLA & MOUCHA, 1971

Fig. 60.

Tabanus confinis auct. nec Zetterstedt, 1838.

Tabanus conformis Frey, 1917, Nat. Unt. Sarakgeb., 4: 681 nom. nov. for *confinis* auct. nec Zett. (nec *T. conformis* Walker, 1848) – mistake.
Hybomitra nitidifrons confiformis Chvála & Moucha, 1971, Notulae ent., 51: 111.

DIAGNOSIS. Generally rather larger species with brownish sidemarkings on anterior three tergites and subcallus in female polished brown on the upper part; dull grey in male. Lower frontal callus brownish, not shining. Palpi light grey to yellowish-brown, short and very stout at base. Male with all facets almost equal in size, dark median stripe on dorsum of abdomen very narrow.

DESCRIPTION. ♀. *Head.* Eyes reddish-brown pubescent, with three bands. Frons greyish dusted, broader, index about 1: 3.5, slightly widened above. Lower callus usually brownish or black and slightly brownish at middle, transversally wrinkled and only slightly shining, narrowly separated from the eye-margins. Median callus black, spindle-shaped, narrowly connected with lower callus. Ocellar tubercle polished brown, oval and distinctly convex. Subcallus more or less polished brown at middle and on the upper part at sides, otherwise yellowish-grey dusted. Face with the same dusting as subcallus at sides, clothed with long greyish to golden-yellow hairs, cheeks with some darker hairs. Basal antennal segments brown in ground colour, densely greyish dusted and predominantly pale haired; segment 3 reddish-brown, terminal flagellar segments black, rather short and broad with a prominent rectangular dorsal tooth. Apical segment of palpi light grey to yellowish-brown, very stout on basal half and pale haired, apically slightly pointed and with some dark hairs.

Thorax black, mesonotum and scutellum slightly shining, mostly pale haired. Notopleural lobes dark to brownish. Pleura greyish dusted, clothed with long, fine light grey to golden-yellow hairs. *Legs* blackish-grey, fore tibiae on basal third dark brown, rest of fore tibiae and fore tarsi black; posterior four tibiae and tarsi brown, apical tarsal segments sometimes darkened. *Wings* clear with brown veins, base of vein R_4 with a slight indication of brownish patch. Halteres dark brown.

Abdomen with yellowish-brown sidemarkings on anterior three or four tergites, dark median stripe rather narrower, occupying on tergite 2 about one quarter or slightly more of tergite. All tergites with narrow posterior margins and a row of median triangles of pale dusting and pubescence. Whole of dorsum short grey-yellow to golden-yellow pubescent. Venter yellowish-brown on sternites 2 to 4 (or to 5), sternite 1 and apical three to two sternites greyish; whole of venter rather densely greyish to golden-yellow pubescent. Sternite 2 with a dark median spot. Cerci rectangular, rounded at sides; subgenital plate as in *H. bimaculata* (Macq.), upper part broadly semiglobular with hardly distinct median excision, lower part nearly square in shape with straight sides.

♂. Eyes with longer dark brown hairs, all facets almost equal in size. Eyes meeting for rather a short distance, no more than one and one-half times height of subcallus. Antennal segment 3 more slender, segment 1 with long black hairs about as long as basal two segments combined. Apical segment of palpi whitish-yellow, very stout, clothed with long, mostly dark hairs. Mesonotum and abdomen rather shining black, former with longer, mostly black hairs. Abdomen with yellowish-brown sidemarkings on anterior three or four tergites, dark median stripe narrow, occupying about 1/5 to 1/8 of tergite 3, posteriorly narrowed. Abdomen mostly dark haired, posterior margins to all tergites with yellowish-grey hairs. Venter as in the ♀.

Length. 14–18 mm.

Variability. Rather a variable species, subcallus more or less polished brown in female at least at middle and on the upper part at sides, but exceptionally there are specimens with only remains of polished brown coloration or specimens with subcallus entirely covered by greyish dusting.

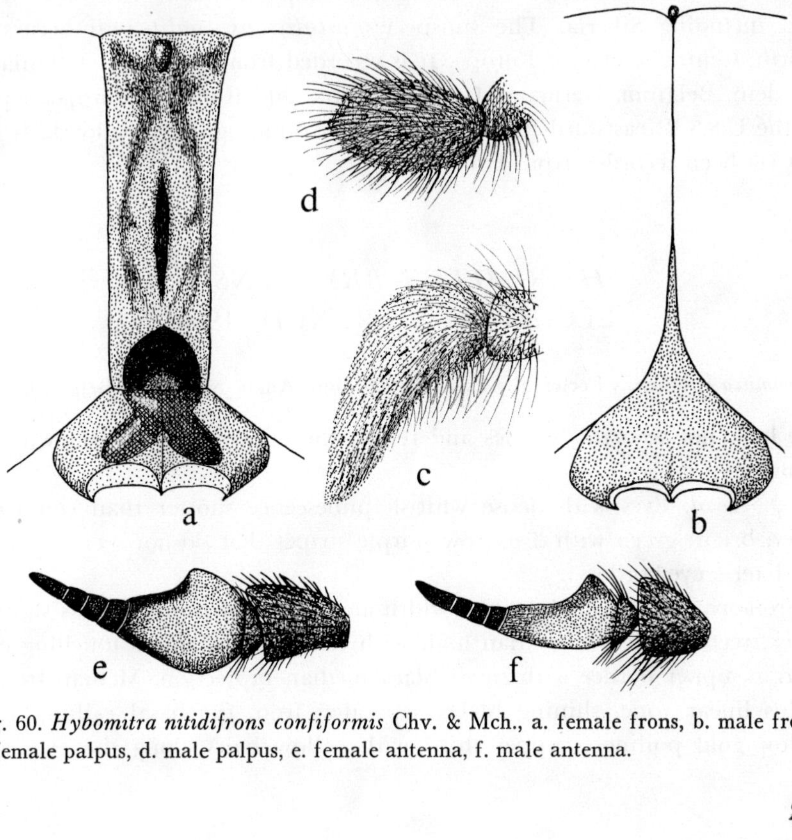

Fig. 60. *Hybomitra nitidifrons confiformis* Chv. & Mch., a. female frons, b. male frons, c. female palpus, d. male palpus, e. female antenna, f. male antenna.

The Asiatic nominate subspecies *H. nitidifrons nitidifrons* Szilády, 1914 (The Nearctic *H. nuda* McDunnough, 1921, is a very closely related species, if not identical with *nitidifrons*) differs in the light grey pubescent eyes, in the distinctly silvery-grey pubescence on face, pleura and abdomen, and the reddish-brown sidemarkings on abdomen are densely silvery-grey dusted. The complicated nomenclature and synonymy of this species has recently been fully discussed by Chvála & Moucha (1971).

Biology. A typical species of taiga and forest taiga but never a common species; it has been collected both in Europe and Siberia but only individually. One of the early spring species in the whole area of distribution, the first specimens are collected in very early May. Females attack man, horned cattle, horses, elks and reindeer.

Dates. From May until August.

Distribution. A species with a wide area of distribution from Scandinavia through Siberia to Japan, it is recorded also from Mongolia, from the eastern regions of the U.S.S.R. and from North East China.

The nominate subspecies *nitidifrons nitidifrons* occurs eastwards from and including Siberia. The subspecies *nitidifrons confiformis* occurs in North, Central and East Europe. It is recorded from Scandinavia (Finland, Sweden), Belgium, Germany, Czechoslovakia, and from the European part of the U.S.S.R. eastwards to Ural, to the surroundings of Sverdlovsk. It has not yet been recorded from Poland.

HYBOMITRA BRYANENSIS LECLERCQ & FRENCH, 1966

Hybomitra bryanensis Leclercq & French, 1966, Bull. Annls. Soc. r. ent. Belg., 102: 265.

We have not seen this species and repeat the original description without comments.

»♀. *Head.* Eyes with dense whitish pubescence shorter than *conformis* Frey, bright green with 3 narrow purple stripes that do not seem reach to the lateral eye-borders.

Frons parallel 3.8 higher than width at base. Basal frontal callus shining black, rectangular, wider than high with entire lateral edges touching eye-margin, upper border with small black median projection. Median frontal callus linear wide, shining black, separated from the basal callus. Frons yellow gold pollinose, upper third with yellow hairs along the eyes and black hairs in the middle and on vertex, longer black and yellow hairs at occiput. Tubercule ocellar callous, grey pollinose not shiny, vestigial ocelli. Postocular rim narrow with dense yellow hair. Frontal triangle entirely pollinose, greyish yellow. Face pollinose, greyish, black hairs along the eyes. Palpi robust, short and thickened with blunt point, 2.5 to 3 longer than wide, basal segment blackish at base with yellow hairs, terminal segment yellowish with many black hairs. Antennae: first and second segments greyish pollinose with short black and yellow hairs, third segment black, base reddish brown, broad.

Thorax. Greyish black slightly shining with black and yellow gold hairs not dense. Notopleural callus reddish yellow with long predominantly black hairs. Pleurae greyish with yellow hairs, mesopleura with predominantly black hairs. Halteres reddish yellow with blackish knob. Scutellum greyish black with long yellow hairs on the posterior border mixed with black hairs at upper side. *Legs* bicolor; coxae greyish with long yellow hairs; femurs greyish black pollinose; F II and F III yellow hairs predominant at inner side, F I black shining at inner side with black and yellow hairs. Knees reddish yellow. Tibias I reddish yellow but blackish at distal third, black hairs. Tibias II and III reddish yellow with black and yellow hairs. Tarsi of leg I black with black hairs, tarsi of legs II and III black with black hairs but reddish at under side.

Abdomen. Not arched and more slender than in *conformis* FREY. It is blackish with reddish yellow pollinosity, yellow gold hairs and sparse black hairs, reddish yellow sidemarkings on tergites 1 to 3, posterior edge of tergites yellow with yellow gold hairs. Tergite I with yellow hairs only, some black hairs on the lateral sidemarkings. Venter blackish with dense reddish yellow pollinosity, dense yellow gold hairs; sternites 1 to 3 reddish yellow laterally, posterior edge of all sternites yellow. Sternites I and II with black middle longitudinal stripe which is less pronounced on other sternites. Genitalia of type IV (LECLERCQ, 1966: fig. 177), similar to those of *conformis* FREY. Cerci (lamelle anale) more or less quadrangular with lateral edges rounded, anterior gonopophyse without median notch.

Wings. Hyaline, costal cell yellow, no recurrent veinlet, venation brownish«.

♂. Unknown.

Length. 18 mm.

DATES. June.

DISTRIBUTION. Described recently from Germany from the single holotype female collected at Grafenwöhr in Hoch Franken, West Germany.

HYBOMITRA SAREPTANA (SZILÁDY, 1914)

Fig. 61.

Tabanus (Therioplectes) sareptanus Szilády, 1914, Annls Mus. nat. hung., 12: 662.
Tabanus (Therioplectes) sareptanus var. *melas* Szilády, 1914, Annls Mus. nat. hung., 12: 664.
Tabanus (Tylostypia) adachii Takagi, 1941, Rep. Inst. Horse-Dis. Manchukuo, no. 2: 49.
Tabanus (Tylostypia) sareptanus tschuensis Olsufjev, 1962, Zool. Zh., 41: 886.

DIAGNOSIS. Larger blackish-grey species with mostly black antennae and very broad pale palpi. Frons broader, parallel, with lower callus wrinkled, not shining. Eyes densely whitish haired. Abdominal pattern as in *T. autumnalis* L., female with at most anterior three tergites light yellowish-brown at sides, male with anterior four tergites broadly reddish-brown at sides. All facets in male equal in size.

DESCRIPTION. ♀. *Head.* Eyes densely and rather longer whitish haired, with three bands. Frons light grey dusted, rather broad, index 1: 3.5, almost parallel-sided or very slightly widened above. Lower callus rectangular, broader than high, usually touching the eye-margins; black or slightly brownish at middle, distinctly wrinkled, not plain and shining. Median callus rather shining black, spindle-shaped, connected with lower callus. Ocellar tubercle oval, polished brown, usually an adjacent part of vertex entirely polished. Subcallus and face whitish-grey dusted, face and cheeks with whitish pubescence. Antennal bows very narrow. Antennae black, segment 3 often yellowish-brown at base; basal segments densely light grey dusted and mostly pale haired; segment 3 rather broad at base, with a distinct, almost rectangular dorsal tooth. Palpi whitish-yellow, apical segment very stout also on apical half, clothed with fine pale hairs, often with some additional black hairs.

Thorax dark grey on mesonotum with distinct light grey longitudinal stripes and rather densely, predominantly pale haired. Notopleural lobes yellowish-brown. Pleura light grey dusted and densely long pale haired. *Legs* with coxae and femora light grey, tibiae yellowish-brown. Fore tibiae on apical third and all tarsi blackish-brown, black haired; otherwise legs whitish haired. *Wings* clear with dark veins. Halteres blackish.

Abdomen blackish-grey with pale greyish pattern as in *Tabanus autumnalis* L., consisting of a row of high (often confluent) median triangles and large oblong sublateral patches; tergites 2 to 6 with a narrow pale posterior margin, anterior three tergites more or less light yellowish-brown at sides leaving median third on tergite 2 blackish; or the brownish coloration restricted to only tergite 2 and a small patch posteriorly on tergite 1. Venter reddish-yellow on anterior sternites with a distinct greyish patch on sternite 2, or venter more or less entirely light grey dusted with rather broad yellowish posterior margins to all sternites.

♂. Eyes covered with long, densely set whitish-grey hairs, all facets almost equal in size. Face and especially cheeks with some additional darker grey hairs. Antennae with segment 3 more slender, basal segment with long darker hairs which are as long as both basal segments combined. Palpi yellowish-grey, short and very stout, broadest on apical third and clothed with longer whitish hairs. Thorax very long haired including on mesonotum, legs mostly dark haired on tibiae. Abdomen broadly yellowish-brown on anterior four tergites, black median stripe narrowest on tergite 3, occupying there at most 1/6 of tergite. Dorsum with the same but less distinct light grey pattern as in the ♀, tergites 2 to 6 distinctly silvery-white pruinose at sides when viewed from behind. Venter often light yellowish-brown including on posterior sternites, pale haired, and only sternite 1 with indefinite greyish patch at middle.

Length. 16–19 mm.

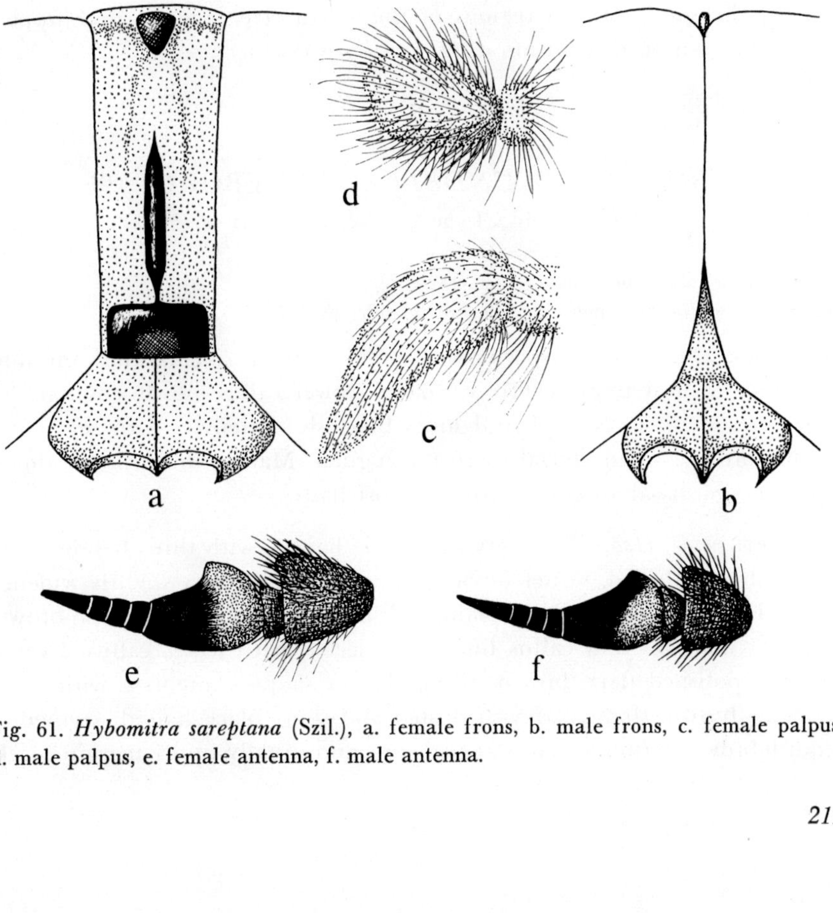

Fig. 61. *Hybomitra sareptana* (Szil.), a. female frons, b. male frons, c. female palpus, d. male palpus, e. female antenna, f. male antenna.

VARIABILITY. Rather a variable species in abdominal coloration, the light yellowish-brown sidemarkings vary in size and number and are often reduced to only tergite 2 in female. The species is, however, very well separated from the other species of the *H. montana* complex in the characters given in the key. The extensively darkened specimens were named by Szilády as var. *melas*.

According to Olsufjev (1969, in litt.) *T. adachii* Takagi, 1941 and *T. sareptanus tschunensis* Olsufjev, 1962 described from Manchuria and Altai respectively, represent distinct subspecies.

BIOLOGY. A species distributed mainly along rivers, often a very common species, the flight period varies in different geographical regions. Females attack man, horses, horned cattle, camels and dogs.

DATES. From May until August.

DISTRIBUTION. The main areas of the distribution are the regions from the northern coast of the Caspian Sea through the district of Omsk and Tomsk eastwards as far as Altai Mts. and the region of Primorye. It is recorded also from Kazakhstan, Mongolia and Manchuria. Westwards it penetrates only to the south eastern regions of the Volga river, having in Europe a similar pattern of distribution to *H. peculiaris* (Szil.).

HYBOMITRA LUNDBECKI LYNEBORG, 1959

Fig. 1d; 4c & f; 5c & f; 62; pl. 2: fig. c.

Tabanus fulvicornis auct., nec Meigen, 1820.
Hybomitra lundbecki Lyneborg, 1959, Ent. Meddr, 29: 127.

DIAGNOSIS. Medium-sized species with reddish-brown sidemarkings on anterior three to four tergites. Frons broader, lower callus mostly circular, polished black, plain. Notopleural lobes blackish. Antennae with segment 3 reddish-brown, broad, dorsal tooth rectangular. Male with all facets almost equal in size, basal antennal segment short haired.

DESCRIPTION. ♀. *Head.* Eyes very short pale haired, with three bands. Frons yellowish-grey dusted, rather broader, index 1: 3.5–4, very slightly widened above. Lower callus distinctly plain, polished black to dark blackish-brown, often circular. Median callus linear, connected with lower callus. Ocellar tubercle polished dark brown, triangular in shape. Antennae with basal segments brown, slightly greyish dusted and short black haired; segment 3 reddish-brown, terminal flagellar segments and usually upper margin blackish; broad at base, dorsal tooth distinct, rectangular. Subcallus and face greyish dusted, face with long yellowish hairs. Apical segment of palpi light brown to yellowish, mostly pale haired, outside with some black hairs.

Thorax black in ground colour and greyish dusted, pleura with yellowish to grey hairs; mesonotum predominantly black haired. Notopleural lobes blackish, only exceptionally translucent dark brown. *Legs* blackish-grey, fore tibiae on basal half and whole of posterior tibiae and metatarsi brown. *Wings* clear, costal cell slightly brown clouded, veins brownish; usually a faint brownish patch at base of vein R_4. Halteres dark brown.

Abdomen reddish-brown to brownish-yellow on anterior three to four tergites at sides, a dark median stripe occupying on tergite 2 at most 1/3 of tergite. Distinct pale median triangles on all tergites reaching anterior margins. Apical tergites blackish-grey with an indication of paler sublateral spots. Venter yellowish-brown on sternites 2 and 3, rest greyish dusted. Sternite 2 with a large grey median spot, sternites 3 and 4 with more or less distinct median stripe.

♂. Eyes with long pale to whitish hairs, all facets almost equal in size. Antennae brownish, basal segments mostly greyish dusted, segment 1 with short black hairs; segment 3 with distinct dorsal tooth and blackish terminal flagellar segments. Apical segment of palpi yellowish-brown, rather

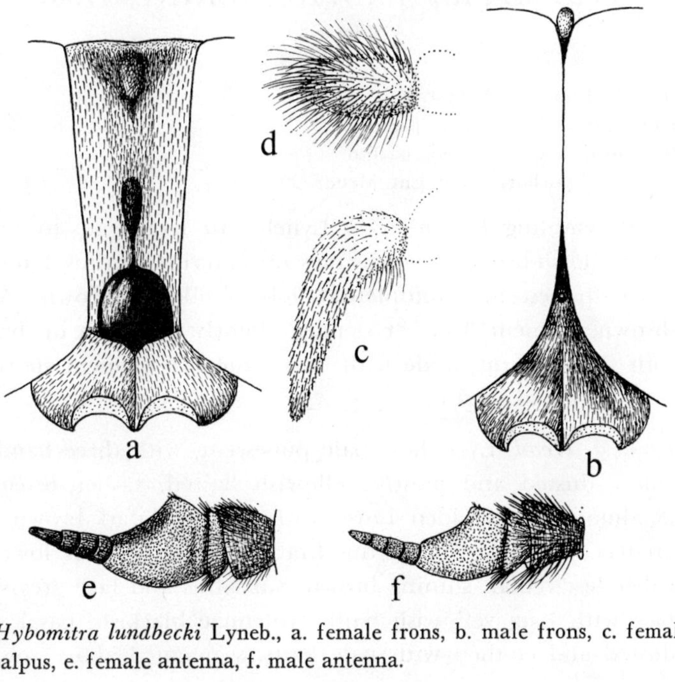

Fig. 62. *Hybomitra lundbecki* Lyneb., a. female frons, b. male frons, c. female palpus, d. male palpus, e. female antenna, f. male antenna.

more slender, slightly oval. Abdomen with reddish-brown sidemarkings on anterior four tergites, pubescence darker than in the ♀, a dark median stripe narrower, occupying about 1/5 of tergite.

Length. 13—17 mm.

Biology. One of the common *Hybomitra* species inhabiting various types of biotopes, often very common in forests near lakes and ponds. Females attack man, horses, horned cattle and dogs. The larva and pupa were described by Chvála & Ježek (1969).

Dates. From May until August.

Distribution. A species with a wide area of distribution known almost throughout the Palaearctic region. It has not yet been recorded from the British Isles; in Scandinavia it penetrates to Torne Lappmark, southwards to the Balkan Peninsula (Jugoslavia, Albania), Italy and France. Eastwards it is distributed throughout Siberia as far as Kamtchatka, Ussuri region and Vladivostock. It has also been recorded from Mongolia and North East China under the name of *fulvicornis* Meig.

HYBOMITRA TROPICA (LINNÉ, 1758)

Fig. 63.

Tabanus tropicus Linné, 1758, Syst. Nat., p. 602.
Tabanus montanus auct. nec Meig. partim.
Tabanus fulvicornis auct. nec Meig. partim.
Hybomitra tuxeni Lyneborg, 1959, Ent. Meddr, 29: 133.

Diagnosis. Resembling *H. lundbecki* Lyneb. but larger, up to 18 mm in length. The reddish-brown sidemarkings on anterior tergites 1 to 4 (or 5) golden-yellow pubescent. Notopleural lobes yellowish-brown. Antennae blackish-brown, segment 3 rather slender, slightly brownish on basal half, dorsal tooth rather blunt. Male with basal antennal segment short haired, all facets almost equal in size.

Description. ♀. *Head.* Eyes short pale pubescent, with three bands. Frons greyish-yellow dusted and mostly yellowish haired, rather broad, index 1: 3.5—4.3, almost parallel-sided. Lower callus polished dark brown to black, almost circular, plain. Median callus linear, connected with lower callus. Ocellar tubercle circular, shining brown. Subcallus and face greyish-yellow dusted, face with long yellowish hairs. Antennae blackish, basal segments greyish dusted and clothed with pale hairs, segment 3 above towards tip with some shorter black hairs; segment 3 rather narrower with blunt dorsal tooth, brownish on basal half, rest including terminal flagellar segments black. Apical segment of palpi greyish-yellow, clothed with yellowish-brown hairs, on the outer side with some short black hairs; only slightly stout.

Thorax blackish-grey, pleura more greyish dusted and long golden-yellow haired. Mesonotum and scutellum with some black hairs. Notopleural lobes almost yellowish-brown, humeri often brownish. *Legs* with coxae and femora greyish, mostly yellowish haired; fore tibiae on basal half and posterior tibiae and metatarsi brown; otherwise legs blackish. *Wings* with dark brown veins which are slightly brownish clouded along anterior margin and on basal third of wings, costal cell tinted brownish. Halteres dark brown.

Abdomen yellowish-brown on anterior four to five tergites at sides, apical tergites greyish; dark median stripe rather narrow, occupying about 1/4 of tergite 2, pale median triangles on all tergites distinct. Abdomen mostly golden-yellow pubescent, dark areas with some black hairs. Venter yellowish-brown on anterior four sternites with more or less distinct grey median stripe, which is often reduced on sternite 2 to a median spot. Apical three sternites greyish with an indicated darker median stripe. Terminalia similar to those of *H. lundbecki* Lyneb.

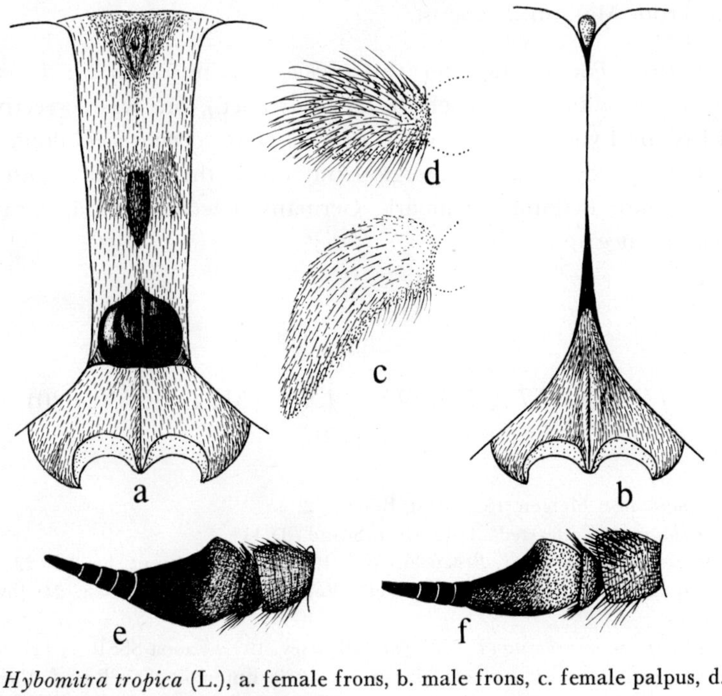

Fig. 63. *Hybomitra tropica* (L.), a. female frons, b. male frons, c. female palpus, d. male palpus, e. female antenna, f. male antenna.

♂. Eyes with long pale to light brown hairs, all facets almost equal in size. Basal antennal segments brownish and distinctly greyish dusted, segment 1 with short black hairs; segment 3 more slender, slightly brownish at base, otherwise black. Apical segment of palpi light brown, often greyish dusted, not so slender as in *H. lundbecki* Lyneb. and mostly long pale haired with some shorter black hairs beneath. Abdomen with yellowish-brown sidemarkings on anterior four tergites, dark median stripe occupying 1/6 to 1/5 of tergite 3. Median triangles high, with distinct golden-yellow pubescence on lower part.

Length. 15.5–18 mm.

SYNONYMY. Most of the recent authors in tabanidology records *H. tropica* (L.) as a subspecies of *H. montana* (Meig.) but this action is, considering the sympatric distribution of both these species, an absurdity demonstrating the ignorance of the subspecific status.

BIOLOGY. In Europe a widely distributed but everywhere uncommon species. One of the earlier spring species with a maximum occurrence in late May and in the beginning of June. Females attack man, horses and horned cattle. The larva and pupa were described by Chvála & Ježek (1969).

DATES. From May until August.

DISTRIBUTION. For a long time this species was mistaken for *H. montana* (Meig.) or *H. lundbecki* Lyneb. (*fulvicornis* auct.), but was correctly recognized first by Lyneborg in 1959 (as *tuxeni*). The species is no doubt widely distributed in the Palaearctic region but up to the present recorded only from England, Belgium, Denmark, Germany, Czechoslovakia, Austria, Jugoslavia, France and Spain.

HYBOMITRA MONTANA (MEIGEN, 1820)

Fig. 64.

Tabanus montanus Meigen, 1820, Syst. Beschr., 2: 55.
Tabanus flaviceps Zetterstedt, 1842, Dipt. Scand., 1: 111.
Therioplectes Mühlfeldi var. *Bezzii* Surcouf, 1924, Annls Soc. ent. Fr., 93: 22 – syn. n.
Sziladynus calluneticola Kröber, 1935, Verh. Ver. naturw. Heimatforsch., 24: 159 – syn. n.
Tabanus (Tylostypia) montanus f. *obscura* Olsufjev, 1937, Fauna SSSR, 7: 127, 378.
Sziladynus montanus var. *alpicola* Muschamp, 1939, Entomologist's Rec. J. Var., 51: 53 – syn. n.

DIAGNOSIS. Smaller to medium-sized species with yellowish-brown sidemarkings on anterior three to four tergites, black median stripe broad. Frons rather broad, lower callus polished black, plain. Resembling *H. lundbecki* Lyneb. and *H. tropica* (L.) but *lundbecki* has dark notopleural calli and reddish-brown antennae, *tropica* is larger and a generally golden-yellow pubescent species with not so slender and black antennal segment 3. Male with basal antennal segment only short haired, facets on the upper part of eyes enlarged, and all specific characters as in the ♀.

DESCRIPTION. ♀. *Head.* Eyes short pale haired with three bands. Frons greyish dusted, rather broad, index 1: 3.5–4, almost parallel-sided. Lower callus polished black and distinctly convex, plain, broadly rectangular to circular, connected with linear median callus. Ocellar tubercle shining brown, triangular in shape and often greyish dusted. Subcallus and face whitish-grey dusted, face and cheeks with long pale hairs. Antennae black, basal segments greyish dusted, above with black, below mostly with pale hairs; segment 3 conspicuously slender, often slightly brownish at base, dorsal tooth slightly developed. Palpi light yellowish-brown, apical segment rather slender and pointed, mostly pale haired, on the outer side predominantly black haired.

Thorax mostly pale greyish dusted and pale haired, mesonotum with some fine black hairs. Notopleural lobes yellowish-brown, humeri often brownish. *Legs* blackish-grey, fore tibiae on basal half and whole of tibiae and metatarsi on posterior two pairs brown. *Wings* clear with slightly brownish clouded costal cell; veins brown; a small brownish patch at base of vein R_4. Halteres blackish-brown.

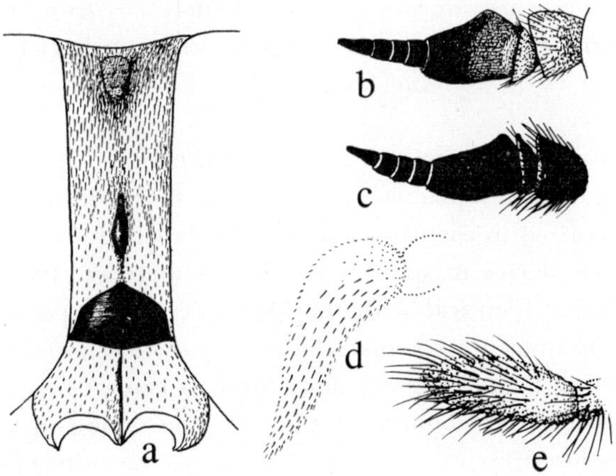

Fig. 64. *Hybomitra montana* (Meig.), a. female frons, b. female antenna, c. male antenna, d. female palpus, e. male palpus.

Abdomen blackish-grey, anterior three or four tergites with yellowish-brown sidemarkings, leaving a broad dark median stripe which occupies at least 1/3 of tergite 2; or abdomen extensively darkened in var. *flaviceps*. Abdomen pale and black pubescent. Venter greyish, anterior three sternites with more or less developed brownish lateral spots which are separated by a broad dark median stripe. Cerci long rectangular, rounded on the inner side; subgenital plate with slight excision above, lower part widened below.

♂. Eyes with long light grey hairs, facets on the upper two-thirds of eyes enlarged but not sharply separated from the lower part with smaller facets. Antennae black except for extreme base of segment 3; segment 1 greyish dusted and clothed with short black hairs, segment 3 slender. Apical segment of palpi yellowish, slender, with somewhat blunt but apically pulled tip, clothed with longer, predominantly black hairs. Notopleural lobes yellowish-brown. Anterior four tergites reddish-brown at sides, a dark median stripe narrow, occupying about 1/5 of tergites.

Length. 12.5–16 mm.

VARIABILITY. Very extensively darkened specimens are known under the name of var. *flaviceps* Zett., differing as follows: 1) the brownish sidemarkings on the first tergites lacking or reduced into very small markings; 2) venter mainly greyish-black, sometimes a faintly reddish-brown coloration at sides of sternites 2 and 3; and 3) antennae still more slender and darker than in the nominate form. This variety is distributed throughout the area of distribution of the nominate form but is rare, and represents only a melanistic variety without taxonomical value. Philip (1956) described var. *manchuriensis* from Manchuria. Some other taxa such as *reinigiana* End., *staegeri* Lyneb. (= *morgani* Surc.), *tuxeni* Lyneb. (= *tropica* L.) and also *flaviceps* Zett. are often mistakenly listed by some authors (e. g. Leclercq, 1967a) as subspecies of *montana* Meig.

SYNONYMY. Three new synonymies are established: 1) We have seen the holotype female of *Therioplectes Mühlfeldi* var. *Bezzii* described by Surcouf in 1924 and deposited in the Museum in Paris, labelled »Marino 14.VIII.12 / TYPE / Therioplectes n. sp. aff. Mühlf., Kröber det. 1922 / mühlfeldi Brauer«; it is quite identical with the above described species. 2) We did not succeed in finding the type material of *Sziladynus calluneticola* Kröber, 1935 but according to the original description it cannot be anything other than a dark form of *H. montana* (Meig.). 3) The same can be said about another unrecognized taxon, *Sziladynus montanus* var. *alpicola* Muschamp, 1939. The type material has obviously been lost and we think that this new synonymy is also quite correct.

Biology. The species inhabits the same types of biotopes as the other »reddish« *Hybomitra* species, and according to Oldroyd (1939: 93) the species is mainly met in mountainous or hilly districts, but is not restricted to such places. Lyneborg (1959: 144), Shevtshenko (1961: 106) and some further authors refer accordingly to a long flight period; Violovič (1968: 157) studied this species in Siberia and recorded it in steppe and forest-steppe from the beginning of June, while in Siberian tundra the species occurs only from the end of July until late August. Females attack man and animals. Olsufjev & Lelep (1935) recorded it as a vector of anthrax.

Dates. From May until August.

Distribution. It is a widely distributed species in the Palaearctic region from the British Isles including Ireland through Europe to as far as the Far East. In Europe it is known from the north of Scandinavia to Spain and France. In Central, West and South Europe rather a rare species, but

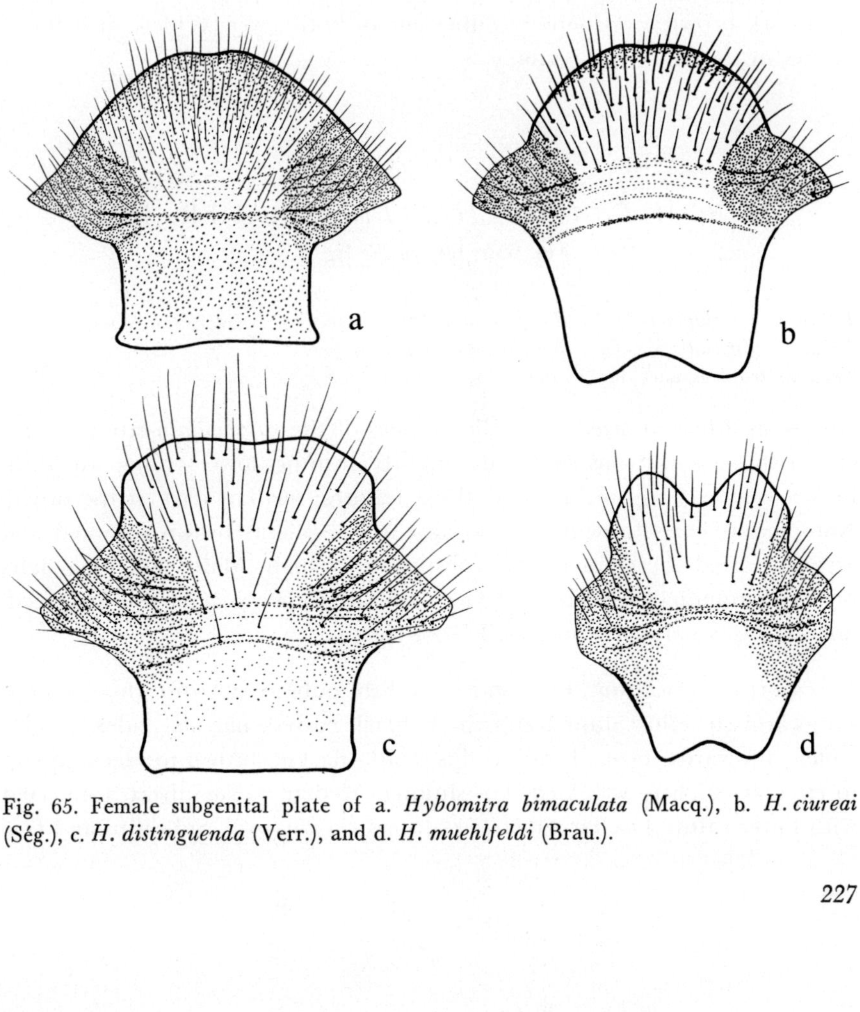

Fig. 65. Female subgenital plate of a. *Hybomitra bimaculata* (Macq.), b. *H. ciureai* (Ség.), c. *H. distinguenda* (Verr.), and d. *H. muehlfeldi* (Brau.).

more frequent in the east; in some suitable localities in Siberia a very common species. Eastwards it is known as far as Kamtchatka and Sakhalin, it has been recorded also from Mongolia, China including Manchuria, Corea and Japan. The North American *H. frontalis* (Walker, 1848) is a very closely related species to *montana*.

BIMACULATA-GROUP

A well defined group of more or less reddish-brown species with narrow frons in female, index 1: 4—6, which is distinctly widened above. Lower callus smaller, usually higher than broad and distinctly wrinkled, not shining. Subcallus always greyish dusted. Palpi whitish-yellow to yellowish-brown or somewhat greyish in male, distinctly stout. Males with long black haired basal antennal segment and very stout, almost globular palpi. Halteres dark brown, eyes densely pubescent in both sexes. Widely distributed species in the Holarctic region.

HYBOMITRA MUEHLFELDI (BRAUER, 1880)

Fig. 65d; 66; pl. 2: fig. g.

Tabanus (Therioplectes) Mühlfeldi Brauer, 1880, Denkschr. Akad. Wiss., Wien, 42: 149.
Tabanus solstitialis auct. nec Meigen, 1820 partim.
Tabanus tropicus auct. nec Linné, 1758 partim.

Diagnosis. Medium-sized to smaller species of the *bimaculata*-group of species with narrow frons and only slightly shining lower callus. Reddish-brown sidemarkings on anterior three tergites, median dark stripe broad. Notopleural lobes brownish, basal antennal segments brown coloured and greyish dusted. Cerci in female conspicuously high. Male with long hairs on basal antennal segment and facets on the upper part of eyes enlarged, not sharply separated from small facets below.

Description. ♀. *Head.* Eyes short reddish pubescent, with three bands. Frons greyish-yellow dusted and finely black haired, narrow, index 1: 5—6, widened towards vertex. Lower callus small, blackish-brown to black, square to circular, slightly wrinkled, not shining. Median callus linear, connected with lower callus. Ocellar tubercle polished brown, oval. Subcallus and face light grey to greyish-yellow dusted, face with long whitish hairs, cheeks with some black hairs. Basal antennal segment brown in ground colour, rather densely greyish dusted and short black haired; segment 3 reddish-brown, darkened towards tip, terminal flagellar segments usually black; dorsal tooth well developed, segment rather broad. Palpi yellowish-brown to greyish-brown, apical segment swollen at base and gently narrowed towards tip, clothed with pale and black hairs.

Thorax blackish-grey, mesonotum and scutellum greyish-yellow dusted with short pale and black hairs, pleura yellowish-grey to whitish pubescent; mesonotum with indefinite greyish longitudinal stripes, notopleural lobes always at least partly brown. *Legs* with coxae and femora grey, tibiae except for apical third of fore tibiae yellowish-brown, fore tarsi and tip of fore tibiae black, posterior tarsi dark brown. *Wings* with blackish-brown to black veins, slightly brownish clouded along costal margin and in basal cells. Halteres dark brown.

Abdomen with yellowish-brown or reddish-brown sidemarkings on anterior three tergites, often with greyish shadows, only exceptionally also tergite 4 slightly brownish anteriorly at sides. The brown areas mostly black haired. A blackish-grey median stripe rather broad, occupying not more than 1/3

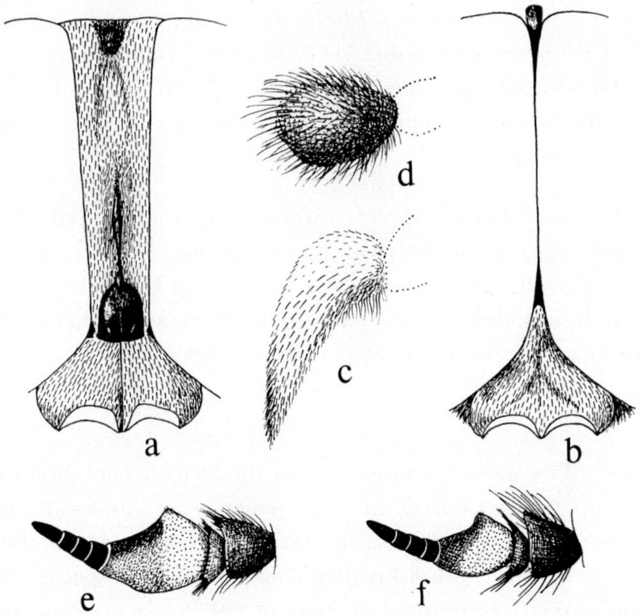

Fig. 66. *Hybomitra muehlfeldi* (Brau.), a. female frons, b. male frons, c. female palpus, d. male palpus, e. female antenna, f. male antenna.

on tergite 2. Distinct light grey median triangles on all tergites, posterior tergites blackish-grey. Venter brownish on anterior four sternites, following sternites greyish; sternite 2 with a rounded greyish median spot at anterior margin, which is sometimes prolonged as far as posterior margin. Venter only short whitish haired, last sternite with long blackish hairs. The female terminalia distinguish this species from all other »reddish« *Hybomitra* species: cerci conspicuously high and narrow, apically rounded; subgenital plate distinctly higher than broad, both upper and lower margin with a deep median excision.

♂. Eyes with long light brown hairs; facets at middle of the eyes distinctly enlarged but not sharply separated from the smaller facets. Basal antennal segments as in the ♀, segment 1 with long black hairs about as long as both basal segments combined; segment 3 more slender, mostly brownish, upper margin and terminal flagellar segments darkened. Apical segment of palpi short and stout, greyish to brown-grey, predominantly long pale haired. Abdomen with yellowish-brown sidemarkings on anterior three tergites, sometimes the brown coloration distinct also on anterior half of tergite 4. Dark median stripe narrow, occupying on tergite 3 1/8 to 1/6 of tergite.

Length. 13–16.5 mm.

Synonymy. The *Hybomitra muehlfeldi* of Brauer has been correctly recognized since 1959 when Lyneborg's revision of the Danish *Hybomitra* species appeared. Until 1959 specimens of *H. muehlfeldi* (Br.) were determined either as *solstitialis* sensu Schin. (= *ciureai* Séguy) or *tropicus* sensu Panz. (= *bimaculata* Macq.).

Biology. A very common species on various biotopes but above all on moisture and foggy meadows near lakes and forests. It is often the commonest species of this genus in the lake districts in Central Europe. Females attack man, horses, horned cattle, camels, dogs and other animals. The larva and pupa were described by Chvála & Ježek (1959).

Dates. From May until August.

Distribution. The species is known from the British Isles, Scandinavia and from all countries of Central Europe, penetrating eastwards through the European part of the U.S.S.R. to its Asiatic part to as far as the region of Magadan and to the Chukotskiy Peninsula. Since the species has only recently been correctly recognized (Lyneborg, 1959), we have no precise data about its distribution in South Europe; we have only seen the documentary material from Jugoslavia.

HYBOMITRA BIMACULATA (MACQUART, 1826)

Fig. 65a; 67; pl. 2: fig. d.

Tabanus tropicus auct., nec Linné, 1758.
Tabanus bimaculatus Macquart, 1826, Ins. Dipt. Nord Fr., 2: 163.
Tabanus confinis Zetterstedt, 1838, Ins. Lapp., p. 516.
Tabanus bisignatus Jaennicke, 1866, Berl. ent. Z., 10: 74.
Therioplectes subguttatus Enderlein, 1925, Mitt. zool. Mus. Berl., 11: 359.
? *Therioplectes borealis* var. *bimaculata* Enderlein, 1925, Mitt. zool. Mus. Berl., 11: 360.
Tabanus (Tylostypia) solstitialis manchuricus Takagi, 1941, Rep. Inst. Horse-Dis. Manchukuo, no. 2: 48.
Hybomitra collini Lyneborg, 1959, Ent. Meddr, 29: 94.

Diagnosis. Medium-sized reddish-brown species with brown sidemarkings on at most anterior three tergites. Notopleural lobes black, frons narrow with lower callus small, wrinkled, not plain. Antennae with basal segment blackish, long haired in male. Male with all facets nearly equal in size.

Description. ♀. *Head.* Eyes densely reddish-brown pubescent, with three bands. Frons greyish-yellow to grey dusted and mostly black haired, rather narrow, index 1: 4.5–5, distinctly widened above. Lower callus small, nearly

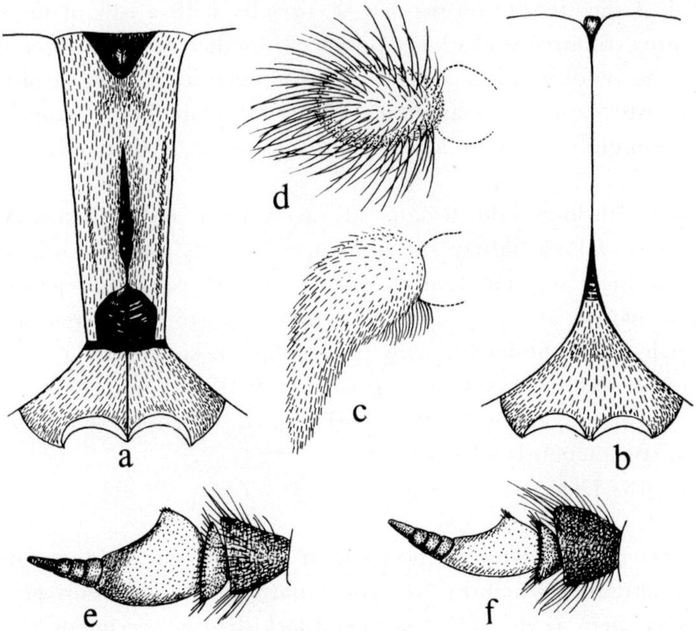

Fig. 67. *Hybomitra bimaculata* (Macq.), a. female frons, b. male frons, c. female palpus, d. male palpus, e. female antenna, f. male antenna.

square in shape and separated from the eye-margins; blackish-brown to black, transversally wrinkled, not shining. Ocellar swelling oval, shining dark brown. Subcallus and face grey to silvery-grey dusted, cheeks black haired, face with somewhat longer yellowish-grey hairs. Basal two antennal segments blackish-grey, covered by grey dust and densely black pubescent; segment 2 sometimes translucent brown in ground colour; segment 3 broad, reddish-brown to blackish-brown, terminal flagellar segments black; dorsal tooth large, rectangular to slightly pointed. Palpi greyish-yellow, apical segment stout at base, clothed with mostly short black hairs.

Thorax blackish-grey, mesonotum mostly fine black haired, scutellum and pleura with light grey hairs. Notopleural lobes blackish-grey, only very rarely slightly dark brown. *Legs* blackish-grey, tibiae brown; apical half of fore tibiae and posterior tibiae apically blackish, tarsi mostly black. Femora sometimes slightly brownish. *Wings* clear, costal margin and especially costal cell slightly brownish; veins blackish-brown. Halteres dark brown.

Abdomen black, anterior three tergites brownish-yellow to reddish-brown at sides, very exceptionally there is a trace of some brown also on tergite 4, on the other hand the reddish sidemarkings are often confined to tergite 1, or abdomen is entirely blackish (f. *bisignata*). The brown sidemarkings are distinctly black haired, black median stripe rather broad, occupying at least one-third of the tergite on segment 2, mesally with a row of more or less distinct grey coloured and silvery pubescent median triangles. Venter blackish-grey, the reddish coloration on anterior sternites is very variable. Cerci conspicuously slender, rectangular; subgenital plate broad, upper margin broadly semiglobular with a small indication of median excision, lower margin straight.

♂. Eyes with long reddish hairs, all facets nearly equal in size. Antennae with segment 1 long haired, the hairs are about as long as both basal segments combined; segment 3 more slender. Apical segment of palpi greyish, slightly brownish at tip, rather short and very stout; covered with long, mostly pale hairs. Abdomen with reddish-brown sidemarkings on anterior three to four tergites, black median stripe broad, narrowest on tergite 3 anteriorly, occupying there 1/5 to 1/4 of tergite. When viewed from behind abdomen conspicuously silvery dusted.

Length. 13—17 mm.

VARIABILITY. A very variable species with regard to the reddish-brown coloration on abdomen which forms a continual series from extensively reddish-brown specimens *(collini)* to entirely blackish-grey specimens *(bisignata)*. The extensively darkened specimens occur in the whole area of distribution of the species but are always rare. The coloured forms have often been described and recorded as distinct species or varieties, Leclercq (1967a: 122) recorded them erroneously as subspecies of *H. tropica* Panz.

BIOLOGY. A common species in foggy biotopes, in forest clearings and near ponds and lakes. The maximal occurrence has been observed in Central Europe in the second half of June, but *H. bimaculata* (Macq.) belongs together with *H. lurida* (Fall.), *H. nitidifrons confiformis* Chv. & Mch. and *H. tropica* (L.) to the typical earlier spring species. In the eastern parts of its area of distribution (Siberia, Kazakhstan) the first specimens occur only in June. Females attack man, horses and horned cattle in Europe. The larva and pupa were described by Chvála & Ježek (1969).

DATES. From May until August.

DISTRIBUTION. A widely distributed species inhabiting almost the whole of the Palaearctic region from the British Isles and Scandinavia as far as East Siberia, Kamtchatka, Sakhalin and the islands of Hokkaido and Honshu, Japan. The species is known throughout Europe including its southern parts.

HYBOMITRA SOLSTITIALIS (MEIGEN, 1820)

Fig. 68.

Tabanus solstitialis Meigen, 1820, Syst. Beschr., 2: 56
nec *Tabanus solstitialis* Meig. sensu Schin. et auct. (= *ciureai* Seg.).

DIAGNOSIS. Similar to *bimaculata* Macq., but smaller, and two basal antennal segments distinctly reddish-brown translucent, i. e. only slightly greyish dusted. Thorax with very pale greyish hairs. Brown sidemarkings of tergites 1—3 paler than in *bimaculata* and the blackish middle stripe narrower, occupying only about 1/3 of tergal width. Never brown sidemarkings on tergite 4 as in *ciureai* and *distinguenda*. Most easily confused with *muehlfeldi,* but shape of cerci and subgenital plate quite different. Male eye-facets of nearly equal size. As in female with paler brownish sidemarkings and narrower middle stripe than in *bimaculata*.

DESCRIPTION. ♀. *Head.* Eyes densely pale brownish pubescent, with three bands. Frons greyish to pale greyish dusted and black haired, index 1: c. 5, distinctly widened above. Lower callus almost square with rounded »shoulders«, separated from eye-margins and strongly wrinkled; colour blackish-brown. Ocellar swelling oval and shiny brownish. Subcallus and face pale greyish dusted; both face and cheeks with pale hairs only. Basal two antennal segments yellowish-brown translucent, i. e. only thinly covered with greyish dust. Segment 3 broad, with a distinct dorsal tooth, reddish-brown with dorsal margin and apex darkened; terminal flagellar segments black. Palpi pale yellowish-white, apical segment rather stout at base, clothed with mainly pale hairs, only short black hairs on apical half.

Thorax greyish-black, paler than in *bimaculata*, mesonotum not distinctly striped and covered with mainly pale greyish hairs. Notopleural lobes often indistinctly brownish translucent posteriorly. Scutellum and pleura pale greyish pubescent, only some black hairs on mesopleura. *Legs* with femora blackish-grey. Tibiae yellowish-brown, fore tibiae blackish in apical third or more, while median and posterior tibiae are not darkened at apices. *Wings* clear. Halteres dark brown.

Abdomen black, anterior three tergites with broad and very bright yellowish-brown sidemarkings. The sidemarkings are mostly pale haired, but black hairs are present laterally. Median stripe parallel-sided, rather narrow, occupying hardly 1/3 of total tergal width, mesally with a row of greyish, pale haired triangles. Sternite 1 and 2 more or less yellowish-brown, following sternites yellowish-brown and blackish to various degree. Cerci and subgenital plate practically as in *bimaculata*.

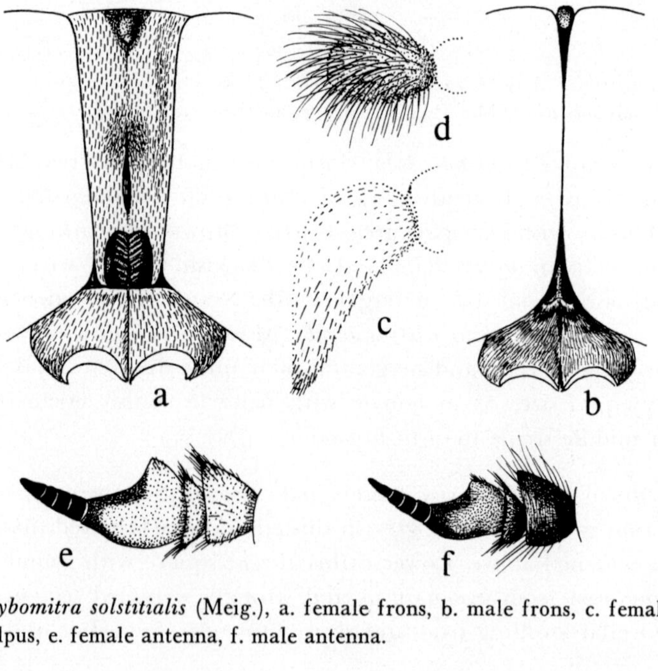

Fig. 68. *Hybomitra solstitialis* (Meig.), a. female frons, b. male frons, c. female palpus, d. male palpus, e. female antenna, f. male antenna.

♂. Eye-facets of equal size, with pale brownish pubescence as in female. Two basal antennal segments greyish-black, much darker than in female, and with long black hairs. Segment 3 more slender and more darkened dorsally and apically. Apical segment of palpi greyish-brown, paler towards the apex. Pubescence mainly pale, only black hairs intermixed apically. Abdomen with practically the same pattern as described for female.

Length. 14–15 mm.

BIOLOGY. Nothing is known about the biology of this obviously rare species. The three known Danish specimens are all from coastal localities.

DATES. June–July.

DISTRIBUTION. A little known species, may be both local and rare. Described from France. We have seen documentary material from England, Denmark and Finland.

HYBOMITRA DISTINGUENDA (VERRALL, 1909)

Fig. 65c; 69; pl. 2: fig. f.

Tabanus distinguendus Verrall, 1909, Brit. Flies, 5: 371.
Tabanus distinguendus f. *rufa* Goffe, 1931, Trans. ent. Soc. S. Engl., 6: 98.
Tabanus distinguendus f. *parva* Goffe, 1931, Trans. ent. Soc. S. Engl., 6: 99.

DIAGNOSIS. Larger, conspicuously reddish-brown species, the reddish-brown sidemarkings on anterior four tergites distinctly golden haired, without any black hairs intermixed. Notopleural lobes brown to black. Frons rather narrow, lower callus small and transversely wrinkled, not shining. Basal antennal segments blackish-grey, with long hairs in male; the upper facets are considerably enlarged in male but the sharp separation from small facets absent.

DESCRIPTION. ♀. *Head.* Eyes densely brownish pubescent, with three bands. Frons yellowish-grey dusted, rather narrow, index 1: 5–6, slightly widened above. Lower callus black, separated from the eye-margin, square in shape or slightly higher than broad, transversely wrinkled. Median callus linear, black, connected with lower callus. Ocellar tubercle shining dark brown. Subcallus and face yellowish-grey to greyish dusted, face and cheeks with long whitish-grey hairs. Antennae with segment 1 densely greyish-black dusted and mostly pale haired; segments 2 and 3 brown to reddish-brown, segment 3 broad with a distinct rectangular dorsal tooth, apical part of segment usually blackish, terminal flagellar segments always black. Palpi greyish-brown to brown, somewhat darker than in other closely related species of this group, apical segment stout at base, covered with short black hairs and longer pale ones.

Thorax blackish-grey, golden and black haired; mesonotum with three indistinct greyish longitudinal stripes and mostly black haired. Notopleural lobes brown to blackish, but often the brown colour occupies a smaller part at middle. *Legs* blackish-grey, tibiae except apical half of fore tibiae brown, tarsi mostly black. *Wings* distinctly brownish clouded along costal margin, veins dark brown to black. Halteres dark brown.

Abdomen with reddish-brown to yellowish-brown sidemarkings on tergites 1 to 4, the rest black. Median stripe on anterior three tergites occupies about 1/4 to 1/5 of tergites. A row of more or less distinct whitish-grey median triangles present. Venter yellowish on anterior four sternites, often also on sternite 5. Sternite 1 with a square dark spot, sternite 2 with triangular to trapeze-shaped spot. Whole of abdomen covered with golden hairs, only black areas on dorsum with black hairs. Anterior four tergites and especially tergite 2 at sides only golden pubescent, without any black hairs. Cerci broadly rectangular with rounded lateral edges; subgenital plate straight on lower margin, upper part rather broad with only a slight excision above.

♂. Eyes with longer brown hairs, upper facets considerably enlarged but not sharply contrasted to the lower and smaller facets. Basal antennal segments densely greyish dusted, segment 1 with long blackish hairs which are about as long as both basal segments combined; segment 3 more slender. Apical segment of palpi brownish coloured, slightly greyish dusted at base; short and stout especially towards tip, the part below tip slightly concave. Abdomen with anterior four tergites yellowish-brown at sides, the blackish median stripe narrowest on tergite 3, occupying there at most 1/8 of tergite. Whitish-grey median triangles on posterior margins rather distinct. Abdomen with golden hairs on brownish areas and on posterior margin of tergite 1, otherwise mostly black haired.

Length. 14.5–18 mm.

Biology. A species inhabiting various types of biotopes, often rather a common species but never in mass occurrence as, for example, *H. muehlfeldi* (Br.), *H. lundbecki* Lyneb. or *H. ciureai* (Ség.). Soboleva (1965) observed oviposition on leaves of trees and shrubs near water, the egg-clusters contain from 383 to 445 eggs. The larva and pupa have not yet been described. Females attack man and animals.

DATES. From May until August.

DISTRIBUTION. A widely distributed species known throughout Europe including England and Ireland. It is recorded from all European countries from Scandinavia to Spain, eastwards it is known through the European part of the U.S.S.R. and Siberia to as far as the Far East and Japan.

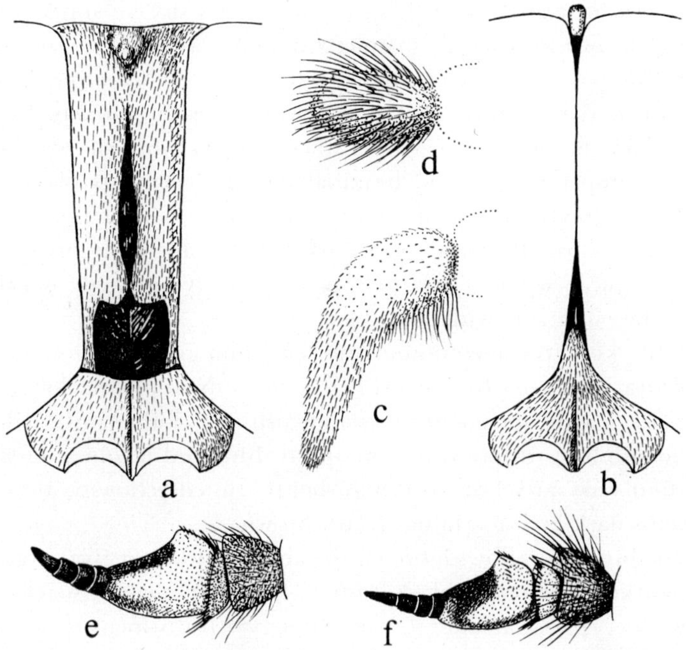

Fig. 69. *Hybomitra distinguenda* (Verr.), a. female frons, b. male frons, c. female palpus, d. male palpus, e. female antenna, f. male antenna.

HYBOMITRA CIUREAI (SÉGUY, 1937)

Fig. 65b; 70; pl. 2: fig. e.

Tabanus solstitialis auct. nec Meigen, 1820.
Tabanus tenuistria Kröber, 1936, Acta Inst. Mus. zool. Univ. athen., 1: 33 (nec Lutz et Neave, 1914) – syn. n.
Sziladynus solstitialis var. *Ciureai* Séguy, 1937, Archs roum. Path. exp. Microbiol., 10: 207.
Hybomitra schineri Lyneborg, 1959, Ent. Meddr, 29: 109.

DIAGNOSIS. Medium-sized to larger species with yellowish-brown sidemarkings on anterior four to five tergites, black median stripe rather narrow. Frons narrow, median callus small, distinctly wrinkled, not shining. Basal antennal segments and notopleural calli distinctly yellowish. Male with upper facets distinctly enlarged and sharply separated from the lower area with small facets; basal antennal segment with long black hairs.

Description. ♀. *Head.* Eyes short reddish pubescent, with three bands. Frons yellowish-grey dusted, rather narrow, index 1: 4—5.5, distinctly widened above. Lower callus small, higher than broad and separated from the eye-margins; brown to blackish, distinctly transversely wrinkled, not shining. Median callus black, linear, connected with lower callus. Ocellar tubercle small, polished dark brown. Antennae entirely reddish-brown, basal two segments black haired; segment 3 rather yellowish-brown with distinct dorsal tooth, upper margin and terminal flagellar segments blackish. Subcallus and face greyish-yellow dusted, face with long whitish-grey to yellowish hairs, cheeks usually with some dark hairs. Palpi light brown to yellowish-grey, apical segment stout at base, apically pointed; mostly pale haired, on the outer side with some black hairs.

Thorax blackish-grey, mesonotum and scutellum greyish-yellow and black haired, pleura with only fine, whitish-grey hairs. Notopleural lobes yellowish-brown. *Legs* with coxae and femora greyish and clothed with pale hairs, tibiae yellowish-brown; fore tibiae on apical third and whole of tarsi black, posterior four tarsi dark brown. *Wings* slightly tinted yellowish along costal margin, veins dark brown. Halteres dark brown.

Abdomen broadly yellowish-brown on anterior four to five tergites, the light sidemarkings pale and black haired. The dark median stripe narrow, on tergite 3 occupying at most 1/5 of tergite, with distinct greyish median triangles which are high and distinct on all tergites. Posterior tergites darker grey. Venter yellowish-brown on anterior four to five sternites, sternite 2 with a small greyish patch anteriorly at middle, posterior two or three sternites grey. Venter whitish-grey to yellowish pubescent, last sternite with a tuft of black hairs. Cerci rectangular with oblique lateral edges, subgenital plate with a deep excision on lower margin, upper part regularly semiglobular.

♂. Eyes with long pale hairs, facets on the upper two-thirds distinctly enlarged and sharply separated from the lower small facets and from the strip with small facets along postocular margin. Basal antennal segments yellowish-brown coloured and thinly greyish dusted, segment 1 with long black hairs which are as long as basal segments combined; segment 3 more slender. Apical segment of palpi yellowish-brown, distinctly stout and mostly dark haired. Abdomen with yellowish-brown sidemarkings on anterior four tergites, dark median stripe very narrow, often indistinct, occupying about 1/8 of tergite 3.

Length. 14—17 mm.

Biology. A species inhabiting various types of biotopes and one of the very common *Hybomitra* species in Europe and Siberia, both in lowlands and in the mountainous regions. In mountainous taiga and in tundra rather a rare species. Females attack man and animals, and are known to be vectors of tularaemia (Olsufjev & Golov, 1935) and anthrax (Olsufjev & Lelep, 1935). The eggs are laid by females on leaves of vegetation near to water or in marshy places. The larva and pupa were described by Chvála & Ježek (1969).

Dates. From May until the beginning of September.

Distribution. Rather a widely distributed species known throughout Europe from England and Scandinavia to Spain and in all countries of Central and South East Europe. From the U.S.S.R. it penetrates far to the north (Archangelsk, North Ural Mts, Jakutia) and south (coast of the Black Sea, Kazakhstan). The species is also recorded from Turkey and it penetrates eastwards as far as Mongolia.

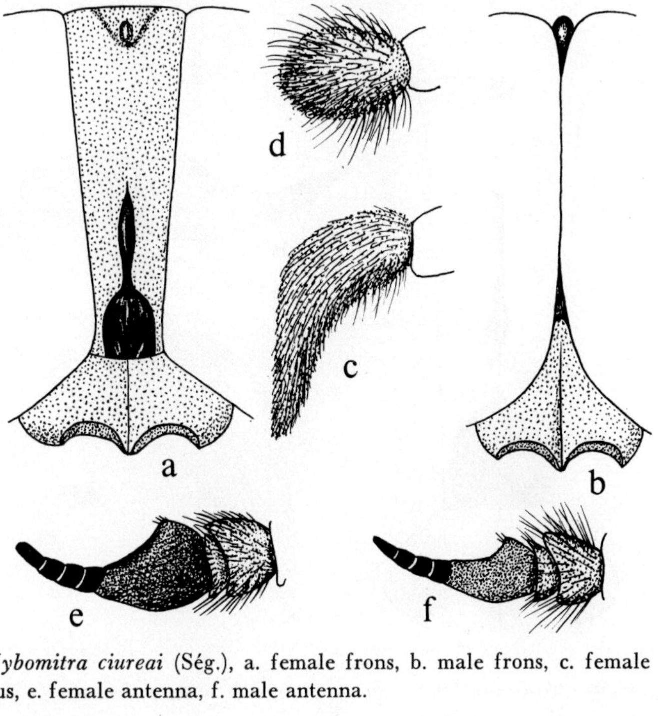

Fig. 70. *Hybomitra ciureai* (Ség.), a. female frons, b. male frons, c. female palpus, d. male palpus, e. female antenna, f. male antenna.

HYBOMITRA UKRAINICA (OLSUFJEV, 1952)

Fig. 71.

Tabanus (Tylostypia) ukrainicus Olsufjev, 1952, Chron. Ent., 32: 311.

DIAGNOSIS. Larger species resembling *H. ciureai* (Ség.) but the apical segment of palpi only pale haired, very stout at base, apical half slender and pointed. Abdomen with yellowish-brown sidemarkings on anterior four tergites, median stripe greyish, narrow. Frons narrow, lower callus wrinkled, only slightly shining. Notopleural lobes yellowish, antennae predominantly light reddish-brown.

DESCRIPTION. ♀. *Head.* Eyes very short but densely pale haired, with three bands. Frons greyish-yellow dusted, narrow, index about 1: 5, slightly widened above. Lower callus black, only slightly shining, distinctly wrinkled; almost square in shape and indistinctly separated by a narrow dusted line from the eye-margins. Median callus black, very linear, connected with lower callus and like an indistinct line usually joined with ocellar tubercle above; latter rather small, dark brown. Subcallus darker grey dusted with rather narrow antennal bows. Face and cheeks lighter grey dusted and clothed with fine whitish hairs. Antennae mostly reddish-brown, terminal

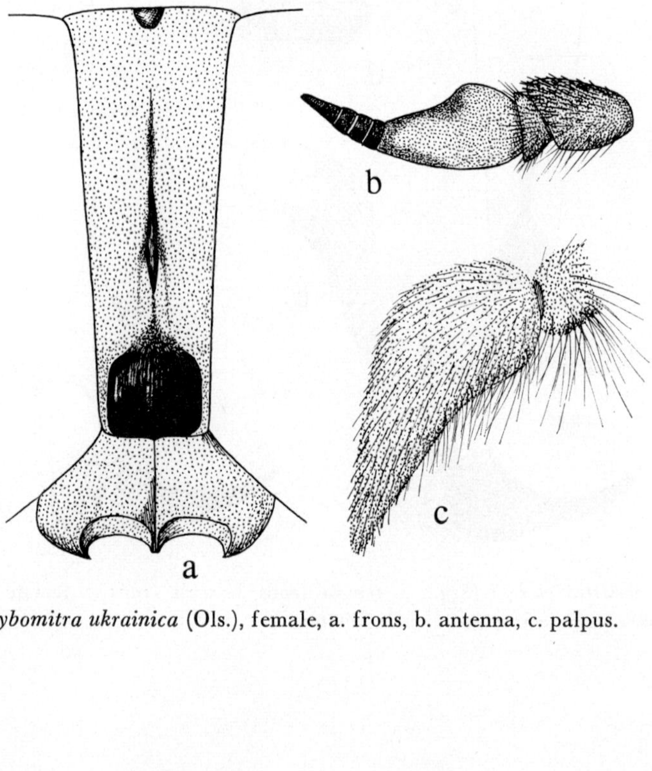

Fig. 71. *Hybomitra ukrainica* (Ols.), female, a. frons, b. antenna, c. palpus.

flagellar segments darkened, usually a slight clouding also on segment 3 towards tip; basal segments silvery-grey dusted, segment 1 above with short black hairs, below with longer pale hairing; segment 3 rather broad with a distinct rectangular dorsal tooth. Palpi whitish-yellow, apical segment very stout on basal half, apically slender and pointed; entirely short whitish haired, exceptionally with several short black hairs.

Thorax darker grey on mesonotum, somewhat bluish-grey dusted when viewed from behind, clothed with short pale and dark hairs. Notopleural lobes light yellowish-brown. Pleura and coxae light grey dusted and very pale haired, pteropleura with some dark hairs. Femora greyish, tibiae and all femora narrowly at tip yellowish-brown. Fore tibiae on apical third and fore tarsi blackish, posterior tarsi extensively darkened. *Wings* clear with brown veins, costal cell slightly yellowish. Halteres dark brown, knob at tip often pale.

Abdomen broadly yellowish-brown at sides on anterior four tergites, dark median stripe very narrow, occupying at most 1/5 on tergites 2 and 3, rather light greyish dusted. Posterior tergites grey with indistinct pale median triangles. Tergite 2 at sides exclusively pale haired, dark areas on abdomen black haired. Venter yellowish coloured and pale haired on anterior four sternites, apical three sternites light grey dusted and mostly dark haired. Sternite 2 with a very small greyish median spot on anterior margin.

♂. Unknown.

Length. 17–19 mm.

DATES. May and June.

DISTRIBUTION. A recently recognized and described species from the Ukraine, where it is a rather common species. It has also been recorded from the adjacent regions, from Moldavia and Rumania (Olsufjev 1969a: 487).

HYBOMITRA VALENCIAE (LECLERCQ, 1957)

Therioplectes valenciae Leclercq, 1957, Bull. Inst. r. Sci. nat. Belg., 33: 5.

We have not seen this species. Owing to the unusual combination of characters we present the following translation of the original description.

♀. *Head.* Eyes green with three red stripes, with sparse but distinct hairs. Frontal stripe yellowish, whitish at the top, 5 to 5.5 times higher than broad, with upwards diverging edges. Lower frontal callus shining black, square-shaped; upper frontal callus shining black, narrow, oblong, distinctly separated from the lower callus. Vertex has a raised area of dull blackish-brown coloration which is longitudinally divided by a depression; some black hairs. Subcallus yellowish dusted, with a number of yellowish hairs mixed with some black hairs at the upper external part of the lateral part. Antennal segments 1–2 greyish dusted, with yellow and black hairs; segment 3 blackish-brown. Terminal flagellar segments dark, basally paler. Palpi long and thin, pointed, yellowish, the second segment has some black hairs.

Thorax greyish with black hairs mixed with tawny hairs. Anterior part with traces of longitudinal bands. Pleura with dense white pile, mixed with black hairs. Scutellum also with black and tawny hairs. *Legs:* Femora blackish-grey (except the knees which are reddish-yellow) with long, yellowish hairs. Femur 1 shows a shining black colour of the whole length of the interior surface. Tibiae reddish-yellow; tibia 1 dark at apex. Tarsi blackish. All tibiae have black and yellowish hairs. *Wings* have a light colour with yellowish costal margin and yellowish stigma.

Abdomen reddish, on the first four tergites with a median longitudinal narrow band of a black colour, covering completely the last tergites; each tergite has a yellowish hairy spot in middle, forming a longitudinal line in the middle of the median black stripe. Venter reddish-yellow; a black median spot on sternites 1 and 2, ending at the middle of sternite 3; the last sternites are lightly darkened.

Length of body 15 mm (from the point of the antennae to the apex of abdomen); wings 12 mm.

♂. Unknown.

DATES. July.

DISTRIBUTION. Described by Leclercq on the basis of a single female specimen originating from Saler, Provincia de Valencia, Spain. Later, Leclercq (1964a: 316) recorded a further female specimen collected in the same area.

ERBERI-GROUP

Rather light yellowish-brown species with whitish-yellow halteres, females with minute and rather indistinctly pubescent eyes; eyes in male always densely haired. Ocellar tubercle in females sometimes reduced into three more or less distinct vestigial ocelli. Antennae extensively blackish with segment 3 rather slender, number of eye-bands sometimes reduced. The species are distributed mainly in the Asiatic part of the Palaearctic region and in southern parts of Europe.

HYBOMITRA EXPOLLICATA (PANDELLÉ, 1883)

Fig. 72.

Tabanus expollicatus Pandellé, 1883, Revue Ent., 2: 218.
Tabanus (Tylostypia) nigrivitta Olsufjev, 1937, Fauna SSSR, 7: 192.
Hybomitra pseuderberi Philip & Aitken, 1958, Memorie Soc. ent. ital., 37: 88.

DIAGNOSIS. Reddish-brown species with whitish halteres, uniformly black antennae, and the reddish-brown sidemarkings at most on anterior three tergites. A broad blackish median stripe on dorsum of abdomen, at middle with another light grey, narrower median line. Venter with a broad dark median stripe on anterior sternites. Male with upper facets slightly enlarged.

DESCRIPTION. ♀. *Head.* Eyes with dense but very minute greyish pubescence, usually with three bands but the upper and lower bands often absent. Frons yellowish-grey dusted, rather narrower, index about 1: 4.5, very slightly widened above. Lower callus black, not shining, usually narrowly separated from the eye-margins; above connected with a linear black median callus. Vertex usually with only slightly shining brown patch substituting ocellar tubercle, or with more or less distinct 3 brown ocelli. Subcallus and face

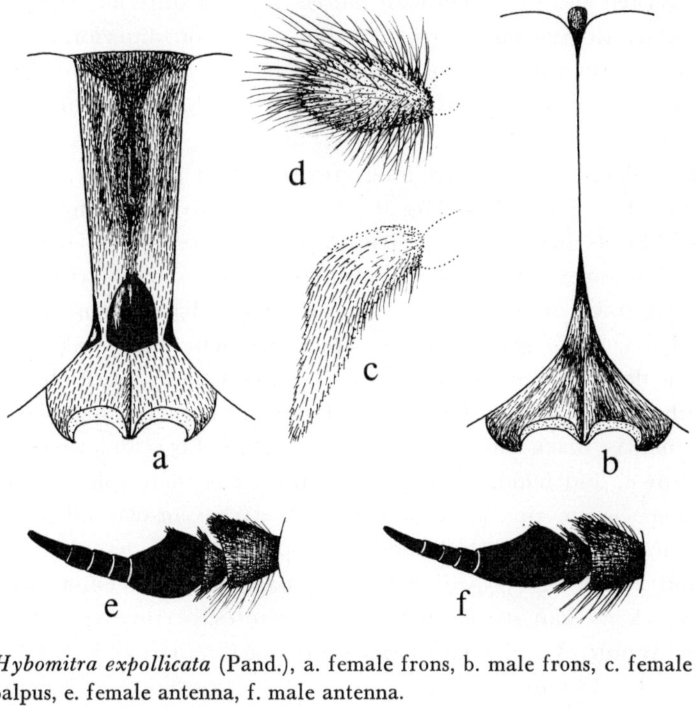

Fig. 72. *Hybomitra expollicata* (Pand.), a. female frons, b. male frons, c. female palpus, d. male palpus, e. female antenna, f. male antenna.

light greyish-yellow dusted, face pale haired. Antennal bows narrow. Antennae entirely black, or segment 3 very slightly translucent brownish at extreme base; basal segments densely light grey dusted and fine pale haired, only upper tip of segment 1 with several black hairs; segment 3 rather slender, dorsal tooth slightly developed, terminal flagellar segments conspicuously long and pointed. Palpi yellowish-white, apical segment long and rather slender, pale haired or with a few black hairs.

Thorax dark grey dusted and mostly pale haired on mesonotum, no longitudinal stripes. Notopleural lobes yellowish-brown. Pleura and coxae lighter grey dusted and densely pale haired. *Legs:* Femora blackish-grey, more or less yellowish-brown apically, especially posterior femora often broadly yellowish-brown on apical third. Basal half of fore tibiae and whole of posterior tibiae except extreme tip yellowish-brown, otherwise legs black. Femora pale haired, especially long beneath, tibiae with pale and black hairs. *Wings* faintly tinted brownish, veins dark brown. Halteres whitish, base yellowish.

Abdomen reddish-brown on anterior three tergites; black median stripe broad, slightly widened posteriorly on each tergite, occupying 1/3 to 1/4 of tergites, at middle with a distinct, narrower greyish dusted and pale haired stripe, dividing the black median stripe into thirds. Posterior tergites blackish-grey dusted and light yellowish haired, likewise anterior tergites at sides. Venter blackish-grey on a broad median stripe on anterior two or three sternites, and on whole of following sternites; sternites 1 and 2 yellowish-brown at sides, sternite 3 usually more darkened. Venter uniformly short pale haired.

♂. Eyes densely and rather long greyish-brown pubescent, facets on the upper two-thirds slightly enlarged, about twice to three times as large as the small facets below, sharp division absent. Ocellar tubercle small but distinct. Antennae entirely black, segment 3 more slender with a long and pointed complex of terminal flagellar segments; basal segment with short greyish hairs. Palpi greyish-brown, apical segment long oval, about twice as long as deep, clothed with long black hairs. Cheeks mostly black haired, face with greyish hairs. Mesonotum darker and finely long black haired, predominantly black hairs also on pteropleura. Legs somewhat darkened, tibiae brown, and femora apically brown on less than apical third. Wings and halteres as in the ♀. Abdomen with darker brown sidemarkings on anterior four tergites, a black median stripe occupying less than 1/4 of tergites, and a paler grey median stripe usually absent. Venter with a very broad, black median stripe on anterior sternites, occupying at least 1/3 of sternites. Whole of abdomen mostly short black haired.

Length. 12—18 mm.

VARIABILITY. Rather a variable species, the eye-bands vary in number from one (central) to three, the reddish-brown sidemarkings vary in size but the broad black median stripe always present.

BIOLOGY. The species occurs in rather isolated localities, but on suitable, usually saline biotopes is often very common. Females attack man, horses, horned cattle and dogs, and the species is known as a vector of *Trypanosoma evansi* causing surra disease.

DATES. From June until August.

DISTRIBUTION. The species is known from a wide area of distribution from Spain to as far as the Far East (Manchuria, China, Mongolia). In Europe distributed along the coast and occurs inland only isolately on saline biotopes. It is recorded from Italy, France, Spain, England, Belgium, Netherlands, Germany (Rügen, Hiddensee in the north, but it is very common inland in the vicinity of Stassfurt), Denmark and Sweden (Öland). The species has not yet been collected in Central Europe (Czechoslovakia, Austria) but its occurrence there is anticipated. In the U.S.S.R. it is known from Moldavia, Ukraine through Siberia, Kazakhstan and Uzbekistan as far as the district of Primorye in the east.

HYBOMITRA MORGANI (SURCOUF, 1912)

Fig. 73.

Tabanus mühlfeldi auct. nec Brauer, 1880.
Tabanus Morgani Surcouf, 1912, Compte Rendu Expéd. Morgan, p. 71.
Therioplectes sibiricus Enderlein, 1925, Mitt. zool. Mus. Berl., 11: 358.
Hybomitra staegeri Lyneborg, 1959, Ent. Meddr, 29: 145 – syn. n.

DIAGNOSIS. Medium-sized to larger species with abdomen broadly light reddish-brown to yellowish-brown on anterior four tergites at sides, dark median stripe very narrow. Halteres whitish, vertex with distinct ocellar tubercle. Sternite 2 with a dark median patch in both sexes. Male with facets on the upper two-thirds enlarged.

DESCRIPTION. ♀. *Head.* Eyes clothed with sparse, minute light grey hairs, three narrow bands present. Frons yellowish-grey dusted, rather narrower, index 1: 4—5, almost parallel-sided or slightly widened above. Lower callus usually polished blackish-brown, rectangular, broader than high with often rounded upper margin, touching the eye-margins. Median callus subshining black, broadly spindle-shaped dilated and often narrowly connected with lower callus. Ocellar tubercle shining reddish-brown, triangular in shape or slightly oval. Subcallus and face yellowish-grey dusted, antennal bows narrow. Face clothed with rather shorter whitish hairs. Antennae black or brownish on basal segments, thinly greyish dusted and clothed with short pale and black hairs; segment 3 slender, mostly black, slightly brownish at base; dorsal tooth rather small but pointed, placed near to base of segment. Palpi whitish-yellow, apical segment stouter at base, pointed on apical half, clothed with short pale and black hairs.

Thorax. Mesonotum blackish-grey dusted, humeri and notopleural lobes yellowish, postalar calli often brown. Pleura densely whitish-grey dusted and mostly pale haired. *Legs:* Femora greyish, yellowish-brown at tip; most of fore tibiae and whole of posterior tibae yellowish-brown, fore tibiae apically and fore tarsi black; posterior tarsi brownish, darkened towards tip. *Wings* clear, veins light brown, distinctly yellowish along anterior margin and at base of wing; sometimes a short appendix to vein R_4. Halteres whitish-yellow.

Abdomen broadly light reddish to yellowish-brown at sides on anterior four tergites, dark median stripe narrow, occupying on tergite 2 and 3 almost 1/8 of tergite, on tergite 4 broader posteriorly. Posterior tergites greyish-black, all tergites with a row of high and distinctly paler median triangles, forming more or less distinct paler median line. Venter yellowish-brown on sternites 1 to 4, sternites 3 and 4 slightly greyish along posterior margin; sternite 2 usually with a square-shaped spot on the posterior half of sternite, also central part of sternite 1 faintly darkened. Posterior three sternites pale greyish, sternite 5 with small yellowish sidemarkings.

♂. We have not seen the male sex and therefore present a translation of the description given by Olsufjev (1937: 191): Eyes with long grey hairs. Facets on the upper two-thirds enlarged (about 2 to 3 times). Ocellar tubercle not very large, reddish-brown, slightly shining. Subcallus grey. Antennae as in the ♀, segment 3 more slender. Segment 1 with short hairs. Face yellowish or greyish dusted and grey haired. Palpi whitish, apical segment more or less stout, clothed with long pale and whitish hairs. Thorax with appendices as in the ♀; mesonotum without longitudinal stripes. Abdomen brownish-yellow, dorsum with a dark median stripe, which is about 1/6—1/10 of the width of abdomen. The stripe is covered by dusting and adpressed grey hairs (latter sometimes denuded). Segment 5 and following segments dark. Sternite 2 with a dark median patch.

Length. 14—18 mm.

SYNONYMY. Through the kindness of Dr. L. Tsacas, Paris we had the opportunity to re-examine the type female of *Tabanus morgani* Surcouf, 1912, labelled »Perse / Ghilan 950 m Alt. (Calhors) / (R. de Mecquenem) / T. de Morgan 1908«. The type specimen is identical with the species recorded by Olsufjev (1937) and subsequent authors as *Tabanus mühlfeldi* Br. and later, when redescribing the true *Hybomitra muehlfeldi* of Brauer, newly described by Lyneborg (1959) as *Hybomitra staegeri*. The latter name becomes a synonym of *H. morgani* (Surc.). There is a female of the Asiatic *H. reinigiana* (Enderlein) labelled: »Zentral-Pamir, VII.–VIII.1928, leg. Reinig«, »Schor-Kul, 17.VII, 3720 m.«, »Cotype«, and »Tylostypia reinigiana ♀ / Cotype / Enderl., Dr. Enderlein det. 1932« in the Zoological Museum, Berlin. The specimen has much in common with *H. morgani* but the eyes are distinctly pubescent, the antennal segment 3 is broader and the dark median stripe on abdomen is much broader, occupying almost one third of the tergites 2 and 3. It should be noted that some recent authors (e. g. Olsufjev, 1962; Leclercq, 1967a) place without foundation *morgani* as a subspecies of *H. montana* (Meig.). According to Olsufjev (in litt. 10.1.1972) *Th. sibiricus* End. is identical with *morgani*.

Biology. A species inhabiting various types of biotopes but it occurs most frequently in forest regions. Shevtshenko (1961: 107) recorded it from Kazakhstan especially from pine forest (forming 56 % of the tabanid population), from birch forest (32 %), but the species is much less common on the shores of lakes (12 %). Violovič (1968: 159) observed oviposition on the leaves of the Common Reed *(Phragmites communis)* in Siberia and recorded the number of eggs in egg-clusters as being between 396 and 519, according to Soboleva (1965) from 492 to 584. The larva and pupa are not yet described.

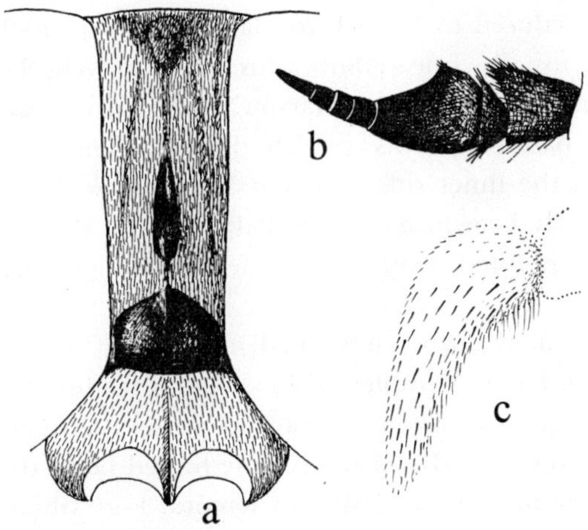

Fig. 73. *Hybomitra morgani* (Surc.), female, a. frons, b. antenna, c. palpus.

DATES. From May until August.

DISTRIBUTION. The area of distribution of this species is not well known because of the confusion in the systematic position of this species and the complicated synonymy. *H. morgani* (Surc.) is known for certain from Denmark and from the European part of the U.S.S.R. (Ukraine) but it is much commoner in the Asiatic part of the U.S.S.R. through Kazakhstan and Siberia to as far as the region of Primorye. It is also recorded from Mongolia and China.

HYBOMITRA ERBERI (BRAUER, 1880)

Fig. 74.

Tabanus (Therioplectes) Erberi Brauer, 1880, Denkschr. Akad. Wiss., Wien, 42: 151.
Therioplectes erberi var. *fuscipennis* Szilády, 1926, Annls Mus. nat. hung., 24: 607.

DIAGNOSIS. Yellowish-brown species on at least anterior four tergites at sides, black median stripe rather broad. Halteres whitish, ocellar tubercle in the form of only 3 small black or blackish-brown ocelli, all femora apically yellowish-brown. Venter of abdomen yellowish-brown, anteriorly with distinct grey median spot on sternite 2. Male with very enlarged and sharply separated facets on the upper two-thirds of eyes.

DESCRIPTION. ♀. *Head.* Eyes only microscopically pale pubescent with three narrow bands. Frons yellowish-grey dusted and short pale haired especially above, rather narrow, index 1: 4—4.5, slightly widened above. Lower callus subshining black, rectangular to triangular in shape, very narrowly separated from the eye-margins and connected above with the elongate, black median callus. Ocellar tubercle reduced to 3 black to blackish-brown small polished ocelli, the upper two usually linear. Subcallus, face and cheeks with similar dusting as on frons, antennal bows narrow. Face with dense pale hairing. Antennae black, basal segments greyish dusted, segment 1 slightly translucent brownish on the inner side; segment 3 slender with an obtuse dorsal tooth, usually slightly brownish at base. Palpi whitish-yellow, apical segment slender and very pointed, clothed with dense pale hairing, some additional black hairs present.

Thorax rather light grey dusted including unstriped mesonotum, latter clothed with short pale and black hairs. Notopleural lobes yellowish-brown. Pleura and coxae with fine, longer whitish hairs, pteropleura with some black hairs. *Legs:* Femora light grey dusted and finely pale haired beneath, apical part yellowish-brown, more broadly on posterior femora. Fore tibiae on basal half and whole of posterior tibiae yellowish; rest of fore tibiae and fore tarsi black, posterior tarsi extensively darkened and short black haired. *Wings* almost clear with dark veins which are yellowish-brown along costal margin and at base of wing. Halteres whitish, stem slightly brownish.

Abdomen yellowish-brown on anterior four to five tergites, black median stripe occupying 1/5 to 1/3 of tergite 2, becoming broader posteriorly. Apical tergites blackish. Venter yellowish-brown on anterior four sternites, apical three sternites light grey; sternite 2 with a large greyish median spot of varying shape.

♂. Eyes densely but short whitish pubescent, facets on the upper two-thirds pale and very enlarged (about six times), sharply separated from the blackish area below with small facets. Subcallus, face and cheeks greyish dusted, face densely pale haired, cheeks with greyish hairs. Antennae often entirely black, or brownish on basal segments, segment 3 more slender; basal segment short black haired. Palpi whitish-yellow, long oval, about twice as long as deep, clothed with longer, pale and black hairs. Mesonotum with long greyish hairs. Legs as in the ♀ with femora yellowish-brown apically, tibiae darker. Abdomen broadly yellowish-brown on anterior five tergites,

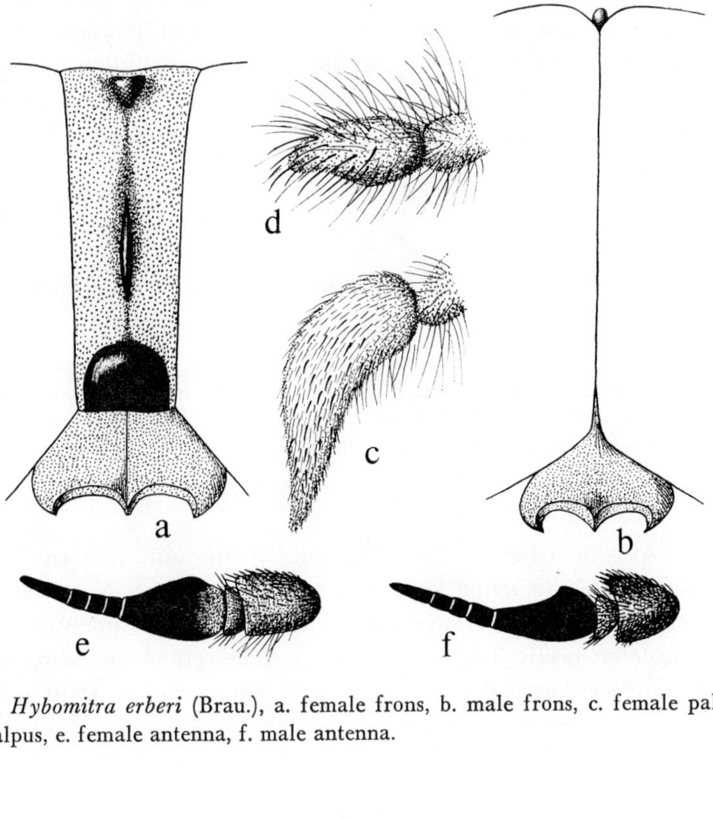

Fig. 74. *Hybomitra erberi* (Brau.), a. female frons, b. male frons, c. female palpus, d. male palpus, e. female antenna, f. male antenna.

median stripe blackish with light grey median line, occupying 1/10 to 1/12 of tergite 2. Apical two tergites blackish-grey. Venter mostly yellowish-brown with a distinct greyish median spot on tergite 2, apical three sternites greyish.

Length. 13–17 mm.

VARIABILITY. Szilády described specimens from China with somewhat clouded wings as var. *fuscipennis,* and Olsufjev (1937: 129) named specimens with brownish sidemarkings present on anterior three tergites only as f. *obscura.*

BIOLOGY. The species is rather common on banks of both fresh-water and salt lakes, much less common along rivers. According to Shevtshenko (1961: 114) the larvae very probably live in soil with some degree of salinity.

DATES. From June until August but according to Shevtshenko (1961) from the end of May until exceptionally the beginning of October in extreme localities in Kazakhstan.

DISTRIBUTION. A Central Asiatic species penetrating from Kazakhstan eastwards to Mongolia, North East China and North Manchuria. It is also recorded from Transcaucasia and Iran. In Europe it is known from the European part of the U.S.S.R., from Italy, France including Corsica, and from Greece and Corfu. The records from Austria (Kröber, 1938: 86) is very uncertain or refers to the old Austrian-Hungarian monarchy.

HYBOMITRA PECULIARIS (SZILÁDY, 1914)

Fig. 75.

Tabanus (Atylotus) peculiaris Szilády, 1914, Annls Mus. nat. hung., 12: 665.
Tabanus inaequatus Austen, 1923, Bull. ent. Res., 13: 384.
Tabanus (Therioplectes) peculiaris var. *Kröberi* Szilády, 1926, Annls Mus. nat hung., 24: 607.
? *Tabanus peculiaris* var. *kashmirianus* Szilády, 1926, Biologica hung., 1 (7): 17.

DIAGNOSIS. Abdomen light yellowish-brown, leaving only posterior two segments greyish, median stripe light grey and very narrow. No dark median spot on sternite 2. Halteres whitish, ocellar tubercle rudimental, in form of three isolated ocelli. Legs extensively orange-yellow including femora. Male with upper facets distinctly enlarged, no greyish median patch on sternite 2.

DESCRIPTION. ♀. *Head.* Eyes with sparse minute pale hairs and with three narrow bands. Frons whitish-grey dusted, narrow, index about 1: 4.5, slightly widened above. Lower callus rather dull brown to blackish, almost rectangular, indistinctly separated from the eye-margins and narrowly connected with spindle-shaped median brownish callus. Ocellar tubercle reduced to 3 shining light brown ocelli, upper two linear, lower one almost circular and much smaller. Subcallus, face and cheeks whitish-grey dusted, face with shorter whitish pubescence. Antennae reddish-brown on basal segments; segment 3 blackish on apical half including terminal flagellar segments, reddish-brown on basal half; slender, with indistinct dorsal tooth. Palpi whitish-yellow, long, slender and apically pointed; clothed with short pale hairs with some additional black ones.

Thorax almost whitish-grey dusted, mesonotum only indistinctly darker grey and rather densely short pale haired. Humeri and notopleural lobes yellowish-brown, latter with fine dark hairs. Pleura and coxae clothed with rather shorter but dense whitish hairing. *Legs* very light yellowish-brown to orange-yellow, femora at most on basal half light grey dusted. Fore tibiae on apical third and whole of fore tarsi blackish with concolorous hairs,

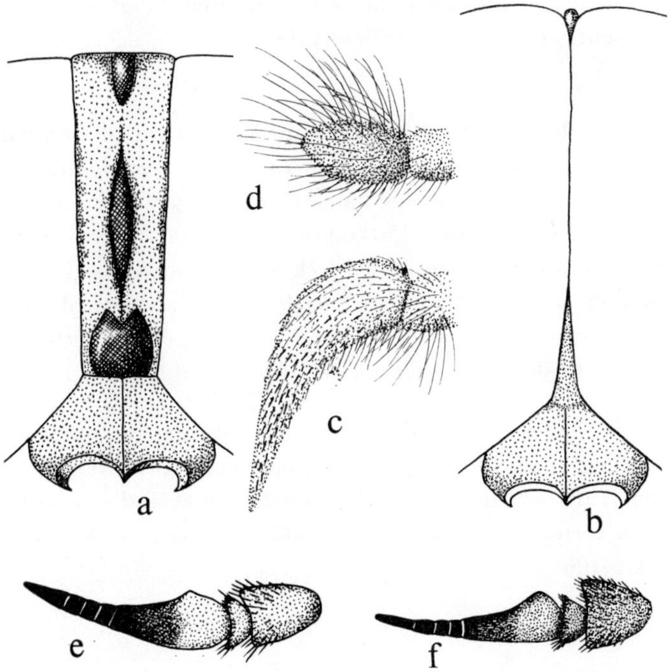

Fig. 75. *Hybomitra peculiaris* (Szil.), a. female frons, b. male frons, c. female palpus, d. male palpus, e. female antenna, f. male antenna.

posterior four tarsi dark brown and black haired; otherwise legs mostly pale haired. *Wings* clear with brown veins. Halteres whitish, stem brownish.

Abdomen broadly light yellowish-brown on anterior four to five tergites at sides, light grey median stripe very narrow, occupying 1/6 to 1/10 of tergite 2, slightly widened posteriorly. Apical two or three tergites greyish dusted and mostly black haired. Venter unicolorous yellowish, apical two sternites (or to four sternites) more or less light grey. No median patch on sternite 2.

♂. Eyes short but densely whitish haired, facets on the upper two-thirds enlarged, about 3 times, distinctly but not sharply separated from the small facets on the lower third of eyes and on a broad stripe along postocular margin. Ocellar tubercle very small. Subcallus light greyish-brown dusted, face and cheeks greyish dusted, cheeks with fine darker hairs. Antennae as in the ♀ but segment 3 more slender and basal segment with only very short dark hairs. Palpi yellowish, apical segment oval but rather slender, almost twice as long as deep; clothed with longer pale and some shorter black hairs. Legs somewhat darkened, femora dark grey on basal half, rest of femora and tibiae rather brown. Abdomen extensively yellowish-brown, extremely narrow median stripe sometimes interrupted on posterior margins of tergites or absent. Venter unicolorous light yellowish-brown, dark median patch on sternite 2 absent, apical two sternites darker grey.

Length. 14.5–17 mm.

Variability. Rather a variable species especially in the abdominal pattern, the light yellowish-brown sidemarkings sometimes very enlarged, in extremely pale specimens a greyish median stripe very narrow or absent. Szilády described var. *kroeberi* from Turkestan. Var. *kashmirianus* Szilády, 1926 has entirely reddish antennae, dull black and rounded lower callus, and is a much smaller species, 13 mm in length — on the basis of the holotype female deposited in the Naturhistorisches Museum, Vienna; the variety was described from Kashmir and represents very probably a distinct species.

Biology. A typical species of desert zone, inhabiting biotopes close to salt lakes and along rivers. Females attack man and both domestic and wild living animals (horses, horned cattle, camels, saigas and also pelicans) and are known as vectors of tularaemia and su-auru disease of horses and camels (Shevtshenko, 1961).

Dates. From May until the beginning of September.

Distribution. The centre of the distribution lies in Central Asiatic republics including Kazakhstan, in Iran and Iraq, from where it penetrates eastwards to Mongolia. In Europe it is known only from the most south eastern parts, from the region of the Volga river (e. g. in the Kuma river basin).

ACUMINATA-GROUP

Reddish-brown species with whitish-yellow halteres and abdomen conspicuously laterally compressed on posterior segments, distinctly pointed apically when viewed from above. Antennae extensively blackish on segment 3, postocular margin on vertex rather deep. Eyes rather densely pubescent in both sexes. The species of this group are often placed into separate genus (or subgenus) *Sipala* End. Species inhabiting southern parts of the Palaearctic region.

HYBOMITRA ACUMINATA (LOEW, 1858)

Fig. 76.

Tabanus acuminatus Loew, 1858, Verh. zool.-bot. Ges. Wien, 8: 590.

DIAGNOSIS. Medium-sized species with pale halteres (more brownish in male) and abdomen distinctly laterally compressed and pointed at tip also in female. Antennae rather broad and mostly black, segment 3 brownish at base, dorsal tooth almost rectangular. Frons rather narrower, lower callus large and mostly shining black. Abdomen with yellowish-brown sidemarkings on tergites 1–4. Male with facets on the upper part of eyes enlarged.

DESCRIPTION. ♀. *Head.* Eyes rather densely but short pale haired, with three bands. Frons and subcallus light grey to greyish-yellow dusted, former rather narrower, index about 1: 4.5, slightly widened above. Lower callus large, almost rectangular or rounded above, slightly shining black and connected with a linear blackish median callus. Ocellar tubercle very small, rounded, subshining brown. Occiput and a deep postocular margin on vertex whitish-grey dusted and very finely pale haired. Face and cheeks paler greyish dusted with pale longer hairs, cheeks above with a few fine black hairs. Antennae dark grey and mostly black haired (at least above) on basal two segments; segment 3 black, brownish at base, rather broad with almost rectangular dorsal tooth. Palpi very pale, predominantly pale haired with some short black hairs, apical segment long but rather stout throughout.

Thorax greyish on mesonotum, mostly pale haired, with three indefinite dark longitudinal stripes. Notopleural lobes yellowish. Pleura paler grey dusted, with some fine black hairs on pteropleura, otherwise with long, almost whitish hairs. *Legs* light grey on coxae and femora, clothed with longer whitish hairs; tibiae and tarsi yellowish-brown, short pale haired and with some black hairs intermixed; fore tibiae towards tip and fore tarsi darkened. *Wings* clear with brown veins, no appendix to vein R_4. Halteres whitish-yellow, stem at tip brownish.

Abdomen with yellow-brown sidemarkings on tergites 1–4, dark median stripe rather lighter grey, occupying on tergites 2 and 3 at most one quarter of tergites, widened on tergite 4. Apical tergites uniformly greyish. Dorsum clothed with short pale and black hairs. Venter yellowish-brown on sternites 1–4, anterior two sternites with indefinite greyish median spots, apical three sternites greyish. Yellowish-brown areas on the venter only pale haired. Abdomen distinctly laterally compressed and pointed at tip when viewed from above.

♂. Eyes with longer and still more dense pale pubescence, facets are distinctly larger on the upper two-thirds but the sharp division absent. Face and cheeks with longer hairs, latter predominantly black haired. Antennae more slender on segment 3 with less developed dorsal tooth and mostly blackish, dark brown at base only. Palpi oval, pale, especially above with long pale and some black hairs. Thorax rather darker grey and all pubescence much longer. Legs and wings as in the ♀, halteres more brownish. Abdomen with the same pattern but the dark median stripe and apical tergites more blackish-grey and slightly shining, venter with greyish spot also on sternite 3; apical sternites greyish.

Length. 13–15 mm.

REMARKS. This species, together with *H. media* (Kröb.) and two further Palaearctic species *H. cuspidata* (Aust.) and *H. aino* (Kono & Tak.), was

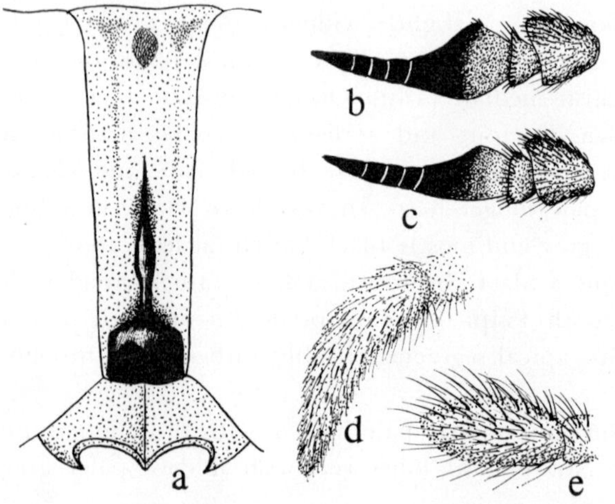

Fig. 76. *Hybomitra acuminata* (Lw.), a. female frons, b. female antenna, c. male antenna, d. female palpus, e. male palpus.

separated as a different genus *Sipala* End. Enderlein (1923) erected this genus originally because of the enlarged and sharply separated facets on the upper two-thirds of eyes in the male sex, a feature which is also present in other *Hybomitra* species. The genus *Sipala* End., or subgenus according to some recent authors, has been adopted by subsequent authors mainly because of the conspicuously pointed and laterally compressed abdomen in the female sex both in *acuminata* and *media*. This character, however, is of no value for separating the species into a different higher category, especially when they are compared with another group of species (*H. vittata* (F.), *H. macularis* (F.)) with extremely broad and dorsoventrally flattened abdomen.

BIOLOGY. The species occurs especially in semi-desert regions, inhabiting localities close to lakes. According to Shevtshenko (1961: 112) the larvae live in soil with a high concentration of salt but the larva has not yet been described. In Central Europe the species occurs similarly in saline localities. Females attack man, domestic and wild animals including birds. A very common species in suitable localities.

DATES. From May until August.

DISTRIBUTION. A species with a wide area of distribution from France as far as the region of Ussuri in east. In Europe it is recorded from France through Central Europe to the Balkan Peninsula (Jugoslavia, Rumania), the northern border in Europe lies in Austria (Neusiedler See), Czechoslovakia (surrounding of Prešov, Slovakia) and Hungary. In the U.S.S.R. it is known from Moldavia and Ukraine through Kazakhstan, Uzbekistan and the region of the Baikal Sea to Ussuri, and it has been recorded also from Iran, North East China and Mongolia.

HYBOMITRA MEDIA (KRÖBER, 1928)

Sipala (Therioplectes) media Kröber, 1928, Zool. Anz., 76: 262.

Described by Kröber (1928) probably from a single female collected at Attica, Greece, the drawings of palpus, antenna and frons are included in the original description. We have not seen this species and therefore present only a translation of the original description including differential diagnosis.

DIAGNOSIS. Resembling very much *acuminatus* and *cuspidatus,* sufficiently differing from both in the laterally compressed abdomen on only segments 6 and 7. Median frontal callus absent. Only knees yellowish-brown.

DESCRIPTION. ♀. *Head.* Frons about 3.5 times as high as deep below, slightly widened above, blackish, with yellowish pubescence. Callus almost square in shape, with rounded edges, purely reddish-brown. Ocellar tubercle hardly convex, reddish-yellow with no trace of ocelli. Some black hairs present near ocellar tubercle. Subcallus somewhat convex, blackish in ground colour and densely yellowish dusted. Face whitish dusted, yellowish pubescent. Palpi slender, whitish-yellow, hardly bent, whitish and finely black pubescent. Antennal segments 1 and 2 reddish, segment 3 with reddish patch on both sides at base. Segments 1 and 2 with short yellowish and some black hairs. Basal part of segment 3 hardly longer than deep, with scarcely developed dorsal tooth, with whitish dusting. Annulation distinctly differentiated, longer than the basal portion, black and indistinctly segmented. Pubescence of eyes very short, faintly yellowish. Eyes green with three fine, red bands. Occiput whitish-grey, postocular margin finely yellowish pubescent.

Thorax and scutellum black, rather dull, with dense yellowish pubescence. Notopleural lobes somewhat brownish. Pleura greyish dusted with long yellowish hairs. *Legs:* Femora black, with a greyish dusting and long silky yellowish pubescence. Knees reddish-yellow, tibiae yellowish-brown, silky yellow pubescent. Fore tibiae black at tip. *Wings* clear with very fine, brown veins. Wing-margin pale yellowish-brown. Squamae yellowish-hyaline. Halteres yellow with darker knob at base.

Abdomen black, somewhat yellowish due to the dusting and pubescence, and with large reddish-yellow lateral patches from segment 1 to segment 3, black median stripe parallel-sided. The denser pubescence forms a paler median line but median triangles are not present. All segments distinctly convex but the apical two somewhat laterally compressed. Sternites 1 to 3 light reddish-yellow, not shining, with black square-shaped median patch on each sternite, leaving only fine posterior margin pale. Sternites 4 to 7 black, somewhat yellowish due to the yellow pubescence and dusting.

♂. Unknown.

Length. 15 mm.

DISTRIBUTION. Described from Greece, later recorded by Kröber (1938) also from Hungary.

VITTATA-GROUP

Uniformly light grey species with distinct brown longitudinal stripes on thorax and abdomen, abdomen conspicuously dorsoventrally flattened, very broad and flat. Frons in female very broad, index 1: 1.5—2, frontal calli strongly reduced. Eyes densely long pubescent, unbanded or with three bands. Halteres dark brown. Rare species in the West Mediterranean.

HYBOMITRA VITTATA (FABRICIUS, 1794)

Fig. 77a–c.

Tabanus vittatus Fabricius, 1794, Ent. Syst., 4: 371.

DIAGNOSIS. A greyish, long haired species with conspicuously broad and flattened abdomen. Frons very broad, frontal calli and eye-bands absent. Antennae greyish on basal segments, long black haired, segment 3 yellowish-brown with shortened terminal flagellar segments. Femora grey, tibiae and tarsi yellowish-brown.

DESCRIPTION. ♀. *Head.* Eyes clothed with long whitish hairs, unbanded. Frons rather light grey to brownish-grey dusted, very broad, index about 1: 1.5, distinctly wider above than below, and densely clothed with mostly blackish, long hairs. No calli, sometimes only a very small patch of dark coloration at middle in front, imitating lower callus. Ocellar swelling oval, light brown and distinctly polished. Occiput light grey dusted and clothed with long whitish hairs. Subcallus greyish dusted, slightly convex, antennal bows high, occupying lower half of subcallus. Face and cheeks greyish, long pale haired beneath, cheeks black haired. Antennae light grey on basal segments and clothed there with fine, long black hairs; segment 3 light brown, rather broad with hardly visible dorsal tooth, slightly darkened near base; terminal flagellar segments dark, rather short and stout. Palpi yellowish-brown, apical segment rather slender at base and apically pointed, clothed with long pale and a few black hairs.

Thorax grey, mesonotum with brownish stripes; the median one very broad, occupying almost whole of scutellum and continuing as a median stripe on abdomen; the sublateral stripes narrower and less distinct. Whole of mesonotum clothed with rather short but densely set pale pubescence, and with sparse longer black hairs. Notopleural lobes dark. Pleura concolorous with mesonotum, long pale and dark haired. *Legs* grey on coxae and femora, long pale haired; tibiae and tarsi yellowish-brown, clothed with shorter black hairs which are longer and erect on tibiae. *Wings* very faintly greyish tinted, veins dark, bifurcations slightly darkened. Halteres blackish-brown.

Abdomen light grey with darker brown median stripe becoming narrower on posterior tergites, another stripe at sides of abdomen reaches lateral edges of tergites. The dark brown stripes black pubescent, light grey areas with pale hairs. Venter uniformly grey and densely clothed with long pale and some black hairs.

♂. We have not seen the male sex, neither have we found any description of it in the literature. The short characteristic given by Kröber (1925a: 73) »♂ gleicht offenbar dem ♀ volkommen« does not clearly show if the author had seen the male sex.

Length. 11.5–12 mm.

Dates. Unknown to us.

Distribution. A West Mediterranean species known from both the African (Morocco, Algeria) and the European parts (Spain, France). In France probably only a coastal species, recorded by Leclercq (1967a: 123) from only two localities, viz. Marseille and Montpellier. A rare species which is only represented in collections by single specimens.

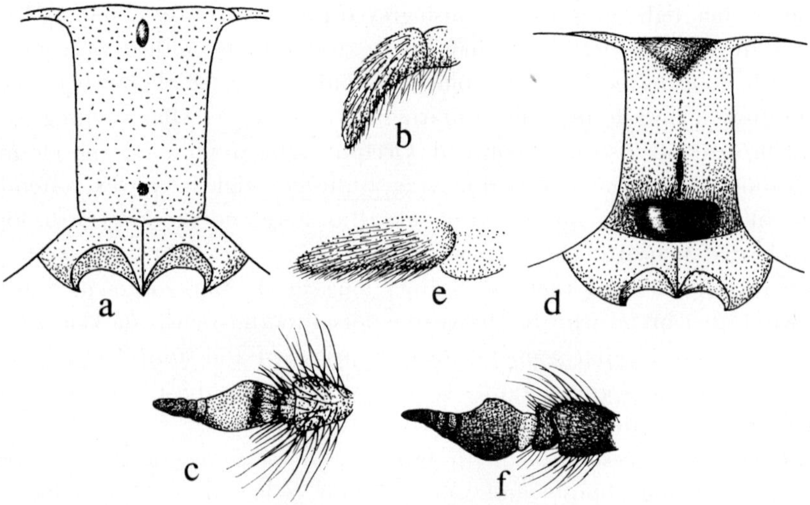

Fig. 77. a–c. *Hybomitra vittata* (F.) and d–f. *H. macularis* (F.). a and d. female frons. b and e. female palpus, c and f. female antenna.

HYBOMITRA MACULARIS (FABRICIUS, 1794)

Fig. 77d–f.

Tabanus macularis Fabricius, 1794, Ent. Syst., 4: 370.
Therioplectes trichocerus Bigot, 1892, Mém. Soc. zool. Fr., 5: 637.

Diagnosis. Similar to *vittata* (F.) in size, shape and general appearance. Frons broader below than above and with a shining blackish lower callus.

DESCRIPTION. ♀. *Head.* Eyes clothed with moderately long pale hairs, with three bands. Frons light greyish dusted, broad, index 1: 1.5, distinctly wider below than above, and clothed with moderately long pale and black hairs. Lower callus broad and low, well separated from eye-margins, colour shining dark brownish. Subcallus, face, cheeks and occiput pale greyish dusted and with exclusively pale hairs. Basal two antennal segments greyish dusted and with moderately long black and pale hairs. Third segment remarkable short, brownish at base, the rest and terminal segments being blackish. Palpi pale yellowish, apical segment hardly curved, blunt tipped, and clothed with pale hairs only.

Thorax, legs and *wings* practically as in *vittata,* but apices of fore tibiae and fore tarsi darkened. Stigma darker brownish than in *vittata.*

Abdomen also mainly coloured as in *vittata,* but the pale greyish stripes lateral to the broad median band are much less distinct than in *vittata,* especially on the posterior segments.

♂. We have not seen this sex which was described by Kröber (1938: 175).

Length. 12—13 mm.

DATES. Unknown to us.

DISTRIBUTION. The species is still known only from Morocco but because of its possible occurrence in South Spain and the general similarity to *H. vittata* (Fabr.), it is included in the present revision of European Tabanidae.

GENUS *ATYLOTUS* OSTEN-SACKEN, 1876

Mem. Boston Soc. Nat. Hist., 2: 426.

Ochrops Szilády, 1915, Ent. Mitt., 4: 93.
Baikalia Surcouf, 1921, Genera Insect., 175: 39.
Dasystypia Enderlein, 1922, Mitt. zool. Mus. Berl., 10: 347.
Surcoufiella Bequaert, 1924, Psyche, 31: 26.
Baikalomyia Stackelberg, 1926, Rev. Microbiol. & Epidémiol. Saratov, 5: 53 (nov. nom. pro *Baikalia* Surcouf, nec Martens).
Abatylotus Philip, 1948, Bull. Soc. Fouad I. Ent., 32: 292.

TYPE SPECIES: *Tabanus bicolor* Wiedemann, 1821.

DIAGNOSIS. Small to medium-sized species, usually greyish, yellowish or yellowish-brown coloured and mostly finely pubescent. Head large, semiglobular, eyes naked or pubescent, sometimes with one narrow band or with a trace of one. Males with lower area of small facets sharply separated from upper part with large facets. Eyes in living specimens yellowish, greenish to greyish, dark brown to brown in dried specimens. Ocellar swelling present only in the male sex. Frontal calli usually very small, circular and very reduced, sometimes missing. Wings hyaline, usually a long appendix to vein R_4. Abdomen greyish or yellowish haired; a pattern, if present, less distinct and consisting of darker haired patches or median stripe.

REMARKS. The genus is distributed mainly in the Holarctic and Ethiopian regions, from where the majority of species is known. 42 species and 6 forms are known from the Palaearctic region, 7 species and 1 form from the Ethiopian region. A further 2 species are recorded from Mexico, and the origin of *Atylotus parvidentatus* (Macquart, 1838) is still unclear. Altogether 60 species and 7 forms are known of the world fauna, 12 species and 1 form of which occur in Europe.

It should be noted that in the genus *Atylotus* Ost.–Sack. many changes in the taxonomic position of individual species and forms should be anticipated inasmuch as most of the species are rather variable and the range of individual variability has been insufficiently studied. It is quite obvious that the majority of the so-called »subspecies«, mostly occurring incidentally with the nominate forms in the same area of distribution, demonstrate only the range of variability of individual taxa.

So far only the larvae and pupae of five Nearctic species have been described (Teskey, 1969) and Ježek (in litt.) has collected the larva and pupa of the European *Atylotus sublunaticornis* (Zett.). Only a little is known about the biology and economic importance of *Atylotus* species, several species are still not known to be blood-sucking, the females are to be found together with males on flowers. The species of *Bembex* (Hymenoptera) have often been observed as preying on adults of *Atylotus* species.

Key to European species of *Atylotus*

Females

1 Eyes distinctly pubescent even if hairs only short 2
– Eyes naked, some minute hairs can be seen only when highly magnified 6
2 (1) Small greyish species (Pl. 3, fig. e), at most 11 mm in length 3
– Larger species (Pl. 3, fig. f), about 14 mm in length 4
3 (2) Frons (Fig. 78a) broad, index 1: 2.3–2.5; palpi (Fig. 78d) stout, about 2.5 times as long as deep. Vertex with a row of long black hairs *sublunaticornis* (Zett.)
– Frons (Fig. 79a) narrower, index 1: 3–3.3; palpi (Fig. 79d) more slender, about three times as long as deep. Vertex with only fine, short pale hairs .... *plebejus* (Fall.)
4 (2) Frontal calli polished brown, enlarged and connected. Palpi short and stout, 1.9 times as long as deep .... *venturii* Lecl.

– Frontal calli (Fig. 80a) small, usually circular and widely separated. Palpi (Fig. 80d) longer, more than three times as long as deep 5

5 (4) Vertex with very short pale hairs. Basal antennal segments with black hairs .... *latistriatus* (Br.)

– Vertex with a row of very long hairs. Basal antennal segments with whitish hairs (after Szilády, 1915) .... *agricola* (Wied.)

6 (1) Vertex with only minute pale hairs 7

– Vertex with a row of distinct, long pale hairs 11

7 (6) Yellowish to yellowish-brown species with golden-yellow to yellowish-brown pubescence 8

– Greyish species (Pl. 3, fig. f) with silvery-grey to grey pubescence 9

8 (7) Yellowish-brown to light brown coloured species; frontal calli (Fig. 81a) very small, sometimes hardly visible. Antennal segment 3 (Fig. 81b) about as long as deep .... *fulvus* (Meig.)

– Mostly golden-yellow species with rather larger, well developed frontal calli (Fig. 82a). Antennal segment 3 (Fig. 82b) at least 1.5 times as long as deep .... *loewianus* (Vill.)

9 (7) Femora entirely greyish-black, only apices yellowish. Frons (Fig. 83a) broader, index 1: 3.5–4 .... *rusticus* (L.)

– Femora yellowish to yellowish-brown, sometimes greyish at base only 10

10 (9) Fore tibiae at tip and whole of fore tarsi black. Abdomen mostly reddish-yellow with dark patches arranged into four longitudinal stripes. Frons (Fig. 84a) narrower, index about 1: 4.5 .... *quadrifarius* (Loew)

– Fore tibiae at tip and whole of fore tarsi yellowish-brown. Abdomen on tergite 2 very indistinctly yellowish at sides. Frons (Fig. 85a) broader, index about 1: 3.5 .... *pallitarsis* (Ols.)

11 (6) Femora greyish, slightly yellowish at tip. Dorsum of abdomen with a broad, black median stripe. Terminal flagellar segments (Fig. 86b) darker than antennal segment 3. Larger species on average, 11.5–16 mm in length .... *flavoguttatus* (Szil.)

– Femora yellowish, sometimes slightly greyish at base. Abdomen mostly greyish with four dark patches on each tergite, forming four longitudinal stripes. Terminal flagellar segments (Fig. 87b) concolorous with antennal segment 3. Smaller species on average, 10–13 mm in length .... *pulchellus* (Loew)

Males

1 Small species, 9.5–11 mm in length, long greyish haired. Venter of abdomen unicolorous greyish 2

– Larger, yellowish to greyish coloured species. Venter of abdomen always at least somewhat yellowish anteriorly 3

2 (1) Vertex with a row of very long black hairs .... *sublunaticornis* (Zett.)

– Vertex with fine, short pale hairs .... *plebejus* (Fall.)

3 (1) Vertex with a row of long whitish-grey hairs 4

– Vertex with only fine, short hairs 5

4 (3) Eyes short grey pubescent, vertex with a row of long greyish hairs. Dorsum of abdomen with a broad, blackish median stripe. Larger species, 13–14 mm in length .... *flavoguttatus* (Szil.)

– Eyes naked, vertex with a row of long whitish hairs. Dorsum of abdomen with four rows of darker patches. Smaller species, about 12 mm in length .... *pulchellus* (Loew)

5 (3) Dorsum of abdomen with a darker, black pubescent median stripe 6

– Dorsum of abdomen pale pubescent with some black hairs, no darker median stripe 7

6 (5) Femora blackish-grey at least on basal half. .... *latistriatus* (Br.)

– Femora yellowish-brown, dark at most at extreme base .. *quadrifarius* (Loew)

7 (5) Ochraceous-yellowish species, abdomen golden-yellow pubescent, sometimes with some additional black hairs 8

– Yellowish-grey to greyish pubescent species 9

8 (7) Head large, semiglobular, eyes short pubescent. Yellowish-brown species with greyish notopleural lobes .... *fulvus* (Meig.)

– Head smaller, eyes with long hairs. Golden-yellow species with yellowish notopleural lobes .... *loewianus* (Vill.)

9 (7) Abdomen yellowish-grey pubescent. Femora yellowish ...... *agricola* (Wied.)

– Abdomen mostly greyish pubescent. Femora grey, at most apical third yellowish .... *rusticus* (L.)

ATYLOTUS SUBLUNATICORNIS (ZETTERSTEDT, 1842)

Fig. 78.

Tabanus sublunaticornis Zetterstedt, 1842, Dipt. Scand., 1: 118.
Tabanus plebejus auct., nec Fallén, 1817.
Baikalia vaillanti Surcouf, 1921, Genera Insect., 175: 39.

Diagnosis. Small greyish species with broad frons in female and very reduced or missing frontal calli. Palpi short and stout, vertex with a row of densely placed, long black hairs in both sexes.

Description. ♀. *Head.* Eyes with fine, pale hairs and one band. Frons and subcallus grey to olive-grey dusted, former broad, index 1: 2.3–2.5, with fine black hairs, especially above, slightly widening below. Frontal calli very reduced, lower callus usually in a form of two, small black points, or both calli missing. Face and cheeks greyish with short pale hairs, cheeks with some black hairs. Vertex with a row of longer black hairs. Antennae unicolorous brownish-yellow to brownish, segment 3 sometimes darker at base; basal two segments with black hairs, segment 3 rather broad with a small dorsal tooth, terminal flagellar segments short and stout. Palpi whitish, apical segment very stout at base, apically pointed, about 2.5 times as long as deep; on the outer side with longer black and pale hairs.

Thorax black, densely grey dusted; mesonotum with short, pleura with longer, whitish-grey hairs. Mesonotum with some black hairs which are more numerous on scutellum. *Legs.* Coxae grey dusted and whitish haired, fore legs predominantly brownish-yellow, fore tibiae on apical third and whole of fore tarsi black. Posterior four femora greyish, brownish-yellow at tip to apical three-quarters. Tibiae and tarsi at base brownish, apical tarsal segments black. Legs short pale and black haired. *Wings* clear, veins blackish-brown, wing at base and in costal cell sometimes slightly yellowish. Usually no appendix to vein R_4 or only a very short one. Squamae pale with pale hairs, halteres dark brown.

Abdomen grey to olive-grey dusted, tergites mostly with pale grey hairs, basad with predominantly black hairs. Sternites only pale haired. Anterior two tergites sometimes very indistinctly brownish at sides.

♂. Eyes densely but short light brown haired, with one band. Lower third with small facets is not sharply separated from the upper two-thirds with large facets. Vertex with a row of very long black hairs. Antennae with segment 3 more slender than in the ♀, apical segment of palpi very small, shortly oval, with longer pale and black hairs. Thorax with longer whitish hairs including mesonotum and scutellum; legs and wings as in the ♀ but femora on basal third beneath with long pale hairs which are nearly twice as long as femur is deep. Abdomen with long hairs, tergites 1–2 (or 3) brownish at sides.

Length. 8–11 mm.

VARIABILITY. The frontal stripe in female is distinctly widened out below but we have seen several specimens with frons narrower above antennae and slightly widened above. The frontal calli are usually very reduced but there are several specimens with a well developed, longitudinal, shining black lower callus. There is usually no appendix to vein R_4 on wing but very exceptionally a long appendix is present.

BIOLOGY. A rather rare species, the larvae live very probably only in Sphagnum and the adults are to be found only locally near peat-bogs. The females have never been observed sucking on man or animals and are collected only on flowers together with the males.

DATES. From June until August.

DISTRIBUTION. A species with a similar area of distribution as *A. plebejus* (Fall.) but not yet recorded from the British Isles. *A. sublunaticornis* (Zett.) is known from West and North West Europe (France, Holland, Belgium, Luxemburg), from the whole of Scandinavia and from Central Europe. The southern border of its area of distribution in Europe lies in Switzerland, North Italy, Austria and North Jugoslavia. Eastwards it penetrates through Siberia to as far as the island of Sakhalin.

ATYLOTUS PLEBEJUS (FALLÉN, 1817)

Fig. 79; pl. 3: fig. e.

Tabanus plebejus Fallén, 1817, Dipt. Suec., Tabani, p. 8.
Therioplectes aethereus Bigot, 1892, Mém. Soc. zool. Fr., 5: 637.
Tabanus (Ochrops) plebejus var. *calvus* Szilády, 1915, Ent. Mitt., 4: 94.

DIAGNOSIS. A small, greyish species resembling *sublunaticornis* (Zett.) but differing in the narrower frons in female with index at least 1: 3, and in the presence of only fine pale hairs on postocular margin in both sexes.

DESCRIPTION. ♀. *Head.* Eyes with one band, fine pale haired. Frons rather narrower, index 1: 3—3.3, slightly widening towards vertex or nearly parallel-sided; greyish to grey-yellow dusted and clothed with fine pale hairs. Lower callus shining black, very small, sometimes divided into two black points; median callus usually well visible, circular to linear, shining black. Vertex with only short and fine pale hairs. Subcallus pale grey to greyish-yellow; face and cheeks densely pale pubescent and with the same dusting as subcallus. Antennae yellowish to brownish-yellow, basal two segments with sparse black hairs, segment 3 rather short and broad with only a small dorsal tooth. Palpi yellowish, thickened at base, slender and pointed on apical half, about three times as long as deep; clothed with longer pale and black hairs.

Thorax blackish-grey, greyish dusted and clothed with pale hairs becoming longer on pleura. *Legs* mostly yellowish-brown but coxae and basal quarter to one-third to all femora greyish, fore tibiae at tip and whole of fore tarsi black, posterior four tibiae at tip and apical tarsal segments on posterior two pairs darkened. Legs only short pale haired, coxae with longer whitish pile. *Wings* clear, veins brown to blackish-brown; often an appendix to vein R_4. Squamae pale with fine pale hairs, halteres brownish-yellow.

Abdomen blackish-grey, olive-grey dusted and mostly short pale haired, all tergites at middle with some additional black hairs. Anterior two tergites sometimes slightly brownish at sides.

♂. Eyes very densely brownish haired, the hairs are longer on the area with larger facets. Lower third of eyes with smaller facets is well separated from the upper two thirds but a sharp division is not present. Vertex with only small, fine pale hairs. Segment 3 of antennae more slender than in the ♀, apical segment of palpi oval, nearly twice as long as deep, and clothed with long pale and black hairs. Thorax with long pale greyish hairs, wings and legs as in the female, except for very long pale hairs on all femora beneath. The coloration of pubescence on abdomen as in the ♀ but all hairs are distinctly longer; tergite 2 brownish at sides.

Length. 9–12 mm.

VARIABILITY. The frontal calli vary both in shape and size as in *sublunaticornis* (Zett.) but generally they are large and more distinct in *plebejus* (Fall.). Abdomen is mostly greyish but in some specimens slightly brownish on anterior two tergites at sides, in the male sex the brownish side markings on tergite 2 are always distinct.

The ssp. *sibericus* described by Olsufjev (1936) from Siberia (as ssp. of *aethereus* Big.) has, according to the original description, much in common with *sublunaticornis* (Zett.) (broad frons and stouter palpi) but the fine pale hairs on vertex are as in *plebejus* (Fall.); ssp. *sibericus* (Ols.) differs also in the mostly golden-yellow pubescence on thorax and abdomen, and represents very probably a distinct species.

BIOLOGY. The larvae live in marshy places near peat-bogs (Lutta, 1965), the females have not yet been observed as blood-sucking. A rather rare species everywhere.

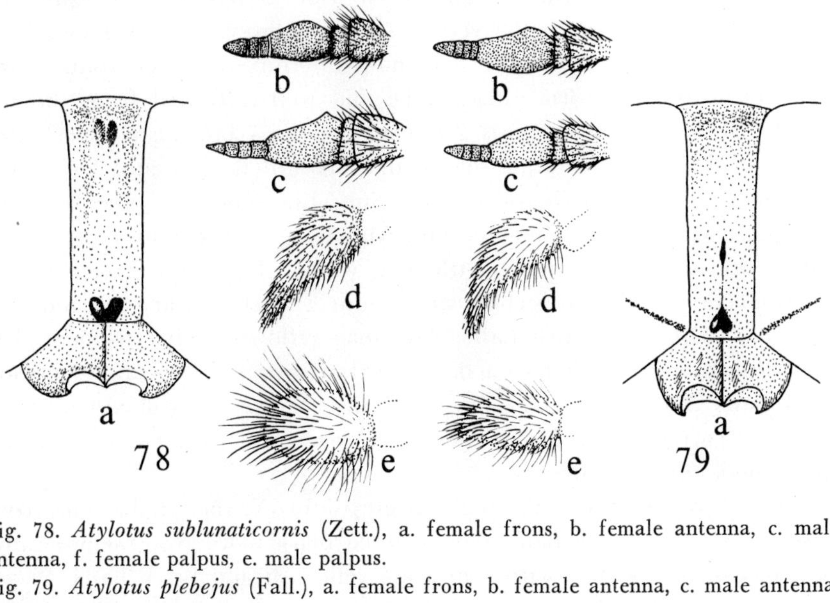

Fig. 78. *Atylotus sublunaticornis* (Zett.), a. female frons, b. female antenna, c. male antenna, f. female palpus, e. male palpus.

Fig. 79. *Atylotus plebejus* (Fall.), a. female frons, b. female antenna, c. male antenna, d. female palpus, e. male palpus.

DATES. July and August.

DISTRIBUTION. A species distributed over a large area in the northern parts of the Palaearctic region, known from the British Isles through Scandinavia to as far as the Far East of the U.S.S.R. The south border of its area of distribution in Europe lies in Germany (Bayern), Austria and Czechoslovakia. The records from Rumania need verification, perhaps the species has been mistaken there for *sublunaticornis* (Zett.). Eastwards *plebejus* (Fall.) penetrates through Siberia as far as North East China and the region of Amur.

ATYLOTUS VENTURII LECLERCQ, 1967

Atylotus venturii Leclercq, 1967, Mém. Inst. r. Sci. nat. Belg., 80 (1966): 33–34.

DIAGNOSIS. Middle sized species with hairy eyes and with frontal calli connected by a narrow line. Palpi short and stout, less than twice as long as broad.

We have not seen this species and present a translation of the original DESCRIPTION.

♀. *Head.* Frontal calli connected. Eyes with scattered and short whitish pubescence. Frons 3.7 times higher than wide at base; the margins very slightly diverging towards the vertex. Its colour greyish, with a short pale yellowish pubescence and a few black hairs intermixed. Lower frontal callus shiny brownish, of a triangular shape and well separated from the eye-margins. It continues above as a line to the shiny brownish upper callus which is as small as a point. Postocular margin narrow and with short whitish hairs; longer hairs on occiput. Subcallus yellowish tomented. Face and genae whitish-grey tomented and with long whitish pubescence. Palpi pale yellowish, basal segment with long whitish hairs, apical segment 1.9 times longer than broad, slender and pointed, thickened at base and with both blackish and whitish hairs. Antennae yellowish. First segment with short, black and pale hairs on dorsal surface. Segment 2 with some short black hairs. Third antennal segment 2.5 times longer than maximal depth, the basal part being 1.2 times longer than deep and with a slightly pronounced hook on basal quarter.

Thorax. Mesonotum and scutellum greyish-black; their pubescence composed of pale yellowish hairs and scattered black hairs. Notopleural callus pale reddish-yellow and with both pale yellowish and black hairs. Pleura whitish-grey and with concolorous long hairs. Halteres yellowish, its stem very pale. *Wings* hyaline with pale yellowish-red veins; vein R_4 without appendix. *Legs* are practically uniformly yellowish-red and have a pubescence of whitish hairs mixed with black hairs. Middle and hind tibiae slightly darkened at extreme base. Coxae brownish-red and covered with tomentum and whitish pubescence. Front tibia at distal end and front tarsus slightly darkened.

Abdomen brownish-black with greyish-yellow tomentum, tergite 2 with large yellowish-red lateral areas, posterior margin of all tergites yellowish-red. Pubescence mainly whitish and not dense; black hairs are intermixed. Venter brownish-black with greyish-yellow tomentum, yellowish-red lateral areas occur on two first sternites, anterior part of sternite 3 is also yellowish-red and so are posterior margins of all sternites. Pubescence mainly whitish and not dense, last sternite also with black hairs.

Length. 13 mm.

♂. Unknown.

DATES. July.

DISTRIBUTION. The species is known from Italy, from the single locality (Lazio: Circeo) recorded in the original description.

ATYLOTUS LATISTRIATUS (BRAUER, 1880)

Fig. 80.

Tabanus (Atylotus) latistriatus Brauer, 1880, Denkschr. Akad. Wiss., Wien, 42: 170.
Tabanus (Atylotus) nigrifacies Gobert, 1881, Mém. Soc. linn. N. Fr., 1881: 30.

DIAGNOSIS. Larger, usually over 15 mm in length, greyish pubescent species. Eyes with short but dense pale pubescence, vertex with only short pale hairs. Females with very reduced frontal calli or without them. Femora extensively brownish-yellow, abdomen with reddish-brown side markings on tergites 1 to 3. Male with mostly greyish femora.

DESCRIPTION. ♀. *Head.* Eyes short but densely pale pubescent, without stripe. Frons grey-yellow dusted, rather broad and nearly parallel-sided, index 1: 3—3.5, above and on vertex densely black pubescent. Vertex with a row of fine, very short pale hairs. Frontal calli very small, often entirely missing. Subcallus, face and cheeks yellowish-grey dusted, lower part of head with long pale yellowish hairs. Antennae yellowish-brown to orange-yellow, basal segments with short black hairs. Segment 3 rather slender with distinct dorsal tooth near base. Palpi long and pointed, thickened on basal half; clothed with short black and longer pale hairs.

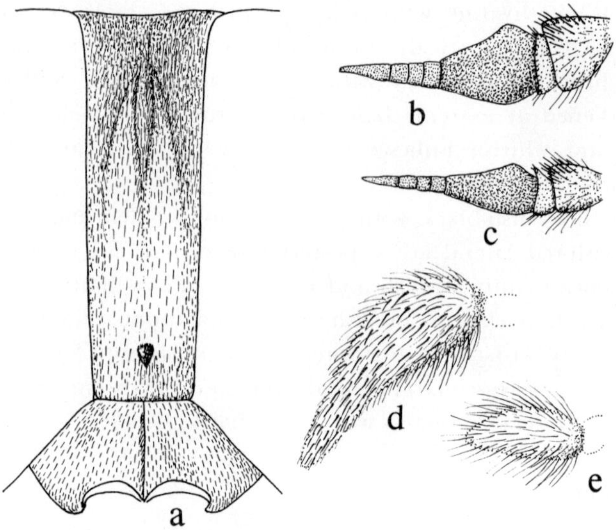

Fig. 80. *Atylotus latistriatus* (Brau.), a. female frons, b. female antenna, c. male antenna, d. female palpus, e. male palpus.

Thorax blackish-grey, mesonotum and scutellum with long yellowish and some black hairs, pleura still longer greyish haired. Notopleural lobes yellowish-brown. *Legs* mostly brownish-yellow, fore tibiae at tip and whole of fore tarsi black, apical segments to four posterior tarsi brown. All coxae and femora near base greyish. Femora with long and dense pale hairs. *Wings* clear or very slightly yellowish clouded; veins brownish, yellow along anterior margin and near base; a long appendix to vein R_4. Halteres yellowish.

Abdomen blackish-grey with dark hairs, anterior three tergites (or four) reddish-brown and mostly pale haired at sides; the dark median longitudinal stripe occupies one-quarter to one-third of the tergites, sometimes it is divided by a very narrow paler median stripe. All tergites narrowly yellowish on posterior margins, the venter is mostly brown with pale hairing, apical three to four sternites dark grey with dark hairs. Sternite 2 with a greyish, small median patch at anterior margin.

♂. Eyes short and densely yellowish-grey pubescent, the lower third with small facets is sharply separated from the upper two-thirds with large facets. Antennae as in the ♀, segment 3 more slender. Palpi yellowish-white with fine pale hairs, apical segment longly oval. Thorax with more densely set pale hairs; legs darker, especially femora greyish at least on basal half, or only tip distinctly yellowish. Wings and abdominal pattern as in the ♀.

Length. 11–18 mm.

VARIABILITY. A rather variable species especially in coloration of abdomen; the femora vary from nearly entirely yellow *(latistriatus* (Br.)) with all intermediates to darker specimens with femora greyish on more than basal half *(nigrifacies* (Gob.)), in male the femora are mostly greyish.

We have had the opportunity to examine a series of both *latistriatus* (Br.) and *nigrifacies* (Gob.) determined by older authors and deposited in the Naturhistorisches Museum, Vienna, but we did not find any specific distinctions between these two species.

DATES. June and July.

DISTRIBUTION. The species is distributed over a wide area but everywhere occurs only singly, and seems to be a rather rare species. It is widely distributed in South West and South Europe (Portugal, Spain, France, Greece, Bulgaria, Rumania), eastwards it penetrates as far as South East Russia and Central Asia, southwards to North Africa (Morocco, Algeria, Tunisia). In West Europe it has been recorded from England (Kent, Essex and Dorset), in Central Europe very rarely in Germany and Czechoslovakia (Bohemia).

ATYLOTUS AGRICOLA (WIEDEMANN, 1828)

Tabanus agricola Wiedemann, 1828, Aussereur. zweifl. Ins., 1: 556.
Tabanus (Ochrops) grisescens Szilády, 1915, Ent. Mitt., 4: 104.

We have not seen this species but present a translation of Szilády's redescription based on a study of the female type from Egypt, deposited in the Museum in Berlin.

♀. *Head.* »Eyes short and densely pubescent, reddish stripe very narrow, nearly disappearing. Posterior eye-margin with long hairs, those at middle being much longer than the eye-pubescence. Frons whitish-grey, above and below yellowish. Lower callus shining brownish-yellow, median callus shining black. Subcallus somewhat wrinkled, convex above antennae, concave on median line, yellowish-grey. Lower part of head of the same coloration and with long whitish hairs. Antennae reddish-yellow, segment 1 paler with whitish hairs. Palpi with apical segment missing, base reddish-yellow. Proboscis (mouth parts) brownish-yellow.

Thorax black, somewhat dirty grey owing to dense pollinosity and whitish hairs, slightly shining on denuded parts, lower part paler, bluish subshining, sides near wing-roots yellowish with long, dense whitish hairs. *Wings* clear with yellow veins; veins on apical half of wing, an appendix and costa, brown. Halteres orange-yellow. *Legs* orange-yellow, all coxae grey, tarsi at tips and fore tibiae at tip blackish-brown.

Abdomen orange-yellow, owing to dusting and whitish hairs whitish subshining. The darker spots on dorsum and venter brownish-grey.«

♂. Unknown to us.

Length. 14 mm.

Variability. *Ochrops grisescens* (Szilády, 1915), described from the female sex from Tripolis, represents only an individual variation, as it was already supposed by Szilády in 1915.

Dates. From June until August.

Distribution. The species is known from North Africa (Egypt, Libya and Morocco), in Egypt, according to Efflatoun (1930), its distribution seems to be limited to the South Eastern coast of the Mediterranean. It is recorded also from Turkey (Leclercq 1966b: 465) but this, as well as further records from Bulgaria and the island of Corsica (Leclercq, 1967a: 126), need to be verified. The occurrence of *agricola* (Wied.) in Europe is rather doubtful but we include it for completeness.

ATYLOTUS FULVUS (MEIGEN, 1820)

Fig. 81.

? *Tabanus ferus* Scopoli, 1763, Ent. Carniol., p. 371.
? *Tabanus rufipes* Meigen, 1820, Syst. Beschr., 2: 59.
Tabanus fulvus Meigen, 1820, Syst. Beschr., 2: 61.
Atylotus bituberculatus Bigot, 1892, Mém. Soc. zool. Fr., 5: 659.
Atylotus aurisquammatus Bigot, 1892, Mém. Soc. zool. Fr., 5: 665.
Dasystypia fulva var. *flavifemur* Enderlein, 1925, Mitt. zool. Mus. Berl., 11: 371.
? *Dasystypia tunesica* Enderlein, 1931, Sber. Ges. naturf. Freunde Berl., 1930, p. 381.
Tabanus (Ochrops) fulvus transcaucasicus Bogatčev & Samedov, 1949, Izv. AN Aserb. SSR, 5: 68.

Diagnosis. Medium-sized yellowish-brown to brownish coloured species with golden-yellow pubescence. Frons in female with only small, sometimes hardly visible, shining black calli; antennal segment 3 very broad, with small, pointed dorsal tooth near base. Head in male conspicuously large, semiglobular, eyes short pubescent.

Description. ♀. *Head.* Eyes naked, sometimes with a narrow band; frons rather narrow, index nearly 1: 4, parallel-sided, yellowish to yellow-brown dusted and clothed with short pale and black hairs. Calli very small, shining black and circular, sometimes hardly visible. Subcallus yellowish-brown, face and cheeks slightly greyish with long pale hairs. Vertex with short, fine pale hairs. Antennae yellowish-brown to reddish-brown, basal two segments with short black hairs; segment 3 conspicuously broad, about as long as deep; the rather pointed dorsal tooth placed near to base of the segment. Palpi long and pointed, clothed with short pale and black hairs.

Thorax dark brown, mesonotum mostly finely black haired, pleura with long golden-yellow hairs. *Legs* yellowish-brown, fore tibiae on apical half and whole of fore tarsi black, apical two segments on posterior four tarsi extensively blackish; all coxae and femora at base greyish. *Wings* clear, veins black, on basal half of wing and along costal margin brownish; a long appendix to vein R_4. Costal cell yellowish, halteres pale yellow.

Abdomen brownish-yellow in ground colour, clothed with black and golden-yellow hairs. Dorsum of abdomen with greyish pattern occupying nearly whole of tergite 1, median third of tergites 2 and 3, and nearly whole of following tergites. Sternites mostly greyish.

♂. Head conspicuously large, semiglobular; eyes short greyish pubescent especially on the area with large facets, which is sharply separated from the lower third with small facets. Subcallus and face yellowish coloured and greyish dusted, vertex with short pale hairs. Antennae with segment 3 more slender than in the ♀, a distinct but rather small dorsal tooth is placed near

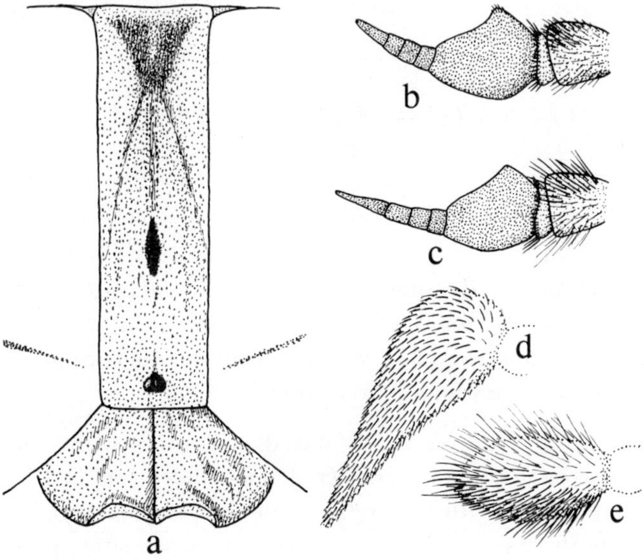

Fig. 81. *Atylotus fulvus* (Meig.), a. female frons, b. female antenna, c. male antenna, d. female palpus, e. male palpus.

base. Palpi longly oval, mostly black haired. Thorax, legs and wings as in the ♀. Notopleural lobes concolorous with mesonotum. Abdomen yellowish-brown, short pale and black haired. Anterior four tergites yellow at sides, the darker median stripe occupying one-fifth to one-quarter of the tergites.

Length. 13–16 mm.

VARIABILITY. The specimens with entirely yellow femora without any grey at base are named in the literature as a form *rufipes* (Meig.), with *flavifemur* (End.) and *transcaucasicus* Bog. & Sam. as synonyms. They have, of course, no taxonomic value.

SYNONYMY. The synonymy of this species is still quite open and urgently needs some solution, since two names *(ferus* (Scop.) and *rufipes* (Meig.)) antedate the commonly used name *fulvus* (Meig.).

BIOLOGY. The females attack man, horses, horned cattle, dogs and elks. It represents in Europe a typical forest species, but contrary to *rusticus* (L.) the adults are never common.

DATES. From June until August.

DISTRIBUTION. One of the species of the genus with a wider area of distribution, known throughout Europe, including Great Britain and all Scandinavian countries. Eastwards it penetrates to as far as Transbaikalia and the island of Sakhalin, in North Africa known only from Morocco.

ATYLOTUS LOEWIANUS (VILLENEUVE, 1920)

Fig. 82.

Ochrops (Atylotus) loewianus Villeneuve, 1920, Annls Soc. ent. Belg., 60: 65.
Tabanus (Ochrops) znojkoi Olsufjev, 1937, Fauna SSSR, 7: 212.

DIAGNOSIS. Medium sized, golden-yellow to yellowish-brown pubescent species closely related to *fulvus* (Meig.) but differing in the larger, shining black frontal calli and the more slender third antennal segment in female; head is smaller and eyes long haired in male.

DESCRIPTION. ♀. *Head*. Eyes nearly naked, sometimes with a narrow dark stripe. Frons parallel-sided and rather slender, index nearly 1: 4, yellowish tomented and clothed with pale yellow hairs, upper part of frons with some black hairs. Both frontal calli not convex but rather large, polished black, circular and nearly equal in size. Subcallus yellowish, face and cheeks slightly greyish with longer pale hairs. Vertex with only short and fine pale hairs. Antennae yellowish, basal segments with short black hairs, segment 3 rather slender with slightly developed dorsal tooth. Palpi yellow, slightly thickened at base, rather long and pointed, clothed with short pale and black hairs; basal segment with long yellowish hairs.

Thorax grey with yellowish dusting, mesonotum and scutellum mostly with short, fine black hairs, and with some yellowish hairs; pleura with long yellowish hairs. All coxae grey and pale haired, femora yellowish, greyish on basal third to half; apical half of fore tibiae and whole of fore tarsi black, tibiae and tarsi on posterior two pairs yellowish. *Wings* clear, slightly yellowish at base and in costal cell. Veins black, whole of subcosta and other veins at base of wing brownish-yellow. A long appendix to vein R_4. Halteres yellowish.

Abdomen yellowish-brown and short golden pubescent, dorsum with some black hairs. Posterior four segments somewhat greyish, tergites 2 and 3 with very narrow darker median stripe.

♂. Head rather smaller and only slightly semiglobular, eyes with rather long greyish to brown hairs. Facets on lower third of eyes and along posterior margin distinctly smaller and sharply separated from larger facets. Antennae still more slender than in the ♀, segment 3 near base with a very small but pointed dorsal tooth. Palpi yellowish, apical segment long oval and bears longer pale and black hairs. Thorax mostly greyish, notopleural lobes distinctly yellow. Abdomen more yellow in colour, usually only last two segments greyish and a narrow median stripe less distinct. Sternite 2 with a large, greyish, circular median spot.

Length. 13.5–16 mm.

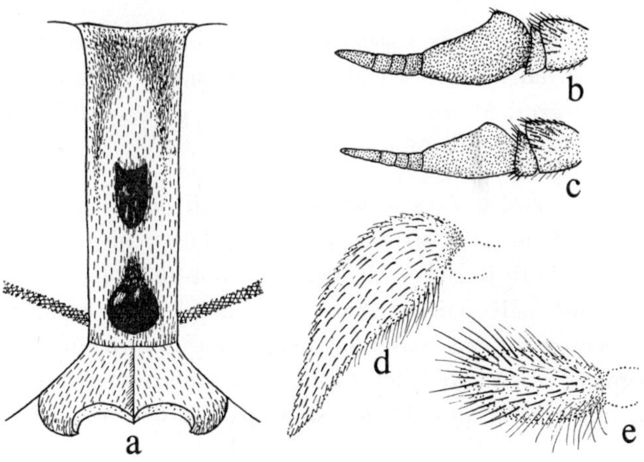

Fig. 82. *Atylotus loewianus* (Vill.), a. female frons, b. female antenna, c. male antenna, d. female palpus, e. male palpus.

VARIABILITY. Some paler specimens have femora extensively yellow, slightly greyish at extreme base only. The frontal calli are very rarely reduced in female in the same way as in *fulvus* (Meig.), the very slender antennal segment 3 then remains as the best diagnostic feature.

DATES. July and August.

DISTRIBUTION. The species is known from South Europe (Spain, France, Italy including Sicily, and Jugoslavia) and North Africa (Morocco), eastwards it penetrates to Transcaucasus but not yet recorded from Turkey. In the Eastern Mediterranean it is known from the Lebanon and Cyprus (One male in the British Museum determined by Kröber as *agricola* Wied.), in South East Europe from Bulgaria and Rumania. The north border of its area of distribution in Europe lies in Central Europe (Hungary, Czechoslovakia, Germany) and north west in Belgium. The precise area of distribution of *loewianus* (Vill.) is still not known considering that the species has often been mistaken, especially by older tabanidologists, for the common *fulvus* (Meig.).

ATYLOTUS RUSTICUS (LINNÉ, 1767)

Fig. 1e; 83; pl. 3: fig. f.

Tabanus rusticus Linné, 1767, Syst. Nat., Ed. 12, p. 100.
Tabanus ruralis Zetterstedt, 1838, Ins. Lapp., p. 517 (*ruraiis*, lapsus).
Tabanus (Ochrops) rusticus parallelifrons Szilády, 1923, Biologica hung., 1 (7): 11.

DIAGNOSIS. Medium-sized greyish coloured and pale pubescent species, vertex with short pale hairs. Frontal calli in female small, shining black. Femora mostly blackish-grey. Males with eyes distinctly pubescent, anterior three to four tergites yellowish-brown at sides.

DESCRIPTION. ♀. *Head.* Eyes nearly naked with one narrow, darker band. Subcallus and frons yellowish-grey dusted, latter narrow, parallel-sided, index 1: 3.5—4; both frontal calli small and polished black, circular. Vertex with small, fine pale hairing. Face and cheeks greyish dusted and pale haired. Antennae brown, basal segments more yellowish and short pale haired, segment 3 with well developed dorsal tooth at about middle. Palpi yellowish, rather long and slender, short pale haired and with some black hairs.

Thorax blackish-grey, densely pale haired, mesonotum and scutellum with some additional black hairs. *Legs* blackish-grey, greyish dusted, only extreme tip on femora, tibiae except tip, and metatarsi, yellowish-brown. Fore tibiae at tip and fore tarsi black, posterior tarsi darkened. Coxae and femora beneath with longer pale hairs. *Wings* clear, veins blackish-brown, brownish at base of wing; a long appendix to vein R_4. Squamae whitish and pale haired, halteres pale yellow.

Abdomen blackish-grey coloured and olive-grey dusted, entirely short pale haired. All tergites with two rather indistinct, darker longitudinal stripes of black pubescence, tergite 2 (exceptionally also tergite 1) sometimes yellowish at sides.

♂. Lower part of eyes with small facets short pale haired, upper two thirds with large facets clothed with longer brown hairs. Vertex with only small, fine pale hairs. Antennae yellowish-brown, segment 3 more slender than in the ♀ and with less developed dorsal tooth. Palpi with rather large apical segment which is oval, about twice as long as deep, yellowish, and with longer pale hairs. Thorax long pale haired, legs and wings as in the ♀. Abdomen light grey dusted and rather short pale haired, anterior three to four tergites with large yellow side markings. Anterior four sternites mostly yellowish with a narrow greyish median stripe, posterior sternites greyish.

Length. 11–16 mm.

VARIABILITY. A very variable species, the yellow side markings on anterior tergites in the female vary from large yellow spots to only an indistinct

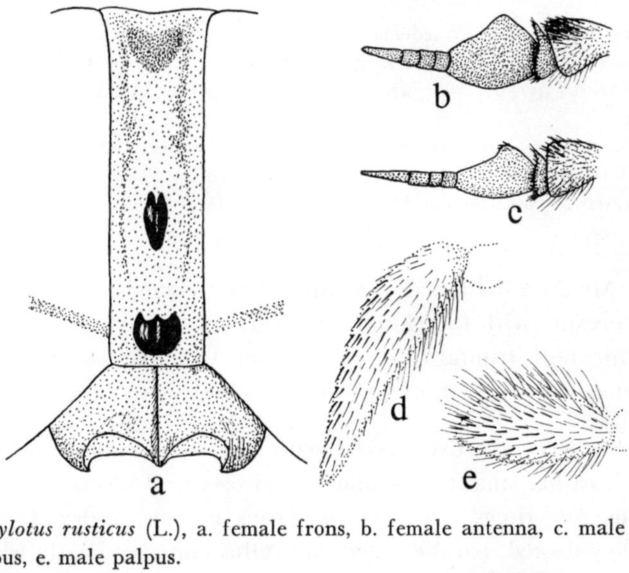

Fig. 83. *Atylotus rusticus* (L.), a. female frons, b. female antenna, c. male antenna, d. female palpus, e. male palpus.

yellowish clouding on tergite 2, or abdomen is entirely greyish; the yellow coloration in the male sex is usually very distinct. The pubescence on thorax and abdomen is silvery-grey to greyish, the specimens with distinct golden-yellow pubescence have been named by Olsufjev & Melnikova (1962) as var. *ochraceus,* which has, of course, no taxonomic value.

BIOLOGY. A widely distributed and in Europe a very common species. Females attack man, horses, horned cattle, elks and wild boars. It has been recorded as a vector of tularaemia, trypanosomiasis and anthrax under laboratory conditions. In Central Europe the species inhabits meadows, fields and banks of lakes and ponds.

DATES. From June until August.

DISTRIBUTION. A species with the largest area of distribution known from the British Isles through Scandinavia as far as Siberia. The southern border of its area of distribution runs from North Africa (Morocco) through Spain, France, Italy including Sicily to Greece and Turkey. In Europe everywhere a common species, the records from North West China need to be verified, they refer very probably to a closely related species *Atylotus miser* (Szil.).

ATYLOTUS QUADRIFARIUS (LOEW, 1874)

Fig. 84.

Atylotus agrestis auct., nec. Wiedemann, 1828.
Tabanus quadrifarius Loew, 1874, Z. ges. Naturwiss. (N. F.), 9: 414.
Tabanus (Ochrops) agrestis var. *rufipes* Szilády, 1915, Ent. Mitt., 4: 106 (nec. Meigen, 1820)–syn. n.
Tabanus (Ochrops) agrestis var. *lattesica* Strand in Kröber, 1925, Arch. Naturgesch., A 90 (1924): 14 (n. n. for *rufipes* Szil. nec Meig.)–syn. n.
Atylotus agrestis afghanistanicus Moucha & Chvála, 1959, Acta ent. Mus. Nat. Pragae, 33: 279–syn. n.

DIAGNOSIS. Medium-sized, pale greyish-yellow to greyish-brown species, abdomen on dorsum with four longitudinal stripes of dark pubescent patches. Frons narrow, both frontal calli well visible; Antennae yellowish to yellow-brown, vertex with fine, short pale hairs in both sexes.

DESCRIPTION. ♀. *Head.* Eyes naked with one narrow band or unbanded. Frontal calli rather smaller, circular but always well visible; shining black, lower callus sometimes dark brown. Frons narrow, index 1: 4–5, light greyish-yellow dusted, parallel-sided. Subcallus and face nearly whitish-grey, lower part of face with fine whitish hairs. Vertex with very short pale hairs. Antennae pale yellowish-grey, segment 3 slightly brownish, rather slender, and with only a small dorsal tooth placed at about the middle of the basal part of segment; terminal flagellar segments darker. Palpi whitish-grey, long and slender, pointed at tip; clothed with short pale and black hairs.

Thorax blackish-grey coloured and light grey dusted, clothed with sparse, short pale hairs, pleura with longer whitish hairs. Notopleural lobes yellowish-brown with fine black hairs. *Legs* pale greyish-yellow to yellowish-brown, four posterior coxae greyish dusted. Fore tibiae at tip and whole of fore tarsi brown to dark brown, apical segments on posterior four tarsi brownish. Legs with fine, short pale hairs, tibiae and tarsi with some more black hairs. *Wings* clear, veins brown, at base of wing and along anterior margin yellowish; a long appendix to vein R_4. Halteres whitish-yellow.

Abdomen yellowish-brown in ground colour, greyish dusted; dorsum with four darker longitudinal stripes; the lateral stripes, often less distinct, are formed of lateral dark pubescent patches; the inner stripes are formed by paired median triangular spots, the space between them is usually more darker haired. Sternites unicoloured greyish-yellow to yellowish-brown, pale pubescent, only last sternite with some black hairs.

♂. Head conspicuously large, semiglobular, eyes with fine pale hairs; the upper part with large facets is sharply separated from the lower part. Vertex with only short, fine pale hairs. Antennae as in the ♀, segment 3 more slender and usually paler. Apical segment of palpi long oval, whitish and pale haired. Otherwise, including the abdominal pattern, as in the ♀.

Length. 12.5—15.5 mm.

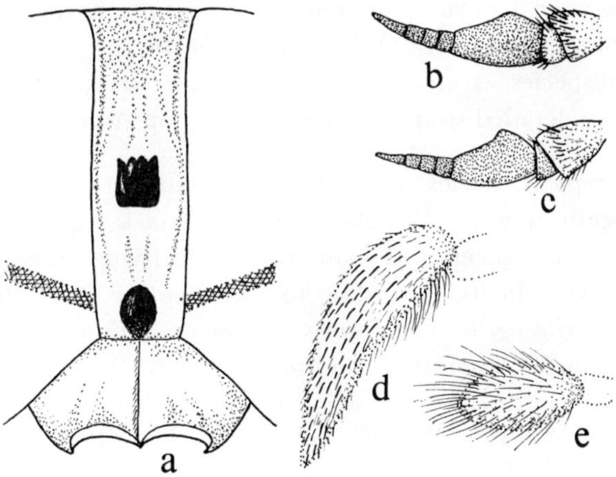

Fig. 84. *Atylotus quadrifarius* (Lw.), a. female frons, b. female antenna, c. male antenna, d. female palpus, e. male palpus.

VARIABILITY. The dark pattern on dorsum of abdomen is rather variable, the inner longitudinal stripes (consisting of paired median triangles) are more or less distinct, but the outer stripes may or may not be present.

SYNONYMY. In the Palaearctic region the species has been commonly known until recently under the name of *A. agrestis* (Wiedemann, 1828), which represented a widely distributed species in the Ethiopian and Palaearctic regions. Ovazza, Camicas & Pichon (1968) divided *A. agrestis* (Wied.) into two different species based on a study of the male terminalia. One, which keeps the original name, occupies the whole Ethiopian region and Egypt. The other is Palaearctic in distribution, known at present from Europe, Asia Minor and Central Asia. For the latter these authors proposed to elevate the subspecies *afghanistanicus* Moucha & Chvála, 1959, to specific rank. From a large number of synonyms available only three belonged to the Palaearctic species, viz. var. *rufipes* Szilády, 1915; var. *lattesica* Strand, 1925; and ssp. *afghanistanicus* Moucha & Chvála, 1959. The authors named the Palaearctic species as *Atylotus afghanistanicus* Moucha & Chvála, considering that *rufipes* Szil. (a junior homonym to *rufipes* Meig.) and *lattesica* Strand (nom.nov. for *rufipes* Szil. nec Meig.) were in fact only named conditionally, without examining type material and without any description, and therefore unavailable.

Prof. N. G. Olsufjev (in litt. 10.1. 1972) has kindly called our attention to the synonymy of *quadrifarius* Lw., the type material of which he has studied. Up to the present time *quadrifarius* was known only from the female sex originating from Asia Minor and Central Asia.

We are still convinced that ssp. *afghanistanicus* Moucha & Chvála, 1959, which is at present known from Iran and Afghanistan, inhabiting the bordering part of the whole area of distribution of the species, should represent a distinct subspecies as given in the original description. This, however, needs a further detailed study of the material from Asia.

BIOLOGY. A typical species of desert and semidesert biotopes, inhabiting especially localities near salt lakes. Females attack man, horses, horned-cattle, dogs, camels, sheep and goats, from wild living animals foxes, spermophiles and wild boars. According to Sachibzadaev (1957) females attack also lizards *Lacerta agilis*. The species has been demonstrated to be a vector of tularaemia under laboratory conditions.

DATES. From May until August.

DISTRIBUTION. The species has a wide area of distribution from the West Mediterranean (Morocco, Portugal, Spain) to as far as Asia Minor and Near and Middle East (Israel, Iraq, Iran and Afghanistan). In the U.S.S.R. it is recorded from its European part (South Ukraine, Crimea), from Central Asiatic republics (e. g. Kazakhstan, Uzbekistan, Turkmenia) and from Siberia.

ATYLOTUS PALLITARSIS (OLSUFJEV, 1936)

Fig. 85.

Tabanus (Ochrops) pallitarsis Olsufjev, 1936, Parasit. sbor. Zool. Inst. AN SSSR, 6: 236.

DIAGNOSIS. Rather smaller, mostly greyish species with naked eyes and vertex with minute pale hairs. Legs very pale yellowish-brown, fore tarsi and tip to fore tibiae only darker yellowish-brown, not darkened.

DESCRIPTION. ♀. *Head.* Eyes naked. Frons, face and cheeks whitish-grey and covered with minute pale hairs, only lower part of occiput above mouth with long pale hairs. Frons rather broader, index 1: 3.5, indistinctly widening below; lower callus shining black to blackish-brown, very small and nearly circular; median callus at most in the form of only a small, rather indistinct blackish patch, sometimes divided. Antennae whitish-yellow dusted and very pale haired on segment 1, segments 2 and 3 more orange-yellow coloured, segment 3 rather broad with distinct dorsal tooth. Palpi very pale with light and some black hairs, rather slender.

Thorax light grey dusted. Mesonotum (except anterior part) and scutellum somewhat darker and mostly short black haired; anterior part of mesonotum and pleura pale haired, latter with longer hairs above. Notopleural lobes usually yellowish. *Legs* unicoloured yellowish and pale haired, only fore tarsi and corresponding tibiae at tip more yellowish-brown and predominantly black haired. Coxae greyish, fore coxae more yellowish-grey with longer hairs. *Wings* clear with yellowish-brown veins, a long appendix to vein R_4. Squamae and halteres whitish-yellow.

Abdomen light grey dusted and pale haired, with indefinite darker median stripe which is covered by short, adpressed black hairs. All tergites are narrowly yellow at side margins, anterior two tergites somewhat yellowish at sides, the yellow patches are more distinct on corresponding sternites.

♂. Unknown.

Length. 9.5—13 mm.

BIOLOGY. A typical steppe species, rather common in steppes of West Siberia, for example it represents nearly 48 % of the tabanid population in the lakes region of Tuva. Females attack man and horses.

Dates. From June until the beginning of October.

Distribution. The species is known from the U.S.S.R. (South and West Siberia, Primoryie), Mongolia and China (Manchuria). It penetrates very probably to adjacent regions of the eastern part of the European S.S.S.R.; Olsufjev (1969a) recorded this species as a member of the European fauna of the U.S.S.R.

ATYLOTUS FLAVOGUTTATUS (SZILÁDY, 1915)

Fig. 86.

Tabanus (Ochrops) flavoguttatus Szilády, 1915, Ent. Mitt., 4: 98.
Tabanus (Ochrops) flavoguttatus var. *quadripunctatus* Szilády, 1915, Ent. Mitt., 4: 99.

Diagnosis. Medium-sized greyish species, vertex with a row of long pale grey hairs, femora mostly greyish. Frons and face whitish-grey, abdomen with a distinct, broad, darker median stripe.

Description. ♀. *Head*. Eyes nearly naked with a single, slender dark band, or unstriped. Frons whitish-grey, parallel, index about 1: 3.5. Lower callus rounded or somewhat elongated or transverse, shining black to dark brown, always distinct. Median callus smaller, circular, shining black, sometimes missing. Subcallus, face and cheeks whitish-grey, face and cheeks with long whitish hairs. Vertex with a row of long and dense pale greyish hairs.

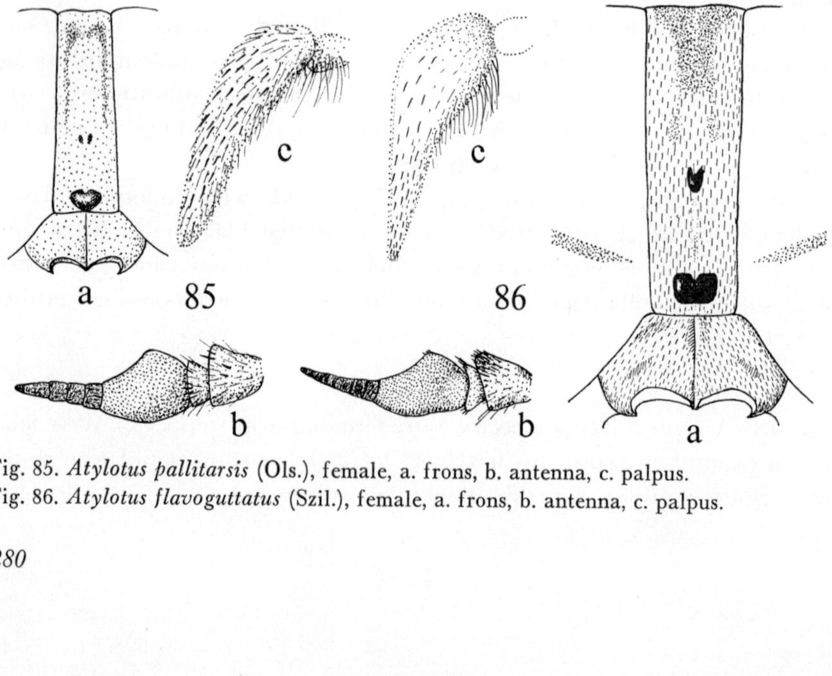

Fig. 85. *Atylotus pallitarsis* (Ols.), female, a. frons, b. antenna, c. palpus.
Fig. 86. *Atylotus flavoguttatus* (Szil.), female, a. frons, b. antenna, c. palpus.

Antennae brownish-yellow, segment 1 paler, both basal segments with short black hairs. Segment 3 rather slender with a blunt dorsal tooth, rest of flagellum usually darker. Palpi whitish, slightly thickened near base but long pointed, mostly pale haired with some black hairs.

Thorax greyish, notopleural lobes yellowish. Mesonotum and scutellum with dense, short greyish pubescence, pleura with longer whitish hairs. *Legs:* Coxae and femora light grey with longer pale hairs, only femora at tip yellowish. Fore tibiae black, somewhat yellowish near base; posterior four tibiae yellowish, brownish at tip. Tarsi black, metatarsi on posterior two pairs brownish. *Wings* clear, veins light brown, a long appendix to vein R_4.

Abdomen grey to blackish-grey, anterior two tergites yellowish at sides, tergite 3 often with a small yellow patch at side. A broad, darker median stripe of black pubescence always more or less distinct, sides of tergites with greyish pubescence. Sternites greyish, anterior two sternites with yellow side markings.

♂. Eyes with minute, sparse greyish hairs, lower third with small facets sharply separated from the upper part. Vertex with a row of long greyish hairs. Antennae slightly more slender than in the ♀, palpi whitish, long oval and whitish haired. Thorax, legs and wings as in the ♀. Abdomen on the dorsum with a distinct, blackish median stripe occupying one-third of the tergite. Tergites 1–3 (or 4) yellowish at sides. Anterior sternites yellowish-brown with greyish median stripe, posterior sternites greyish.

Length. 11.5–16 mm.

Variability. A very variable species (as is usual in this genus) both in abdominal pattern and in coloration of legs and sides of abdomen. Szilády's var. *quadripunctatus* also belongs to the range of variability of this species.

Dates. From May until July or possibly August.

Distribution. A Mediterranean species with its center of distribution lying very probably in Central Asia (Kazakhstan, Tadjikistan). In Europe it is known from the European part of the U.S.S.R., Rumania, South France (Eastern Pyrenees, mouth of the river Rhone) and from the single female, examined by Prof. Olsufjev, also from Austria (Apetlon 28.VII.1967, H. Malicky). The occurrence in Turkey, including its European part (Edirne), has been recently verified by new findings (Leclercq, 1966b: 466). Moucha & Chvála (1965) also recorded this species from North Africa (Algeria).

Lectotype designation. This species was described from a series of females deposited in the Zoological Museum, Berlin. They were collected in May and June at »Araxestal« (the Valley of Araxes-river), U.S.S.R. Through the kindness of Dr. H. Schumann we have studied two syntypic females with the same datas. A female labelled »S. Caucasus, Araksfluss, 30.V.1905, Wolowadow S.«, »Type« and »flavoguttatus m., det. Szilády« is hereby designated as lectotype, and has been labelled accordingly. This female quite corresponds with the above description. The second female was labelled as paralectotype.

ATYLOTUS PULCHELLUS (LOEW, 1858)

Fig. 87.

Tabanus pulchellus Loew, 1858, Verh. zool.-bot. Ges. Wien, 8: 597.
Tabanus cyprianus Ricardo, 1911, Rec. Indian Mus., 4: 248.

DIAGNOSIS. Rather smaller, pale greyish to greyish-yellow species, about 12 mm in length. Dorsum of abdomen with four longitudinal stripes of smaller dark patches of black pubescence. Vertex in both sexes with a row of long whitish hairs; femora yellowish, slightly darker at base.

DESCRIPTION. ♀. *Head.* Eyes naked, sometimes with a narrow band. Frons whitish-grey dusted, rather narrow, index 1: 3.5—4, parallel or indistinctly widened towards vertex. Both frontal calli small, circular, brownish or median callus sometimes black. Subcallus and face whitish dusted, latter with long whitish hairs. Vertex with a row of long whitish hairs. Antennae yellowish, basal segments paler; segment 3 rather slender with small dorsal tooth, basal part of segment 3 about twice as long as deep. Palpi whitish, slightly thickened at base and long pointed, clothed with fine white hairs.

Thorax pale greyish and densely whitish pubescent, more densely on pleura. Mesonotum, especially on posterior half, with indistinct longitudinal stripes; scutellum darker. Notopleural lobes yellowish. *Legs* pale yellowish but apical half of fore tibiae and whole of fore tarsi black, distal segments to posterior four tarsi somewhat whitish. Coxae and sometimes femora just at base greyish. *Wings* clear, veins blackish-brown, on basal part of wing and along costal margin yellowish-brown; a long appendix to vein R_4. Halteres whitish.

Abdomen light grey, anterior four tergites slightly yellowish at sides. All tergites with four triangular spots on anterior margin which are in fact small blackish pubescent areas, reaching to middle of the tergite; between the inner pair there is a darker median stripe occupying one-quarter to one-third of the tergite. Sternites mostly yellowish-grey, posterior sternites greyish, often with indistinct darker median stripe.

♂. Head large, semiglobular. Eyes naked, the area with small facets on lower third of eyes is sharply separated from the upper two-thirds with large facets. Vertex with a row of long, densely set whitish hairs. Subcallus and face whitish-grey dusted, antennae as in the ♀ but more slender. Palpi whitish, apical segment finely pale pubescent, long oval. Thorax, legs and wings as in the ♀. Abdomen yellowish-grey with darker median stripe occupying nearly one-third of the tergites, posterior 3 to 4 tergites darkened. All tergites with four darker triangular patches reaching posterior margin on each tergite.

Length. 10—13 mm.

Variability. The yellowish coloration on sides of abdomen is restricted sometimes to only tergite 1, sometimes the whole of the abdomen is yellowish at sides, including apical tergites. The antennae vary from yellowish to nearly brown.

Biology. The species is known as a vector of trypanosomiasis of camels under laboratory conditions.

Dates. From April until August.

Distribution. The center of its area of distribution lies in Transcaucasia and in the Central Asiatic republics of the U.S.S.R. from where it penetrates west to the European part of the U.S.S.R. and far south to Jordan, Iraq and Iran. In the Mediterranean region it is known from North Africa (Algeria), Egypt, Cyprus and Sardinia.

Lectotype designation. Described from material taken by Loew on the seacoast near the outrun of the river Xanthus, Turkey. We have seen a pair in rather good condition in the Zoological Museum, Berlin. They were

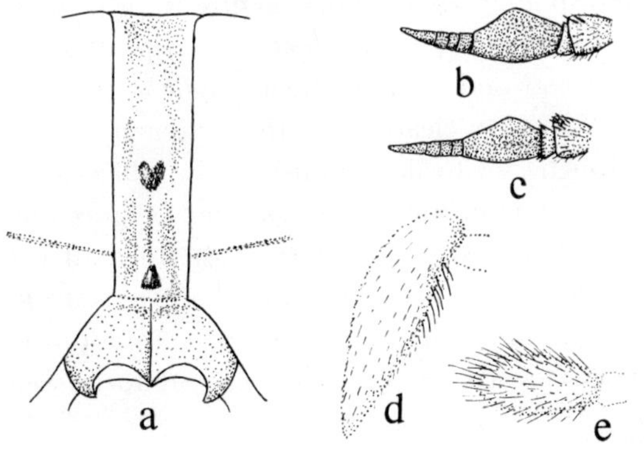

Fig. 87. *Atylotus pulchellus* (Lw.), a. female frons, b. female antenna, c. male antenna, d. female palpus, e. male palpus.

labelled »Klein-Asien, coll. Loew«, »9423«, »Coll. H. Loew« and »Type«. The male bears an additional label in Loew's handwriting »Tabanus pulchellus Lw.«. The female is hereby designated as lectotype and has been labelled accordingly. The male was labelled as paralectotype.

GENUS *THERIOPLECTES* ZELLER, 1842

Isis, 2: 819.

Brachytomus Costa, 1857, Giambatt. Giorn. Napol., 22: 445.
Sziladya Enderlein, 1923, Dt. ent. Z., 1923: 545.

TYPE SPECIES: *Therioplectes tricolor* Zeller, 1842.

DIAGNOSIS. Very large, more than 20 mm in length, densely pale and black haired species, which look very like humble-bees. Eyes unstriped, rather densely haired, all facets of the same size in the male sex. Head rather small, frons in female parallel-sided with index about 1: 2.5, ocellar swelling not developed in female and only vestigial in male. Antennae rather slender, segment 3 with only slightly developed dorsal tooth. Legs stout and densely pubescent, all tibiae distinctly thickened. Wings always more or less clouded at least in central part. Males closely resemble the females and all species and forms are distinguished mainly by the differently coloured pubescence.

REMARKS. The systematic position of this genus has been unclear for a long time, the older authors included in *Therioplectes* all recently known *Hybomitra* species or other uncertain species. This confusion has been caused by the fact that in 1842 Zeller erected a new genus *Therioplectes* with *Therioplectes tricolor* Zeller as type species; this was partly followed by Enderlein, but the latter author erected in 1925 another new genus *Sziladya* with type species *Tabanus gigas* Herbst, placing by mistake *Therioplectes tricolor* both in the genus *Therioplectes* and, as a form of *Sziladya gigas,* in the genus *Sziladya.* Olsufjev (1937) first cleared up the systematic position of *Therioplectes,* and Moucha & Chvála published in 1958—1964 several papers on the taxonomy and faunistics of the species in question. The separation of the species of this genus is rather difficult since all the species are very closely related and the best distinguishing characters are in the coloration of the pubescence on face, thorax and abdomen. In addition to their great resemblance the species are rather variable, and form well separated geographic subspecies.

Altogether 7 species with 2 subspecies and 1 form of the genus *Therioplectes* Zeller are known at present; 3 species with 2 subspecies and 1 form are known from Europe.

The geographic distribution of the genus is very interesting. The centre of distribution undoubtedly lies in the East Mediterranean and the species penetrate rather far north westwards and eastwards. The north west border lies in the Netherlands, Belgium and France *(gigas* Herbst), the east border in Central Asiatic republics of the U.S.S.R. and in Iran *(carabaghensis* Portsch.). The south border of the area of distribution lies in Israel *(tunicatus* Szil.); the genus has not yet been recorded from the Palaearctic North Africa. Nothing is known about the distribution of *griseus* (End.), known at present only from the unlabelled type pair deposited in the Zoologisches Museum, Berlin.

The larvae and pupae of *Therioplectes* species are still unknown. Females attack horses and horned cattle and cause the same injuries as the large species of the genus *Tabanus;* they do not attack man. The flight period is from spring until the early summer.

Key to European species of *Therioplectes*

1	Face with black hairs, at most with only some additional paler hairs. Tergite 2 at most with pale hairs at middle and (or) along posterior margin	2
–	Face with greyish-yellow to yellowish-brown hairs. Anterior two tergites with distinct pale hairs	5
2 (1)	Whole of the mesonotum including anterior third with yellowish-grey hairs. At most posterior two abdominal segments with indication of rust coloured pubescence	*gigas* (Herbst)
–	At least anterior third of mesonotum mostly black haired, or the pale pubescence forms a median stripe on anterior third. Posterior 3 to 4 abdominal segments densely rust coloured or yellowish-grey pubescent	3
3 (2)	Only tergite 1 whitish or yellowish-grey pubescent, tergite 2 entirely black haired	4
–	The whitish-grey pubescence also distributed on tergite 2 at middle and along posterior margin	*tricolor kirchbergi* Mch. & Chv.
4 (3)	Mesonotum on anterior two-thirds with only black hairs, apical abdominal segments rust coloured pubescent	*tricolor tricolor* Zell.
–	Anterior part of mesonotum with some additional paler hairs, apical abdominal segments yellowish-grey pubescent	*tricolor pallidicaudus* (Ols.)
5 (1)	Face with yellowish-grey hairs, the pubescence on thorax and on anterior two tergites greyish-yellow	*tunicatus* Szil.
–	Face with yellowish-brown hairs, the pubescence on thorax and on anterior two tergites reddish-yellow	*tunicatus* Szil. f. *rufescens*

THERIOPLECTES GIGAS (HERBST, 1787)

Pl. 4: fig. a

Tabanus gigas Herbst, 1787, Naturg. Tier. Ins., 8: 12.
Tabanus ignotus Rossi, 1790, Fauna Etrusca, 2: 320.
Tabanus albipes Fabricius, 1794, Ent. Syst., 4: 364.
Tabanus grossus Thunberg, 1827, Nova Acta R. Soc. Scient. upsal., 9: 57.
Brachytomus ursus Costa, 1857, Giambatt. Giorn. Napol., 2: 454.

DIAGNOSIS. Face and cheeks black haired, whole of mesonotum densely yellowish-grey to rufuous-brown pubescent. Abdomen shining black and black haired, but whole of tergite 1 and tergite 2 at middle or along posterior margin with yellowish-brown to rufuous-brown hairs; posterior 2 or 3 tergites with some reddish hairs.

DESCRIPTION. ♀. *Head.* Eyes clothed with dense, short yellowish-brown to reddish-brown hairs. Frons black in ground colour and dark brown dusted, parallel-sided, index about 1: 2–2.5. Lower callus slightly shining, black, somewhat triangular and connected above with short, linear median callus. Lower half of frons black haired, upper half and occiput with mostly brownish hairs. Subcallus distinctly convex but rather low, black with dark grey dusting. Antennae black, only segment 1 at tip and on the inner side sometimes slightly brownish, basal segments short black haired. Segment 3 with only slightly developed dorsal tooth, terminal flagellar segments rather short and thick. Face and cheeks long and densely black haired, often some pale hairs on lower part of face. Palpi brown to dark brown, on the outer side with short but densely set black hairs; apical segment rather long and stout, blunt ended.

Thorax. Whole of mesonotum densely yellowish-grey to rufuous-brown pubescent, some longer paler hairs on scutellum, on notopleural lobes and near roots of wings. Lower part of pleura with black hairs. All coxae and femora black with concolorous hairs. Fore tibiae on basal third whitish with pale hairs, apical two-thirds and fore tarsi black. Posterior four tibiae whitish with concolorous hairs, tibiae at tip and tarsi dark brown with short, black hairs. All knees yellowish, tibiae distinctly stout. *Wings* yellowish with pale veins on basal half, apical half brown clouded mesally and with dark brown veins. Sometimes a short appendix to vein R_4. Halteres pale yellowish-brown.

Abdomen black with concolorous hairs except for pale pubescent tergite 1 and central part of tergite 2, posterior 2 or 3 tergites with some reddish hairs.

♂. Eyes more densely reddish-brown pubescent, all facets equal in size.

Antennae more slender than in the female, especially on segment 3. Palpi brownish, very short, oval in shape but pointed at tip, with longer black hairs everywhere. Otherwise as in the female.

Length. 20–23 mm.

VARIABILITY. The coloration of pale hairs on abdomen varies from pale yellowish-grey to reddish-brown. Tergite 2 with pale hairs more often only at middle but sometimes also along posterior margin. Face usually with only black hairs but sometimes also some paler hairs are present. The varieties *trigonellum* and *rufula* described by Sziládу (1927) are identical with *Therioplectes tunicatus* Szil., for the synonymy see Moucha & Chvála (1964).

DATES. From May until July.

DISTRIBUTION. *T. gigas* (Herbst) is known from the Balkan Peninsula (Jugoslavia, Bulgaria, Greece) and Italy, from where it penetrates north to Central Europe. The northern border of its area of distribution lies in Hungary, Czechoslovakia (Slovakia, South Moravia) and Austria. Several records are known also from Switzerland and Germany. From Germany recorded mainly in older literature (e. g. Kittel and Kriechbaumer, 1872; Kröber, 1932b, 1938) but only three specimens are deposited in collections (Bayerische Alpen, Peterbergergasten, 24.V.1948, 1 ♂ in coll. München; Stuttgart, VI.1915, 1 ♂, leg. Gerstner; and Würtenberg, Böblinger Wald, 13.VI.1915, 1 ♀, both in coll. Stuttgart). The species penetrates north west through France to Belgium and the Netherlands. The precise southern border is still not well known since the species has been until recently misidentified with the closely related *tunicatus* Szil. and all records from Syria and Palestine (Kröber, 1938) very probably refer to this species. *T. gigas* (Herbst) has not yet been found on the territory of the U.S.S.R.

THERIOPLECTES TUNICATUS SZILÁDY, 1927

Therioplectes tunicatus Sziládу, 1927, Zool. Anz., 74: 204.
Therioplectes gigas var. *trigonellum* Sziládу, 1927, Zool. Anz., 74: 204.
Therioplectes gigas var. *rufula* Sziládу, 1927, Zool. Anz., 74: 204.
Tabanus alazanicus Hauser, 1953, Ent. Obozr., 33: 247.

DIAGNOSIS. Resembling *gigas* (Herbst) but frons, face and palpi pale pubescent, and abdominal segment 2 covered with whitish-grey dusting and pale hairs.

DESCRIPTION. ♀. *Head*. Eyes densely clothed with short yellowish-grey hairs, frons parallel-sided, index 1: 2–2.5, predominantly brown dusted and light brown pubescent. Lower callus shining black, slender, triangular shaped and connected with a linear median callus. Subcallus distinctly convex, black, with yellowish-grey dusting. Face and cheeks long yellowish-grey to yellowish-brown haired. Antennal segment 1 brownish with pale and black hairs; segment 3 black, sometimes slightly brownish at base, dorsal tooth only slightly developed. Palpi long and stout, brownish, clothed with long pale and short black hairs.

Thorax. Mesonotum, scutellum and pleura above with long, dense, yellowish-grey pubescence, lower part of pleura with long paler hairs. Coxae and femora black and greyish dusted, with long pale hairs. Tibiae whitish-yellow and densely whitish haired, fore tarsi and fore tibiae at tip black with concolorous hairs; posterior tarsi dark brown and clothed with short black and reddish hairs. *Wings* on basal half yellowish to yellowish-brown with pale veins; central part of wing with distinct dark clouding reaching along veins to base of vein R_4, veins in apical half of wing dark brown; sometimes a short appendix to vein R_4. Halteres yellowish.

Abdomen shining black, tergites and sternites of anterior two segments yellowish-grey pubescent, segment 2 on both sides more or less distinctly whitish-grey dusted along posterior margin. Posterior three segments with sparse reddish hairs.

♂. Eyes densely reddish haired, all facets of equal size. Third antennal segment more slender than in the female. Palpi very short and oval shaped, mostly black haired. Otherwise as in the female.

Length. 20–23 mm.

VARIABILITY. The intensity of whitish-grey dusting on second abdominal segment is rather variable but at least the posterior margin on both tergite and sternite is somewhat whitish-grey dusted. The specimens with distinct reddish-brown pubescence on head, thorax and anterior two abdominal tergites, were named by Szilády (1927) as form *rufescens*.

DATES. From March (Israel) until early July but mostly in May.

DISTRIBUTION. This species is distributed from South East Europe through Turkey to as far as Transcaucasus. It is known from Albania, Jugoslavia, Greece and Italy (Sicily) but the record from Hungary (Szilády, 1927) has not been verified even though we have revised all the accessible material from this country. *T. tunicatus* is recorded from the East Mediterranean from Syria and Israel but we have no records from Lebanon and Jordan where its occurrence is rather probable. The eastern border of the area of distribution lies in the Azerbaijan SSR from where is was first recorded in 1953 under the name of *T. alazanicus* (Hauser).

The form *rufescens* Szil. occurs together with the nominate form in the whole area of distribution but, on the other hand, only this form has been found on Sicily, the single male collected by Schultz is deposited in the Zoologisches Museum, Berlin. The form *rufescens* has also been collected in Jugoslavia, in the surroundings of Beograd and Niš; this apparently forms part of the northern border of the area of distribution of *T. tunicatus,* unless Szilady's Hungarian record can be verified.

THERIOPLECTES TRICOLOR TRICOLOR (ZELLER, 1842)

Tabanus tricolor Zeller, 1842, Isis, 2: 819.
Sziladya tricolor var. *ruficauda* Enderlein, 1925, Mitt. zool. Mus. Berl. 11: 368.
Sziladya tricolor var. *albifascia* Enderlein, 1925, ibid., 11: 368.

Diagnosis. Conspicuously many coloured species, mesonotum on anterior two-thirds black, laterally and on posterior third pale whitish-grey pubescent. Abdomen black haired but tergite 1 with whitish-grey hairs, and posterior three tergites very densely and conspicuously reddish pubescent.

Description. ♀. *Head.* Eyes with fine but densely set brown to reddish-brown hairs. Frons parallel-sided, index 1: 2–2.5, black, finely brownish dusted, and with brown to reddish-brown hairing. Lower callus rather plain, triangular in shape, more or less shining black, connected above with a narrow black median callus. Subcallus rather low and convex, black with brownish dusting, short black pubescent at sides. Face and cheeks black with concolorous hairs, latter sometimes with additional pale hairs. Antennae black to brown-black, basal two segments with short black hairs, segment 3 with only slightly developed dorsal tooth. Palpi black to blackish-brown with short black hairs, long and rather stout, blunt ended.

Thorax. Mesonotum black in ground colour, anterior two-thirds black haired, posterior third including scutellum and pleura with long whitish-grey hairs. *Legs.* Coxae and femora black with concolorous hairs, knees whitish. Fore tibiae on basal half whitish with pale hairs, apical half and fore tarsi black with concolorous hairs. Posterior four tibiae whitish with pale hairs, tarsi dark brown with short black and reddish hairs. *Wings* faintly greyish clouded, paler towards base. Sometimes a short appendix to vein R_4. Halteres light brown, knobs whitish.

Abdomen shining black with concolorous hairs except for a somewhat greyish dusted tergite 1 which bears whitish-grey hairs, and posterior three segments are very densely reddish pubescent. Venter except for posterior three sternites black with black hairs.

♂. Eyes with longer brownish hairs, all facets equal in size. Antennae somewhat more slender than in the female, palpi blackish-brown, short, oval in shape, and clothed with longer black hairs. Otherwise as in the female.

Length. 20–25 mm.

VARIABILITY. Some specimens vary in coloration of the pubescence on anterior part of mesonotum, where sometimes a few pale hairs may also be present, but the general black appearance of anterior two-thirds of mesonotum is always distinct. The coloration of hairs on thorax and abdomen is not the same in all specimens over the whole area of distribution of this species and, on the basis of this character, two distinct subspecies were separated in South East Europe.

DATES. From May until July.

DISTRIBUTION. Described from »Südrussland«, the centre of its area of distribution lies probably in Trans- and Ciscaucasus, from where it penetrates west to as far as South Europe (Italy including Sicily). The species is also recorded from South East Rumania from the Dobrogea region (Comarova), which represents the most northern border, and from Bulgaria and Turkey.

THERIOPLECTES TRICOLOR PALLIDICAUDUS (OLSUFJEV, 1937)

Tabanus (Therioplectes) tricolor var. *pallidicaudus* Olsufjev, 1937, Fauna SSSR, 7: 230, 397.

DIAGNOSIS. This subspecies differs from the nominate form in the yellowish-grey pubescence on tergite 1 and on posterior three abdominal segments. The anterior part of the mesonotum, which is entirely black haired in the nominate form, bears black and pale hairs in ssp. *pallidicaudus*.

DATES. From May until June.

DISTRIBUTION. The subspecies was described from the Crimea and from the northern parts of the Caucasus (Kuban, Pjatigorsk). The area of distribution of ssp. *pallidicaudus* is probably restricted to the Crimea Peninsula and to the northern slopes of the Caucasus between the coast of the Black Sea and Pjatigorsk.

THERIOPLECTES TRICOLOR KIRCHBERGI MOUCHA & CHVÁLA, 1959

Therioplectes tricolor kirchbergi Moucha & Chvála, 1959, Acta ent. Mus. Nat. Pragae, 33: 103.

Diagnosis. This subspecies differs from the nominate form in the pubescence on the abdomen, where, in addition to tergite 1, tergite 2 is also whitish-grey pubescent in the central part and along posterior margin. Anterior black part of mesonotum often with numerous additional pale hairs, forming in extremely pale specimens (especially in males) a distinct pale median stripe right up to anterior margin of mesonotum. Apical abdominal segments with reddish hairs as in the nominate form. The halteres are darker in ssp. *kirchbergi*, usually very dark brown, leaving only apices of knobs somewhat paler.

Dates. May.

Distribution. An island subspecies described from the Greek island of Samos which lies close to Turkey in the archipelago Dodecanese. We have not seen any other material from the other Greek islands but the occurrence of this subspecies there is very probable.

GENUS *TABANUS* LINNÉ, 1758

Syst. Nat., p. 601.

Bellardia Rondani, 1864, Arch. Zool. Anat. Fisiol. Genova, 3: 81 (preoccupied by Robineau-Desvoidy, 1863).
Neotabanus Lutz, 1909, Instituto Oswaldo Cruz, em Manguinos, Rio de J., p. 30.
Macrocormus Lutz, 1913, Braz.-méd., 27: 487.
Chelotabanus Lutz, 1913, Braz. méd., 27: 487.
Odontotabanus Lutz, 1918, in Lutz, Aranjo et Fonseca, Mems Inst. Oswaldo Cruz, 10: 166.
Brachypsalidia Enderlein, 1922, Mitt. zool. Mus. Berl., 10: 344.
Phyrta Enderlein, 1922, Mitt. zool. Mus. Berl., 10: 344.
Chelommia Enderlein, 1922, Mitt. zool. Mus. Berl., 10: 345.
Styporhamphis Enderlein, 1922, Mitt. zool. Mus. Berl., 10: 346.
Hybostraba Enderlein, 1923, Dt. ent. Z., 1923: 545.

Straba Enderlein, 1923, Dt. ent. Z., 1923: 545.
Gymnochela Enderlein, 1925, Mitt. zool. Mus. Berl., 11: 388.
Callotabanus Szilády, 1926, Biologica hung., 1 (7): 10.
Lophotabanus Szilády, 1926, Biologica hung., 1 (7): 25.
Bellaria Strand, 1928, Arch. Naturgesch., 92 (1926) A. 8: 48, nom. nov. for *Bellardia* Rond.
Taeniotabanus Kröber, 1931, Zool. Anz., 94: 68.
Astigmatophthalmus Kröber, 1931, Revista Ent., Rio de J., 1: 297.
Alliomma Borgmeier, 1934, Revista Ent., Rio de J., 4: 222.

TYPE SPECIES: *Tabanus bovinus* Linné, 1758.

DIAGNOSIS. Medium-sized to large, mostly black to greyish-black species, either with pale abdominal pattern of median triangles and sublateral patches, or with more or less distinct brown sidemarkings. Eyes naked or haired, unbanded or with one to four bands. Males with facets equal in size, or more or less sharply separated large facets on the upper part of eyes. Female with usually well developed and large frontal calli of specific shape and arrangement; no ocellar swelling. Frons broad to very narrow. Wings mostly clear, without pattern. Antennae with more or less distinct dorsal tooth to segment 3, four terminal flagellar segments. Basicosta pubescent.

REMARKS. The genus *Tabanus* L. is known from all over the world, and from a large number of described species, of which about 1050 species are probably valid; in addition about 30 subspecies and about 30 forms are accepted by recent authors.

The taxonomy and nomenclature of the genus is very complicated since most of the species were described in older literature as »*Tabanus*« and many of them are placed at present not only in other genera of the tribe *Tabanini,* but also in the tribe *Diachlorini,* including several European species *(Philipomyia).* The same complicated situation exists in the homonymy, some subgenera were raised up to generic rank, some genera (especially Neotropical) were synonymized with *Tabanus,* etc. Recently only the subgenus *Pseudobolbodimyia* Mackerras, 1962, with three Oriental species is generally accepted, while *Glaucops* Szilády, 1923, is considered in the present work as a distinct genus.

Altogether less than 200 species are recorded at present from the Palaearctic region – according to Olsufjev (1969b) 173 species – of which 47 species have been found in Europe. Even this number does not seem to be certain, though it will hardly increase as may be anticipated in the Oriental and Neotropical regions.

Unfortunately little is known about the immature stages of *Tabanus*-species and if the larvae or pupae have been described, this is mentioned under the respective species. The biology is also poorly known and the records available from Japan or Asia (Siberia, Kazakhstan) cannot be automatically adopted for the European fauna. In general females are bloodsucking and males are to be found on flowers, near water, or flying in forest clearings and path-ways similar to hover-flies.

The economic and epidemiological importance of at least the common species is obvious, especially in those species in which mass occurrence is often observed. Some data is summarized in the corresponding chapter in the general part.

The genus *Tabanus* L. can be subdivided into several more or less natural groups of species. The separation is based mainly on the female sex but the males will also fit into these subdivisions. However, it is much better to use another classification when determining the males, and therefore the differential key for the male sex does not quite agree with the grouping of species used in females. Altogether six different groups of species are represented in the European fauna, viz. *quatuornotatus*-group, *glaucopis*-group, *cordiger*-group, *bromius*-group, *bovinus*-group and *chrysurus*-group. The species are arranged in the following text in the corresponding groups of species.

Key to European species of *Tabanus*

Females

1 Eyes haired. Smaller to medium-sized species usually with 3 eye-bands (*quatuornotatus*-group) 2

– Eyes naked, the hairs are not visible under a magnification of 25 diameters; if microscopically haired (*brunneocallosus* Ols.), then eyes unbanded and subcallus polished brown at sides 11

2 (1) Abdomen (Pl. 3, fig. b) black with grey or silvery-grey pattern 3

– Abdomen olive-grey or brownish with paler or black pattern of concolorous hairs 6

3 (2) Subcallus (Fig. 88a) polished black; frons with 3 separated black calli, nearly equal in size. Eyes with 3 bands .... *quatuornotatus* Meig.

– Subcallus dull grey 4

4 (3) Median callus (Fig. 90a) linear, connected with a large lower callus. Antennae (Fig. 90b) black, eyes unbanded or with 1 (sometimes incomplete) band .... *rupium* Br.

– Frontal calli separated, median callus oval in shape. Eyes with 3 bands 5

5 (4) Lower callus (Fig. 89a) broad, touching the eye-margins. Frons broader, index 1: 3–4. Abdomen entirely black with greyish pattern. Antennae (Fig. 89b) black or reddish-brown on segment 3 .... *nemoralis* Meig.

– Lower callus broadly separated from the eye-margins. Frons narrower, index 1: 4–5. Abdomen with brownish sidemarkings on tergites 2 and 3. Antennae reddish-brown .... *decipiens* (Kröb.)

6 (2) Median callus (Fig. 92a) absent, lower callus brownish-yellow. Larger species about 15–17 mm in length; frons (Fig. 92a) very narrow, index 1: 5–6. Eyes with 3 bands .... *simovae* (Lecl.)

– Median callus present, always separated from lower callus. Generally smaller species. Frons broader 7

7 (6) Eyes (Fig. 93a) with 1 band. Femora reddish-brown on apical third .... *rousselii* Macq.

– Eyes with 3 bands. Femora unicolorous blackish-grey 8

8 (7) Palpi (Fig. 94d) stout, about 3 times as long as deep, pointed. Abdomen usually brown on anterior 4 tergites at sides. Lower callus polished black or blackish-brown .... *lunatus* F.

– Palpi longer and more slender, about 4 times as long as deep. Lower callus yellowish-brown 9

9 (8) Palpi (Fig. 91c) black haired. Frontal index 1: 4–5 .... *marianii* (Lecl.)

– Palpi mostly pale haired 10

10 (9) Frons (Fig. 95a) narrower, index 1: 5–5.5. Palpi (Fig. 95d) somewhat blunt ended, clothed with pale and some black hairs. Abdominal pattern consists of pale median triangles and oblong lateral patches .... *bifarius* Loew

– Frons (Fig. 96a) broader, index 1: 4. Palpi (Fig. 96c) very pointed and clothed with only pale hairs. Abdomen with black haired linear patches arranged in 4 longitudinal stripes .... *tenuicornis* (End.)

11 (1) Smaller to medium-sized species (Pl. 3, figs. c & d), only exceptionally at most 18 mm in length. Eyes with bands or unbanded 12

– Large species (Pl. 3, fig. a), about 20 mm in length, eyes unbanded 33

12 (11) Median callus in form of oval or transverse patch, quite separated from lower callus 13

– Median callus more or less linear, connected with lower callus (*bromius*-group) 25

13 (12) Subcallus dusted, if polished (*brunneocallosus* Ols.), then eyes unbanded. Frons usually broad, lower callus large, rather broader than high, touching subcallus. Eyes with bands or unbanded (see also paragraph 39) (*cordiger*-group) 14

– Subcallus polished, at least on the upper part. Frons narrower with lower callus usually higher than broad, separated from subcallus. Eyes always with 3 bands (*glaucopis*-group) 20

14 (13) Eyes without bands 15

– Eyes with 1 or more bands 18

15 (14) Frons (Fig. 104a) narrow, index 1: 5. Posterior femora yellowish-brown. Abdomen with brownish sidemarkings on anterior tergites .... *cuculus* Szil.

– Frons much broader, index at most 1: 4. All femora greyish-black. Abdomen with light grey pattern, in very pale species with black pattern 16

16 (15) Subcallus (Fig. 109a) polished brown at sides. Frons very broad, index 1: 2–2.5. Wings slightly milk-white, a long appendix to vein R_4. Light grey species .... *brunneocallosus* Ols.

– Subcallus dulled by greyish dust. Frons not so broad and wings clear, no appendix to vein R_4. Darker species 17

17 (16) Frons (Fig. 105a) rather broad, index 1: 2.5–3.3. Palpi (Fig. 105d) very stout at base, about twice as long as deep. Notopleural lobes yellowish-brown .... *cordiger* Meig.

– Frons (Fig. 106a) narrower, index 1: 3.7–4. Palpi (Fig. 106d) more slender and notopleural lobes dark grey .... *smirnovi* Ols.

18 (14) Eyes with 1 band, parafacial band distinct. Wings clear, no appendix to vein R_4 19

– Eyes (Fig. 110a) with 4 bands, no parafacial band. Wings milk-white, a long appendix to vein R_4 .... *sabuletorum* Loew

19 (18) Frons (Fig. 107a) rather broader, index 1: 2.7–3.5; median callus less developed, often indistinct .... *leleani* Aust.

– Frons (Fig. 108a) narrower, index 1: 3.5–4; median callus distinct, black .... *unifasciatus* Loew

20 (13) Larger species, 15.5–18 mm in length. Subcallus (Fig. 98a) entirely polished black or blackish-brown above antennal bows .... *glaucopis* Meig.

– Smaller species, at most 15 mm in length 21

21 (20) Subcallus entirely polished black or brown above antennal bows 22

– Subcallus more or less polished on the upper part, or with a small shiny patch in upper corner 24

22 (21) Scutellum conspicuously whitish-grey dusted, very pale in contrast to dark mesonotum. Abdomen very dark brown with yellowish-brown sidemarkings, and very large, light grey median triangles on tergites 3–5 *shannonellus* Kröb.

– Scutellum dark, concolorous with mesonotum. Median triangles smaller, equal in length on all tergites 23

23 (22) Abdomen rather brownish, sidemarkings yellowish-brown. Frons (Fig. 100a) narrow, index more than 1: 5, distinctly widened above .... *obsolescens* Pand.

– Abdomen unicolorous olive-grey dusted with paler greyish pattern. Frons (Fig. 101a) broader, index 1: 3.5–4, parallel-sided .... *caucasius* Kröb.

24 (21) Abdomen mostly blackish-grey with grey or brown sidemarkings .... *exclusus* Pand.

– Abdomen extensively reddish-brown on anterior tergites. .... *fraseri* Aust.

25 (12) Eyes unbanded 26

– Eyes with bands 31

26 (25) Frons (Fig. 111a) broad, index 1: 3. Larger species, 16–18 mm in length. Median callus elongated but rather broader, not linear .... *briani* Lecl.

– Frons not so broad, generally smaller species. Median callus distinctly linear 27

27 (26) Frons (Fig. 115a) very narrow, index 1: 5–6 28

– Frons (Fig. 113a) broader, index at most hardly 1: 5 29

28 (27) Femora dark grey. Antennae (Fig. 115b) black or reddish-brown .... *regularis* Jaenn.

– Femora reddish-yellow except tip. Antennae (Fig. 116b) very pale, reddish-yellow .... *darimonti* Lecl.

29 (27) Postocular margin on vertex with longer black and pale hairs. Frons (Fig. 113a) narrower, index 1: 4–5. Abdomen usually reddish-brown at sides and on venter, dorsum with indistinct *bromius*-like pattern, or abdomen extensively darkened .... *miki* Br.

– Postocular margin on vertex with only minute, mostly pale hairs 30

30 (29) Frons (Fig. 114a) narrower, index 1: 4.5–5. Abdomen usually more or less reddish-brown at sides and on venter (or extensively darkened); dorsum with conspicuously pale, silvery-grey pattern. Antennae (Fig. 114b) brownish at least on segment 3 at base .... *indrae* Haus.

– Frons (Fig. 112a) broader, index 1: 3.5–4. Abdomen blackish with less distinct pale pattern, antennae (Fig. 112b) black .... *armeniacus* Kröb.

31 (25) Eyes (Fig. 119a) with 3 bands. Frons very narrow, index 1: 6. Larger species, 15–18 mm in length, abdomen reddish-brown at sides .... *tergestinus* Egg.

– Eyes with 1 band. Frons broader, index 1: 4–4.5, smaller species 32

32 (31) Postocular margin on vertex narrow and only short pale haired. No black hairs alongside base of antennae. Abdomen with smaller sublateral patches and usually brownish at sides .... *bromius* L.

– Postocular margin on vertex conspicuously broad and with a row of longer pale hairs. A small patch of black hairs beside base of antennae. Abdomen blackish with rather indefinite greyish pattern, sublateral patches larger. Antennae (Fig. 118b) unicolorous brownish .... *maculicornis* Zett.

33 (11) Antennae (Fig. 134b) with prominent, hooked dorsal tooth directed forward. Antennae, palpi and legs orange-yellow, abdomen black with conspicuous golden-yellow pattern *(chrysurus*-group) .... *barbarus* Coq.

– Antennae with »tabanine«-like, rather smaller and usually rectangular dorsal tooth *(bovinus*-group) 34

34 (33) Posterior tibiae black, at most translucent brownish on the inner side 35

– Posterior tibiae brown at least on basal half 37

35 (34) Frons (Fig. 120a) narrower, index 1: 5. Palpi (Fig. 120d) black haired, tergites black. Posterior tibiae entirely black 36

– Frons (Fig. 125a) broader, index 1: 4. Palpi (Fig. 125d) clothed with pale and black hairs, tergites dark chestnut-brown. Posterior tibiae translucent brownish on the inner side .... *spodopteroides* Ols., Mch. & Chv.

36 (35) Tergites with distinct pale median triangles and narrow lateral borders on posterior margin. Antennal bows very high, occupying lower half of subcallus .... *paradoxus* Jaenn.

– Abdomen black with only very small median triangles on tergites 2–5. Antennal bows not so conspicuously high .... *subparadoxus* Ols.

37 (34) Abdomen broadly silvery-grey, pinkish to reddish-grey at sides, leaving only median stripe black; no pale median triangles .... *spectabilis* Loew

– Pale median triangles always more or less distinct. Lateral patches, if present, never fused into stripes 38

38 (37) Abdomen with 3 rows of light grey patches. Mostly blackish-grey species .. 39

– Abdomen with only a row of pale median triangles, tergites mostly brown to reddish-brown at sides 41

39 (38) Frons very broad (index 1: 2.5) with large brown calli broadly separated as in the *cordiger*-group. Subcallus polished brown at sides and abdomen laterally compressed towards tip .... *martinii* Kröb.

– Frons narrower (index at least 1: 4) with median callus linear and connected with lower callus as is usual in this group of species. Subcallus dusted and abdomen broad 40

40 (39) Abdominal pattern whitish and very conspicuous, lateral patches situated on posterior margin of each tergite. Palpi (Fig. 123d) black haired, notopleural lobes blackish .... *rectus* Loew

– Abdominal pattern greyish, sublateral oval patches not reaching posterior margins of tergites. Palpi (Fig. 124d) mostly pale haired, notopleural lobes yellowish-brown .... *autumnalis* L.

41 (38) Palpi grey to brown, densely clothed by short black or greyish hairs. Antennae black or blackish-brown with black terminal flagellar segments 42

– Palpi whitish-yellow to yellowish-brown, clothed with pale or black hairs. At least basal antennal segments brown to yellowish-brown, only rarely antennae black 44

42 (41) Femora black and greyish dusted. Venter of abdomen with distinct and sharply separated dark brown to reddish-brown median stripe, sides thinly silvery dusted. Pale median triangles very distinct with straight sides 43

– Posterior femora usually more or less dark brown. Venter with indistinct median stripe or entirely unicolorous brown. Pale median triangles less distinct, sides concave .... *prometheus* Szil. (= *capito* Ols.)

43 (42) Sternites pale haired at sides. Median triangles on tergites 2 and 3 occupy at least lower half of tergite .... *spodopterus spodopterus* Meig.

– Sternites mostly black haired at sides, only posterior margins with pale hairs. Median triangles on tergites 2 and 3 occupy at most lower third of tergite .... *spodopterus ibericus* Ols., Mch. & Chv.

44 (41) Lower frontal callus (Figs. 130a, 131a) more or less triangular, broadest at base. Venter of abdomen brownish on anterior half with blackish-brown median stripe, or posterior margins to all sternites whitish 45

– Lower callus (Figs. 132a, 133a) longly oval, broadest at middle. Venter of abdomen mostly reddish-yellow or light brown. Median stripe, if present, reddish or brownish 46

45 (44) Venter blackish-brown with broad whitish posterior margins to all sternites. Median triangles with more or less straight sides, not reaching foregoing tergites .... *sudeticus* Zell.

– Venter brownish to yellowish-brown, with distinct dark brown median stripe. Median triangles with rather concave sides, usually touching foregoing tergites .... *bovinus* L.

46 (44) Antennae with segment 3 reddish-brown, terminal flagellar segments darkened .... *tinctus* Walk. (= *mixtus* Szil.)

– Antennae with segment 3 entirely black, at most slightly brownish at extreme base 47

47 (46) Abdomen reddish-brown at sides. Median triangle on tergite 2 more or less equilateral. Mesonotum light bluish-grey dusted .... *spodopterus ponticus* Ols., Mch. & Chv.

– Abdomen more reddish-yellow at sides. Median triangle on tergite 2 elongated, base the shortest. Mesonotum brownish dusted .... *eggeri* Schin.

Males.

1 Eyes distinctly haired (*quatuornotatus*-group) 2

– Eyes naked or with minute hairs visible only under a magnification of 20 diameters 10

2 (1) Subcallus polished black at least on the upper half .... *quatuornotatus* Meig.

– Subcallus dulled by greyish dust 3

3 (2) Eyes unbanded or with one (often incomplete) band 4

– Eyes with 2 bands. Posterior tibiae brownish 5

4 (3) Posterior tibiae extensively blackish. Femora blackish-grey .... *rupium* Br.

– Posterior tibiae yellowish-brown; posterior femora yellowish-brown at least at tip, usually dorsally on the whole length .... *rousselii* Macq.

5 (3) Antennae (Fig. 89c) black, segment 3 sometimes brownish at base. Palpi (Fig. 89e) long and pointed. Eyes with long, light brown hairs. Facets on the upper 2/3 only slightly larger, vertex with long black hairs .... *nemoralis* Meig.

– Antennae reddish-brown to orange-yellow, terminal flagellar segments usually darkened 6

6 (5) Upper area with larger facets only slightly differentiated from the lower area with smaller facets; upper facets about twice as large as lower facets 7

– Upper area with large facets sharply separated from the lower area with small facets; upper facets usually more than 4 times as large as lower facets 8

7 (6) Palpi (Fig. 94e) broadly oval, about twice as long as deep, blunt ended. Eyes clothed with densely set, longer whitish hairs. Vertex with longer black hairs .... *lunatus* F.

– Palpi (Fig. 97b) slightly longer and pointed at tip. Eyes clothed with shorter and less densely set whitish hairs. Vertex with fine black hairs *holtzianus* End.

8 (6) Palpi rather short, ovoid and mostly black haired. Vertex with long black and white hairs. Abdomen blackish-grey with 3 rows of whitish patches, the lateral ones on tergites 2 and 3 large and reddish .... *marianii* (Lecl.)

– Palpi longer, about 3 times as long as deep, mostly pale haired. Abdomen olive-grey dusted 9

9 (8) Palpi (Fig. 95e) longly oval, slightly pointed at tip. Eyes with sparse, minute pale hairs. Abdomen brownish on tergites 2 and 3 at sides, dorsum with pale pattern of median triangles and sublateral patches. Vertex with longer dark hairs .... *bifarius* Loew

– Palpi (Fig. 96d) more slender and very pointed at tip. Eyes with short but densely set pale hairs. Abdomen with 4 rows of black haired patches. Vertex with longer pale hairs .... *tenuicornis* (End.)

10 (1) Smaller to medium-sized species; if larger species up to 18 mm in length, then eyes with bands 11

– Large species about 20 mm in length, eyes always without bands 25

11 (10) Facets on the upper 2/3 or 3/4 of eyes distinctly enlarged and sharply separated from the lower area with small facets. Head large or small 12

– Facets nearly equal in size, sharp division between larger and smaller facets absent. Head always smaller 23

12 (11) Subcallus more or less polished, at least in upper corner. Eyes with 2 bands (*glaucopis*-group) 13

– Subcallus entirely dulled by greyish dust. Eyes with bands or unbanded (*cordiger*- and *bromius*-groups) 16

13 (12) Large species, more than 15 mm in length. Subcallus entirely polished black or dark brown .... *glaucopis* Meig.

– Smaller species, less than 14 mm in length 14

14 (13) Subcallus at most only slightly polished at tip. Vertex with longer, mostly pale hairs .... *exclusus* Pand.

– Subcallus entirely polished black or brown 15

15 (14) Scutellum conspicuously whitish-grey, tergites 3 and 4 with large, pale median triangles. Vertex with long dark hairs .... *shannonellus* Kröb.

– Scutellum dark, concolorous with mesonotum. All median triangles less distinct and nearly equal in size. Vertex with short pale hairs ..... *obsolescens* Pand.

16 (12) Vertex with a row of longer hairs on postocular margin 17

– Vertex with only minute hairs on postocular margin 21

17 (16) Wings milk-white, a long appendix to vein R_4. Eyes with 3 bands .... *sabuletorum* Loew

– Wings clear, no appendix to vein R_4 or only a trace of it. Eyes unbanded or at most with 1 band 18

18 (17) Eyes unbanded; a distinct dark parafacial band. Head very large, semiglobular. Palpi (Fig. 105e) very stout, nearly globular .... *cordiger* Meig.

– Eyes with 1 band 19

19 (18) A distinct dark parafacial band. Head very large, semiglobular. Palpi (Fig. 107e) very stout, nearly globular .... *leleani* Aust.

– No parafacial band on each side of antennae. Palpi (Fig. 113e) oval, rather slender 20

20 (19) Head rather smaller, not broader than thorax. Vertex with black and pale hairs, palpi (Fig. 113e) mostly dark haired. Rather brownish species *miki* Br.

– Head very large, distinctly broader than thorax. Vertex with pale hairs, palpi (Fig. 118e) mostly pale haired. Extensively blackish-grey species .... *maculicornis* Zett.

21 (16) Head very large, much broader than thorax. Vertex with minute pale hairs, palpi mostly pale haired. Eyes with 1 band .... *regularis* Jaenn.

– Head smaller, at most slightly broader than thorax. Vertex with minute dark hairs, palpi with pale and black hairs 22

22 (21) Eyes with 1 band. Abdominal pattern greyish, rather indefinite, anterior side-markings brown .... *bromius* L.

– Eyes unbanded. Abdominal pattern whitish-grey, very distinct; sublateral patches reddish-brown .... *indrae* Haus.

23 (11) Vertex with long, mostly black hairs; a distinct dark parafacial band on each side of antennae. Palpi (Fig. 108e) short and very stout. Rather smaller, greyish-black species 24

– Vertex with short pale hairs, no parafacial band. Palpi (Fig. 119e) oval, not very stout. Larger brownish species, 15–18 mm in length. Eyes with 2 bands .. .. *tergestinus* Egg.

24 (23) Eyes unbanded. Legs extensively darkened, posterior tibiae brownish at base only. Small species, 11–14 mm in length .... *smirnovi* Ols.

– Eyes with 1 band, posterior tibiae brown. Generally larger species, 14–16 mm in length .... *unifasciatus* Loew

25 (10) Antennae (Fig. 134c) with prominent, hooked dorsal tooth directed forward. Antennae, palpi and legs orange-yellow. Abdomen black with conspicuous golden-yellow pattern. Eyes with facets nearly equal in size *(chrysurus*-group) .... *barbarus* Coq.

– Antennae with »tabanine«-like, rather small and at most rectangular dorsal tooth *(bovinus*-group) 26

26 (25) Facets on the upper 2/3 or 3/4 of eyes distinctly larger than on the lower area (at least 3 to 4 times) 27

– All facets nearly equal in size, those on the upper area at most twice as large as facets on the lower area 35

27 (26) Posterior tibiae black, at most slightly translucent brownish on the inner side 28

– Posterior tibiae brown at least on basal half 29

28 (27) Antennal bows very high, occupying lower half of subcallus. Abdomen mostly black, tergite 2 slightly brownish at sides. Tibiae entirely black .... *paradoxus* Jaenn.

– Antennal bows narrow. Abdomen mostly brown on anterior four tergites, leaving only a narrow black median stripe. Posterior tibiae translucent brownish on the inner side .... *spodopteroides* Ols., Mch. & Chv.

29 (27) Abdomen broadly silvery-grey to reddish-grey at sides, only a median stripe black; no pale median triangles .... *spectabilis* Loew

– Pale median triangles always more or less distinct. Lateral patches, if present, never fused into stripes 30

30 (29) Abdomen with 3 rows of light grey patches, sublateral patches distinct 31

– Abdomen with only a row of pale median triangles, no sublateral patches. Abdomen usually brown at sides 32

31 (30) Blackish species; abdomen with conspicuous whitish pattern, lateral patches situated on posterior margin of each tergite. Notopleural lobes blackish .... *rectus* Loew

– Abdomen brownish at sides; pattern greyish, sublateral oval patches not reaching posterior margins of tergites. Notopleural lobes yellowish-brown .... *autumnalis* L.

32 (30) The area with large facets sharply separated from small facets, large facets 5 to 6 times as large as the small ones. Abdomen at sides chestnut-brown ... 33

– The area with large facets indistinctly separated from small facets, large facets about 3 to 4 times as large as the small ones. Sides of abdomen reddish-brown to reddish-yellow 34

33 (32) Venter of abdomen blackish-brown with more or less distinct yellowish to whitish posterior margins to all sternites. Posterior femora black .... *sudeticus* Zell.

– Venter of abdomen uniformly brown, without paler posterior margins. Posterior femora more or less brownish .... *prometheus* Szil.

34 (32) Antennal segment 3 (Fig. 133c) black, sometimes brownish at base. Tergites reddish-yellow at sides .... *eggeri* Schin.

– Antennal segment 3 (Fig. 132c) reddish-brown, terminal flagellar segments darkened. Tergites reddish-brown at sides .... *tinctus* Walk.

35 (26) Abdomen yellowish-brown at sides. Pale median triangles rather slender with more or less concave sides. Venter brownish to yellowish-brown, median stripe dark brown .... *bovinus* L.

– Abdomen reddish-brown at sides. Pale median triangles broader, rather equilateral, with straight sides. Venter reddish-brown and densely silvery-grey dusted at sides, median stripe reddish to yellowish-brown 36

36 (35) Palpi yellowish-brown to greyish, clothed with long black hairs. Median stripe on venter of abdomen reddish-brown and densely black haired .... *spodopterus spodopterus* Meig.

– Palpi whitish-yellow with pale and black hairs. Venter with an indefinite yellowish-brown median stripe, which is pale haired at least on anterior sternites .... *spodopterus ponticus* Ols., Mch. & Chv.

QUATUORNOTATUS-GROUP

Medium-sized species with hairy eyes in both sexes. Frons rather narrower with broadly separated calli (except *rupium* Br.). Lower callus narrowly separated from both subcallus and the eye-margins, median callus mostly oval, higher than broad. Eyes with 3 bands in female and 2 bands in male (except *rupium* Br. and *rousselii* Macq.).

This group is closely related to the *glaucopis*-group but regarding the hairy eyes, the *quatuornotatus*-group should be separated subgenerically from the other *Tabanus*-species.

TABANUS QUATUORNOTATUS MEIGEN, 1820

Fig. 88; pl. 3: fig. b.

Tabanus quatuornotatus Meigen, 1820, Syst. Beschr., 2: 51.
Atylotus quatuornotatus var. *cherbottae* Muschamp, 1939, Entomologist's Rec. J. Var., 51: 54.

Diagnosis. Medium-sized blackish species with eyes densely pale haired, with 3 bands in female and 2 bands in male. Frons in female with three, rather dull black calli, subcallus polished black in both sexes. Antennae extensively darkened, abdomen somewhat shining black with greyish pattern. Male with facets nearly equal in size, vertex with a row of long black hairs.

Description. ♀. *Head.* Eyes densely clothed with longer pale hairs, and with three bands. Frons yellowish-grey dusted, rather broader, index 1: 3—4, nearly parallel-sided. Lower callus square in shape, rather dull black and longitudinally wrinkled, broadly separated from subcallus and rather narrowly from the eye-margins. Median callus as dulled and wrinkled as lower callus, somewhat higher, broadly separated from lower callus. Frons towards vertex with another, rather oval black patch simulating ocellar swelling. Postocular margin on vertex light grey, not very narrow, and clothed with longer black hairs. Subcallus polished black, antennal bows yellowish, very high, occupying lower half of the subcallus. Face and cheeks whitish-grey dusted and whitish haired; a distinct, nearly blackish, parafacial band on each side of antennae. Antennae black or segment 3 brownish except terminal flagellar segments. Basal segments more or less thinly greyish dusted and finely black haired; segment 3 not very broad, with a distinct but small dorsal tooth at very base. Palpi light grey, rather stout basally, apically pointed, and clothed with short pale and black hairs.

Thorax. Mesonotum blackish-grey dusted with indefinite paler longitudinal stripes, clothed with short whitish-yellow adpressed pubescence and with longer, fine blackish hairs. Notopleural lobes dark grey. Pleura light grey dusted and densely, long whitish haired. *Legs.* Coxae concolorous with pleura and with the same hairing; femora grey, covered with long, fine pale hairs beneath. Fore tibiae on apical half and whole of fore tarsi black; the rest of fore tibiae and posterior four tibiae brown to dark brown, tarsi extensively darkened or entirely black. *Wings* clear with very dark veins and distinct brown stigma, sometimes a short appendix to vein R_4. Halteres blackish-brown with brownish base to stem.

Abdomen rather shining black and black haired when viewed from above, the light grey pattern with concolorous hairing consists of a row of large sublateral patches, of narrow margins on each tergite posteriorly, and of a row of high median triangles which are very indistinct on posterior tergites. Abdomen rather densely greyish dusted when viewed from behind. Venter uniformly light grey dusted and pale haired, last sternite darkened and long black haired. A darker median stripe rather inconspicuous.

♂. Head not very large, about as deep as thorax at middle. Eyes densely clothed with longer pale hairs, all facets nearly equal in size, no distinct division present. Lower part with somewhat smaller facets bears two bands. Vertex with a row of long black hairs. Cheeks with predominantly greyish hairs, antennae more slender on segment 3, with indistinct dorsal tooth, basal segments with longer black hairs above. Apical segment of palpi yellowish, shortly oval (about 1.5 times as long as deep) and blunt ended, covered with longer, mostly dark hairs. Thorax longer haired, pteropleuron with predominantly dark grey hairs. Legs usually darker, abdomen with

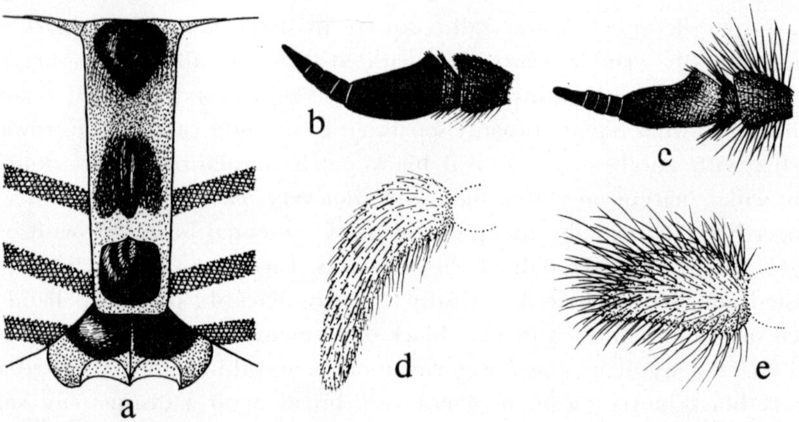

Fig. 88. *Tabanus quatuornotatus* Meig., a. female frons, b. female antenna, c. male antenna, d. female palpus, d. male palpus.

smaller pale sublateral patches, the black pubescence is longer, and tergite 2 slightly brown at sides.

Length. 12.5–15 mm.

VARIABILITY. Rather a variable species in coloration of antennae and legs, antennal segment 3 varies from reddish-brown (except terminal flagellar segments) to entirely black, and legs are sometimes extensively blackish, leaving only hind tibia dark brown. The variety *cherbottae* Muschamp described from France (Haute-Savoie) comes well within the range of variability and it cannot be accepted as a distinct subspecies as did Leclercq (1967a: 165).

BIOLOGY. A typical spring species, in Central Europe usually the first species which is on the wing. Females attack horses and horned cattle but sometimes also man. Males are to be found in forest clearings and on roads and on forest paths.

DATES. From the end of April until the beginning of August, mainly in May and June.

DISTRIBUTION. Central and South Europe, occurring from Spain and France through Italy and the Balkan Peninsula to Turkey and Iran, and through Rumania and Ukraine to the Caucasus, Armenia and Azerbaijan. From Spain it penetrates to North Africa, Morocco. It seems to be a commoner Species in Central Europe (Switzerland, Austria, Hungary, Czechoslovakia), the north border of its area of distribution in Europe lies in Belgium, Germany, Poland and Ukraine.

TABANUS NEMORALIS MEIGEN, 1820

Fig. 89.

Tabanus nemoralis Meigen, 1820, Syst. Beschr., 2: 50.
Tabanus barbarus Thunberg, 1827, Nova Acta R. Soc. Scient. upsal., 9:60 (nec Coquebert, 1804).
Therioplectes Batnensis Bigot, 1892, Mém. Soc. zool. Fr., 5: 639.
Therioplectes calopsis Bigot, 1892, Mém. Soc. zool. Fr., 5: 639.
Tabanus nemoralis var. *ruficornis* Surcouf, 1920, Bull. Soc. ent. Fr., 19: 268.
Therioplectes algericus Enderlein, 1931, Sber. Ges. naturf. Freunde Berl., 1930: 378.

DIAGNOSIS. Rather smaller, mostly shining black species with three rows of greyish patches on abdomen; resembling *T. quatuornotatus* Meig. but subcallus is dulled by greyish dust. Eyes haired with 3 bands in female, frontal calli separated, and lower callus very large, black. Palpi slender in both sexes. Male with 2 eye-bands and very slightly differentiated facets, vertex with a row of very long black hairs.

Description. ♀. *Head.* Eyes short but densely pale haired, with three bands. Frons pale greyish dusted, rather broader, index 1: 3–4, nearly parallel-sided. Lower callus shining black, large and nearly square in shape, narrowly separated from subcallus and usually touching the eye-margins. Median callus large and very broad, rather dull black; larger than, and broadly separated from, the lower callus. Frons at vertex with another broad blackish patch. Postocular margin on vertex broader than usual, whitish-grey, and clothed with longer pale or greyish hairs. Subcallus greyish dusted, face and cheeks whitish-grey with long whitish hairs below, a distinct blackish parafacial band on each side of antennae. Antennae entirely black, or segment 3 extensively reddish-brown with all intermediates to entirely black. Basal segments with fine black hairs; segment 3 rather slender, with only slightly developed dorsal tooth near base. Palpi yellowish-grey, apical segment rather long and slender, about 4 times as long as deep and only indistinctly thickened at base, predominantly black haired.

Thorax mostly blackish, mesonotum with distinct, paler longitudinal stripes and scattered pale hairing. Pleura paler grey dusted with denser pale hairing, notopleural lobes always blackish. *Legs* greyish on coxae and femora, finely pale haired. Tibiae brownish with predominantly black hairs towards tip, fore tibiae on apical half and fore tarsi black, posterior four tibiae at tip and posterior tarsi extensively darkened. *Wings* clear with blackish-brown veins, and distinct brown stigma before apex of subcosta. Exceptionally a very short appendix to vein R_4. Halteres very dark brown, knobs paler at tip.

Abdomen rather shining black, clothed with densely set, short, adpressed black hairs; greyish pattern rather distinct, consisting of a row of slender median triangles which are broader on anterior tergites; of large, oval and distinctly oblique sublateral patches; and of narrow pale borders on posterior margins. Venter uniformly light grey dusted and short pale haired, posterior two sternites darker and black haired. A darker median stripe very indistinct.

♂. Head broad, distinctly broader than thorax, but not very deep when viewed from above. Eyes clothed by rather longer, dense pale pubescence; facets on the upper three-quarters slightly larger, about twice as large as smaller facets on lower quarter, no distinct division between large and small facets. Vertex with a row of very long blackish hairs. Antennae more slender on segment 3 with a small dorsal tooth, basal segments with long, fine black hairs especially above. Face and cheeks more greyish, latter with predominantly blackish hairs. Apical segment of palpi yellowish-brown, long and slender, about 3 times as long as deep, mostly dark haired. Thorax including mesonotum and femora beneath with very long pale hairs. Abdomen with the same pattern as in the ♀ but tergite 2 (and sometimes also 3) largely yellowish-brown at sides.

Length. 10—14 mm.

VARIABILITY. Surcouf described a variety *ruficornis* which is rather common in southern parts of the area of distribution, differing from the nominate form in the more or less reddish-brown antennae on segment 3 and in the somewhat blackish-brown lower frontal callus. Leclercq (1967a: 161) raised this paler form by mistake to a subspecific rank; firstly all intermediate forms are present, and secondly, var. *ruficornis* occurs inside the area of distribution of *nemoralis* Meig., representing in this way a sympatric distribution with the nominate form.

DATES. From May until August.

DISTRIBUTION. A Mediterranean species, known especially from South West Europe (Portugal, France, Spain, Italy including the islands of Corsica and Sicily, and Jugoslavia) and North Africa (Morocco, Algeria, Tunisia, and Libya). Eastwards it is recorded from Israel. The north border of the area of distribution in Europe lies in North Jugoslavia, Italy and Switzerland; the record from Luxemburg needs verification and the recorded occurrence in Czechoslovakia (Bohemia) has been disproved (Chvála, 1964: 374).

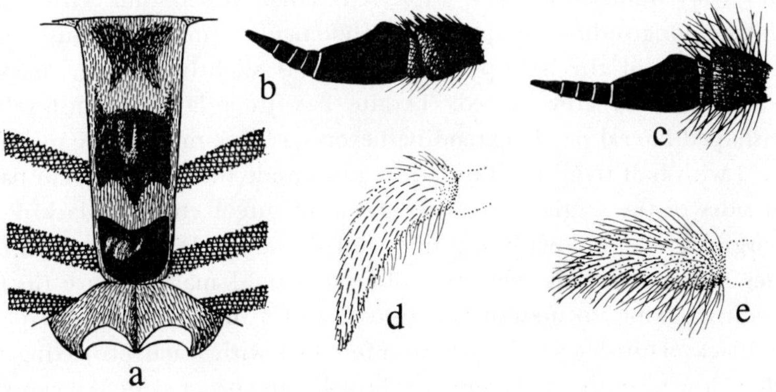

Fig. 89. *Tabanus nemoralis* Meig., a. female frons, b. female antenna, c. male antenna, d. female palpus, e. male palpus.

TABANUS DECIPIENS (KRÖBER, 1928)

Atylotus decipiens Kröber, 1928, Zool. Anz., 76: 265.

DIAGNOSIS. A species very closely related to *nemoralis* Meig. differing in the narrower frons, in the entirely reddish-yellow antennae, smaller lower frontal callus, and the abdomen being distinctly brownish on tergites 2 and 3.

REMARKS. We have not seen this species, recorded recently by Leclercq (1967c) from Turkey, but it may be a very pale form of *nemoralis* Meig., even more reddish-brown coloured than var. *ruficornis* Surc. We have seen several specimens of var. *ruficornis* with somewhat narrower frons than in the nominate form, but we have never seen specimens of *nemoralis* with antennae also reddish on basal segments or with abdomen brownish on anterior tergites. We are, of course, not entitled to synonymize this species with *nemoralis* Meig. and we therefore present a translation of the modified original description published by Kröber (1938: 214). Kröber (1928: 265) compared this species with *nemorius* Meig. (which is a lapsus) and in the later modified description changed also some details.

DESCRIPTION. ♀. Resembling *nemoralis* Meig. but eyes with 3 very fine purple bands. Frons about 4–5 times higher than broad, slightly widened above. Lower callus square-shaped, broadly separated from eyes, polished brown. Median callus represented by an oval patch, hardly deeper than the lower callus. Parafacial band at sides of antennae hardly visible. Antennae light red-yellow. Segments 1 and 2 with fine black pubescence, segment 3 with very small dorsal tooth and with terminal flagellar segments rather stout and indistinctly segmented. Palpi rather stout at base, distinctly curved and with numerous, black adpressed hairs. Mesonotum with hardly visible pale longitudinal stripes. The abdomen distinguishes this species from all others of this group of species. It is slightly shining, black in ground colour and grey dusted. Tergite 2 with a large, reddish-yellow, square-shaped lateral patch, extending beyond a black median square patch. Tergite 3 with half reddish-yellow patch just beside the black median patch, so that sides of the tergite are black again. Tergite 1 entirely black. Posterior margin faintly yellowish and fine whitish haired. Whitish-grey median triangles form a median line. The oblique lateral markings are distinct, more whitish, lying on margin of tergite 2 and 3 in a yellowish-red patch. Venter black, whitish-grey dusted. Sternites 1–4 with usual projecting pale reddish-yellow median patch, which is broadly greyish at sides. All posterior margins distinctly paler. No appendix to vein R_4. 13.6 mm. – Peloponnes. (Kröber, 1938).

♂. Unknown.

Distribution. A species for a long time only known from the original type locality from Peloponnes, Greece but lately also recorded from Turkey.

TABANUS RUPIUM BRAUER, 1880
Fig. 90.

Tabanus pusillus Egger, 1859, Verh. zool-bot. Ges. Wien, 9: 393 (nec Macquart, 1838) – syn. n.
Tabanus (Atylotus) rupium Brauer, 1880, Denkschr. Akad. Wiss. Wien, 42: 163.
Tabanus abazus Bigot, 1886, Annls Soc. ent. Fr., 10: 146.
Atylotus alazinus Bigot, 1892, Mém. Soc. zool. Fr., 5: 647.
Atylotus lasios Surcouf, 1924, Tab. de France, p. 139 (nom. nov. for *pusillus* Egger nec Macquart) – syn. n.
Tabanus hadjinicolaoui Kröber, 1936, Acta Inst. Mus. Zool. Univ. athen., 1: 39 – syn. n.
Atylotus lowei Muschamp, 1939, Entomologist's Rec. J. Var., 51: 54.

Diagnosis. Medium-sized blackish species, eyes rather densely whitish haired; unbanded, or with 1 band, sometimes only a trace of one. Frons rather broader, median callus linear and connected with lower callus. Palpi stouter, mostly black haired, antennae black. Posterior four tibiae extensively darkened in both sexes.

Description. ♀. *Head.* Eyes short but rather densely whitish haired, with one band, sometimes with only a trace of one, or entirely unbanded. Frons greyish dusted and finely dark haired, rather broader, index about 1: 3.5, nearly parallel-sided. Lower callus large, nearly square in shape; somewhat shining black, touching subcallus and the eye-margins. Median callus very

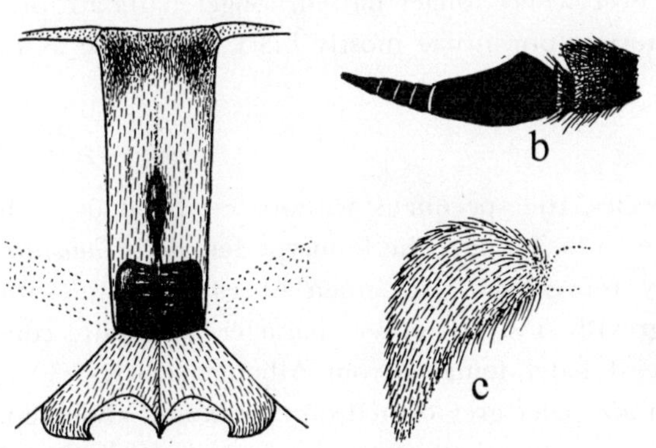

Fig. 90. *Tabanus rupium* Brau., female, a. frons, b. antenna, c. palpus.

linear, connected with lower callus. Postocular margin on vertex broad, light grey dusted and with a row of long, predominantly black hairs. Subcallus black in ground colour, densely greyish dusted. Face whitish-grey dusted and whitish haired, cheeks finely black spotted and mostly dark grey haired; a darker parafacial band usually well visible. Antennae black, basal segments greyish dusted and short black haired above, below with longer pale hairs; segment 3 sometimes slightly brownish at extreme base, dorsal tooth nearly rectangular, large. Palpi yellowish-grey, densely clothed with predominantly black hairs, rather longer and not very stout basally.

Thorax dark grey dusted on mesonotum and pteropleuron, and covered with rather long, fine black and pale hairs. Pleura except pteropleuron lighter grey dusted and finely whitish haired. Mesonotum with indistinct paler longitudinal stripes, notopleural lobes dark. *Legs.* Coxae light grey like pleura, otherwise legs mostly black and black haired, posterior four femora with longer pale hairs beneath. Femora thinly greyish dusted, all tibiae only slightly brownish at base. *Wings* clear or very indistinctly greyish clouded, veins blackish; no appendix to vein R_4. Halteres blackish.

Abdomen predominantly black and black haired, rather shining when viewed from above. Dorsum with indefinite greyish dusted and pale haired pattern, consisting of three rows of patches: a row of small oval sublateral patches, and a row of median triangles, which are longer and often more or less confluent; the grey pattern is more distinct on tergite 2, the greyish dusting is more spread out at sides. Each tergite bears a very narrow pale border on posterior margin. Venter dark grey dusted, laterally pale haired and densely black haired on median stripe.

♂. Eyes rather long and densely yellowish-brown haired, usually only a trace of one band on the lower third with smaller facets. Vertex with a row of long black hairs. Antennae black, basal segments with longer black hairs, segment 3 much more slender. Palpi rather short and oval, clothed with longer black hairs. Thorax everywhere longer haired, longer hairs are present also on abdomen. Posterior four tibiae mostly black, otherwise as in the ♀.

Length. 12—14.5 mm.

Variability. A variable species, the specimens without eye-band or with only a trace of one are often to be found. The holotype female of *hadjinicolaoui* Kröb. undoubtedly represents a specimen of *rupium* Br. with median callus covered by greyish dust, all other characters are quite conspecific. We have seen several paler females from Albania (Durrës, 3.VI. 1959, leg. J. Moucha) which are paler grey dusted on thorax and abdomen, palpi black haired towards tip only, tibiae are extensively brownish, and tergite 2 slightly translucent brown at sides. The specimens collected on mountains are in general darker coloured and mostly black haired, with extensively blackish tibiae.

BIOLOGY. Rather a common species in South Europe, more often in mountainous regions, where it can be found at altitudes above 2000 m. Females attack man, horses and horned cattle.

DATES. From June until August.

DISTRIBUTION. A Mediterranean species known from Spain, France, Italy, Albania, Greece and Jugoslavia, eastwards from Turkey, Armenia, Azerbaijan and the Caucasus. The north border of its area of distribution lies in Switzerland, Austria and in Bayern, Germany. In the last mentioned country the species has been taken several times recently, on Wallberg, 1500 m, on 13.VIII.1966, at Bad Reichentall on 30.VI.1968 and at Weissbach near Inzell on 26.VI. and 30.VI.1968, all the material having been collected by Mr. Schacht. The species has not yet been recorded from North Africa.

TABANUS SIMOVAE (LECLERCQ, 1959)

Fig. 92.

Therioplectes simovae Leclercq, 1959, Fragm. balcan., 2: 182.

DIAGNOSIS. Medium sized species with short hairy eyes and three eye-bands. Median callus absent. Posterior four femora yellowish-brown and only slightly darkened at apices. Abdomen greyish, never brownish laterally.

DESCRIPTION. ♀. *Head.* Eyes with sparse, minute pale hairs; with three bands. Frons light yellowish-grey dusted, on ocellar area more whitish-grey dusted. Frontal index 1: 5–6. Lower callus yellowish-brown and well separated from both subcallus and eye-margins. Median callus absent. Subcallus yellowish-grey dusted as frons. Rest of head more whitish-grey dusted and with exclusively pale hairs. Postocular margin on vertex with pale hairs only. Antennae reddish-yellow, first and second segments palest and slightly dusted, hairs short and pale, terminal flagellar segments darkened. Segment 3 narrow with a low dorsal tooth. Palpi whitish-yellow, long and slender, apically blunt ended, exclusively pale haired.

Thorax light grey dusted, mesonotum with indefinite longitudinal darker stripes and with both pale and black hairs. Notopleural lobes grey with pale and black hairs. Pleura with long whitish hairs. *Legs* with all coxae and femora grey, only extreme apices of femora yellowish-brown. Fore tibiae on basal two-thirds yellowish-brown, apical third blackish. Other tibiae yellowish-brown with slightly darkened apices. Fore tarsi black, other tarsi brownish-black. *Wings* clear with stigma pale brownish. Knob of halteres whitish apically, dark brownish dorsally and ventrally.

Abdomen light olive-grey dusted, with three rows of paler grey patches, clothed with both pale and black hairs. Venter uniformly light grey dusted and pale haired except for last sternite which has erect black hairs.

Length. 15–17 mm.

♂. Unknown.

DATES. May–July.

DISTRIBUTION. The species is known only from Jugoslavia and Turkey.

TABANUS ROUSSELII MACQUART, 1838

Fig. 93.

Tabanus rousselii Macquart, 1838, Dipt. exot., 1 (2): 181.
Sziladynus laticornis Enderlein, 1931, Sber. Ges. naturf. Freunde Berl., 1930: 377.

DIAGNOSIS. Medium-sized species with hairy eyes, closely related to *bifarius* Meig. but the eyes with only 1 band, tergites 2 and 3 largely reddish-brown

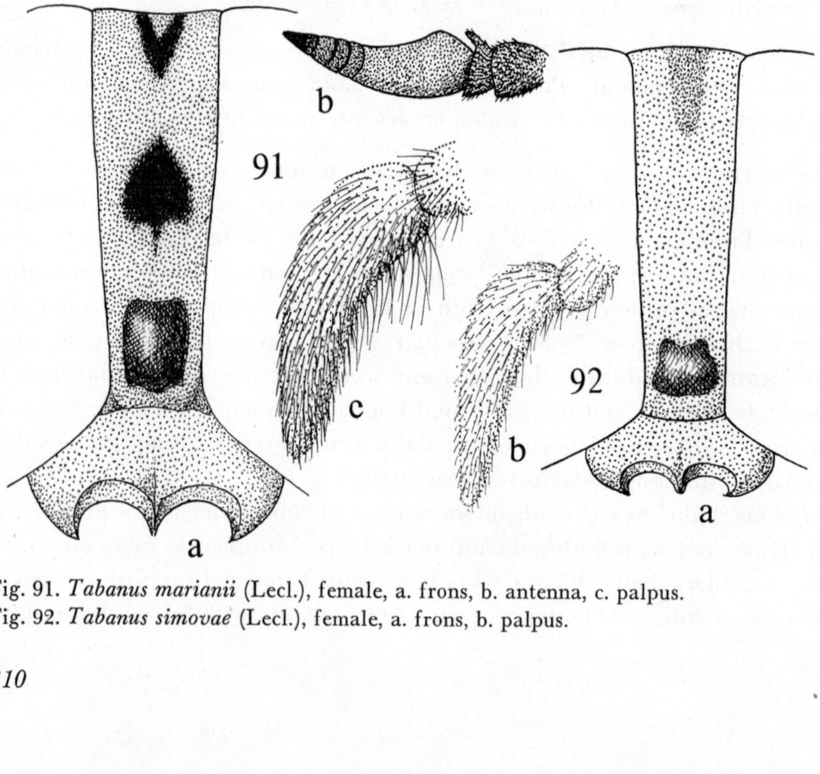

Fig. 91. *Tabanus marianii* (Lecl.), female, a. frons, b. antenna, c. palpus.
Fig. 92. *Tabanus simovae* (Lecl.), female, a. frons, b. palpus.

at sides, and posterior four femora more or less reddish towards tip. Male with upper facets larger (about 3 times) and sharply separated from the small facets, which bear one band as in ♀. Vertex with only short pale hairs, and abdomen largely yellowish-brown on anterior four tergites.

DESCRIPTION. ♀. *Head.* Eyes with sparse, minute pale hairs, with one band. Frons rather light greyish dusted, narrower, index about 1: 4—4.3, slightly widened above. Lower callus dull yellowish-brown, slightly oval, small, broadly separated from subcallus and the eye-margins. Median callus black, usually somewhat longer but at most as deep as lower callus, from which it is broadly separated. Frons on vertex with another larger blackish patch imitating ocellar swelling. Subcallus densely light grey dusted, face and cheeks more whitish-grey with fine whitish hairs. Postocular margin on vertex with a row of short pale and dark hairs. Antennae reddish-brown, basal segment silver-yellow dusted, terminal flagellar segments extensively darkened; segment 3 very broad, dorsal tooth not very large but the lower edge of segment 3 is distinctly convex. Palpi whitish-yellow, long and rather slender, apically blunt ended; clothed with pale hairs, sometimes with a few black hairs towards tip.

Thorax light grey dusted, mesonotum with indefinite darker longitudinal stripes and mostly short pale haired. Notopleural lobes grey with fine black hairs. Pleura densely clothed with longer whitish hairs. *Legs* greyish on coxae and partly on femora, pale haired. Posterior four femora extensively yellowish-brown at least near apex, sometimes on the whole apical half. Fore tibiae on basal two-thirds and whole of posterior tibiae yellowish-brown; fore tibiae towards tip and fore tarsi nearly blackish, posterior tarsi

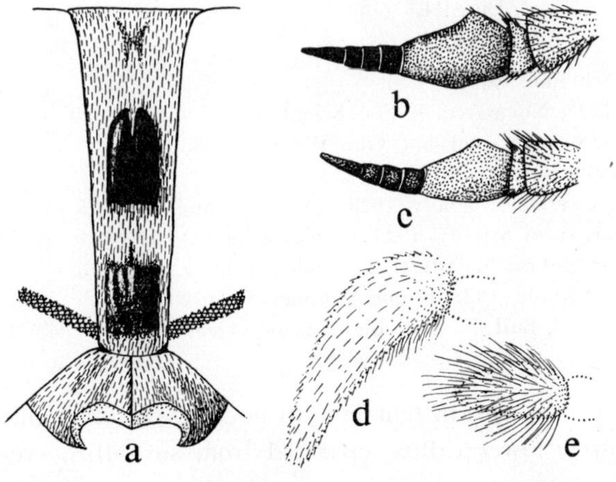

Fig. 93. *Tabanus rousselii* Macq., a. female frons, b. female antenna, c. male antenna, d. female palpus, e. male palpus.

dark brown. *Wings* clear with lighter brown veins especially along costa; rather a longer appendix to vein R_4, usually as long as the basal portion of vein R_4. Halteres whitish, stem brownish.

Abdomen olive-grey dusted and mostly pale haired, with three rows of very indefinite paler patches; tergite 2 (usually also 3) largely yellowish-brown at sides. Venter uniformly light grey dusted and pale haired except for last sternite which is black haired.

♂. Head slightly broader than thorax, eyes clothed with minute pale hairs, with one band. Large facets on the upper two-thirds about 3 times as large as small facets, and rather sharply separated from the lower area with small facets. Vertex with a row of short pale and some dark grey hairs. Antennae with much more slender segment 3, basal segment mostly pale haired. Apical segment of palpi long oval, about twice as long as deep, clothed with longer whitish hairs, apically very slightly pointed. Thorax with denser and longer whitish pubescence. Posterior four femora usually yellowish-brown on the whole length on dorsum. Abdomen largely yellowish-brown on anterior four tergites, corresponding sternites translucent yellowish-brown at sides. Otherwise as in the ♀, abdominal pubescence longer.

Length. 12–13 mm.

DATES. Unknown to us.

DISTRIBUTION. A little known species occurring in North Africa (Morocco, Algeria, Tunisia), Asia Minor (Turkey) and in Jugoslavia. We have seen documentary material from Algeria and Tunisia.

TABANUS LUNATUS FABRICIUS, 1794

Fig. 94.

Tabanus lunatus Fabricius, 1794, Ent. Syst., 4: 370.
Tabanus algiricus Thunberg, 1827, Nova Acta R. Soc. Scient. upsal., 9: 60.
Tabanus anthophilus Loew, 1858, Verh. zool.-bot. Ges. Wien, 8: 593.
Tabanus Wideri Jaennicke, 1866, Berl. ent. Z., 10: 72.
Tabanus (Atylotus) lunatus var. *syriacus* Szilády, 1923, Biologica hung., 1 (1): 5.
Tabanus (Atylotus) lunatus var. *rufus* Szilády, 1923, Biologica hung., 1 (1): 6.
Tabanus (Atylotus) lunatus var. *politus* Szilády, 1923, Biologica hung., 1 (1): 6.
Tabanus lunatus var. *farinosus* Szilády, 1923, Biologica hung., 1 (1): 20.
Tabanus danubicus Dinulescu, 1953, Bull. St. Sect. Biol., Agron., Geol. & Geogr. 5: 556 (nomen nudum).

DIAGNOSIS. Medium-sized species, eyes in female with microscopic hairs and three bands. Frons narrower, lower callus separated from subcallus, eye-margins and median callus, black or brownish. Palpi stout, abdomen usually brownish on anterior four tergites. Male with densely hairy eyes with 2 bands; the upper, slightly enlarged facets indistinctly separated from lower facets. Palpi broadly oval, blunt ended.

DESCRIPTION. ♀. *Head.* Eyes only microscopically short pale haired, with three bands. Frons greyish-yellow dusted, narrow, index 1: 4—5, sometimes distinctly widened above or nearly parallel-sided. Lower callus slightly oval to nearly rectangular, polished black to brown, broadly separated from subcallus and narrowly from the eye-margins. Median callus less shiny black, broadly separated from lower callus, rather large. Subcallus more light grey dusted, face whitish-grey with concolorous long hairs, cheeks finely greyish spotted. Vertex with a row of slightly longer pale to greyish hairs. Antennae mostly reddish-yellow, terminal flagellar segments usually extensively blackish; basal segments with sparse black hairing; segment 3 rather broad with only small, blunt dorsal tooth. Apical segment of palpi very stout on basal two-thirds, slightly pointed towards tip; pale yellowish and clothed with predominantly whitish hairs, some short black hairs near tip.

Thorax dark grey on mesonotum, paler greyish dusted on pleura. Mesonotum with indefinite paler longitudinal stripes and mostly short yellowish-grey haired, pleura with long and rather dense whitish pubescence. Notopleural lobes yellowish to dark grey. *Legs* dark grey on femora, beneath with longer pale hairs; coxae concolorous with pleura, long whitish haired. Knees, basal half of fore tibiae, and posterior four tibiae, yellowish-brown; fore tibiae on apical half and fore tarsi black, posterior tarsi darkened and

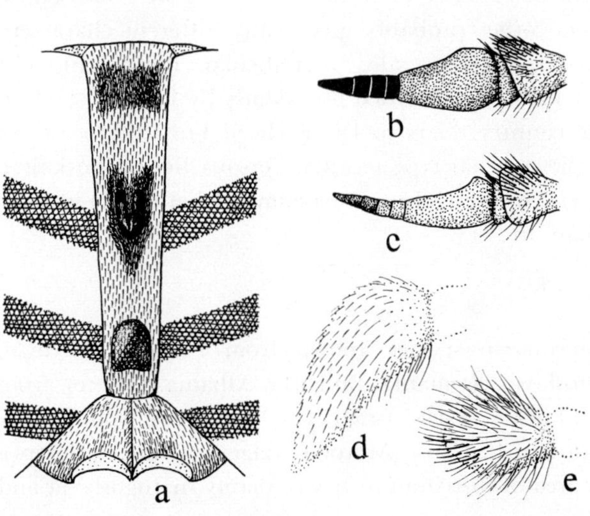

Fig. 94. *Tabanus lunatus* F., a. female frons, b. female antenna, c. male antenna, d. female palpus, e. male palpus.

mostly black haired. *Wings* clear with dark veins, no appendix to vein R_4. Halteres light brown to yellowish, with whitish apex of knob.

Abdomen olive-grey dusted on median stripe and on posterior tergites, anterior four tergites largely yellowish-brown at sides. Dorsum with more or less distinct paler pattern consisting of a row of median triangles, of sublateral oval patches, and narrow posterior margins. In more greyish specimens the pattern remains usually brownish. The dark and pale areas with concolorous hairs. Venter mostly yellowish-brown and short pale haired, apical sternites greyish; last sternite (and often the foregoing one) densely black haired.

♂. Head not very large, about as deep as thorax. Eyes densely whitish haired, upper two-thirds with somewhat larger facets (about twice as large as smaller facets) indistinctly separated from the lower area with small facets. Two distinct bands are on the area with small facets. Vertex with a row of long blackish hairs. Antennae similarly coloured but more slender. Palpi whitish-yellow, shortly oval, about twice as long as deep, blunt ended and mostly pale haired. Mesonotum with long pale hairing, tibiae usually darker brown; otherwise as in the ♀ including the abdominal pattern, the dark median stripe on anterior tergites narrower.

Length. 12–16 mm.

VARIABILITY. A very variable species in coloration of antennae, of lower frontal callus, and in abdominal pattern. The range of variability of this species is very wide, covering all described varieties, which were recorded by Leclercq (1967a) as subspecies. All these taxa have only an infrasubspecific status with no taxonomic value. *T. bactrianus* Olsufjev, 1937, originally described as a subspecies of *lunatus* F. from the Near East and Central Asia, has longer palpi and other probably specifically different characters, and represents a distinct species (see also Shevtshenko, 1961: 136). The variety *farinosus* Szilády, 1923, was recorded mistakenly by Leclercq (1967a: 157) from Finland. The country refers to Dr. Richard Frey, the owner of the type specimen, but the original type locality Tersoka lies in Turkestan or Transcaspia, the material in the Helsinki Museum is labelled »Tersok.or., leg.Ahnger« (Dr. Hackman, in litt.).

DATES. From May until July.

DISTRIBUTION. A Mediterranean species known from Europe (Portugal, Spain, France, Italy, Jugoslavia, Rumania, Bulgaria, Albania, Greece), from Near and Middle East (Turkey, Syria, Israel, Lebanon, Iraq, Iran) as far as Central Asia and from North Africa (Morocco, Algeria, Tunisia, Egypt). The north border of its area of distribution lies probably in Jugoslavia and

Rumania, the records from Poland are undoubtedly a mistake and refer to another species.

TABANUS MARIANII (LECLERCQ, 1956)

Fig. 91.

Therioplectes marianii Leclercq, 1956, Bull. Inst. r. Sci. nat. Belg., 32: 4.

DIAGNOSIS. Resembling *T. bifarius* Loew very much having also the same abdominal pattern but palpi mostly black haired, vertex with minute pale hairs, antennae unicolorous light yellowish-brown, being only faintly brownish apically.

DESCRIPTION. ♀. *Head.* Eyes with very fine and scattered pale hairs, with three narrow bands. Frons and face pale to whitish-grey dusted, former rather narrow, index about 1: 4—5. Lower callus yellowish to brownish, rectangular and only narrowly separated from subcallus and eye-margins. Median callus usually of the same size, blackish, and broadly separated from lower callus. Vertex with distinct blackish patch. Subcallus and upper parts of face dark greyish dusted, most of the face very pale dusted and fine whitish haired. Postocular margin on vertex indistinctly whitish pubescent. Antennae almost unicolorous yellowish-brown, terminal flagellar segments more brownish; plate of segment 3 not very broad, dorsal tooth obtuse and placed near base. Palpi longer, about 4 times as long as deep, predominantly short black haired.

Thorax dark grey dusted, mesonotum with rather short, pleura with longer pale hairs. Notopleural lobes dark, mostly dark haired. *Legs.* Coxae and femora blackish-grey, tibiae yellowish-brown but apical third of fore tibiae and fore tarsi blackish. Posterior tarsi darkened, brownish. *Wings* clear, veins yellowish-brown (in one female paratype) to almost black (in another female paratype). A very short appendix to vein R_4. Halteres yellowish-brown, with a whitish knob in one female paratype.

Abdomen light olive-grey dusted, with the same pattern as in *T. bifarius,* posterior margins to all tergites narrowly paler. Venter light grey dusted and mostly pale haired except posterior two sternites which are black haired; all posterior margins narrowly paler.

♂. Head distinctly wider than thorax. Eyes greenish with two purple bands on lower third. Facets on upper two-thirds of eyes 3 to 4 times larger than lower facets. Subcallus greyish-yellow dusted. Antennae yellowish with terminal flagellar segments darkened. First and second antennal segments with long blackish hairs mixed up with some whitish hairs. Third segment with a distinct tooth dorsally. Postocular margin with long black hairs and some whitish hairs which are bent forwards. Palpus yellow, egg-shaped and pointed, with long black hairs mixed up with whitish hairs. Genae with numerous long black hairs. Thorax shining, greyish with indistinct longitudinal bands. Hairing long and black with a few whitish hairs intermixed. Pleura and scutellum with long yellowish hairing. Legs and wings as in female. Abdomen greyish-black with three rows of spots. The median row composed of whitish indistinct spots. The lateral rows composed of large reddish spots on tergites 2–3 and of whitish and much smaller spots on the following tergites. Posterior margins of tergites yellowish. Venter as in female. (Translated from the original description).

Length. 14–15 mm.

Dates. June.

Remarks. We have seen two female paratypes, both labelled »Alcamo (Trapani) 3.6.56«. The species differs somewhat from *bifarius* but since the latter is known to be a very variable species, we can only solve the systematical position of *T. marianii,* when larger series from South Europe are available.

Distribution. Described from Sicily. Later (Leclercq, 1967a: 158) also recorded it from Greece.

TABANUS BIFARIUS LOEW, 1858

Fig. 95.

Tabanus bifarius Loew, 1858, Verh. zool.-bot. Ges. Wien, 8: 595.
Tabanus Kervillei Surcouf, 1911, Bull. Soc. Amis Sci. nat. Rouen, p. 6.
Dasystypia rustica var. *nigra* Enderlein, 1925, Mitt. zool. Mus. Berl., 11: 370.
Dasystypia longicornis Enderlein, 1932, Mitt. dt. ent. Ges., 3: 63.
Dasystypia taurica Enderlein, 1932, Mitt. dt. ent. Ges., 3: 64.
? *Tabanus bifarius* ssp. *tarjukini* Hauser, 1941, Izv. Azerb. Fil. AN SSSR, 2: 73.
? *Tabanus bifarius* ssp. *kurensis* Djafarov, 1960, Zool. Zh., 34: 714.

Diagnosis. Medium-sized, greyish to olive-grey coloured species with rather narrow frons in female and well separated calli; lower callus brownish. Apical segment of palpi long and slender, more than 4 times as long as deep in female, nearly 3 times as long as deep and apically pointed in male. Eyes haired and with 3 or 2 bands, antennae reddish-brown with dark apex.

Description. ♀. *Head.* Eyes clothed with sparse, fine pale hairs, with 3 (or very exceptionally with only 2) bands. Frons narrow, index 1: 5–5.5, greyish-yellow dusted and very indistinctly widening above. Frontal calli separated, lower callus brown to yellowish-brown, elongated and narrowly separated from the eye-margins. Median callus black, long oval and usually larger than lower callus. Subcallus dull light grey. Face and cheeks pale with fine whitish hairs. Vertex with a row of short black hairs. Antennae reddish-brown to yellowish-brown, except for blackish terminal flagellar segments. Basal two segments with short black hairs, segment 3 rather broader (ratio of plate 3: 2.5) with only slightly developed dorsal tooth near base. Palpi whitish, long and slender, rather blunt ended and clothed with short pale and black hairs.

Thorax black, greyish dusted; mesonotum with indistinct paler longitudinal stripes and short pale and black hairs. Notopleural lobes blackish-grey, pleura with longer pale hairs. *Legs.* Coxae and femora greyish with pale hairs, tibiae yellowish-brown; apical half of fore tibiae and fore tarsi black, tibiae at tip and tarsi on posterior two pairs blackish-brown. *Wings* clear, veins dark brown; sometimes a short appendix to vein R_4. Halteres dark brown, knob usually paler.

Abdomen blackish in ground colour and olive-grey dusted; the pale pattern of pale hairs formed by indistinct median triangles and more distinct small sublateral patches on each tergite. Venter unicolorous blackish-grey.

♂. Eyes clothed with sparse, fine pale hairing. Facets on the upper two-

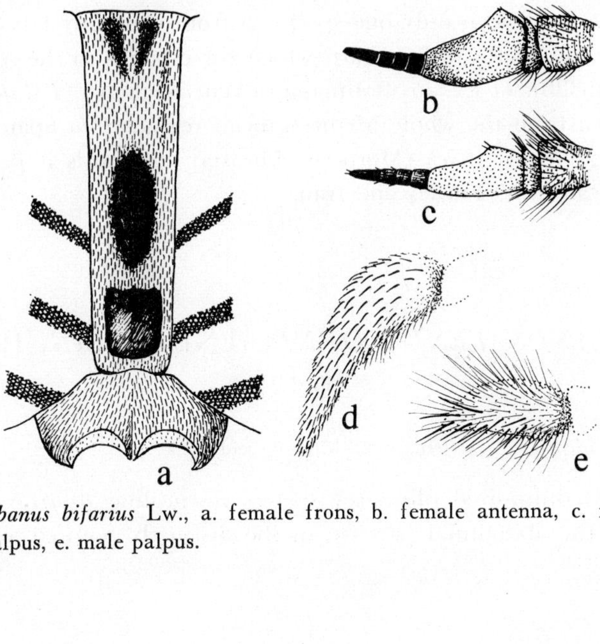

Fig. 95. *Tabanus bifarius* Lw., a. female frons, b. female antenna, c. male antenna. d. female palpus, e. male palpus.

thirds are very large, more than 4 times larger, and sharply separated from the lower area with small facets, which bears 2 bands. Vertex mesally with a row of longer dark brown to black hairs, laterally only short haired. Antennal segment 3 slender with very small dorsal tooth near base, basal segments with longer black hairs. Coloration of antennae as in the ♀. Apical segment of palpi yellowish to yellowish-grey, mostly pale haired but with some additional black hairs towards tip; long oval, about 3 times as long as deep, slightly but distinctly pointed at tip. Thorax and legs on coxae and femora with longer hairs. Wings and abdomen as in the ♀ but tergites 2 and 3 brownish at sides.

Length. 12—17 mm.

VARIABILITY. A very variable species, especially in coloration of antennae and in abdominal pattern. The species is often mistaken for *tenuicornis* (End.) and the systematic position of the subspecies *tarjukini* Hauser and *kurensis* Djafarov described from Azerbaijan is rather unclear; considering their occurrence inside the area of distribution of the nominate species, they both should represent only an infrasubspecific category. We have not seen these subspecies.

DATES. From May until August.

DISTRIBUTION. A rather common species in the Mediterranean region, the northern border of its area of distribution in Europe lies in Central Europe (Hungary, Czechoslovakia, Austria and Germany). In suitable localities a rather common species in South Moravia and South Slovakia, Czechoslovakia, but we have seen only one specimen from Germany labelled »Bothnang, coll. Ertle, 1881« in Stuttgart, which corresponds to the record given by Kröber (1932b): »1 Ex. aus Bothnang in Württemberg«. *T. bifarius* Loew is well known from the whole Mediterranean region from Spain to Bulgaria including North Africa (Morocco, Tunisia), eastwards it penetrates as far as Transcaucasus, Turkey and Iran.

TABANUS TENUICORNIS (ENDERLEIN, 1932)

Fig. 96.

Dasystypia tenuicornis Enderlein, 1932, Mitt. dt. ent. Ges., 3: 63.

DIAGNOSIS. Medium-sized olive-grey species resembling *bifarius* Loew but differing in the abdominal pattern, in the distinctly pointed and entirely pale haired palpi in both sexes; the female differs also in the broader frons and the narrower antennal segment 3.

Description. ♀. *Head.* Eyes with 3 bands and clothed with short, sparse pale hairs. Frons rather broader, slightly diverging above, index about 1: 4; yellowish-grey dusted and short pale haired, near vertex with some black hairs. Lower callus yellowish-brown, slightly shining, rectangular and narrowly separated from the eye-margins. Median callus dull black, long oval and widely separated from the lower callus. Vertex with rather shorter pale hairing. Subcallus and face whitish-yellow dusted, face below with long whitish hairs. Antennae reddish-brown, basal segments thinly silvery dusted and clothed with fine pale hairs; segment 3 rather narrower (ratio of plate 3: 2), dorsal tooth very small; terminal flagellar segments usually darkened. Palpi whitish-yellow and clothed with only pale, short hairs; long and rather slender, very pointed at tip.

Thorax dark grey on mesonotum and mostly short pale haired, pleura more whitish-grey dusted and covered with longer whitish hairs. Notopleural lobes greyish. *Legs.* Coxae concolorous with pleura and similarly haired, femora greyish with fine pale hairs; fore femora black beneath. Knees and tibiae yellowish-brown, fore tibiae on more than apical third, posterior four tibiae at tip, and all tarsi, black. *Wings* clear, veins blackish-brown, yellowish-brown near base of wing and along costal margin; a long appendix to vein R_4. Halteres dark brown with paler knob.

Abdomen olive-grey dusted and golden-yellow to silvery-grey (from some point of view) short haired, dorsum with four more or less distinct longitu-

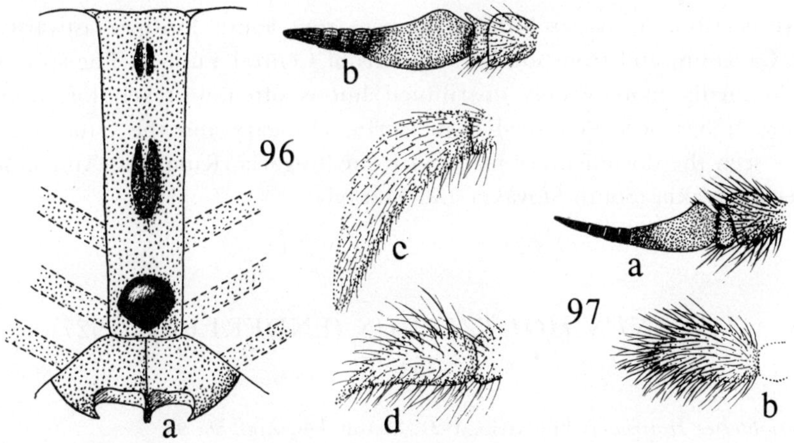

Fig. 96. *Tabanus tenuicornis* (End.), a. female frons, b. female antenna, c. female palpus, d. male palpus.
Fig. 97. *Tabanus holtzianus* End., male, a. antenna, b. palpus.

dinal stripes of black pubescence, dividing each tergite into five areas with pale hairing. Venter unicolorous olive-grey dusted and pale haired, only last sternite with black hairs.

♂. Eyes with 2 bands, short but densely pale haired. Facets on the upper two-thirds very large and sharply separated from the small facets below. Vertex with a row of longer pale hairs. Palpi rather slender, about 3 times as long as deep, pointed at tip and clothed with only pale longer hairs. Thorax with long and densely set pale hairs on mesonotum and scutellum, otherwise as in the ♀. Abdomen with the same pattern and only greyish coloured on anterior tergites at sides.

Length. 12–16 mm.

VARIABILITY. The antennae are usually reddish-brown including terminal flagellar segments but we have seen specimens with antennae extensively darkened on segment 3 at tip and on terminal flagellar segments. The abdominal pattern seems to be very constant.

REMARKS. The species has not been well recognized by students of tabanidology since Enderlein, and all the specimens that we have seen in various collections were usually arranged among material of *bifarius* Loew. *T. tenuicornis* (End.) is, however, a very distinct and easily recognizeable species. We have not seen the type material but according to the original description there is no doubt that the species is correctly recognized and redescribed in the present work.

DATES. From June until August.

DISTRIBUTION. A species hitherto known from South Europe eastwards to the Caucasus, and from southern regions of Central Europe. The species is undoubtedly more widely distributed but is often mistaken for *bifarius* Loew. It has been described from Corfu, Hungary and the Caucasus; we have seen the documentary material from Bulgaria, Rumania, Austria and Czechoslovakia (South Slovakia and Moravia).

TABANUS HOLTZIANUS (ENDERLEIN, 1927)

Fig. 97.

Therioplectes Holtzianus Enderlein, 1927, Stettin. ent. Ztg., 88: 99.

DIAGNOSIS. Male: Eyes with 2 bands, very densely whitish-grey haired; larger facets indistinctly separated from smaller facets. Vertex with longer blackish hairs. Antennae reddish-brown, palpi nearly three times as long as deep, apically pointed. Resembling *lunatus* F. but specifically distinct.

♀. Unknown.

DESCRIPTION. ♂. Head hardly deeper than thorax, eyes with 2 bands, meeting on two-thirds in front and densely whitish-grey haired. Facets on the upper two-thirds not very large, only about twice as large as smaller facets, and they are not sharply separated from the latter. Vertex with a row of longer dark grey hairs becoming longer and blackish towards middle. Subcallus and face greyish dusted, latter with long whitish hairs becoming greyish-brown on cheeks. Antennae reddish-brown, terminal flagellar segments somewhat darkened; basal two segments with longer dark hairs, segment 3 slender, with a small, but distinctly pointed dorsal tooth near base. Palpi yellowish, basal segment extensively darkened; apical segment rather slender, nearly three times as long as deep, apically pointed, clothed with predominantly dark hairs.

Thorax. Mesonotum unstriped, blackish-grey dusted and armed with fine but long, dark grey hairs becoming rather blackish posteriorly and on scutellum. Notopleural lobes dark. Pleura lighter grey dusted and more densely whitish-grey to whitish-yellow haired. *Legs*. Coxae concolorous with pleura and whitish haired; femora much darker, blackish-grey dusted and with predominantly dark hairs beneath. Tibiae brownish, fore tibiae on apical half, posterior four tibiae at tip, and all tarsi, nearly blackish. *Wings* very indistinctly tinted brownish or nearly clear, veins brown. Sometimes a short appendix to vein R_4. Halteres brown.

Abdomen blackish, olive-grey (or rather silvery-grey when viewed from behind) dusted, with three rows of very indefinite paler to silvery dusted patches. Tergite 2 broadly yellowish-brown to brown at sides, tergite 3 only anteriorly at sides. Venter unicolorous greyish dusted and covered by pale hairs becoming blackish on apical 2 sternites.

Length. 13—14 mm.

REMARKS. The species is still known only from the male sex; apart from the holotype we have seen two males collected on 12.—16.V.1956 by Fr. Borchmann on the same locality as the holotype male and they all undoubtedly represent a distinct species from both *lunatus* F. and *bifarius* Loew. The differences are given in the key. It is surprising that the female sex is still unknown but, considering the shape of palpi, *holtzianus* (End.) should be very closely related to, if not identical with, *bactrianus* Olsufjev, 1937. The latter is still known only from the female sex, originally described as a variety of *lunatus* F., but it has not yet been collected in Europe.

DATES. May.

DISTRIBUTION. Greece; all the material, including the holotype male, was collected at Euböa, Chalkis.

GLAUCOPIS-GROUP

Medium-sized to larger species. Eyes naked with 3 bands in female and 2 bands in male. Frons rather narrower, median callus oval, usually higher than broad and broadly separated from lower callus; latter is narrowly separated from both subcallus and the eye-margins. Subcallus more or less polished black to brown.

TABANUS GLAUCOPIS MEIGEN, 1820

Fig. 98.

Tabanus ferrugineus Meigen, 1804, Klass., p. 169; Syst. Beschr., 2: 60.
Tabanus glaucopis Meigen, 1820, Syst. Beschr., 2: 48 (nom. nov. for *ferrugineus).*
Tabanus lunulatus Meigen, 1820, Syst. Beschr., 2: 49.
Tabanus chlorophthalmus Meigen, 1820, Syst. Beschr., 2: 58.
Tabanus flavicans Zeller, 1842, Isis, 2: 819.
Tabanus cognatus Loew, 1858, Verh. zool.-bot. Ges. Wien, 8: 602.
Tabanus glaucopis var. *castellanus* Strobl, 1906, Mems. R. Soc. esp. Hist. nat., 3 (1905): 279.
Straba glaucopis ab. *rubra* Muschamp, 1939, Entomologist's Rec. J. Var., 51: 51.

DIAGNOSIS. Larger species, 15.5–18 mm in length, with naked eyes with 3 bands in female and entirely polished black to blackish-brown subcallus. Frontal calli mostly oval, widely separated. Abdomen usually chestnut-brown with three rows of yellowish-brown to grey patches. Male with naked eyes with 2 bands and sharply separated large facets on more than upper two-thirds.

DESCRIPTION. ♀. *Head.* Eyes naked with 3 bands. Frons rather narrow, index 1: 4–5, yellowish-grey dusted and only slightly widened above. Lower callus rectangular to oval, polished black to dark brown, rather broadly separated from subcallus and from the eye-margins. Median callus at least equal in size, oval, subshiny black or dulled, broadly separated from the lower callus. Frons above slightly darkened and distinctly black haired. Subcallus convex, entirely polished black or dark brown, antennal bows yellowish, deep. Face and cheeks whitish-grey with long whitish hairs especially on face below, a dark parafacial band usually distinct. Antennae yellowish-brown on basal segments, black haired and with mostly pale hairs below; segment 3 reddish-brown or extensively darkened, rather broad at base and with only small tooth near base. Palpi rather narrower and pointed on apical segment, which is mostly black haired.

Thorax dark grey on mesonotum with rather distinct paler longitudinal stripes, mostly short pale haired. Pleura light grey dusted and with longer whitish hairing. Humeri and notopleural lobes usually brownish. *Legs* light grey dusted and fine pale haired on coxae and femora; tibiae light brown with predominantly black hairs; fore tibiae on apical half and posterior four tibiae at tip extensively blackish; tarsi mostly black, especially on front pair. *Wings* clear with dark veins, sometimes a short appendix to vein R_4. Halteres brownish with paler tip of knob.

Abdomen blackish to chestnut-brown on anterior four tergites, posterior tergites always dark greyish-black. Abdominal pattern yellowish-brown to greyish, consisting of a row of median triangles (which are usually more greyish), of two rows of sublateral, oval oblique patches, and narrow posterior margins. Abdomen mostly short black haired, pale areas with concolorous hairs. Venter mostly light brown on anterior sternites, with indefinite greyish markings at middle and laterally, posterior sternites light grey; all sternites pale haired except last sternite which is clothed with dense, black hairing.

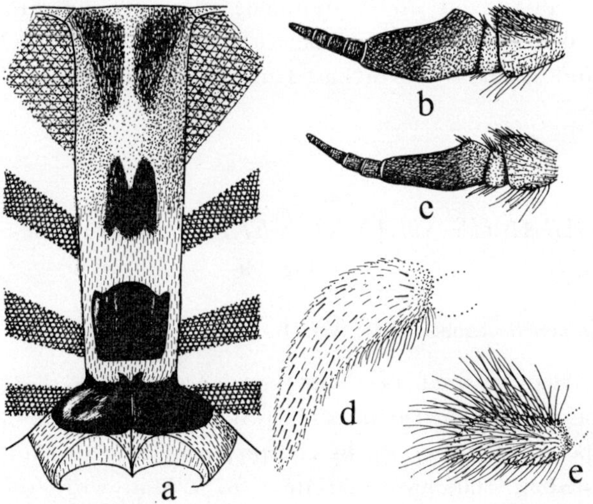

Fig. 98. *Tabanus glaucopis* Meig., a. female frons, b. female antenna, c. male antenna, d. female palpus, e. male palpus.

♂. Eyes naked with 2 bands on the lower area with small facets, the large facets on more than upper two-thirds of the eyes are sharply separated. Vertex with a row of longer dark hairs. Subcallus entirely polished black to dark brown, cheeks with predominantly dark grey hairs. Antennae more slender on segment 3, and with smaller and more pointed dorsal tooth. Palpi small, oval, slightly pointed at tip and mostly black haired on apical two-thirds. Thorax longer haired; notopleural lobes, posterior part of mesonotum and pteropleura, mostly dark haired. Otherwise as in the ♀.

Length. 15.5–18 mm.

VARIABILITY. A very variable species, especially in coloration of polished subcallus and coloration including shape of frontal calli. The abdominal coloration and pattern vary from blackish-grey to reddish-brown, some specimens have the abdomen mostly brownish. All the names such as *cognatus, castellanus, rubra,* etc., represent only a range of variability and have no taxonomic value.

BIOLOGY. A widely distributed species especially on steppe and forest-steppe biotopes; in mountains it has been collected up to an altitude of 1800 m. The females attack man, horses and horned cattle, the species is known as a vector of *Trypanosoma theileri* Laveran. A detailed description of the immature stages does not exist.

DATES. From June to September.

DISTRIBUTION. A species of Eurasiatic distribution, it is known from Great Britain (except Ireland) and Scandinavia as far as South Europe, eastwards to Transbaikalia and Primorie District. It is recorded from Turkey, Transcaucasus and as far as North East China, but not yet known from North Africa.

TABANUS SHANNONELLUS KRÖBER, 1936

Fig. 99.

Tabanus shannonella Kröber, 1936, Acta Inst. Mus. zool. Univ. athen., 1: 36.

DIAGNOSIS. Medium-sized species of the *glaucopis*-group. Eyes naked with 3 bands, subcallus polished blackish-brown. The species is well distinguished from all species of this group by conspicuously whitish scutellum and very enlarged median triangles on tergites 3 to 5. Male with eyes naked with 2 bands, upper large facets sharply separated from small facets, vertex with a row of long grey hairs.

DESCRIPTION. ♀. *Head.* Eyes naked with three bands. Frons yellowish-grey dusted, rather narrow, index about 1: 5, distinctly widened towards vertex. Lower callus black to brown, more or less shining, long rectangular in shape and distinctly separated from both subcallus and the eye-margins. Median callus broadly oval, dull black, broadly separated from the lower callus. Subcallus with high, yellowish antennal bows occupying nearly lower half of the subcallus, the rest of subcallus entirely polished black to blackish-brown. Face whitish-grey dusted and finely whitish haired, a brown parafacial band on each side of antennae slightly visible. Postocular margin on vertex narrow with rather short but densely set pale hairs. Antennae entirely brown to reddish-brown, terminal flagellar segments slightly darkened. Basal segments thinly greyish dusted and mostly black haired; segment 3 rather slender with a slightly developed dorsal tooth near base. Palpi light grey, slightly stouter basally and sharply pointed apically, clothed with predominantly black hairs.

Thorax. Mesonotum blackish-grey dusted and pale haired, with three narrow, more or less distinct, light grey longitudinal stripes. Notopleural lobes and humeri yellowish-brown. Pleura whitish-grey dusted and long, finely pale haired. Scutellum conspicuously densely, whitish-grey dusted and pale haired, much paler in contrast to darker mesonotum. *Legs.* Coxae and femora blackish-grey, rather densely grey dusted and whitish haired, posterior four coxae and femora sometimes slightly brownish at base. Fore tibiae on basal half to two-thirds, and whole of posterior four tibiae, yellowish with slight greyish dusting and pale hairs; apical part of fore tibiae and whole of fore tarsi black and black haired; hind tibiae at extreme tip and corresponding tarsi brown with short black pubescence. *Wings* clear, veins dark

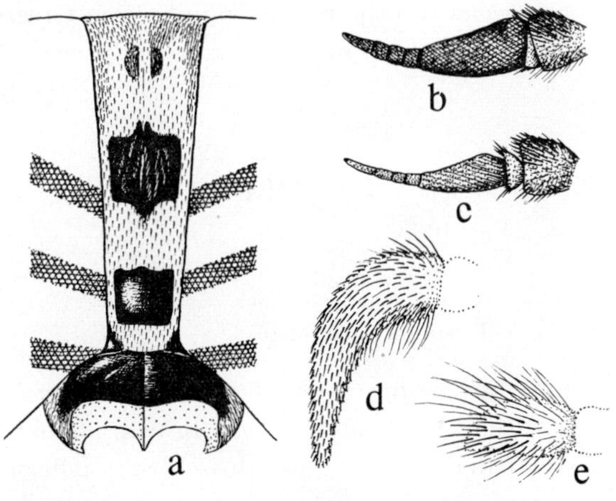

Fig. 99. *Tabanus shannonellus* Kröb., a. female frons, b. female antenna, c. male antenna, d. female palpus, e. male palpus.

brown, no appendix to vein R_4. Halteres yellowish-brown with darkened knob.

Abdomen more or less shining black and black haired, with very distinct pale pattern; the sublateral oval patches do not reach the anterior margin of the tergites, on tergites 2 to 4 brownish, on following tergites greyish. The median triangles are very light grey, conspicuously large on tergites 3 to 5 (or 6), nearly equilateral, reaching the foregoing tergite. Tergite 2 with only a small median triangle at posterior margin. All tergites bear a narrow light border on posterior margin which is pale haired, as well as the three rows of patches. Anterior four sternites reddish-brown, laterally slightly greyish dusted, posterior sternites grey with a blackish-grey median stripe of black pubescence.

♂. Eyes naked with 2 bands, facets on the upper three-quarters large and sharply separated from the lower quarter with small facets. Subcallus polished brown, vertex with a row of long greyish hairs. Antennae as in the ♀, brownish-yellow and much more slender on segment 3. Apical segment of palpi oval in shape, whitish-grey, with long pale hairs and with some black hairs towards tip. Thorax with long whitish-grey hairs including on mesonotum, scutellum similarly conspicuously whitish. Otherwise as in the ♀ but anterior three tergites extensively brown at sides.

Length. 12—15 mm.

BIOLOGY. A species occurring in late summer, females attack man, horses and horned cattle.

DATES. August and September.

DISTRIBUTION. The species has been described by Kröber (1936a) from three females from Greece, the male sex has been described only recently by Moucha & Chvála (1963a). The species is hitherto known only from Greece, Bulgaria and Jugoslavia including the island of Hvar.

TABANUS OBSOLESCENS PANDELLÉ, 1883

Fig. 100.

Tabanus obsolescens Pandellé, 1883, Revue ent., 2: 207.
Tabanus obsoletus; Kertész, 1900, Catal. Tabanid., p. 63, lapsus.

DIAGNOSIS. Medium-sized, rather brownish species of the *glaucopis*-group with naked eyes with 3 bands in female. Antennae light brown, abdomen mostly brownish with 3 rows of paler patches. Subcallus entirely polished dark brown in both sexes. Eyes in male with sharply differentiated facets and only small, fine pale hairs on vertex.

Description. ♀. *Head.* Eyes naked with three bands. Frons dark yellowish-grey dusted, narrow, index 1: 5–6, and distinctly widened above. Lower callus polished dark brown, rectangular, broadly separated from subcallus and very narrowly from, or nearly touching, the eye-margins. Median callus subshiny black, long oval and longitudinally wrinkled, about twice as long as deep, and broadly separated from lower callus. Subcallus entirely polished dark brown, antennal bows yellowish dusted, only narrow. Postocular margin on vertex narrow, dark grey, clothed with minute pale hairs. Face and cheeks grey to dark grey dusted, former clothed with long pale hairs below. Antennae unicolorous brown to yellowish-brown, terminal flagellar segments sometimes darkened. Basal segment with minute black hairs apically above, segment 3 rather slender, with blunt ended dorsal tooth in basal third. Palpi greyish, apical segment slightly stouter basally and very pointed at tip; clothed with short, predominantly black hairs.

Thorax dark grey on mesonotum, clothed with mostly short pale hairs becoming longer posteriorly and on scutellum. Humeri, mesonotal lateral margin including notopleural lobes, and pteropleuron near root of wing, brownish to yellowish-brown. Pleura more greyish dusted, with longer but fine pale pubescence. *Legs* greyish on coxae and femora, mostly long pale haired, all coxae and hind femora usually translucent brownish, similarly like lower parts of pleura. Tibiae and posterior tarsi brownish, fore tibiae on apical half and fore tarsi blackish or extensively darkened. *Wings* clear with dark veins, no appendix to vein R_4. Halteres yellowish-brown with paler knob at tip.

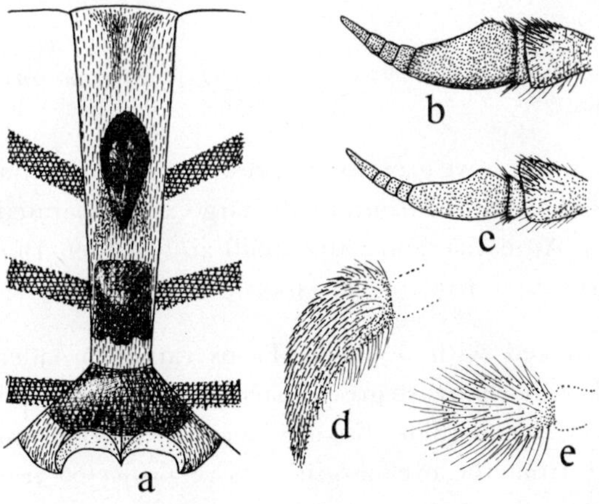

Fig. 100. *Tabanus obsolescens* Pand., a. female frons, b. female antenna, c. male antenna, d. female palpus, e. male palpus.

Abdomen yellowish-brown in ground colour; each tergite with yellowish, oval sublateral patches; rather narrow but high, greyish median triangles which reach anterior margin of each tergite; and a narrow, yellowish posterior border. The pale pattern including extreme sides of tergites pale haired, otherwise abdomen black haired and rather dark brown coloured. Venter mostly reddish-yellow with some greyish areas, uniformly pale haired; apical two sternites greyish, last sternite long black haired, some black hairs also at middle on the foregoing sternite.

♂. Head large, broader than thorax. Eyes naked with two bands, large facets on less than apical two-thirds of eyes are sharply differentiated from the lower area with small facets. Vertex with short, fine pale hairs.. Subcallus entirely polished dark brown. Face and cheeks rather whitish-grey dusted and whitish haired. Antennae more yellowish-brown, segment 3 very slender, with small tooth near base. Palpi whitish-yellow, apical segment oval, hardly twice as long as deep, slightly pointed and mostly whitish haired, only several darker hairs towards tip. Thorax with longer and paler hairs, mesonotum with indistinct greyish longitudinal stripes. Abdomen with the same pattern as in the ♀ but the greyish median triangles often confluent, forming a distinct light grey median stripe. Venter more whitish and longer haired.

Length. 12–14 mm.

DISTRIBUTION. The species was described and is still known only from Greece, from Macedonia and Attica.

TABANUS CAUCASIUS KRÖBER, 1925

Fig. 101.

Tabanus caucasius Kröber, 1925, Arch. Naturgesch., Abt. A, 90 (1924): 183 *(caucasicus* – misspelling of subsequent authors).

DIAGNOSIS. Smaller to medium-sized, olive-grey species, resembling somewhat *glaucopis* Meig. Eyes naked with 3 bands, frontal calli large and separated, subcallus polished black above. Antennae and palpi small and slender. Dorsum of abdomen olive-grey with three rows of pale spots.

DESCRIPTION. ♀. *Head.* Eyes naked with 3 bands. Frons rather broader, index 1: 3.5–4, parallel-sided, and yellowish-grey dusted. Lower callus polished black or blackish-brown, rectangular, broadly separated from subcallus and only very narrowly from the eye-margins; above projected into three distinct points. Median callus black and oval, well separated from lower callus. Vertex with a row of somewhat longer brownish hairs. Subcallus yellowish-grey dusted, polished black above or with two polished patches near upper margin. Face and cheeks paler yellowish-grey dusted and clothed with longer pale hairs. Antennae brownish-yellow, slender, segment 3 darkened and with only a slightly visible dorsal tooth. Palpi brownish-yellow, slightly stout near base, long pointed at tip; clothed with longer pale and some additional black hairs.

Thorax blackish-grey, mesonotum slightly shining with five, narrow, paler longitudinal stripes. Notopleural lobes dark. Pleura rather dark grey dusted and finely pale haired. *Legs.* Coxae and femora greyish, tibiae brown to yellowish-brown; apical third to half of fore tibiae and whole of fore tarsi black. Posterior four tibiae at tip and posterior tarsi darker. *Wings* clear, veins brownish, sometimes a short appendix to vein R_4. Halteres brown.

Abdomen blackish-grey coloured and densely olive-grey dusted, with three rows of paler patches, a median row of often confluent triangles, and two sublateral rows of oval spots. Sternites unicolorous olive-grey dusted and pale haired.

♂. Unknown.

Length. 10—13 mm.

DATES. July and August.

DISTRIBUTION. An endemic species in the Caucasus including its European part.

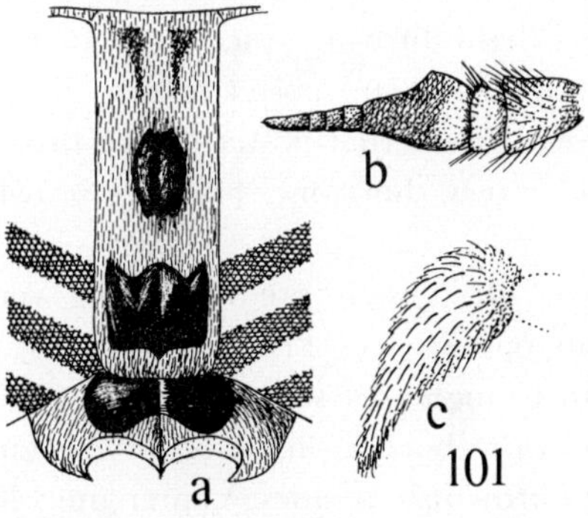

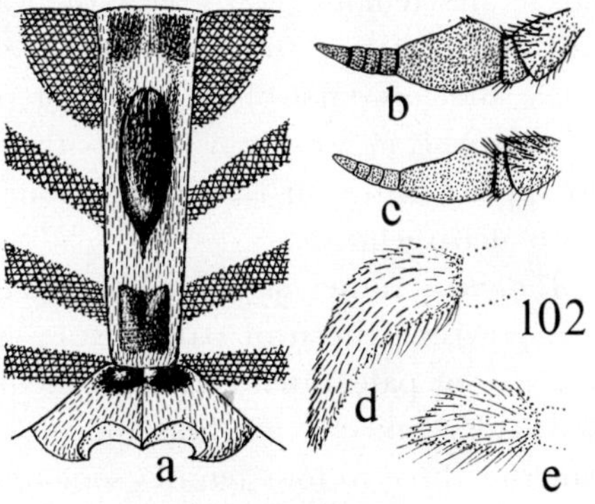

Fig. 101. *Tabanus caucasius* Kröb., female, a. frons, b. antenna, c. palpus.

Fig. 102. *Tabanus exclusus* Pand., a. female frons, b. female antenna, c. male antenna, d. female palpus, e. male palpus.

TABANUS EXCLUSUS PANDELLÉ, 1883

Fig. 102.

Tabanus exclusus Pandellé, 1883, Revue ent., 2: 208.

DIAGNOSIS. A smaller, slender greyish species; abdomen with three rows of distinct pale patches, sometimes brownish at sides. Eyes with 3 bands, frons narrow, lower square callus separated both from subcallus and an elongated median callus; subcallus usually polished black above. Antennae entirely yellowish-brown to reddish. Head in male conspicuously large, large facets sharply separated from the area with small facets, which bears 2 bands.

DESCRIPTION. ♀. *Head.* Eyes naked, with three bands. Frons pale greyish, narrow and slightly widened above, index 1: 5—5.5. Lower callus nearly square-shaped, slightly shining black or brownish, broadly separated from subcallus and median callus, the latter being rather broad, long oval, dull black. Subcallus greyish, usually polished black on the upper half, or at least with a small polished patch in upper corner. Face and cheeks whitish-grey dusted and whitish haired, a blackish-brown parafacial band on each side of antennae distinct. Vertex with small pale hairs. Antennae entirely yellowish-brown to reddish-brown, basal segments densely black haired, segment 3 rather slender, with a small dorsal tooth near base. Palpi whitish to whitish-grey, stouter in basal third and very narrowed and pointed towards tip; mostly with black hairs anteriorly.

Thorax blackish-grey, mesonotum with three narrow, pale grey longitudinal stripes, mostly short pale haired. Notopleural lobes dark, or exceptionally brownish. Pleura paler grey dusted and fine whitish haired. *Legs.* Coxae and femora light grey dusted and pale haired; fore tibiae on basal half and posterior tibiae except tip very light brown; apical half of fore tibiae and fore tarsi black, posterior tibiae at tip and posterior tarsi blackish-brown. *Wings* entirely clear with brown veins; first posterior cell broad, no appendix to vein R_4 or exceptionally a very short one. Halteres brown, knob at tip whitish.

Abdomen rather slender, blackish-grey, often with predominating very pale greyish pattern of pale dusting and pubescence. The pattern consists of a row of pale, often confluent median triangles; of sublateral, and often also lateral rows of patches; and of a narrow border on posterior margin. Anterior three to four tergites sometimes brownish at sides. Venter unicolorous light grey dusted and pale haired, with a darker median stripe. In brownish coloured specimens at least anterior four sternites unicolorous light brown or with only an indication of a brownish median stripe.

♂. Eyes naked and with 2 bands on the lower area with small facets, which are sharply separated from the upper three-quarters with large facets. Vertex with a row of long, mostly pale hairs. Subcallus polished dark brown on the upper half, or at least brownish and somewhat shining at tip. Antennae slender, entirely yellowish-brown. Apical segment of palpi slender, more than twice as long as deep, pointed, whitish-yellow and clothed with long whitish hairs, only rarely with some additional black hairs. Otherwise as in the ♀ but the abdominal pattern is less distinct, especially the median triangles; at least tergites 2 and 3 dark reddish to chestnut-brown coloured at sides.

Length. 11—14 mm.

VARIABILITY. A very variable species, especially in abdominal pattern, resembling in this way *bromius* L. The abdomen varies from entirely blackish-grey with more or less distinct pale pattern, to very reddish-brown at sides on anterior tergites. Also the size of the polished area on subcallus is rather variable.

DATES. From the end of May until August.

DISTRIBUTION. A Mediterranean species especially known from South France but recorded also from Spain, Italy, and from all countries of South East Europe (Jugoslavia, Albania, Greece, Bulgaria) including Turkey.

TABANUS FRASERI AUSTEN, 1925

Fig. 103.

Tabanus fraseri Austen, 1925, Bull. ent. Res., 16: 17.

DIAGNOSIS. Medium-sized species of the *glaucopis*-group resembling *exclusus* Pand. but apical segment of palpi rather short and stout, and abdomen extensively brown.

DESCRIPTION. ♀. *Head.* Eyes naked, with 3 bands. Frons greyish dusted, narrow at base and distinctly widening towards vertex, index about 1: 5—6. Lower callus elongated, rectangular and polished brown, well separated from subcallus and from the eye-margins. Median callus long oval, larger than lower callus and widely separated from it, subshining black. Vertex with fine pale hairs. Subcallus greyish dusted, polished dark brown above, at least slightly at tip. A dark parafacial band more or less distinct. Face and cheeks whitish-grey, former with longer whitish hairs. Antennae yellowish-brown, tip of terminal flagellar segments sometimes slightly darkened;

basal segments silvery dusted and covered with short black hairs above; segment 3 rather broad with blunt tooth at base. Palpi whitish, apical segment short and stout, shortly pointed; pale haired, anteriorly with some black hairs.

Thorax blackish-grey with indistinct paler stripes on mesonotum, pleura more greyish dusted and with longer whitish hairs. Mesonotum clothed with rather short, mostly pale hairs; notopleural lobes dark. *Legs* blackish-grey on coxae and femora and finely pale haired. Fore tibiae on basal half and posterior four tibiae except tip yellowish-brown; apical half of fore tibiae and whole of fore tarsi black, posterior tarsi with corresponding tips of tibiae very darkened. Tibiae and tarsi mostly black haired. *Wings* clear with dark brown veins, no appendix to vein R_4. Halteres yellowish, knobs somewhat brownish at base.

Abdomen yellowish-brown to reddish-brown on anterior three to four tergites, leaving only a broad median stripe black. Posterior tergites blackish, all tergites with short black and pale hairs. Dorsum of abdomen with indistinct pale pattern of silvery-grey dusted median triangles, oval sublateral patches, and narrow posterior margins. Venter brown, apical three sternites blackish-grey.

♂. Unknown.

Length. 12.5–14 mm.

DATES. June and July.

DISTRIBUTION. The species was described from the Asiatic shore of the Dardanelles, Turkey, later recorded also from Albania and Bulgaria.

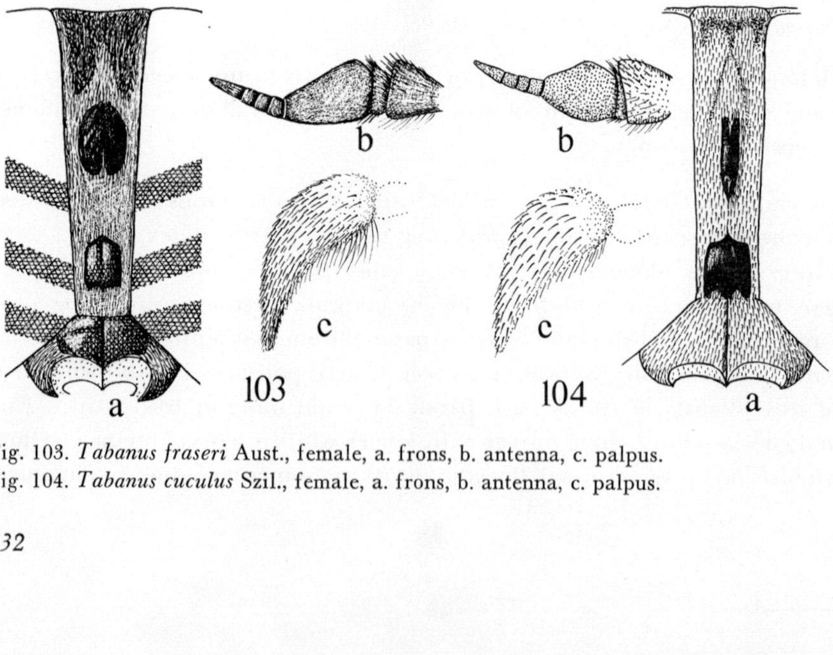

Fig. 103. *Tabanus fraseri* Aust., female, a. frons, b. antenna, c. palpus.
Fig. 104. *Tabanus cuculus* Szil., female, a. frons, b. antenna, c. palpus.

CORDIGER-GROUP

Smaller to medium-sized greyish species, eyes naked, unbanded or with bands. Frons rather broad with median callus large and broad, usually broader than high, sometimes more or less covered by greyish dusting, and broadly separated from lower callus. Latter large, square in shape or broadly rectangular, touching subcallus and usually also the eye-margins. A distinct subgroup of species with milk-white clouded wings and with a long appendix to vein R_4 is represented in Europe by only 2 species but is more distributed in Asia. Subcallus dusted except in *brunneocallosus* Ols.

TABANUS CUCULUS SZILÁDY, 1923

Fig. 104.

Tabanus cuculus Szilády, 1923, Biologica hung., 1 (1): 2.

DIAGNOSIS. Smaller blackish-grey species with a brownish pattern on abdomen as in *bromius*. Eyes naked and unbanded, frons narrow, frontal calli separated. Antennae reddish-yellow, legs yellowish-brown except for darker tarsi.

DESCRIPTION. ♀. *Head*. Eyes naked and unbanded. Frons and subcallus yellowish-grey dusted. Frons narrow, slightly diverging above, index about 1: 5. Lower callus shining black or dark brown, square in shape, touching the subcallus but narrowly separated from the eye-margins. Median callus black and rather narrow, separated from the lower callus or with a slight indication of the joining. Postocular margin narrow, whitish-grey and with a row of short greyish hairs. Face and cheeks whitish-grey dusted, face with fine, densely set whitish hairs. Antennae entirely reddish-yellow, segment 1 greyish dusted, above with small black hairs, below longer pale haired. Segment 3 with blunt ended dorsal tooth. Palpi whitish-yellow, apical segment rather stout at base and long pointed at tip, covered with short pale and black hairs.

Thorax blackish-grey, mesonotum short pale and black haired and with three indistinct paler longitudinal stripes. Pleura pale greyish dusted and covered with rather short but densely set pale hairs. Notopleural lobes yellowish-brown. *Legs* predominantly yellowish-brown and thinly whitish dusted; fore femora above, fore tibiae at tip, whole of fore tarsi, and posterior four tarsi apically, blackish. Coxae and femora with fine whitish hairs, tibiae and tarsi mostly with black hairs. *Wings* clear, veins dark brown, no appendix to vein R_4. Halteres light brown.

Abdomen blackish-grey dusted and black haired, dorsum with three rows of pale haired greyish spots: a row of median triangles, which are large and distinct only on tergites 2 and 3, and two rows of sublateral oval patches, which are large and brown to reddish-brown on tergites 2 to 4. All tergites bear a narrow pale border on posterior margin. Sternites mostly uniformly light reddish-brown coloured and short pale haired, sternites 2 to 5 somewhat greyish at sides, apical two sternites mostly blackish-grey with denser black pubescence.

♂. Unknown.

Length. 12—13.5 mm.

DATES. July.

DISTRIBUTION. The species is known for certain only from the Balkan Peninsula, from Greece and Jugoslavia. The specimens from Soviet Central Asia recorded in the literature are according to Olsufjev (1937: 414), identical with *T. laetitinctus* Beck.

TABANUS CORDIGER MEIGEN, 1820

Fig. 105.

Tabanus cordiger Meigen, 1820, Syst. Beschr., 2: 47.
Tabanus atricornis Meigen, 1838, Syst. Beschr., 7: 59.
Tabanus latifrons Zetterstedt, 1842, Dipt. Scand., 1: 106.
Tabanus vicinus Egger, 1859, Verh. zool.-bot. Ges. Wien, 9: 391.
Tabanus Braueri Jaennicke, 1866, Berl. ent. Z., 10: 83 (nom. nov. for *vicinus* Egger, nec Macq.).
Tabanus megacephalus Jaennicke, 1866, Berl. ent. Z., 10: 82.

DIAGNOSIS. Medium-sized blackish-grey species with eyes naked and unbanded; frons in female broad, median callus black, transverse, widely separated from lower callus; latter being large, polished black and touching the subcallus. Antennae black. Head in male very large, large facets sharply separated from small facets, vertex in both sexes with long pale and black hairs.

DESCRIPTION. ♀. *Head.* Eyes naked, unbanded. Frons and subcallus yellowish-grey dusted, former broad, index 1: 2.5—3.3, slightly widening towards vertex. Lower callus square in shape, very large and polished black, touching the subcallus and the eye-margins. Median callus black but rather dulled, large, transverse, oval in shape and broadly separated from the lower callus. Vertex with a row of long pale and some black hairs. Face and cheeks whitish-grey dusted and long pale haired, cheeks with distinct dark brown parafacial band on each side of antennae. Antennae black, basal two segments with short black hairs, segment 3 broad with well developed, nearly rectangular dorsal tooth. Palpi whitish-yellow, very stout at base, apically pointed; mostly whitish haired, with some additional small black hairs.

Thorax blackish-grey, mesonotum with indefinite paler longitudinal stripes and mostly fine black haired, pleura light grey dusted and clothed with long whitish hairs. Notopleural lobes yellowish-brown with black hairs. *Legs.* Coxae and femora black with greyish dusting and with mostly fine pale hairs; tibiae yellowish-brown, fore tibiae on apical third and posterior four tibiae at tip black. Tarsi black, slightly brownish near base. *Wings* clear, veins blackish-brown; no appendix to vein R_4. Halteres dark brown.

Abdomen black, blackish-grey dusted and black haired; each tergite with a pair of small, greyish, oval sublateral patches, a pale median triangle and paler posterior margin. The greyish pattern on dorsum of abdomen is pale haired, median triangles are less visible on posterior tergites. Tergite 2 sometimes indistinctly brownish at sides. Venter unicolorous light grey dusted and pale haired, last sternite darker and black haired.

♂. Head conspicuously large, semiglobular and distinctly broader than thorax. Eyes naked and unbanded, facets on the upper three-quarters very large and sharply separated from the small facets on lower quarter. Postocular margin very narrow and with a row of long, mostly pale hairs. A distinct dark parafacial band on each side of antennae, palpi whitish-yellow

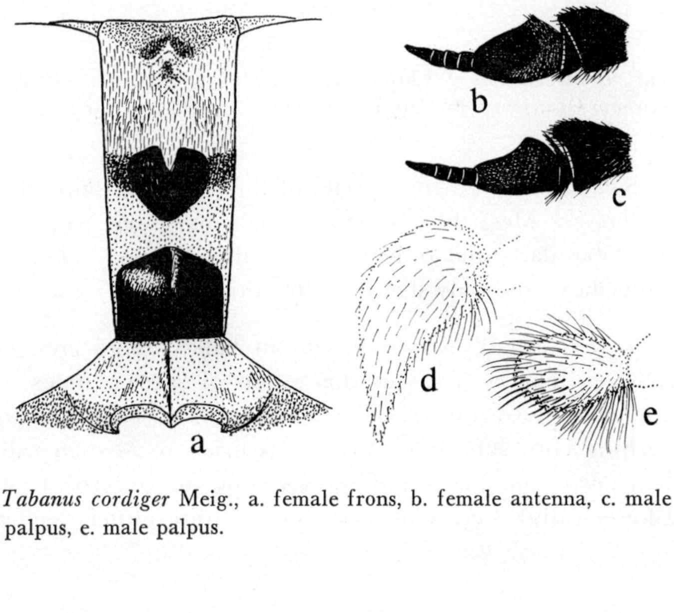

Fig. 105. *Tabanus cordiger* Meig., a. female frons, b. female antenna, c. male antenna, d. female palpus, e. male palpus.

and mostly whitish haired, apical segment stouter towards tip. Thorax with longer, mostly pale hairs on mesonotum; otherwise as in the ♀ including the abdominal pattern but tergites 2 and 3 (or to 4) always brown at sides.

Length. 12–17 mm.

VARIABILITY. A little variable species; the pale grey abdominal pattern is sometimes less distinct, especially a row of median triangles, and frontal median callus varies often both in shape and the intensity of black coloration.

BIOLOGY. A widely distributed but never common species, females attack man and domestic animals (horses and horned cattle). The larva was described by Marchand (1920), the pupa by the same author and by Picard & Blanc (1913).

DATES. From the end of May until August.

DISTRIBUTION. A species with a large area of distribution known from Great Britain through Scandinavia and the Leningrad region as far as the Ural Mts., it is recorded from most countries in Europe, from North Africa (Morocco), Turkey, Armenia and Iran. The older literary records of *T. cordiger* from the Far East and Japan refer in fact to *T. kinoshitai* Kono & Takahasi, 1939.

TABANUS SMIRNOVI OLSUFJEV, 1962

Fig. 106.

Tabanus tauricus Olsufjev, 1952, Chron. Ent., 32: 312 (nec Enderlein, 1932).
Tabanus smirnovi Olsufjev, 1962, Ént. Obozr., 41: 577 (nom. nov. for *tauricus* Olsufjev nec Enderlein).

DIAGNOSIS. Smaller blackish-grey species of the *cordiger*-group, eyes unbanded as in *cordiger* Meig. but frons in female narrower, palpi less stout, notopleural lobes dark, and in general a smaller species. The male differs in the smaller head and only slightly differentiated facets.

DESCRIPTION. ♀. *Head.* Eyes naked, without bands. Frons greyish dusted, rather narrower than is usual in this group of species, index 1: 3.7–4, slightly widened above. Lower callus shining black, large and square in shape, touching both subcallus and the eye-margins. Median callus oval, higher than deep, dull black and usually bifid above, broadly separated from the lower callus. Vertex on postocular margin rather slender with a row of long black and grey hairs. Subcallus greyish dusted, face and cheeks whitish-grey, finely whitish haired. Parafacial band on each side of antennae dark brown and distinct. Antennae black, basal two segments black haired, segment 3 rather broad with somewhat blunt dorsal tooth. Palpi whitish, apical segment only slightly stouter near base, long pointed apically and clothed with mostly whitish and some additional black hairs.

Thorax blackish-grey, mesonotum unstriped, pleura more greyish dusted and paler haired. Notopleural lobes dark grey. *Legs* blackish-grey coloured and grey dusted, femora finely pale haired. Fore tibiae whitish-yellow on basal half, apical half and fore tarsi black. Posterior four tibiae yellowish-brown, apically darkened, as well as tarsi. *Wings* clear, veins dark brown; no appendix to vein R_4. Halteres whitish with brownish base to stem.

Abdomen blackish-grey dusted and black haired, tergites with oblique, oval pale haired lateral patches which do not reach the tergal margins, and with a row of usually only slightly visible pale median triangles. Tergite 2 very indistinctly brownish anteriorly and at sides, all tergites very narrowly paler on posterior margin. Venter light grey dusted and pale haired, sometimes with an indefinite darker median stripe, posterior two sternites with black hairs.

♂. Head rather smaller, eyes naked and unbanded. Facets on the upper part of eyes only indistinctly larger, no distinct separation from smaller facets. Vertex with a row of long black hairs, subcallus dark, greyish dusted. Face and cheeks whitish-grey dusted as in the ♀ but cheeks mostly with long blackish hairs. Antennae black, segment 3 rather broad with well developed dorsal tooth, terminal flagellar segments long and slender. Apical segment of palpi whitish-yellow, short and stout, apically pointed and down-

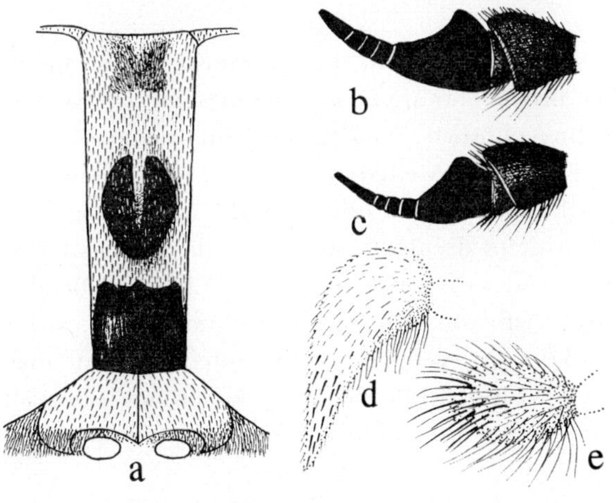

Fig. 106. *Tabanus smirnovi* Ols., a. female frons, b. female antenna, c. male antenna, d. female palpus, e. male palpus.

curved; mostly long whitish haired, with some black hairs before tip. Thorax more or less shining blackish-brown, mesonotum clothed with rather long black and whitish hairs, pleura mostly whitish-grey haired. Legs extensively darkened, posterior four tibiae brownish at base only. Halteres blackish-brown with stem and knob at tip pale. Abdomen with the same pattern, median triangles still less visible but tergite 2 with more distinct brown side markings. Venter greyish dusted, sternites with paler posterior margins and, except posterior three sternites, pale haired.

Length. 11–14 mm.

VARIABILITY. The shape and size of the frontal median callus in the female are rather variable, the callus is very elongated in some specimens, and rather narrowly separated from the lower callus.

DATES. From June until August.

DISTRIBUTION. *T. smirnovi* Ols. is still known only from the Crimea.

TABANUS LELEANI AUSTEN, 1920

Fig. 107.

Tabanus leleani Austen, 1920, Bull. ent. Res., 10: 312.

DIAGNOSIS. Smaller blackish-grey species of the *cordiger*-group. Eyes naked with 1 band, frons in female broad with only indistinct median callus. Antennae black with rather slender segment 3, palpi whitish and very stout. Head in male large, semiglobular, eyes with 1 band and very enlarged facets on upper three-quarters.

DESCRIPTION. ♀. *Head*. Eyes naked with one conspicuously broad band. Frons greyish dusted, rather broad and slightly widening towards vertex, index 1: 2.7–3.5. Lower callus polished black, large, square-shaped, touching the subcallus and eye-margins. Median callus dull black, broadly separated from the lower callus; sometimes only slightly visible, more or less covered by the greyish dusting or divided into two smaller dark patches. Vertex rather narrow, whitish, and with a row of long pale hairs. Subcallus greyish dusted; face and cheeks whitish with long concolorous hairs, a distinct dark brown parafacial band on each side of the antennae. Antennae black, segment 3 rather slender with small dorsal tooth, sometimes brownish at base. Palpi whitish, apical segment very stout and sharply pointed at tip, clothed with whitish hairs.

Thorax blackish-grey, mesonotum mostly fine pale haired, unstriped. Pleura light grey dusted and densely whitish haired. Notopleural lobes yellowish-brown coloured and clothed with black hairs. *Legs* grey on coxae and femora, sometimes also tibiae extensively greyish; fore tibiae yellowish-brown on basal half, apical half of fore tibiae and all tarsi blackish. Posterior four tibiae brownish to brownish-grey, with darkened tip. *Wings* clear with dark veins, no appendix to vein R_4. Halteres whitish, brownish at base.

Abdomen blackish-grey with small, oval, oblique pale patches at sides and a very indistinct median row of paler triangles. Sternites blackish-grey with rather broad but indistinct darker median stripe.

♂. Head large, semiglobular, much broader than thorax. Eyes naked with one band, facets on the upper three-quarters very large and sharply separated from the lower quarter with small facets. Vertex with a row of long greyish hairs. Antennae more slender, segment 3 with well developed dorsal tooth, usually brownish on basal half. Palpi whitish, very stout, nearly circular with slightly pointed apex. Otherwise as in the ♀ but thorax bears longer hairs and hind tibiae usually more brownish. Halteres brownish.

Length. 11.5—15 mm.

VARIABILITY. *T. leleani turkestanicus* Olsufjev, 1970 (nom.nov. for *T. leleani pallidus* Olsufjev, 1937; nec Palisot de Beauvois, 1809) was described by Olsufjev as a distinct subspecies from the south eastern regions of the area of distribution of *T. leleani* Aust., viz. from Iran, Iraq, Armenia and Turkmenia. It differs from the nominate form in the general paler coloration, in

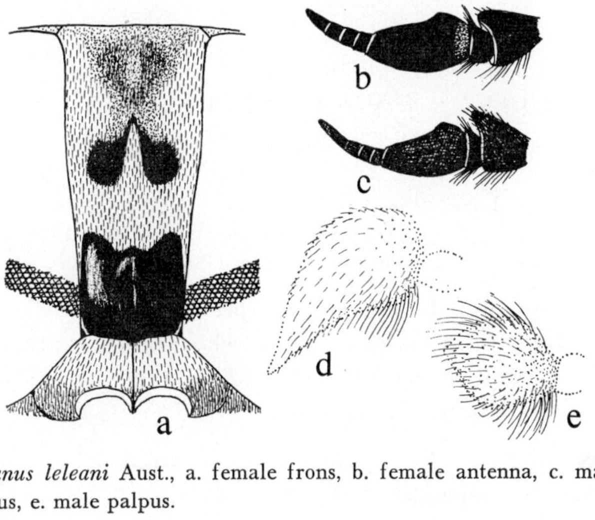

Fig. 107. *Tabanus leleani* Aust., a. female frons, b. female antenna, c. male antenna, d. female palpus, e. male palpus.

the brownish sidemarkings on tergites 1 to 3 (or 4), in the more distinct paler abdominal pattern, and in yellowish posterior four tibiae. Only when more precise data on the distribution of the paler form is available, can the taxonomic position of the ssp. *turkestanicus* Ols. be solved. It seems, however, to be sympatric in distribution with the nominate »subspecies« at least in Iran, Iraq and the Nachitchevan ASSR, and if intermediate forms are found, ssp. *turkestanicus* will be only a pale infrasubspecific variety. It is also probably identical with an unnamed form recorded by Kröber (1925a: 118) from Algeria.

BIOLOGY. Rather a common species with a wide area of distribution, in mountains it is known at altitudes up to 2200 to 2500 m. Males are to be found sucking on *Ferula karatvica* and *F. penninervis* (Shevtshenko, 1961: 148). Females attack man, horned cattle, horses and camels.

DATES. From April until August.

DISTRIBUTION. A species inhabiting a wide area of distribution, it is known in Europe from Greece including the islands of Crete and Cyprus, from Near and Middle East, eastwards as far as North West China and Mongolia, and from an adjacent part of the Oriental region (Punjab, Kangra valley). It is recorded from Turkey, Israel, Iraq, Iran, Afghanistan, in the U.S.S.R. from the Caucasus, Transcaucasus, and from some Central Asiatic republics (Kazakhstan, Uzbekistan, Tadjikistan), it has been recorded as far as Siberia in the region of Altai. In North Africa it is recorded from Morocco through Algeria as far as Tunisia. It will be found very probably also in other countries of South East Europe.

TABANUS UNIFASCIATUS LOEW, 1858

Fig. 108.

Tabanus unifasciatus Loew, 1858, Verh. zool.-bot. Ges. Wien, 8: 600.
Tabanus unifasciatus var. *albescens* Kröber, 1928, Dt. ent. Ztg., 1928: 430.
Tabanus unifasciatus pallidus Hauser, 1960, Ént. Obozr., 39: 647.

DIAGNOSIS. Medium-sized blackish-grey species of the *cordiger*-group, eyes with 1 band. It differs from *leleani* Aust., which possesses also one eye-band, in the narrower frons in female, index 1: 3.5–4, and in the small head in male with all facets nearly equal in size.

DESCRIPTION. ♀. *Head.* Eyes naked with one band. Frons greyish dusted, rather narrow in comparison with other species of this group, index 1: 3.5

to 4, slightly diverging towards vertex. Lower callus shining black, large and square in shape, touching both subcallus and the eye-margins. Median callus large, rather dull black, oval in shape and often bifid above, broadly separated from the lower callus. Vertex rather narrow with a row of long black and pale hairs. Subcallus dull, greyish dusted, face and cheeks whitish-grey dusted and densely whitish haired. A parafacial band on each side of antennae dark brown. Antennae black, segment 3 rather broad with blunt dorsal tooth. Palpi whitish, very stout at base and apically pointed, pale haired, with some additional black hairs.

Thorax blackish-grey, pleura distinctly whitish-grey dusted and pale haired. Mesonotum with very indefinite paler longitudinal stripes. Notopleural lobes dark, exceptionally brownish. *Legs.* Coxae and femora grey, tibiae yellowish-brown; fore tibiae on apical third, posterior tibiae at tip, and all tarsi, mostly blackish. *Wings* clear with dark veins, no appendix to vein R_4. Halteres dark brown, knob paler at tip.

Abdomen blackish-grey dusted and black haired; the pale pattern consists of a row of rather indistinct median triangles, and of small but more distinct oval sublateral spots. Each tergite bears a narrow pale posterior margin. Venter uniformly blackish-grey dusted and pale haired, last sternite with black hairs.

♂. Head conspicuously small, eyes naked with one band. All facets nearly equal in size. Vertex narrow with a row of long, predominantly blackish-grey hairs. Antennae black, segment 3 more slender. Palpi whitish, apical segment very short and nearly globular, mostly black haired on apical half.

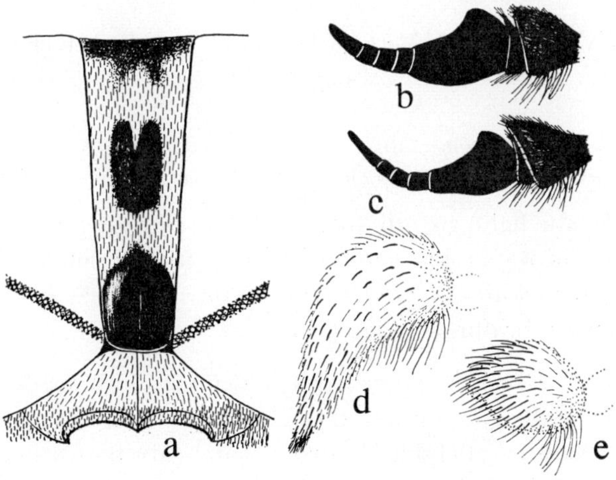

Fig. 108. *Tabanus unifasciatus* Lw., a. female frons, b. female antenna, c. male antenna, d. female palpus, e. male palpus.

Abdominal pattern as in the ♀ but median triangles still less distinct or missing, tergite 2 (or also tergite 3) light chestnut-brown at sides.

Length. 14—16 mm.

VARIABILITY. Rather a variable species, the legs are often extensively darkened, tibiae sometimes blackish-grey. The light specimens with conspicuous silver pubescence were named by Kröber as a variety *albescens*. This form was described from Turkey, and the subspecies *pallidus* described by Hauser from Nachitschevan, represents very probably only a junior synonym.

BIOLOGY. The males have been collected by one of the authors (Chvála, 1964: 380) in larger numbers in the morning on a sun-lit cottage in a forest clearing in North East Slovakia, Czechoslovakia.

DATES. From June until August.

DISTRIBUTION. The species is known throughout South Europe from Portugal and Spain through France, Italy, Jugoslavia, Greece, Albania, Bulgaria and Rumania to South Ukraine, Crimea and the Caucasus including Transcaucasus (Armenia, Azerbaijan). It has also been recorded from Asia Minor, Iran, Syria, Israel and North Africa. The north border of its occurrence in Europe lies in southern parts of Central Europe, where it has been recorded from Hungary, Austria and Czechoslovakia. Kröber (1932b) recorded it from Germany (Württemberg) probably by mistake, as we have not found any documentary material even in the Museum at Stuttgart.

TABANUS BRUNNEOCALLOSUS OLSUFJEV, 1936

Fig. 109.

Tabanus gerckei Brauer; Kröber, 1914, Arch. Naturgesch., Abt. A, 90 (9): 174.
Tabanus brunneocallosus Olsufjev, 1936, Trudy Kazachstan. Fil. AN SSSR, 2: 167.

DIAGNOSIS. Small, light greyish species of the *cordiger*-group with a long appendix to vein R_4. From the other species with the same combination of characters, *brunneocallosus* Ols. differs in the unstriped eyes and in the polished brown subcallus at sides.

DESCRIPTION. ♀. *Head.* Eyes unstriped, sometimes with sparse microscopic hairing. Frons light grey dusted, broad, index 1: 2—2.5, slightly widening out on lower half, parallel-sided above. Frontal calli brownish; lower callus broad, nearly touching the eye-margins or very narrowly separated, polished and slightly convex. Median callus broadly oval, longitudinally wrinkled.

Subcallus dusted at middle, broadly polished brown at sides. Face and cheeks unicolorous very pale whitish-grey dusted and with whitish hairs. Antennae blackish or brownish on basal segments and on segment 3 at base; segment 3 slender, with only indistinct dorsal tooth. Palpi whitish with concolorous hairs, rather stout at base and sharply pointed at tip. Postocular margin deep, with fine and closely set whitish hairs.

Thorax light grey dusted and covered by whitish hairs, those on pleura more numerous and longer. Mesonotum with four, darker longitudinal stripes, notopleural lobes yellowish-brown. *Legs* light grey on coxae and femora; knees, tibiae and tarsi yellowish-brown but fore tibiae on apical half and whole of fore tarsi extensively darkened. Legs pale haired, only blackish parts on fore legs with dark hairs. *Wings* slightly milk-white, veins brown, lighter at base and on costal half; a long appendix to vein R_4. Halteres whitish-yellow.

Abdomen very pale greyish dusted, dorsum with dark median longitudinal stripe of paired, narrow dark spots on each tergite, sometimes another row of indistinct darker spots at side. Posterior margins to all tergites narrowly yellowish-grey. Venter unicolorous light grey. Short pubescence whitish, only dark areas with blackish hairs.

♂. Unknown.

Length. 10–12 mm.

Variability. According to Shevtshenko (1961) a little variable species, antennal segment 3 brownish or entirely black, and notopleural lobes sometimes darkened.

Biology. A typical species of steppes and heaths, according to Olsufjev (1937: 262) the adults inhabit the regions near salt lakes. Females attack camels and horses.

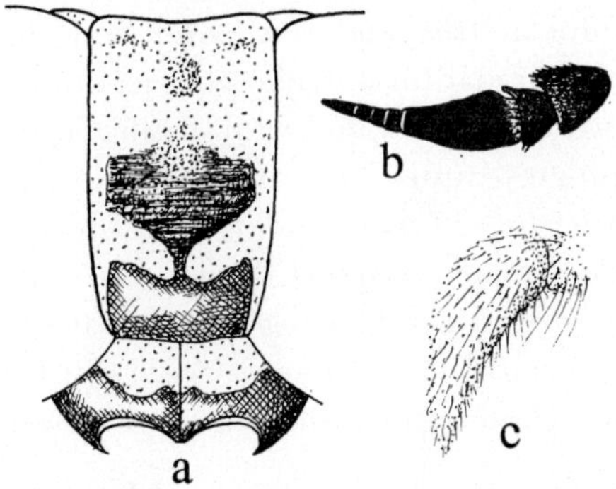

Fig. 109. *Tabanus brunneocallosus* Ols., female, a. frons, b. antenna, c. palpus.

DATES. From the end of May until August.

DISTRIBUTION. A species with rather limited area of distribution, known from Kazakhstan, North West China and Mongolia. According to Olsufjev (in litt. 31.XII. 1969) the species penetrates west to adjacent regions of the European part of the U.S.S.R.

TABANUS SABULETORUM LOEW, 1874

Fig. 110.

Tabanus sabuletorum Loew, 1874, Z. ges. Naturwiss. (N. F.), 9: 414.
Tabanus (Tabanus) Gerkei Brauer, 1880, Denkschr. Akad. Wiss. Wien, 42: 205.
Tabanus lama Portschinsky, 1892, Horae Soc. ent. ross., 26: 201.

DIAGNOSIS. Smaller whitish-grey species of the *cordiger*-group with four eye-bands. Frons broad in female; antennae slender, brownish at base, segment 3 mostly dark; no parafacial band. Male with very large head, eyes with three bands and sharply differentiated large and small facets. The only one European species of this group with more than one eye-band.

DESCRIPTION. ♀. *Head.* Eyes naked with four bands. Frons light grey dusted, broad, index 1: 2.3–3, slightly widened above. Lower callus narrow, in the form of a transverse rectangle, shining black to dark brown, touching the eye-margins. Median callus black and only slightly polished, in the form of a transverse patch, quite separated from lower callus. Vertex whitish, deep above and distinctly narrowed on postocular margin laterally, with a row of long whitish-grey hairs. Subcallus, face and cheeks whitish-grey dusted, face and cheeks with long whitish hairs. Antennae very slender, segment 3 with hardly visible dorsal tooth. Basal two segments brownish, pale greyish dusted and pale haired, segment 3 mostly blackish or dark brownish. Palpi whitish, apical segment very stout at base and very pointed at tip, clothed with whitish hairs and some additional black hairs on apical third.

Thorax blackish-grey, mesonotum whitish haired and with distinct whitish longitudinal stripes. Pleura whitish-grey dusted and finely whitish haired, notopleural lobes yellowish-brown. *Legs.* Coxae and femora greyish, femora at tip and tibiae yellowish; fore tibiae on apical third to half and fore tarsi black, posterior four tibiae at tip darker. Tarsi dark, basal segment yellowish at base. *Wings* slightly milk-white clouded with distinct dark veins, a long appendix to vein R_4. Halteres whitish, somewhat brownish at base.

Abdomen blackish-grey with conspicuous, large whitish patches in three rows; the sublateral patches very large and oblique, occupying the whole width of the tergites; median triangles nearly as large, reaching anterior margin of each tergite. Posterior margins to all tergites with distinct border. Sternites whitish-grey dusted, with whitish border on posterior margin, and an indistinctly darker median stripe.

♂. Head large and distinctly semiglobular. Eyes naked with three bands, facets on the upper two-thirds very enlarged and distinctly separated from the lower third with small facets. Vertex with a row of long pale greyish, forward directed hairs. Antennae more slender on segment 3; palpi short and stout, whitish with concolorous hairs. Otherwise as in the ♀ but anterior three to four tergites brownish-yellow at sides.

Length. 9–15 mm.

VARIABILITY. A little variable species but some pale specimens have antennal segment 3 mostly brownish except black terminal flagellar segments, and tergites 2 and 3 are slightly translucent brownish at sides. In the female there are sometimes only 3 bands on eyes instead of the usual four bands.

BIOLOGY. A common species, especially in Asia, inhabiting steppes and forests; more common near salt lakes but also on sand dunes. Females attack camels, horses, horned cattle, less often also sheep, goats and man. The adults have also been collected in mountains at altitudes up to 1800 m in the Zailijskij Alatau (Shevtshenko, 1961: 141).

DATES. From May until August, on the coast of the Caspian Sea until the end of September.

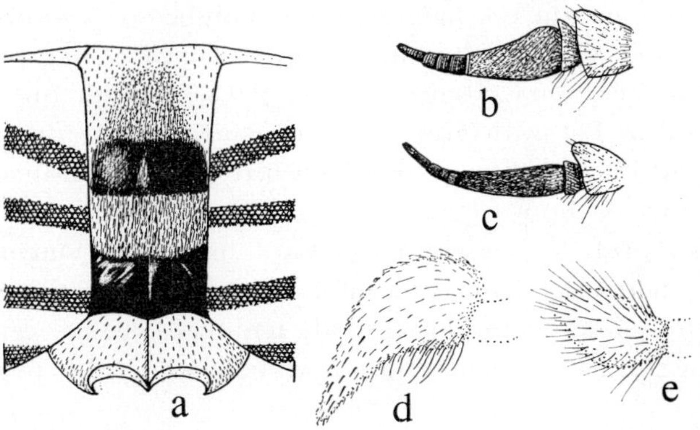

Fig. 110. *Tabanus sabuletorum* Lw., a. female frons, b. female antenna, c. male antenna, d. female palpus, e. male palpus.

Distribution. A Central Asiatic species penetrating eastwards as far as Mongolia and Transbaikalia, a common species in Kazakhstan and Iran from where it penetrates through Azerbaijan to the adjacent European parts of the Caucasus, to Crimea and South Ukraine. It has not yet been recorded from Turkey.

BROMIUS-GROUP

Generally medium-sized species, eyes naked with bands or unbanded. Frons rather narrow, median callus narrow and connected with lower callus. Latter usually only narrowly separated from subcallus and from the eye-margins, globular to nearly rectangular, and then higher than broad. Subcallus dusted.

TABANUS BRIANI LECLERCQ, 1962

Fig. 111.

Tabanus briani Leclercq, 1962, Bull. Inst. agron. Stns. Rech. Gembloux, 30: 135.
Tabanus carpathicus Chvála, 1964, Acta Soc. ent. Čechoslov., 61: 381.

Diagnosis. Medium-sized to rather larger species; eyes without bands, frons rather broad (index 1: 3), antennal segment 3 brown, and palpi stout, whitish-yellow. Median frontal callus elongated and narrowly connected with lower callus. Abdomen blackish-grey with pale pattern as in *cordiger* Meig.

Description. ♀. *Head.* Eyes naked, without bands. Frons greyish dusted and short black haired especially on the upper part; rather broad, index 1: 3, and nearly parallel-sided. Lower callus nearly square, narrowly separated from subcallus and the eye-margins, mostly polished dark brown at middle, blackish at sides. Median callus shining black, elongated and connected with lower callus. Vertex on postocular margin whitish with fine concolorous hairs. Subcallus flat with grey tomentum, on the lower part sometimes slightly brownish. The brown coloration becomes more distinct below and forms a transverse brown parafacial band on each side of antennae. Face and cheeks whitish, former with long whitish hairs. Basal antennal segments black with short black hairs, segment 1 with greyish tomentum; segment 3 brown with well developed dorsal tooth, terminal flagellar segments blackish towards tip. Palpi stout, yellowish-white, clothed with pale and black hairs.

Thorax. Mesonotum greyish dusted, with indefinite paler longitudinal stripes (a median and two sublateral), notopleural lobes brownish. Mesonotum with fine, short black hairs, pleura more greyish dusted and with longer whitish hairs. *Legs.* Coxae and femora greyish, tibiae brownish; fore tibiae at tip and whole of tarsi black. *Wings* clear, veins blackish, brownish along costal margin and near base of wing; no appendix to vein R_4. Halteres blackish-brown.

Abdomen blackish-grey, the paler pattern on dorsum consists of a row of median triangles and two rows of rounded sublateral spots, and each tergite bears a narrow border on posterior margin. Venter paler than dorsum, unicolorous greyish, with only indefinite darker median stripe.

♂. Unknown.

Length. 16–18 mm.

BIOLOGY. A typical species of woodlands in hilly countries. The species has been described from Czechoslovakia as *T. carpathicus* Chvála from a single holotype female taken in Poloninské Karpaty Mts., Slovakia, in the morning on the sun-lit canvas of a tent, but in the following years the species has been found to be common in the same locality, attacking man and horses.

DATES. From June until August.

DISTRIBUTION. The species was described only recently and its area of distribution is still not very well known. It has been recorded throughout South Europe (Spain, France, Italy, Jugoslavia, Bulgaria and Turkey) and in an isolated locality in North East Slovakia.

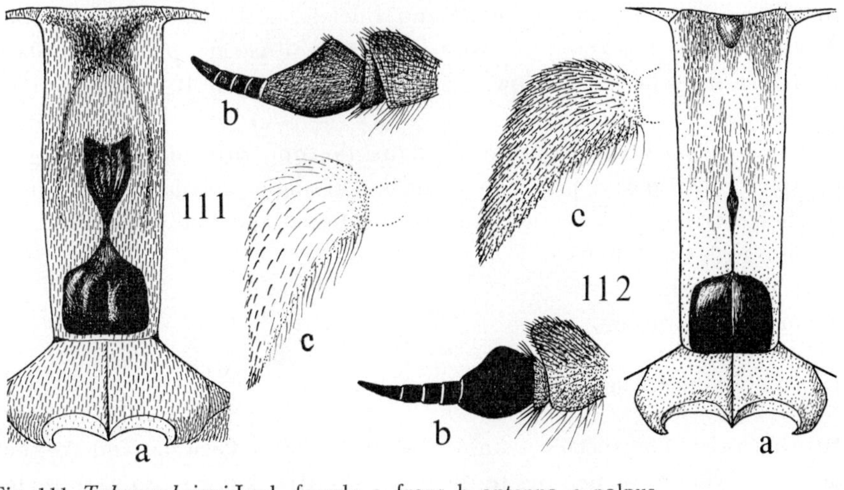

Fig. 111. *Tabanus briani* Lecl., female, a. frons, b. antenna, c. palpus.
Fig. 112. *Tabanus armeniacus* Kröb., female, a. frons, b. antenna, c. palpus.

TABANUS ARMENIACUS (KRÖBER, 1928)

Fig. 112.

Atylotus armeniacus Kröber, 1928, Zool. Anz., 76: 267.

DIAGNOSIS. Medium-sized blackish-grey species, eyes naked, unbanded. Antennae black, palpi pale and thickened, densely black haired. Frontal index 1: 3.5—4, lower callus polished black, large and square, connected with a linear median callus.

DESCRIPTION. ♀. *Head.* Eyes naked, unbanded, whole of the head pale greyish dusted. Frons parallel-sided, index 1: 3.5—4, black haired on upper two-thirds. Lower callus large, shining black, square, touching the subcallus and only narrowly separated from the eye-margins. Median callus linear, connected with lower callus. Postocular margin rather narrow and with only short pale and dark brown hairs, frons with some longer black hairs above. Subcallus dulled, cheeks with shorter, face with longer, whitish hairs. Antennae black, basal two segments greyish dusted and clothed with short black and pale hairs. Segment 3 broad at base, dorsal tooth rectangular; terminal flagellar segments long and slender. Palpi whitish-yellow to very light brownish, thickened at base, pointed at tip; densely black haired and with some pale hairs at base.

Thorax black in ground colour, only thinly greyish dusted; mesonotum with indistinct, narrow, pale longitudinal stripes, finely black haired and with pale hairs at margins. Pleura more greyish dusted and clothed mostly with whitish, fine longer hairs. Notopleural lobes dark. *Legs* blackish-grey, coxae and femora greyish dusted and finely, mostly pale haired. Tibiae dark grey, short black and whitish haired. Fore tibiae at tip and tarsi black. *Wings* clear, veins dark brown; no appendix to vein R_4. Halteres dark brown.

Abdomen black with concolorous hairs, dorsum with three rows of greyish spots consisting of pale haired median triangles and large oval lateral patches. Sternites unicolorous pale greyish dusted and fine pale haired, last sternite with black hairs.

♂. Unknown.

Length. 15—16 mm.

DATES. July and August.

DISTRIBUTION. The species is known from Armenia, Georgia, and Azerbaijan, from where it penetrates to the Caucasus Mts., known also from higher altitudes. Olsufjev (1969a) did not record this species from the European part of the U.S.S.R. but we have seen the documentary material, collected by P. Starý on 31.VII.1966, from Elbrus near the glacier Irik, 2500 m above sea level.

TABANUS MIKI BRAUER, 1880

Fig. 113.

Tabanus graecus Meigen, 1820, Syst. Beschr., 2: 53 (nec Fabricius, 1794).

Tabanus (Tabanus) Mikii Brauer, 1880, Denkschr. Akad. Wiss. Wien, 42: 195.

Tabanus velutinus Kröber, 1936, Acta Inst. Mus. zool. Univ. athen., 1: 38 (nec Surcouf, 1906) – syn. n.

Tabanus miki niger Olsufjev, 1937, Fauna SSSR, 7: 275, 413 (nec Palisot de Beauvois, 1806 and Casablou, 1904) – syn. n.

Tabanus miki niger f. australis Hauser, 1960, Ént. Obozr., 39: 657 – syn. n.

Tabanus postvelutinus Moucha, 1962, Acta faun. ent. Mus. Nat. Pragae, 8: 32 (nom. nov. for *velutinus* Kröb. nec Surc.) – syn. n.

Tabanus miki colchidicus Olsufjev, 1970, Ént. Obozr., 49: 684 (nom. nov. for *niger* Ols. nec Palisot de Beauvois and Casablou) – syn. n.

DIAGNOSIS. Medium-sized species with abdominal pattern resembling *bromius* L. Anterior four tergites more or less reddish-brown at sides or abdomen entirely dark grey including on venter. Eyes in female naked and unstriped, frons rather narrow. Head in male not broader than thorax, vertex with a row of long black hairs. Eyes naked with one band and sharply differentiated large and small facets.

DESCRIPTION. ♀. *Head.* Eyes naked, unbanded, frons and subcallus greyish-yellow dusted. Frons narrow, index 1: 4—5, lower callus long rectangular to triangular-shaped, black to blackish-brown, slightly shining and narrowly separated from the eye-margins. Median callus black, spindle-shaped, connected with lower callus. Face and cheeks greyish dusted and especially below finely greyish haired. Vertex on postocular margin slightly deeper with somewhat longer mostly pale hairs, in dark specimens with nearly black hairs. Antennae brownish on basal two segments and on segment 3 except tip, or antennae nearly black, leaving only extreme base of segment 3 brownish. Dorsal tooth blunt ended, segment 3 rather broader. Palpi greyish-yellow to yellowish, distinctly stout in basal third, apically pointed; mostly black haired.

Thorax. Mesonotum greyish-black, short yellowish and black haired, with distinct darker longitudinal stripes. Notopleural lobes brownish to dark. Pleura more greyish dusted and densely yellowish-grey haired. *Legs.* The ground colour of coxae and femora black, coxae similarly grey dusted as pleura, femora blackish-grey dusted and finely pale haired. Fore tibiae on basal half and posterior four tibiae brownish, apical half of fore tibiae and fore tarsi black, posterior four tarsi dark brown. *Wings* clear with dark brown veins, sometimes a short appendix to vein R_4. First posterior cell sometimes slightly narrower towards tip. Halteres dark brown, knob at tip whitish.

Abdomen with reddish-brown side markings on anterior three to four tergites, otherwise blackish-grey with three rows of pale patches, a row of median triangles and sublateral oval patches. The lateral patches are in very brownish specimens concolorous with reddish-brown sidemarkings on anterior tergites, or abdomen extensively darkened, leaving in very dark specimens only anterior margin of tergite 2 translucent brownish at sides. Venter usually reddish-brown to yellowish-brown on anterior four sternites, or venter mostly blackish-grey in dark specimens, always only finely pale haired.

♂. Head not very broad, at most as broad as thorax. Eyes naked with sharply separated large facets on the upper two-thirds of eyes, and with one purple band on the border between large and small facets. Vertex with a row of longer black and pale hairs. Antennae smaller and segment 3 usually more brownish. Apical segment of palpi yellowish to yellowish-grey, shortly pointed at tip, downcurved and clothed with longer, mostly dark hairs. Thorax with dense and longer, mostly pale hairs, especially on mesonotum. Legs and wings as in the ♀, abdomen usually more brownish at sides, lea-

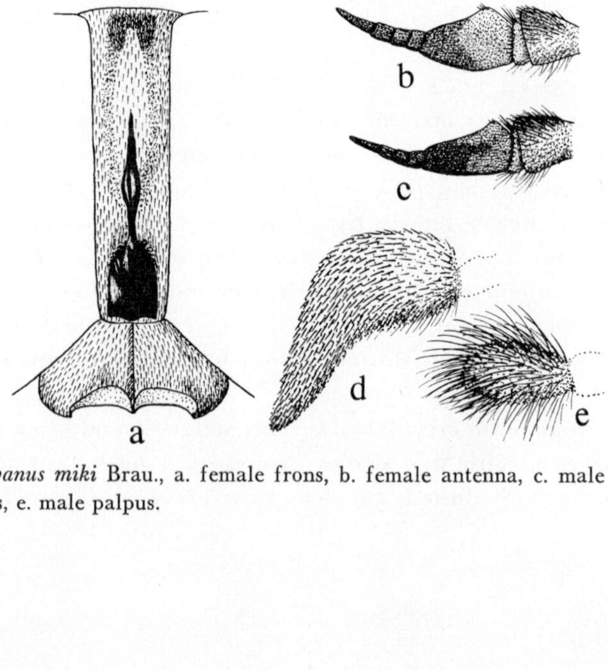

Fig. 113. *Tabanus miki* Brau., a. female frons, b. female antenna, c. male antenna, d. female palpus, e. male palpus.

ving only a narrow, blackish median stripe on dorsum, venter blackish-grey usually only on posterior three sternites.

Length. 13–17 mm.

Variability. A very variable species especially in coloration on abdomen, in the shape and coloration of lower frontal callus in female, in coloration of antennae and the pubescence on postocular margin. Dark, mostly blackish coloured specimens, which were described as *T. velutinus* Kröber (with *postvelutinus* Moucha nom. nov.) and *T. miki niger* Olsufjev (with *miki colchidicus* Olsufjev nom. nov.) cannot have either specific or subspecific status and come within the range of variability of *T. miki* Br.

Synonymy. *T. velutinus* Kröber, according to the original description, can only be the same dark form described a year later by Olsufjev as *T. miki niger*. Kröber described his *velutinus* from a single female from Laia, Greece and no other record is available until 1961, when Moucha & Chvála recorded this species also from Varna, Bulgaria. The Bulgarian »*velutinus*« were represented partly by a dark form of *T. miki* Br., and partly by *T. briani* Lecl., at that time still unrecognised.

Biology. A typical species of forest and forest-steppe biotopes, occurring also in taiga. An uncommon species in western parts of its area of distribution, especially in Europe, but very common in eastern parts, forming for instance nearly 30 % of the tabanid fauna in the Region of Kemerovsk, Siberia (Gomojunova, 1967). Nothing is known about the immature stages.

Dates. From June until August.

Distribution. A widely distributed species known throughout Europe (not recorded from Ireland, Holland, Norway, Finland); its north border of distribution lies in Sweden, Carelia and the Leningrad region, penetrating eastwards as far as the river Jenisej, Siberia. It is known also from North Kazakhstan and from Turkmenia (Askhabad), but not yet recorded from North Africa. The dark forms are commoner in South Europe, in the Caucasus, Crimea, Azerbaijan and Iran.

TABANUS INDRAE HAUSER, 1939

Fig. 114.

Tabanus indrae Hauser, 1939, Trudy zool. Inst. Azerb. Fil. AN SSR, 10: 142.
Tabanus vappa Bogačev & Samedov, 1949, Izv. AN Azerb. SSR, 5: 70.
Tabanus indrae montivagus Olsufjev, 1970, Ént. Obozr., 49: 684 – syn. n.

Diagnosis. Medium-sized species with naked, unbanded eyes, closely related to *miki* Br. but postocular margin armed with only short, densely set pale (greyish in male) hairs, and dorsum of abdomen with striking silvery-grey to silvery-brown pattern.

Description. ♀. *Head.* Eyes naked, unbanded. Frons rather narrow, index 1: 4.5 to 5, indistinctly widened above or nearly parallel; yellowish-grey dusted, likewise subcallus. Lower callus polished yellowish-brown to black, rather large, circular to slightly rectangular, narrowly joined with linear black median callus. Face and cheeks more whitish-grey dusted, clothed with long whitish hairs especially on lower part of face. Postocular margin densely but short, usually pale haired, the hairs are not visible when viewed from in front. Antennae reddish-brown or extensively blackish in dark specimens, leaving only base to segment 3 narrowly brownish. Basal segments clothed with short black hairs, segment 1 with pale hairs beneath; segment 3 not very stout, with well developed, nearly rectangular, dorsal tooth. Palpi whitish-yellow, apical segment stouter on basal half, and mostly short black haired.

Thorax blackish-grey on mesonotum, with rather distinct pale longitudinal stripes and short pale and black pubescence. Notopleural lobes yellowish-brown to blackish. Pleura whitish-grey dusted and clothed with rather long, dense whitish pubescence. *Legs* grey on coxae and femora, pale haired, fore femora black beneath with dark hairing. Tibiae yellowish-brown to dark brown, mostly black haired on posterior two pairs; apical half of fore tibiae and whole of fore tarsi black, posterior four tarsi including tips of tibiae darkened, nearly black in dark specimens. *Wings* clear with dark veins, no appendix to vein R_4. Halteres brown.

Abdomen entirely blackish-grey or distinctly reddish-brown on anterior tergites, dorsum with very distinct pale silvery-grey pattern, consisting of a row of large median triangles and oblique, oval sublateral patches, which are large on tergites 2 to 4. Each tergite bears a narrow yellowish posterior margin at sides. Whole of dorsum densely clothed with short black pubescence, pale pattern with concolorous light hairs. In brown specimens the large sublateral patches on anterior tergites are yellowish to reddish-brown. Venter mostly yellowish-brown and pale haired in pale specimens, posterior tergites at least at sides greyish; posterior sternites predominantly black haired with indication of darker median stripe. The dark specimens have venter uniformly greyish, pale haired at sides, black haired on a distinct darker median stripe.

♂. Described first by Olsufjev (1970: 684) as follows: Head rather large, slightly broader than thorax. The facets on the upper two-thirds of eyes distinctly larger than those on lower part, about 4 times larger; the border between large and small facets distinct. Vertex very narrow, with short grey hairs. Subcallus and face greyish dusted. Antennae: Segment 1 yellowish with black hairs above, segment 3 reddish-brown, very slender, dorsal tooth blunt. Apical segment of palpi yellowish, blunt ended, about twice as long as its maximal depth, covered with comparatively long pale and black hairs. Thorax, mesonotum, legs, wings and abdomen as in the ♀. (The description was based on a pale specimen named by Olsufjev as ssp. *vappa* Bog. & Sam.).

Length. 14—16 mm.

Variability. A very variable species especially in coloration of abdomen, legs and antennae; all these variable characters are discussed in the above description. The dark specimens of *T. indrae* Hauser resemble very much the dark specimens of *miki* Br. (known as *velutinus* Kröb. or *niger* Ols.), the best differential features remain the distinct pale pattern on dorsum of abdomen and the shorter pubescence on vertex.

Olsufjev (1970) described the very dark specimens from the Caucasus and Crimea as ssp. *montivagus* and in the same paper named the very pale brownish specimens as ssp. *vappa* Bog. & Sam. In the same paper, however, Olsufjev recorded *T. vappa* Bogačev & Samedov, 1949, as a new synonym of *T. indrae* Hauser (l. c., p. 683). Considering that all intermediate forms are known between these two »subspecies«, from very light brown *(vappa)*

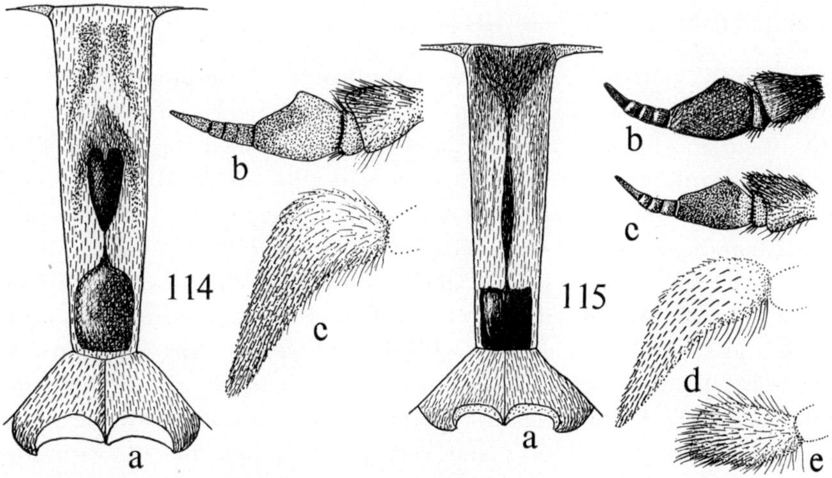

Fig. 114. *Tabanus indrae* Hauser, female, a. frons, b. antenna, c. palpus.
Fig. 115. *Tabanus regularis* Jaen., a. female frons, b. female antenna, c. male antenna, d. female palpus, e. male palpus.

to extensively blackish *(montivagus)*, the extreme forms only represent the range of variability of *T. indrae* Hauser. Also Olsufjev (1970: 684) mentioned that »among the three subspecies intermediate forms are present«, so that only infrasubspecific categories, without any taxonomic value, and sympatric in distribution, are involved.

DATES. From the end of June until August.

DISTRIBUTION. Originally described from Azerbaijan (incl. Nachitchevan ASSR), later also recorded from Armenia, Georgia, Iran, Crimea and Bulgaria, eastwards as far as Central Asiatic republics (Tadjikistan, Uzbekistan). We have also seen a single female of the nominate form from Jugoslavia (Starigrad b. Zadar, Küstengebiet, 25.VII.1967 leg. H. Freude).

TABANUS REGULARIS JAENNICKE, 1866
Fig. 115.

Tabanus regularis Jaennicke, 1866, Berl. ent. Z., 10: 85.
Tabanus regularis var. *rufus* Szilády, 1923, Biologica hung., 1 (1): 20.

DIAGNOSIS. Smaller to medium-sized species resembling *bromius* L. but frons in female very narrow, lower callus elongated, and eyes unbanded. Antennae black, or segment 3 brown, or antennae entirely brownish. Head in male very large, eyes naked with one band on the border between large and small facets. Vertex with only short hairs.

DESCRIPTION. ♀. *Head.* Eyes naked and unbanded. Frons and subcallus yellowish-grey to brownish-grey dusted, frons very narrow, index 1: 5–6, usually slightly widened above. Lower callus polished brown to black, long rectangular, beneath touching the subcallus and only very narrowly separated from the eye-margins, or nearly touching the eyes. Median callus black, spindle-shaped and connected with lower callus. A darker brown parafacial band on each side of antennae separates the darker dusted subcallus from whitish dusted and whitish haired face and cheeks. Postocular margin on vertex rather narrow, with densely set but short pale hairs. Antennae black, or segment 3 brown, or antennae entirely brown. Segment 3 rather slender with a blunt ended dorsal tooth near base. Palpi whitish, stouter near base, apically narrower and very pointed; pale haired, with some additional black hairs towards apex.

Thorax. Mesonotum blackish-grey, mostly black haired, with an indication of three narrow, light grey longitudinal stripes. Notopleural lobes usually yellowish-brown with black hairs, only scarcely dark. Pleura light grey dusted and finely whitish haired. *Legs.* Coxae and femora light grey dusted and pale haired. Fore tibiae except tip and whole of posterior tibiae yellowish, apex of fore tibiae and fore tarsi black, posterior four tarsi brown. *Wings* clear, veins brown; no appendix to vein R_4. First posterior cell broad. Halteres brown, knob whitish at tip.

Abdomen blackish-grey with light grey pattern which is formed by pale dusting and pubescence. The triangular spots in median row reach the anterior margin of each tergite, the oval sublateral patches at sides are often enlarged and confluent, forming in this way paler sublateral stripes on the dorsum of abdomen. Tergites 2 and 3 sometimes slightly translucent brownish at sides or abdomen distinctly brownish at sides (var. *rufus*). Venter blackish-grey with greyish dusting and pale hairs, a darker median stripe only slightly visible and mostly black haired.

♂. Head very large, semiglobular, much broader than thorax. Eyes naked with one band between the large facets on the upper three-quarters and small facets on lower quarter. Vertex with a row of only short pale hairs. Antennae more slender on segment 3; palpi whitish, apical segment oval, slender, with pointed and downwards curved tip, mostly densely pale haired. Thorax, legs and wings as in the ♀, abdomen with similar pattern but lateral patches are usually larger and tergites 2 and 3 distinctly brownish at sides. The brown coloration is visible also on corresponding sternites.

Length. 12—15 mm.

VARIABILITY. A variable species in coloration of antennae and in abdominal pattern. The specimens with paler, brown colour on abdomen and entirely brownish antennae including basal segments, were described by Szilády (1923) as a variety *rufus* from Tunisia, Cyprus and Jerusalem. The pale form, or at least its intermediates with slightly reddish basal segments and translucent brownish anterior tergites, occur also in South Europe; Leclercq (1967a: 166) raised this form without justification to a subspecific rank.

BIOLOGY. A common species in southern regions, females attack man, horses and horned cattle. Nothing is known about the immature stages.

DATES. July and August.

DISTRIBUTION. A Mediterranean species known from the European part (Portugal, Spain, France, Italy including the islands of Corsica and Sicily, Greece, Jugoslavia, Bulgaria), from the North Africa (Morocco, Algeria, Tunisia), eastwards through Turkey and Cyprus to Israel, Iraq and Iran. It has also been recorded from Transcaucasus and Azerbaijan including the Nachitchevan ASSR. The species has not yet been recorded from Rumania and Hungary, but we have seen a single female taken at Štúrovo in South Slovakia, Czechoslovakia, on the river Dunaj on Czechoslovak-Hungarian border. This capture also represents the most northern locality known up to the present.

TABANUS DARIMONTI LECLERCQ, 1964

Fig. 116.

Tabanus darimonti Leclercq, 1964; Mems Estud. Mus. zool. Univ. Coimbra, no. 288: 6.

Diagnosis. Similar to *regularis* Jaen. and *miki* Br., but differs in shape of frontal calli, in the postocular margin being with short pale hairs and in yellowish-brown coloured femora.

Description. ♀. *Head.* Eyes naked and unbanded. Frons and subcallus brownish-grey dusted, on upper part of occiput more pure greyish. Frons very narrow, index 1: 5–6, slightly widened above. Lower callus polished blackish, high and narrow, well separated from eye-margins and subcallus. Median callus black, narrow and connected with lower callus. Parafacial areas on each side of antennae brownish-grey as subcallus, but not forming distinct bands. Rest of head whitish-grey dusted and with exclusively whitish hairs. Postocular margin on vertex rather narrow and with short pale hairs. Antennae reddish-brown, first and second segments slightly darkened by a dark brownish-grey dust and short black hairs. Segment 3 short and rather broad, dorsal tooth low and obtuse, terminal flagellar segments only slightly darkened.

Thorax. Mesonotum whitish-grey to pale greyish dusted, with indistinct darker longitudinal stripes; notopleural lobes yellowish-brown translucent. Pubescence composed of both pale and black hairs. Pleura pale greyish with whitish hairs. *Legs.* Coxae and femora are much less dusted than pleura, therefore the yellowish-brown ground coloration is distinctly seen, and especially prominent on posterior four femora. Fore femora darkened at apex of dorsal and anterior surfaces. Tibiae yellowish-brown, fore tibiae darkened in apical fourth. Fore tarsi black. Other tarsi not much darker than corresponding tibiae. *Wings* clear, veins brownish to blackish; no appendix to vein R_4. Knob of halteres yellowish-white.

Abdomen dark greyish with three rows of patches. The middle row is composed of paler greyish triangles which are not sharply demarcated, while the lateral rows consist of more roundish spots where the yellowish-brown ground coloration is clearly visible, and is especially distinct on tergites 2–4. Pubescence mainly blackish, pale hairs mainly to be found laterally. Venter mostly yellowish-brown, though thinly greyish dusted all over. The dust covers the ground coloration more laterally and on posterior sternites.

♂. Unknown.

Length. 12.5–14 mm.

DATES. July.

DISTRIBUTION. The species is hitherto known only from Portugal, Spain, North Africa (Morocco) and Turkey.

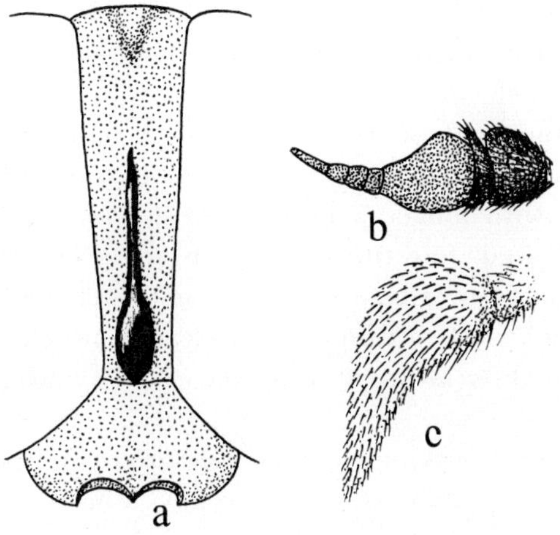

Fig. 116. *Tabanus darimonti* Lecl., female, a. frons, b. antenna, c. palpus.

TABANUS BROMIUS LINNÉ, 1758

Fig. 117; pl. 3: fig. c.

Tabanus bromius Linné, 1758, Syst. Nat., p. 602.
Tabanus maculatus De Geer, 1776, Mém. Ins., 6: 221.
Tabanus scalaris Meigen, 1820, Syst. Beschr., 2: 38.
Tabanus glaucus Meigen, 1820, Syst. Beschr., 2: 51.
Tabanus bronicus Gimmerthal, 1847, Bull. Soc. Nat. Moscou, 20: 182 (? lapsus).
Tabanus connexus Walker, 1850, Ins. Saunders., Dipt., 1: 62.
Tabanus glaucescens Schiner, 1862, Fauna Austriaca, Dipt., 1: 36 (nov. nom. pro *glaucus* Meig., nec Wied.).
Tabanus bromius var. *flavofemoratus* Strobl, 1909, Verh. zool.-bot. Ges. Wien, 59: 292.
Tabanus bromius var. *nigricans* Szilády, 1914, Annls Mus. nat hung., 12: 668.
Straba bromius ab. *simplex* Muschamp, 1939, Entomologist's Rec. J. Var., 51: 51.

DIAGNOSIS. Medium-sized greyish species, eyes naked with one band. Lower frontal callus connected with linear median callus. Antennae mostly blackish-brown, dorsum of abdomen with three rows of paler patches. Head in male not very large, upper large facets sharply separated from small facets; vertex with short hairs.

DESCRIPTION. ♀. *Head.* Eyes naked, with one band. Frons greyish-yellow dusted, rather narrow and parallel-sided, index 1: 4—4.5; lower callus polished black, nearly rectangular, narrowly separated from the eye-margins and narrowly connected with linear median callus. Subcallus small, greyish-yellow dusted, face and cheeks whitish-grey dusted and long pale haired. Postocular margin slender, clothed with short pale hairs. Antennae blackish-brown, basal two segments and segment 3 at base usually dark brown, terminal flagellar segments black; segment 3 with distinct rectangular dorsal tooth. Palpi whitish, apical segment slightly stouter near base and very pointed at tip, clothed with short pale and black hairs.

Thorax blackish-grey, mesonotum with short pale and black hairs, and with rather distinct paler longitudinal stripes. Notopleural lobes brownish. Pleura more greyish dusted and with longer pale hairs. *Legs.* Coxae and femora greyish dusted and pale haired; fore tibiae brownish, black on apical third including tarsi. Posterior four tibiae dark brown to yellowish-brown, usually darker at tip, tarsi dark brown. *Wings* clear, veins dark brown, no appendix to vein R_4. Alula as broad as axillary lobe of wing. Halteres blackish-brown.

Abdomen blackish-grey with three rows of paler greyish to grey-yellow coloured and haired patches. The median triangles occupy usually the whole width of the tergites, lateral spots being oval to rounded; tergites 2 and 3 sometimes brownish at sides. Venter unicolorous blackish-grey, sternites 2 and 3 sometimes with brownish sidemarkings.

♂. Head not very large, eyes naked and with one band. The facets on the upper two-thirds of eyes large and sharply separated from the lower area with small facets. Vertex with only short brownish hairs. Antennae as in the ♀ but segment 3 more slender, with small, nearly rectangular dorsal tooth at base. Apical segment of palpi yellowish-grey, small and oval, clothed with longer pale and black hairs. Mesonotum with fine but long, mostly black hairs. Abdomen more brownish on anterior segments, otherwise as in the ♀.

Length. 11—16 mm.

VARIABILITY. A very variable species in all respects, which is demonstrated by the long list of synonyms. The variability of this species, especially of the frons in female, has been studied by Roman (1959). The very pale (brownish) specimens which occur mostly in southern regions of the area of distribution, were named by Strobl as var. *flavofemoratus*, the subsequent authors quite incorrectly raised this form to subspecific rank.

Biology. *T. bromius* L. is very widely distributed and one of the commoner species of the family. It has been studied from many points of view and its mass occurrence in suitable localities is fairly well known. It is a vector of tularaemia, both in Europe including the Near East and in North Africa (Leclercq, 1952: 38), and of anthrax (Olsufjev, 1937: 280). Sachibzadaev (1957) recorded this species as a vector of trypanosomiasis of horses and camels. Females attack man and both domestic and wild animals. Males are often to be found on flowers (e. g. *Angelica silvetris* L., *Allium cepa* L., *Allium ampellopasum* L.) as recorded from France by Surcouf (1921a). *Neoitamus cyanurus* L. (Dipt., Asilidae) and *Bembex rostrata* F. (Hym., Sphecidae) are recorded as predators. The larva was described by Beling (1875), Marchand (1920), Surcouf & Fischer (1924), Stammer (1924) and Skufin (1967); the pupa was described by Beling (1875), Surcouf & Ricardo (1909), Marchand (1920) and Surcouf & Fischer (1924).

Dates. From the end of May until the beginning of September.

Distribution. A widely distributed species known throughout Europe from the British Isles (except Ireland) and Scandinavia to North Africa (Algeria, Morocco). Eastwards it penetrates as far as the river Ob, to North and East Kazakhstan and to all countries of the Near and Middle East. The north

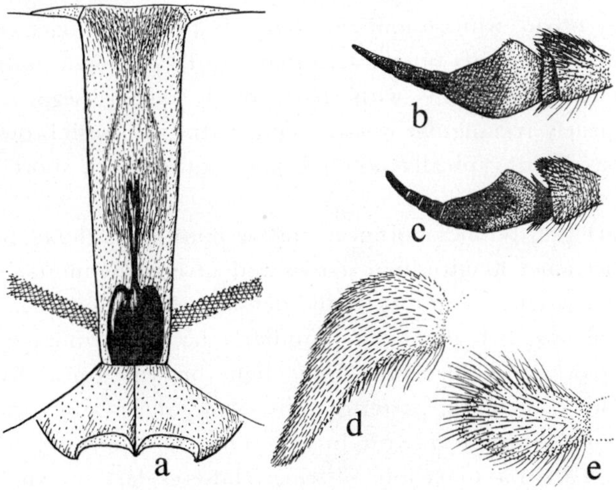

Fig. 117. *Tabanus bromius* L., a. female frons, b. female antenna, c. male antenna, d. female palpus, e. male palpus.

border of its area of distribution lies in Lapland, Carelia and North Ural. In mountains it occurs at altitudes over 2000 m, e. g. in the Swiss Alps.

TABANUS MACULICORNIS ZETTERSTEDT, 1842

Fig. 118.

Tabanus maculicornis Zetterstedt, 1842, Dipt. Scand., 1: 117.
Tabanus nigricans Egger, 1859, Verh. zool.-bot. Ges. Wien, 9: 392.

DIAGNOSIS. Rather smaller to medium-sized, blackish-grey species resembling *bromius* L. but antennae broader on segment 3 and uniformly brown, eye-band deeper and darker, postocular margin on vertex very broad, dorsum of abdomen with larger and more indefinite greyish patches in three rows. Male with sharply differentiated facets, with a row of long pale hairs on vertex, and abdomen mostly blackish.

DESCRIPTION. ♀. *Head.* Eyes naked with one broad, dark band. Frons greyish, rather narrower, index 1: 4—4.5, usually slightly widening above. Lower callus dull black and distinctly wrinkled, rectangular, very narrowly separated from subcallus and from the eye-margins. Median callus rather linear, narrowly connected with lower callus. Subcallus black in ground colour, thinly greyish dusted, rather black when denuded; antennal bows rather broad, yellowish. Face and cheeks whitish-grey, clothed with whitish hairs becoming longer below; laterally to antennal bases a group of black hairs. Usually a distinct dark brown parafacial band. Postocular margin on vertex conspicuously broad, whitish and clothed with a row of longer concolorous hairs. Antennae uniformly brown, terminal flagellar segments only exceptionally darker. Basal segments with sparse black hairing, segment 3 rather broad with nearly rectangular dorsal tooth. Palpi yellowish-brown, slightly stouter on basal half, apically pointed, and clothed with short black and pale hairs.

Thorax dark grey on mesonotum including notopleural lobes, mesonotum with indistinct paler longitudinal stripes and covered by mostly pale, short hairing. Pleura paler greyish dusted and densely whitish-yellow haired. *Legs.* Coxae concolorous with pleura and similarly haired. Femora darker grey dusted and pale haired beneath, tibiae light brown. Apical half of fore tibiae and fore tarsi black, posterior four tibiae at tip and corresponding tarsi darkened. Wings clear with brown veins, no appendix to vein R_4. Alula narrower than axillary lobe of wing. Halteres dark brown.

Abdomen blackish-grey coloured and greyish dusted, dorsum with rather indefinite greyish pattern of large median triangles and still larger, oval sublateral patches. Posterior margins to all tergites paler. Whole of dorsum covered with scattered black hairs, tergite 2 anteriorly at sides translucent brownish. Venter unicolorous grey with fine pale pubescence, darker median stripe hardly visible.

♂. Head large, distinctly broader than thorax, eyes naked with one band. Facets on the upper three-quarters large and sharply separated from small facets. Vertex with a row of long pale hairs, postocular margin rather narrower, whitish. Antennae more slender and basal segments densely short black haired. Palpi yellowish-brown, oval and rather slender, distinctly pointed; clothed with longer pale and black hairs, especially anteriorly. Legs and thorax including mesonotum with much longer pale hairs, abdomen densely and longer black haired. Tergite 2 (sometimes also tergite 3) with more distinct dark brown sidemarking anteriorly.

Length. 10–14.5 mm.

VARIABILITY. Only a little variable species, the antennae vary in coloration from brown to dark brown.

BIOLOGY. A common species on peat-bogs, moist meadows and everywhere near ponds and lakes, but it has been collected also in valleys high in the mountains. In suitable localities it represents sometimes over 20 % of the tabanid population. Females attack man and both domestic and wild living animals. The larva was described by Stammer (1924), the pupal stage by Kröber (1910) and Séguy (1926).

DATES. From the end of May until September.

DISTRIBUTION. The species is known throughout Europe, eastwards as far as

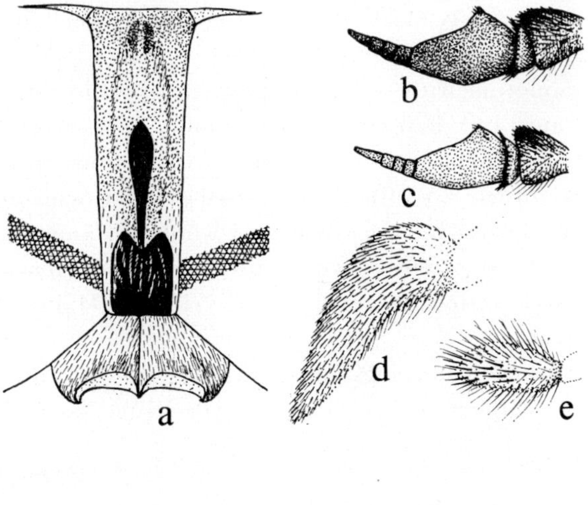

Fig. 118.
Tabanus maculicornis Zett., a. female frons, b. female antenna, c. male antenna, d. female palpus, e. male palpus.

Transcaucasus, North Kazakhstan and in Siberia to the region of Lake Baikal. Not yet recorded in Europe from Ireland and Lapland, but it is known from the Kola Peninsula. In the south it has been recorded from Spain, but not from Portugal or North Africa. We have no records from Greece and Turkey but its occurrence there is very probable, especially in the mountainous regions.

TABANUS TERGESTINUS EGGER, 1859

Fig. 119; pl. 3: fig. d.

Tabanus tergestinus Egger, 1859, Verh. zool.-bot. Ges. Wien, 9: 391.

DIAGNOSIS. Medium-sized to larger species with eyes naked and 3 banded, frons in female narrow, median callus linear and connected with lower callus; abdomen reddish-brown at sides in both sexes. Male with very slightly differentiated facets, eyes naked with 2 bands, and only small pale hairs on vertex.

DESCRIPTION. ♀. *Head.* Eyes naked with three bands. Frons greyish dusted, very narrow, index about 1: 6, slightly diverging above. Lower callus oval and small, blackish-brown; narrowly separated from both subcallus and the eye-margins. Median callus black, linear, connected with lower callus. Frons at vertex with blackish, occasionally double path, simulating ocellar swelling; postocular margin on vertex narrow, short pale haired. Subcallus greyish dusted, antennal bows deeper, yellowish. Face and cheeks rather whitish-grey dusted, with longer whitish hairs. Antennae reddish-brown, basal segments usually more orange-yellow coloured and short black haired; segment 3 rather deep with rectangular dorsal tooth, terminal flagellar segments extensively darkened or entirely black. Palpi greyish-yellow, long and only slightly stout at base, clothed with short pale and black hairs.

Thorax dark grey on mesonotum with indefinite paler longitudinal stripes, covered by short pale and black hairs. Notopleural lobes dark. Pleura paler grey dusted and only whitish haired. *Legs.* Coxae concolorous with pleura, femora darker grey dusted and fine pale haired. Fore tibiae on apical half and fore tarsi black, rest of fore tibiae and whole of posterior four tibiae yellowish-brown. Tarsi extensively darkened and mostly black haired. *Wings* clear with dark veins, no appendix to vein R_4. Halteres brownish, knob mostly whitish.

Abdomen with reddish-brown sidemarkings on tergites 1–4 (or including tergite 5), dark median stripe with indistinct paler and pale haired median triangles, posterior tergites uniformly greyish. Each tergite bears a distinct paler, narrow posterior margin. Dorsum of abdomen short black haired except for pale haired pale pattern, brownish sidemarkings black and pale haired. Venter light reddish-brown coloured and mostly pale haired, posterior two sternites greyish and longer black haired.

♂. Head not very large, facets on the upper two-thirds only slightly larger, no distinct border between larger and smaller facets. Eyes naked with two bands, vertex with a row of only short pale hairs. Antennae more slender especially on segment 3, palpi yellowish-grey with longer pale and dark hairs; apical segment oval, slightly pointed at tip. Thorax and legs longer haired. Otherwise, including abdominal pattern, as in the ♀.

Length. 15–18 mm.

VARIABILITY. Only a little variable species, the reddish-brown sidemarkings vary in size and number.

BIOLOGY. A common species on suitable dry biotopes, the females are common on pastures and pasture-meadows, attacking mainly horses and horned cattle.

DATES. From June until August.

DISTRIBUTION. A southern species, in South Europe from Spain and France through Italy, Jugoslavia, Greece, Albania, Bulgaria and Rumania to Ukraine, and through the Caucasus as far as to Transcaucasus (Daghestan,

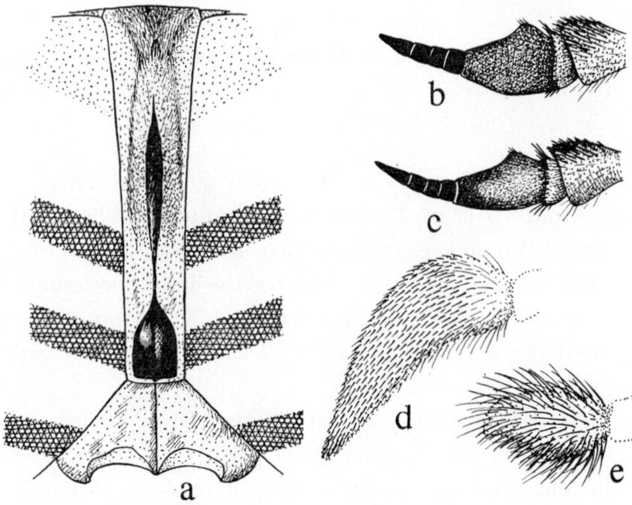

Fig. 119. *Tabanus tergestinus* Egg., a. female frons, b. female antenna, c. male antenna, d. female palpus, e. male palpus.

Armenia, Azerbaijan). In Central Europe only in its southern parts, the north border lies in South Germany and South Czechoslovakia (Moravia, Slovakia), it is recorded also from Austria, Switzerland and Hungary.

BOVINUS-GROUP

Large species, eyes naked and unbanded. Frons rather narrower (except *martinii* Kröb.) with median callus linear, connected with lower callus. Latter oval to triangular, usually very indistinctly separated from subcallus and more broadly from the eye-margins. Subcallus dusted (except *martinii* Kröb.), and antennae with moderately large, tabanine-like, dorsal tooth to segment 3.

T. martinii Kröb., which we have not seen, has much more in common with the *cordiger*-group and is placed here provisionally, in fact only because of its very large size.

TABANUS MARTINII KRÖBER, 1928

Tabanus martinii Kröber, 1928, Dt. ent. Z., 1928: 430.

Diagnosis. A very remarkable, large black species with three rows of pale patches on abdomen, resembling in this way *autumnalis* L., but frons very broad (index 1: 2.5) with large and broadly separated brown frontal calli. Subcallus polished brown and abdomen distinctly pointed in female; male unknown. The structure of the head and shape of frontal calli resemble somewhat *brunneocallosus* Ols. of the *cordiger*-group.

Kröber described this species from a single holotype female collected at Aidin in the Asiatic part of Turkey, and Dinulescu (1958) without doubt correctly recorded this species from Ineu in the Oradea region of Rumania. Kröber gave the unusual size of 26 mm for the holotype female. Dinulescu recorded the size of Rumanian specimens as 20–21 mm; considering that Kröber recorded the length of wing as 19.4 mm, the given strange size of the body is probably not a misprint.

We have not seen this very interesting species and therefore we present a translation of the detailed original description:

»Length 26 mm. Antenna 1.9 mm. Length of wing 19.4 mm. Width of wing 4.9 mm. A very conspicuous species which does not fit into any group of species. I name this species after the collector Prof. E. Martini.

The best position for this species is, with regard to the size and the whitish rows of patches, in the *autumnalis*-group. The abdominal segments 5–7 are still more laterally compressed than in *acuminatus,* forming a long ovipositor. The entirely clear wings bear distinct blackish patches on the anastomosis. Frons with square median callus. Subcallus polished brown and very convex, as in *uniciactus.*

Eyes dark purple. Frons broad, hardly 2.5 times as high as broad below, yellowish-grey dusted. Vertex with false ocellar tubercle, with a small, dull blackish-brown tubercle with black hairs. Lower callus polished reddish-brown, narrowly separated from the eye-margins; above straight, scarcely somewhat convex. Median callus brown, nearly dull, broadly oval and touching the eyes, above and below with a small tongue-like projection. Vertex slightly broader than frons. Subcallus polished reddish-brown, prominent, smooth and very polished with a deeper median furrow. Antennae entirely deep black; segment 3 with a small dorsal tooth. Terminal flagellar segments form a long, pointed complex. Face densely woolly snow-white haired. Palpi snow-white, whitish haired, stout, finely pointed just at tip and there finely black haired. Occiput on postocular margin whitish-yellow, with dense yellowish pubescence and some black hairs.

Thorax yellowish whitish-grey, dull, with three black and somewhat shining longitudinal stripes. The central one anteriorly wedge-shaped forked, forming a distinct stripe only just in front of scutellum. The two lateral ones are finely incised on notopleural depression. Behind this incision there is an isolated longitudinal patch on the outside, on the inner side another not sharply limited black transverse patch. Scutellum entirely black. The pubescence is long and densely whitish, especially on lateral margins and on scutellar margin. Humeri and notopleural lobes whitish-yellow. The erect thoracal pubescence faintly black. Whole of pleura densely and long whitish-grey haired, so that the ground colour is not visible. Femora black; fore femora on the inner side shining, otherwise densely white haired. Knees and tibiae yellowish-brown but densely white haired; fore and mid tibiae snow-white on basal half, otherwise deep black including tarsi. The black parts are black haired. Apical segments on tarsi with particularly long black hairs. Squamae clear whitish, halteres black with paler tip to knob.

Abdomen deep black, not shining, with sharply differentiated whitish, yellowish-grey pattern. Tergites 2–4 with median triangles, that on tergite 2 reaching the anterior margin with its prolonged apex, those on following tergites are indistinct anteriorly, but well differentiated when viewed from behind. Lateral patches on tergites 1–4 bright and distinct, oblique, nearly S-shaped, reaching from anterior margin to posterior margin. No pale margins. At extreme side there is another whitish-grey S-shaped patch leaving outside a similar black design. Tergite 2 somewhat translucent brown anteriorly, laterally from the oblique pale patch. Segment 5 roof-like compressed, about half as broad as segment 4, with three indistinct, whitish-grey longitudinal stripes. Segments 6 and 7 as long as segment 3 but hardly of one-quarter breadth, forming really an ovipositor which I have never seen before in any tabanid. On segments 4—7 the border between tergites and sternites somewhat yellowish-brown. Venter whitish-grey, with fine yellowish posterior margins. The white and black pubescence on abdomen corresponds with the abdominal pattern. Wings entirely clear. Veins faintly black. All bifurcations finely black spotted, not very intensively but still distinctly, especially on crossveins. Appendix to vein R_4 about as long as basal portion of R_4. Fourth posterior cell broadly open.

Type: Tropenhyg. Inst. Hamburg.«

REMARKS. Dinulescu (1958: 213) on the basis of the Rumanian material figured the frons, antenna, palpus and abdominal pattern, which all correspond quite well to Kröber's original description.

DATES. Not recorded.

DISTRIBUTION. Turkey and Rumania.

TABANUS PARADOXUS JAENNICKE, 1866

Fig. 120.

Tabanus paradoxus Jaennicke, 1866, Berl. ent. Z., 10: 83.
Tabanus paradoxus var. *macedonicus* Kröber, 1936, Acta Inst. Mus. zool. Univ. athen., 1: 35.

DIAGNOSIS. Large black species with naked and unstriped eyes. Tergites with distinct pale median triangles and narrow lateral borders on posterior margins. Posterior four tibiae black, antennae blackish-grey, palpi dark brown and densely black haired. Subcallus with conspicuously high antennal bows. Head in male large, eyes with upper two-thirds with large facets sharply separated from lower third with small facets.

DESCRIPTION. ♀. *Head.* Eyes naked, unbanded. Frons greyish-yellow dusted, narrow, index about 1: 5, slightly widened above and with a light brown patch on vertex simulating ocellar tubercle. Lower callus black, only slightly shining, longly rectangular to oval, only narrowly separated from the eye-margins and narrowly connected with linear median callus. Subcallus greyish with conspicuously high yellowish antennal bows, occupying the whole of lower half of the subcallus. Face and cheeks more greyish dusted and clothed with long, fine dark brown to nearly blackish hairs. Antennae blackish-brown, segment 1 short but densely black haired, segment 3 with well developed dorsal tooth. Palpi dark brown, short black haired; long and slender, blunt ended.

Thorax blackish-grey dusted and mostly black haired, pleura more greyish dusted and clothed with long, fine blackish-brown hairs, becoming paler below. Posterior half of mesonotum at sides and scutellum on margin with longer pale hairs. Notopleural lobes dark and black haired. *Legs* black and mostly finely black haired, except for yellowish-brown basal third on fore tibiae, which bears pale hairs. Posterior four tibiae translucent brownish at extreme base. All coxae greyish dusted and clothed with fine pale and black hairs. *Wings* clear or indistinctly faintly brownish clouded, with distinct dark veins. No appendix to vein R_4, first posterior cell slightly narrowed towards tip. Halteres dark brown.

Abdomen black, tergite 2 at sides very indistinctly translucent brownish. All tergites with conspicuous whitish coloured and pale haired median

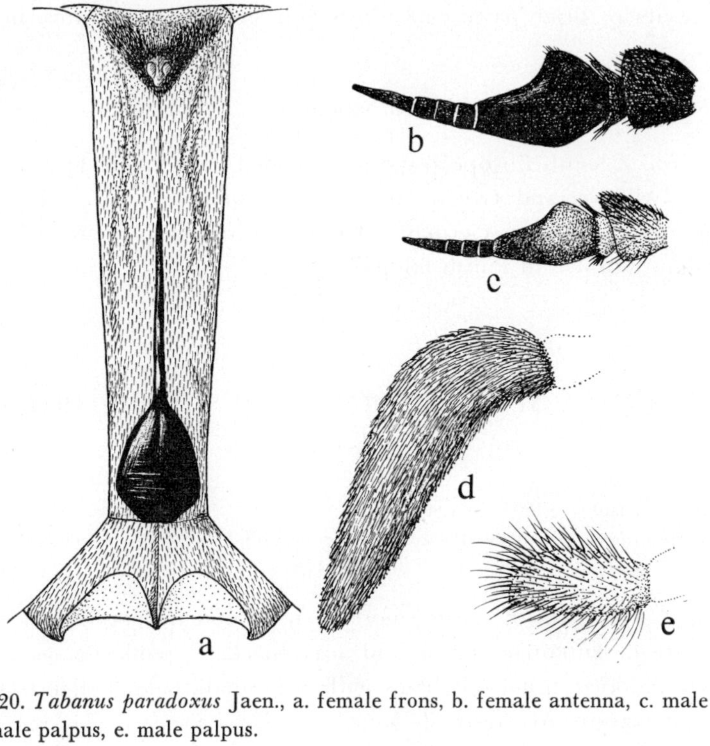

Fig. 120. *Tabanus paradoxus* Jaen., a. female frons, b. female antenna, c. male antenna, d. female palpus, e. male palpus.

triangles and narrow lateral patches on posterior margins. The median triangles reach anterior half of each tergite, the lateral patches are widened towards lateral margin of the tergite. Otherwise abdomen short but densely black haired. Venter black, slightly silvery dusted at sides and with distinct paler lateral patches on posterior margin to each sternite; the black median stripe broad and distinct.

♂. Head very large, broader than thorax. Eyes naked and unbanded, facets on the upper two-thirds very enlarged and sharply separated from the lower third with small facets. Antennae blackish-brown, segment 3 more slender and with only small dorsal tooth. Palpi brownish, apical segment darkened towards tip, oval and longly black haired. Otherwise as in the ♀.

Length. 18–21 mm.

Variability. The paler haired specimens occurring in South Europe were described by Kröber (1936) as var. *macedonicus.*

Biology. Nothing is known about the immature stages but the adults are well known as typical evening insects. The females attack horses and horned cattle only after sunset, they fly very low over the ground in late evening during dusk and early after nightfall, somewhat resembling humble-bees. A typical species of drier pasture-meadows and steppes, more often in hilly countries.

Dates. August and the beginning of September.

Distribution. A South European species recorded from Spain, France, Italy, Jugoslavia, Albania and Greece, penetrating north to Central European countries, viz. Switzerland, Germany, Austria, Hungary, Czechoslovakia and South Poland (Zabrze in Polish Silesia).

TABANUS SUBPARADOXUS OLSUFJEV, 1941

Fig. 121.

Tabanus morio Olsufjev, 1937, Fauna SSSR, 7: 304.
Tabanus subparadoxus Olsufjev, 1940, Acad. Sci. URSS Fil. Géorg., zool., 3: 45 (nom. nov. for *morio* Olsufjev, 1937, nec Fabricius, 1794).

Diagnosis. Large blackish species more than 20 mm in length, eyes naked and unstriped. Antennae, palpi and legs black. Resembling *paradoxus* Jaenn. but abdomen is entirely black with only small, pale median triangles on posterior margins to tergites 2–5.

DESCRIPTION. ♀. *Head.* Eyes naked, unstriped. Frons and face rather pale greyish dusted; former narrow, very slightly widening above, index about 1: 5. Lower callus shining black, oval, higher than broad, and connected with the linear, shining black median callus. Subcallus with the same dusting as on the face, antennal bows yellowish, rather high. Face and lower part of cheeks with black hairs, upper half of cheeks with predominantly whitish hairs. Antennae entirely black, segment 3 sometimes very indistinctly brownish at extreme base, dorsal tooth nearly rectangular. Basal segments clothed with short, adpressed black hairs. Palpi long and rather slender, black, with short concolorous hairing.

Thorax black in ground colour but with a distinct, though thin, greyish tomentum. Mesonotum with whitish hairs, pleura mostly dark haired. *Legs.* Coxae greyish dusted like pleura, black haired, only fore coxae with long whitish hairs anteriorly above. Otherwise legs entirely black with fine black hairs, ventral side of tarsi with short rufous hairing. *Wings* faintly greyish clouded, costal cell slightly brownish. Veins dark, brownish along costal margin, no appendix to vein R_4. Squamae dark brown, halteres blackish-brown.

Abdomen entirely black with only very small pale median triangular spots

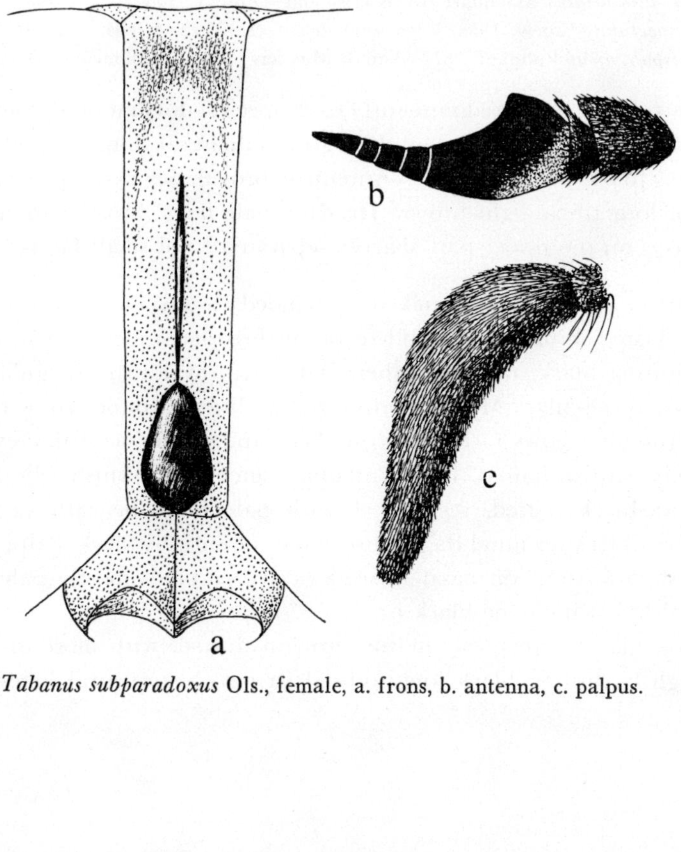

Fig. 121. *Tabanus subparadoxus* Ols., female, a. frons, b. antenna, c. palpus.

on posterior margin of tergites 2—5, the triangle on tergite 5 the smallest and sometimes missing altogether. Basal segment sometimes indistinctly greyish dusted on both sides.

♂. Unknown.

Length. 21—25 mm.

Variability. The abdomen is sometimes entirely black with only an indication of pale median triangle on tergite 2.

Biology. In comparison with the closely related *paradoxus* Jaenn. the females of *subparadoxus* Ols., according to Olsufjev (1940: 79), attack horses in full day-light.

Distribution. A mountainous species described and so far known only from the Caucasus, where it also occurs in its European part.

TABANUS SPECTABILIS LOEW, 1858

Fig. 122.

Tabanus lateralis Brullé, 1832, Exped. Sci. Morée, 3: 304 (nec Meigen, 1820).
? *Tabanus albivittatus* Macquart, 1834, Hist. nat. Dipt., 1: 206.
Tabanus spectabilis Loew, 1858, Verh. zool.-bot. Ges. Wien, 8: 605.
Tabanus ispahanicus Rondani, 1873, Annali Mus. civ. Stor. nat. Giacomo Doria, 4: 300.

Diagnosis. Large and predominantly dark species, dorsum of abdomen with conspicuous whitish-grey to pinkish-grey sublateral longitudinal stripes, separating dark median stripe. Antennae brown, segment 3 often black. Posterior four tibiae light brown. Head in male large, broader than thorax, large facets on the upper part sharply separated from small facets.

Description. ♀. *Head.* Eyes naked, unbanded. Frons and subcallus yellowish-grey dusted. Frons parallel-sided, rather broader, index 1: 3.5—4. Lower callus shining black, usually higher than deep, oval to rectangular, sometimes nearly circular. Median callus black, linear, connected with lower callus. Antennal bows rather narrow. Face and cheeks whitish-grey dusted and finely whitish haired. Basal antennal segments brownish-yellow dusted and short black haired, segment 1 with pale hairs beneath; segment 3 brown with black terminal flagellar segments or entirely black. Palpi whitish-yellow, slightly stout on basal third, apically pointed; mostly pale haired, on apical half with some black hairs.

Thorax blackish-grey, mesonotum greyish dusted, with more or less distinct slightly shining black longitudinal stripes. Notopleural lobes yellowish-brown and mostly black haired. Pleura light grey dusted and whitish haired. *Legs.* Coxae and femora black, light grey dusted and whitish haired. Fore tibiae on basal half whitish-yellow and pale haired, the rest of tibiae including tarsus black with concolorous hairs. Posterior four tibiae yellowish-brown, darker at tip, tarsi blackish-brown. *Wings* clear with dark brown veins, first posterior cell narrowed towards tip. No appendix to vein R_4, but there is an indication of a brownish patch at base of R_4. Halteres whitish-yellow, stem brownish.

Abdomen with conspicuous pattern on dorsum, tergites silvery-grey or somewhat pinkish and pale haired at sides, separating a broad black median stripe. The pale side markings are formed by a coalescence of oval sublateral patches. The blackish median stripe is somewhat widened on posterior margin of each tergite. Venter whitish-grey dusted and pale haired at sides, median stripe distinct, black with concolorous hairs to nearly reddish with mostly pale hairs.

♂. Head large, broader than thorax. Eyes naked and unbanded, facets on the upper two-thirds enlarged and sharply separated from the lower third with small facets. Subcallus brownish above, antennae as in the ♀ but segment 3 more slender and usually brown. Palpi greyish to light brown, oval, pale haired, apex mostly black haired. Cheeks predominantly with dark hairs. Otherwise as in the ♀ including abdominal pattern.

Length. 16–21 mm.

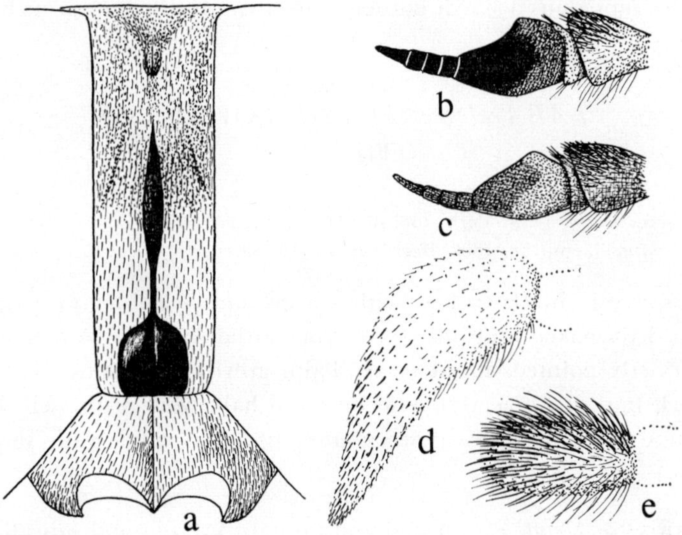

Fig. 122. *Tabanus spectabilis* Lw., a. female frons, b. female antenna, c. male antenna, d. female palpus, e. male palpus.

VARIABILITY. Rather a variable species but different varieties have not been described. The pale side markings on abdomen vary from nearly whitish to reddish-brown; in the reddish specimens the light lateral patches are rather separated, not so confluent as in very pale specimens. The same colour variation is to be seen on the median stripe on the venter, which varies from entirely black to reddish-brown, in extremely pale specimens it is densely covered by greyish dust. The coloration of antennal segment 3 and shape of lower frontal callus are also very variable.

SYNONYMY. *T. albivittatus* Macq., which antedates Loew's description, is very probably identical with *T. spectabilis* Loew and the latter name should be replaced by the former.

BIOLOGY. Never a common species occurring rather in higher altitudes, females attack horses and horned cattle.

DATES. From June until August.

DISTRIBUTION. A widely distributed species known from North Africa (Morocco), from Spain and France through South Europe (Italy including Sicily, Jugoslavia, Greece including the island of Corfu, Albania, Rumania and Bulgaria) to Turkey, Ukraine and the Caucasus including Transcaucasus, eastwards penetrating to as far as to Turkmenia, Kazakhstan, Iraq, Iran and Afghanistan. The species has been recorded also from Hungary, its occurrence there represents a north border of its area of distribution in Europe.

TABANUS RECTUS LOEW, 1858

Fig. 123.

Tabanus rectus Loew, 1858, Verh. zool.-bot. Ges. Wien, 8: 603.
Tabanus ornatus Jaennicke, 1866, Berl. ent. Z., 10: 84.

DIAGNOSIS. Large black species with conspicuous whitish-grey pattern on abdomen. Eyes naked and unstriped, frons rather broader. Antennae black with distinctly pointed dorsal tooth. Palpi greyish with short black hairs. Legs black but all tibiae yellowish on basal half. Male with well differentiated large facets on eyes, postocular margin on vertex with short pale pubescence.

DESCRIPTION. ♀. *Head.* Eyes naked and unstriped. Frons and subcallus light grey dusted, former rather broad, index 1: 4 or slightly more, nearly parallel-sided. Lower callus more or less polished black, oval but somewhat narrower and pointed above, distinctly separated from the eye-margins. Median callus black, linear, connected with lower callus. Antennal bows rather narrow, face and cheeks light grey dusted and densely pale haired. Antennae black, segment 1 thinly greyish dusted and short black haired, segment 3 with distinct pointed dorsal tooth, terminal flagellar segments long and slender. Palpi greyish, apical segment long and blunt ended, rather slender, clothed by short pale and black hairs. Vertex on postocular margin with short, dense pale pubescence.

Thorax black, greyish dusted and pale haired. Pleura with longer and denser pale pubescence. Mesonotum with four more or less polished black longitudinal stripes, which are distinctly black haired. The two median stripes are narrow and rather close, the two lateral ones are broad and wide apart. Notopleural lobes dark and densely black haired. *Legs* black but all tibiae on basal half light yellowish-brown coloured and pale haired. Femora blackish-grey dusted and mostly pale haired, coxae paler, concolorous with pleura and with the same pubescence. Otherwise legs black haired. *Wings* clear with blackish-brown veins, first posterior cell narrower apically, no appendix to vein R_4. Halteres blackish-brown with brownish knob.

Abdomen more or less shining black and black haired on dorsum, with

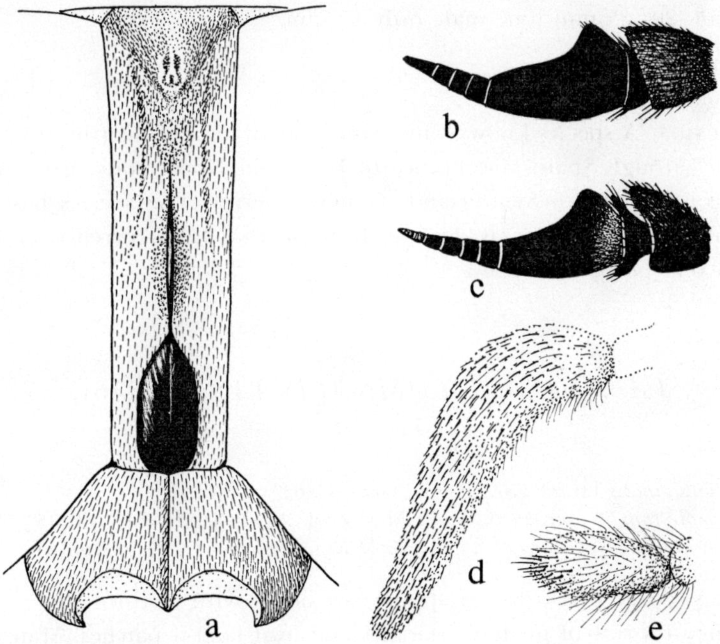

Fig. 123. *Tabanus rectus* Lw., a. female frons, b. female antenna, c. male antenna, d. female palpus, e. male palpus.

a very distinct whitish-grey pattern which is formed by very pale dusting and pubescence. The median triangles are very large and nearly equilateral, reaching anterior half of the tergites on anterior tergites, and occupying nearly the whole tergites posteriorly. Each tergite bears at sides a large patch on posterior margin, the patches are distinctly widened laterally, occupying on posterior tergites nearly the whole side margin of the tergite. Venter whitish-grey dusted and pale haired with a broad, black median stripe of black pubescence.

♂. Head not very large, eyes naked and unbanded. Facets on the upper two-thirds large and sharply separated from the small facets on lower third. Subcallus blackish-brown in ground colour and thinly pale greyish dusted, vertex with minute pale hairs. Face and cheeks darker greyish dusted and mostly greyish haired. Antennae more slender, segment 3 with smaller but distinct dorsal tooth. Palpi brownish, covered with fine, long dark hairs, predominantly whitish haired beneath; oval in shape, with slightly produced tip. Thorax with longer hairs everywhere, the hairs on mesonotum somewhat darker. Legs with longer hairs on femora and not so yellowish tibiae. Abdominal pattern as in the ♀ but the median triangles usually higher, forming (at least posteriorly) a more or less continuous pale median stripe.

Length. 20–25 mm (one male only 17 mm).

DATES. From June until August.

DISTRIBUTION. A species known only from a small area of distribution, from Portugal through Spain and France to West and North Italy, from where it penetrates north to Switzerland (Genève, Sierre). The species has been collected eastwards as far as Trieste, Italy, so that its occurrence in Jugoslavia is very probable.

TABANUS AUTUMNALIS LINNÉ, 1761

Fig. 124.

Tabanus autumnalis Linné, 1761, Fauna Suec., p. 462.
Tabanus molestans Becker, 1913, Annls Mus. Zool. Akad. Sci. St. Petersb., 18: 77.
Tabanus brunnescens Szilády, 1914, Annls Mus. nat. hung., 12: 671 partim.

DIAGNOSIS. Large blackish-grey species, abdomen with distinct grey pattern consisting of a row of median triangles and oval lateral patches. Male with basal four tergites brownish at sides. Antennae black or brownish at base of segment 3, palpi whitish. Hind tibiae brownish.

Description. ♀. *Head.* Eyes naked, unbanded. Frons nearly parallel-sided, greyish to grey-yellow dusted, index 1: 4—5. Frontal calli black, slightly shining; lower callus oval, connected with linear median callus. Vertex with short black hairs, occiput on postocular margin with a row of short pale hairs. Subcallus and face whitish-grey, latter with long whitish hairs. Antennae black, segment 3 sometimes indistinctly brownish, segment 3 slender with distinct and nearly rectangular dorsal tooth near base. Palpi whitish to whitish-yellow, short pale haired with some additional black hairs.

Thorax blackish-grey dusted, mesonotum with five indistinct, paler longitudinal stripes and clothed with short pale and black hairs. Notopleural lobes brownish with black hairs. Pleura densely pale haired. *Legs.* Femora greyish with pale hairs; tibiae yellowish-brown, fore tibiae on apical third and posterior four tibiae at tip blackish; tarsi black. *Wings* clear with dark brown veins, no appendix to vein R_4. Wings sometimes very slightly clouded at base. Halteres light yellow, brownish at base.

Abdomen black, dark grey dusted, with distinct light grey pattern consisting of three rows of pale haired patches, of median triangular spots occupying the whole width of tergites, and of large oval patches at sides. Sternites greyish with somewhat darker median stripe.

♂. Head rather large, as broad as or slightly broader than thorax. Eyes bare and unstriped, facets on the upper two-thirds of eyes large and sharply

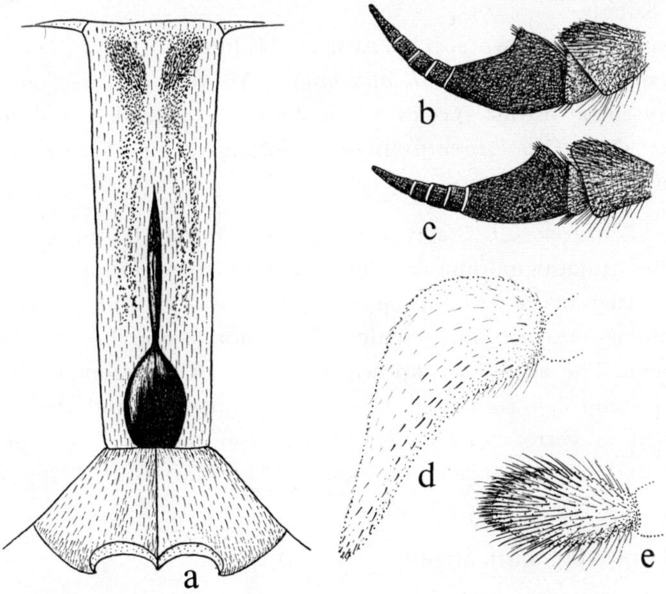

Fig. 124. *Tabanus autumnalis* L., a. female frons, b. female antenna, c. male antenna, d. female palpus, e. male palpus.

separated from the lower third with small facets. Vertex on postocular margin with very short pale hairs. Antennae black, segment 3 more slender and with rather pointed dorsal tooth near base. Apical segment of palpi longly oval, yellowish-grey and clothed with fine pale and black hairs. Thorax mostly black haired, legs darker. Wings and abdominal pattern as in the female but the median triangles are somewhat smaller and anterior four tergites chestnut-brown at sides. Anterior four sternites brownish, following sternites greyish with distinct darker median stripe.

Length. 17—22 mm.

VARIABILITY. In the southern part of the area of distribution (South Europe, North Africa and Near East) the specimens of *autumnalis* L. are often more brownish in the female sex; anterior tergites in females are brownish at sides, or at least the side markings are somewhat brownish; the males are more reddish-brown on abdomen. These specimens were first described by Becker as *T. molestans* and a year later by Szilády as *T. brunnescens.* Both these names represent only brownish varieties, with all intermediates to the dark nominate form, well known up to present as ssp. *brunnescens* Szil. These specimens, of course, cannot have subspecific status. We have seen three paratypes of *brunnescens* Szil. in the British Museum (Nat. Hist.), London from Cyprus and Algeria, and a single female in the Zoological Museum, Berlin, labelled »Cipro«, »Coll. Loew«, »Type« and »brunnescens m., det. Szilády«.

The very light brown specimens from Middle East (Iraq, Iran, Afghanistan), commonly known as *T. autumnalis brunnescens* Szil., are different and represent a distinct species which should be named *T. polygonus* Walker, 1854, with *T. polyzonatus* Bigot, 1892 and partly *T. brunnescens* Szil. as junior synonyms.

BIOLOGY. *T. autumnalis* is a typical species of lowlands and hilly countries, it does not inhabit mountains; the adults are to be found rather sporadically, and they never occur in large numbers as is typical for the large species of the *bovinus*-group. Females attack horses and horned cattle, only rarely man. The adults are known as vectors of tularaemia, anthrax and various trypanosomiasis under laboratory conditions, and they have been ascertained as vectors of tularaemia infection in water reservoirs (Schevtchenko, 1961: 166). The larva was described by Marchand (1920) and Skufin (1967).

DATES. From May until August.

DISTRIBUTION. A widely distributed species known throughout nearly all of Europe including Great Britain (not yet recorded from Ireland), Sweden,

Denmark and Finland. It is known from the whole of South Europe including Portugal and Spain, from North Africa (Morocco, Egypt) and from many islands in the Mediterranean, viz. Balearic Islands, Corsica, Sardinia, Sicily, Corfu, Cyprus, etc. Eastwards it penetrates through Siberia (except the most northern parts) as far as the vicinity of Khabarovsk. It has also been recorded from Transcaucasus, Central Asia (Tadjikistan, Uzbekistan and Kazakhstan) including Iraq and Iran.

TABANUS SPODOPTEROIDES OLSUFJEV, MOUCHA & CHVÁLA, 1969

Fig. 125.

Tabanus spodopteroides Olsufjev, Moucha & Chvála, 1969, Angew. Parasit., 10: 37.

Diagnosis. Large dark brown species resembling *spodopterus* Meig. and *paradoxus* Jaenn. but differing from both in the broader frons in female and in the partly pale haired palpi. Posterior four tibiae mostly black, abdomen chestnut-brown, tergites 1 to 5 with very small, pale median triangles, sternites brown and only a darker median stripe is black haired. Head

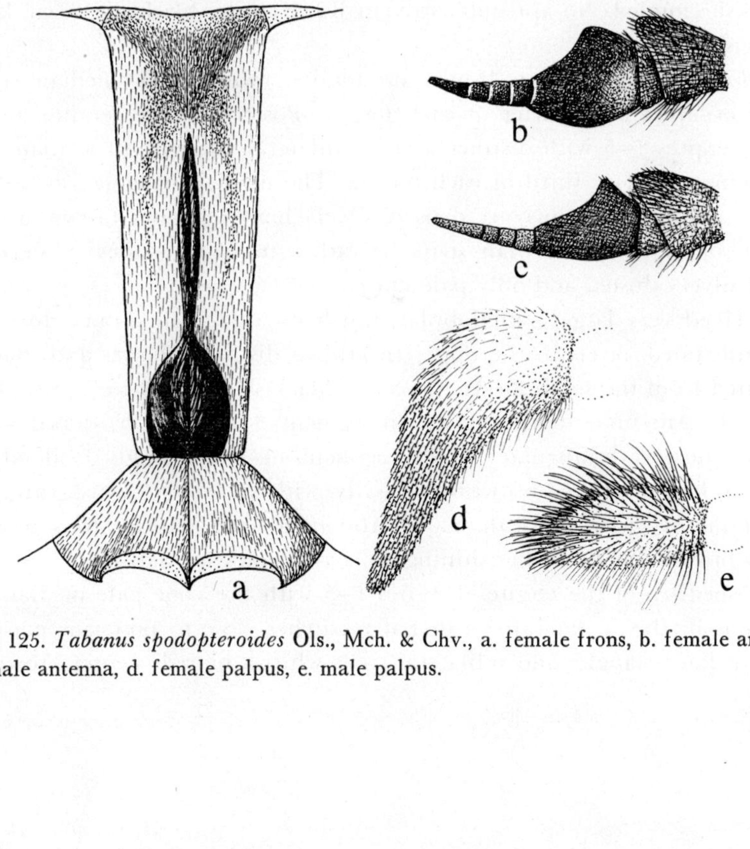

Fig. 125. *Tabanus spodopteroides* Ols., Mch. & Chv., a. female frons, b. female antenna, c. male antenna, d. female palpus, e. male palpus.

in male conspicuously large; large facets on the upper two-thirds of eyes sharply separated from small facets.

DESCRIPTION. ♀. *Head.* Eyes naked, without bands. Frons greyish-yellow dusted, rather broad, index 1: 4, slightly widened above. Subcallus dark brown, greyish dusted. Lower callus dull black, oval, narrowly separated from the eye-margins, but somewhat broader below and touching the subcallus. Median callus slightly shining, elongated, connected with lower callus. Face whitish-grey, slightly brownish above and wholly clothed with densely set yellowish-grey hairs. Antennal bows rather narrow. Antennae black but segment 3 slightly brownish at base, dorsal tooth nearly rectangular. Palpi yellowish-brown, apical segment stout at base, clothed with short pale and black hairs.

Thorax blackish-grey dusted and short reddish-brown and black haired on mesonotum and scutellum. Mesonotum with four distinctly darker longitudinal stripes, notopleural lobes brown, black haired. Pleura greyish-white dusted and densely reddish-brown haired, mostly whitish haired on lower part. *Legs* predominantly black, only basal third of fore tibiae brownish and posterior four tibiae are slightly translucent brownish on the inner side. Femora blackish-grey dusted, coxae paler. *Wings* clear with distinct dark veins, costal cell brownish, and veins on basal two-thirds of wing brownish clouded. No appendix to vein R_4. Halteres blackish-brown, knob yellowish.

Abdomen dark chestnut-brown on tergites, with black median stripe which occupies one-quarter of each tergite. Posterior three tergites mostly black, tergites 1–5 with distinct silver equilateral triangles in median row, occupying posterior third of each tergite. The median triangles, as well as narrow posterior margins, are densely silvery haired. Venter brown, a dark brown, black haired median stripe is rather indistinct; sides of sternites rather silvery dusted and only pale haired.

♂. Head very large, semiglobular, much broader than thorax. Eyes naked, unbanded, facets in the upper two-thirds distinctly larger and sharply separated from the small facets. Subcallus blackish-grey dusted, upper third brownish. Antennae more slender on segment 3 and darker, dorsal tooth distinct, nearly rectangular. Apical segment of palpi longly oval, about twice as long as deep, brownish; basally with mostly brownish, apically predominantly with blackish, hairs. Abdomen with anterior four tergites mostly brown and somewhat shining, a narrow black median stripe occupies about one-fifth of the tergite. Tergites 1–5 with the same pale median triangles as in the ♀, laterally with paler patches close to posterior margin; both median triangles and sublateral spots whitish haired. Venter brown to light brown, clothed with fine greyish hairs, only darker median stripe with black hairs. Apical two sternites darkened.

Length. 21—21.5 mm.

DATES. August.

DISTRIBUTION. Italy. It is only a recently described species from the Italian Alps where it has been repeatedly collected by Mr Schacht at the same locality in August 1966 and 1968.

TABANUS SPODOPTERUS SPODOPTERUS MEIGEN, 1820

Fig. 126.

Tabanus spodopterus Meigen, 1820, Syst. Beschr., 2: 46.

DIAGNOSIS. Large reddish-brown species with entirely black antennae and greyish palpi, which are only short black haired. Tergites with large, equilateral whitish median triangles. Venter of abdomen silvery dusted and pale haired, median stripe dark reddish-brown with black hairs. Head in male smaller, at most as broad as thorax, all facets nearly equal in size.

DESCRIPTION. ♀. *Head.* Eyes naked, unbanded. Frons rather narrow, index 1: 5, slightly diverging towards vertex, greyish to greyish-yellow dusted. Lower callus black and only indistinctly shining, longly oval in shape and narrowly connected with linear black median callus. Subcallus greyish dusted, yellow antennal bows narrow. Face and cheeks yellowish-grey dusted and densely whitish-grey haired. Vertex with short pale and some black hairs. Antennae black, segment 3 rather slender, with small but rectangular or slightly pointed dorsal tooth at base. Palpi greyish-yellow to grey, stouter at base, densely clothed with short black hairs, only dorsally at base with a few additional pale hairs.

Thorax black, mesonotum blackish-grey dusted with three indistinct, narrow, greyish longitudinal stripes, and wholly short pale and black haired; some longer pale hairs posteriorly at margins and on scutellum. Notopleural lobes brown to dark, black haired. Pleura greyish dusted and mostly densely and finely whitish haired. *Legs.* Coxae with the same dusting and pubescence as pleura. Femora dark greyish, basal half of fore tibiae and whole of posterior four tibiae brown with black hairs, all tarsi and rest of fore tibiae black. *Wings* clear, slightly greyish clouded along anterior margin, veins brown to dark brown; no appendix to vein R_4. First posterior cell very narrowed towards tip, sometimes closed. Halteres dark brown, tip of knob whitish.

Abdomen reddish-brown on anterior 3 to 4 tergites and mostly black haired there, with only a narrow black median stripe. Apical tergites black. Tergites 2–5 with large, distinct, nearly equilateral whitish coloured and pale haired median triangles; they are larger on tergites 4 and 5, reaching anterior margin of the tergite. All tergites with a narrow pale posterior border which is widened laterally. Venter reddish-brown in ground colour, silvery dusted and pale haired at sides. A dark median stripe rather broader, occupying nearly one-third of the sternites, reddish-brown and densely black haired.

♂. Head not very large, at most as broad as thorax. Eyes naked, without bands. Facets on the upper two-thirds only very slightly larger and hardly distinguishable from the lower facets. Antennae with still more slender segment 3, black. Palpi yellowish-brown to greyish, apical segment narrowly oval, very pointed at tip and clothed with long black hairs. Mesonotum with longer dark hairs, otherwise resembling female.

Length. 17–23 mm.

VARIABILITY. A very variable species; two very well separated geographical subspecies are known from Europe, and specimens from Central Europe with conspicuously golden-yellow pubescence on face, thorax and light areas on abdomen were named by Olsufjev, Moucha & Chvála (1967) as f. *slovacus*.

BIOLOGY. A typical species of pasture meadows, more often in higher altitudes; in Bulgaria it has often been collected in about 2000 m (Rila). Females attack horses, horned cattle and other large animals.

DATES. From the end of June until August.

DISTRIBUTION. A South and Central European subspecies known from Jugoslavia, Greece, Bulgaria, Rumania and Moldavia, in Central Europe from Switzerland, Austria, South Germany, Hungary and Czechoslovakia.

TABANUS SPODOPTERUS IBERICUS OLSUFJEV, MOUCHA & CHVÁLA, 1967

Fig. 127.

Tabanus spodopterus ibericus Olsufjev, Moucha & Chvála, 1967, Acta ent. bohemoslov., 64: 305.

DIAGNOSIS. ♀. The thoracic and abdominal pattern distinctly darker than in the nominate form. Antennae and palpi as in the nominate form, face with paler hairs. The median triangles on abdomen are whitish but distinctly smaller, reaching on tergites 2 and 3 hardly basal third of the tergite. Posterior borders to all tergites are golden-yellow haired, whitish haired at sides only. Sternites are darker than in the nominate form: the black hairs not only on the median stripe but they are spread all over the venter except for posterior margins which are pale haired. Tibiae blackish-brown with black pubescence. Mesopleuron blackish haired at middle.

♂. Unknown.

Length. 21–24 mm.

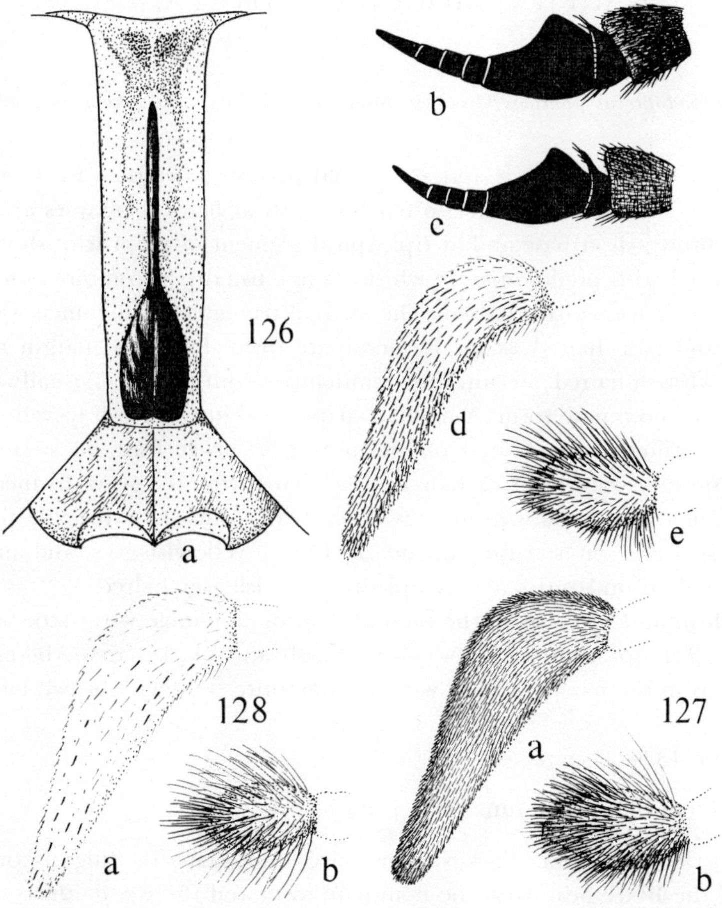

Fig. 126. *Tabanus s. spodopterus* Meig., a. female frons, b. female antenna, c. male antenna, d. female palpus, e. male palpus.

Fig. 127. *Tabanus spodopterus ibericus* Ols., Mch. & Chv., a. female palpus, b. male palpus.

Fig. 128. *Tabanus spodopterus ponticus* Ols., Mch. & Chv., a. female palpus, b. male palpus.

Dates. July.

Distribution. Spain and France. The subspecies has only recently been separated from the nominate form on the basis of the material from Spain and France but probably the records from Portugal of *spodopterus* Meig. also refer to this subspecies.

TABANUS SPODOPTERUS PONTICUS OLSUFJEV, MOUCHA & CHVÁLA, 1967

Fig. 128.

Tabanus spodopterus ponticus Olsufjev, Moucha & Chvála, 1967, Acta ent. bohemoslov., 64: 305.

Diagnosis. ♀. The thoracic and abdominal pattern paler than in the nominate form. Antennal segment 3 often brownish at base, sometimes also segment 1 brownish at base and at tip. Apical segment of palpi whitish-yellow and clothed with predominantly whitish hairs, usually in combination with black hairs. Face whitish haired. The median triangles on abdomen whitish dusted and pale haired as in the nominate form. Posterior margin to all tergites whitish haired. Sternites predominantly reddish-yellow, usually paler than in the nominate form. A median stripe on venter reddish to yellowish-brown, distinctly pale haired on sternites 2–4, or at least on sternite 2. Apical sternites mostly black haired. A median stripe is not so distinct and dark as in the nominate form, this effect being caused by its pale pubescence especially on sternites 2 and 3. Tibiae yellowish-grey and mostly whitish haired on basal half. Mesopleuron whitish-grey haired.

♂. Head and facets as in the nominate form, antennae with dark brown segment 3. Palpi whitish-yellow with whitish and black hairs. Abdominal pattern as in the female, venter with an indefinite, yellowish-brown median stripe.

Length. 18.5–23 mm.

Dates. From the end of June until July.

Distribution. Bulgaria, Turkey. This subspecies occurs in Bulgaria on the coast of the Black Sea. Both the nominate form and the ssp. *ponticus* occur in Bulgaria; the nominate form is found inland where the east border of its area of distribution lies, on the other hand the occurrence of ssp. *ponticus* on Bulgarian coast represents its western border. From Rumania we have seen specimens of *spodopterus* Meig. only from the Transsylvanian Alps, they all belonged to the nominate form.

TABANUS PROMETHEUS SZILÁDY, 1923

Fig. 129.

Tabanus Eggeri var. *Prometheus* Szilády, 1923, Biologica hung., 1 (1): 12.
Tabanus capito Olsufjev, 1937, Fauna SSSR, 7: 299, – syn. n.

DIAGNOSIS. Large, reddish-brown to deeply brown species with more or less brownish posterior four femora. Antennal bows rather high, palpi mostly black haired with some additional pale hairs. Head in male only slightly broader than thorax, facets on the upper two-thirds large and sharply separated from the small facets.

DESCRIPTION. ♀. *Head.* Eyes naked, unstriped. Frons yellowish-grey dusted, rather narrower, index 1: 5.5, slightly widening above. Lower callus black, longly oval and joined with a linear median callus. Subcallus with rather high yellowish antennal bows, occupying nearly one-third of the subcallus. Face and cheeks greyish dusted and densely pale haired. Antennae blackish-brown to brown, segment 3 black at tip; dorsal tooth well developed, nearly

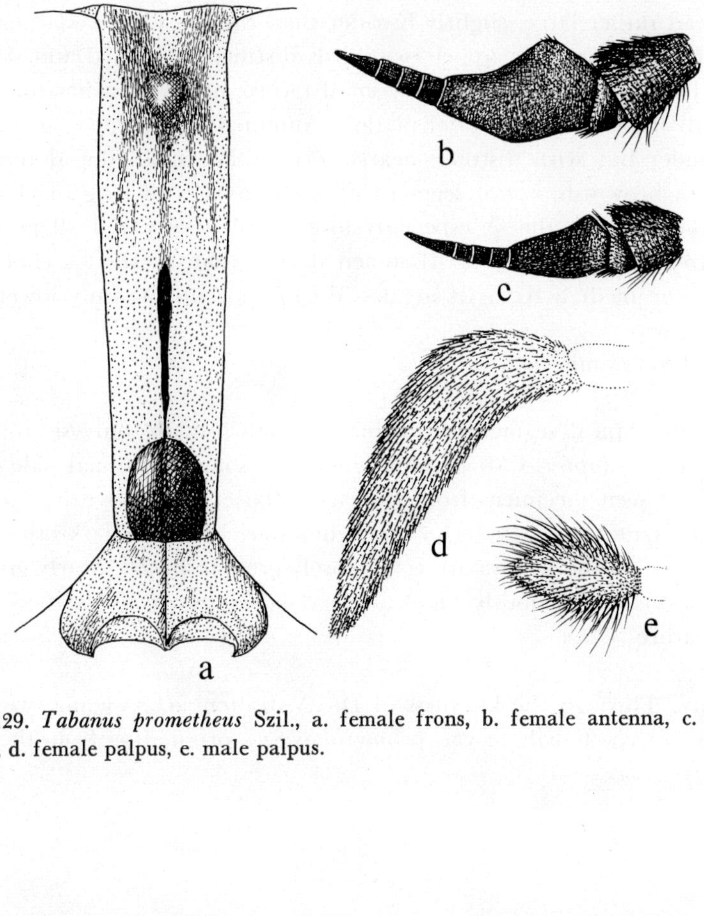

Fig. 129. *Tabanus prometheus* Szil., a. female frons, b. female antenna, c. male antenna, d. female palpus, e. male palpus.

rectangular. Palpi yellowish-brown, clothed with short black hairs and with some additional pale hairs.

Thorax blackish-grey, mesonotum with short pale and black hairs, pleura greyish and long whitish haired. Notopleural lobes usually brown and mostly black haired. *Legs*. Fore femora blackish-grey with pale hairs; fore tibiae whitish, apical half to two-thirds including tarsi black. Posterior four femora brown in ground colour, more or less greyish dusted; posterior tibiae brown, tarsi blackish-brown and mostly black haired. *Wings* clear with blackish-brown veins, no appendix to vein R_4; first posterior cell narrowed towards apex but always open. Halteres brown, knobs whitish at tip.

Abdomen dark reddish-brown in ground colour but an indistinct median stripe on dorsum and apical two or three tergites blackish. Anterior five tergites with usually large and distinct pale greyish median triangles, reaching by their tips posterior margin of foregoing tergites. All tergites with narrow, pale haired borders on posterior margin at sides, otherwise tergites short black haired. Venter unicolorous brown and pale haired except for apical two sternites which are darker and black haired, some black hairs also on other sternites at sides; the darker, reddish median stripe hardly visible.

♂. Head rather large, slightly broader than thorax. Face naked and unstriped, the facets on the upper two-thirds distinctly enlarged and sharply separated from the lower area with small facets, and from a narrow stripe with small facets along occipital margin. Antennae dark brown, segment 3 more slender but with distinct, nearly rectangular, small dorsal tooth at base. Palpi brownish, apical segment narrowly oval with long black hairs. Legs darker than in the ♀, especially fore tibiae basally and all posterior tibiae brown to dark brown. Abdomen darker than in the ♀, chocolate-coloured, the median triangles are less distinct, occupying only lower half of the tergites.

Length. 20—23 mm.

VARIABILITY. Apical segment of palpi in female usually only short black haired as in *spodopterus* Meig., sometimes with some additional pale hairs, but we have seen specimens from Bulgaria (Zlatje Piasecy) with palpi predominantly pale haired. Posterior four femora are brown to dark brown but sometimes, when the femora are very densely greyish dusted, nearly grey; in such cases the conspicuously high antennal bows remain as the best differential feature.

SYNONYMY. Through the kindness of Dr. A. Kaltenbach, Vienna, we have seen a single type female of var. *prometheus* Szil. originating from the type series of 1 male and 3 females described from the Caucasus. The type female, deposited in the Naturhistorisches Museum, Vienna was identical with the species hitherto known as *T. capito* Ols.; it was also re-examined by Prof. Olsufjev, Moscow. Szilády, when describing this species as a variety of *T. eggeri* Schin., already noted that »it may be regarded even as a distinct species«. Unfortunately he did not mention in the original description the distinctly brown middle and hind femora and conspicuously high antennal bows.

Dates. July and August.

Distribution. The species is known from Transcaucasus and Iran, recently it has also been recorded from Bulgaria (Olsufjev, Moucha & Chvála, 1967: 308) from several localities especially on the coast of the Black Sea.

TABANUS SUDETICUS ZELLER, 1842

Fig. 130; pl. 3: fig. a.

Tabanus sudeticus Zeller, 1842, Isis, 2: 815.
Tabanus sudeticus var. *perplexus* Verrall, 1909, Brit. Flies, 5: 399.
Tabanus sudeticus f. *meridionalis* Goffe, 1931, Trans. ent. Soc. S. Engl., 6: 74.
Tabanus sudeticus f. *confusus* Goffe, 1931, Trans. ent. Soc. S. Engl., 6: 76.
Tabanus sudeticus f. *distinctus* Goffe, 1931, Trans. ent. Soc. S. Engl., 6: 77.
Tabanus verralli Oldroyd, 1939, in Edwards, Oldroyd et Smart, 1939, Brit. Bloodsucking Flies, p. 103 (nom. nov. for *perplexus* Verr.).

Diagnosis. Large blackish-brown species with distinct yellow posterior borders to all tergites and sternites, venter of abdomen with hardly visible darker median stripe. Lower frontal callus longly triangular. Antennae reddish-brown on basal segments, segment 3 apically blackish, broad, with well developed, pointed dorsal tooth; antennal bows high. Palpi yellowish-brown with short black hairs. Head in male rather smaller, upper facets distinctly enlarged but not sharply separated from smaller facets below.

Description. ♀. *Head.* Eyes naked, unbanded. Frons yellowish-brown dusted and black haired, rather narrow, index 1: 4—4.5, parallel-sided. Lower callus elongated, triangular in shape, below with four minute projections; slightly shining black, connected with rather shortened and broader linear median callus. Subcallus yellowish-grey dusted, antennal bows yellow, rather high, occupying lower third of subcallus. Face and cheeks paler yellowish-grey dusted and clothed with long golden-yellow hairs. Basal antennal segments reddish-brown and short black haired, segment 3 reddish-brown on basal part including dorsal tooth, apically blackish-brown, terminal flagellar segments black; distinctly broad, lower edge conspicuously convex, dorsal tooth prominent, pointed. Palpi long and slender, blunt ended; yellowish-brown and clothed with short black hairs, dorsally at base with some paler hairs.

Thorax blackish-grey, mesonotum with hardly visible greyish longitudinal stripes, covered by short black and yellowish hairs. Notopleural lobes dark brown, densely blackish haired beneath. Pleura densely yellowish haired, pteropleuron predominantly with black hairs. *Legs:* Femora blackish-grey, finely black haired and slightly shining. Tibiae yellowish and pale haired, extreme tip of fore tibiae and fore tarsi black, posterior four tarsi brown and black haired. *Wings* clear or slightly brownish clouded along costal margin, veins dark brown, no appendix to vein R_4. First posterior cell narrowed towards tip. Halteres brown, knob paler at tip.

Abdomen mostly black and black haired, anterior three tergites dark brown at sides. Dorsum with pale pattern of yellowish dusting and pale hairing consists of a row of distinct median triangles which occupy posterior half of each tergite, and of yellow posterior borders to each tergite, the

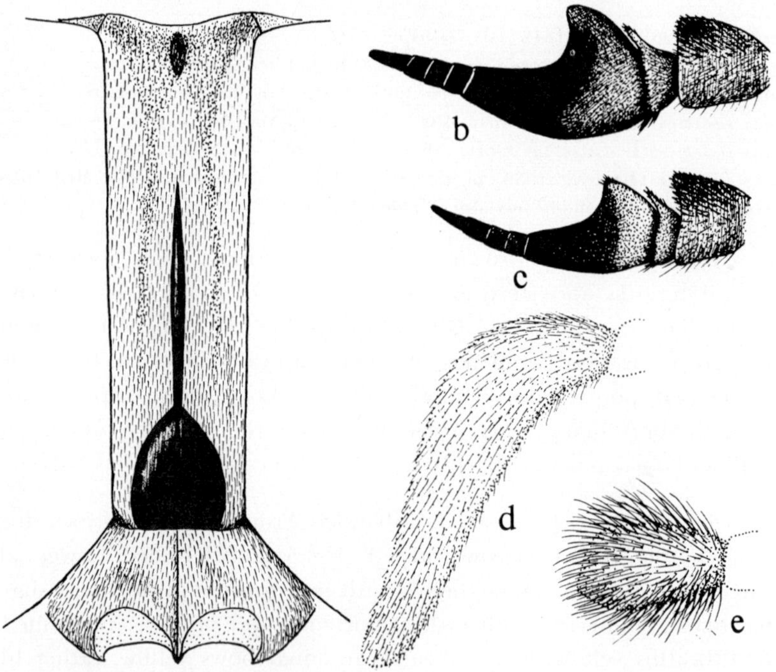

Fig. 130. *Tabanus sudeticus* Zell., a. female frons, b. female antenna, c. male antenna, d. female palpus, e. male palpus.

borders are broader laterally and interrupted mesally. Venter blackish, especially laterally greyish dusted, with indistinct darker median stripe and very distinct, broad, yellowish-grey border posteriorly to each sternite; the borders are somewhat narrower at middle.

♂. Head not larger than in the ♀, not broader than thorax. Eyes naked and unbanded. Facets on the upper two-thirds distinctly larger than on lower third, about 4 times as large as small facets below, but the sharp division is not present. Vertex with small, fine pale hairs. Cheeks on the upper part mostly black haired, antennae with more slender segment 3. Palpi yellowish-brown, apical segment longly oval and mostly short black haired. Abdomen with the same pattern as in the ♀ but both median triangles and posterior margins are less distinct, and tergite 2 broadly chestnut-brown at sides. Venter mostly shining black.

Length. 20–27 mm.

VARIABILITY. A very variable species; Goffe named three forms from England and the systematic position of var. *perplexus* Verrall has been unclear for a long time. The abdominal pattern and coloration vary from extensively dark specimens (described above) to paler specimens with somewhat chestnut to reddish-brown coloration on anterior tergites, with elongated and mostly greyish median triangles, with narrower pale posterior margins to each tergite, and the median stripe on the venter being distinctly darkened. Specimens with such a combination of characters resembles specimens of *bovinus* L. The pale specimens of *sudeticus* Zell. differ from *bovinus* L. in the enlarged upper facets in male sex, in the female sex in the mostly black haired palpi, in the higher antennal bows and in the different shape of antennal segment 3, which is more slender and with less distinct dorsal tooth in *bovinus* L.

The paler form is commoner in west parts of the area of distribution, it was described from England as var. *perplexus* Verrall and is fairly well known under the name of *verralli* Oldroyd. The whole range of variability between the nominate form and the variety *perplexus* Verr. is known, the variety *perplexus* Verr. inhabits a large area from England through Central Europe as far as South East Russia (Volgograd). Of course, it cannot be taken for a different subspecies as did Leclercq (1967a: 172).

DATES. From June until August.

BIOLOGY. Rather a common species on pastures; females attack horses and horned cattle.

DISTRIBUTION. A species known throughout Europe including its north parts (Sweden, Finland), eastwards it penetrates as far as Ural, West Siberia

(Omsk), in south through Asia Minor to Azerbaijan. It has also been recorded from Morocco, North Africa.

TABANUS BOVINUS LINNÉ, 1758

Fig. 131.

Tabanus bovinus Linné, 1758, Syst. Nat., p. 601.
Tabanus auratus Ghidini, 1936, Archo zool. ital., 22: 439.

DIAGNOSIS. Large reddish-brown species with antennae brown on basal two segments, segment 3 black. Palpi yellowish with pale hairs. Abdominal tergites mostly reddish-brown with a row of pale median triangles. Sternites with distinct blackish-brown median stripe. Facets in male nearly equal in size.

DESCRIPTION. ♀. *Head.* Eyes naked, unbanded. Frons greyish-yellow dusted, parallel-sided and rather narrow, index 1: 4–5. Lower callus black, only slightly shining, triangular in shape, apically connected with linear, black median callus. Vertex with short dark hairs. Subcallus and face greyish

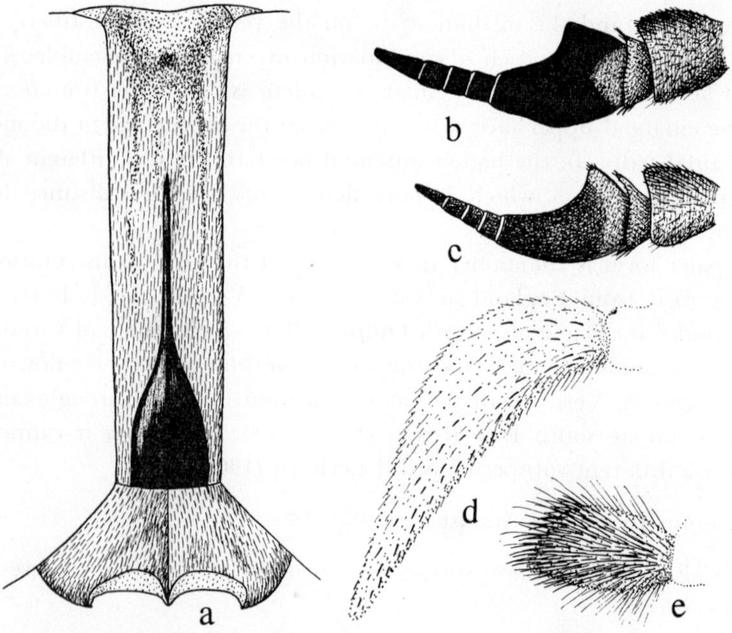

Fig. 131. *Tabanus bovinus* L., a. female frons, b. female antenna, c. male antenna, d. female palpus, e. male palpus.

dusted, latter with longer pale hairs. Antennae black, basal two segments and sometimes segment 3 narrow brownish at base; segment 3 rather broad with distinct rectangular dorsal tooth. Palpi large and long, whitish-yellow to yellowish-brown, short pale haired, sometimes with some additional black hairs.

Thorax blackish-grey, mesonotum with indistinct paler longitudinal stripes, notopleural lobes brownish. Pleura more greyish dusted and long yellowish-brown haired. *Legs* with femora greyish with pale hairs, femora at tip and tibiae yellowish-brown; fore tibiae on apical third and fore tarsi black, tip on posterior four tibiae and tarsi darkened. *Wings* clear or very indistinctly greyish tinted, slightly yellowish along costal margin. Veins blackish-brown, brownish near wing-base; no appendix to vein R_4. Halteres blackish-brown, knob paler.

Abdomen reddish-brown to chestnut-brown on anterior three to four tergites, distinct pale haired median triangles reaching apical third of the tergites. Apical tergites darkened, all tergites with more or less distinct pale posterior margin. Sternites greyish-yellow dusted, brownish anteriorly, and with distinct, broad, dark median stripe.

♂. Head not very large, eyes naked, unbanded and all facets nearly equal in size. Antennae with narrower segment 3, apical segment of palpi yellowish-brown, shortly oval and somewhat pointed, mostly black haired. Otherwise as in the ♀.

Length. 19–24 mm.

Variability. The brown coloration on abdomen varies from reddish-brown to dark chestnut-brown, likewise the distinctness of pale median triangles and posterior borders to all tergites is rather variable. The dark median stripe on the venter is usually more distinct in the males, sometimes more or less confluent with brown coloration anteriorly.

Biology. A very well known species, the adults are common on various biotopes, the larvae live in banks of rivers, ponds and lakes. Females attack especially horned cattle and horses, often a considerable way, 4 to 5 km according to Violovič (1968: 98), from places where the larvae live. A typical species of pasture-meadows where the females cause serious damage to horned cattle by sucking much blood and disturbing the feeding animals. The same may be said about other large species of the *bovinus*-group. The females are known as vectors of tularaemia, anthrax and trypanosomiasis of camels under laboratory conditions. The larva has been described by Marchand (1920) and Skufin (1967).

Dates. From the end of May until August.

Distribution. A widely distributed species known throughout Europe including North Scandinavia (Åsele Lappmark and South Carelia) but not yet recorded from Ireland. Eastwards it penetrates as far as Altai, the north border of its area of distribution in the east lies in the Transcaucasia and Kazakhstan; recorded also from North Africa (Algeria and Morocco).

TABANUS TINCTUS WALKER, 1850

Fig. 132.

Tabanus tinctus Walker, 1850, Ins. Saunders., Dipt., 1: 9.
Tabanus mixtus Szilády, 1914, Annls Mus. nat. hung., 12: 672.

Diagnosis. Large reddish-brown species of the *bovinus*-group with brown antennae, only terminal flagellar segments darkened; segment 3 broad with distinct, nearly pointed dorsal tooth. Palpi yellowish and pale haired, only a few black hairs intermixed. Abdomen reddish-brown on anterior five tergites, venter entirely brownish and pale haired with indistinct darker median stripe. Head in male rather small, not broader than thorax, upper facets only slightly enlarged, no distinct division.

Description. ♀. *Head.* Eyes naked and unbanded. Frons yellowish-grey dusted, rather narrow, index 1: 5. Lower callus longly oval, black and only slightly shining, connected with a linear black median callus. Vertex with a row of very short black hairs. Subcallus yellowish-grey dusted, antennal bows rather narrow, occupying at most one-quarter of subcallus. Face and cheeks light grey dusted and long pale haired. Antennae brown, terminal flagellar segments darkened or nearly black; basal segments short black haired, segment 3 with well developed rectangular to pointed dorsal tooth, broad. Palpi yellowish, long, distinctly thickened in basal third, blunt ended; clothed with short pale hairs, some black hairs towards tip and beneath.

Thorax blackish-grey, pleura light grey dusted and densely whitish-grey haired. Mesonotum distinctly darker, covered by short pale and black hairs. Notopleural lobes brown, occasionally dark and always black haired. Femora except tip black and greyish dusted, finely pale haired. *Legs.* Coxae light grey dusted and clothed with long pale hairs. Fore tibiae on basal half and whole of posterior four tibiae except tip brown; rest of fore tibiae and fore tarsi black, posterior tarsi blackish-brown. Posterior tibiae more or less densely black haired. *Wings* slightly greyish tinted with blackish-brown veins, somewhat brownish anteriorly. First posterior cell narrowed apically; no appendix to vein R_4, only exceptionally a trace of it. Halteres blackish-brown, knob whitish at tip.

Abdomen reddish-brown on anterior four tergites and mostly black haired, a narrow median stripe widened on posterior tergites, which are often entirely blackish. All tergites with a narrow posterior border and a row of equilateral median triangles, which do not reach anterior margin; the pale pattern is formed by greyish dusting and pale hairing. Sternites reddish-brown and pale haired, posterior sternites with greyish lateral patches, and last sternite entirely dark grey. A median stripe is more distinct when viewed from behind, it is formed by short blackish hairs and lack of silver-grey dusting.

♂. Head rather small, not broader than thorax. Facets on the upper two-thirds slightly larger but the sharp division between them and small facets is not present. Antennal segment 3 more slender and usually darker. Apical segment of palpi longly oval, yellow with greyish dust, clothed with longer pale hairs, dorsally and towards tip with some black hairs. Otherwise as in the ♀.

Length. 19–24 mm.

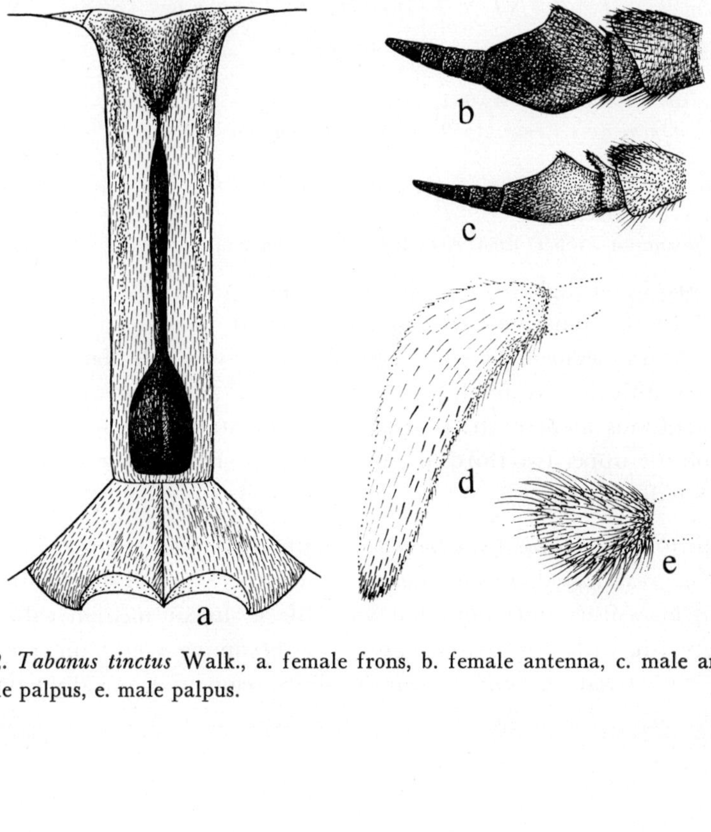

Fig. 132. *Tabanus tinctus* Walk., a. female frons, b. female antenna, c. male antenna, d. female palpus, e. male palpus.

VARIABILITY. The pale abdominal pattern is rather variable, the light grey median triangles are usually very distinct on tergites 2 to 6, in some specimens, however, missing on tergites 2 and 3, so that a narrow black median stripe is more distinct.

SYNONYMY. This species is commonly known in the literature under the name of *mixtus* Szil., the change of name has been made by Moucha (1971) who has revised the type of Walker's *T. tinctus* in the British Museum (Nat. Hist.) and who at last found out the origin of the type specimen; the holotype female of *tinctus* Walk. originates from Greece. Fairchild (1956) synonymized *tinctus* Walk. by mistake with *eggeri* Schin., and this has been followed also by Leclercq (1967a).

DATES. July and August.

DISTRIBUTION. This species is known from South Europe (Italy, Jugoslavia, Albania, Greece and Bulgaria), eastwards to Turkey, Cyprus, the Caucasus and Azerbaijan. It is recorded also from North Africa from Morocco, Algeria and Tunisia.

TABANUS EGGERI SCHINER, 1868

Fig. 133.

Tabanus tinctus auct., nec Walker, 1850.

Tabanus intermedius Egger, 1859, Verh. zool.-bot. Ges. Wien, 9: 389 (nec Walker, 1848).

Tabanus eggeri Schiner, 1868, Novara Reise, Dipt., p. 81 (nom. nov. for *intermedius* Egger nec Walker).

Phyrta lavandoni Kröber, 1938, Acta Inst. Mus. Zool Univ. athen., 2: 101, 244 – syn. n.

DIAGNOSIS. Large light reddish species of the *bovinus*-group. Antennal segment 3 black, sometimes slightly brownish at base, basal two segments brown. Apical segment of palpi whitish-yellow and pale haired. Venter of abdomen unicolorous reddish-yellow coloured and short pale haired, a darker rufuous median stripe hardly visible. Male with somewhat larger facets on the upper two-thirds of eyes, which are not sharply separated from lower, smaller facets.

DESCRIPTION. ♀. *Head.* Eyes bare and without bands; frons and subcallus yellowish-grey dusted, former narrow, index 1: 5–5.5. Lower callus oval-shaped, brownish, and connected with black, linear median callus. Face more greyish, with short whitish-grey hairs becoming longer on cheeks. Antennae with basal segments brownish-yellow, segment 1 apically with black hairs; segment 3 black, sometimes just at base slightly brownish, dorsal tooth rectangular. Palpi rather long and slender, pointed at tip, whitish-yellow coloured and short pale haired, at most with a few black hairs. Vertex with fine pale hairing.

Thorax greyish, thinly brownish dusted; mesonotum with short, pleura with long, pale hairs. Notopleural lobes brownish-yellow, black haired below. *Legs* with femora blackish-brown, greyish dusted, and densely pale haired. All femora at tip brownish. Tibiae light yellow, black haired towards tip; fore tibiae on apical third and whole of fore tarsi black, posterior four tarsi brown with short black pubescence. *Wings* clear with distinct brown veins, no appendix to vein R_4. First posterior cell narrowly open or closed. Halteres brown with knobs yellowish.

Abdomen reddish to yellowish-brown, tergites 2–5 with a black, narrow median patch and a pale median triangle, which reaches anterior half of the tergite. Apical two or three tergites sometimes black. Sternites unicolorous reddish to yellowish-brown, very short pale haired and more densely at sides, leaving mesally a somewhat darker rust coloured stripe.

♂. Head comparatively large, semiglobular, slightly broader than thorax is deep. Facets on the upper two-thirds of eyes larger than on the lower

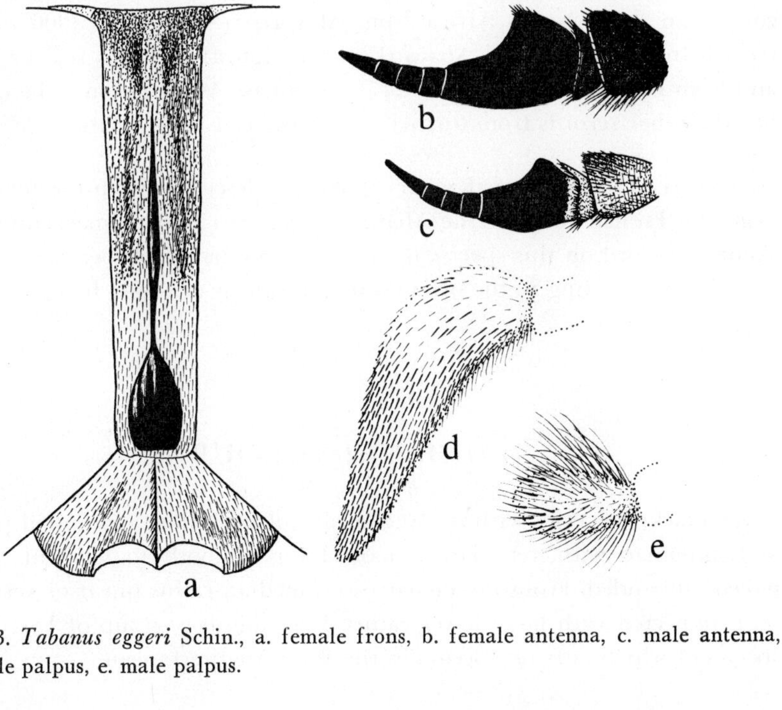

Fig. 133. *Tabanus eggeri* Schin., a. female frons, b. female antenna, c. male antenna, d. female palpus, e. male palpus.

third, the sharp division is, however, not present. Antennae with darker and black haired basal two segments, segment 3 more slender. Palpi long oval, whitish-yellow with longer pale hairs, some black hairs at tip. Otherwise as in the ♀ but notopleural lobes usually darker, first posterior cell on wing open, and apical abdominal segments usually darker.

Length. 18–23 mm.

VARIABILITY. The abdomen is always distinctly rust-coloured but the pattern varies, especially in the size and shape of the pale median triangles; they are sometimes very large in pale specimens and the black median patches are hardly visible, on the other hand some specimens have distinct blackish median patches and the pale triangles are very small, hardly visible. The var. *prometheus,* described by Szilády in 1923 from the Caucasus, represents a distinct species known for a long time under the name *capito* Ols.

BIOLOGY. The adults are rather common in suitable localities, females attack horned cattle and horses.

DATES. July and August.

DISTRIBUTION. A Mediterranean species; we have seen the documentary material from South France, Italy (Trieste), Jugoslavia, Albania and Bulgaria, and from North Africa from Morocco (Atlas Mts., 1900 m). The records from Portugal and Spain (Leclercq, 1967a: 174 – as *tinctus* Walk.), and from Israel (Theodor, 1965: 247 – as *tinctus* Walk.) seem to be reliable, but the other records from further countries need to be verified.

SYNONYMY. *T. lavandoni* (Kröber, 1938) was described from the female sex from the French coast of the Mediterranean Sea (»Mittelmeerküste«) and no other record on this species is available. We have not seen the type specimen but according to the original description it can only be *eggeri* Schin.

CHRYSURUS-GROUP

Large blackish species with conspicuously golden-yellow abdominal pattern, and antennae with very large, hooked dorsal tooth to segment 3. Eyes naked, unbanded. Frons rather narrower, median callus linear or very reduced, connected with large lower callus. It is mainly a group of East Asiatic species of which only one occurs in the West Mediterranean.

TABANUS BARBARUS COQUEBERT, 1804

Fig. 134.

Tabanus barbarus Coquebert, 1804, Illustr. Icon. Ins., 3: 111, pl. 25, fig. 2.
Tabanus taurinus Meigen, 1804, Klass., p. 165.
Tabanus maroccanus Fabricius, 1805, Syst. Ant., p. 93.
Tabanus auricinctus Macquart, 1838, Dipt. exot., 1 (1): 130.

DIAGNOSIS. Large species with conspicuously orange-yellow antennae, palpi and legs. Antennal segment 3 with a large, forward directed, pointed dorsal tooth. Abdomen black with golden-yellow pattern consisting of large median triangles and interrupted posterior margin to each tergite.

DESCRIPTION. ♀. *Head.* Eyes naked, unbanded. Frons parallel-sided, greyish dusted and clothed with longer reddish-golden hairs, index more than 1: 4. Frontal calli dulled brown, lower callus rectangular, above gradually confluent with a narrower median callus. Vertex with a row of short reddish hairs. Subcallus reddish coloured and golden dusted, distinctly convex. Face and cheeks dark grey dusted, clothed with long reddish hairs, face with some additional black hairs. Antennae unicolorous reddish-yellow to orange, basal two segments short reddish above and with longer black hairs beneath.

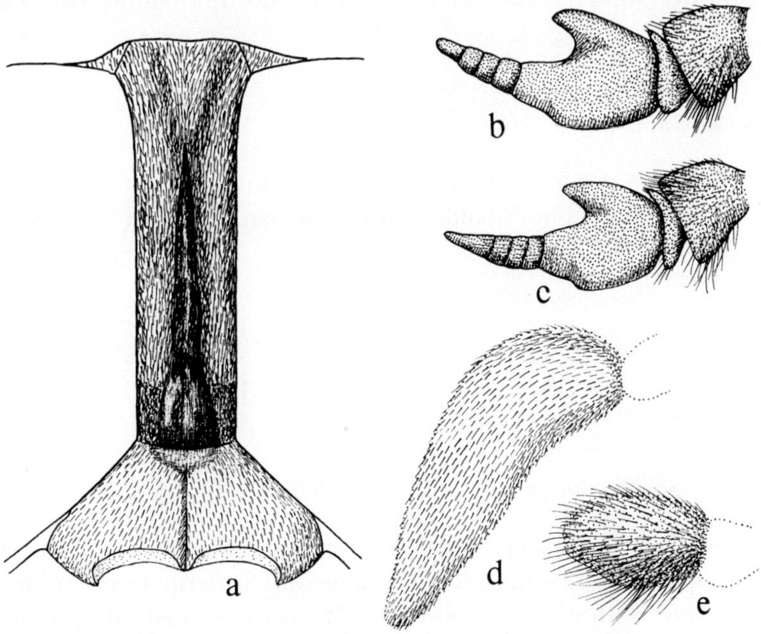

Fig. 134. *Tabanus barbarus* Coq., a. female frons, b. female antenna, c. male antenna, d. female palpus, e. male palpus.

Segment 3 with conspicuously large and forward directed dorsal tooth, reaching by its apex to base of the terminal flagellar segments. Palpi long and rather broad, blunt ended, entirely reddish-yellow coloured and covered by short concolorous hairs.

Thorax blackish-grey, mesonotum and scutellum with short reddish hairs, notopleural lobes light brownish. Pleura mostly black haired. *Legs* unicolorous reddish-yellow and clothed with concolorous hairs, only femora with a few black hairs, posterior four tarsi and tibiae nearly yellowish. *Wings* faintly yellowish tinted, more distinctly along costal margin. Veins yellowish-brown, no appendix to vein R_4. Halteres dark brown.

Abdomen black with distinct golden-yellow pattern. Tergite 1 with a small double patch at middle, following tergites with broad median triangles and lateral patches on posterior margins. The lateral patches become larger on posterior tergites so that apical tergites are nearly entirely golden-yellow. Venter black with concolorous hairs except to sternite 1 which bears a broad golden-yellow border on posterior margin.

♂. Eyes naked, unbanded, all facets nearly equal in size. Head rather smaller, not deeper than thorax. Vertex with a row of rather short reddish hairs. Subcallus, face and antennae as in the ♀, but the dorsal tooth to antennal segment 3 slightly shorter. Apical segment of palpi rather broad and short oval in shape, reddish, with rather short concolorous hairs. Otherwise as in the ♀.

Length. 19–22 mm.

Dates. May and June.

Distribution. A West Mediterranean species known from North Africa (Morocco, Algeria, Tunisia) and from the Iberian Peninsula (Portugal and Spain).

GENUS *GLAUCOPS* SZILÁDY, 1923

Biologica hung., 1 (1): 17.

Type species: *Tabanus hirsutus* Villers, 1789.

Diagnosis. Small blackish-grey species resembling somewhat a larger *Haematopota*-species but wings clear without any pattern. Frons in female rather broader with well developed and broadly separated calli, no ocellar swelling. Eyes naked with three bands, male with sharply separated large and small facets and with two eye-bands. Antennae with three terminal flagellar segments which form a short and stout complex. Dorsal tooth to segment 3 well developed. Basicosta bare.

REMARKS. The genus is closely related to *Tabanus* L. and is usually considered only as a subgenus of *Tabanus*. The great affinity of *Glaucops* to *Tabanus* has been pointed out already by Chvála (1964: 379) and later by Olsufjev (1969b: 119), on the other hand *Glaucops* cannot be arranged as a subgenus of *Hybomitra* End. as it was proposed by Leclercq (1967a). In the present work we place *Glaucops* as a distinct genus for two different reasons: first it is better to work with isolated genera than with subgenera, in the latter case it would be necessary still to use binominal generic names; secondly, when omitting the presence of three terminal flagellar segments, the bare basicosta represents such an important character which separates different tribes *Tabanini* and *Diachlorini,* that the generic status followed here should be tolerated.

The genus *Glaucops* Szil. includes only three species, viz. *G. hirsutus* (Villers) known from mountains of Central Europe; *G. fratellus* (Williston) from North America; and finally *G. chusanensis* (Ouchi) from China.

All the three above mentioned species are very rare and occur only locally, almost nothing is known about their biology and immature stages.

GLAUCOPS HIRSUTUS (VILLERS, 1789)

Fig. 135.

Tabanus hirsutus Villers, 1789, Car. Linn. Ent., 3: 561.
Tabanus haematopoides Jaennicke, 1866, Berl. ent. Z., 10: 77.

DIAGNOSIS. Small greyish species resembling somewhat a *Haematopota*-species but wings clear without any clouding. Eyes in female naked with three

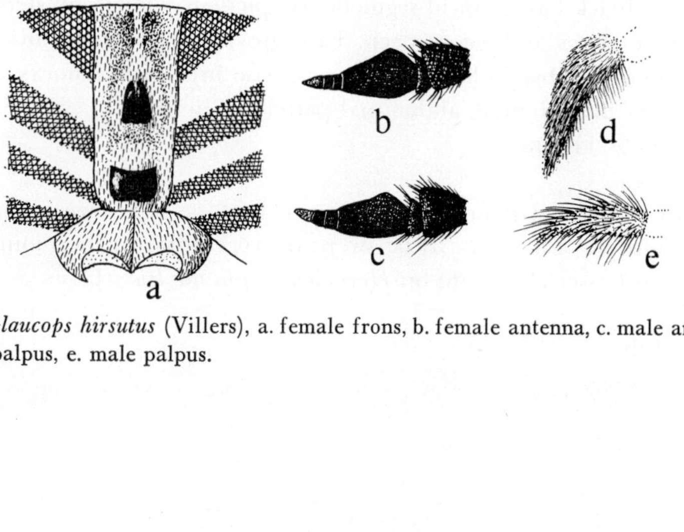

Fig. 135. *Glaucops hirsutus* (Villers), a. female frons, b. female antenna, c. male antenna, d. female palpus, e. male palpus.

bands. Frons in female with separated calli. Male with two eye-bands and sharply separated larger facets.

DESCRIPTION. ♀. *Head.* Eyes naked with three bands. Frons greyish dusted and short black haired, rather broader, index about 1: 3, nearly parallel-sided. Lower callus shining brown to black, nearly circular with straighter upper margin, narrowly separated from subcallus and more broadly from the eye-margins. Median callus blackish, slightly oval in shape, usually only indicated in the grey fundamental tomentum and broadly separated from the lower callus. Postocular margin on vertex with somewhat longer dark hairs. Subcallus greyish dusted, face and cheeks whitish-grey dusted and long whitish haired. Antennae dark brown to blackish, basal segments with short black hairs; segment 3 with blunt dorsal tooth on basal third. Terminal flagellar segment with hardly visibly indicated incision on the upper side as if two segments originally fused. Palpi brownish with short pale and black hairs, apical segment long and slender.

Thorax blackish-grey on mesonotum and scutellum, former with three light longitudinal stripes. Pleura lighter grey dusted and whitish haired. *Legs* blackish-brown, fore tibiae at base and posterior four tibiae on basal two-thirds yellowish-brown, tarsi black. *Wings* clear with dark brown veins, no appendix to vein R_4. Halteres dark brown.

Abdomen on dorsum shining black, the grey pattern consists of a row of median triangles, of a pair of sublateral spots and of pale posterior margins to each tergite. Tergites with black hairs which are more greyish along posterior margin. Venter paler, blackish-grey, with indefinite darker median stripe.

♂. Head large, eyes naked with two bands. Facets on the upper two-thirds larger and distinctly separated from the lower third with small facets. Vertex with a row of long black hairs; subcallus greyish dusted, on the upper half blackish. Antennae black, otherwise as in the ♀. Palpi light brown with long black hairs, apical segment conspicuously long and slender, more than three times as long as deep. Face greyish and densely black haired. Legs extensively blackish, only tibiae at base brownish. Thorax and abdomen longer black haired, abdominal pattern as in the ♀.

Length. 9—11 mm.

BIOLOGY. A typical mountainous species; nothing is known about the life history but the adults are to be swept on vegetation in the mountains, according to Keiser (1947: 46) on *Heracleum sphondylium* L.

DATES. July.

DISTRIBUTION. A rare species in mountains of Central Europe, recorded so far from the Alps (France, Switzerland, Austria) and from Krkonoše Mts. (Czechoslovakia, Poland).

TRIBE HAEMATOPOTINI

GENUS HEPTATOMA MEIGEN, 1803

Illig. Mag. Ins., 2: 266.

Hexatoma Meigen, 1820, Syst. Beschr., 2: 83.

TYPE SPECIES: *Tabanus pellucens* Fabricius, 1776.

DIAGNOSIS. Medium sized, 10—13.5 mm in length, species resembling somewhat a honey-bee. Eyes only very microscopically pubescent, especially in female, with four bands. Frons very broad, polished and densely clothed with adpressed hairs, ocellar tubercle absent. Antennae black, conspicuously long and slender, segment 3 more than twice as long as basal two segments together; followed by 3 distinct segments which together are as long as segment 3; antennae thus look like 6-segmented. Legs slender, posterior four tibiae whitish, hind tibiae without apical spurs. Wings clear, without any pattern, no appendix to vein R_4.

REMARKS. The genus *Heptatoma* Meig. is monotypic. The single known species *H. pellucens* (F.) which is known almost throughout the Palaearctic region including the extreme north. The East Asiatic population from the Altai Mts. was described by Olsufjev (1962) as a distinct subspecies *orientalis* Ols.

HEPTATOMA PELLUCENS (FABRICIUS, 1776)

Fig. 136; pl. 4: fig. d.

Tabanus pellucens Fabricius, 1776, Gen. Ins., p. 307.
Tabanus albipes Schrank, 1781, Enum. Ins. Austr., p. 480.
Heptatoma bimaculata Meigen, 1804, Klass., p. 156.

DIAGNOSIS. Blackish species, head, thorax and anterior two tergites densely golden-yellow to yellowish-brown haired. Antennae black, basal two segments light grey dusted, antennae more than twice as long as head is deep. Frons polished black to blackish-brown, densely clothed by adpressed yellowish hairs. Wings clear.

Description. ♀. *Head.* Eyes with hardly visible minute hairs, almost bare, and with 4 bands which are widened and upcurved laterally. Frons very broad, broader than high, polished black or very blackish-brown, only anterior corners greyish dusted, wholly clothed by long, yellowish adpressed hairs. Subcallus polished black with a few fine yellowish hairs. Face and cheeks whitish dusted and, especially below, long and densely yellowish-grey haired. Antennae black, basal two segments light grey dusted and with minute pale hairs, segment 3 rather dull black; segment 1 very slender, segment 2 of the same stoutness but only half as long as segment 1; segment 3 more than twice as long as basal two segments combined; three very distinct terminal flagellar segments which are as long as segment 3; the whole flagellum evenly cylindrical, not stouter at base, basal two segments distinctly narrower. Palpi black, dark grey dusted, above with longer adpressed yellowish hairs, at sides and below shorter black haired. Proboscis stout, blackish, twice as long as palpi.

Thorax black in ground colour, thinly greyish dusted, more densely on pleura. Whole of thorax densely and rather long golden-yellow to yellowish-brown haired, mesonotum with shorter hairs. *Legs* black but fore tibiae on basal third and posterior four tibiae except tip whitish with concolorous hairs. Posterior metatarsi brownish at base, coxae and femora more or less

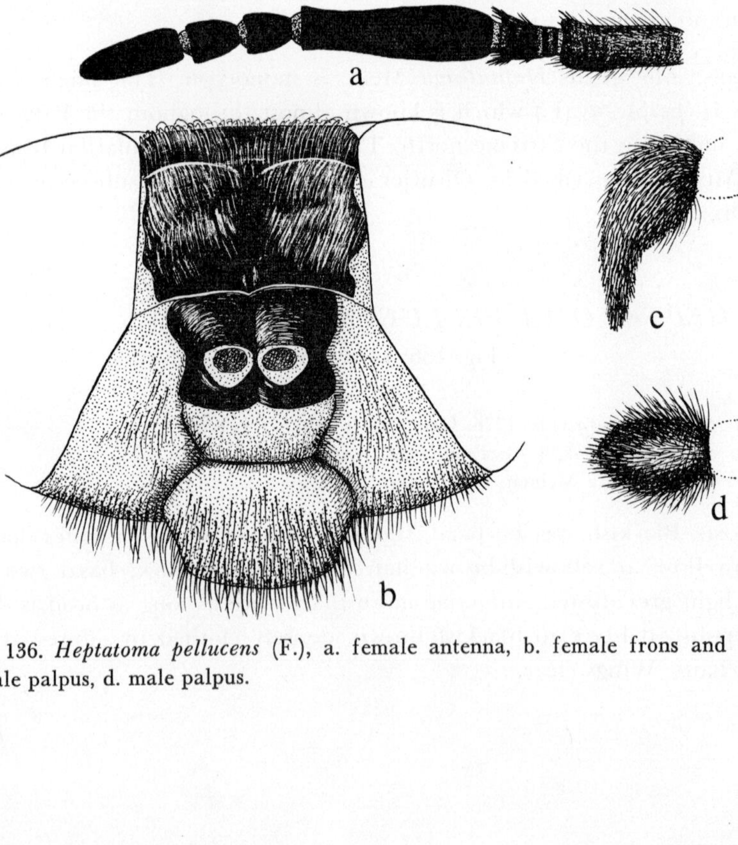

Fig. 136. *Heptatoma pellucens* (F.), a. female antenna, b. female frons and face, c. female palpus, d. male palpus.

greyish dusted and finely pale haired. *Wings* clear with brown veins, no appendix to vein R_4. Halteres dark brown, knob paler towards tip.

Abdomen black in ground colour, anterior two tergites greyish dusted, tergite 2 rather whitish-grey at sides, and densely golden-yellow to yellowish-brown haired. Tergites 3 to 5 subshining black with black hairs, apical two tergites yellowish-grey haired. Venter whitish-grey dusted and pale haired at sides, mesally with a broad black stripe with concolorous hairs.

♂. Eyes with short and very fine brownish hairs, facets on the upper two-thirds of eyes slightly enlarged and only indistinctly separated from the lower third with smaller facets. Subcallus polished black, cheeks broadly polished blackish-brown, finely pale haired, upper corner with only black hairs. Face greyish dusted on a small part and rather greyish-yellow haired. Antennae as in the ♀, but basal two segments with fine, long black hairs above. Palpi blackish, very short and stout, almost globular, mostly short black haired. Thorax, legs and wings as in the ♀, abdomen with the same coloration and pubescence, the hairs, however, longer; tergite 2 slightly translucent brown at sides.

Length. 10—13.5 mm.

Biology. The species inhabits various types of biotopes. It never occurs in large numbers. The flight period is very long, but the maximal occurrence is in June and July. The larva was described by Brauer (1883), Stammer (1924), Bischoff (1925) and Ježek (1971); the pupa by Brauer (1883) and Ježek (1971).

Dates. From May until the beginning of September.

Distribution. A widely distributed species in Europe, in Sweden up to 64° N. (Forsslund, 1956). Not yet recorded from the British Isles, Portugal and Spain. Eastwards it penetrates as far as to the Siberian Altai Mts. and Sajan Mts., from where the ssp. *orientalis* Ols. was described. According to Violovič (1968: 73) in the U.S.S.R. up to 66° N. (Turuchansk). Not yet recorded from Mongolia.

GENUS *HAEMATOPOTA* MEIGEN, 1803

Illig. Mag. Ins., 2: 267.

Chrysozona Meigen, 1800, Nouv. Classif., p. 23, 24 (suppressed by I. C. Z. N.).
Holcoceria Grünberg, 1906, Zool. Anz., 30: 357.
Parhaematopota Grünberg, 1906, Zool. Anz., 30: 360.
Austenia Surcouf, 1909, Bull. Mus. Hist. nat., Paris, 15: 454.
Potisa Surcouf, 1909, Bull. Mus. Hist. nat., Paris, 15: 454.

Sterrhocera Enderlein, 1922, Mitt. zool. Mus. Berl., 10: 350.
Tylopelma Enderlein, 1922, Mitt. zool. Mus. Berl., 10: 350.
Chrysopota Travassos S. Dias & Sousa Junior, 1958, Alguns novos dados, Mocambique, no. 89–92: 86.
Ricardomisa Travassos S. Dias, 1958, An. Inst. Med. trop. Lisboa, 15: 726.

TYPE SPECIES: *Tabanus pluvialis* Linné, 1761.

DIAGNOSIS. Generally smaller and slender, uniformly greyish species, from 7 to 13 mm in length. Eyes more or less haired, most densely in the male, with several undulating bands; upper area with large facets in male usually sharply separated from small facets. Frons almost square in shape, anterior frontal callus polished, narrow, occupying usually lower quarter of frons. Usually paired velvety black spots at sides and a smaller spot at middle. Neither ocellar tubercle nor ocelli present. Antennae usually longer than head (at least in female), segment 1 oval or slender and cylindrical, usually several times longer than broad, much shorter in male. Segment 2 very small; segment 3 long and slender, dorsal tooth not developed, three terminal flagellar segments. Wings brownish to greyish with whitish pattern of spots or rosettes, a long appendix to vein R_4. Abdomen blackish-grey with light grey pattern, usually with more or less developed paired sublateral spots on tergites.

REMARKS. The genus *Haematopota* Meig. is distributed mostly in the Ethiopian region, altogether 238 species with 6 described forms. Only 83 species and 5 forms are known from the Oriental region but many new species will surely be discovered (Philip and Stone, in litt.). Less than 60 species and about 10 forms are known so far from the Palaearctic region and only 5 species from the Nearctic region. The genus has not yet been found in the Neotropical region, Australia and New Zealand. The origin of two species is still uncertain.

About 380 species of *Haematopota* are thus known in the world fauna, of these only 20 have been found in Europe. On the basis of some recent studies by Lyneborg & Chvála (1970) the number of valid European species decreased since some of the species were known only from the original descriptions and a study of the type material enabled to synonymize them with well known common species. Moreover, most of the *Haematopota* species are very variable and some of the described taxa represent only varieties of well known and common species.

The adults inhabit various types of biotopes but they predominantly live along banks of rivers, lakes and ponds, on meadows and on foggy biotopes. The adults do not fly far from the places where the larvae live. Females attack man and both domestic and wild living animals. The swarming of some species, but especially of *H. pluvialis* (L.) in Europe, is well known. Some of the species are known as vectors of various diseases.

Several larvae and pupae are described in the older literature, but the descriptions are usually useless because of the very complicated synonymy and nomenclature in the genus, and also because of wrong identifications. The most useful descriptions of larvae and pupae of some of the European *Haematopota* species were published by Ježek (1971).

The Palaearctic *Haematopota* species are usually separated into two groups of species, viz., *italica*-group and *pluvialis*-group. This subdivision is used also in the following text.

Key to European species of *Haematopota*

Females

1 Antennal segment 1 long, cylindrical and rather slender, at least 4 times as long as deep, always entirely greyish dusted; when viewed from above about as long as frons is high *(italica*-group) 2

– Antennal segment 1 shorter, usually conical to oval, at most 3 times as long as deep, more or less polished, only seldom entirely dusted; distinctly shorter than frons is high when viewed from above *(pluvialis*-group) 8

2 (1) A velvety black spot on subcallus absent, clypeus without a pair of small black patches. Frons as broad as one-half the width of head. Antennal segment 1 densely haired, not constricted. Wings greyish, posterior margin broadly whitish. Smaller species, 7 mm in length .... *caenofrons* (Kröb.)

– A velvety black spot on subcallus present, clypeus with a pair of small black patches. Frons narrower, as broad as one-third of the width of head 3

3 (2) Greyish sublateral spots on tergites 2 to 6, sometimes a small spot also on tergite 1 4

– Greyish sublateral spots (Pl. 4, fig. e) at most on tergites 3 to 6, usually only on posterior two or three tergites, or absent 6

4 (3) Posterior wing-margin (Pl. 8, fig. a) broadly whitish. Antennal segment 1 (Fig. 137a) usually with several constrictions; segment 3 dark, very slender, distinctly narrower than segment 1. Frons (Fig. 137d) higher than broad .... *pallens* Loew

– No whitish border to posterior wing-margin, or if present, then antennal segment 3 extensively yellow and very broad. Antennal segment 1 with only a subapical constriction; segment 3 broader, at least as broad as segment 1 .. 5

5 (4) Antennal segment 3 (Fig. 138a) rather slender, about as broad as segment 1. Apical band on wing (Pl. 8, fig. b) very narrow and indistinct. Larger species, 11.5–13.5 mm in length .... *grandis* Meig.

– Antennal segment 3 (Fig. 142b) very broad, almost twice as broad as segment 1. Apical band on wing (Pl. 8, fig. o) very broad, occupying almost whole apex of wing. Smaller species, 7.5–8 mm in length .... *lambi* Vill.

6 (3) Antennal segment 1 (Fig. 139a) yellowish-brown, without a subapical constriction, or only a very small one. Mostly brownish species with conspicuously narrow frons (Fig. 139 c) .... *pandazisi* (Kröb.)

– Antennal segment 1 blackish-grey, with more or less distinct subapical constriction. Generally blackish-grey species with broader frons, which is at most only slightly higher than broad 7

7 (6) Frons (Fig. 140c) slightly higher than broad, paired velvety black spots large, circular. Antennae with segment 1 (Fig. 140a) about 4 times as long as deep, segment 3 more or less brownish at base .... *italica* Meig.

– Frons (Fig. 141a) very broad, distinctly broader than high; paired velvety black spots rather smaller, semicircular. Antennal segment 1 (Fig. 141b) very long and slender, about 5 times as long as deep, segment 3 entirely black .... *longeantennata* (Ols.)

8 (1) Antennal segment 1 entirely greyish dusted, at most very slightly subshining before tip 9

– Antennal segment 1 polished black, at least distinctly polished on apical quarter 12

9 (8) Frons (Fig. 146a) very broad, distinctly broader than high. Frontal callus narrow and distinctly separated at sides from eye-margins .... *turkestanica* (Kröb.)

– Frons narrow, distinctly higher than broad. Callus broader and touching eye-margins at least at anterior corners 10

10 (9) Clypeus unicolorous whitish-grey, without a pair of small black patches on upper third. Antennae (Fig. 147b) shortened and stout, segment 3 at least as broad as segment 1 .... *csikii* Szil.

– Clypeus with a pair of small black patches. Antennae longer, segment 1 at least 2.5 times as long as deep, segment 3 narrower than segment 1 11

11 (10) Antennal segment 1 (Fig. 143b) brownish, with more or less distinct subapical constriction. Femora yellowish-brown, sublateral grey spots on abdomen absent or indistinctly present on posterior tergites .... *gallica* Szil.

– Antennal segment 1 (Fig. 145b) blackish and not constricted. Femora blackish-grey, at most very indistinctly pinkish at middle. Abdomen with distinct grey sublateral spots on all tergites .... *latebricola* Aust.

12 (8) Antennal segment 1 greyish dusted at least on basal quarter above 13

– Antennal segment 1 entirely polished black. Frons always broad, broader than high; antennal segment 1 not constricted 18

13 (12) Frons broad, distinctly broader than high. Antennae entirely black, segment 3 broad 14

– Frons narrower, distinctly higher than broad, or at most square in shape. Antennae at least slightly brown on segment 3 at base, latter rather slender .. 15

14 (13) Antennal segment 1 (Fig. 148b) very short and stout, less than twice as long as deep, thinly greyish dusted on less than basal half. Femora more or less brownish at middle .... *pseudolusitanica* Szil.

– Antennal segment 1 (Fig. 149a) cylindrical, more than twice as long as deep, greyish dusted on more than basal half above. Femora blackish-grey .... *ocelligera* (Kröb.)

15 (13) Antennal segment 1 (Fig. 150a) of irregular shape, with a deep constriction before tip. Generally olive-grey dusted species. Wings brown to dark brown, femora blackish-grey .... *pluvialis* (L.)

– Antennal segment 1 evenly oval to cylindrical, at most with a slight constriction before tip. Generally blackish or light grey species 16

16 (15) Rather blackish species, scutellum with a large whitish-grey patch. Paired velvety black spots on frons conspicuously large, usually touching callus and eye-margins. Wings (Pl. 8, fig. i) dark brown. Antennal segment 1 (Fig. 151a) polished black at least on apical half .... *scutellata* (Ols., Mch. & Chv.)

– Generally light greyish species, scutellum without a pale patch, concolorous with mesonotum. Paired velvety black spots on frons smaller, separated from callus and eye-margins. Wings light grey, antennal segment 1 polished black only on apical quarter 17

17 (16) Antennal segment 1 (Fig. 152a) black, all femora blackish-grey. Abdomen with distinct but rather small grey sublateral spots on tergites 3 to 7, sometimes a small spot also on tergite 2 .... *subcylindrica* Pand.

– Antennal segment 1 (Fig. 153a) more or less brownish at base, femora extensively yellowish-brown. Abdomen with conspicuously large, whitish-grey sublateral spots on all tergites, rarely absent on tergite 1 ....
.... *bigoti* Gob. and *graeca* Szil.

18 (12) Antennae (Fig. 154a) entirely black. Wings (Pl. 8, fig. m) dark brown, posterior margin clouded. All femora blackish-grey, anterior two tergites without sublateral grey spots .... *crassicornis* Wahlbg.

– Antennal segment 3 reddish-brown on basal half. Wings light grey, broadly whitish on posterior margin. Posterior four femora more or less yellowish, sublateral greyish spots on all tergites including the first ... *pallidula* (Kröb.)

Males

Males of *H. csikii* Szil. (if known), *H. pseudolusitanica* Szil. and *H. ocelligera* (Kröb.) are not included, since we have not seen them. Males of *H. caenofrons* (Kröb.), *H. gallica* Szil., *H. latebricola* Aust., *H. graeca* Szil., *H. pallidula* (Kröb.) and *H. longeantennata* (Ols.) are still unknown.

1 Antennal segment 1 entirely greyish dusted, long oval, about twice as long as deep or longer 2

– Antennal segment 1 polished black at least on apical third 4

2 (1) Generally smaller species, 7.5–8 mm in length. Antennal segment 1 dark brown in ground colour, segment 3 conspicuously broad .... *lambi* Vill.

– Generally larger species, usually about 10 mm in length. Antennal segment 3 slender 3

3 (2) Antennal segment 1 (Fig. 139b) brown in ground colour, long oval but stout, at most twice as long as deep .... *pandazisi* (Kröb.)

– Antennal segment 1 (Fig. 138b) black in ground colour, oblong oval, more than twice as long as deep .... *grandis* Meig.

4 (1) Subcallus with a small, narrow velvety black spot at middle, which is broadly separated from eye-margins 5

– Subcallus with a large velvety black spot, touching or almost touching eye-margins 6

5 (4) Antennal segment 1 short oval, about 1.5 times as long as deep. Femora brownish .... *turkestanica* (Kröb.)

– Antennal segment 1 (Fig. 137b) long oval, about twice as long as deep. Femora blackish-grey .... *pallens* Loew

6 (4) Antennal segment 1 elongated, oblong oval, more than twice as long as deep 7

– Antennal segment 1 shorter, more egg-shaped, at most twice as long as deep 8

7 (6) Antennal segment 1 (Fig. 140b) mostly polished black, densely whitish-grey dusted on basal third above. Wings brownish-grey .... *italica* Meig.

– Antennal segment 1 (Fig. 152b) densely whitish-grey dusted above on more than basal half. Wings light grey .... *subcylindrica* Pand.

8 (6) Antennae (Fig. 154b) entirely black including segment 3, segment 1 entirely polished without greyish dust. Wings darker brown .... *crassicornis* Wahlbg.

- Antennae at least slightly brownish on segment 3 at base, segment 1 whitish-grey dusted at least at base 9

9 (8) Scutellum with a distinct whitish-grey patch at middle. Cheeks subshining black on upper margin. Wings dark brown .... *scutellata* (Ols., Mch. & Chv.)

– Scutellum without a greyish patch, concolorous with mesonotum. Cheeks black spotted, not black 10

10 (9) Femora blackish-grey. Wings darker brown, grey sublateral spots on tergites rather indistinct .... *pluvialis* (L.)

– Femora extensively yellowish-brown. Wings light grey, sublateral spots on tergites conspicuously large and whitish-grey .... *bigoti* Gob.

ITALICA-GROUP

HAEMATOPOTA CAENOFRONS (KRÖBER, 1922)

Chrysozona caenofrons Kröber, 1922, Arch. Naturgesch., Abt. A, 88 (8): 141.

Diagnosis. Small species of the *italica*-group with antennal segment 1 long, without any constriction. Subcallus without velvety black spot, clypeus without the usual paired blackish patches. Frons very broad. Wings whitish with brown pattern, first basal cell and posterior wing-margin whitish.

We have not seen this species, the type of which should be in Kröber's Collection, and therefore we present only a translation of the original description:

♀. *Head.* Frons more than one-half of the width of head, somewhat narrower above, dark ashy-grey, mesally with a whitish-grey line directed downwards. Apically this line is knob-like widened on the place where the velvety spot usually is present. Both lateral velvety spots very small, placed on a whitish-grey square. A narrow, slightly polished black transverse band on the border to the face. A velvety black spot between antennae absent. Face entirely whitish-grey with some indistinct dark spots. Clypeus without spots, and with long whitish pubescence as on frons, but also with scattered black hairs. Apical segment of palpi slender, whitish-yellow, only whitish haired. Occiput grey, short yellowish pubescent. Antennae blackish-brown, segment 1 long cylindrical (1 cm!), at least 4 times as long as broad. Segment 2 very short. Both (Binde = misprint) wholly short yellowish haired. Segment 3 missing.

Thorax blackish-brown with three whitish longitudinal stripes. Lateral stripes and pleura light grey. Black parts chocolate-brown dusted. Pubescence fine and whitish. Squamae brownish. Halteres whitish, base of knob brown. *Abdomen* whitish-grey. Sublateral spots deep brown bordered to tergite 3 inclusively. Posterior margins pale, whitish pubescent. Venter light ashy-grey, whitish haired. *Legs* with coxae and femora blackish-brown, grey due to dusting, fore tibiae pale on basal third, other tibiae with two pale rings. Tarsi black, metatarsi of mid and hind tarsi yellowish. *Wings* milk-white with coarse brown pattern which is denser towards anterior margin. First basal cell and whole of posterior margin almost without pattern. Appendix very long, reaching as far as to discal cell.

Length. 7 mm. Wing length 7 mm, wing breadth 2.7 mm.

♂. Unknown.

DATES. Unknown.

DISTRIBUTION. Only a little known species described by Kröber from the Caucasus (Kasiko). Olsufjev (1937: 339) did not see this species.

HAEMATOPOTA PALLENS LOEW, 1870

Fig. 137; pl. 8: fig. a.

Haematopota pallens Loew, 1870, Schrift. Ges. Freund. Nat. Moscou, p. 54
id., 1871, Beschr. Europ. Dipt., 2: 61.
Chrysozona caucasica Kröber, 1922, Arch. Naturgesch., Abt. A, 88 (8): 142.
Haematopota Araxis Szilády, 1923, Biologica hung., 1 (1): 33.

DIAGNOSIS. Antennae with segment 1 long and entirely greyish dusted, usually with several constrictions; segment 3 long and very slender. Wings light grey with a broad whitish border along posterior margin. Frons broader than high, abdomen with large greyish sublateral spots on all tergites except the first. Male with antennal segment 1 rather shorter and stout, mostly polished black, subcallus with only a small and narrow velvety black spot.

DESCRIPTION. ♀. *Head.* Frons very light grey, broad, slightly broader than high, parallel-sided or slightly narrower above. Paired velvety black spots rather larger, semicircular, distinctly separated from callus and eye-margins. Median spot small, blackish-brown. Callus polished black, occupying about lower quarter of frons and touching the eye-margins at anterior corner. Subcallus with a large velvety black oval spot. Face whitish with concolorous hairs, cheeks finely blackish spotted above. Antennae black but segment 3 slightly brownish at base; segment 1 long and slender, about 4 times as long as deep, greyish dusted, distinctly constricted before tip and usually with several less distinct constrictions or somewhat stouter at middle; segment 3 long and very slender, much more slender than segment 1. Palpi whitish-yellow with whitish hairs.

Thorax brownish-grey on mesonotum, side margins and three narrow longitudinal stripes light grey. Scutellum dark, paler at tip. Pleura whitish-grey dusted and whitish haired. *Legs* light grey on coxae and femora, posterior four coxae and femora on basal two-thirds sometimes translucent brownish. Fore tibiae whitish-yellow on basal third, apical part and fore tarsi black. Posterior tibiae pale yellowish with three dark rings, the basal one the narrowest. Tarsi dark except metatarsi. *Wings* light grey with whitish pattern, apical band double and posterior margin broadly whitish. Halteres brownish with pale knob.

Abdomen blackish-brown with distinct whitish-grey pattern which consists of a median stripe, narrow posterior borders and very large sublateral oval spots on tergites 2–7; the spots are often confluent with the broadly whitish-grey sides and posterior margins. Venter very light grey dusted, pale haired, often with a broad, indefinite darker median stripe.

♂. Eyes long and densely whitish haired, facets on the upper three-quarters very large and sharply separated from small facets. Subcallus with only a small and narrow velvety black spot situated on the median line, broadly separated from the eye-margins. Cheeks more distinctly blackish

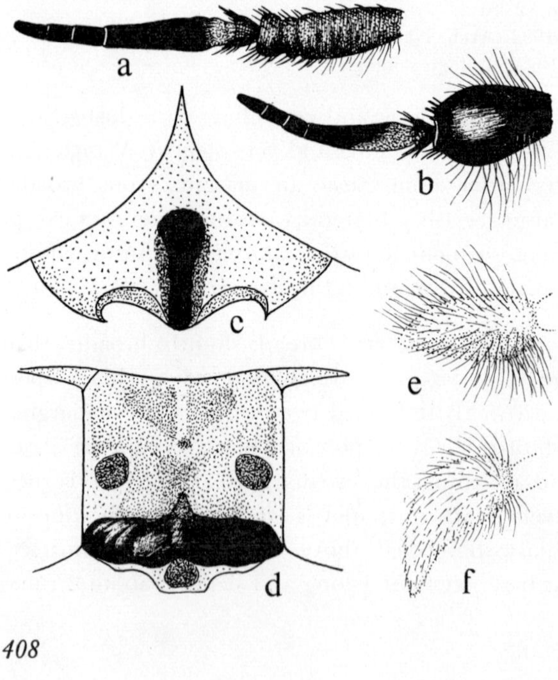

Fig. 137. *Haematopota pallens* Lw., a. female antenna, b. male antenna, c. male subcallus, d. female frons, e. male palpus, f. female palpus.

spotted and black haired. Antennal segment 1 rather stout, broadest on apical third, about twice as long as deep, mostly polished black, densely whitish-grey dusted on basal third to half above and on the inner side. Legs with long whitish hairs on femora beneath, hind tibiae anterodorsally and ventrally densely long black haired. Abdomen yellowish-brown on tergite 2 at sides and usually slightly brownish also on tergite 3, greyish pattern as in the ♀ but less distinct. Venter darker grey and conspicuously long whitish haired, apical two sternites with black hairs.

Length. 7.5–12 mm, averaging usually from 9 to 10 mm.

Biology. According to Shevtshenko (1961) often occurring near salt lakes and along small rivers in mountains. Females attack horned cattle, horses, donkeys, camels, but less often man.

Dates. From June until September.

Distribution. A common species in Central Asia, eastwards to the Tian-Šan Mts. and north of the Caspian Sea. It is recorded from Transcaucasia, Iraq and Iran, west to the northern coast of the Black Sea. In Europe it is known from Ukraine, especially in the south, and from the Caucasus and Crimea.

HAEMATOPOTA GRANDIS MEIGEN, 1820

Fig. 138; pl. 8: fig. b.

Haematopota grandis Meigen, 1820, Syst. Beschr., 2: 79.
Haematopota fraseri Austen, 1925, Bull. ent. Res., 16: 9.

Diagnosis. One of the larger species of the genus in Europe. Antennal segment 1 more or less brownish, very long and with rather a distinct subapical constriction; segment 3 about as deep as segment 1. Abdomen with large grey sublateral spots usually on all tergites including the first. Frons slightly higher than broad. Male with antennal segment 1 very long oval, black and wholly densely greyish dusted, tergites 2 and 3 largely brown at sides.

Description. ♀. *Head.* Frons light grey to somewhat yellowish-grey, slightly higher than broad and slightly converging above. Paired velvety spots small, kidney-shaped or narrow; median spot small and oval. Callus polished black, rather deep, more than one-quarter as high as frons is high in middle, touching the eye-margins. Face whitish with concolorous hairs. Antennae more or less brown, segment 1 sometimes black only at tip beyond the constriction, or entirely blackish-grey and translucent brown on the inner side at base only; segment 3 brownish on basal third, otherwise black. Segment 1 very long and rather stout, about 4.5 times longer than deep, with rather distinct subapical constriction, black haired above and thinly greyish dusted throughout; segment 3 about as deep as segment 1. Palpi greyish to light brownish, rather pale, clothed with pale and black hairs.

Thorax dark greyish-brown on mesonotum, light grey longitudinal stripes very distinct, narrow. Pleura and coxae very light grey dusted and whitish haired. *Legs:* Femora pinkish-grey dusted except for dark tips, longer whitish haired beneath. Fore tibiae at least on basal half yellowish, apically and whole of fore tarsi black. Posterior tibiae and metatarsi yellowish, tibiae with three indefinite dark rings, tarsi blackish. *Wings* brownish with whitish pattern, rosettes rather minute, apical streak narrow, posterior margin clouded. Halteres whitish-yellow, knob darkened at base.

Abdomen with a distinct light grey pattern which consists of a row of high median triangles (the one on tergite 2 distinctly longer and broader), of narrow posterior margins, and of large circular to oval sublateral spots on all tergites; the spots on tergite 1 usually smaller or absent. Venter light grey dusted and pale haired. Anterior two tergites and sternites often translucent yellowish on extreme lateral margins.

♂. Eyes rather long and very densely whitish to very light brown haired, upper facets distinctly enlarged and sharply separated from lower quarter with small facets. Subcallus with a large velvety black spot. Antennae often

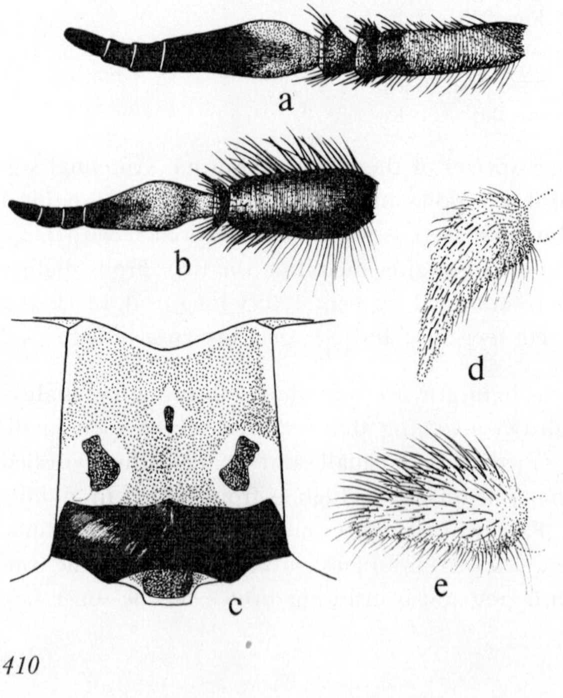

Fig. 138. *Haematopota grandis* Meig., a. female antenna, b. male antenna, c. female frons, d. female palpus, e. male palpus.

extensively light brown on segment 3. Segment 1 enlarged, oblong oval, more than twice as long as deep, black in ground colour and entirely and rather densely greyish dusted. Palpi yellowish, conical, clothed with fine whitish hairs, often with some additional small dark hairs. Cheeks black spotted and mostly black haired. Mesonotum and scutellum long whitish haired, legs extensively yellowish and long, predominantly whitish haired. Tergite 1 except extreme yellow sides deep blackish-brown, tergite 2 with a large whitish median triangle, otherwise a greyish abdominal pattern less distinct. Tergites 2 and 3 broadly yellowish-brown at sides, leaving on tergite 3 only a dark median patch anteriorly. Dorsum rather long and densely blackish haired, venter densely whitish haired, light grey dusted, anterior three sternites yellowish haired at sides.

Length. 11.5—13.5 mm.

Variability. Rather a variable species in the yellow-brown coloration of first antennal segment. Abbassian-Lintzen (1960) described a ssp. *iranica* which should differ from the nominate form in the wing pattern, posterior margin being narrowly whitish. We have not seen material of this Iranian subspecies.

Biology. The adults inhabit foggy biotopes on shores of lakes and rivers. The immature stages are not yet described.

Dates. From June until October, but mainly occurring in September.

Distribution. A South European species which penetrates northwards along the large rivers to Ukraine and to southern parts of Central Europe: Hungary, Czechoslovakia (Moravia), Austria and Switzerland. In South Europe it is known from Bulgaria, Rumania, Jugoslavia, Albania, Greece, Italy, France and Spain, from where it penetrates along the Atlantic coast to England and Denmark (Lyneborg & Chvála 1970). Also in Sweden it seems to occur, as a female labelled »Småland« is present in the »Diptera Scandinavia« collection of Zetterstedt in Lund. The species has not yet been recorded from the Asiatic part of the U.S.S.R., but it is known from the Asiatic part of Turkey and as ssp. *iranica* Abb.-Lintz. also from Iran.

HAEMATOPOTA PANDAZISI (KRÖBER, 1936)

Fig. 139; pl. 8: fig. c.

Haematopota variegata auct. nec Fabricius, 1805 (= *Silvius*).
Chrysozona pandazisi Kröber, 1936, Acta Inst. Mus. zool. Univ. athen., 1: 43.

Haematopota romanica Dinulescu, 1953, Bul. St. Sect. St. Biol., Agron., Geol., Geogr., 5: 556 (nomen nudum).

DIAGNOSIS. Rather a smaller, generally more brownish coloured species of the *italica*-group. Antennal segment 1 long and slender, not constricted before apex, entirely yellowish-brown. Frons conspicuously narrow, distinctly higher than broad, abdomen with sublateral greyish spots usually on posterior three tergites, exceptionally also up to tergite 3, but here always rather indistinct. Male with antennal segment 1 long oval, at most twice as long as deep, brown in ground colour and entirely thinly greyish dusted.

DESCRIPTION. ♀. *Head.* Frons yellowish-grey dusted, very narrow, distinctly higher than broad. Paired velvety black spots rather large, almost circular, only indistinctly separated from callus and eye-margins. Median spot small, circular, velvety black. Callus rather narrow, polished black, touching the eye-margins at sides at least on anterior half. Subcallus with a large velvety black spot. Face whitish-grey dusted and whitish haired, cheeks finely black spotted, with sparse whitish hairs. Antennae very long and slender, yellowish-brown, segment 3 darkened towards tip, terminal flagellar segments black; segment 1 more than 4 times as long as deep, at most with a slight and hardly visible subapical constriction, short black haired and with some fine whitish hairs on basal half beneath; segment 3 about as deep as segment 1. Palpi rather slender, whitish-grey to yellowish-white, clothed with short black and pale hairs.

Thorax rather blackish-brown on mesonotum, with distinct light grey longitudinal stripes, humeri and notopleural lobes yellowish; scutellum thinly greyish dusted. Pleura rather brown in ground colour, greyish dusted and whitish haired. *Legs* including coxae yellowish coloured and thinly greyish dusted, fore tibiae on apical two-thirds and posterior tarsi extensively darkened, fore tarsi black. Posterior tibiae with three more or less distinct darker rings. *Wings* brownish-grey clouded with whitish pattern, apical band narrow, posterior margin clouded. Halteres whitish, base of knob brownish.

Abdomen blackish-brown in ground colour, sternites with high, distinct light grey median triangles which are often confluent on median line. Posterior margins and sides of tergites greyish-yellow to yellowish-brown, anterior three tergites often lighter brown at sides. Indistinct greyish sublateral spots on posterior three tergites, exceptionally also on tergites 4 and 3; pubescence concolorous. Venter light grey dusted and paler haired, apical two sternites with black hairs; ground colour usually somewhat yellowish, a broad indistinct median stripe often darker brown.

♂. Eyes densely long whitish haired. Facets on the upper three-quarters very enlarged and sharply separated from small facets. Face densely whitish haired, cheeks distinctly blackish spotted and mostly black haired. Subcallus largely velvety blackish-brown. Antennal segment 1 brown in ground colour, long oval but rather stout, at most twice as long as deep, above with black hairs, and mostly whitish haired beneath; entirely thinly greyish dusted. Segment 3 more evenly brown including on terminal flagellar segments. Palpi whitish-yellow, conical and pointed, predominantly long whitish haired. Thorax and abdomen rather brown in ground colour, mesonotum with fine, long whitish hairs. Legs and wings as in the ♀, but legs predominantly long whitish haired. Abdomen yellowish-brown on anterior three tergites at sides, median triangles on tergites 2 to 4 distinctly light grey, very broad and rather low, occupying at most posterior half of tergites. Venter yellowish-brown coloured and very densely and long whitish haired, last sternite with black hairs.

Length. 8–11 mm, usually about 10 mm.

SYNONYMY. The species has been for a long time known under the name of *H. variegata* Fabr. The synonymy was fully discussed by Chvála & Lyneborg (1970: 554) in a revision of the Fabrician types of Tabanidae, and in a revision of North European *Haematopota* (Lyneborg & Chvála, 1970: 34). *H. variegata* var. *rotundata* described by Szilády in 1923 from Algeria is very probably a distinct species allied to *H. pallens* Loew.

DATES. From June until September.

DISTRIBUTION. A South European species recorded also from North Africa

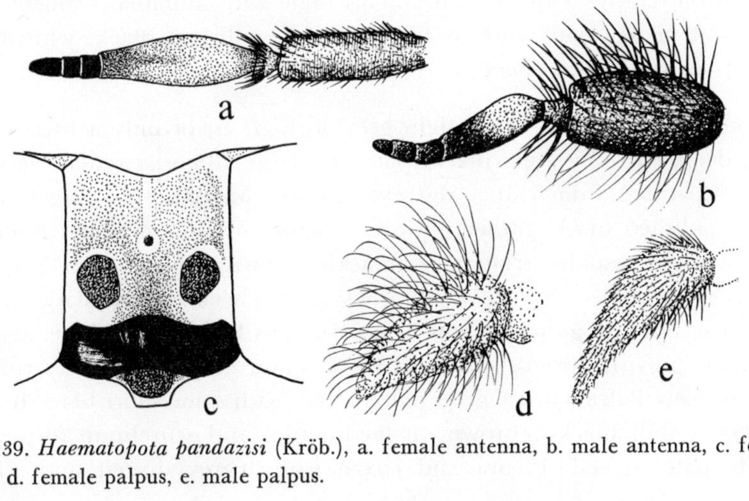

Fig. 139. *Haematopota pandazisi* (Kröb.), a. female antenna, b. male antenna, c. female frons, d. female palpus, e. male palpus.

(Morocco, Tunisia) and Asia Minor, eastwards it penetrates to Transcaucasia (Olsufjev, 1937: 336). In Europe it is known from Rumania, Bulgaria, Jugoslavia, Albania, Italy including Sicily, France and Spain, but not yet recorded from the European part of the U.S.S.R. The species is very common on the Black Sea coast in Bulgaria. The northern border in Europe lies south of the Alps. The record from Austria was a mistake, all the material determined as *H. variegata* belonged to the closely allied species *H. grandis* Meig., and the recorded occurrence in Poland should also be a mistake.

HAEMATOPOTA ITALICA MEIGEN, 1804

Fig. 140; pl. 4: fig. e; pl. 8: fig. d.

Haematopota italica Meigen, 1804, Klass., p. 163.
Haematopota elongata LePeletier & Serville, 1827, Enc. Méth., 10: 543.
Haematopota gymnonota Brullé, 1832, Exp. Sci. Morée, 3: 306.
Haematopota longicornis Macquart, 1834, Hist. Nat. Dipt., 1: 211.
Haematopota tenuicornis Macquart, 1834, Hist. Nat. Dipt., 1: 210.
? *Haematopota lusitanica* Guérin, 1835, Icon. Règne Anim., 7: 452.
? *Haematopota nigricornis* Gobert, 1881, Mém. Soc. linn. N. Fr., 1881: 38.
? *Chrysozona italica* var. *argyrophora* Kröber, 1922, Arch. Naturgesch., Abt. A, 88 (8): 148.

Diagnosis. Large blackish-grey species with frons as high as broad or slightly narrower, paired velvety black spots very large, circular. Antennae blackish-grey, segment 3 brownish at base, segment 1 constricted before tip, 4 times as long as deep and entirely greyish dusted. Abdomen with sublateral spots at most on tergites 4 to 7, often absent. Male with antennal segment 1 oblong oval, more than twice as long as deep, polished black, whitish-grey dusted on basal third above.

Description. ♀. *Head.* Frons light grey, as high as, or only a little higher than, deep. Paired velvety black spots very large, almost circular, very narrowly separated from callus and eye-margins. Median spot larger, black. Callus polished black, rather narrow, touching the eye-margins. Subcallus with a large, usually triangular, blackish-brown velvety spot. Face and cheeks whitish dusted with concolorous hairs, cheeks finely black spotted. Antennae blackish-grey, segment 3 more or less brownish at base; segment 1 densely greyish dusted, subapical constriction distinct, about 4 times as long as deep. Palpi whitish-grey, pale haired, with some short black hairs.

Thorax dull blackish-brown on mesonotum and scutellum, former distinctly pale striped. Pleura and coxae whitish-grey dusted and whitish haired. *Legs:* Femora light grey, usually broadly brownish mesally on posterior two pairs. Tibiae yellowish-brown, posterior tibiae with three dark rings, fore tibiae black on apical half or with two blackish rings at middle and at tip; fore tarsi black, posterior four tarsi extensively darkened except for base. *Wings* brownish-grey with whitish pattern, apical band very narrow, posterior margin dark. Halteres whitish with darkened knob at base.

Abdomen blackish in ground colour, light grey pattern consisting of narrow posterior borders and high but narrow median triangles, forming often a narrow pale median stripe. Grey sublateral spots either absent or indistinct on posterior two to four tergites (only very exceptionally reaching tergite 4). Sides of tergites only narrowly greyish. Venter unicolorous light grey dusted and pale haired, posterior two sternites with black hairs, sometimes sternites slightly darkened at middle.

♂. Eyes densely whitish haired, facets on more than upper three-quarters enlarged and sharply separated from small facets below. Subcallus with a large, velvety black oval spot, cheeks with some darker hairs. Antennae black, segment 3 often indistinctly brownish at base; segment 1 oblong oval, more than twice as long as deep, mostly polished black but densely whitish-grey dusted on basal third above, clothed with long black hairs above, mostly whitish haired below. Palpi whitish-yellow, very long and densely whitish haired. Mesonotum and femora with long whitish hairs, femora less brown mesally than in the ♀. Abdomen very narrowly brownish on tergite

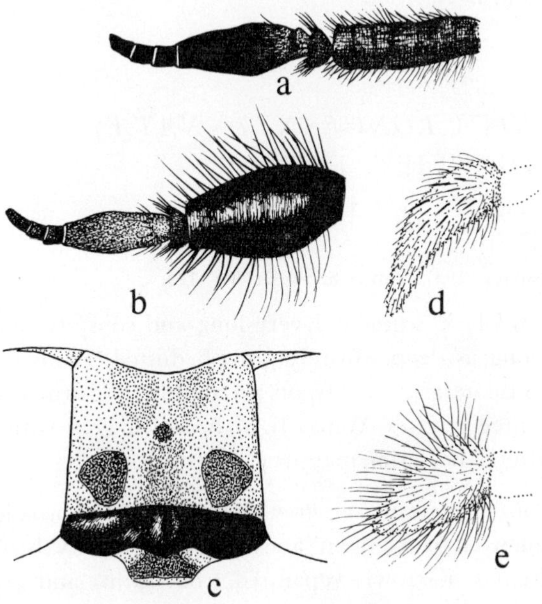

Fig. 140. *Haematopota italica* Meig., a. female antenna, b. male antenna, c. female frons, d. female palpus, e. male palpus.

2 at sides, otherwise as in the ♀; the pubescence very long, venter with only whitish hairs.

Length. 9—12.5 mm.

VARIABILITY. Rather a variable species in the abdominal pattern, tergites usually without any sublateral greyish spots but sometimes indefinite spots are present on apical two or three tergites. The systematical position of so-called »subspecies« *lusitanica* Guérin, *nigricornis* Gob. and *argyrophora* Kröb. is still unclear and we have not seen the type material of them. *Haematopota gallica* Séguy, often recorded by subsequent authors as a subspecies of *H. italica* Meig., represents a distinct species of the *pluvialis*-group.

BIOLOGY. The species occurs on the same biotopes together with *H. pluvialis* (L.), but is never a common species. The larva and pupa were described by Folco (1934).

DATES. From June until August.

DISTRIBUTION. A European species distributed eastwards to the Sverdlovsk region in the U.S.S.R., it has not been found in the eastern parts of Siberia and in Kazakhstan. In North Europe it is known from Denmark, and in Sweden and the European part of the U.S.S.R. up to 60° N; not yet known from Norway and Finland. Most of the records from England refer to *H. grandis* Meig. *H. italica* Meig. is known from almost all countries of Central and South Europe including the Mediterranean islands but the occurrence in North Africa needs to be verified.

HAEMATOPOTA LONGEANTENNATA (OLSUFJEV, 1937)

Fig. 141; pl. 8: fig. n.

Chrysozona longeantennata Olsufjev, 1937, Fauna SSSR, 7: 338, 426.

DIAGNOSIS. Antennae entirely black, segment 1 very long and conspicuously slender, about 5 times as long as deep, entirely greyish dusted. Frons distinctly broader than high. Sublateral greyish spots on abdmen indistinct, at most present on posterior three tergites. Wings light brownish-grey with a little developed whitish pattern, posterior margin clouded.

DESCRIPTION. ♀. *Head.* Frons rather darker grey dusted, slightly broader than high and usually somewhat convergent above. Paired velvety black spots rather larger, semicircular, narrowly separated from callus and eye-margins. Median spot black, circular, very small. Callus polished black, narrow, touching the eye-margins at anterior corner. Subcallus with a large, circular velvety black spot. Face whitish-grey dusted and long whitish haired, cheeks distinctly black spotted, with short whitish hairs. Antennae entirely black including the base of segment 3; segment 1 very long and slender, about 5 times as long as deep, entirely greyish dusted and short black haired; segment 3 almost as deep as segment 1. Palpi yellowish-grey, covered with whitish and some black hairs.

Thorax rather blackish on mesonotum, usually with three indistinct and very narrow longitudinal stripes; scutellum concolorous. Pleura and coxae light grey dusted and rather long whitish haired. *Legs:* Femora grey coloured, with whitish hairs beneath; fore tibiae yellowish on basal third to fourth, rest of tibiae and fore tarsi deep black. Posterior tibiae yellowish with three dark rings, tarsi almost blackish, brownish at base. *Wings* very light brown-grey, whitish spots minute; apical band very narrow, not reaching posterior margin; latter entirely clouded, without pale spots in apices of posterior cells. Halteres whitish, knobs brownish at base.

Abdomen subshining black, greyish median stripe rather indistinct, forming a high, paler median triangle on tergite 2. Posterior margins narrowly pale; indistinct sublateral spots on posterior two or three tergites, sometimes a trace of an oval spot also on tergite 4. Venter unicolorous grey dusted and short whitish haired, apical two sternites with black hairs.

♂. Unknown.

Length. 9—11 mm.

Dates. May.

Distribution. Described by Olsufjev (1937) on the basis of a single female specimen from Kutaisi in Georgia. Olsufjev (1969a) did not record it from the European part of the U.S.S.R., but we have seen females from Albania (Mali Dajti, 28.V.1959, leg. J. Moucha, examined by N. G. Olsufjev) and Greece (Stehni-Euböa, 4.—11.V.1956, leg. Fr. Borchman).

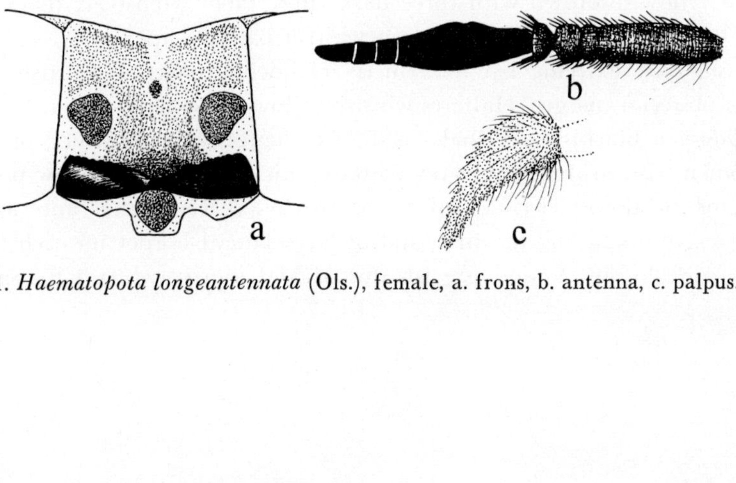

Fig. 141. *Haematopota longeantennata* (Ols.), female, a. frons, b. antenna, c. palpus.

HAEMATOPOTA LAMBI VILLENEUVE, 1921

Fig. 142; pl. 8: fig. o.

Haematopota lambi Villeneuve, 1921, Annls Soc. ent. Belg., 61: 157.
Chrysozona planicornis Kröber, 1922, Arch. Naturgesch., Abt. A, 88 (8): 144.

DIAGNOSIS. Small species about 8 mm in length with yellowish antennae, segment 1 very long and slender, segment 3 laterally flattened, much broader than segment 1. Frons slightly higher than broad, apex of wing almost whitish. Abdomen with greyish sublateral spots on all tergites. Male with antennal segment 1 blackish-brown coloured and entirely whitish-grey dusted, long oval, more than twice as long as deep.

DESCRIPTION. ♀. *Head.* Frons light grey, slightly higher than broad. Paired velvety black spots not very large, almost circular, separated from callus and eye-margins. Median spot very small, in the shape of a small black point. Callus polished black, rather narrow, touching the eye-margins at anterior corner. Subcallus with a large velvety black spot. Face whitish-grey dusted with sparse whitish hairs, cheeks distinctly black spotted. Antennae extensively yellowish-brown, leaving only tip blackish, or somewhat darkened apically on segment 1 and on whole of terminal flagellar segments. Segment 1 very long and slender, more than 4 times as long as deep, thinly silvery-grey dusted, at most with a slight constriction before tip; segment 3 distinctly laterally compressed, very broad when viewed from the side, about twice as broad as segment 1 on basal half. Palpi very light greyish-yellow, clothed with pale hairs, and with several short black hairs towards tip.

Thorax brownish-grey on mesonotum except for on anterior part and on lateral margins, scutellum apically greyish; light longitudinal stripes on mesonotum distinct. Pleura whitish-grey dusted and densely whitish haired. *Legs:* Coxae and femora light grey, posterior femora usually translucent yellowish-brown except tip. Fore tibiae very spindle-shaped dilated, pale yellowish on basal third, rest of tibiae including fore tarsus black. Posterior tibiae yellowish-brown with three dark rings, tarsi extensively blackish except for base. *Wings* pale grey with whitish pattern, apex of wing broadly whitish, only extreme tip indistinctly clouded; a narrow whitish border along posterior margin. Halteres whitish-yellow, knob darkened at base.

Abdomen blackish-grey, pale median triangles very indistinct, otherwise abdomen with distinct light grey pattern which consists of narrow posterior margins, of almost circular sublateral patches placed rather anteriorly on each tergite including the first, and of large lateral border on each tergite; hairs concolorous. Venter greyish dusted and mostly whitish haired with more or less distinct, very broad, darker brown and rather subshining median stripe.

♂. Described recently by Salom (1967). We have not seen the male sex but according to Salom (l.c.: 17) antennal segment 1 is more than twice as long as deep, dark brown or almost black coloured and entirely whitish-grey dusted, slightly shining only on the outer side at base, and black haired. Segment 3 yellowish-brown, darkened apically, terminal flagellar segments black; only slightly more slender than segment 1. Facets on the upper three-quarters sharply separated from small facets. Femora reddish-yellow coloured, greyish dusted and whitish haired. Abdomen with grey sublateral spots on tergites 2 to 7, anterior tergites distinctly yellowish coloured at sides, not reddish. Salom unfortunately did not mention the wing pattern.

Length. 7.5–8 mm.

Dates. July and August. Salom (1961: 85) recorded 1 ♀ from April.

Distribution. A West Mediterranean species known so far only from France and Spain.

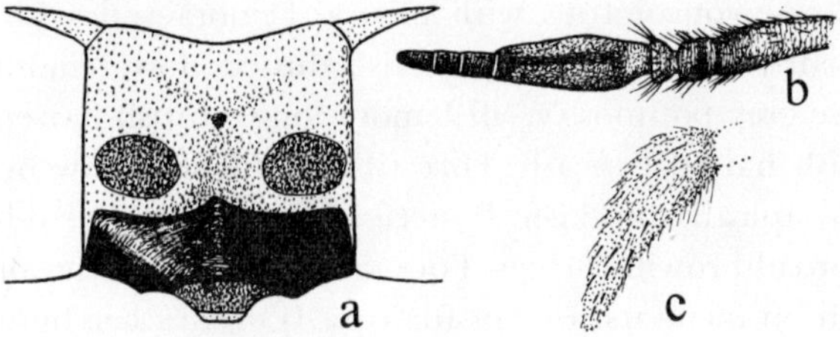

Fig. 142. *Haematopota lambi* Vill., female, a. frons, b. antenna, c. palpus.

PLUVIALIS-GROUP

HAEMATOPOTA GALLICA SZILÁDY, 1923

Fig. 143.

Haematopota gallica Szilády, 1923, Biologica hung., 1 (1): 37.

Diagnosis. Larger species of the *pluvialis*-group closely resembling *H. italica* Meig. in having rather narrow frons with large, circular velvety black spots and abdomen without greyish sublateral spots on tergites, but antennal segment 1 is distinctly shorter and extensively brownish, and all femora brown to yellowish-brown in ground colour.

Description. ♀. *Head.* Frons greyish dusted, rather dark grey above and on a broad median stripe below, more whitish along eye-margins and around the large, circular, velvety black spots at sides. Whole of frons covered with dense and rather long greyish hairs. Median velvety black spot small, slightly oval. Frons narrow, higher than broad. Callus polished dark brown, quite straight on the upper margin, touching the eye-margins. Subcallus with a large velvety black spot. Face and cheeks whitish dusted and clothed with long concolorous hairs, cheeks distinctly black spotted. Antennal segment 1 brown, darker towards tip, rather yellow-brown at base and on inner side on the whole length, segment 2 blackish, segment 3 dark brown, paler at base, terminal flagellar segments black. Segment 1 rather long and cylindrical, less than 3 times as long as deep, with a rather distinct but not very deep constriction before tip; covered with short black hairs above, and with longer whitish hairs beneath except for tip; segment 3 almost as broad as segment 1. Palpi yellowish and thinly greyish dusted, rather long and pointed, clothed with longer white and shorter black hairs.

Thorax black in ground colour, mesonotum densely grey dusted, pale longitudinal stripes rather indistinct on anterior half in front of notopleural depression, humeri slightly brownish; whole of mesonotum covered by dense, short, whitish-grey pubescence. Pleura more whitish-grey dusted and long pale haired. *Legs:* Coxae concolorous with pleura. Femora yellowish-brown on posterior two pairs, and very thinly greyish dusted; fore femora darkened due to very dense grey pollinosity; all femora long whitish haired beneath. Fore tibiae whitish haired beneath. Fore tibiae whitish-yellow on basal third, brown mesally, apically blackish. Posterior four tibiae light yellowish-brown with three broad brownish rings. Fore tarsi blackish, posterior four tarsi brown, yellowish on metatarsi except for tips. *Wings* rather light grey with not very distinct whitish pattern of small spots and rosettes, posterior margin broadly greyish clouded. Halteres whitish-yellow, knob brownish except for tip.

Abdomen dull blackish-brown, light grey pattern consists of narrow posterior borders and of very narrow median triangles which form a distinct median stripe; greyish sublateral spots absent. Pubescence short and concolorous, posterior three tergites with rather long greyish hairs especially at sides. Venter rather pinkish-grey anteriorly and darker grey on posterior tergites, densely whitish-grey dusted and short pale haired, last sternite with longer black hairs.

♂. Unknown.

Length. 11 mm.

VARIABILITY. According to Szilády (1923) there are sometimes very small and faint sublateral spots on posterior abdominal tergites, and the light border of the wings may be scarcely developed or absent.

Szilády (1923) described this species on the basis of females (not males as wrongly stated by Leclercq (1967a)) collected at Rambouillet, France of Villeneuve and determined by him as *nigricornis* Gobert. Szilády mentioned in the original description also further two females, probably from Dalmatia, and deposited in the Vienna Museum. We have seen one of these females. It is labelled »italica, det. Schiner / Schiner, 1869 / H. gallica m., det. Szilády«, and the above given description is based on this specimen. *H. gallica* Szil. has for a long time been recorded by all authors as a form or subspecies of *H. italica* Meig., but it undoubtedly represents a quite distinct species of the *pluvialis*-group.

DATES. Unknown to us.

DISTRIBUTION. A South European species originally described from France and Jugoslavia (Dalmatia). Leclercq (1967a) recorded it also from Italy, Greece and Spain.

NOTE. *Haematopota sewelli* Austen, 1920 is a closely related species to *H. gallica* Szil., differing from the latter in having distinct light grey sublateral spots on all abdominal tergites including the first. Furthermore the paired velvety black spots (Fig. 144a) on frons are smaller and semicircular, median spot black, callus polished black and wings rather brownish-

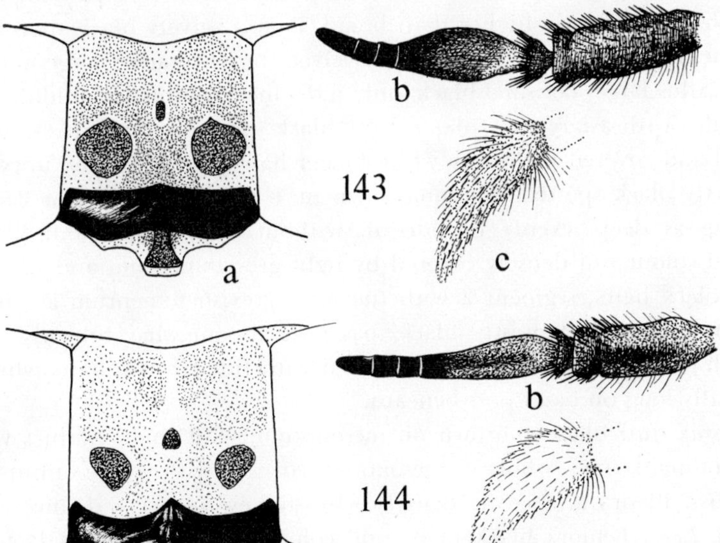

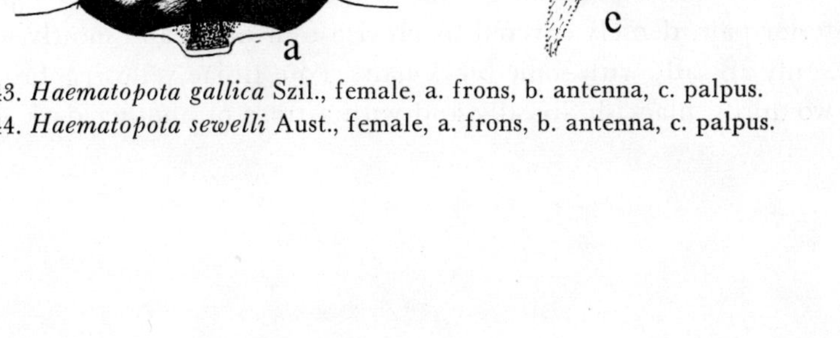

Fig. 143. *Haematopota gallica* Szil., female, a. frons, b. antenna, c. palpus.
Fig. 144. *Haematopota sewelli* Aust., female, a. frons, b. antenna, c. palpus.

grey clouded with posterior margin only slightly paler. Antennae (Fig. 144b), legs and shape of frons as in *H. gallica* Szil. *H. sewelli* Aust. is, according to Theodor (1965: 243), the commonest species of the genus in Israel. Abbassian-Lintzen (1964: 300) recorded it also from Iran, but the occurrence in Greece (Shannon & Hadjinicolaou, 1936: 169) is, following all subsequent authors, doubtful and we therefore not accept this species as being European. We have seen specimens of *H. sewelli* Aust. from Israel, Jordan and Syria.

HAEMATOPOTA LATEBRICOLA AUSTEN, 1925

Fig. 145.

Haematopota latebricola Austen, 1925, Bull. ent. Res., 16: 11.

DIAGNOSIS. Medium-sized species with antennal segment 1 black and entirely greyish dusted, cylindrical, about 2.5 times as long as deep, and not constricted before tip. Frons narrower, slightly higher than broad, paired velvety black spots not very large, almost circular. Wings light grey, abdomen with greyish sublateral spots on all tergites except the first.

DESCRIPTION. ♀. *Head.* Frons whitish-grey dusted and clothed with minute whitish hairs, slightly higher than broad. Paired velvety black spots almost circular, not very large. Median spot velvety brown, rather large and elongate. Callus large, polished black, only indistinctly pointed at middle above. Subcallus with a large, circular velvety black spot. Face and cheeks whitish dusted and covered with only white longer hairs, cheeks on the upper part distinctly black spotted. Antennal segment 1 rather long, almost 2.5 times as long as deep, evenly cylindrical, without any constriction; black in ground colour but densely covered by light grey tomentum and with some short black hairs; segment 2 with the same greyish tomentum as on basal segment; segment 3 mostly black, basal third somewhat brownish. Palpi whitish-pink, rather conical, and covered with fine whitish hairs which are especially long on basal part beneath.

Thorax dull blackish-brown on mesonotum, with three distinct whitish longitudinal stripes, whole of mesonotum covered with sparse minute whitish hairs. Pleura and coxae densely whitish-grey dusted and long whitish haired. *Legs:* Femora black in ground colour, or very indistinctly pinkish on posterior pair, densely covered by greyish tomentum and mostly whitish haired, only apically with some black hairs. Fore tibiae yellowish-brown on basal two-thirds, blackish apically and with a trace of another dark ring at middle. Fore tarsi black. Mid tibiae and tarsi broken (only right femur present). Hind tibiae yellowish-brown with three dark rings, hind metatarsi yellowish-brown except for tip, otherwise tarsi black. *Wings* light grey with rather large whitish rosettes, veins dark brown. Squamae whitish, halteres yellowish with base of knob brownish.

Abdomen greyish-black, tergites somewhat darkened with distinct whitish-grey sublateral spots on tergite 2 and following tergites, the spots are larger on posterior tergites. Whitish median triangles very narrow, forming a narrow median line, each tergite with a pale posterior margin. Venter entirely whitish-grey dusted and short whitish haired, last sternite with longer black hairs.

♂. Unknown.

Length. 10.5 mm.

REMARKS. This species is still known only from the female holotype described by Austen from the Asiatic shore of the Dardanelles. We have seen the type in the British Museum (Nat. Hist.). The specimen is labelled »*Haematopota latebricola* Austen, Type / on horse / Dardanelles (Asiatic Shore): nr. Chanak., Summer 1923, major A. D. Fraser, D.S.O., M.O., R.A.M.C., B.M. 1923 – 471.« and the above description and the figures are based on this specimen.

H. latebricola Aust. is closely related to the Asiatic *H. sewelli* Aust. and to the European *H. gallica* Szil.; the latter differs, inter alia, in the brownish antennal segment 1, and in the absence of grey sublateral spots on abdomen.

DATES. »Summer«.

DISTRIBUTION. The species is still known only from the Asiatic shore of the Dardanelles.

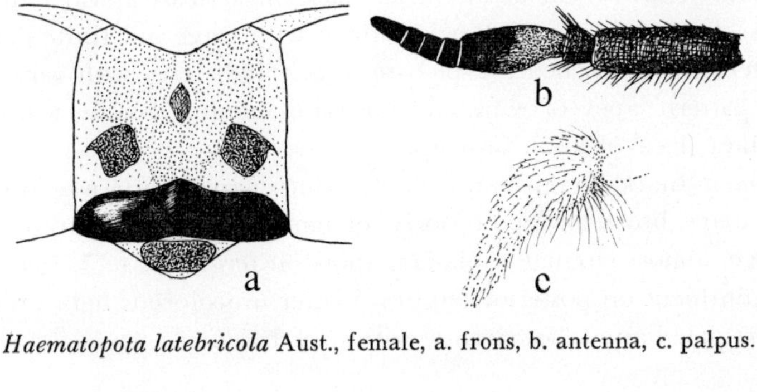

Fig. 145. *Haematopota latebricola* Aust., female, a. frons, b. antenna, c. palpus.

HAEMATOPOTA TURKESTANICA (KRÖBER, 1922)

Fig. 146; pl. 8: fig. e.

Chrysozona turkestanica Kröber, 1922, Arch. Naturgesch., Abt. A, 88 (8): 151.

DIAGNOSIS. Frons very broad, parallel-sided, paired velvety black spots rather small, almost as large as the enlarged median spot. Callus very narrow, with a distinct extension at middle and broadly separated from eye-margins. Antennal segment 1 brownish and entirely greyish dusted, with a distinct subapical constriction. Wings greyish with posterior margin broadly whitish. Greyish sublateral spots very large on tergites 2 to 7. Male with only a narrow black spot on subcallus.

DESCRIPTION. ♀. *Head.* Frons light grey dusted, very broad, distinctly broader than high. Paired velvety black spots rather small, triangular in shape to almost circular, broadly separated from callus and eye-margins. Median spot black, conspicuously large, almost as large as paired lateral spots. Callus polished black, very low, occupying about one-fifth of frons, with a distinct extension at middle and broadly separated at sides from the eye-margins. Subcallus with a distinct velvety black spot. Face and cheeks whitish-grey dusted and whitish haired, cheeks black spotted. Antennae mostly brownish, apical part of segment 3 darkened, tip and terminal flagellar segments black; segment 1 rather long and cylindrical, 2.5—3 times as long as deep, deeply constricted before tip and entirely densely greyish dusted; usually blackish towards tip; segment 2 brownish; segment 3 long and slender, distinctly narrower than segment 1. Palpi yellowish, thinly light grey dusted and clothed with black and pale hairs.

Thorax blackish on mesonotum, anteriorly greyish dusted, otherwise rather dull brownish-black, short pale pubescent. Humeri and notopleural lobes yellowish, scutellum concolorous with mesonotum. Pleura light grey dusted and whitish haired. *Legs:* Coxae light grey, femora brownish in ground colour and densely greyish dusted, usually darkened at tip. Fore tibiae pale yellowish on basal third, black on at least apical half and on fore tarsi. Posterior tibiae yellowish-brown with three indefinite dark rings, tarsi extensively darkened except base. *Wings* light grey with very enlarged whitish pattern, apex of wing and posterior margin broadly whitish. Halteres yellow, base of knob brownish.

Abdomen black in ground colour, whitish-grey pattern consists of a median stripe broadened posteriorly, of narrow posterior margins, and of very large, almost circular sublateral spots on tergites 2 to 7, the spots are almost confluent on posterior tergites. Venter unicolorous light grey dusted and short pale haired, last sternite with dark hairs.

♂. We have not seen this sex and therefore present a translation of the description given by Olsufjev (1937: 344). Eyes with rather long, light grey hairs. Facets on the upper three-quarters of eyes distinctly larger than the facets below; demarcation very sharp. Postocular margin on vertex with a row of rather long light grey hairs. Subcallus greyish dusted, with a small velvety black spot at middle. Its upper corners rounded and broadly separated by greyish pollinosity from the eye-margins. Antennae mostly black; segment 3 brownish on basal half. Segment 1 very stout, short oval (about $1^1/_2$ times as long as deep), clothed with moderately long black hairs, on basal part with grey hairs. Apical third of the segment polished black, the rest thinly greyish dusted. Face with white, upper margin of cheeks with black, hairs. Apical segment of palpi yellowish-white, stouter at base, apically evenly narrowed, clothed with moderately long whitish hairs. Thorax black, mesonotum with narrow, grey, indistinct stripes. Halteres yellow; knob brownish on basal half. Legs and wings as in the ♀. Abdomen black, with not very large brown spots at sides of tergite 2, and partly also of tergites 1 and 3. Tergite 2 with smaller, tergite 3 and following tergites with comparatively large, distinct silvery-grey spots at sides. These tergites with a narrow grey border at posterior margin. Tergites 4 to 6 with a grey median stripe. Venter blackish-grey, densely light dusted.

Length. 8–11 mm.

Biology. One of the more common *Haematopota* species in Central Asia, often occurring near water in steppe and desert regions. The larvae have been found in banks of rivers but are not yet described. Females attack man, domestic and wild living animals, and also birds. According to Shevtshenko (1961) both males and females suck the nectar of flowers. The females are known as vectors of tularaemia (Olsufjev & Golov, 1935).

Dates. From May until September.

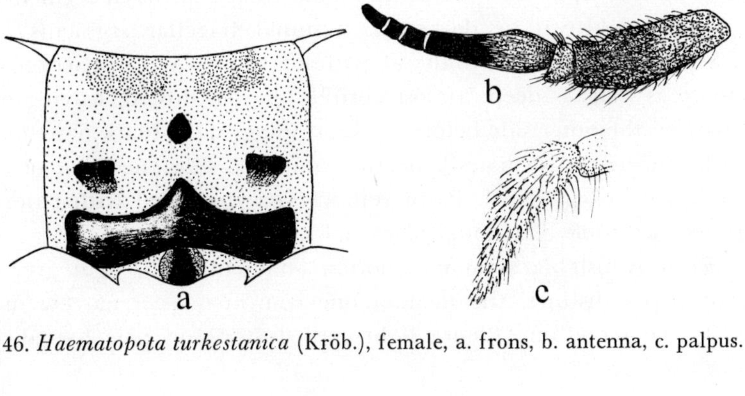

Fig. 146. *Haematopota turkestanica* (Kröb.), female, a. frons, b. antenna, c. palpus.

DISTRIBUTION. An Asiatic species known from Kazakhstan through Transbaikalia to as far as China and Mongolia. Towards the West it penetrates through West Siberia to the Dnepr river and to the south of the European part of the U.S.S.R. We have seen documentary material only from Altai and Mongolia.

HAEMATOPOTA CSIKII SZILÁDY, 1922

Fig. 147; pl. 8: fig. p.

Haematopota Csikii Szilády, 1922, Balkan-Kutat. Tud. Eredm., 1: 68.
? *Haematopota perisi* Salom, 1961, Boln R. Soc. esp. Hist. nat. (B), 59: 102.

DIAGNOSIS. Smaller species with frons slightly higher than broad, clypeus without a pair of small black patches as is usual in other species (except *caenofrons* and partly *turkestanica*). Antennae short and stout, segment 1 black and almost entirely greyish dusted, not constricted; segment 3 at least as broad as segment 1. Wings light greyish, posterior margin clear, femora more or less pinkish. Abdomen with distinct sublateral greyish spots on tergites 3 to 7.

DESCRIPTION. ♀. *Head.* Frons grey, often slightly higher than broad or almost square in shape, usually slightly narrowed above. Paired velvety black spots circular, not very large, distinctly separated from callus and eye-margins. Median spot blackish, very small or absent. Frontal callus polished black, touching the eye-margins at anterior corners, upper margin often more or less convex or with a slight median extension. Subcallus with a large velvety black spot. Clypeus in contrary to other species of the genus without a pair of blackish spots on anterior third at sides. Face and cheeks whitish-grey dusted and densely whitish haired, cheeks distinctly black spotted. Antennae conspicuously short and stout, black on basal segments, segment 3 reddish-brown or darkened, terminal flagellar segments always black. Segment 1 evenly cylindrical without subapical constriction, more than twice as long as deep; almost entirely greyish dusted, leaving only a small part on the outer side before tip subshining; short black haired above, and with longer whitish hairs beneath. Segment 3 shortened and broad, at least as broad as segment 1. Palpi yellowish-grey, clothed with pale hairs, sometimes with some additional black hairs.

Thorax brownish-black on mesonotum and scutellum, light grey longitudinal stripes distinct, the median one continues as a narrow median stripe also on scutellum. Pleura light grey dusted and pale haired. *Legs:*

Coxae unicolorous with pleura, femora brownish to pinkish in ground colour but densely greyish dusted, blackish-grey at tips. Usually more than basal third of fore tibiae yellowish, rest of tibae and tarsus black. Posterior tibiae yellowish-brown with three dark rings, tarsi very darkened except for base. *Wings* light grey to pale greyish-brown, whitish pattern rather indistinct, posterior margin whitish. Halteres with brown knob, only extreme tip of knob and almost whole of stem whitish-yellow.

Abdomen blackish-grey, rather subshining on dorsum. Light grey pattern consists of pale posterior borders on tergites 2 to 6, distinct narrow median triangle on tergite 2, anterior border on tergite 2, and of distinctly circular sublateral spots on tergites 3 to 7, the spots are distinctly situated anteriorly, often partly hidden by the foregoing tergite. Venter unicolorous grey, often broadly darker at middle, pale and black haired.

♂. Unknown to us. Both Szilády (1922, 1923) and Salom (1961) did not know the male sex, but Kröber (1936b: 52) gave a short diagnosis in his key as follows: »f_2 und f_3 fast ganz gelb. Kleine Art von 7–9 mm. Nur das 6. Tergit mit hellen Seitenflecken«. According to Leclercq (1967a: 94) the male sex is known but he did not include it in his key. We have not found any description of the male sex in the literature.

Length. 7–10.5 mm.

SYNONYMY. Salom (1961) described from Spain *H. perisi* on the female sex, but the differential characters seem insignificant to us and the synonymy with *H. csikii* is very likely. We have not seen the type material of *H. perisi* Salom, but specimens from Aguas Amarguas, collected by V.S.v.d. Goot on 24.VII.1965 and labelled as *perisi,* are identical with *H. csikii* Szil. On the other hand, we have seen a specimen from Arag. Noguera, Algeciras, 9.–10.VII.1924, collected by Zerny and determined by Szilády as *csikii* Szil., which quite agrees with the description and figures of *perisi* given by Salom. The small differences given by Salom can, however, hardly justify a specific separation.

DATES. From July until September.

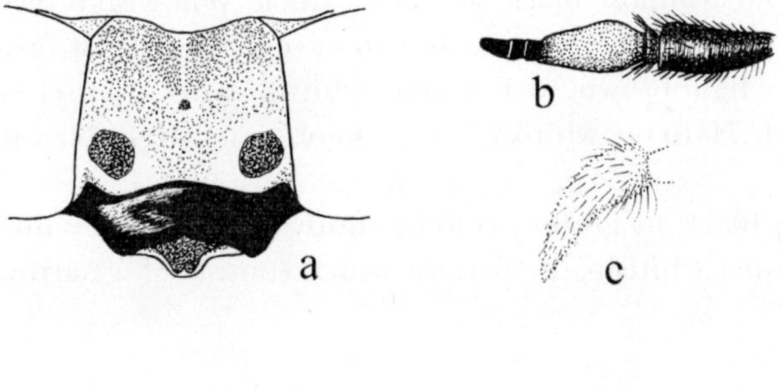

Fig. 147. *Haematopota csikii* Szil., female, a. frons, b. antenna, c. palpus.

DISTRIBUTION. A rare European species recorded so far only from Rumania, Bulgaria, Albania, Austria and Spain. We have seen the documentary material only from Spain.

HAEMATOPOTA PSEUDOLUSITANICA SZILÁDY, 1923

Fig. 148; pl. 8: fig. f.

Haematopota pseudolusitanica Szilády, 1923, Biologica hung., 1 (1): 37.

DIAGNOSIS. Larger blackish species with very broad frons, and rather smaller, almost circular, paired velvety black spots. Antennae entirely black, segment 1 conspicuously short and stout, polished black at least on apical half; segment 3 very broad at base. Wings brownish with distinct whitish pattern, posterior margin clouded. Dorsum of abdomen with distinct light grey sublateral spots, which are rather wide apart on tergites 2 to 6.

DESCRIPTION. ♀. *Head.* Frons darker greyish dusted, broad, distinctly broader than high. Paired velvety black spots not very large, almost circular, distinctly separated from callus but usually touching the eye-margins. Median spot blackish, very small, shaped as a small point. Callus polished blackish-brown, usually brownish at middle, rather narrow, occupying lower quarter of frons, touching the eye-margins at sides. Subcallus with a distinct, oval, velvety black spot. Face and cheeks whitish-grey dusted and densely whitish haired, cheeks finely black spotted. Antennae entirely black, segment 1 very short and stout, stouter on apical third and without any constriction; mostly polished black, thinly greyish dusted at most on basal half; segment 3 rather short and conspicuously stout at base, but usually still narrower than the very stout segment 1. Palpi yellowish-grey, clothed with black and whitish hairs.

Thorax blackish on mesonotum and scutellum, very short but rather densely pale haired, greyish longitudinal stripes distinct. Sides of mesonotum and pleura rather darker grey dusted and clothed with light grey hairs. *Legs:* Coxae greyish, femora usually darker grey dusted, translucent brown to pinkish mesally, pale haired. Fore tibiae yellowish-brown on basal third, rest of tibiae and fore tarsi almost black. Posterior tibiae yellowish-brown with three broad dark rings, metatarsi light brown except tip, rest of tarsi blackish. *Wings* brown to light brown, with distinct whitish pattern, posterior margin broadly clouded. Halteres whitish-yellow, knob extensively brownish except tip.

Abdomen subshining black in ground colour, thinly brownish-grey dusted; dorsum with a distinct whitish-grey pattern which consists of a narrow median stripe, narrow posterior margins, and large, almost circular sublateral spots on tergites 2 to 6; the spots are rather wide apart from the median line and placed more anteriorly, especially on posterior tergites. Sides of abdomen only narrowly greyish. Venter unicolorous light grey dusted and fine pale haired, last sternite with longer black hairs.

♂. Unknown to us.

Length. 10–12 mm.

NOTE. Szilády (1923) described this species on the basis of specimens which Ricardo and Kröber incorrectly recorded as *H. lusitanica* Guérin. We have seen a female paratype from Portugal collected by O. Thomas.

DATES. Unknown to us.

DISTRIBUTION. A West Mediterranean species known from Morocco, Portugal, Spain and France (Ariège). We have seen the documentary material from Portugal and from Andalusia, Spain.

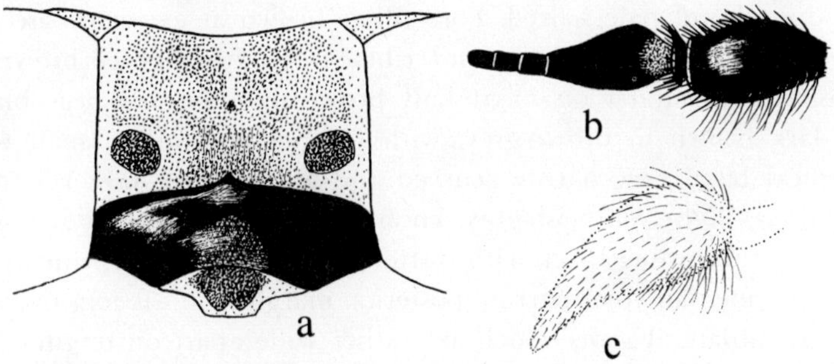

Fig. 148. *Haematopota pseudolusitanica* Szil., female, a. frons, b. antenna, c. palpus.

HAEMATOPOTA OCELLIGERA (KRÖBER, 1922)

Fig. 149; pl. 8: fig. g.

Chrysozona Bigoti var. *ocelligera* Kröber, 1922, Arch. Naturgesch., Abt. A, 88 (8): 161.
Haematopota pluvialis var. *hispanica* Szilády, 1923, Biologica hung., 1 (1): 38.
Haematopota belligera Austen, 1925, Bull. ent. Res., 16: 13.
? *Haematopota crassicornis* var. *maculata* Ghidini, 1936, Archo zool. ital., 22: 420.

DIAGNOSIS. Blackish species with entirely black antennae, segment 1 long oval, polished black and thinly grey dusted on basal half; segment 3 entirely black, almost as broad as segment 1. Frons slightly broader than high, paired velvety black spots large. Palpi grey, darkened. Legs extensively blackish, wings dark brown with whitish pattern. Abdomen with distinct greyish sublateral spots from tergite 3, sometimes indistinct small spots also on tergite 2.

Description. ♀. *Head.* Frons lighter grey dusted, slightly broader than high, usually only indistinctly converging above. Paired velvety black spots large, circular to oblong oval, very narrowly separated from callus and eye-margins. Median spot usually very small, hardly visible. Callus polished black, conspicuously broad, occupying almost lower third of frons. Face light grey dusted with concolorous hairs, cheeks finely black spotted and pale haired. Antennae entirely black, segment 1 long oval, more than twice as long as deep, sometimes with a slight constriction before tip; polished black, thinly grey dusted on basal half to basal two-thirds, finely black haired; segment 3 rather broad, almost as broad as segment 1. Palpi grey or greyish-brown, mostly black haired.

Thorax blackish-brown on mesonotum, light grey longitudinal stripes distinct, scutellum usually thinly greyish dusted. Pleura densely light grey dusted and whitish haired. *Legs:* Coxae and femora black, rather densely greyish dusted and pale haired. Fore tibiae brown at extreme base, otherwise including tarsi black. Posterior tibiae with two lighter brown rings and posterior metatarsi on basal half brownish, otherwise legs blackish. *Wings* dark brown to brown-grey, with distinct but rather small whitish spots, apical band very narrow, curved and abbreviated, posterior margin dark. Halteres light yellowish-grey, knob extensively darkened at base.

Abdomen subshining black with distinct light grey pattern which consists of a narrow median line, narrow posterior margins on all tergites, and of large, oval sublateral spots which are rather wide apart on tergites 3 to 6; last tergite unicolorous grey, tergite 2 sometimes with a small greyish spot at each side. Sides of tergites only narrowly greyish. Venter unicolorous light grey dusted and short pale haired, sometimes an indefinite, broad, darker median stripe; apical two sternites with predominantly black hairs.

♂. We have not seen the male sex of this species and the descriptive information available refers probably at least partly to the Central and North European *H. subcylindrica* Pand. (= *H. hispanica* auct.).

Length. 9–11 mm.

Synonymy. The very complicated synonymy of this species has been fully discussed by Lyneborg & Chvála (1970). The species was not for a long period differentiated from *H. hispanica* auct. nec Szil. (= *H. subcylindrica* Pand.).

Dates. From June until August.

Distribution. A South European species which is widely distributed on a large area from Turkey as far as to Spain. It occurs also in North Africa (Morocco, Algeria). The species has been correctly separated from *H. subcylindrica* Pand. only recently (Olsufjev, 1969a; Lyneborg & Chvála, 1970) and is probably a very common species in South Europe. Hitherto we have seen the documentary material from Turkey, Rumania, Albania, Italy, France and Spain.

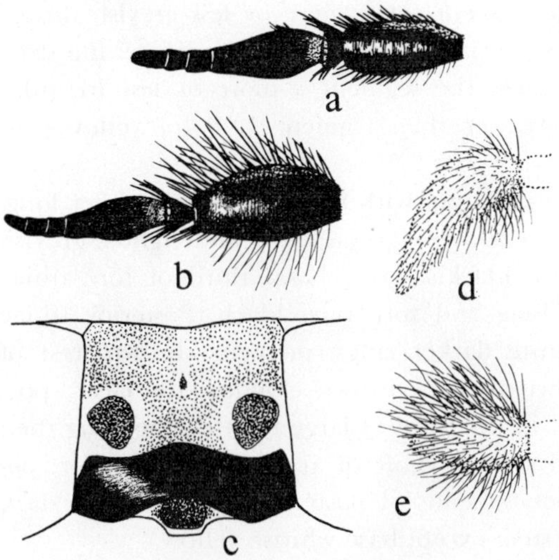

Fig. 149. *Haematopota ocelligera* (Kröb.), a. female antenna, b. male antenna, c. female frons, d. female palpus, e. male palpus.

HAEMATOPOTA PLUVIALIS (LINNÉ, 1758)

Fig. 1b; 150; pl. 8: fig. h.

Tabanus pluvialis Linné, 1758, Syst. Nat., p. 602.
Tabanus equorum Fabricius, 1794, Ent. Syst., 4: 370.
Tabanus hyetomantis Schrank, 1803, Fauna Boica, 3: 155.
Haematopota serpentina Wiedemann, 1828, Aussereur. Zweifl. Ins., 1: 219.
Chrysozona pluvialis minima Ghidini, 1936, Archo zool. ital., 22: 425.

Diagnosis. Blackish coloured and densely olive-grey dusted species with antennal segment 1 mostly polished black and always with a deep constriction before tip, which gives the segment a somewhat irregular shape. Frons narrow, paired velvety black spots large. Femora greyish-black, wings brown to dark brown, whitish pattern usually distinct. Abdomen olive-grey dusted with indefinite sublateral spots on tergites 2 to 7. Male with antennal segment 1 more evenly conical, mostly polished black.

Description. ♀. *Head.* Frons grey, rather narrow, distinctly higher than broad, usually slightly convergent above. Paired velvety black spots large, circular, only very narrowly separated from callus and eye-margins. Median spot often larger, circular. Callus polished black, rather high, occupying more than one-quarter of frons. Subcallus with a large velvety black spot. Face and cheeks whitish-grey dusted, whitish haired, cheeks distinctly black spotted. Antennae black, segment 3 usually brown at least on basal third, but in northern populations often extensively darkened or entirely black; segment 1 mostly polished black except for a more or less greyish dusted basal part, about twice to almost thrice as long as deep, always with a deep constriction before tip, which gives the segment a more or less irregular shape; segment 3 distinctly narrower than segment 1. Palpi yellow-grey, with pale and black hairs.

Thorax blackish-brown on mesonotum, with rather indefinite paler longitudinal stripes, pleura dark grey to olive-grey dusted and lighter greyish haired. *Legs:* Coxae and femora blackish-grey; basal third of fore tibiae yellowish-brown, the rest of tibiae and fore tarsi black. Posterior tibiae light brown with three indefinite darker rings, metatarsi brown, rest of tarsi black. *Wings* usually brown to dark brown clouded, the clear spots often small, sometimes enlarged in the form of large rosettes, the wing then being paler. Apical band broad above, whole of apex somewhat paler; posterior margin with whitish spots at ends of posterior cells. Halteres dark brown, extreme tip of knob and stem except base whitish-yellow.

Abdomen blackish in ground colour but usually covered with dense olive-grey pollinosity. The greyish sublateral spots, which are very small on tergite 2 and larger on following tergites, rather indistinct, likewise paler sides of tergites, a broader median stripe and narrow posterior margins on all tergites. Venter uniformly dark grey to olive-grey dusted, mostly short pale haired.

♂. Eyes densely brownish haired, large facets on more than upper three-quarters of eyes sharply separated from small facets below. Subcallus with a large velvety black spot, cheeks black haired. Antennae with segment 1 more evenly conical without any constriction before tip, usually broadest at base, the whitish-grey pollinosity restricted to at most basal third. Palpi brownish with grey dust, finely long whitish haired. Mesonotum and scutellum mostly long pale haired, abdominal pattern usually lighter grey and more distinct; otherwise as in the ♀ but tergites 2 and 3 narrowly brownish at sides.

Length. 8—12 mm.

VARIABILITY. A very variable species both in shape and coloration of antennae, in size and in coloration of abdominal pattern.

Biology. *H. pluvialis* (L.) inhabits various types of biotopes but the adults are very common especially near water and on foggy biotopes, where the larvae live. In Europe, and especially in Central Europe, usually the commonest species of the family. Females attack very actively man and animals not only in the middle of the day, when it is hot, but also in the evening and in cloudy and showery weather. The females are known as vectors of tularaemia and anthrax. The immature stages were described in details by Cameron (1934). Later Skufin (1967) described the larva and Ježek (1971) both larva and pupa.

Dates. From May until October, the maximal flight period is in July and August.

Distribution. A very common European species known throughout Europe including the extreme north, in Scandinavia up to 70° N. It is known in South Europe from Portugal and Spain to Ukraine, and from Ireland eastwards as far as to East Siberia. The occurrence in North Africa and in the southern parts of Asia needs verification; only literary records are available from these areas. Unfortunately a large number of different species were identified and recorded in the past under the name of *pluvialis* L.

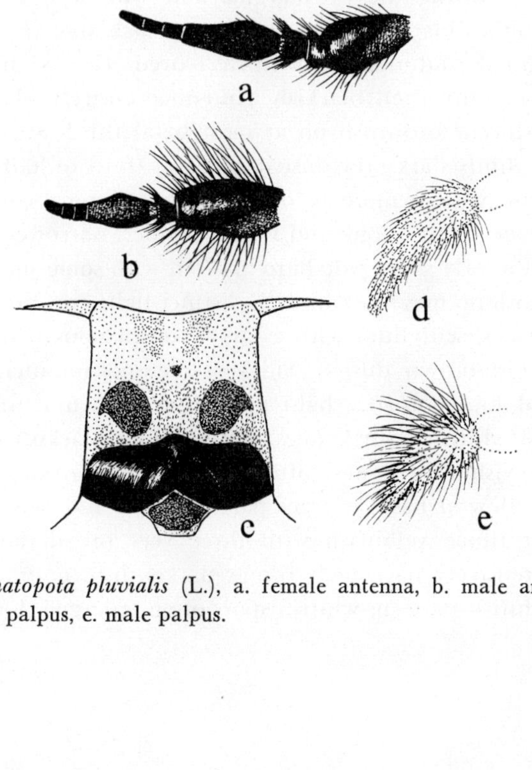

Fig. 150. *Haematopota pluvialis* (L.), a. female antenna, b. male antenna, c. female frons, d. female palpus, e. male palpus.

HAEMATOPOTA SCUTELLATA (OLSUFJEV, MOUCHA & CHVÁLA, 1964)

Fig. 151; pl. 8: fig. i.

Chrysozona scutellata Olsufjev, Moucha & Chvála, 1964, Acta Soc. ent. Čechoslov., 61: 284.

DIAGNOSIS. Black species with a large, whitish-grey patch on scutellum. Frons slightly narrower than broad or almost square in shape, parallel or slightly spots conspicuously large, usually confluent with callus and eye-margins, median spot large. Antennae extensively blackish, segment 1 often with a slight subapical constriction, polished black, thinly grey dusted on about basal third above. Wings brown with distinct pale pattern, sublateral greyish spots usually only on posterior three tergites. Male with antennal segment 1 broadly oval, mostly polished black.

DESCRIPTION. ♀. *Head.* Frons light grey to bluish-grey dusted, usually slightly narrower than broad or almost square in shape, parallel or slightly convergent above. Paired velvety black spots conspicuously large, often with a narrow extension above and on the outer side, often broadly confluent with callus and touching the eye-margins. Median spot large, of various shape. Callus polished black and rather broad, occupying almost lower third of frons, touching the eye-margins and with a large extension at middle above. Subcallus with a large velvety black spot. Face and cheeks whitish-grey dusted and densely whitish haired, cheeks distinctly black spotted, upper margin often blackish. Antennae entirely black, segment 3 sometimes translucent brownish on at most basal third. Segment 1 mostly polished black, thinly dark grey dusted on basal third to half above, rather cylindrical, about twice or more as long as deep, subapical constriction only slight or absent; segment 3 long and rather slender, narrower than segment 1. Palpi greyish, mostly short pale haired, often with some short black hairs.

Thorax blackish on mesonotum, with distinct light grey and rather broad longitudinal stripes, scutellum with a large, conspicuous whitish-grey spot, only sides blackish-brown dusted. Sides of mesonotum including humeri and notopleural lobes broadly light grey dusted. Pleura and coxae light grey dusted and whitish haired. *Legs:* Fore femora blackish-grey, posterior four femora greyish dusted and often brownish in ground colour. Fore tibiae whitish-yellow at base, a larger part of tibiae and whole of fore tarsi black; posterior tibiae yellowish with three very broad dark rings, tarsi except base extensively darkened. *Wings* darker brown to brownish-grey, with distinct whitish pattern, whitish spots often enlarged, forming distinct rosettes, posterior margin often with pale spots at apices of posterior cells. Halteres yellowish-brown on stem, knob often extensively greyish-black.

Abdomen blackish, a light grey pattern consists of a narrow median stripe, of narrow posterior margins on all tergites, and of almost circular sublateral spots on posterior three to four tergites, only very rarely a very indefinite patch also on tergite 3. Venter light grey dusted, with a broad, more or less distinct, darker median stripe; pubescence pale, some blackish hairs on a median stripe and on last sternite.

♂. Eyes with fine brownish hairs, facets on more than upper three-quarters of eyes very enlarged and sharply separated from small facets below. Subcallus with a large, triangular velvety black spot, cheeks velvety black on the upper inner corner, black haired. Antennal segment 1 very large, evenly broad oval, about twice as long as deep at middle; polished black, rather densely greyish dusted on only a small part on the inner side at base, black haired; segment 3 slightly brownish at base, rather short and very slender. Palpi greyish, clothed with long pale greyish hairs. Thorax as in the ♀ with the same conspicuous grey patch on scutellum, mesonotum long pale haired. Posterior femora very long pale haired beneath, hind tibiae with long dark hairs ventrally and anterodorsally (the latter almost black). Abdomen with the same, but less distinct pattern as in the ♀, dorsum mostly long black haired, venter with shorter pale hairs except on last sternite, which bears long black hairs.

Length. 9–10.5 mm.

Biology. An uncommon species but on suitable biotopes near ponds or on

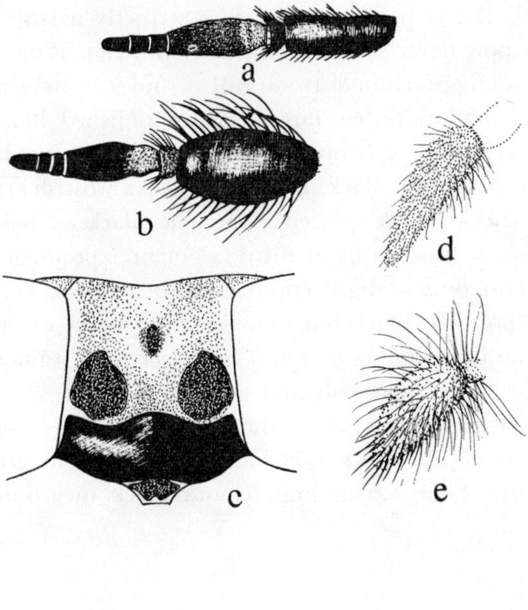

Fig. 151. *Haematopota scutellata* (Ols., Mch. & Chv.), a. female antenna, b. male antenna, c. female frons, d. female palpus, e. male palpus.

foggy localities in forests, especially in hilly regions, often in large number. The larva and pupa were described by Ježek (1971).

DATES. From the end of June until the beginning of September.

DISTRIBUTION. A Central and South European species described only recently and known so far from Austria, Czechoslovakia, Germany, Switzerland, Italy and France. Olsufjev (1964) described a subspecies *pontica* from the Caucasus.

HAEMATOPOTA SUBCYLINDRICA PANDELLÉ, 1883

Fig. 152; pl. 8: fig. k.

Haematopota hispanica auct. (nec Szilády, = *ocelligera* Kröb.).
Haematopota pluvialis var. *subcylindrica* Pandellé, 1883, Revue ent. 2: 196.
Haematopota elbrusiensis Abbassian-Lintzen, 1960, Bull. Soc. Path. exot., 53: 825.

DIAGNOSIS. Rather larger, light grey species of the *pluvialis*-group with antennal segment 1 prolonged, evenly oval to cylindrical, sometimes with a slight constriction before tip; densely light grey dusted above, leaving only apical quarter polished black. Frons conspicuously narrow, paired velvety black spots not very large, usually narrowed. Wings very light grey, femora grey. Greyish sublateral spots distinct on tergites 2 to 7 or 3 to 7. Male with antennal segment 1 long oval, polished black, densely whitish-grey dusted on more than basal half above.

DESCRIPTION. ♀. *Head.* Frons lighter grey dusted, conspicuously narrow, distinctly higher than broad, almost parallel-sided or indistinctly narrowed above. Paired velvety black spots never very large, usually rather half-moon shaped and narrowed, distinctly separated from callus and eye-margins. Median black spot oval to circular, rather larger. Callus polished black, higher, occupying almost lower third of frons, median extension above distinct. Subcallus almost entirely velvety black. Face and cheeks whitish-grey dusted and whitish haired, cheeks black spotted. Antennae black on basal segments, segment 3 brownish at least on basal third; segment 1 prolonged, rather cylindrical with at most only a slight constriction before tip, more than twice as long as deep; polished black but densely whitish-grey dusted especially above on more than basal half; segment 3 narrower than segment 1. Palpi greyish-yellow, clothed with short pale and some black hairs.

Thorax dull brown-black on mesonotum and scutellum, pale longitudinal stripes not very distinct; mesonotum short pale haired. Pleura light grey dusted with concolorous hairs. *Legs:* Coxae and femora black in ground colour, very densely light grey dusted and pale haired beneath. Fore tibiae yellowish at least on basal half, apically black likewise tarsi. Posterior tibiae yellowish-brown with three faintly dark rings, metatarsi brown, apical tarsal segments blackish. *Wings* very light greyish, with rather indefinite whitish pattern, posterior margin usually broadly clouded. Halteres whitish-yellow, basal half of knobs dark brown.

Abdomen blackish with distinct light grey pattern which consists of a distinct median stripe, narrow posterior margins, and not very large, circular sublateral spots, which are absent or only small on tergite 2, but more prominent on following tergites. All tergites broadly greyish at sides. Venter light grey dusted and mostly pale haired, a broad darker median stripe (with darker hairs) more distinct when viewed from behind.

♂. Eyes densely brownish haired, facets on the upper three-quarters very large and sharply separated from small facets below. Subcallus almost entirely velvety black. Cheeks mostly black haired, palpi yellowish-brown coloured and long whitish haired. Antennal segment 1 conspicuously elongated, about 3 times as long as deep, polished black but densely whitish-grey dusted above on more than basal half, long black haired also on apical half beneath; segment 3 more reddish-brown, not longer than segment 1. Thorax with long light grey hairs everywhere. Posterior four femora and hind tibiae beneath very long whitish haired, hind tibiae anterodorsally with a row of longer black hairs. Abdomen very densely and long haired, tergites 2 and 3 narrowly brown at sides.

Length. 9–12 mm.

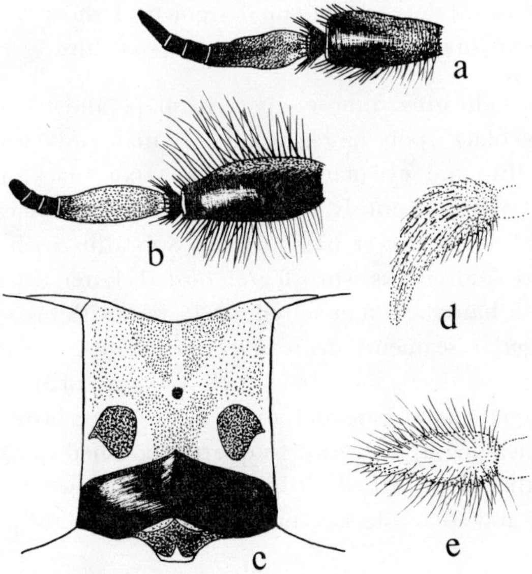

Fig. 152. *Haematopota subcylindrica* Pand., a. female antenna, b. male antenna, c. female frons, d. female palpus, e. male palpus.

Biology. The species inhabits the same biotopes as *H. pluvialis* (L.), but is less common than this species. Females attack man and animals. The larva and pupa were described recently by Ježek (1971).

Dates. From the end of May until the beginning of September.

Distribution. Central and East Europe as far as West Siberia, in West Europe known from Belgium and Holland, northwards to Denmark and South Sweden. Not recorded from England. The species is known from the European part of the U.S.S.R., from the Caucasus and North Kazakhstan. *H. subcylindrica* Pand. does not occur in South and South West Europe, where it is replaced by *H. ocelligera* (Kröb.) (= *H. hispanica* Szil. nec auct.).

HAEMATOPOTA BIGOTI GOBERT, 1881

Fig. 153; pl. 8: fig. 1.

Haematopota Bigoti Gobert, 1881, Mém. Soc. linn. N. Fr., 1881: 38.
Haematopota Bigoti var. *monspellensis* Villeneuve, 1921, Annls Soc. ent. Belg., 61: 157.

Diagnosis. An extensively brownish species on legs and antennae. Frons almost square in shape, paired velvety black spots large, circular; black median spot usually very large. Antennal segment 1 more evenly oval, densely whitish-grey dusted on at least basal half, on the inner side basally and above often brown. Abdomen with distinct large whitish-grey sublateral spots on all abdominal tergites. Male with antennal segment 1 short oval and mostly polished black, whitish-grey dusted at most on basal third.

Description. ♀. *Head.* Frons light grey, almost square in shape and rather parallel-sided. Paired velvety black spots large, usually circular, only very narrowly separated from callus and eye-margins. Median spot black, in comparison with other species conspicuously large. Callus polished black, touching the eye-margins at least on lower half at sides. Subcallus with a large, velvety black spot. Face and cheeks whitish-grey dusted, latter finely black spotted and only whitish haired. Antennae reddish to yellowish-brown on segment 3, terminal flagellar segments deep black. Segment 1 evenly oval, more than twice as long as deep, sometimes with a slight subapical constriction; black, on the inner side at base and above more or less brown, densely whitish-grey dusted, leaving apical third to quarter polished black; longer whitish haired beneath, above with short black hairs. Palpi whitish-yellow, clothed with whitish and some black adpressed hairs, distinctly pointed.

Thorax dull blackish-brown dusted on mesonotum, light longitudinal stripes distinct, scutellum sometimes slightly darker grey dusted. Pleura and coxae whitish-grey dusted and densely whitish haired. *Legs* extensively yellowish-brown to pinkish-brown on femora, leaving only apices greyish. Tibiae yellowish-brown, posterior four tibiae with three dark rings, fore tibiae black on apical half. Fore tarsi black, posterior tarsi extensively darkened, metatarsi brownish at base. *Wings* very pale greyish with usually enlarged clear pattern, which gives the wing a very pale appearance. Apical band broad and curved, posterior margin clouded or with enlarged clear patches in apices of posterior cells. Halteres whitish, both knob and stem brownish at base.

Abdomen black in ground colour and rather dulled by greyish dust, with conspicuous whitish-grey pattern on dorsum which consists of narrow posterior margins on all tergites, high and narrow median triangles, and conspicuously large, rounded sublateral spots on all tergites, sometimes absent on tergite 1. The sublateral spots are situated close to median triangles, blackish bordered on the inner side and below, often confluent with anterior margin and grey coloration at side. Venter uniformly dark grey dusted and short pale haired, last sternite with longer black hairs.

♂. Eyes long whitish haired, facets on the upper three-quarters very large and sharply separated from small facets. Subcallus with a large, triangular, velvety black spot. Cheeks long black haired. Antennal segment 1 very stout, short oval, polished black with concolorous hairs, covered with whitish-grey tomentum only on basal third above and on the inner side,

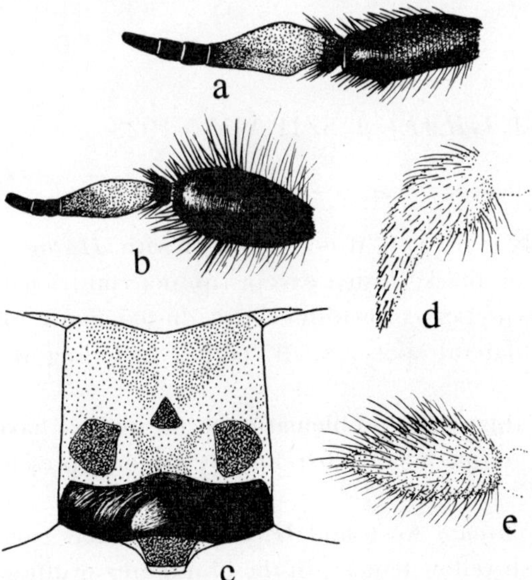

Fig. 153. *Haematopota bigoti* Gob., a. female antenna, b. male antenna, c. female frons, d. female palpus, e. male palpus.

and there mostly whitish haired; segment 3 slender, yellowish-brown, terminal flagellar segments blackish. Palpi yellowish-grey, conical, with dark hairs above, below mostly whitish haired. Mesonotum rather long whitish haired, legs long haired especially on femora and hind tibiae. Otherwise as in the ♀ including the distinct whitish abdominal pattern, tergites 2 and 3 narrowly brown at sides. Venter with very long, fine whitish hairs.

Length. 9.5–11 mm.

SYNONYMY. *H. bigoti* var. *monspellensis* Villeneuve, 1921 is distinguished from the nominate form by the enlarged clear rosettes on wings, but has probably no taxonomic value and may be listed at most only as a form. Salom (1961: 98) recorded it from Spain as a distinct species based on a description of the male sex, but the figured narrow female frons (on p. 99) with rather small paired velvety spots indicates a distinct, unknown species to us. The possible synonymy with *H. graeca* Szil. (see below) is still open.

DATES. From May until middle of September.

DISTRIBUTION. A South European species known from all countries from Rumania to Spain, in North Africa from Morocco and Algeria. The north border of its area of distribution lies in southern parts of Central Europe, in Hungary and Czechoslovakia (Slovakia) and it is also known from an isolated locality in Germany (Stassfurt). The species is again more frequent in England, from where it penetrates as a coastal species to Denmark, South Sweden and North Poland (see also Lyneborg & Chvála, 1970). The species has not yet been found in Austria, South Germany (Bavaria) and Switzerland.

HAEMATOPOTA GRAECA SZILÁDY, 1923

Haematopota graeca Szilády, 1923, Biologica hung., 1 (1): 35.

DIAGNOSIS. The species is closely related to, if not identical with, *H. bigoti* Gob. Antennal segment 1 shining black, dusted except tip, not constricted; segments 2 and 3 reddish-brown. Legs brownish-yellow, dusted, posterior wing-margin whitish. Grey sublateral spots on all tergites including the first.

Only a little is known about this rather problematic species, and we have not seen any specimen labelled as *graeca* Szil. Therefore we can only present the short original description.

♀. »A form between *H. innominata* Aust. and *H. Csikii.* It differs from the former species in its brownish yellow femora, in the bluish grey pruinose lateral borders of its abdomen, etc. From the latter species is differing in its form of antennae, yellow fore femora, and in having the two characteristic black spots of the clypeus at least in the form of small dots.

In general similar to our *H. pluvialis,* but differs from it as follows:

1. The first segment of the antennae much swollen before its end, short, oval, shining, black; pruinose, except its tip; preapical groove wanting. The third, reddish brown segment without appendix, nearly just as long as the first one. Second segment reddish brown with black pubescence.

2. The two large velvet spots of the parallel and at the vertex somewhat impressed frons are round and equal to one quarter of the frons.

3. The light spots of the wing mostly round and partially fused leave larger parts of the wings dark; the bordering is an uninterrupted, light band with serrate incisions at the veins. Preapical band undulated, sometimes interrupted.

4. Legs pruinose brownish yellow.

5. On the dorsum of every segment of the abdomen two rather large, round, pruinose side spots and a narrow middle stripe are to be seen.

Types, from the Poros Island, are in the collection of the Hungarian National Museum«.

♂. Unknown.

Length. 9—10 mm.

NOTE. The type specimens in the Hungarian National Museum, Budapest have obviously been destroyed in 1956.

DATES. Unknown.

DISTRIBUTION. Greece. Leclercq (1967a: 181) recorded this species in addition to the island of Poros also from the Greek Macedonia.

HAEMATOPOTA CRASSICORNIS WAHLBERG, 1848

Fig. 154; pl. 8: fig. m.

? *Haematopota globulifera* Schummel, 1838, Arb. Schles. Vaterl. Kultur, p. 108.
Haematopota crassicornis Wahlberg, 1848, Öfvers. K. VetenskAkad. Förh., 5: 200.
? *Chrysozona flavopilosa* Kröber, 1922, Arch. Naturgesch., Abt. A, 88 (8): 155.

DIAGNOSIS. Blackish species with entirely black antennae, segment 1 short oval in both sexes, not constricted and entirely polished black without any greyish dusting. Frons distinctly broader than high, paired velvety black spots large. Wings rather dark brown with enlarged clear patches. Abdomen black with rather small but distinct sublateral greyish spots on tergites 3 to 7, the spots are situated close to median line.

DESCRIPTION. ♀. *Head.* Frons grey to dark grey, broad, distinctly broader than high. Paired velvety black spots large, of irregular shape, narrowly separated from callus but often with a slight outer projection above and touching the eye-margins. Median spot black, circular and very small. Callus polished black, rather low, occupying lower quarter of frons. Face and cheeks whitish-grey dusted and whitish haired, cheeks black spotted. Antennae entirely black including whole of segment 3; segment 1 entirely polished black, more or less evenly oval, stouter at middle, twice as long as deep or slightly longer, not constricted; segment 3 very slender. Palpi greyish to pinkish-grey, pale and black haired.

Thorax rather dull black, pleura dark grey dusted and light greyish haired. Mesonotum with distinct light grey longitudinal stripes, scutellum often dark grey dusted at tip. *Legs:* Coxae concolorous with pleura, femora black, thinly grey dusted and rather long pale haired beneath. Fore tibiae yellowish-brown on basal third, rest of tibia and whole of fore tarsus black. Posterior tibiae light brown with three broad blackish rings, tarsi extensively blackish, paler at base. *Wings* rather dark brown to brownish-grey, whitish patches enlarged. Posterior margin always clouded. Halteres very dark brown on knob, base of stem paler.

Abdomen mostly blackish, paler median stripe on dorsum indistinct, light grey borders on posterior margins of all tergites narrow and distinct. Whitish-grey sublateral spots on tergites 3 to 7 small but distinct, in comparison with other species situated closer to median line, not in the centre of each of tergites as usual. Venter blackish-grey dusted and finely pale haired, apical sternite with longer black hairs.

♂. Eyes densely and rather shorter dark brown haired, upper facets only slightly enlarged and gradually becoming smaller below, sharp division absent. Subcallus with a large velvety black spot, postocular margin on vertex with a row of long dark hairs. Cheeks extensively blackish and long black haired, face pale haired. Antennae black, segment 1 entirely polished black and rather long black haired, almost twice as long as deep; segment 3 rather short and very slender, about as long as segment 1. Palpi brownish-grey, mostly long pale haired, and with some additional black hairs. Mesonotum with longer black and brownish hairs, pleura darker grey haired. Halteres almost black. Dorsum of abdomen long black haired with the same but less distinct pattern as in the ♀, venter mostly yellowish-grey haired.

Length. 8–11 mm (usually about 9 mm).

SYNONYMY. The synonymy has been discussed by Lyneborg & Chvála (1970: 36). *H. flavopilosa* (Kröb.) was described only from the male sex and is very probably identical with *H. crassicornis* Wahlbg.

Biology. The adults occur always only individually and are one of the early spring species. The larva was described by Brindle (1961), and both larva and pupa by Ježek (1971).

Dates. From the beginning of May until July.

Distribution. A European species recorded eastwards as far as to the Ural Mts., according to Violovič (1968: 69) in Siberia to the Ob river, southwards to Transcaucasia. The species is well known from West Europe including the British Isles and from all countries of North and Central Europe. It is known from all Scandinavian countries up to 60°–61° N. The recorded occurrence in South Europe and North Africa needs verification since the species has probably been confused here with *H. ocelligera* (Kröb.) (= *H. hispanica* Szil. nec auct.), because this species and *H. subcylindrica* Pand. (= *H. hispanica* auct. nec Szil.) were not recognized as distinct species until recently. Salom (1967) recorded *H. crassicornis* Wahlbg. from Spain but it seems more likely that this species is replaced in the southern European regions by *H. ocelligera* (Kröb.).

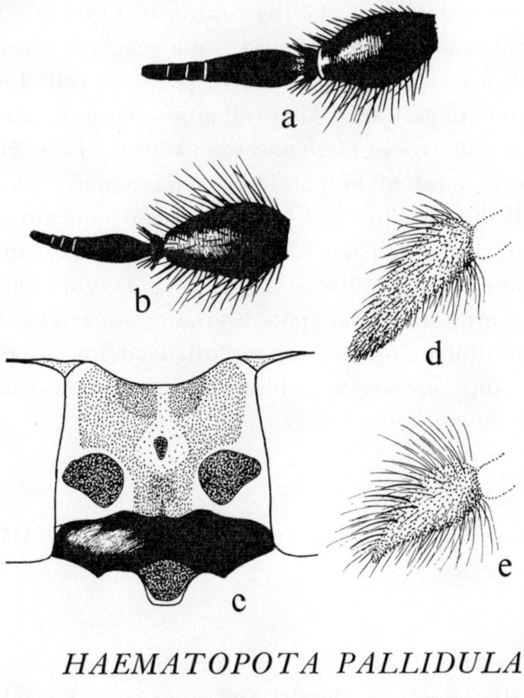

Fig. 154. *Haematopota crassicornis* Wahlb., a. female antenna, b. male antenna, c. female frons, d. female palpus, e. male palpus.

HAEMATOPOTA PALLIDULA (KRÖBER, 1922)

Chrysozona pallidula Kröber, 1922, Arch. Naturgesch., Abt. A, 88 (8): 152.

Diagnosis. Larger species of the *pluvialis*-group with antennal segment 1 entirely polished black, without subapical constriction; segment 3 reddish-brown on basal half. Frons slightly broader than high, converging above, median spot usually absent. Wings light grey with very enlarged whitish pattern, posterior margin whitish. Grey sublateral patches on all tergites including the first.

Unfortunately we have not seen this species which was recorded as European by Olsufjev (1969a). Kröber (1922) described it in details. A shorter description with figures of frons, antennae, palpus and wing gave Olsufjev (1937: 346). Since Olsufjev's description is shorter and gives the most important differential characters, we present a translation of it.

♀. Eyes very short haired. Frons broad, slightly broader at base than high, yellowish-grey dusted. Paired velvety spots black, not very large, triangular in shape. Median spot absent or present as a minute point. Frontal callus polished black, about 4 times as broad as deep. Antennae black but basal half of segment 3 reddish-brown. Segment 1 polished black, stouter, about twice as long as deep, no subapical constriction. Apical segment of palpi yellowish, rather slender, clothed with mostly pale hairs. Mesonotum with distinct grey longitudinal stripes. Wings light grey with strongly developed pale pattern. The pale spots in central part of wing confluent, forming distinct rosettes. Apical crossband not very broad, curved, not reaching posterior wing-margin. Latter with a broad whitish band in posterior cells forming a row of circular spots, one in each cell. Anal cell almost entirely pale. Veins brownish. Halteres brownish, tips of knob and stem whitish. Legs: Femora blackish-grey, densely greyish dusted, mid and hind femora more or less yellowish, fore tibiae on basal third yellow, rest black, mid and hind tibiae yellow with three blackish-brown rings. Tarsi black, base of mid and hind tarsi yellow. Abdomen elongated, usually olive-grey coloured. Tergites with large but not sharply defined grey sublateral spots beginning on tergite 1. The spots are more or less confluent into two longitudinal lateral stripes. A grey median stripe distinct only on tergite 2. Posterior margins unclear. Venter unicolorous grey with olive coloured tinge.

♂. Unknown.

Length. 9—11 mm.

Biology. Only a little known species, but according to Olsufjev (1937: 347) it deals with a typical spring species.

Dates. April and May.

Distribution. Described by Kröber (1922) from Orenburg. Olsufjev (1937) recorded new captures from the Orenburg District and from West Kazakhstan. Later (Olsufjev, 1969a: 499) collected it also in the south of the European part of the U.S.S.R.

TRIBE DIACHLORINI

GENUS *PHILIPOMYIA* OLSUFJEV, 1964

Bull. Mosk. Obšč. Isp. Prir., 69: 74.

TYPE SPECIES: *Tabanus graecus* Fabricius, 1794.

DIAGNOSIS. Medium-sized, rather robust *Tabanus*-like species with flat, broad abdomen. Eyes bare, unstriped. Frons in female moderately broad, frontal calli joined into a keel-shaped callus. Head in male rather smaller, all facets nearly equal in size. Antennae with well developed dorsal tooth to segment 3, ocelli or ocellar swelling absent. Wings clear, no appendix to vein R_4, basicosta bare.

REMARKS. The last mentioned character in addition to the very long and slender spermathecae in female, was the main reason why Olsufjev (1964) detached the species *Tabanus apricus* Meig., *Tabanus graecus* F. and *Tabanus rohdendorfi* Ols. from the genus *Tabanus* L. and erected for them a new genus *Philipomyia,* which was placed together with the genus *Dasyrhamphis* End. in the tripe *Diachlorini* Enderlein, 1922.

Altogether only 3 species of the genus *Philipomyia* Ols., originally included by Olsufjev in this genus, are known so far and they all occur also in Europe. *P. aprica* (Meig.) has the largest area of distribution from Spain to as far as Transcaucasus, northwards to Belgium; *P. graeca* (F.) inhabits nearly the same large area but prefers dry and warm localities, reaching at its northern border only Central Europe (South Slovakia); finally *P. rohdendorfi* (Ols.) is an endemic species in the Caucasus.

Nothing is known of the life history of *Philipomyia* species, the larva and pupa have not been hitherto described. Females attack horses, horned cattle but also man.

Key to European species of *Philipomyia*

1 Antennal segment 3 with a large, pointed, hook-like dorsal tooth directed forwards, orange-yellow; terminal flagellar segments darkened. Anterior three tergites yellowish-brown at sides with usually narrow black median stripe; abdomen mostly golden-yellow haired. Halteres yellowish .... *graeca* (F.)

– Antennal segment 3 darker, and with a smaller, rectangular, tabanine-like dorsal tooth which is not directed forwards. Anterior tergites rather brownish or extensively darkened with broader black median stripe; abdomen rather darker haired. Halteres darker 2

2 (1) Antennal segment 3 reddish-brown. Abdomen with anterior three tergites brownish at sides. Halteres brownish-yellow .... *aprica* (Meig.)

- Antennal segment 3 entirely black. Abdomen with only two anterior tergites chestnut-brown at sides, tergite 3 mostly black, brownish along posterior margin only. Halteres brown .... *rohdendorfi* (Ols.)

PHILIPOMYIA APRICA (MEIGEN, 1820)

Fig. 155; pl. 4: fig. b.

Tabanus apricus Meigen, 1820, Syst. Beschr., 2: 37.
Tabanus infuscatus Loew, 1858, Verh. zool.-bot. Ges. Wien, 8: 608.

DIAGNOSIS. Medium-sized dark species with anterior three tergites chestnut-brown at sides; antennae reddish-brown with black terminal segments, dorsal tooth to segment 3 rectangular. Eyes unstriped, both frontal calli joined and club-shaped as it is usual in this genus.

DESCRIPTION. ♀. *Head.* Eyes bare, unstriped. Frons nearly parallel-sided or slightly widened above, rather narrow, index nearly 1: 5. Both frontal calli shining black and joined, club-shaped, slightly widening out below. Frons and subcallus yellow to golden-yellow dusted, face and cheeks sometimes slightly greyish with long pale hairs. Antennae reddish-brown, only terminal flagellar segments and extreme apex of segment 3 black. Basal two segments sometimes slightly greyish dusted and always black haired, dorsal tooth to segment 3 rectangular. Palpi yellowish, rather slender and pointed at tip, clothed with short, densely set pale hairs, sometimes with several black hairs.

Thorax blackish-brown, mesonotum and scutellum with pale and black hairs, pleura greyish dusted and with densely set paler hairs. *Legs:* Coxae and femora blackish-grey with pale hairs, femora brownish at tip. Tibiae and tarsi mostly yellowish, fore tibiae at tip and fore tarsi darkened, apical tarsal segments on posterior two pairs nearly black. *Wings* clear or very slightly greyish clouded, somewhat yellowish along costal margin and especially in costal cell, slightly brownish to yellowish at base. No appendix to vein R_4. Halteres brownish-yellow.

Abdomen rather broad, anterior three tergites brown to chestnut-brown, with a broader, shining black median stripe on tergites 2 and 3, apical segments shining black. The pale pubescence on posterior margins of all tergites forms on posterior tergites more or less distinct paler median triangular spots. Anterior three to four sternites yellowish-brown, sternite 2 sometimes with central greyish spot, apical sternites dark grey with pale posterior margins.

♂. Eyes bare, unstriped, meeting for a long distance; all facets of the same size. Occiput with only short pale hairs. Antennal segment 3 very slender, generally darker coloured than in the female and with distinct but small dorsal tooth near base. Segment 1 usually mostly blackish-grey. Palpi brownish-yellow, apical segment oval, twice as long as deep, clothed with longer pale hairs, apex with mostly black hairs. Legs are darker than in the female; coxae, femora and tarsi predominantly black, fore tibiae brownish towards base only. Abdomen rather slender, otherwise as in the female.

Length. 14—19 mm.

VARIABILITY. The brown lateral spots on tergites 1 to 3 vary from a reddish-brown to a dark chestnut-brown colour. The black median stripe is very wide in some specimens, occupying nearly one-third of the tergites; also the intensity of the pale median triangles on posterior tergites is variable.

DATES. July and August.

DISTRIBUTION. A species with a large area of distribution. Known from Portugal and Spain through France and Italy to as far as South East Europe, Turkey and Transcaucasus, sometimes rather a common species. *P. aprica* (Meig.) has been recorded from all countries of Central Europe (Switzerland, Austria, Hungary, Czechoslovakia, Poland and Germany), the northern border of its occurrence lies in Belgium (Leclercq, 1967a), and from all countries of South East Europe. Its occurrence in Iran (Olsufjev, 1937) has not been recently verified. It is a typical species of hilly countries but is known also from mountains at an altitude of about 2000 m, e. g. Rila

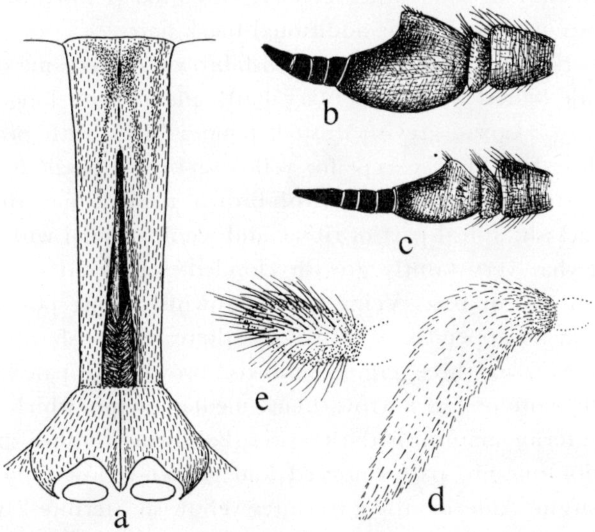

Fig. 155. *Philipomyia aprica* (Meig.), a. female frons, b. female antenna, c. male antenna, d. female palpus, e. male palpus.

Planina 2000 m (Gregor), Sierra Alba 1800 m and Alpes Maritimes 2000 m (Hesselbarth), Bases Alpes 2250 m (Leclercq).

PHILIPOMYIA GRAECA (FABRICIUS, 1794)

Fig. 156.

Tabanus graecus Fabricius, 1794, Ent. Syst., 4: 368.
Tabanus ferrugineus Meigen, 1820, Syst. Beschr., 2: 60.
Tabanus infusus Walker, 1851, Ins. Saunders. Dipt., 1: 23.
Tabanus segmentarius Brullé, 1832, Expéd. Sci. Morée, 3: 304.
Tabanus propinquus Palm, 1875, Verh. zool.-bot. Ges. Wien, 25: 411.

Diagnosis. Medium-sized, golden-yellow pubescent species resembling *Philipomyia aprica* (Meig.) but antennae paler, rather orange-yellow on segment 3, which bears a large, hooked dorsal tooth directed forwards. Sides of anterior three tergites more yellowish-brown with narrower black median stripe.

Description. ♀. *Head.* Eyes bare, unstriped. Frons, subcallus and face yellowish-brown dusted; frons parallel-sided, index 1: 4—5.5, golden-yellow pubescent with some black hairs. Both frontal calli joined, club-shaped and shining black. Face and cheeks with longer golden-yellow hairs. Antennae orange-yellow to yellowish-brown, only terminal flagellar segments (sometimes only apically) dark. Basal two segments with short black hairs, segment 1 sometimes greyish dusted. Segment 3 rather broad with very distinct, apically pointed, hooked dorsal tooth, which is directed forwards. Palpi yellowish-brown, long and rather slender, somewhat pointed at tip; golden-yellow pubescent or with some additional black hairs.

Thorax dark brown, entirely yellowish-brown dusted, mesonotum and scutellum pale haired with some black hairs, pleura with longer yellowish-grey hairs. *Legs:* Coxae greyish dusted, femora black with predominantly pale hairs; fore legs black except for yellowish-brown basal third of tibiae. Tibiae on posterior two pairs yellowish-brown, tip of tibiae and tarsi dark brown to blackish; apical part of tibiae and whole of tarsi with black hairs. *Wings* somewhat very faintly greyish clouded, somewhat yellowish along costal margin and at base. Veins black, brownish along posterior margin and near base; no appendix to vein R_4. Halteres yellowish.

Abdomen. Anterior three tergites yellowish-brown with pale hairs, tergites 2 and 3 with more or less narrow, black median stripe, which is more distinct near anterior margin of the tergites. Following tergites shining black along anterior margin, pale coloured and golden-yellow pubescent along posterior margin. Anterior three sternites yellowish, sternite 2 with greyish median spot, following sternites greyish; all sternites with only short, pale greyish hairs.

♂. Eyes meeting for a long distance, all facets nearly of the same size; occiput with short pale hairs. Antennae narrower, yellowish-brown, only terminal flagellar segments dark. Palpi yellowish-brown with longer black hairs, oval shaped, about twice as long as deep. Abdomen yellowish-brown on tergites 1 to 3 (or to 4) with very narrow black median stripe, which is often interrupted on posterior margins of each tergite. Following tergites shining black, only narrowly pale pubescent along posterior margins. Otherwise as in the female.

Length. 14–20 mm.

VARIABILITY. The black median stripe on tergites 1 to 3 in female varies from rather broad, occupying nearly one-third of the tergite, to a very narrow and sometimes interrupted stripe as in the male sex. The width of frontal stripe in female is also rather variable.

Leclercq (1967a: 41) described very briefly a ssp. *zizaniae* from the Asiatic part of Turkey. The value of this subspecies is very problematic since Leclercq does not treat *aprica* and *graeca* as distinct species.

DATES. From May until July.

DISTRIBUTION. A Mediterranean species known from Spain to as far as Turkey, not yet recorded from Portugal. In South West Europe it is recorded from France and Italy; a very common species in South East Europe (Alba-

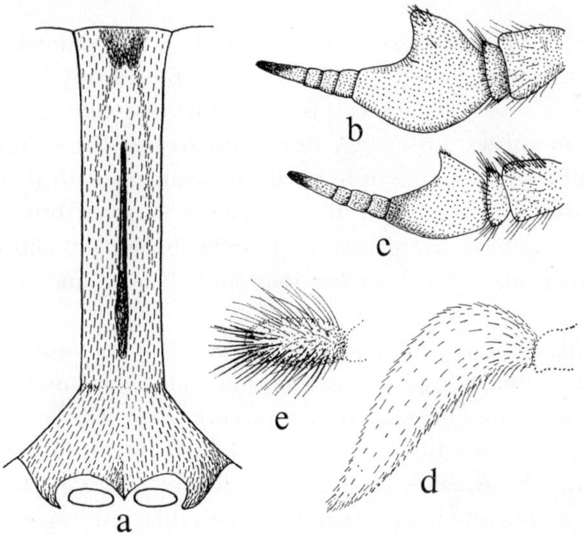

Fig. 156. *Philipomyia graeca* (F.), a. female frons, b. female antenna, c. male antenna, d. female palpus, e. male palpus.

nia, Jugoslavia, Greece, Bulgaria), where it occurs also at higher altitudes (e. g. Kožuf Planina, Macedonia 1400 m, J. Thurner). Both the nominate form and the ssp. *zizaniae* Lecl. are known from Turkey. The north border of the area of distribution of this species lies in Central Europe, from where it is recorded from Switzerland, Austria, Hungary and Czechoslovakia. In the last mentioned country *graeca* occurs only in South Slovakia, inhabiting the very dry localities in the warmest regions along the Donau river, quite unlike those localities inhabited by *aprica* (Meig.), which are margins of forests, forest clearing, etc. *P. graeca* is not yet recorded from the U.S.S.R. There are some literary records from Germany (Kröber, 1932b; Leclercq, 1967a) but we did not succeed in finding this species either in nature or in any existing collections; the species should be deleted in the meantime from the list of German species.

PHILIPOMYIA ROHDENDORFI (OLSUFJEV, 1937)

Fig. 157.

Tabanus rohdendorfi Olsufjev, 1937, Fauna SSSR, 7: 291, 415.

DIAGNOSIS. Resembling *Philipomyia aprica* (Meig.) but differs in the entirely black antennal segment 3, in the longer pale greyish hairs on face, and in the darker coloured abdomen. Sternites are unicolorous blackish-grey in female.

DESCRIPTION. ♀. *Head.* Eyes bare, unstriped. Frons yellowish-grey, hardly widening out towards vertex, index 1: 4—4.5. Both frontal calli joined into a club-shaped, shining black callus. Subcallus and face greyish-yellow dusted, face and cheeks with long, fine, pale greyish hairs. Antennae black, only segment 2 slightly brownish, basal two segments with short black hairs, segment 1 also with some pale hairs, segment 3 rather broad with rectangular dorsal tooth as in *aprica.* Palpi yellowish-brown, short pale haired and with some black hairs, rather long and slender, and somewhat blunt ended.

Thorax. Mesonotum and scutellum shining blackish-brown coloured and mostly black haired, margins of mesonotum and pleura covered with greyish dust and more dense, longer pale pubescence. *Legs:* Coxae black with grey dusting, femora mostly black, sometimes slightly brownish at tip, fore tibiae on basal third brownish, apical two-thirds and fore tarsi black. Posterior four tibiae yellowish-brown, tarsi brown to blackish-brown. Legs mostly pale haired, coxae and femora with much longer hairs. *Wings* clear or very slightly greyish clouded, veins dark brown, brownish on basal half of wing;

wings very slightly yellowish along costal margin and near base, no appendix to vein R_4. Halteres brown.

Abdomen broad, flat and blunt ended, anterior two tergites brown to chestnut-brown at sides with golden-yellow hairs. The black median stripe is not sharply separated from the brown coloration, occupying about one-third of the tergites. Tergite 3 slightly brownish only on posterior margin, following tergites black with distinct pale haired posterior margins. Sternites unicolorous blackish-grey, mostly with pale greyish hairs and with pale posterior margins.

♂. Eyes bare and unstriped, facets equal in size. Vertex with short pale hairs. Antennal segment 3 more slender than in the female and likewise black. Palpi oval shaped, brown, with black and grey hairs. Abdomen pointed, the brown lateral spots on tergites 1 to 3 are only very narrowly separated by a black median stripe, following tergites shining black with pale hairs on posterior margins. Anterior three sternites brownish-yellow, sternite 2 with large greyish median spot, posterior sternites black with paler posterior margins.

Length. 16–19 mm.

Dates. July and August.

Distribution. The species has been described from the Caucasus including its promontory, the region of Kuban, and is supposed to be an endemic species in the Caucasus.

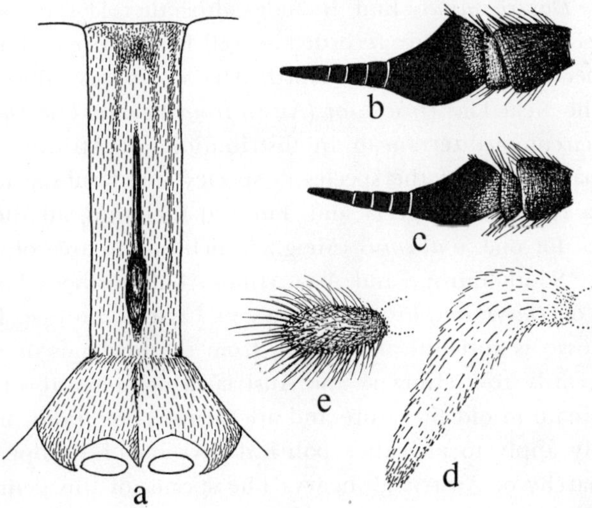

Fig. 157. *Philipomyia rohdendorfi* (Ols.), a. female frons, b. female antenna, c. male antenna, d. female palpus, e. male palpus.

GENUS *DASYRHAMPHIS* ENDERLEIN, 1922

Mitt. zool. Mus. Berl., 10: 346.

Efflatounanus Philip, 1948, Bull. Soc. Fouad I. Ent., 37: 79.

Type species: *Tabanus ater* Rossi, 1790.

Diagnosis. Medium-sized to large, mostly robust blackish species with more or less clouded wings. Eyes usually at least microscopically pubescent, facets in males at most slightly differentiated, never sharply separated in parts with small and large facets. Frons in female rather narrower with well developed calli. Proboscis about as long as head is high. Basicosta bare, antennal segment 3 with more or less developed dorsal tooth.

Remarks. The type species of the genus belongs to a group of species with a very large, forward pointed, hooked dorsal tooth. Philip (1948) separated the species with small, tabanine-like dorsal tooth on antennal segment 3 and proposed for them the genus *Efflatounanus* with *Tabanus alexandrinus* Wied. (syn. of *Tabanus nigritus* F.) as type species. We do not separate the genus *Efflatounanus* Philip as distinct from *Dasyrhamphis* End. since almost the same situation is found, for example, in the genus *Tabanus* L. (a group of large Asiatic *Tabanus* species have the same type of very hooked antennae as in *Dasyrhamphis* s. str.) but this problem will need to be solved in the future.

The genus *Dasyrhamphis* End. includes altogether 11 species and 1 subspecies, 8 species of which are recorded as well from Europe. The three non European species are known from North Africa (*villosus* (Macq.), *goleanus* (Szil.)) and the Near East (*insecutor* (Aust.) from Israel). The *Dasyrhamphis* species are circummediterranean in distribution on African, Asiatic and European coasts. Most of the species (9 species and 1 subspecies) occur in North Africa (Morocco, Algeria and Tunisia) including all the European species except for one, *umbrinus* (Meig.), which has an area of distribution covering only South Europe and Asia Minor. The northern border of the distribution of *Dasyrhamphis* species lies in Central Europe, from where only *ater* (Rossi) is authentically known from the lowlands of Switzerland. The other records from Hungary and Austria, which refer also to *umbrinus* (Meig.), originate in old literature and are misinterpretations, because they very probably apply to an ealier political division of Europe, namely to the old monarchy of Austria-Hungary. The species of this genus have not been found in the European part of the U.S.S.R., and only *umbrinus* (Meig.) is recorded from its Asiatic part (Transcaucasus, Turkmenia).

Nothing is known of biology and life history of *Dasyrhamphis* species but the adults (especially males) are often to be found on flowers, sometimes in large numbers.

Key to European species of *Dasyrhamphis*

1 Legs bicoloured, tibiae brownish. Palpi greyish dusted and short pale haired .... *tomentosus* (Macq.)

– Legs unicolorous black, palpi black with black hairs 2

2 (1) Antennal segment 3 with marked excision and a very long, pointed dorsal tooth directed forward 3

– Antennal segment 3 with less developed, at most only rectangular dorsal tooth, without any excision *(Efflatounanus* Phil.) 4

3 (2) Subcallus entirely shining black in ♀, sometimes extensively dusted in ♂. Wings uniformly dark brown clouded; squamae dark with very darkened margin and black fringes. Generally larger species, 14–18.5 mm .. *ater* (Rossi)

– Subcallus in both sexes shining black only mesally. Wings brownish clouded, central part from base to apex of discal cell semihyaline. Squamae somewhat yellowish with pale fringes. Generally smaller species, 14–16.5 mm .... *anthracinus* (Meig.)

4 (2) Subcallus entirely polished black or blackish-brown; if dusted at sides *(umbrinus)* then wings mostly clear and antennae slender on segment 3 5

– Subcallus entirely dusted; if somewhat polished at middle *(algirus)* then wings uniformly brownish and antennae with distinct and rather pointed dorsal tooth 7

5 (4) Wings clear with distinct dark brown patch close to anterior margin at middle and near base of discal cell. Subcallus often largely dusted at sides .... *umbrinus* (Meig.)

– Wings more or less uniformly brown clouded, subcallus always entirely polished 6

6 (5) Wings in male rather clear, in female dark brown clouded with hyaline area at apex between veins R_4 and R_5, and along posterior margin. Frons in female broader, index 1: 3, lower callus narrowly separated from the eye-margins .... *nigritus* (F.)

– Wings uniformly dark brown clouded in both sexes, without any hyaline areas. Frons in female narrower, index about 1: 4, lower callus touching the eye-margins .... *carbonarius* (Meig.)

7 (4) Pubescence on mesonotum pale. Abdomen black with anterior two tergites thinly greyish dusted and pale haired, apical two segments with pale hairs; rest of abdomen black haired .... *algirus* (Macq.)

– Mesonotum black haired with some greyish hairs. Abdomen black with concolorous hairs, posterior margin on tergites 1–5 at sides, and on tergite 6–8 on the whole length, yellowish haired .... *denticornis* (End.)

DASYRHAMPHIS ATER (ROSSI, 1790)

Fig. 158; pl. 4: fig. c.

Tabanus ater Rossi, 1790, Fauna Etrusca, 2: 320.
Tabanus ater Meigen, 1820, Syst. Beschr., 2: 32 (nom. nov. for *T. morio* L. sensu F.).
Tabanus fuscatus Macquart, 1826, Ins. Dipt. Nord Fr., 2: 152.
Tabanus transiens Walker, 1848, List Dipt. Brit. Mus., 1: 174.

DIAGNOSIS. Large blackish species, with antennae, palpi and legs entirely black. Antennal segment 3 with a large, hooked, forward pointed dorsal tooth, subcallus often entirely shining black. Thorax more or less greyish pubescent, wings nearly uniformly dark brown clouded.

DESCRIPTION. ♀. *Head.* Frons rather broad, index about 1: 3.5, slightly widening below; pale greyish dusted and black haired. Calli shining black, lower callus large, touching the eye-margins, and broadly connected with elongated median callus. Subcallus entirely polished black or blackish-brown, often extensively dulled at sides. Face and cheeks dull black with concolorous hairs. Antennae black, basal two segments with short black hairs, segment 3 with a very acute and forward prolonged dorsal tooth. Palpi black with short black hairs, only slightly stouter at base, rather blunt ended.

Thorax black, mesonotum and scutellum dark greyish dusted and clothed with dense but short pale grey hairs, usually also with some black hairs. Pleura densely black haired. *Legs* black with concolorous hairs. *Wings* entirely dark brown clouded, sometimes with indefinite semihyaline areas near apex, along posterior margin or in discal cell. No appendix to vein R_4. Squamae black with black hairs, halteres blackish-brown.

Abdomen shining black and mostly black haired, tergite 1 on posterior margin at sides and following tergites on posterior margins at middle with greyish hairs, apical one or two tergites paler haired.

♂. The facets on lower third somewhat smaller but not sharply separated from the upper two-thirds. Postocular margin with short black hairs becoming longer towards middle. Antennal segment 3 very slender but with a very well developed pointed and forward directed dorsal tooth. Palpi black, apical segment shortly oval, about one and one half times as long as deep, with longer black hairs. Thorax, legs and wings as in the female but mesonotum and scutellum mostly black haired. Abdomen with pale greyish pubescence on posterior margins usually only at sides.

Length. 15–20 mm.

Variability. The pubescence on mesonotum and scutellum varies in females from very whitish-grey to nearly black, similarly as in the males. Abdomen often uniformly black haired without any paler triangles at middle to each tergite. The wings are mostly uniformly dark brown clouded with only an indication of somewhat paler area near apex of wing, but in some specimens (especially from Spain) the posterior wing margin is nearly hyaline.

Dates. From May until August.

Distribution. *D. ater* (Rossi) is, together with *umbrinus* (Meig.), one of the species of this genus with a wider area of distribution. It has been recorded from North Africa (Morocco, Algeria), from Turkey (Dardanelles) and from all countries of South and South East Europe from Portugal to as far as Greece. The northern border of the area of distribution lies in Central Europe in Switzerland and North Jugoslavia. The literary records from Hungary and Rumania were not confirmed by new findings. *D. ater* (Rossi) has been collected also on the islands of Sardinia and Corsica, including some smaller islands along the Jugoslavian coast; often a very common species, e. g. in South France.

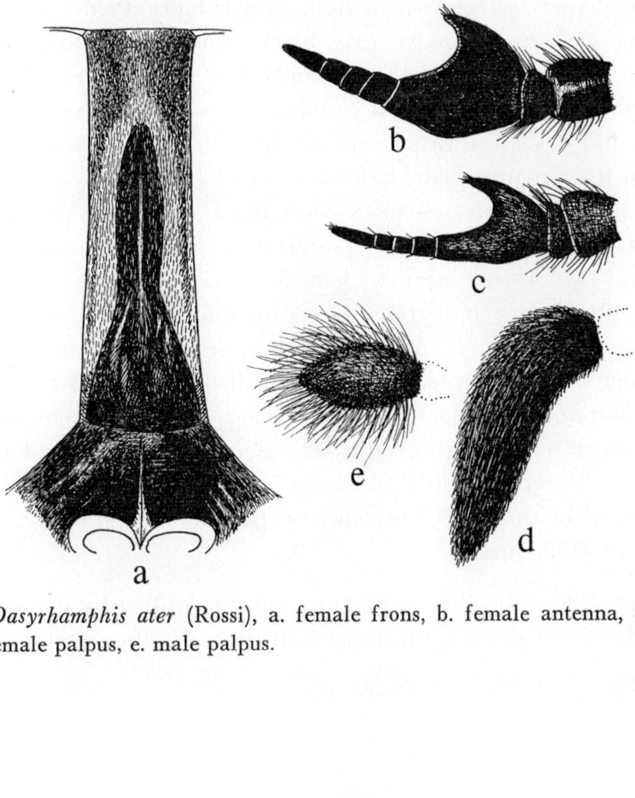

Fig. 158. *Dasyrhamphis ater* (Rossi), a. female frons, b. female antenna, c. male antenna, d. female palpus, e. male palpus.

DASYRHAMPHIS ANTHRACINUS (MEIGEN, 1820)

Fig. 159.

Tabanus anthracinus Meigen, 1820, Syst. Beschr., 2: 36.
Tabanus corsicanus Macquart, 1883, Revue Ent., 2: 216.
Tabanus obscurus Loew, 1858, Verh. zool.-bot. Ges. Wien, 8: 612.
Tabanus atropos Jaennicke, 1866, Berl. ent. Z., 10: 87.

DIAGNOSIS. Medium-sized black species with antennae, palpi and legs black. Antennal segment 3 with a large, forwards directed, hook-like dorsal tooth. Subcallus dulled, on the upper half sometimes polished black. Wings faintly brownish clouded, hyaline in central part.

DESCRIPTION. ♀. *Head.* Eyes with fine microscopic pubescence. Frons and face black in ground colour, more or less dark grey dusted. Frons parallel-sided, index about 1: 3—3.5, lower callus polished black, usually not touching the eye-margin, broadly connected with a slender polished median callus. Subcallus convex, mostly dulled, sometimes polished above. Face and cheeks with longer greyish-brown hairs. Antennae black, basal two segments short black pubescent, segment 3 sometimes brownish near base, with distinct, pointed, forward hooked dorsal tooth as in *ater* (Rossi). Palpi black, finely black haired, rather long and slender.

Thorax black, slightly shining, mesonotum rather dulled and clothed with short, densely set greyish to light brown hairs. Pleura and scutellum with longer dark brown hairs. *Legs* black; femora with long, other parts with short, dark grey to black hairs, only fore coxae anteriorly with long greyish hairs. *Wings* light brown clouded, subhyaline in central part, both basal cells and discal cell often entirely clear. Veins dark brown, no appendix to vein R_4. Squamae pale, halteres blackish-brown.

Abdomen mostly polished black with black hairs, the pale pubescence forming on each tergite a narrow posterior border and a small median triangle, apical two or three sternites with paler hairs.

♂. Eyes short dark pubescent, facets on lower third smaller. Subcallus rather silvery-grey dusted. Antennae black, segment 3 usually brownish, more slender than in the female but with distinct pointed dorsal tooth of the same shape as in the female. Palpi black, apical segment oval shaped and only short haired. Wings and legs as in the female, abdomen black with tergites 2 and 3 slightly brownish at sides, otherwise with the same pattern caused by the pale pubescence on posterior margins.

Length. 14—16.5 mm.

VARIABILITY. The subcallus varies from entirely dulled by silvery-grey dust to distinctly polished black on upper half, and also the intensity of brownish clouding on wings is rather variable. The median part of wing is sometimes only very slightly translucent in some specimens, in others entirely clear; the darker posterior wing-margin is, however, always distinct.

DATES. May and June.

DISTRIBUTION. A West Mediterranean species known from North Africa (Morocco, Algeria) but above all from South Europe both from the Continent and the islands. It has been recorded from South France, Italy, Greece and from the islands of Sicily, Sardinia and Corsica.

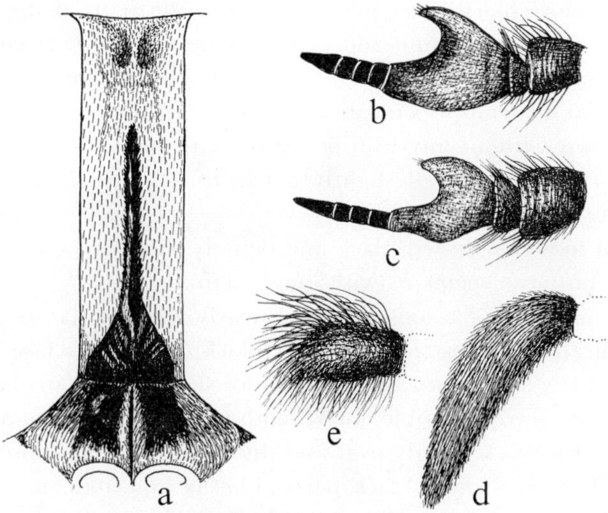

Fig. 159. *Dasyrhamphis anthracinus* (Meig.), a. female frons, b. female antenna, c. male antenna, d. female palpus, e. male palpus.

DASYRHAMPHIS CARBONARIUS (MEIGEN, 1820)

Fig. 160.

Tabanus carbonarius Meigen, 1820, Syst. Beschr., 2: 33.
Tabanus gagates Loew, 1858, Verh. zool.-bot. Ges. Wien, 8: 609.

DIAGNOSIS. Medium-sized to larger, shining black species. Wings unicolorous dark brown clouded. Antennae black, segment 3 slightly brownish, palpi and legs black. Subcallus entirely polished black, frons rather narrower.

DESCRIPTION. ♀. *Head.* Eyes naked, frons parallel-sided, narrower than in other species of the genus, index about 1: 4; frons nearly entirely polished black with hardly distinguishable frontal calli. Lower callus rectangular and touching the eye-margins, median callus elongated and more wrinkled. Subcallus rather convex and polished black as face and cheeks, which bear rather long and fine black hairs. Occiput more or less whitish-grey dusted, especially on posterior ocular margin, and with very short black hairs becoming more numerous and longer below. Basal antennal segments black and blackish pubescent, segment 3 somewhat brownish, blackish towards tip and on terminal flagellar segments, more slender than in *nigritus* (F.), with a small, blunt dorsal tooth. Palpi black and with short blackish hairs, somewhat thickened on basal third and pointed apically.

Thorax entirely black except for the brownish humeral calli, rather shiny, with short black hairs on mesonotum, the hairs being longer and more numerous on scutellum and especially on pleura. *Legs* entirely black and somewhat shiny, with dense, short black pubescence, only fore coxae anteriorly and all femora beneath with long black hairs. *Wings* intensively blackish-brown without any hyaline areas, veins blackish. No appendix to vein R_4. First posterior cell slightly narrower towards tip. Squamae dark brown, halteres blackish-brown.

Abdomen mostly polished black and densely short black pubescent, lateral parts of posterior segments with longer hairs.

♂. Eyes meeting for a long distance, nearly bare, all facets about equal in size. Subcallus convex and polished black, as well as face and cheeks which bear long dark hairs. Antennae more slender than in the female on segment 3, with scarcely visible dorsal tooth near base, segment 3 extensively brownish. Palpi black, longly oval and distinctly pointed, more than twice as long as deep, with long black hairs. Thorax and abdomen with longer and more dense black hairs. Wings very intensively blackish-brown as in the female, only along posterior margin indistinctly paler, but still smoky brownish. Otherwise as in the female.

Length. 16–18 mm.

Synonymy. *D. carbonarius* (Meig.) has for a long time been known and recorded in the literature under the name of *D. nigritus* (F.) with *D. carbonarius* as a synonym. This mistake was originally caused by Meigen (1820) who, without seeing the Fabrician type material, made a revision of this complicated group of species only on the basis of inadequate and incorrect notes on the Fabrician material sent to him by Wiedemann. The synonymy of this species has been fully discussed by Chvála & Lyneborg (1970) and as a result, the originally »literary« name *carbonarius* Meig. has been adopted for this species by the action of selecting a neotype female from Adapazari, Turkey.

Dates. May and June.

DISTRIBUTION. A rather rare species known so far authentically from Tunisia, North Africa, and from Turkey, Syria and Israel. All other records from North Africa and Europe (Bulgaria, Italy) need to be verified.

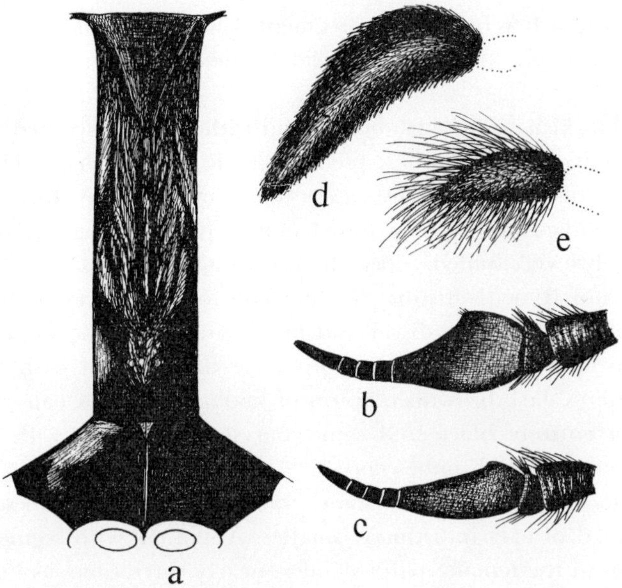

Fig. 160. *Dasyrhamphis carbonarius* (Meig.), a. female frons, b. female antenna, c. male antenna, d. female palpus, e. male palpus.

DASYRHAMPHIS NIGRITUS (FABRICIUS, 1794)

Fig. 161.

Tabanus nigritus Fabricius, 1794, Ent. Syst., 4: 367.
Tabanus alexandrinus Wiedemann, 1830, Aussereur. zweifl. Ins., 2: 624.
Tabanus carbonatus Macquart, 1834, Hist. nat. Dipt., 1: 199.
Sziladya apicalis Enderlein, 1925, Mitt. zool. Mus. Berl., 11: 367.

DIAGNOSIS. Medium-sized blackish species with subcallus polished black, and antennae, palpi and legs entirely black. Antennal segment 3 with a very small dorsal tooth. Wings dark brown clouded with a hyaline area in apex of wing between the veins R_4 and R_5, and often with further hyaline areas along posterior margin and at base.

DESCRIPTION. ♀. *Head.* Eyes with scarcely visible minute pale hairs. Frons rather broad, index about 1: 3, mostly more or less polished black with scarcely differentiated, large lower callus, which is connected with a narrow median callus. Occiput somewhat shiny blackish-brown, covered with dense, dark brown, short pubescence. Subcallus rather low and as well as face and cheeks polished black or blackish-brown, lower part of face with longer dark brown hairs. Antennae entirely black, basal two segments with greyish tomentum and a few black hairs; segment 3 with a distinct but blunt dorsal tooth. Palpi blackish-brown, apical segment long and slender, shortly pubescent.

Thorax blackish to blackish-brown and rather shiny, covered with small fine black hairs on mesonotum; pleura with long black hairs. Humeri and postalar calli distinctly brownish. *Legs* black, more or less shiny and exclusively black pubescent, anterior four femora with fine longer hairs beneath. *Wings* dark brown clouded, especially on costal half, apex of wing between fork of R_4 and R_5 with distinct hyaline spot, other hyaline or semihyaline areas are often present in discal and both basal cells, and along posterior margin. No appendix to vein R_4. Squamae dark brown with long black fringes, halteres dark brownish, apices of knobs sometimes paler.

Abdomen entirely black and somewhat shiny, covered with short, but rather densely set, black pubescence.

♂. Eyes meeting for a short distance, rather densely pale pubescent, facets on lower third of eyes indistinctly smaller. Antennae with segment 3 more slender than in the female; palpi slender, nearly three times as long as deep and long blackish pubescent. Mesonotum and especially pleura with longer and more dense black hairs, anterior part of mesonotum with a few whitish hairs intermixed. Wings rather clear with brown veins, only brownish clouded on costal half and especially along longitudinal veins.

Length. 12–16 mm.

SYNONYMY. *D. nigritus* (F.) has for a long time been well known under the name of *alexandrinus* (Wied.) with the rather well known *apicalis* (Meig.) as a junior synonym. On the other hand, the species which is recorded here as *carbonarius* (Meig.) has been erroneously named by all authors as *nigritus* (F.). Only as a result of the revision of the Fabrician type material of *Tabanus nigritus* and the selection of a lectotype (see Chvála & Lyneborg, 1970), is the Fabrician *nigritus* now correctly recognized.

BIOLOGY. The adults have been observed in Algeria on *Ferula communis* L., *Ferula vesceritensis* Coss., *Chrysanthemum segetum* L., *Chrysanthemum coronarium* L., *Anacyclus elevatus* Pers. and *Astericus maritimus* Moench.

DATES. April and May.

DISTRIBUTION. A typical species of the South and East Mediterranean, having a wide area of distribution from Morocco, Algeria and Tunisia through Libya and Egypt to as far as Israel and Syria. In Europe it is recorded from Spain, France and Italy including Sicily, but some of these records need verification inasmuch as misidentification by older authors is possible.

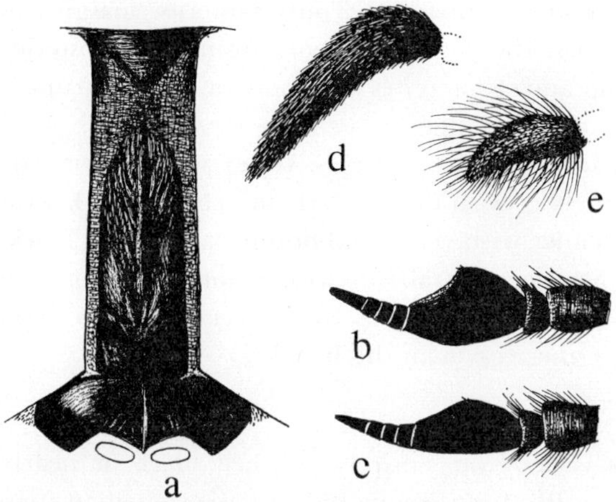

Fig. 161. *Dasyrhamphis nigritus* (F.), a. female frons, b. female antenna, c. male antenna, d. female palpus, e. male palpus.

DASYRHAMPHIS UMBRINUS (MEIGEN, 1820)

Fig. 162.

Tabanus umbrinus Meigen, 1820, Syst. Beschr., 2: 35.
Tabanus istriensis Meigen, 1820, Syst. Beschr., 2: 36.
Tabanus maculipennis Brullé, 1832, Exped. Sci. Morée, 3: 305.
Sziladya atavina Enderlein, 1925, Mitt. zool. Mus. Berl., 11: 368.

Diagnosis. Medium-sized to smaller, blackish species with greyish pattern. Antennae, palpi and legs black, antennal segment 3 with only a small dorsal tooth. Subcallus extensively polished black; wings clear, with brown pattern at anterior margin.

Description. ♀. *Head.* Frons greyish dusted, rather broad, index about 1: 2,5, slightly narrowed towards vertex. Frontal calli shining black, lower callus triangular shaped, not reaching the eye-margins and very broadly connected with oval median callus. Subcallus polished black, sometimes dull grey at sides. Face and cheeks dark grey dusted with pale hairs. Antennae black, segment 3 with only slightly developed, blunt dorsal tooth. Palpi blackish-grey, clothed with sparse black hairing, long and rather slender.

Thorax black in ground colour, mesonotum and scutellum short black pubescent, former with whitish-grey hairs at sides. Pleura with longer yellowish-grey hairs. *Legs* entirely black and short black haired, only fore coxae anteriorly with longer pale hairs. *Wings* mostly clear, slightly brownish near base, along anterior margin and in central part behind discal cell. Both basal cells and discal cell always clear, at most very slightly yellowish. Veins dark brown, no appendix to vein R_4. Halteres blackish-brown.

Abdomen black with short black pubescence, only posterior margins to all tergites with pale grey hairs; the pale pubescence forms pale posterior margins which are broader on anterior tergites and more or less interrupted at middle, forming distinct median triangles.

♂. Facets slightly smaller on lower third of eyes, vertex with longer pale hairs. Subcallus black and finely greyish dusted, face and cheeks black with pale hairs. Antennae more slender with very small dorsal tooth. Palpi black, rather small and slender, apical segment about twice as long as deep, with longer black hairs. Thorax more densely pubescent, especially the hairs on mesonotum long and black. Otherwise as in the female.

Length. 11–16 mm.

Variability. The subcallus varies from entirely polished black or nearly brown to mostly dulled by greyish dust, leaving only a narrow median strip polished. The wings are in some specimens also nearly clear along anterior margin.

Dates. From May until July.

Distribution. A very widely distributed species known from the East Mediterranean, eastwards as far as Turkey, Israel, Lebanon and Iran. It is known also from the Asiatic part of the U.S.S.R. from Transcaucasus and Turkme-

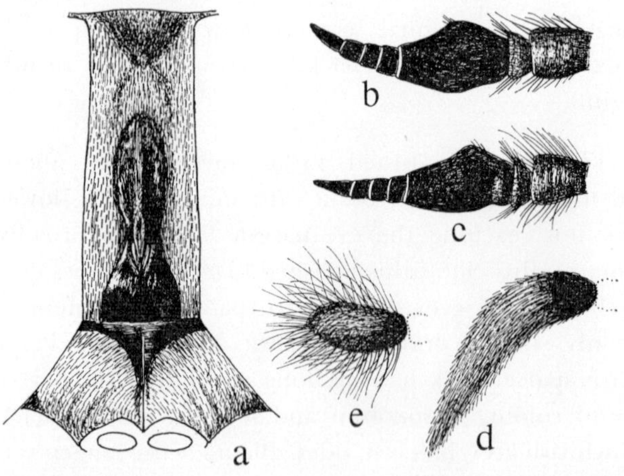

Fig. 162. *Dasyrhamphis umbrinus* (Meig.), a. female frons, b. female antenna, c. male antenna, d. female palpus, e. male palpus.

nian SSR (Askhabad, Karakala) where it is the only representative of the genus. Not recorded from North Africa. The northern border of its area of distribution lies in North Jugoslavia (Istria). The records from Austria given first by Brauer (1880) are, as with *ater* (Rossi), mistakes, since at that time Dalmatia was also a part of the Austrian-Hungarian empire. Moucha observed this species to be very common in Albania (surroundings of Durrës), where both males and females have been collected in large numbers on flowers.

DASYRHAMPHIS TOMENTOSUS (MACQUART, 1845)

Fig. 163.

Tabanus tomentosus Macquart, 1846, Dipt. exot., Suppl. 1: 30.
Tabanus apiarius Jaennicke, 1866, Berl. ent. Z., 10: 68.
Atylotus Letourneuxi Bigot, 1892, Mém. Soc. zool. Fr., 5: 643.

DIAGNOSIS. Medium-sized greyish haired species, with brownish-yellow tinted wings. The only European species of the genus with bicoloured legs, all tibiae being brownish-yellow, other parts of legs black.

DESCRIPTION. ♀. *Head.* Frons pale greyish dusted, rather broader, index 1: 3, parallel-sided. Frontal calli shining black, lower callus rather small, triangular shaped and broadly connected with a narrow median callus. Occiput including postocular margin with only very short pale hairs. Subcallus dulled by pale greyish dust; face and cheeks light grey, with long pale hairs. Basal antennal segments greyish dusted and short pale haired. Segment 3 blackish-brown on basal half, black towards apex, very broad with a distinct rectangular dorsal tooth. Palpi blackish-grey with greyish dusting and short pale hairs, long, slightly thickened at base.

Thorax black in ground colour, mesonotum slightly greyish dusted and short pale haired, pleura more intensively greyish dusted and with longer yellowish-grey hairs. *Legs:* Coxae and femora blackish-grey, pale haired; all tibiae yellowish-brown, darkened at tip, fore tarsi and tip of fore tibiae blackish, posterior four tarsi blackish-brown to black. *Wings* very slightly yellowish to yellowish-brown tinted, more intensively along anterior margin. Veins brown, somewhat yellowish near base and along anterior margin, no appendix to vein R_4. Halteres yellowish-brown, knob darkened.

Abdomen black, dorsum thinly greyish dusted and short pale haired, sternites more yellowish-grey dusted with narrow paler posterior margins.

♂. Eyes with short pale hairs, facets on the lower third of eyes smaller and more or less distinctly separated from the upper part. Vertex with long yellowish-grey hairs. Subcallus dulled, pale yellowish-grey dusted and distinctly convex. Face and cheeks with long greyish-yellow hairs. Antennae black except for brownish base of segment 3, which is distintly narrower than in the female. Palpi dark with greyish tomentum, apical segment short and slender, hardly twice as long as deep, pointed and clothed with long pale hairs. Thorax long greyish-yellow haired, mesonotum with some additional black hairs. Legs and wings as in the female. Abdomen with longer pale hairs, segment 2 (or also 3) sometimes slightly brownish at sides.

Length. 12–15 mm.

DATES. May and June.

DISTRIBUTION. A North African species known from Morocco, Algeria and Tunisia, from where it penetrates to Provence, South France.

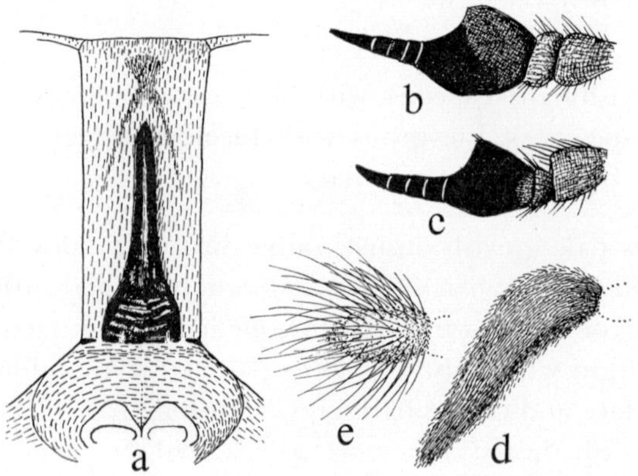

Fig. 163. *Dasyrhamphis tomentosus* (Macq.), a. female frons, b. female antenna, c. male antenna, d. female palpus, e. male palpus.

DASYRHAMPHIS DENTICORNIS (ENDERLEIN, 1925)

Sziladya denticornis Enderlein, 1925, Mitt. zool. Mus. Berl., 11: 367.

The species is in fact still known only from the original description given by Enderlein. Other authors (e. g. Kröber, 1925a; Leclercq, 1961, 1967a) based their data on *denticornis* (End.) on the original description or repeated it in full. We have not seen the type material or any other specimens which could belong to this species and, therefore, we present only the translation of the original description:

»♂♀. The distinctions from *S. alexandrinus* (Wied., 1830) are as follows: Antennal segment 3 above with very strong, somewhat pointed forward tooth. Wings slightly brown clouded, costal and subcostal cells light brown.

Head with whitish-grey tomentum, dark grey pubescence, frons with shorter whitish hairs. Mesonotum thinly greyish dusted, abdomen still more thinly. Mesonotum with some grey hairs among black hairing. Some sparse and short yellowish hairs at sides on posterior margins to tergites, the hairs are more numerous and cover the whole posterior margin on tergites 6, 7 and 8. Second segment of palpi somewhat greyish dusted, in the female broad and hardly pointed. Body larger and stouter.

Body length ♂ 14.5 mm, ♀ 16 mm. Wing length ♂ 13.5 mm, ♀ 15.5 mm. Südspanien, Prov. Constantine, Algeciras, gesammelt von G. Seitz«.

DISTRIBUTION. Described from South Spain from »Constantine« and Algeciras, new records are not available. Kröber (1938) and Leclercq (1961, 1967a) also recorded this species from Algeria, probably considering the original »Constantine« to be the Algerian Constantine. One can, however, doubt this decision, since Enderlein could have recorded in the original description the true South Spanish Constantina. We have seen a pair labelled »Sardinia: Macromer. June 1931. Mrs. O. Grey. B. M. 1932–62« sent to us from the British Museum together with the type female of *D. eatoni* Ric. Both specimens are unfortunately without antennae but they correspond otherwise with *D. denticornis* except for silvery-grey pubescence at sides of abdomen and on posterior tergites.

DASYRHAMPHIS ALGIRUS (MACQUART, 1839)

Fig. 164.

Tabanus algirus Macquart, 1838, Dipt. exot., 1 (2): 180.
Atylotus Eatoni Ricardo, 1905, Ann. Mag. nat. Hist., 16: 198.

DIAGNOSIS. Medium-sized blackish species with uniformly brownish tinted wings, antennae with segment 3 brownish at base and a distinct, rather pointed dorsal tooth. Palpi and legs black, face and pleura with dark hairs, mesonotum and anterior two tergites pale pubescent.

DESCRIPTION. ♀. *Head.* Eyes with microscopic pile, unstriped. Frons dull black, index 1: 2.5, broader at base, slightly narrowed above; lower callus dark brown, wrinkled and triangular shaped, joined above with the very long, linear and somewhat shining black median callus. Frons clothed with sparse whitish hairs. Subcallus dark brown, dulled by silvery-grey dust, sometimes slightly polished at middle and more dark reddish-brown there. Face and cheeks blackish-brown, thinly silvery-grey dusted, dark brown haired, only cheeks above with some pale hairs. Antennae mostly dark blackish-brown, more brownish on segment 3, with apex and terminal flagellar segments black. Dorsal tooth distinct, rectangular to slightly pointed, basal segments with short black hairs. Palpi black and short black haired, rather broader at base, pointed at tip.

Thorax black on mesonotum, only sides, including humeri and postalar calli, narrowly brownish; whole of mesonotum clothed with pale hairs becoming longer anteriorly and on scutellum. Pleura dark brown with concolorous hairs, sternopleura thinly greyish dusted and with some paler hairs. *Legs* black or very indistinctly blackish-brown, black haired, femora with long hairs, tarsi with somewhat reddish pubescence beneath. *Wings* uniformly brownish clouded with brown veins, no appendix to vein R_4. Squamae very pale with minute pale marginal pubescence, and with a tuft of long whitish hairs anteriorly. Halteres dark brown with blackish knobs, paler only at extreme tip.

Abdomen black and slightly shining, anterior two tergites distinctly but only thinly greyish dusted and pale haired, following tergites black pubescent except for apical two segments which bear longer pale hairs. Venter, except apical two sternites, uniformly black with short concolorous hairs.

♂. We have not seen the male sex but according to Macquart's original description only the wings are paler brown (brun rousatre), otherwise as in the female.

Length. 15–17 mm.

VARIABILITY. Surcouf (1913) described a distinct subspecies *tunisiensis* from Tunisia and Algeria which differs from the nominate form in the smaller size, in the longer and distinctly pale haired pleura, in the more whitish pubescent anterior two tergites and the mesonotum bears broad greyish longitudinal stripes.

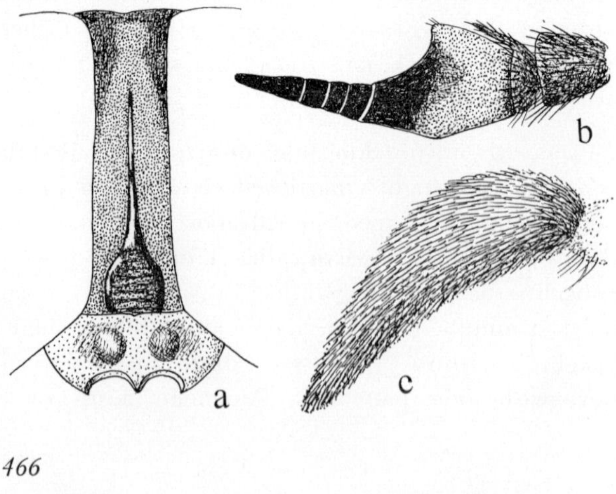

Fig. 164. *Dasyrhamphis algirus* (Macq.), female, a. frons, b. antenna, c. palpus.

Synonymy. *D. eatoni* (Ric.) is generally taken for a synonym of *algirus* (Macq.). We can confirm this synonymy on the basis of examination of the female type labelled »Nr. Algiers, Algeria, 5.V.1893, Rev. A. E. Eaton« and deposited in the British Museum (Nat. Hist.), London.

Biology. According to Surcouf (1921a) both males and females were collected in North Africa on *Ferula communis* L. and *Ferula vesceritensis* Coss.

Dates. May and June.

Distribution. A North African species known from Morocco and Algeria (from Tunisia as ssp. *tunisiensis* Surc.) but recorded also from Sardinia (Leclercq 1961, 1967a). Its occurrence in Europe needs to be verified by new findings.

Literature

Abassian-Lintzen, R., 1960: Tabanidae (Diptera) of Iran. V. Descriptions of three new subspecies of the genus *Haematopota*. *Bull. Soc. Path. exot.*, 53: 824–828.

– 1964: Tabanidae of Iran. X. List, keys and distribution of species occurring in Iran. *Annls Parasit. hum. comp.*, 39: 285–327, 4 figs.

Anthony, D. W., 1958: Pyrethrum emulsion for surveys of Tabanid larvae. *J. econ. Ent.*, 50: 740–742.

– 1960: Tabanidae attracted to an ultraviolet light trap. *Fla Ent.*, 43: 77–80.

Aradi, M. P., 1956: Tabanids from the Carpathian-Basin in the collections of the Hungarian Natural History Museum. *Folia ent. hung.* (N.S.), 9: 431–458, 1 map.

– 1957: Revision der Tabaniden-Fauna des Karpaten-Beckens. *Ibid.* (N.S.), 10: 227–234.

– 1958: Diptera I. Bögölyök – Tabanidae. *Fauna Hung.*, 14 (9): 1–44, 26 figs.

Arias, J., 1912: Datos par el conociemento de la distribucion geográfica de los Dipteros de España. *Mems. R. Soc. esp. Hist. nat.*, 7: 61–246.

– 1914: Dipteros de España. Fam. Tabanidae. *Trab. Mus. nac. Cienc. nat., Madr., Ser. Zool.*, 19: 1–173.

Austen, E. E., 1906a: Horse-flies (Tabanidae), and disease. *J. trop. Med. Hyg.*, 9: 98–99.

– 1906b: Illustrations of British bloodsucking flies, with notes. British Museum Natural History, 74 pp., 34 pls., London.

– 1920: A contribution to the knowledge of the Tabanidae of Palestine. *Bull. ent. Res.*, 10: 277–321, 18 figs.

– 1922a: Further notes on the Tabanidae of Palestine with descriptions of new species. *Ibid.*, 13: 151–160, 4 figs.

– 1922b: New and little-known Mesopotamian blood-sucking Diptera (Families Simuliidae and Tabanidae). *Ibid.*, 13: 275–290, 7 figs.

– 1924: Additional records of Palestine Tabanidae, with descriptions of new species. *Ibid.*, 14: 421–432, 4 figs.

– 1925: A contribution to knowledge of the blood-sucking Diptera of the Dardanelles. *Ibid.*, 16: 1–23, 6 figs.

Bachmann, M., 1911–12: Beobachtungen über blütenbesuchende Insekten in der Eichstätter Alp. *Mitt. münch. ent. Ges.*, 2: 74–80, 91–94; 3: 14–16, 28–32, 41–48, 59–64, 96–105.

Bailey, N. S., 1948a: A mass collection and population survey technique for larvae of Tabanidae. *Bull. Brooklyn ent. Soc.*, 43: 22–29, 2 pls.

– 1948b: The hovering and mating of Tabanidae. A review of the literature with some original observations. *Ann. ent. Soc. Am.*, 41: 403–412.

Baratov, S., 1961: Protection of cattle against Tabanidae. *Selskie chozjajstvo Tadžikistana*, 7: 25–26. [In Russian].

Bau, A., 1909a: Über die Lebensweise der *Tabanus paradoxus* Jännicke. *Wien. ent. Ztg.*, 28: 339–340.

– 1909b: Beitrag zur Kenntnis der Dipteren-Fauna Vorarlbergs. *Landesmus. f. Vorarlberg*, 46. Jahresbericht, Bregenz, pp. 294–325.

Becker, Th., 1887: Beiträge zur Kenntnis der Dipteren-Fauna von St. Moritz. *Berl. ent. Z.*, 31: 93–141.

Beling, Th., 1875: Beitrag zur Metamorphose der zweiflügeligen Insecten. *Arch. Naturgesch.*, 41: 31–57.
– 1882: Beitrag zur Metamorphose zweiflügeliger Insecten aus den Familien Tabanidae, Leptidae, Asilidae, Empidae, Dolichopodidae und Syrphidae. *Ibid.*, 48: 187–240.
– 1888: Beitrag zur Metamorphose einiger zweiflügeliger Insecten aus den Familien Tabanidae, Empidae und Syrphidae. *Verh. zool.-bot. Ges. Wien*, 38: 1–4.

Berezantzev, Ya. A., 1952: Apparatus for catching biting flies. *Zool. Zh.*, 31: 467–470, 2 figs. [In Russian].

Bertrand, H., 1954: Les insectes aquatiques d'Europe. Vol. II. Trichoptères, Lepidoptères, Diptères, Hymenoptères. *Encycl. ent.*, Paris (A), 31: 1–547, 495 figs.

Bessalov, V. S., 1968: Tularemia focus on the Biryuchi Islands of the Kherson region. *Zh. Mikrobiol. Epidem. Immunobiol.*, 12: 97–102. [In Russian].

Bezzi, M., 1892: Contribuzione alla Fauna Ditterologica della provincia di Pavia, Parte II. *Boll. Soc. ent. ital.*, 24: 97–151.
– 1893: I ditteri del Trentino. Saggio di un elenco delle specie di Ditteri finora osservate nel Trentino. *Atti Soc. veneto-trent. scient. nat.* (Ser. IIa), 1: 1–145. [Reprint].
– 1895, 1898 & 1900: Contribuzioni alla Fauna ditterologica italiana. *Boll. Soc. ent. ital.*, 27: 39–78, 30: 19–50 & 32: 77–102.
– 1912: Diptera peninsulae ibericae. *Broteria*, 10: 114–156, 16 figs.
– 1918: Studi sulla ditterofauna nivale delle Alpi italiane. *Memorie Soc. ital. Sci. nat.*, 9: 1–164, 2 pls.

Bigot, J. M. F., 1856: Essai d'une classification générale et synoptique de l'ordre des Insectes Diptères. *Annls Soc. ent. Fr.* (Sér. 3), 4: 51–91.
– 1859: Dipterorum aliquot nova genera. *Revue Mag. Zool.* (Sér. 2), 11: 305–315, 1 pl.
– 1860: Diptères de Sicile recueillis par M. Bellier de la Chavignerie et description de onze espèces nouvelles. *Annls Soc. ent. Fr.* (Sér. 3), 8: 765–784.
– 1880a: Diptères nouveaux ou peu connus. XX. Quelques Diptères de Perse et du Caucase. *Ibid.*, 10: 139–154.
– 1880b: Diptères nouveaux ou peu connus. XXII. Notes et mélanges. *Ibid.*, 10: 369–376.
– 1891a: Diptères nouveaux ou peu connus. Genre *Haematopota. Bull. Soc. zool. Fr.*, 16: 74–79.
– 1891b: Diptères nouveaux ou peu connus. Tabanidi. Tableau dichotomique des genres publiés jusqu'à ce jour (Octobre 1891). *Mém Soc. zool. Fr.*, 4: 408–419.
– 1892a: Déscriptions de Diptères nouveaux. *Ibid.*, 5: 602–691.
– 1892b: Nova Genera Dipterorum. *Wien. ent. Ztg.*, 11: 161–162.

Bischoff, W., 1925: Über die Kopfbildung der Dipterenlarven. III. Teil. Die Köpfe der Orthorrhapha-Brachycera-Larven. *Arch. Naturgesch.*, 90A: 1–105.

Blickle, R. L., 1955: Observations on the habits of Tabanidae. *Ohio J. Sci.*, 55: 308–310.
– 1959: Observations on the hovering and mating of *Tabanus bishoppi* Stone. *Ann. ent. Soc. Am.*, 52: 183–190, 2 figs.

Bogačev, A. V., 1951: Diptera in: Zivotnyj mir Azerbajdzana. *Izv. An Azerb. SSR*, Baku. [In Russian].

Bogačev, A. V. & N. G. Samedov, 1949: Materials on studies on the fauna of parasites of Nakhichevan ASSR. *Izv. AN Azerb. SSR*, 5: 66–75, 2 figs. [In Russian].

Boško, G. V., 1948: Horse-flies of the Central part of Pelssie (Ukraine), their dynamics and importance. *Tezisy dokl. 6 nauc. sess. Kievskogo gos. Instituta,* Kiev, pp. 10–13. [In Russian].

– 1968: Ecology and early stages of *Chrysops (Heterochrysops) italicus* Meig., 1804. *Vestnik zool. An USSR,* 3: 37–43, 5 figs., Kiev. [In Russian].

Bouvier, G., 1940a: Contribution à l'étude des Tabanidés de la Suisse. *Mitt. schweiz. ent. Ges.*, 18: 15–47, 20 figs.

– 1940b: Note sur l'armature génitale des Tabanidés. *Ibid.*, 18: 57–61, 3 figs.

– 1941: Quelques observations biologiques sur les Tabanidés. *Ibid.*, 18: 280–285, 13 figs.

– 1945: Les Tabanidés de la Suisse. *Ibid.*, 19: 409–466, 35 figs.

Boženko, V. P., 1941: Horse-flies *(Chrysops)* as vectors of tularemia. *Zh. Mikrobiol. Épidom. Immunobiol.*, 12: 21–25. [In Russian].

Bradescu, V., 1963: Données nouvelles sur deux Diptères Roumains rares. *Trav. Mus. Hist. nat. Gr. Antipa,* 4: 315–317, 1 fig.

Brauer, F., 1869: Kurze Charakteristik der Dipteren-Larven zur Bekräftigung des neuen von Dr. Schiner entworfenen Dipteren-Systems. *Verh. zool.-bot. Ges. Wien,* 19: 843–852.

– & J. E. Bergenstamm, 1880: Die Zweiflügler des keiserlichen Museums zu Wien. I. *Denkschr. Akad. Wiss., Wien,* 42 (Abt. 1): 105–216, 6 Tafeln.

– 1883: Die Zweiflügler des kaiserlichen Museum zu Wien. III. Systematische Studien auf Grundlage der Dipteren-Larven nebst einer Zusammenstellung von Beispielen aus der Literatur über dieselben und Beschreibung neuer Formen. *Ibid.*, 47: 1–100, 5 Tafeln.

Breev, K. A., 1950: The behaviour of blood-sucking Diptera and Bot-flies when attacking Reindeer and the responsive reactions of the Reindeer. I. The behaviour of blood-sucking Diptera and Bot-flies when attacking Reindeer. *Parazit. Sb.*, 12: 167–198, 9 figs. [In Russian].

– 1951: Id op. II. Herding together in Reindeer as a factor in protection from the attacks of blood-sucking flies and Bot-flies. *Ibid.*, 13: 342–354. [In Russian].

Brindle, A., 1961: Taxonomic notes on the larvae of British Diptera. I. The genus *Haematopota* Meigen (Tabanidae). *Entomologist,* 94: 121–124, 13 figs.

– 1963: Terrestrial Diptera larvae. *Entomologist's Rec. J. Var.*, 75: 47–62, 19 figs.

Burtt, B. D., 1924: The distribution of *Tabanus glaucopis* Meig. on the Streatley Downs; with special reference to the breeding-grounds of the insect. *Entomologist's mon. Mag.*, 60: 17–18.

Cameron, A. E., 1930: Oviposition of *Haematopota pluvialis* Linné. *Nature,* 126: 601–602.

– 1934: The life-history and structure of *Haematopota pluvialis* Linné (Tabanidae). *Trans. R. Soc. Edinb.*, 58: 211–250, 28 figs.

Castellani, O. & G. Crivaro, 1967: Materiali per la conoscenza della distribuzione dei Tabanidi in Italia. *Boll. Ass. romana Ent.*, 22: 52–58.

Chvála, M., 1964: Some new or little known Tabanidae in Czechoslovakia. *Acta ent. bohemoslov.*, 61: 374–383, 17 figs.

– 1969: Einige neue oder wenig bekannte Bremsen (Diptera, Tabanidae) von Nepal. *Ibid.*, 66: 39–54, 24 figs., 1 Tafel.

– & Jan Ježek, 1969: Immature stages of five European *Hybomitra* species of the *bimaculata-* and *montana-*groups. (Diptera, Tabanidae). *Folia parasitol.*, 16: 329–347.

– & L. Lyneborg, 1970: A revision of Palearctic Tabanidae (Diptera) described by J. C. Fabricius. *J. Med. Entomol.*, 7: 543–555, 11 figs.
– & J. Moucha, 1971: Zur Taxonomie von *Hybomitra nitidifrons* (Szilády, 1914) (Diptera, Tabanidae). *Notulae ent.*, 51: 109–112.
Ciurea, I., E. Séguy & T. Stefanescu, 1937: Sur une espèce de Taon *(Sziladynus solstitialis* var. *Ciureai* nov. Séguy, 1937) qui attaque impétuesement l'homme et les animaux dans le Delta du Danube. *Archs roum. Path. exp. Microbiol.*, 10: 207–210, 3 pls.
Coe, R. L., 1958: Diptera taken in Jugoslavia from May to July, 1955, with localities and notes. *Glasnik prirod. Muz. Beogr.* (B), 12: 181–206.
– 1960: A further collection of Diptera from Jugoslavija, with localities and notes. *Ibid.*, 16: 43–67, 1 map.
Collart, A., 1950: Notules diptèrelogique. II. *Bull. Inst. r. Sci. nat. Belg.*, 26 (no. 46): 8 pp., 1 fig.
Collin, J. E., 1932: A review of Mr. E. Rivenhall Goffe's paper on Tabanidae. *Entomologist's Rec. J. Var.*, 44: 37–39.
– 1940a: Review of »British Blood-sucking Flies«. By F. W. Edwards, H. Oldroyd and J. Smart. *Entomologist's mon. Mag.*, 76: 70–72.
– 1940b: A note on certain structural distinctions between the females of *Therioplectes tropicus* L., *solstitialis* Mg. and *distinguendus* Verr. (Dipt. Tabanidae). *Ibid.*, 76: 178–179, 1 plate.
– 1945: Correction of a mistake of long standing concerning the identity of *Atylotus plebeius* Fallén. *Proc. R. ent. Soc. Lond.*, (B), 14: 89–90.
Compte-Sart, A., 1958: Los Tabánidos de Mallorca. *Boln Soc. Hist. nat. Baleares,* 4: 13–22.
Coquebert, A. J., 1798–1804: Illustratio Iconographica Insectorum, quae in musaeis parisinis observavit . . . , 142 pp., 30 pls. Paris.
Coquillett, D. W., 1905: The Linnaean genera of Diptera. *Proc. ent. Soc. Wash.*, 8: 66–70.
Corbet, P. S., 1964: Nocturnal flight activity of sylvan Culicidae and Tabanidae (Diptera) as indicated by light-traps: a further study. *Proc. R. ent. Soc. Lond.*, 39: 53–67, 17 figs.
– & A. J. Haddow, 1962: Diptera swarming above the forest canopy in Uganda, with speciel reference to Tabanidae. *Trans. R. ent. Soc. Lond.*, 114: 267–284, 6 figs.
Costa, A., 1857: Contribuzione alla Fauna ditterologica italiana. *Il Giambatt. Vico,* Napoli, 2: 438–460.
– 1893: Ditteri, in: Miscellanea Entomologica. Memoria quarta. *Rc. Accad. Sci. fis. mat., Napoli,* (Ser. 2), 5 (Nr. 15): 1–30, 1 plate.
Cziżek, K., 1906: Beiträge zu einer Dipterenfauna Mährens. *Z. mähr. Landesmus.*, 6: 182–234.
Čepelák, J., 1959: Die Sammelergebnisse der höheren Fliegen aus der Umgebung von Velké Meziříčí (Diptera, Brachycera). *Vlastivěd. sborník Vysočiny, odd. věd přir. Havlíčkův Brod,* 3: 95–103.
Danielová, V., 1960: Diptéres albanais des familles Tabanidae, Hippoboscidae et Hypodermatidae recueillis par l'expédition de l'Académie Tchécoslovaque des Sciences. *Čsl. Parasit., Praha,* 7: 37–40. [In Russian with French summary].
Demjančenko, G. F., 1959a: Data on horse-flies in Belorussian wooded districts. *Trudy vses. nauchno-issled. Inst. Vet. Sanit.*, 15: 99–101. [In Russian].

– 1959b: Horse-flies of Belorussian SSR, White Russia. *Tezisy Dokl. 10. Sovesc. Parazit. Probl. & Prirodoočag. Bolez.*, 2: 62–63. [In Russian].
– 1960: Tabanids of the Central zone of White Russia and methods of controlling them. *Trudy naucno-issled. Vet. Inst.*, 1: 110–115. [In Russian].
– , R. P. Demjančenko, L. S. Južakova & Z. G. Serguševa, 1965: Horseflies of Grodnensk region, White Russia. *Tezisy Dokl. nauc. sessii 25. letiju Grodnenskogo Pedag. Inst., Minsk*, pp. 144–147. [In Russian].
– , E. N. Samujlo & Z. M. Pronina, 1962: Tabanids of the Minsk region, White Russia. *Tezisy Dokl. 2. zool. Konf.. Belorussian SSR, Minsk*, pp. 130–131. [In Russian].

Dinulescu, G., 1958: Familia Tabanidae. *Fauna Repub. pop. rom.*, Insecta, vol. 11, fasc. 2, 276 pp.

Drenowski, K. A., 1936: Beitrag zur Insektenfauna Bulgariens und Mazedoniens II. (Lepidoptera, Hymenoptera, Diptera und Orthoptera). *Mitt. bulg. ent. Ges.*, 9: 237–256.

Drenski, P., 1929a: Die bisher aus Bulgarien, Thrazien und Mazedonien bekannt gewordenen Tabaniden. *Sber. Ges. naturf. Freunde Berl.*, 1928: 233–235.
– 1929b: Blutsaugende Fliegen aus der Familie des Tabanidae (Bremsen) in Bulgarien. *Mitt. naturwiss. Inst. Sofia*, 2: 55–128, 11 figs.
– 1931: Kleine entomologische Mitteilungen. *Mitt. bulg. ent. Ges. Sofia*, 6: 123–141.
– 1942: Über die Insekten-Fauna des Küstengebietes nördlich von Warna (Ökologische Notizen). *Ibid.*, 12: 15–44, 5 figs.

Duncan, J., 1836: Characters and descriptions of the Dipterous insects indigenous to Britain. *Magaz. zool.-bot.*, 1: 145–167, 359–368, 453–459.

Džafarov, Š. M., 1957: Tabanids of Azerbaijan. *Tezisy Dokl. III. sovesc. Vses. ent. Obsc., Tbilisi*, 2: 34–35. [In Russian].

Edwards, F. W., H. Oldroyd & J. Smart, 1939: British blood-sucking flies. British Museum (Natural History), London, VIII + 156 pp., 64 figs., 45 pls.

Efflatoun, H. C., 1930: A monograph of Egyptian Diptera, Part III. Family Tabanidae. *Mém. Soc. ent. Égypte*, 4: 1–114, 128 figs., 2 pls.

Egger, J., 1859: Dipterologische Beiträge. *Verh. zool.-bot. Ges. Wien*, 9: 387–407.

Enderlein, G., 1908: Biologisch-faunistische Moor- und Dünenstudien. *Ber. westpreuss. bot.-zool. Ver.*, 30: 54–238, 7 Abb.
– 1923: Vorläufige Diagnosen neuer Tabanidengenera. *Dt. ent. Z.*, 1923: 544–555.
– 1925: Studien an blutsaugenden Insekten. I. Grundlagen eines neuen Systems der Tabaniden. *Mitt. zool. Mus. Berl.*, 11: 253–409, 5 figs.
– 1927: Die von Holtz in Griechenland gesammelten Tabaniden. *Stettin. ent. Ztg.*, 88: 99–101.
– 1932: Einige neue paläarktische Tabaniden. *Mitt. dt. ent. Ges.*, 3: 63–64.

Everett, R. & J. L. Lancaster, 1968: A comparison of animal- and dry-icebaited traps for the collection of Tabanids. *J. econ. Ent.*, 61: 863–864.

Evlachova, V. F., G. A. Serbienko & N. N. Potapov, 1954: Blood-sucking flies in the region of the Kakhovsk water basin and their control. *3. ekol. Konf., Kiev*, 1: 68–72. [In Russian].

Fairchild, G. B., 1956: Synonymical notes on Neotropical flies of the family Tabanidae. *Smithson. misc. Collns*, 131, no. 3: 38 pp.
– 1966: Some new synonymies in Tabanidae. *Proc. ent. Soc. Wash.*, 68: 94–96.
– 1969: Climate and the phylogeny and distribution of Tabanidae. *Bull. ent. Soc. Am.*, 15: 7–11, 1 fig.

Fallén, G. F., (1814–) 1817: Diptera Sueciae. Tabanii et Xylophagei, pp. 3–14. Lundae (Lund).

Fischer, H., 1966: Die Tierwelt Schwabens, 14. Teil: Bremsen-Tabanidae. *Ber. naturf. Ges. Augsburg,* 18: 133–142.

Folco, G. B., 1934: Osservazioni sullo sviluppo di *Chrysozona (Haematopota) italica* Meigen. *Memorie Soc. tosc. Sci. nat.*, 44: 1–11, 4 figs.

Forsslund, K., 1951: Fynd av vattenbromsen, *Heptatoma pellucens* Fabr. *Opusc. ent.*, 16: 96.

Fourcroy, A. F., 1785: Entomologia parisiensis, sive catalogus Insectorum, quae in agro parisiensi reperiuntur. Vol. 1: 1–231, vol. 2: 233–544. Paris.

Francis, E., 1921: Tularaemia Francis, 1921, I. The occurrence of Tularaemia in nature as a disease of man. *Publ. Hlth Rep., Wash.*, 36: 1731–1738.

– 1929: Arthropods in the transmission of Tularaemia. *4th Int. Congr. Ent.*, Ithaca, N. Y., 2: 929–944, 7 figs.

Franz, H., 1952: Bemerkenswerte in den Nordostalpen gemachte Dipterenfunde. *Z. wien. ent. Ges.*, 37: 38–43.

Fraser, A. D., 1920: Notes on blood-sucking flies in North Russia during the summer of 1919. *Bull ent. Res.*, 11: 195–198.

Frauenfeld, G., 1860: Weiterer Beitrag zur Fauna Dalmatiens. *Verh. zool.-bot. Ges. Wien,* 10: 787–794.

Frey, R., 1911: Zur Kenntnis der Dipterenfauna Finnlands. *Acta Soc. Fauna Flora fenn.*, 34: 1–57.

– 1915: Résultats scientifiques de l'expédition polaire Russe en 1900–1903, sous la direction du Baron E. Toll, Section E: Zoologie, vol. II. Livr. 10. Diptera-Brachycera aus den arktischen Küstengegenden Sibiriens. *Ross. Akad. Nauk Petrograd, Zap. Fiz.-Mat. Otd.*, ser. 8, 29: 1–35, 2 pls.

Gabova, E. N., 1960: Observations on blood-sucking flies and their day-activity on the territory of the Komi ASSR. *Trudy Komi Fil. Akad. Nauk SSSR,* 9: 92–95. [In Russian].

Galli-Valerio, B., 1922: Beobachtungen über Culiciden, nebst Bemerkungen über Tabaniden und Simuliiden. *Zentbl. Bakt. Parasitkde,* Abt. I, 87: 557–560.

– 1923: id. op. *Ibid.*, 90: 38–40.

– 1924: id. op. *Ibid.*, 92: 101–104.

– 1925: id. op. *Ibid.*, 94: 309–313.

– 1926: id. op. *Ibid.*, 98: 97–99.

– 1927: id. op. *Ibid.*, 102: 224–226.

– 1929: id. op. *Ibid.*, 110: 100–101.

– 1930: Observations sur les Culicidés, les Tabanidés, les Simulidés et les Chironomidés. *Ibid.*, 116: 220–224.

– 1932: id. op. *Ibid.*, 123: 485–490.

– 1934: id. op. *Ibid.*, 131: 487–490.

– 1936: id. op. *Ibid.*, 137: 91–95.

– 1938: id. op. *Ibid.*, 141: 198–201.

– 1940: id. op. *Revue suisse Hyg.*, pp. 200–203.

Gaunitz, S., 1965: Fynd av bromsar Tabanidae. *Ent. Tidskr.*, 86: 270–271.

Ghidini, G. M., 1936: Tabanidi d'Italia. *Archo zool. ital.*, 22: 371–493, 72 figs.

– 1937: Tavole per la determinazione dei Tabanidi d'Italia. *Memorie Soc. ent. ital.*, 69 (1936): 129–175, 72 figs.

– 1942: Prima esplorazione entomologica del Parco Nazionale del Circeo, Diptera: Tabanidae. *C. N. R. Inst. Naz. Biol., Salerno,* pp. 179–180.

Gimmerthal, B. A., 1832: Catalogus systematicus Dipterorum Livoniae. *Bull. naturf. Ges. Moscou,* 4: 343–352.

– 1842a: Übersicht der Zweiflügler (Diptera) Livlands und Curlands. *Ibid.,* 15: 639–659.

– 1842b: Bemerkungen dazu und Berichtigungen zu dem früheren Verzeichnisse. *Ibid.,* 15: 660–686.

– 1847: Dritter Beitrag zu einer künftig zu bearbeitenden Dipterologie Russlands. *Ibid.,* 20: 175–223.

Gobert, E., 1880–81: Diagnoses de Tabaniens nouveaux. *Bull. Soc. Linn. N. Fr.,* 5: 29–32.

Goetghebuer, M., 1926: Catalogue des Tabanides de Belgique. *Bull. Annls Soc. r. ent. Belg.,* 66: 109–114.

Goffe, E. R., 1931: British Tabanidae. With an account of the principal variation, with descriptions of a number of new forms, and of some additions to the British list. *Trans. ent. Soc. S. Engl.,* 6 (1930): 43–114, 2 pls.

Gomojunova, N. P., 1967: Species composition and phenology of Gadflies from the foot-hill forest steppe. *In:* Results of investigations on the problem in the control of blood-sucking Diptera. Novosibirsk, pp. 187–190. [In Russian].

Grobov, O. F., 1961: Horse-flies of the region of Kaliningrad. *Trudy vses. Inst. éksp. veter.,* 27: 178–184. [In Russian].

Gunárová, V., 1965: Further contributions to the dynamics and ecology of Horse-flies attacking cattle. *Sb. vys. Šk. poľnohospod. Nitre,* 11: 175–182. [In Czech].

Hagmann, L., G. Barber, E. Starnes & O. Starnes, 1948: Evening flight habits of a male Tabanid. *Ent. News.,* 59: 257–258.

Haines, F. H., 1933: *Therioplectes (= Sziladynus) montanus* Meig. taken in Hampshire. *J. ent. Soc. S. Engl.,* 1: 39.

Hamm, A. H., 1933: *Therioplectes micans* Mg., and other Tabanidae in and near Oxford. *J. ent. Soc. S. Engl.,* 1: 66–67.

Harant, H. & E. Brygoo, 1949: Note préliminaire sur quelques Tabanides africaines. *Bull. Soc. Path. exot.,* 42: 370–371.

– & M. Leclercq, 1955: Tabanidae de France II. Récoltes du Départment de l'Hérault. *Bull. mens. Soc. linn. Lyon,* 24: 5–6.

Haseman, L., 1943: The courting flights of Tabanids. *Science,* 97: 285–286.

Hauser, E. G., 1939: Notes on Tabanidae of Chanlarskij rajon. *Trudy zool. Inst., Baku,* 10: 135–159. [In Russian].

Hennig, W., 1952: Die Larvenformen der Dipteren. Eine Übersicht über die bisher bekannten Jugendstadien der zweiflügeligen Insekten. 3. Teil, pp. I–VIII + 1–628, 338 Abb., 21 Taf., Berlin.

Hine, J. S., 1923: Horse-flies collected by J. M. Aldrich in Alaska in 1921. *Can. Ent.,* 55: 143–146.

Hoffman, R. A., 1960: Laboratory evaluation of several insecticides against *Chrysops* larvae. *J. econ. Ent.,* 53: 262–263.

Isaac, P. V., 1924: Papers on Indian Tabanidae. A practical and simple method for rearing Tabanid larvae. *Mem. Dep. Agric. India ent. Ser.,* 8: 53–57, 2 pls.

– 1925: id op. Part VIII. The bionomics and life-histories of some common Tabanidae of Pusa. *Ibid.,* 9: 21–28, 6 pls.

Jaennicke, F., 1866: Beiträge zur Kenntnis der Tabaniden Europa's. *Berl. ent. Z.*, 10: 65–91, 237.

Ježek, J., 1970: Larvae and pupae of four European *Chrysops* species (Diptera, Tabanidae). *Acta ent. bohemoslov.*, 67: 375–383, 32 figs.

– 1971: Larven und Puppen der Art *Heptatoma pellucens* (Fabr.) und vier europäischer Arten der Gattung *Haematopota* Meig. (Diptera, Tabanidae). *Ibid.*, 68: 341–351, 9 Tafeln.

Jones, C. M. & D. W. Anthony, 1964: The Tabanidae of Florida. *Tech. Bull. U.S. Dep. Agric.*, no. 1295: 85 pp., 18 figs.

Kabos, W. J., 1960: Tweevleugelige Insekten – Diptera VI. De Nederlandse Dazen (Tabanidae) en Horzels (Oestridae). *Wet. Meded. K. ned. natuurh. Veren.*, no. 38: 1–16, 21 figs.

Kalugin, S. G., 1945: Contribution to the study of gadflies of the central part of the northern slopes of the Caucasian Mountain range. *Trav. Sta. biol. Caucase*, Dzaužikau, 4: 21–25. [In Russian].

Karvonen, Jaakko, 1969: On Finnish Tabanids (Diptera). *Annls Ent. Fenn.*, 35: 176–183.

Kauri H., 1951: Bemerkungen über schwedische Tabaniden. *Opusc.* ent., 16: 97–109, 8 figs.

– 1954: Bemerkungen über schwedische Tabaniden II. *Ibid.*, 19: 239–244, 1 fig.

– 1958: Über zwei für Europa und Nord-Amerika gemeinsame Tabaniden-Arten. *Ibid.*, 23: 95–104, 3 figs.

– 1964: Über die nordskandinavischen Tabaniden. *Ibid.*, 29: 99–108, 1 fig.

– 1968: Über die norwegischen Tabaniden. *Norsk ent. Tidsskr.*, 15: 63–64.

– 1969: Über Bremsen von Südwest-Häme, Finnland II. *Lounais-Hämeen Luonto*, Forssa, 15: 39–45.

Keiser, F., 1947: Die Fliegen des schweizerischen Nationalparks und seiner Umgebung. Pars I: Brachycera Orthorhapha; Ergebnisse der wissenschaftlichen Untersuchung des schweiz. Nationalparks. Herausgegeben von der Kommission der schweiz. Naturforschenden Gesellschaft zur wiss. Erforschung des Nationalparks, Band. 2, 198 pp., 9 Karten, 23 Abb. Verlag Lündin, Liestal.

Kertész, K., 1900: Catalogus Tabanidarum orbiae terrarum universi, 79 pp., Budapest.

– 1908: Catalogus Dipterorum, Vol. 3: 1–348, Budapest.

Kidd, L. N. & A. Brindle, 1959: Tabanidae, *in:* The Diptera of Lancashire and Cheshire. Part I: 11–112, Market Place.

Kittel, G. & A. Kriechbaumer, 1872: Systematische Übersicht der Fliegen, welche in Bayern und in der nächsten Umgebung vorkommen. *Abh. naturhist. Ges. Nürnberg*, 5: 1–90.

Knuth, P. & G. Rauchbaar, 1910: Weitere Nachforschungen nach Trypanosoma beim Rinde im Kreise Oberwesterwald nebst einem Beitrag zur Kenntnis der deutschen Stechfliegen (Spezies: *Tabanus* und *Haematopota)* parasitierenden Flagellaten. *Z. InfektKrankh. parasit Krankh. Hyg. Haustiere,* 8: 140–154, 2 pls.

Kowarz, F., 1873: Beitrag zur Dipteren-Fauna Ungarns. *Verh. zool-bot. Ges. Wien*, 23: 453–464.

Kramář, J., 1929: Kopulace ovádů *Tabanus sudeticus* Zell. při východu slunce. *Časopis čsl. spol. ent.*, 26: 96.

Kröber, O., 1910a: Fauna Hamburgiensis. Verzeichnis der in der Umgegend von Hamburg gefundenen Dipteren. *Verh. Ver. naturw. Unterh. Hamb.*, 14 (1907–1909): 3–113, 1 Karte.

– 1910b: Die Tabaniden des Niederelbgebietes. *Ibid.*, 14: 114–176.
– 1920: Die *Chrysops*-Arten der paläarctischen Region nebst den Arten der angrenzenden Gebiete. *Zool. Jb. (Syst.)*, 43: 41–160, 12 figs., 2 pls.
– 1921: Die paläarctischen Arten der Gattung *Pangonia* Latr. Versuch einer Auseinandersetzung. *Arch. Naturgesch.* (Abt. A), 87 (1): 1–67, 20 figs.
– 1922: Beiträge zur Kenntnis paläarktischer Tabaniden. Teil I. *Surcoufia, Heptatoma, Silvius* und *Chrysozona. Ibid.*, 88: (8): 114–164.
– 1924a: Beiträge zur Kenntnis palaearktischer Tabaniden. II. Teil: Die Untergattung *Therioplectes* Zell. nebst Bemerkungen zu den mir bekannt gewordenen Bigot'schen Tabaniden-Typen der Collectionen Mr. Collin's in Newmarket. *Ibid.*, 89 (12): 55–118.
– 1924b: Beiträge zur Kenntnis paläarktischer Tabaniden. Teil III: *Ochrops, Atylotus, Tabanus* s. str., *Baikalia, Isshikia. Ibid.*, 90 (9): 1–195.
– 1925a: Tabanidae, *in* E. Lindner: Die Fliegen der palaearktischen Region, Lieferung 8, 146 pp., 70 figs., Stuttgart.
– 1925b: Egyptian Tabanidae. *Bull. Soc. ent. Égypte,* 18: 77–137, 22 figs.
– 1926: Neue Dipteren aus Aegypten. *Ibid.*, 19 (1925): 232–243, 1 fig.
– 1928a: Neue palaearktische Tabaniden. *Zool. Anz.*, 76: 261–272, 13 figs.
– 1928b: Neue Beiträge zur Kenntnis der Thereviden und Tabaniden. *Dt. ent. Z.*, 1928: 417–434, 19 figs.
– 1929: Neue Dipteren aus Aegypten aus den Familien Tabanidae, Therevidae, Omphralidae und Conopidae. *Bull. Soc. ent. Égypte,* 1929: 73–81, 4 figs.
– 1930: Dipterenfauna von Schleswig-Holstein und den benachbarten westlichen Nordseegebieten. *Verh. Ver. naturw. Heimatforsch.*, 22: 19–78.
– 1932a: Dipterenfauna von Schleswig-Holstein und den benachbarten westlichen Nordseegebieten. *Ibid.*, 23: 63–113.
– 1932b: Familie Tabanidae (Bremsen). *Tierwelt Dtl.*, 26: 55–99, 92 figs.
– 1935a: Dipterenfauna von Schleswig-Holstein und den benachbarten westlichen Nordseegebieten. *Verh. Ver. naturw. Heimatforsch.*, 24: 45–156.
– 1935b: Eine neue deutsche Tabanide. *Ibid.*, 24: 159–160.
– 1936a: Einige griechische Tabaniden. *Acta Inst. Mus. zool. Univ. athen.*, 1: 33–40, 19 figs.
– 1936b: Bestimmungstabelle der palaearktischen *Chrysozona*-Arten *(Haematopota). Ibid.*, 1: 43–52.
– 1937: I. Nachtrag zur Dipterenfauna Schleswig-Holsteins. *Verh. Ver. naturw. Heimatforsch.*, 26: 85–93.
– 1938: Katalog der palaearktischen Tabaniden nebst Bestimmungstabelle und Zusätzen zu einzelnen Arten sowie Neubeschreibungen. *Acta Inst. Mus. zool. Univ. athen.*, 2: 57–245.
– 1949: Die Dipterenfauna des Eppendorfer Moores im Wechsel der Zeiten. *Verh. Ver. naturw. Heimatforsch.*, 30: 69–89.
– 1953: Nachträge zur Dipterenfauna Schleswig-Holsteins und Niedersachsens (1933–35). *Ibid.*, 33: 39–96.

Kuntze, A., 1913: Dipterologische Sammelreise in Korsika des Herrn W. Schnuse in Dresden im Juni und Juli 1899. *Dt. ent. Z.*, 1913: 544–552.

Landrock, K., 1907: Mährische Zweiflügler; Achter Bericht des Lehrerklubs für Naturkunde über das Jahr 1906, pp. 50–71, Brno.

Latreille, P. A., 1802: Histoire naturelle, générale et particulière, des Crustacés et des Insectes; vol. 3: 12 + 467 pp. *in:* Sonnini, C. S. (ed.): Histoire naturelle par Buffon, Paris.

Lécaillon, A., 1912: Nouvelles recherches sur la ponte des oeufs et la vie larvaire de *Tabanus quatuornotatus* Meig. *Annls Soc. ent. Fr.*, 80: 487–491.

Leclercq, M., 1951: Notes sur la faune des Hautes-Fagnes en Belgique XX. Diptera: Tabanidae. *Bull. Annls Soc. r. ent. Belg.*, 87: 78–81.

– 1952: Introduction à l'étude des Tabanides et révision des espèces de Belgique. *Mém. Inst. r. Sci. nat. Belg.*, 123: 1–80, 30 cartes.

– 1955a: Tabanidae de France I. *Bull. Annls Soc. r. ent. Belg.*, 91: 76–83.

– 1955b: Tabanidae de France II. See: Harant, H. & M. Leclercq, 1955.

– 1955c: Tabanidae de France III. *Bull. mens. Soc. linn. Lyon*, 24: 248–250.

– 1956a: Suite de Tabanidae (Dipt.) d'Italie, I. Récoltes de Sicile, *Therioplectes marianii* nova species. *Bull. Inst. r. Sci. nat. Belg.*, 32: 1–6.

– 1956b: Tabanidae de France IV. *Bull. Annls Soc. r. ent. Belg.*, 92: 328–337.

– 1957a: Tabanidae paléarctiques et africains I. *Verh. naturf. Ges. Basel*, 68: 65–67.

– 1957b: Tabanidae paléarctiques et africains II. *Bull. Annls Soc. r. ent. Belg.*, 93: 161–167.

– 1957c: Révision systématique et biogéographique des Tabanidae de France I. *Annls Parasit. hum. comp.*, 32: 303–327.

– 1957d: Révision systématique et biogéographique des Tabanidae de France II. *Ibid.*, 32: 398–431.

– 1957e: Faune entomologique du Grand-Duché de Luxembourg, V. Tabanidae. *Archs Inst. gr.-duc. Luxemb., Sect. Sci. nat., phys. mathém.*, 24: 61–64.

– 1957f: Tabanidae d'Espagne I. *Therioplectes valenciae* n. sp. *Bull. Inst. r. Sci. nat. Belg.*, 33 (no. 50): 1–8, 1 fig.

– 1958a: Tabanidae d'Espagne II. *Ibid.*, 34 (no. 34): 1–4.

– 1958b: Tabanidae d'Espagne III. *Bull. Annls Soc. r. ent. Belg.*, 94: 321–322.

– 1958c: Mission E. Janssens en Grèce, 1957. 2e note: Diptera: Tabanidae. *Ibid.*, 94: 75–78.

– 1959: Tabanidae de Yougoslavie I. Récoltes de Macédoine, *Therioplectes simovae* n. sp. *Fragm. balcan.*, 2: 181–184.

– 1960a: Révision systématique et biogéographique des Tabanidae paléarctique. Vol. I: Pangoniinae et Chrysopinae. *Mém. Inst. r. Sci. nat. Belg.*, 63: 1–77, 10 pls., 28 cartes.

– 1960b: Tabanidae d'Espagne IV. Tableaux dichotomique des *Pangonius* Latreille. *Bull. Inst. r. Sci. nat. Belg.*, 36 (no. 9): 1–10.

– 1960c: Tabanidae (Diptera) de Yougoslavie II. *Fragm. balcan.*, 3: 183–188.

– 1961: Révision des Diachlorini: *Stypommia* Enderlein, *Dasyrhamphis* Enderlein, *Nanorrhynchus* Olsoufiev (Tabanidae paléarctiques). *Bull. Annls Soc. r. ent. Belg.*, 97: 87–98.

– 1964a: Tabanidae d'Espagne VI. *Bull. Inst. agron. Stns Rech. Gembloux*, 32: 315–318.

– 1964b: Tabanidae du Portugal I. Diagnose de *Tabanus Darimonti* n. sp. *Mems Estud. Mus. zool. Univ. Coimbra*, no. 288: 1–15, 1 fig.

– 1965a: Tabanidae des Balkans et de Sicile. *Bull. Inst. agron. Stns Rech. Gembloux*, 33: 128–131.

– 1965b: Tabanidae d'Italie II. *Ibid.*, 33: 132–134.

– 1966a: Tabanidae d'Espagne VII. *Bull. Rech. agron. Gembloux,* 1: 458–462.

– 1966b: Tabanidae de Turquie. Diagnoses d'*Atylotus hendrixi, Haematopota coolsi, Haematopota delezi* n. spp. *Ibid.*, 1: 463–477, 5 figs.

– 1966c: Tabanidae de Suisse. *Mitt. schweiz. ent. Ges.*, 38: 241–246.

– 1967a: Révision systématique et biogéographique des Tabanides paléarctiques. Vol. II: Tabaninae. *Mém. Inst. r. Sci. nat. Belg.*, 80 (1966): 1–237, 19 pls., 179 figs.

– 1967b: Tabanidae de Turquie II. Diagnoses d'*Hybomitra okayi, Atylotus hendrixi* et *Haematopota hennauxi* n. spp. *Bull. Rech. agron. Gembloux,* 2: 106–127, 3 figs.

– 1967c: Tabanidae de Turquie III. *Ibid.*, 2: 707–710.

– 1967d: Tabanidae des iles de la Mediterranée. *Ibid.*, 2: 264–272.

– 1967e: Tabanidae des Pays-Bas. *Zool. Bijdr.*, no. 9: 1–34, 24 cartes.

– 1968: Tabanidae des Balkans. *Ent. Ber.*, 28: 21–23.

– 1970: Tabanidae (Diptera) des Pyrénées (Étude préliminaire). *Pirineos,* 95: 75–90.

Lewis, T. & L. R. Taylor, 1965: Diurnal periodicity of flight by insects. *Trans. R. ent. Soc. Lond.*, 116: 393–479, 18 figs.

Loew, H., 1840: Bemerkungen über die in der Posener Gegend einheimischen Arten mehrere Zweiflügler-Gattungen. *Programm des königl. Friedrich-Wilhelm Gymnasiums zu Posen,* 40 pp., 1 pl.

– 1856: Neue Beiträge zur Kenntnis der Dipteren, 4. Beitrag, 57 pp., Berlin.

– 1857: Nachricht über syrische Dipteren. *Verh. zool.-bot. Ges. Wien,* 7: 79–86.

– 1858a: Zur Kenntnis der europäischen *Tabanus*-Arten. *Verh. zool-bot. Ges. Wien,* 8: 573–612.

– 1858b: Versuch einer Auseinandersetzung der europäischen *Chrysops*-Arten. *Ibid.*, 8: 613–634.

– 1858c: Ueber die europäischen Arten der Gattung *Silvius. Wien. ent. Monatschr.*, 2: 350–352.

– 1859: Neue Beiträge zur Kenntnis der Dipteren, 6. Beitrag, 50 pp., Berlin.

– 1862a: Über griechische Dipteren. *Berl. ent. Z.*, 6: 69–89.

– 1862b: Über einige bei Varna gefangene Dipteren. *Wien. ent. Monatschr.*, 6: 161–175.

– 1863: Über bei Sliwno in Balkan gefangene Dipteren. *Ibid.*, 7: 33–35.

– 1868: Cilicische Dipteren und einige mit ihnen concurrirende Arten. *Berl. ent. Z.*, 12: 369–386.

– 1870: Ueber von Herrn Dr. G. Seidlitz in Spanien gesammelte Dipteren. *Berl. ent. Z.*, 14: 137–144.

– 1874: Diptera nova a Hug. Theod. Christopho collecta. *Z. ges. Naturwiss.*, (N. F.), 9: 413–420.

Lundbeck, W., 1907: Tabanidae. *Diptera Danica,* 1: 85–132, figs. 31–40. København.

Lutta, A. S., 1947: Tabanidae of Kara-Kalpak region. Materialy k sist., biol., ekol. slepnej Niž. Delty Amu-Darja. *Izv. AN Uzb. SSR,* 5: 99–114. [In Russian].

– 1965: Larvae of Tabanidae in water. In: Fauna ozer Karelii, Moskva-Leningrad, pp. 300–310. [In Russian].

– 1970: Slepni (Diptera, Tabanidae) Karelii, 313 pp., Leningrad. [In Russian].

Lyneborg, L., 1959: A revision of the Danish species of *Hybomitra* End. with description of five new species. *Ent. Meddr,* 29: 78–150, 23 figs.

– 1960: Tabanidae, klæger. *Danm. Fauna,* 66: 157–222, figs. 119–162. København.

– 1961: On *Tabanus tropicus* and other Linnean species of Palaearctic Tabanidae (Diptera). *Ent. Meddr,* 31: 97–103.

– 1968: A comparative description of the male terminalia in *Thereva* Latr., *Dialineura* Rond., and *Psilocephala* Zett. (Diptera, Therevidae). *Ent. Meddr,* 36: 546–559.
– 1970: On some Stratiomyidae, Rhagionidae, Tabanidae, Acroceridae, Therevidae, and Nemestrinidae from Southern Spain (Diptera), with description of a new species. *Ibid.,* 37: 262–271, 8 figs.
– & M. Chvála, 1970: Revision of *Haematopota* Meig. in North Europe (Dipt. Tabanidae). With appendix on the *hispanica*-group. *Ent. Scand.,* 1: 30–40.
Mackerras, I. M., 1954: The classification and distribution of Tabanidae I. General Review. *Aust. J. Zool.,* 2: 431–454, 10 figs.
– 1955a: The classification and distribution of Tabanidae II. History, morphology, classification, subfamily Pangoniinae. *Ibid.,* 3: 439–511, 39 figs.
– 1955b: The classification and distribution of Tabanidae III. Subfamilies Scepsidinae and Chrysopinae. *Ibid.,* 3: 583–633, 26 figs.
– 1956: The Tabanidae of Australia I. General review. *Ibid.,* 4: 376–407, 1 pl., 8 figs.
Macquart, J., 1826: Insectes Diptères du nord de la France. Asiliques, Bombyliers, Xylotomes, Leptides, Stratiomydes, Xylophagites et Tabaniens. *Soc. des Sci., de l'Agr. et des Arts, Lille, Rec. des Trav.,* 1825: 324–499, 3 pls.
– 1834: Histoire naturelle des Insectes, Diptères. Tome premier, 578 pp., 12 pls., Paris.
– 1838: Diptères exotiques nouveaux ou peu connus. Vol. 1, pt. 1, pp. 5–221, 25 pls., Paris.
– 1846: Diptères exotiques nouveaux ou peu connus. Supplément, pp. 5–238, 20 pls., Paris.
– 1847: Diptères exotiques nouveaux ou peu connus. 2e supplement, pp. 5–104, 6 pls., Paris.
Maevskij, A. G., 1956: Some notes on the Horse-flies of the Byelorussian SSR. *Izv. ANN BSSR, ser. biol.,* 3: 113–117. [In Russian].
Mann, J., 1854: Über das Eierlegen von *Tabanus. Sber. Akad. Wiss. Wien,* 13: 351.
Marchand, W., 1920: The early stages of Tabanidae (Horse-flies). *Monogr. Rockefeller Inst. med. Res.,* 13: 203 pp., 15 pls.
Marino, M. T. P., 1949: La distribuzione geografica dei *Chrysops* s. lat. in Italia e regioni contermini e appunti biologici. *Redia,* 34: 313–337, 8 maps, 1 pl., 9 figs.
– 1951: Pangonini italiani e loro rapporti con la fauna palearctica. *Ibid.,* 36: 277–290, 5 figs., 1 pl., 4 maps.
Meigen, J. W., 1800: Nouvelle classification des mouches à deux ailes (Diptera L.), d'après un plan tout nouveau, 40 pp., Paris.
– 1804: Klassifikazion und Beschreibung der europäischen zweiflügeligen Insecten (Diptera). 1. Band (1. Abt.): 28 + 152 pp., 8 pls., (2. Abt.): 6 + 153 pp., 7 pls., Braunschweig.
– 1820: Systematische Beschreibung der bekannten europäischen zweiflügeligen Insekten. Vol. 2: X + 365 pp., pls. 12–21, Aachen.
– 1830: id op. Vol. 6: IV + 401 pp., pls. 55–66, Hamm.
– 1838: id op. Vol. 7 (oder Supplementband): XII + 434 pp., pls. 67–74, Hamm.
Mik, J., 1864: Dipterologische Beiträge. Mit einem Vorworte von J. R. Schiner. *Verh. zool.-bot. Ges. Wien,* 14: 785–798.
– 1898: Ueber eine Suite mediterraner Dipteren. *Wien. ent. Ztg.,* 17: 157–166.
Mikolajczyk, W., 1963: Review of the Polish species of the genus *Chrysozona* Meigen. *Annls zool., Warsz.,* 21: 93–107, 41 figs.

Minář, J., 1962: The influence of meteorological factors on the activity of some parasitic Diptera (Ceratopogonidae, Simuliidae, Tabanidae). *Čsl. Parasit.*, 9: 331–341, 2 figs.

Mirouse, R., 1955: Quelques Tabanides des Pyrénées ariégeoises. Essai sur leur répartition en altitude. *Entomologiste,* 11: 98–100.

– 1958: Tabanidés des Pyrénées orientales et ariégeoises: récoltes et observations. *Ibid.*, 14: 33–37, 7 figs.

Moucha, J., 1959a: Zur Kenntnis der Tabaniden der Kaukasusländer. *Acta Soc. ent. Čechoslov.*, 56: 129–136.

– 1959b: Zur Kenntnis der Tabanidenfauna Jugoslawiens. *Acta faun. ent. Mus. Nat. Pragae,* 5: 17–28.

– 1962: Tabanidae und Asilidae aus Albanien. *Ibid.*, 8: 21–36, 4 figs.

– 1964: Die Tabaniden-Fauna Österreichs. *Ibid.*, 10: 13–22.

– 1965: Zur Kenntnis der Tabaniden-Fauna Jugoslawiens 2. *Ibid.*, 11.: 71–78.

– 1969: Zum Stand der faunistischen Erforschung der Tabaniden Mitteleuropas. *Abh. Ber. NaturkMus. Görlitz,* 44: 129–132.

– 1970a: Tribus Chrysopini (Diptera, Tabanidae). *Acta ent. Mus. Nat. Pragae,* 38: 237–265.

– 1970b: Die Tabaniden-Fauna Österreichs (Diptera, Tabanidae). *Annln naturh. Mus. Wien,* 74: 211–219.

– 1971: Type-specimens of Palaearctic Tabanidae (Diptera) in the British Museum (Natural History). *Acta faun. ent. Mus. Nat. Pragae,* 14: 21–31.

Moucha, J. & M. Chvála, 1955: Revision der Tabaniden der Tschechoslowakei (I. Teil: Chrysopinae). *Folia zool. ent.*, 4: 227–238, 5 figs.

– 1957a: Beitrag zur Kenntnis der Gattung *Chrysops* nebst Beschreibung einer neuen Untergattung *Pseudochrysops* n. subgen. *Acta ent. Mus. Nat. Pragae,* 31: 159–162, 1 fig.

– 1957b: Beitrag zur Kenntnis der Bremsen-Fauna (Tabanidae) des östlichen Mittelmeergebietes. *Ent. Z. Frankf. a. M.*, 67: 180–184, 199–201.

– 1959: Revision der Gattung *Nemorius* Rond. *Acta Soc. ent. Čechoslov.*, 56: 137–141.

– 1960: Contribution à la répartition des Diptères Tabanidae en France et en Espagne. *Bull. Soc. ent. Mulhouse,* 1960: 17–19.

– 1961: A contribution to knowledge of Tabanidae of Bulgaria. *Acta faun. ent. Mus. Nat. Pragae,* 7: 31–41, 7 figs.

– 1963a: Die Beschreibung des Männchens von *Tabanus shannonellus* Kröber, 1936. *Acta ent. Mus. Nat. Pragae, 35*: 397–399.

– 1963b: Ergebnisse der Albanien-Expedition 1961 des Deutschen Entomologischen Institutes, 5. Beitrag: Diptera, Tabanidae. *Beitr. Ent.*, 13: 25–39.

– 1964: Notes on the genus *Therioplectes* Zeller, 1842. *Acta Soc. ent. Čechoslov.*, 61: 100–105, 8 figs.

– 1965: Contribution à la répartition des Diptères Tabanidae en Espagne et en Afrique du Nord. *Bull. Soc. ent. Mulhouse,* Sept.-Oct. 1965: 75–77.

– 1967a: Beschreibung des Männchens von *Haematopota scutellata* nebst Bemerkungen über die Gattung *Haematopota* Meig. in der Tschechoslowakei. *Acta ent. bohemoslov.,* 64: 224–231

– 1967b: Contribution à la répartition des Diptères Tabanidae en France et en Italie. *Bull, Soc. ent. Mulhouse,* Avril-Mai 1967: 28–30.

– 1967c: Zur Kenntnis der Tabanidenfauna Griechenlands. *Acta ent. Mus. Nat. Pragae,* 37: 269–273.
– 1968: Die Gattung *Hybomitra* Enderlein, 1922 in der Tschechoslowakei. *Acta faun. ent. Mus. Nat. Pragae,* 12: 263–294, 16 figs.
– 1969: Zur Kenntnis der Bremsengattung *Atylotus* Osten-Sacken in der Tschechoslowakei. *Acta ent. bohemoslov.,* 66: 321–329, 2 figs.

Muschamp, P. A. H., 1939: Gadflies in the Savoy Alps, 1938. *Entomologist's Rec. J. Var.,* 51: 49–55.

Neuhaus, G. M., 1886: Diptera marchica. Systematische Verzeichnis der Zweiflügler (Mücken und Fliegen) der Mark Brandenburg, 371 pp., 6 pls., Berlin.

Novikov, G. A., 1958: Diptera, *in:* Gory Kolskogo poluostrova. *Životnyj Mir SSSR,* 5: 559–562. [In Russian].

Oldroyd, H., 1939: Tabanidae, *in:* F. W. Edwards, H. Oldroyd & J. Smart: British blood-sucking flies, VIII + 156 pp., 45 pls., London.
– 1947: Results of the Armstrong College Expedition to Siwa Oasis (Libyan Desert) 1935. Diptera: Tabanidae, Asilidae, Therevidae and Bombyliidae. *Bull. Soc. Fouad I. Ent.,* 31: 113–120.
– 1952: The horse-flies (Diptera: Tabanidae) of the Ethiopian Region, Vol. I: *Haematopota* and *Hippocentrum,* XI + 226 pp., 318 figs., British Museum (Natural History), London.
– 1954: The horse-flies (Diptera: Tabanidae) of the Ethiopian Region. Vol. II: *Tabanus* and related genera, X + 341 pp., 238 figs., 5 pls., 31 maps, British Museum (Natural History), London.
– 1957: The horse-flies (Diptera: Tabanidae) of the Ethiopian Region. Vol. III: Subfamilies Chrysopinae, Scepsidinae and Pangoniinae and a revised classification, XII + 489 pp., 13 pls., 340 figs., 26 maps, British Museum (Natural History), London.
– 1962: South African Horse-flies of the tribe Pangoniinae. *J. Ent. Soc. S. Africa,* 25: 51–55, 1 fig.
– 1964: The Natural History of Flies, 324 pp., 40 figs., 32 pls., Weidenfeld & Nicolson, London.
– 1970: Family Tabanidae. *Handbk Ident. Br. Insects,* 9 (4): 46–68, figs. 124–192.

Olivier, A. G., 1789: Encyclopédie méthodique, vol. 4, Paris.

Olsufjev, N. G., 1934: Beiträge zur Tabanidenfauna des Leningrad Gebietes. *Mag. Parasit. Inst. Zool. Acad. Sci. URSS,* 4: 111–201, 19 figs.
– 1935: Diptera-Tabanidae, *in:* Praktikum medicinskoj parazitologii, pp. 159–180, E. N. Pavlovskij editor. [In Russian].
– 1936: Beiträge zur Tabanidenfauna Westsibiriens. *Mag. Parasit. Inst. Zool. Acad. Sci. URSS,* 6: 201–245, 11 figs. [In Russian].
– 1937: Tabanidae. *Fauna SSSR,* 7: 433 pp., 216 figs., Moskva-Leningrad. [In Russian and German].
– 1940: To the fauna of Tabanidae in Caucasus. *Acad. Sci. URSS, Fil. Géorgienne, sect. zool., Tbilisi,* 3: 45–90, 4 figs. [In Russian].
– 1962: On the horse-flies in Altai Territory. *Zool. Zh.,* 41: 882–892, 2 figs. [In Russian].
– 1964: A study of the fauna of Tabanidae in the West part of Great Caucasian Mountains, with a description of a new genus. *Bull. Mosk. Obšč. Ispit. Pritody, otd. biol.,* 69: 73–76. [In Russian].

– 1967: New species of horse-flies from Palaearctic. *Ént. Obozr.*, 46: 379–390, 12 figs. [In Russian].
– 1969a: Tabanidae – Slepni, *in:* Opredelitel nasekomych Evropejsko, časti SSSR, 5: 481–500, figs. 292–303, Leningrad. [In Russian].
– 1969b: On the taxonomy and distribution of Tabanidae (Diptera) of the Palaearctic region. *Acta ent. bohemoslov.*, 66: 115–121.
– 1970: New and little known Tabanidae (Diptera) from the fauna of the USSR and neighbouring countries. *Ent. Obozr.*, 49: 683–687. [In Russian].
– & D. A. Golov, 1935: On the importance of horse-flies and especially of the cleg Haematopota pluvialis in the epidemiology of tularaemia. *Med. Zh. Kazach.*, 4–5: 29–40. [In Russian].
– & T. G. Melnikova, 1962: On the fauna of horse-flies in the Crimea. *Ént. Obozr.*, 41: 576–578, 1 map. [In Russian].
– & P. P. Lelep, 1935: Über die Bedeutung der Bremsen bei der Verbreitung des Milzbrandes (Anthrax). Parasites, transmetteurs, anim. venimeux, 25e Anniv. Trav. Sci. Pavlovskij, 1909–1934, pp. 145–197, 9 figs., Moskow. [In Russian].
– , J. Moucha & M. Chvála, 1967: Zur Taxonomie und Verbreitung der europäischen und kleinasiatischen Arten der *Tabanus bovinus*-Gruppe. *Acta Soc. ent. Čechoslov.*, 64: 303–313, 6 figs.

Osten-Sacken, C. R., 1858: Umriss der gegenwärtigen Kenntnis der entomologischen Verhältnisse der Fauna der Umgebungen von St. Peterburg. *Journ. Minist. Volksaufklärungen,* Separatum, 166 pp., St. Petersburg.

Ovazza, M., J. L. Camicas & L. Pichon, 1968: Notes pour une révision systématique de l'espèce *Atylotus agrestis* Wiedemann, 1828. *Cah. O.R.S. T.O.M., sér. Ent. méd.*, 6: 3–14, 3 pls.
– & R. Tauflieb, 1954: Les genitalia femalles des Tabanidés et leur importance systématique. *Annls Parasit. hum. comp.*, 29: 250–264, 8 figs.

Palm, J., 1869: Beitrag zur Dipterenfauna Tirols. *Verh. zool.-bot. Ges. Wien,* 19: 395–454.
– 1876: Beitrag zur Dipteren-Fauna Oesterreichs. *Ibid.*, 25: 411–422.

Pandellé, L., 1883: Synopsis des Tabanidés de France. *Revue ent.*, 2: 165–228.

Paramonov, S. J., 1925: Zur Kenntnis der Insektenfauna (hauptsächlich Diptera) von Bessarabien und der Ukraine. *Societas ent.*, 40: 21–23.
– 1929: Dipterological Fragments. *Zbirn. Prats zool. Mus.*, 7: 179–193.
– 1961: Dipterologische Fragmente XXXVII. *Eos*, 37: 71–76.

Pavlova, R. P., 1968: The fecundity of females of *Tabanus bovinus* and *Hybomitra solstitialis* in relation to their physiological state. *Zool. Zh.*, 47: 1103–1106, 2 figs. [In Russian].

Pavlovskij, E. N., 1941: Protection against blood-sucking flies (Culicidae, Simuliidae, Tabanidae), 65 pp., Moskva-Leningrad. [In Russian].
– , G. S. Pervomajskij & K. P. Čagin, 1951: Gnus – Blood-sucking flies, their importance and control. *Medgiz. Moskva,* 118 pp.

Pechuman, L. L. & A. Stone, 1968: A new synonymy in *Hybomitra. Proc. ent. Soc. Wash.*, 70: 302.

Philip, C. B., 1941: Comments on the supra-specific categories of Nearctic Tabanidae. *Can. Ent.*, 73: 2–14.
– 1947: A cataloque of the blood-sucking fly family Tabanidae (horse-flies and deerflies) of the Nearctic region North of Mexico. *Am. Midl. Nat.*, 37: 257–324.

– 1948: Notes on Egyptian Tabanidae with comment on certain supraspecific categories of Old World Tabanidae. *Bull. Soc. Fouad I. Ent.*, 32: 77–83.
– 1950: Corrections and addenda to a catalogue of Nearctic Tabanidae. *Am. Midl. Nat.*, 43: 430–437.
– 1953: The genus *Chrysozona* Meigen in North America. *Proc. ent. Soc. Wash.*, 55: 247–251.
– 1956: Records of horseflies in Northeast Asia. *Jap. J. sanit. Zool.*, 7: 221–230, 1 fig.
– 1959: Some records of Tabanidae from Iran. *Mitt. schweiz. ent. Ges.*, 32: 333–336.
– 1960: Another Holarctic species of Tabanidae. *Can. Ent.*, 92: 697–699.
– 1961: Notes on Palaearctic *Nemorius* with description of one new species. *Bull. Annls Soc. r. ent. Belg.*, 97: 225–236, 9 figs.
– 1965: Family Tabanidae, *in:* A catalog of the Diptera of America North of Mexico, pp. 319–342, Washington.
– & T. H. G. Aitken, 1958: Records of Tabanidae from Sardinia and Corsica. *Memorie Soc. ent. ital.*, 37: 87–97, 2 figs.
Picard, F. & G. R. Blanc, 1913: Sur les moeurs lignicoles de la larve de *Tabanus cordiger* Meig. *Bull. Soc. ent. Fr.*, 18: 318–321.
Pleske, T., 1910: Beschreibung des noch unbekannten Männchens des *Chrysops divaricatus* Loew. *Ann. Mus. Zool. St. Petersburg*, 15: 430–435.
Pokorny, E., 1887: III. Beitrag zur Dipterenfauna Tirols. *Verh. zool.-bot. Ges. Wien*, 37: 381–420, 7 figs.
Poljakov, V. A., 1965: Protection of reindeer against Tabanids. *Veterinariya*, 42: 91–92. [In Russian].
– 1968: Protection of reindeer against Tabanids. *Ibid.*, 45: 91–94, 1 fig. [In Russian].
Poppius, B., C. Lundström & R. Frey, 1917: Dipteren aus dem Sarekgebiet. *Naturwiss. Untersuch. Sarekgeb., Swedish Lappland*, 4: 665–696.
Portevin, G., 1904: Contribution au Cataloque des Diptères de Normandie. *Feuille jeun. Nat.*, 4e sér., 34: 209–213.
– 1915: id op. *Ibid.*, 35: 40–43.
Portschinsky, J. A., 1871: Entomological notes on my stay in the Gubernia of St. Petersburg, Ujezd Gdovsk. *Trudy russ. K. ént. Obshch.*, 7: 44–54.
– 1915: Die Bremsen (Tabanidae) und die einfachsten Mittel zu ihrer Bekämpfung, 6. Auflage. *Trudy ent. ucen. Kom.*, St. Petersburg, 63 pp., 21 figs.
Preyssler, J. D. E., 1790: Verzeichnis böhmisher Insekten. Erstes Hundert, 108 pp., 2 pls., Praha.
Puls, J. C., 1865: Catalog der Dipteren aus der Berliner Gegend gesammelt von J. F. Ruthe. *Berl. ent. Z.*, 8: 1–14.
Rageau, J. & J. Mouchet, 1968: Les Arthropodes hématophages de Camargue. *Cah. O.R.S.T.O.M., sér. Ent. méd.*, 5: 263–281.
Rapp, O., 1942: Die Fliegen Thüringens unter besonderer Berücksichtigung der faunitisch-oekologischen Geographie. *Schr. Mus. Naturk. Stadt Erfurt*, 574 pp., mimeographed.
Rasnitsyn, S. P., 1963: A review of methods employed to control horseflies. *Medskaya Parazit.*, 32: 611–616. [In Russian].
Rateau, J., 1948: Sur la nymphe du *Dasystipia (Ochrops) nigrifacies* Gobert. *Entomologiste*, 4: 209–210, 1 fig.
Remm, H., 1953: Tabanidae of Estonia, with notes on collecting and classification. *Abiks Loodusevaat.*, Tartu, 13: 1–28, 6 figs.

– 1957: Notes on blood-sucking flies in the Transcarpathic region, USSR. *Dokl. Soobsc., ser. biol. Uzg. Gos. Univ., Uzgorod,* 1: 69–71.
– 1959a: Zur Kenntnis der Dipterenfauna von Avaste-Moor. *Ent. Kogumik Tartu,* 1: 102–113, 2 figs.
– 1959b: Zur Kenntnis der Ökologie der Tabaniden Estlands. *Ibid.,* 1: 181–188.
– 1961: On two species of horse-flies in Estonia. *Faun. Märkmeid,* Tartu, 1: 138–140.
Ringdahl, O., 1914: Fyndorter för Diptera. *Ent. Tidskr.,* 35: 69–77.
– 1915: Entomologiska dagboksanteckningar från västra Jämtland. *Ibid.,* 36: 1–18.
– 1931: Flugor – Diptera Brachycera, *in:* Insektfaunan inom Abisko Nationalpark III. *K. svenska VeterskAkad. Skr. Naturskydd.,* 18: 1–36.
Roberts, R. H., 1966a: A technique for rearing the immature stages of Tabanidae. *Ent. News,* 77: 79–82, 1 fig.
– 1966b: Biological studies on Tabanidae I. Induced oviposition. *Mosquito News,* 26: 435–438, 2 figs.
– 1967: Feeding of horse-flies on plant juices. *Ent. News,* 78: 250–251.
– 1968: A feeding association between *Hippelates* (Dipt.: Chloropidae) and Tabanidae on cattle: its possible role in transmission of Anaplasmosis. *Mosquito News,* 28: 236–237.
– & R. J. Dicke, 1959: Wisconsin Tabanidae. *Trans. Wis. Acad. Sci. Arts Lett.,* 47 (1958): 23–42.
– 1964: The biology and taxonomy of some immature Nearctic Tabanidae. *Ann. ent. Soc. Am.,* 57: 31–40, 22 figs.
Röder, V., 1884: Dipteren von der Insel Sardinien. *Wien. ent. Ztg,* 3: 40–42.
– 1887: Uebersicht der beim Dorf Elos bei Kisamos auf der Insel Kreta von Herrn E. v. Oertzen gesammelten Dipteren. *Berl. ent. Z.,* 31: 73–75.
Roman, E., 1926: Distribution géographique de quelques Tabanidae dans le Sud-est de la France – localité nouvelle de *Cyrtopogon mayerduri. Bull. mens. Soc. linn. Lyon,* 18: 121–122.
– 1959: Contribution à la répartition en France des Diptères Tabanidae avec remarques critiques sur quelques espèces et variétés. *Cah. Nat.,* Paris, 15: 3–20, 4 figs.
Rondani, C., 1856: Dipterologicae Italicae prodromus. Tomus 1: 1–226, Parmae.
– 1868: Diptera aliqua in America meridionali lecta a Prof. P. Strobel annis 1866–1867. *Ann. Soc. Nat.,* 3: 24–40.
Roser, V., 1834: Verzeichniss der in Würtemberg vorkommenden zweiflüglichen Insecten. *Correspondenzbl. Landwirthsch. Ver. Würtemberg (Stuttgart),* 1: 19 pp. – Nachtrag. *Ibid.,* 1: 49–64 (1840).
Rossi, F. W., 1849: Systematisches Verzeichniss der zweiflügeligen Insecten (Diptera) des Erzherzogthums Oestreich etc., 10 + 86 pp., Wien.
Rossi, P. (= Rossius), 1790: Fauna Etrusca, sistens Insecta, quae in provinciis Florentina et Pisana praesertim collegit, vol 1: 272 pp., vol. 2: 348 pp., Liburni (= Livorno).
Sachibzadaev, K. S., 1957: On the faunistics and ecology of horse flies in the region of Trans-Ili Alatau. *Tezisy Dokl. sovéšč. zool. Sibiri,* Novosibirsk, pp. 67–68. [In Russian].
Sahlberg, J., 1905: De finska arterna af diptersläktet *Chrysops. Meddn. Soc. Fauna Flora fenn.,* 31: 103–105.
Salom, F., 1961: Las *Haematopota* de la Peninsula Ibérica (Dipt., Tabanidae). *Boln R. Soc. esp. Hist. nat. (B),* 59: 73–108, 15 figs.
– 1967: Las *Haematopota* de la Peninsula Ibérica II. *Ibid.,* 65: 17–20, 4 figs.

Schaerffenberg, B., 1939: Beobachtungen über die Widerstandfähigkeit der Tabanidenlarven. *Anz. Schädlingsk.*, 15: 94–95.

Schiner, J. R., 1857: Dipterologische Fragmente. *Verh. zool.-bot. Ges. Wien*, 7: 3–20.

– 1868: Reise der Österreichischen Fregatte Novara um die Erde, etc. Zool. Teil, Diptera, 6 + 388 pp., 4 pls., Wien.

Scholtz, H., 1850: Beiträge zur Kunde schlesischen Zweiflügler. *Z. Ent.*, 4: 35–40.

Schrank, F., 1781: Enumeratio Insectorum Austriae indigenorum. August. Vindelicor., Klett, 9 + 548 pp., 4 pls.

– 1803–04: Fauna Boica, vol. 3, teil 1: 272 pp., teil 2: 372 pp., Nürnberg.

Schummel, T. E., 1838: Diptera Schlesiens. *Arbeit. schles. Ges. vaterl. Kultur*, 1836: 107–110.

Scopoli, J. A., 1763: Entomologia Carniolica exhibens Insecta Carnioliae indigena et distributa in ordinis, genera, species, varietates, methodo Linneana. 36 + 420 pp. Vindobonae (= Wien).

Séguy, E., 1926: Diptères Brachycéres: Tabanidae. *Faune Fr.*, 13: 308 pp., Paris.

– 1929: Étude systématique d'une collection de Diptères d'Espagne, formée par le R. P. Longin Navas S. J. *Méms. Soc. ent. Esp.*, 3: 1–30.

– 1934: Diptères d'Espagne. Étude systématique basée principalement sur les collections formées par le R. P. Longin Navas, S. J. *Mems Acad. Cienc. exact. fis.-quim. nat. Zaragoza*, 3: 1–54, 7 figs.

– 1936: Diptères de Açores. Voyage de M. M. L. Chopard et A. Méguignon aux Açores, 1930. *Annls Soc. ent. Fr.*, 105: 11–26.

– 1950: La Biologie des Diptères. *Encycl. ent.*, 26: 1–609, Paris.

Shannon, R. C. & J. Hadjinicolaou, 1936: List of Tabanidae of Greece. *Acta Inst. Mus. zool. Univ. athen.*, 1: 160–172.

Shevtshenko, V. V., 1957: The infraspecific variability of some palaearctic horse-flies. *Tezisy Dokl. 3. sovešč. Vses. ent. Obšč.*, Moskva-Leningrad, 1: 29–30. [In Russian].

– 1959: The importance of morphology of genitalia in horse-flies in taxonomic research. *Tezisy Dokl. 10. sovešč. parazit. probl.*, Moskva-Leningrad, 2: 137–138. [In Russian].

– 1960: The morphology of genitalia in some palaearctic species of the subfamily Chrysopinae. *Trudy Inst. zool. AN Kaz. SSR*, Alma-Ata, 11: 157–172, 14 figs. [In Russian].

– 1961: Tabanidae of Kazakhstan. *Izd. AN Kaz. SSR*, 327 pp., 125 figs., 55 maps, Alma-Ata. [In Russian].

– 1962: On the morphology of genitalia in some palaearctic species of *Haematopota*. *Trudy Inst. zool. AN Kaz. SSR*, Alma-Ata, 18: 224–234, 8 figs. [In Russian].

Siebke, H., 1863: Beretning om en i Sommeren 1861 foretagen entomologisk Reise. *Nyt Mag. Naturvid.*, 12: 105–192.

– 1866: Entomologisk reise i Romsdals Amt i Sommeren 1864. *Ibid.*, 14: 375–388.

– 1877: Enumeratio Insectorum Norvegicorum. Fasc. IV, III–XIV + 255 pp., 1 map. Christianiae (= Oslo).

Skufin, K. V., 1938: Contribution to the knowledge of the horse-flies of the Karachayevsk region. *Izv. Voronezh. gosud. Pedag. Inst.*, Voronež, 2: 73–80. [In Russian].

– 1967: Notes on the morphology of larvae of some Tabanids. Vrednye i poleznye nasekomye. *Izd. gosud. Univ. Voronež*, pp. 168–206, 12 figs. [In Russian].

Smith, G. E., S. G. Breeland & E. Pickard, 1965: The Malaise trap – a survey tool in medical entomology. *Mosquito News,* 25: 398–400, 1 fig.

Soboleva, R. G., 1956: Tabanids as ectoparasites on domestic animals. *Veterinariya,* 33: 71–77, 3 figs. [In Russian].

– 1965: Contribution to the knowledge of ecology of the most abundant species of the horse-flies in the southern part of the region of Primorye. *Tezisy Dokl. Dalnevost. Fil. SO AN SSSR,* Vladivostok, pp. 18–21. [In Russian].

– 1968: On the morphology and biology of some rare and little-known horse-flies of the Primorye Territory. *Fauna i ekologia nasekomych Dalnego Vostoka,* Vladivostock, pp. 161–169, 3 figs. [In Russian].

– , N. I. Uvarova & B. K. Gavrilova, 1962: Control of Tabanidae and Muscidae. *Soobšž. Fil. Sibiris. Otd. AN SSSR,* Vladivostock, 16: 105–110. [In Russian].

Speiser, P., 1905a: Ergänzungen zu Czwalinas »Neuem Verzeichnis der Fliegen Ost- und Westpreussens«. *Z. wiss. InsektBiol.,* 1: 405–409, 461–467.

– 1905b: Einen für unsere Fauna neu gefundenen *Tabanus* und die Familie der Tabaniden im allgemeinen. *Schr. phys.-ökon. Ges. Königsb.,* 46: 161–164.

– 1909: Dipterologische Ergebnisse eines Besuches im Samland, Juni 1909: *Ibid.,* 50: 301–302.

– 1912: Bemerkungen und Notizen zur geographischen Verbreitung einiger blutsaugenden Insekten. *Trans. 2nd Int. Congr. Ent.,* pp. 205–207.

Spuris, Z., 1961: New data on the fauna of horse-flies in the Latvian SSR. *Latv. Ent.,* 3: 51–58.

– 1962: Étude sur la faune des Diptères de Lettonie. *2. zool. Konf. Lit. SSR,* Vilnijus, pp. 121–123.

Stackelberg, A. A., 1926a: Notes on the genus *Chrysops. Bull ent. Res.,* 16: 325–328, 1 fig.

– 1926b: Tabanidae, in: Keys for identification of blood-sucking flies. *Vest. Mikrobiol. Épidem. Parazit.,* Saratov, 5: 43–56, 24 figs. [In Russian].

– 1933: Les mouches de la partie européenne de l'URSS. Tabl. analit., Leningrad, 742 pp., 309 figs.

– 1950: Diptera, in: Životnyj mir SSSR III. Zona stepoj, pp. 162–213, figs. 112–143, Moskva-Leningrad. [In Russian].

– 1953: Diptera, in: Životnyj mir SSSR IV. Lesnaja Zona, pp. 227–318, figs. 103–155, Moskva-Leningrad. [In Russian].

– 1954: Contribution to the knowledge of Diptera in the region of Leningrad. *Trudy zool. Inst. AN SSR,* 15: 199–228. [In Russian].

– 1958: Diptera, in: Životnyj mir SSSR V. Gornye oblasti Evropejakoj časti SSSR, pp. 288–318, figs. 122–136, Moskva-Leningrad. [In Russian].

– & A. E. Terterjan, 1953: On the morphology of the female genitalia of Tabanidae. *Dokl. Akad. Nauk armyan. SSR,* Erevan, 16: 53–64, 9 figs. [In Russian].

Stammer, H. J., 1924: Die Larven der Tabaniden. *Z. Morph. Ökol. Tiere,* 1: 121–170, 2 pls., 20 figs.

Starke, H., 1954: Beitrag zur Dipteren-fauna der Oberlausitz, Familien: Syrphidae, Tabanidae und Asilidae. *Abh. naturk. Mus. Görlitz,* 34: 85–100.

Steyskal, G. C., 1953: A suggested classification of the lower brachycerous Diptera. *Ann. ent. Soc. Am.,* 46: 237–242.

– & S. El Bialy, 1967: A list of Egyptian Diptera with a bibliography and key to families. *U. Arab. Rep., Min. Agric. techn. Bull.,* 3: 1–87, 16 figs.

Stone, A., 1941: The generic names of Meigen, 1800 and their proper application (Diptera). *Ann. ent. Soc. Am.*, 34: 404–418.

Strand, E., 1925: *Ochrops lattesica* Strand n. n., in: O. Kröber: Beiträge zur Kenntnis der palaearktischen Tabaniden. Teil III. *Arch. Naturgesch.*, Abt. A., 90 (1924): 14.

– 1927: Animaux divers (à l'exclusion des Arachnides, Lépidoptères et Hyménoptères) nommés jusqu'en 1926 dans les travaux de M. le Professeur Embrik Strand. *Ibid.*, 91 (1925): 62–66.

– 1928: Miscellanea nomenclatorica zoologica et palaeontologica. *Ibid.*, 92 (1926): 30–75.

– 1932: Miscellanea nomenclatorica zoologica et palaeontologica III, IV. *Folia zool. hydrobiol.*, 4: 133–147.

Strobl, G., 1880: Dipterologische Funde um Seitenstetten. Ein Beitrag zur Fauna Niederösterreichs. *XIV Programm des K.-K. Ober-Gymnasiums der Benedictiner in Seitenstetten,* 65 pp.

– 1898: Spanische Dipteren 1. Teil. *Wien. ent. Ztg,* 17: 294–302.

– 1906: Spanische Dipteren, II. Beitrag. *Mems. R. Soc. esp. Hist. nat.*, 3 (1905): 271–422.

Strohm, K., 1933: Diptera, in: Der Kaiserstuhl. Eine Naturgeschichte des Vulkangebirges am Oberrhein. Freiburg i. Br., pp. 321–322, 1 fig.

Surcouf, J. M. R., 1908: Sur une nouvelle division des Tabanides du genre *Pangonia. Bull. Mus. natn. Hist. nat.*, Paris, 1908: 282–85.

– 1913: Note sur les Tabanidae d'Algérie et de Tunesie. *Arch. Inst. Pasteur Tunis,* 3–4: 183–186, 1 pl.

– 1914: Note sur les variations du *Tabanus algirus* Macquart en Algérie et en Tunisie. *Bull. Mus. natn. Hist. nat.*, Paris, 1914: 123–126.

– 1920a: Sur une critique récente de J. Villeneuve. *Bull. Soc. ent. Fr.*, 1920: 249–251.

– 1920b: Note sur les variations du *Tabanus nemoralis* Meig. *Ibid.*, 1920: 268–269.

– 1921a: Diptera, fam. Tabanidae. *Genera Insect.*, 175: 182 pp.

– 1921b: Note synonymique sur la *Diachlorus maroccanus* Bigot. *Bull. Soc. ent. Fr.*, 1921: 143.

– 1921c: Note sur un accouplement aberrant chez les Dipteres. *Ibid.*, 1921: 46–47.

– 1922: Diptères nouveaux ou peu connus. *Annls Soc. ent. Fr.*, 91: 237–244.

– 1923: Note sur un Diptère à vie larvaire littorale, *Tabanus (Ochrops) seurati* n. sp. *Bull. Soc. ent. Fr.*, 1922: 297–299.

– 1924a: Les Tabanides de France et des pays limitrophes. *Encycl. ent.*, sér. A5, Paris, Lechevalier, 261 pp., 133 figs.

– 1924b: Description d'une espèce nouvelle de *Pangonia* paléarctique. *Encycl. ent.*, sér. B2, Dipt. 1: 65, Paris.

– 1924c: Note diptérologique sur les variations du *Theriopectes* [sic] *muhlfeldi* Brauer. *Annls Soc. ent. Fr.*, 93: 22.

– & E. Fischer, 1924: Notes sur la vie larvaire et nymphale du *Tabanus bromius* L. *Bull. Soc. ent. Fr.*, 1924: 232–237, 7 figs.

– & G. Ricardo, 1909: Étude monographique des Tabanides d'Afrique (groupe des Tabanus), Masson Paris, 260 pp., 26 figs., 22 cartes, 3 pls.

Szilády, Z., 1914: Neue und wenig bekannte paläarktische Tabaniden. *Annls Mus. nat. hung.*, 12: 661–678, 8 figs.

– 1915: Subgenus *Ochrops*, eine neue Untergattung der Gattung *Tabanus* L., 1761. *Ent. Mitt.*, 4: 93–107, 2 pls.

– 1922: Die Familie Tabanidae (Bremsen), in: Explorationes zoologicae ab E. Ssiki in Albania peractae IV. *Balkán-Kutat. Tud. Eredm.*, Budapest, 1: 67–70.
– 1923: New or little known Horseflies (Tabanidae). *Biologica hung.*, 1 (1): 1–39, 29 figs., 1 pl.
– 1927: Über Enderleins Bremsengattung *Sziládya* und *Sziladynus*. *Zool. Anz.*, 74: 202–205.
Takahasi, H., 1962: Tabanidae, in: *Fauna japonica*, Biogeographical Society of Japan, Tokyo, 143 pp., 74 figs., 12 pls.
Tamarina, N. A., 1951: On the life-history of *Chrysops relictus* Meig. *Vest. mosk. gos. Univ.*, Moskva, 6: 101–108. [In Russian].
– 1956: On the morphology of larvae and pupae of the species *Chrysops relictus* Meig. and *C. rufipes* Meig. *Trudy vses. ént. obšč.*, Moskva-Leningrad, 45: 167–192, 19 figs. [In Russian].
Tashiro, J. & H. H. Schwardt, 1949: Biology of the major species of Horse-flies in Central New York. *J. econ. Ent.*, 42: 269–272, 3 figs.
Terterjan, A. E., 1954: Aufsammlungen der Tabaniden an verschiedenen Körperteilen der Haustiere. *Izv. AN Armen. SSR*, Jerevan, 7: 71–78.
– 1962: Zur Ökologie der Larven und Puppen einiger in Armenien verbreiteter Tabaniden. *Verh. XI. Int. Kongr. Ent. Wien*, 1: 192–193.
Teskey, H. J., 1969: Larvae and pupae of some Eastern North American Tabanidae. *Mem. ent. Soc. Canada*, 63: 1–147, 148 figs.
Thalhammer, J., 1899: Tabanidae, in: *Fauna Regni Hungariae*, Budapest, pp. 23–24.
Theodor, O., 1965: Tabanidae of Israel. *Israel J. Zool.*, 14: 241–257, 2 figs.
Thompson, P. H., 1969: Collecting methods for Tabanidae. *Ann. ent. Soc. Am.*, 62: 50–57.
Thomson, C. G., 1868: Diptera, in: Kongliga Svenska Fregatten Eugenies Resa omkring jorden under befäl af C. A. Virgin åren 1851–53, Zool. 6, 443–614, 1 pl., Stockholm.
Thornley, A., 1933: Diptera Tabanidae from Cornwall. *J. ent. Soc. S. Engl.*, 1: 60–62.
Thorsteinson, A. J., 1958: The orientation of horse-flies and deer-flies I. The attractance of heat to Tabanids. *Entomologia exp. appl.*, 1: 191–196.
– 1962: Sensory regulation of feeding behaviour and orientation to the host on biting flies. *Verh. XI. Int. Kongr. Ent. Wien*, 2: 426.
– , G. K. Bracken & W. Hanec, 1964: The Manitoba horse-fly trap. *Can. Ent.*, 96: 166.
– G. K. Bracken & W. Hanec, 1965: The orientation behaviour of horse-flies and deer-flies III. The use of traps in the study of orientation of Tabanids in the field. *Entomologia exp. appl.*, 8: 189–192, 1 fig.
– G. K. Bracken & W. Tostowaryk, 1966: The orientation behaviour of horse-flies and deer-flies V. The influence of the number and inclination of the reflecting surfaces of attractiveness to Tabanids of glossy black polyhedra. *Can. J. Zool.*, 44: 275–279, 1 fig.
Thunberg, C. P., 1827: Tabani septendecim novae species descriptae. *Nova Acta R. Soc. Scient. upsal.*, 9: 53–62, 63–75, 1 pl.
Timon-David, J., 1937: Recherches sur le peuplement des hautes montagnes. Diptères de la vallée de Chamonix et du Massif du Mont Blanc. *Annls Fac. Sci. Marseille*, 10: 1–54, 14 figs.
– 1950: Diptères des Pyrénées Ariégeois. Notes écologiques et biogéographiques. *Bull. Soc. Hist. nat. Toulouse*, 85: 11–25, 5 figs.

Tóth, S., 1964: Angaben über die Dipteren des Tardi-Tales I. Bombyliidae und Tabanidae. *Folia ent. hung.*, 17: 67–73.
– 1966: Neue Angaben zur Dipteren-Fauna des Theistales. *Tiscia,* Szeged, 2: 107–112, 1 fig.
– 1967: Angaben über die Dipteren-Fauna des Tisca-Tales (Tabanidae, Stratiomyiidae, Rhagionidae). *Folia ent. hung.*, 20: 37–45.
Trojan, P., 1955: Tabanidae of the surroundings of Warszawa. *Fragm. faun.*, 7: 199–207.
– 1956: Metodyka badan ekologicznych Tabanidae. Some methodics for the investigation of the ecology of the horse-flies. *Ekologia Polska,* ser. B: 41–46, Warszawa.
– 1959: Tabanidae, in: Klucze do oznaczania owadów Polski, part 28, 1–69, 209 figs., Warszawa.
Van Gaver, F. & J. Timon-David, 1930: Observations sur la faune diptérologique du Haut-Queyras. *Annls Fac. Sci. Marseille,* 4: 1–13.
Vapnik, E. E. & T. T. Senčuk, 1959: Importance des Arthropodes hématophages comme vecteurs de tularémie dans les foyers naturels de Bielorussie. *10. sovešč. Parazit. Probl. Prir. Bolez.*, 2: 38–39.
Venturi, F., 1958: Notulae dipterologicae XIX. Sul maschio di *Chrysops melicharii* Mik. *Frustula ent.*, 5: 1–6, 4 figs.
Verrall, G. H., 1883: Diptera in Arran. *Entomologist's mon. Mag.*, 19: 222–226.
– 1909: British Flies V, 780 + 34 pp., 407 figs., London.
Villeneuve, J., 1904: Contribution au catalogue des Diptères de France: Tabanidae. *Feuille jeun. Nat.*, 34: 225–229.
– 1920: Sur *Ochrops (Atylotus) fulvus* Meig. *Annls Soc. ent. Belg.*, 60: 65–66.
– 1921: Description des Diptères nouveaux. *Ibid.*, 61: 157–161.
Villers, C. J. de, 1789: Caroli Linnaei entomologia, etc., vol. 3: 656 pp., 4 pls., Lugduni, Piestro et Delamolliere.
Vimmer, A., 1925: Larvy a kukly dvojkřídlého hmyzu středoevropského se zvlaštním zřetelem na škúdce rostlin kulturních. Česká grafická Unie Praha, 349 pp., 59 pls.
– 1926: O metamorphose ovádu (Tabanus). *Časopis čes. spol. ent.*, Praha, 23: 15–17.
Violovič, N. A., 1956: New species of Tabanidae from Far East of the USSR. *Paraz. Sbor. zool. Inst. AN SSSR,* Moskva-Leningrad, 16: 152–154, 2 figs. [In Russian].
– 1968: The Tabanidae (horse-flies) of Siberia. *Sib. Otd., Biol. Inst. AN SSSR,* Novosibirsk, 283 pp., 69 figs. [In Russian].
Walker, F., 1848: List of the specimens of Dipterous Insects in the collection of the British Museum London, part 1: 229 pp., London.
– 1850a: Insecta Saundersiana, or Characters of undescribed Insects in the collection of W. W. Saunders, Diptera, part 1: 75 pp., 1 pl.
– 1850b: Characters of undescribed Diptera in the British Museum. *Newman's Zoologist,* 8, appendix: pp. LXV, XCV and CXXI.
– 1854: List of the specimens of Dipterous Insects in the collection of the British Museum London, part 5 (Suppl. 1): 330 pp., London.
– 1857a: Catalogue of the Dipterous Insects collected at Singapore and Malacca by Mr. A. R. Wallace, with descriptions of new species. *J. Linn. Soc., Zool.,* 1 (1856): 4–39, 2 pls.
– 1857b: Characters of undescribed Diptera in the collection of W. W. Saunders. *Trans. ent. Soc. Lond.*, 4 (1856–58): 119–158, 190–235.
– 1859: Catalogue of the Dipterous Insects collected in the Aru Islands by Mr. A. R. Wallace, with descriptions of new species, *J. Linn. Soc., Zool.,* 3: 77–131.

– 1860: Characters of undescribed Diptera in the collection of Mr. W. W. Saunders. *Trans. ent. Soc. Lond.,* 5 (1858–61): 268–334.
– 1871: List of Diptera collected in Egypt and Arabia, by J. K. Lord, Esq., with description of the species new to science. *Entomologist,* 5: 255–263.
Weidner, H., 1962: Dem Hamburger Dipterologen Dr. h. c. Otto Kröber zum 80. Geburtstag. *Ent. Mitt. zool. StInst. zool. Mus. Hamb.,* 37: 214–220. [Bibliography].
Weinberg, M., 1960: Beiträge zur Verbreitung der Tabaniden in der Rumänischen Volksrepublik. *Trav. Mus. Hist. nat. Gr. Antipa,* 2: 411–413.
Wentges, H., 1952: Zur Biologie von *Tabanus sudeticus sudeticus* Zell. *NachrBl. bayer. Ent.,* 1: 78–79.
Wiedemann, C. R. W., 1828: Aussereuropäische zweiflügeligen Insekten, 1: XXXII + 608 pp., 7 pls., Hamm.
Wooton, A., 1967: Observations on the insect life of Czechoslovakia, together with some notes on other fauna and flora. *Entomologist,* 100: 202–212, 1 fig.
Wu, C., 1939: Family Tabanidae. *Catalogus Insectorum Sinensium,* 5: 173–200.
Wyniger, R, 1953: Beiträge zur Ökologie, Biologie und Zucht einiger europäischer Tabaniden. *Acta trop.,* 10: 310–347, 19 figs.
Zajcev, V. F. & A. E. Terterjan, 1966: *Villa ventruosa* Loew (Diptera, Bombyliidae) parasite de la larve et de la pupe des Tabanidae de la RSS d'Arménie. *Biol. Zh. Arm.,* Jerevan, 19: 83–89, 3 figs.
Zajonc, I., 1959: Beitrag zur Kenntnis der Bremsen in der Slowakei. *Acta Univ. agric. Nitra,* 3: 205–212.
Zangheri, P., 1949: Fauna di Romagna – Ditteri. *Memorie Soc. ent. ital.,* 28: 21–23.
Zeller, P. C., 1842: Beitrag zur Kenntnis der Dipteren aus den Familien der Bombylier, Anthracier u. Asiliden. *Isis,* 1: 807–848.
Zerny, H., 1920: Diptera, in: Beiträge zur Kenntnis der Fauna Dalmatiens, besonders der Insel Brazza. *Zool. Jh.,* (Syst), 42: 205–212.
Zetterstedt, J. W., 1838: Insecta Lapponica descripta. Diptera, pp. 477–868, Lipsiae.
– 1842–60: Diptera Scandinaviae disposita et descripta, Vols. 1–14, Lund.
Zumpt, F., 1949: Medical and veterinary importance of Horse-flies. *S. Afr. med. J.,* 23: 359–362.
– 1966: The Arthropod parasites of vertebrates in Africa south of Sahara (Ethiopian Region), vol. III: Insecta by E. Haeselbarth, J. Segerman and F. Zumpt. *Publs. S. Afr. Inst. med. Res.,* 13: 1–283, 140 figs.
– 1968: Human- und veterinärmedizinische Entomologie, in: Handbuch der Zoologie, IV. Band: Arthropoda, 2. Hälfte: Insecta, 49 pp., 54 figs., Berlin.

Index

All valid names are in italics. The page number in italics under the valid names of European species refers to the main treatment of the species in question. Reference to figures can be found in the text under the heading of each species.

Corrections

p. 17: The correct number of species for Norway is 31, and for Sweden 46.
p. 377, line 1: replace »and« with »but not«.
p. 384, line 20: replace »Face« with »Eyes«.
p. 386, line 17: replace »consists« with »consisting«.
p. 389, line 1: add »brown« after »segments«.
p. 395, line 18: add »haired« after »reddish«.
p. 399, line 19: add »is« after »species«.

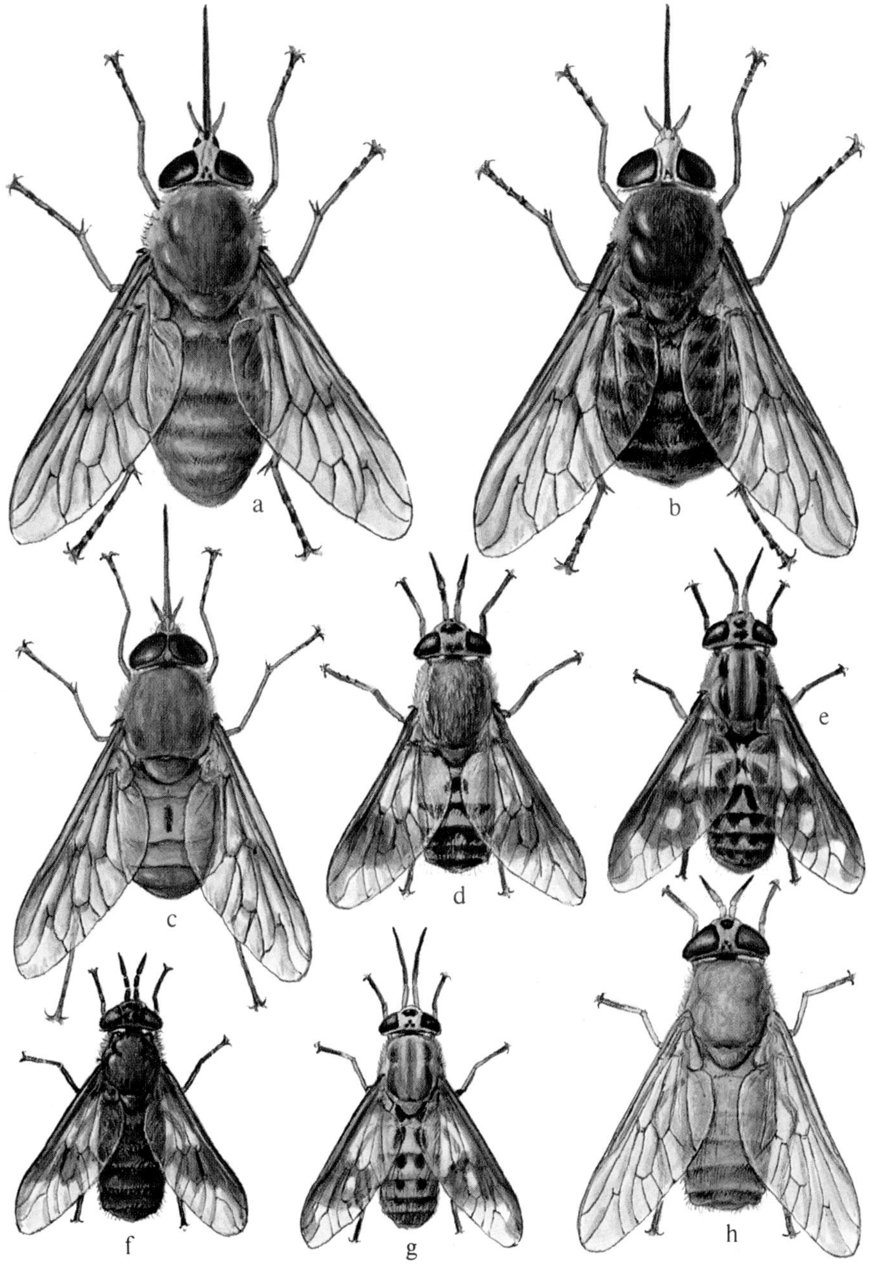

PLATE 1

a. *Pangonius (P.) pyritosus* Lw. ♀, b. *Pangonius (Melanopangonius) micans* Meig. ♀, c. *Pangonius (P.) mauritanus* (L.) ♂, d. *Chrysops viduatus* (F.) ♀, e. *Chrysops italicus* Meig. ♀, f. *Chrysops sepulcralis* (F.) ♀, g. *Chrysops flavipes* Meig. ♀, h. *Silvius alpinus* (Scop.) ♀.

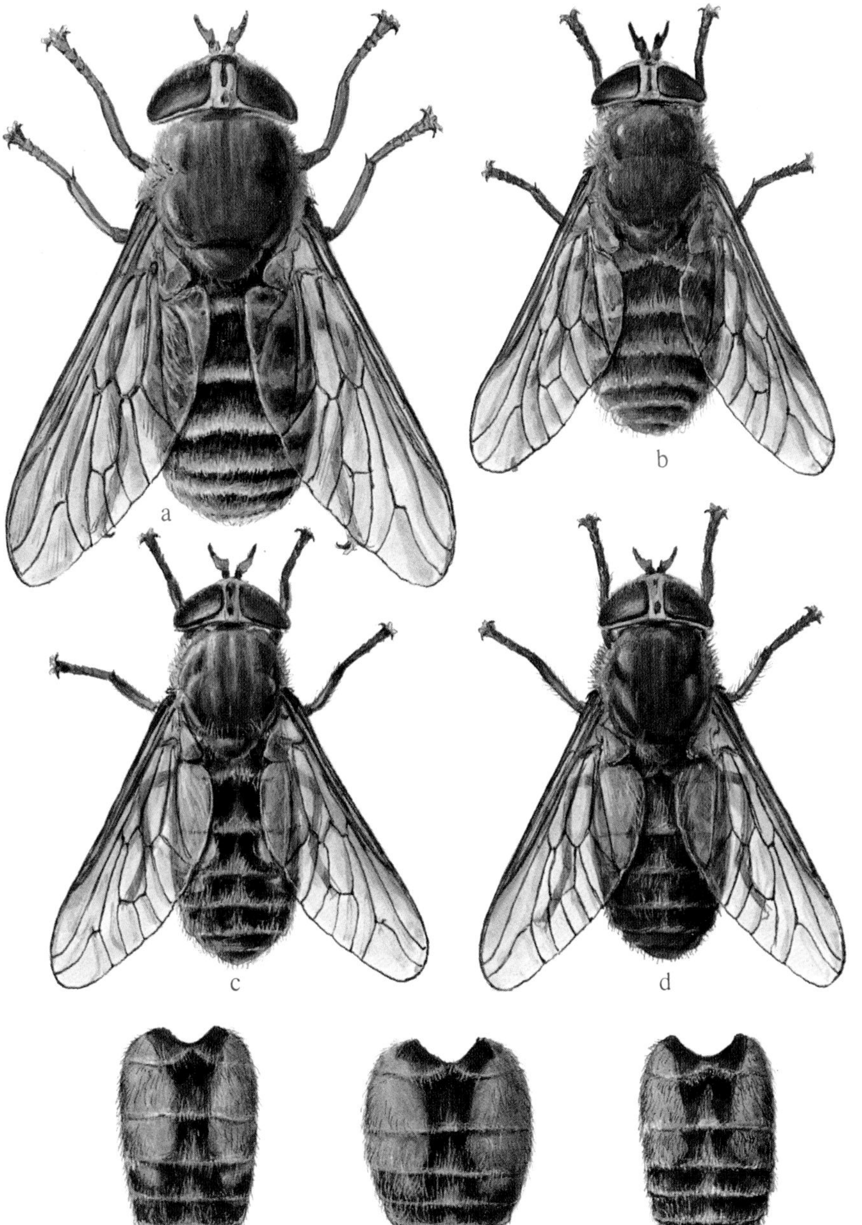

PLATE 2

a. *Hybomitra tarandina* (L.) ♀, b. *Hybomitra auripila* (Meig.) ♀, c. *Hybomitra lundbecki* Lyneb. ♀, d. *Hybomitra bimaculata* (Macq.) ♀, e. *Hybomitra ciureai* (Ség.) ♀ abdomen, f. *Hybomitra distinguenda* (Verr.) ♀ abdomen, g. *Hybomitra muehlfeldi* (Brau.) ♀ abdomen.

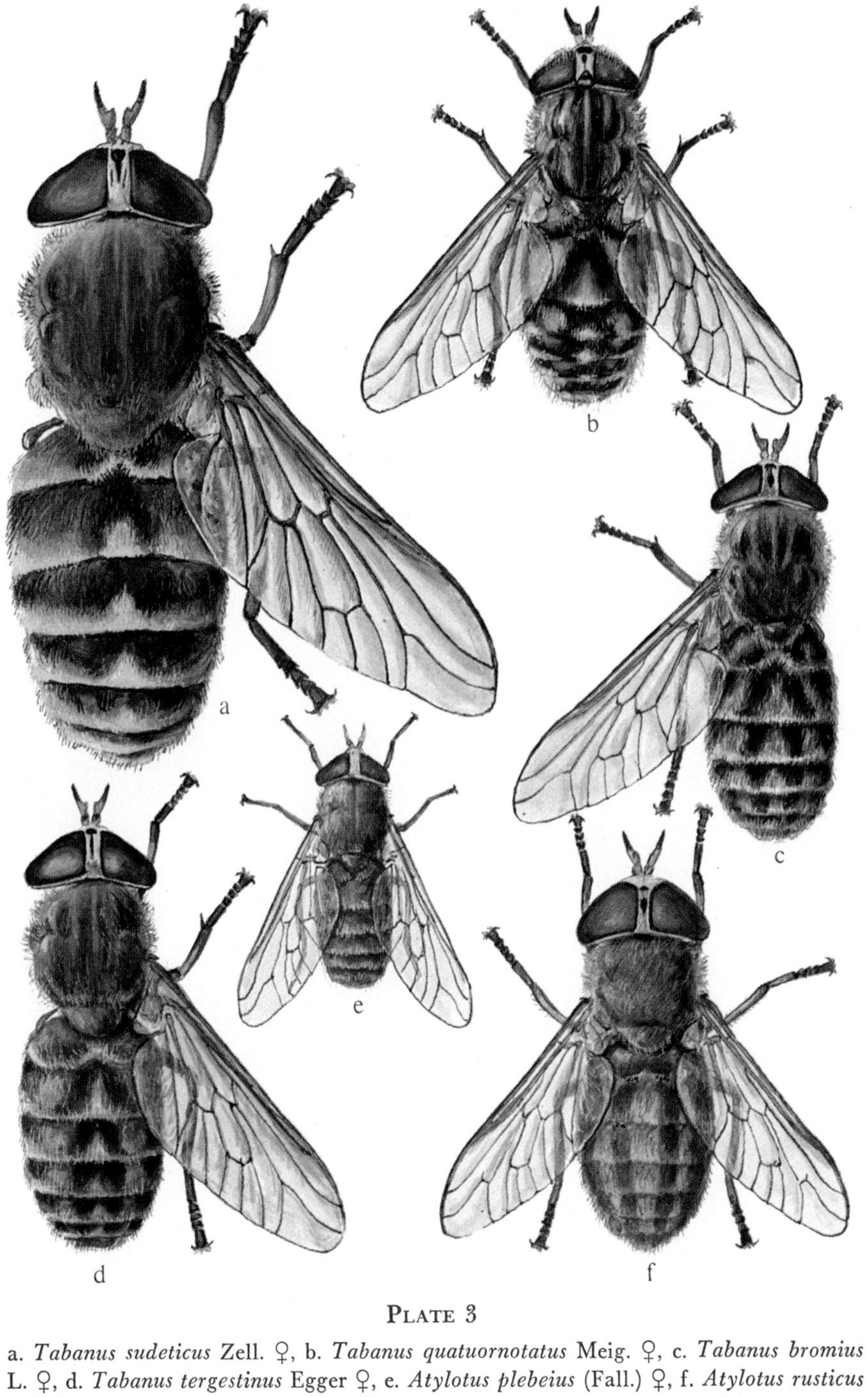

PLATE 3

a. *Tabanus sudeticus* Zell. ♀, b. *Tabanus quatuornotatus* Meig. ♀, c. *Tabanus bromius* L. ♀, d. *Tabanus tergestinus* Egger ♀, e. *Atylotus plebeius* (Fall.) ♀, f. *Atylotus rusticus* (L.) ♀.

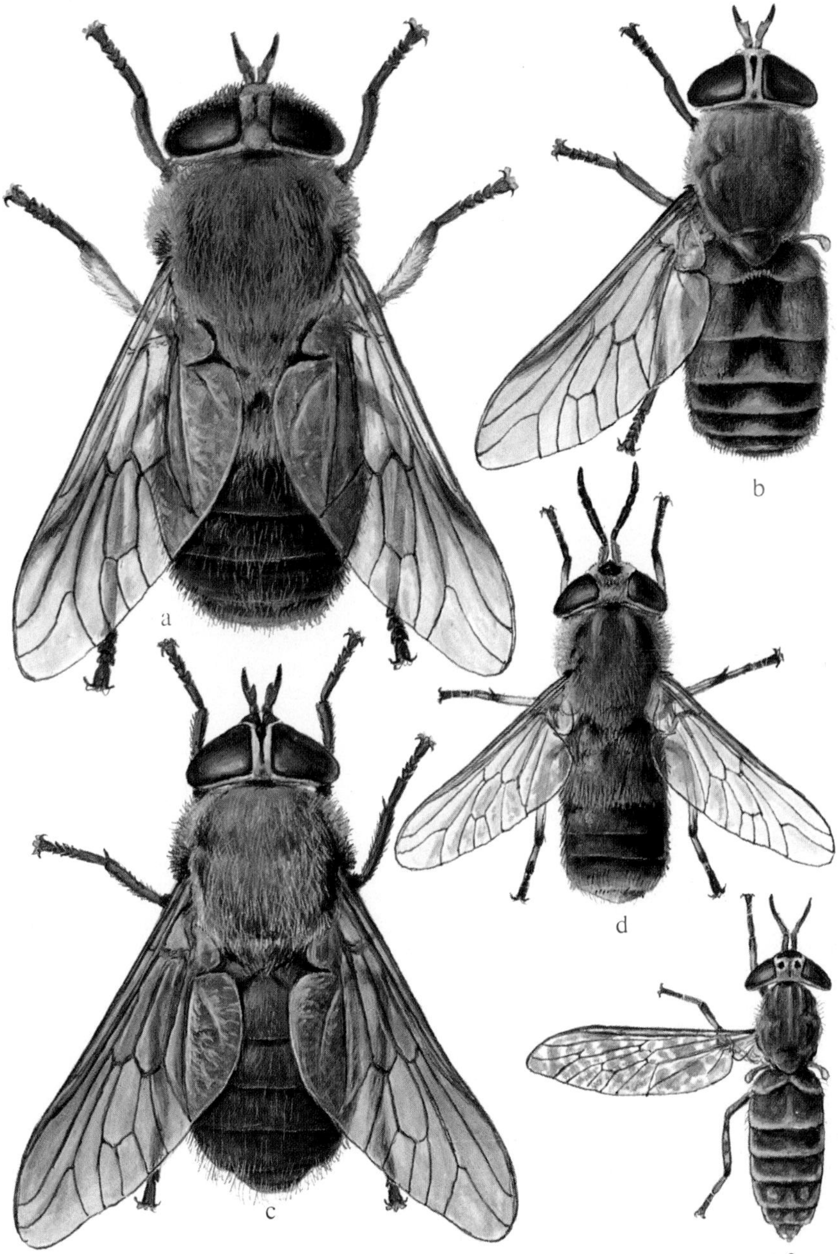

Plate 4

a. *Therioplectes gigas* (Herbst) ♀, b. *Philipomyia aprica* (Meig.) ♀, c. *Dasyrhamphis ater* (Rossi) ♀, d. *Heptatoma pellucens* (F.) ♀, e. *Haematopota italica* Meig. ♀.

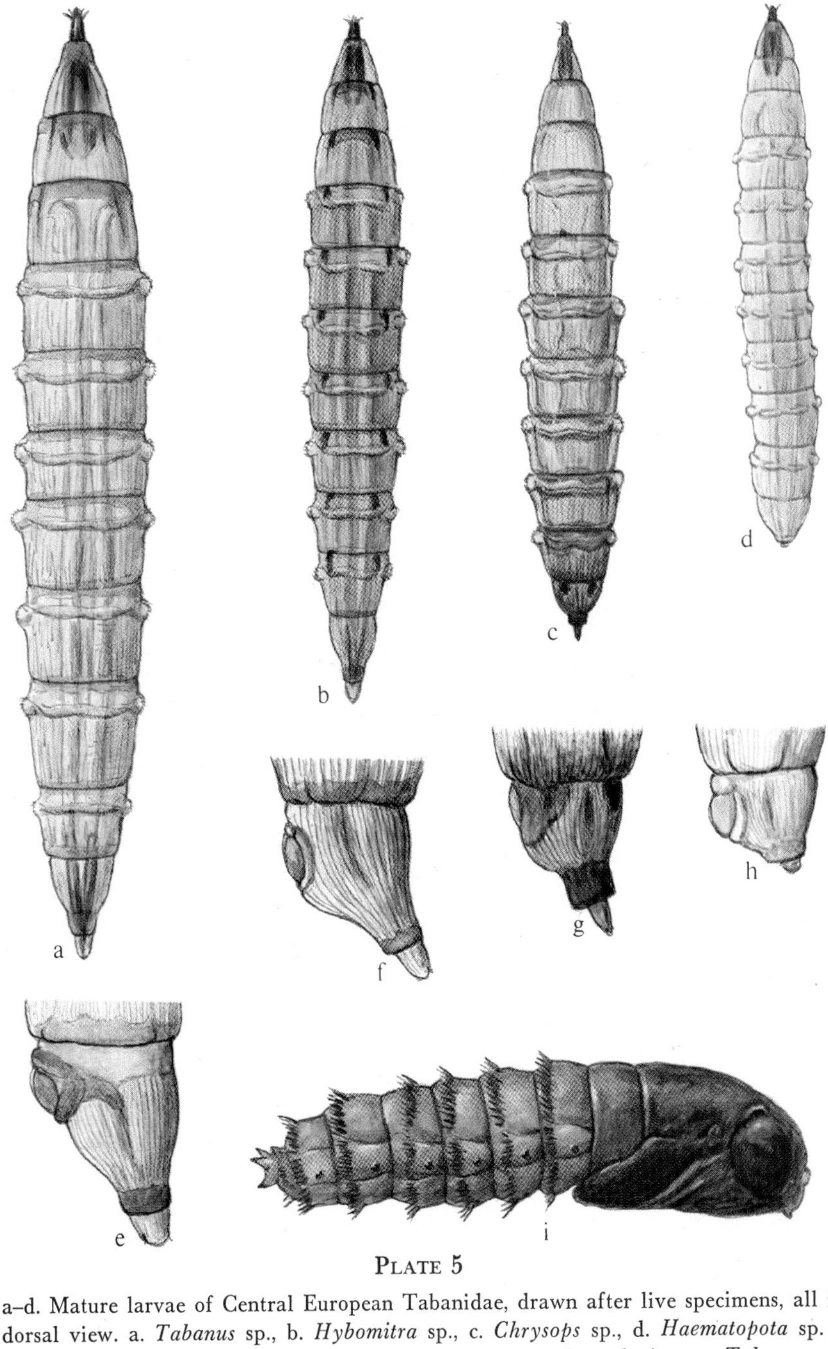

PLATE 5

a–d. Mature larvae of Central European Tabanidae, drawn after live specimens, all in dorsal view. a. *Tabanus* sp., b. *Hybomitra* sp., c. *Chrysops* sp., d. *Haematopota* sp. – e–h. Terminal segments of same larvae as in a–d, all in lateral view. e. *Tabanus* sp., f. *Hybomitra* sp., g. *Chrysops* sp., h. *Haematopota* sp. – i. Pupa of *Hybomitra* sp., lateral view.

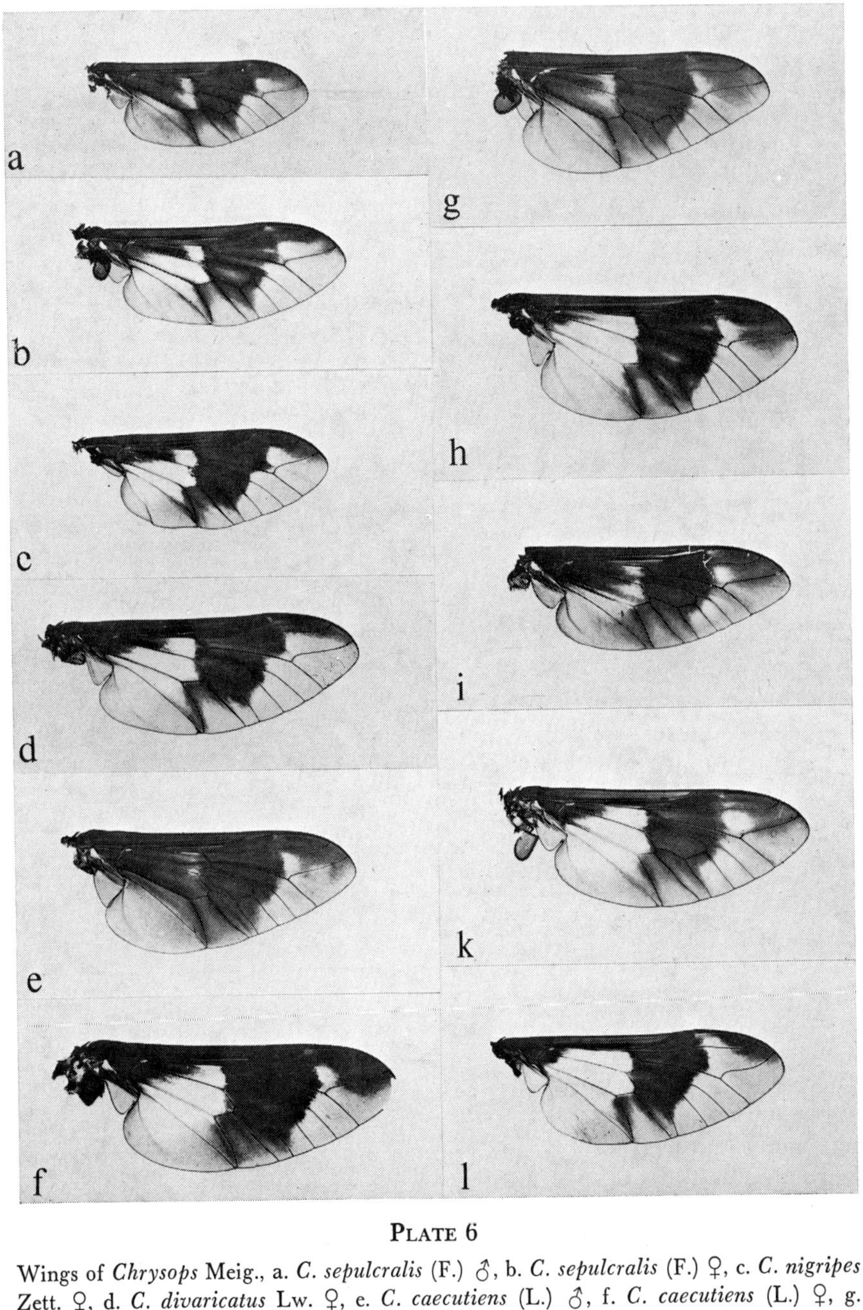

PLATE 6

Wings of *Chrysops* Meig., a. *C. sepulcralis* (F.) ♂, b. *C. sepulcralis* (F.) ♀, c. *C. nigripes* Zett. ♀, d. *C. divaricatus* Lw. ♀, e. *C. caecutiens* (L.) ♂, f. *C. caecutiens* (L.) ♀, g. *C. viduatus* (F.) ♂, h. *C. viduatus* (F.) ♀, i. *C. relictus* Meig ♂, k. *C. relictus* Meig. ♀, l. *C. ricardoae* Pleske ♀.

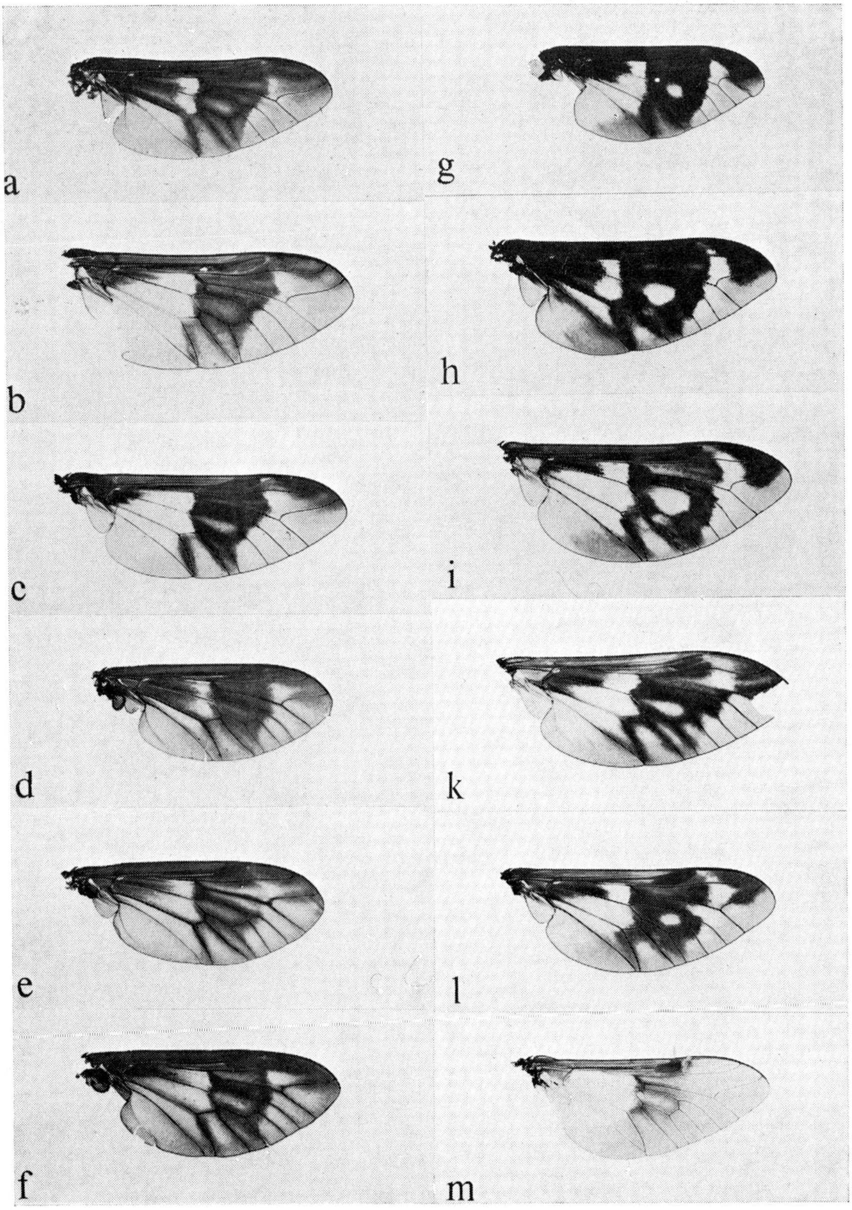

PLATE 7

Wings of *Chrysops* Meig., a. *C. parallelogrammus* Zell. ♂, b. *C. parallelogrammus* Zell. ♀, c. *C. concavus* Lw. ♀, d. *C. rufipes* Meig. ♂, e. *C. rufipes* Meig ♀, f. *C. melichari* Mik ♀, g. *C. flavipes* Meig. ♂, h. *C. italicus* Meig. ♂, i. *C. italicus* Meig. ♀, k. *C. connexus* Lw. ♀, l. *C. mauritanicus* Costa ♀, m. *C. (Petersenichrysops) hamatus* Lw. ♀.